Pynchon's California

THE NEW AMERICAN CANON

The Iowa Series in Contemporary Literature and Culture

Samuel Cohen, series editor

PYNCHON'S CALIFORNIA

EDITED BY SCOTT McCLINTOCK AND JOHN MILLER

UNIVERSITY OF IOWA PRESS | IOWA CITY

University of Iowa Press, Iowa City 52242

www.uiowapress.org

Printed in the United States of America

Design by April Leidig

The University of Iowa Press is a member of Green Press Initiative and is committed to preserving natural resources.

Printed on acid-free paper

Library of Congress Cataloging-in-Publication Data

Pynchon's California / edited by Scott McClintock and John Miller.

pages cm. — (The New American Canon: The Iowa Series in Contemporary Literature and Culture)

Includes bibliographical references and index.

ISBN 978-1-60938-273-5 (pbk)

ISBN 978-1-60938-294-0 (ebk)

1. Pynchon, Thomas — Criticism and interpretation. 2. California — In literature. I. McClintock, Scott. II. Miller, John, 1959 July 2–

PS3566.Y55Z84 2014

813'.54—dc23 2014010227

Contents

Acknowledgments

The editors would like to express their gratitude to the contributors to this volume, all of whom responded quickly and cheerfully to our various requests at every stage of the project, and to Catherine Chilton, Elisabeth Chretien, Catherine Cocks, Samuel Cohen, Charlotte Wright, and the staff at the University of Iowa Press for their encouragement and careful attention throughout.

An earlier version of "Pynchon's Coast: Inherent Vice and the Twilight of the Spatially Specific," by Bill Millard, was originally published in *College Hill Review* 4 (fall 2009). This revised version is published here within by permission.

Pynchon's California

Introduction. Surveying Pynchon's California

SCOTT McCLINTOCK AND JOHN MILLER

The publication of Thomas Pynchon's third "California novel," *Inherent Vice*, in 2009, following *The Crying of Lot 49* (1966) and *Vineland* (1990), inevitably suggests the possibilities of considering these novels as members of a group and the significance of their shared setting within the body of Pynchon's work as a whole. In addition to their setting—California in the 1960s through 1980s—the "California novels" share some other distinguishing features: they are the shortest of his novels; their plots, generally organized around a single protagonist, tend to be more linear than the baroquely interlaced plots of the longer works; they all invoke a genre often associated with Southern California, the detective story; and two of them center largely on female characters.[1]

All four of the longer works, with the partial exception of his first novel, *V.*, and a few pages at the end of *Gravity's Rainbow*, are set in the historical past, although two of them make their circuitous ways to California in their final pages. The California novels, by contrast, are set in a time in which Pynchon and many of his readers actually lived and in a place in which Pynchon lived and that is a part of the contemporary world of his readers, even if experienced solely through media and popular culture. Pynchon's only real foray into journalistic writing also deals with California in the 1960s. For an author so interested in the workings of history and legacies of power and resistance to that power, the contemporary setting suggests that these novels may offer a different perspective on those recurring themes, one perhaps from which the determinist implications of historical fiction, even fantastical[2] historical fiction, are less powerful.

The narrator of *Mason & Dixon* suggests that the unmapped western frontier of 18th-century America—still available to be imagined because unmapped—represents, at least temporarily, a "realm of the Subjunctive" (543), a geographical and temporal space in which the possibility of alternative futures can at least be imagined:

> Does Britannia, when she sleeps, dream? Is America her dream?—in which all that cannot pass in the metropolitan Wakefulness is allow'd Expression away in the restless Slumber of these Provinces, and on West-ward, wherever 'tis not yet mapp'd, nor written down, nor ever, by the majority of Mankind, seen,—serving as a very Rubbish-Tip for subjunctive Hopes, for all that *may yet be true.* (345)

In the cultural imagination, California has often played an analogous role; as essayist Richard Rodriguez has written, "California has for so long played America's America. The end of the road. Or a second shot at the future" (273). Teddy Roosevelt similarly (if somewhat gnomically) described California as "west of the West" (a quotation that has provided a title for at least two different books on the state). The idea that California, and especially Southern California, holds out a promise of reinvention, of second chances, of alternative lifestyles is a cultural stereotype; and the betrayal of that promise has become a literary convention, most distinctly articulated in the "noir" stance from the 1930s fiction of Cain, Chandler, Himes, and others, and the Hollywood fiction of Fitzgerald, West, and Schulberg, to the sun-blasted ennui of Joan Didion's early essays, in one of which she describes California as a place "in which the mind is troubled by some buried but ineradicable suspicion that things had better work here, because here, beneath that immense bleached sky, is where we run out of continent" (172).

What critical attention has been paid to Pynchon's use of California as a setting has tended to invoke familiar postmodern dialectics of surface and emptiness, promise and despair that echo the noir critique. Typically, California is seen as representing in Pynchon's fiction what it so often represents in popular culture: "postmodern America," a place of sleek beauty manufactured to mask inescapable corruption, disillusionment, or mere emptiness—what Judith Chambers describes, quoting *Vineland*, as "a land of surfaces and underbellies where 'the fog . . . [lifts] to reveal not the borderlands of the eternal after all, but only quotidian California again'" (94). In an essay focusing on the representation of California as a touchstone in postmodern fiction, Rachel Adams writes that "Pynchon depicts California as . . . a testament to the exhaustion of the westering impulse once seen as so vital to the nation's manifest destiny. . . . a place that values superficiality over depth" (252, 254). However, just as there is ongoing disagreement about how pessimistic Pynchon's postmodern vision really is, so is there room for a less conventionally despairing understanding of what the California setting represents and thus why it is significant in his novels. David Cowart, for example, suggests that *Vineland* "retains a myth that its author celebrates rather than deconstructs. Pynchon's setting is a representation of the American land; and he refuses to surrender the myth of American promise" (*Thomas Pynchon* 118).

Cowart's phrase "the myth of American promise" is conveniently equivocal, suggesting that the "promise" may be no more than a myth. But many of the particular historical, geographical, and cultural features of the contemporary California setting help make it an apt and important device for suggesting a subjunctive voice in these novels. Though a relatively young state, California has a complex history of repeated settlement and resettlement, of successive uses of the land superseding and attempting to erase preceding uses. The state is often represented as a place in which the new is privileged over what little history there might be, and this process of erasure and reconstruction always seems to resurface in Pynchon's California, like the fermented dandelions blooming in their bottles of Genghis Cohen's wine long after the cemetery in which they had been picked had been paved over for a new freeway. Both Oedipa Maas and Doc Sportello discover that the suburban landscape so easily taken for granted has been the site of long histories of conflict that inform the conflicts they observe taking place today. Near the end of *Inherent Vice*, Doc, just offshore on a boat, looks back at the beach where he lives and, seeing a "cop chasing a longhaired kid along the beach . . . Doc flashed how this was the time machine": the beach had been the scene of recurring conflicts of authority and resistance and of attempts at transcendence, "'come to think of it, not unlike the hippie freaks of our present day,'" as his friend and nemesis Bigfoot Bjornsen points out (355). Oedipa's investigations lead her to stumble on stories of obscure 19th-century sea fights and robberies, along with complex transfers of property ownership. While Doc's drug use and general hippie attitude suggest a preference for living in the present, he is challenged to rethink his understanding of his environment by myths that tie it to ancient cataclysms and ongoing conflict flowing from them. During an LSD trip, he sees that the war in Vietnam is simply the latest iteration of "a karmic loop as old as the geography of those oceans . . . going back, back" to the exile of the Lemurians "fleeing the terrible inundation which had taken their homeland" (109). The central plot of *Vineland* follows Prairie Wheeler's uncovering of her mother's secret history, which involved the cover-up of a crime that occurred two decades before at a college located along the "brief but legendary Trasero County coast," the adjectives potentially modifying the county itself as well as its coastline. This mythical county is "bracketed by the two ultraconservative counties of Orange and San Diego," which in real life are contiguous with one another, and the college is squeezed between the sea and a military base whose situation, we are told, resembles that of the real Camp Pendleton "in the world at large" (204). Vineland itself is threatened by invasion by forces both governmental and commercial, but these are merely the latest manifestation of an ongoing conflict going back at least to the dispossession of the Yurok tribes by the first Europeans; and in fact, the Yuroks themselves have legends of an even earlier people who were themselves dispossessed "when the first humans came" (186). Subsequent influxes of explorers, fishermen, loggers, hippies, pot farmers, and now the government and developers, encountered varying degrees of resistance from those already there; each wave of invaders succeeded only partially in erasing the traces of those they displaced.

California's vast, varied, and open landscape provides a kind of blank slate on which developers and visionaries continue to project new designs: in all three novels, it is particularly the frontiers of suburban development that represent the site of struggles to assert control and independence, to write and rewrite both history and the future. When, in the book's most quoted passage, Oedipa Maas senses "a hieroglyphic sense of concealed meaning" in "a vast sprawl of houses which had grown up all together, like a well-tended crop, from the dull brown earth" in San Narciso, she is describing an archetypal California scene (24). The landscape itself is a particularly apt medium on which to inscribe such "hieroglyphics." The "dull brown earth" presents a blank page on which the developer, in this case Oedipa's ex-boyfriend

Pierce Inverarity, the founding father of San Narciso, tries to write his "legacy" on the land. As Southern California cultural historian Mike Davis has written, to the developer that landscape is no more than an "abstraction of dirt and dollar signs" (*City of Quartz* 4). Thus San Narciso, "Like many named places in California . . . was less an identifiable city than a grouping of concepts—census tracts, special purpose bond-issue districts, shopping nuclei, all overlaid with access roads to its own freeway" (Pynchon, *Crying* 24). There is something ephemeral about such a recently built landscape, as ephemeral as the vanity that is its motivation: a "need to possess, to alter the land, to bring new skylines, personal antagonisms, growth rates into being" (178). Twenty years later, Edenic Vineland is under similar threat: "Developers in and out of state had also discovered this shoreline in the way of the wind, with its concealed tranquillities and false passages, this surprise fish-trap in the everyday coast. All born to be suburbs, in their opinion, and the sooner the better" (Pynchon, *Vineland* 319). These distant commercial interests, as much as the threat of federal agents descending from the sky, threaten the refuge that Vineland has offered its motley inhabitants. In his book *Pynchon and the Political*, Samuel Thomas argues that Pynchon proposes a politics of "fugitive space," local and temporary enclaves that the powers of oppression cannot find or into which they cannot reach (128). Judith Chambers uses a similar metaphor to describe how characters in Vineland resist their oppressors by "establishing local enclaves of mystery that disperse the hardened systems of order and that reassert the animate" (185). Thus the struggle between power and resistance becomes mapped onto a landscape particularly suited to both interests and to the representation of that struggle. As in *Vineland*, we see similar struggles taking place in—and for—some of the state's wilder, less settled geography, and in *Inherent Vice*, the Pacific shore, the edge between land and sea, becomes a symbol of an ever-present potential for apocalyptic or transcendent transformation.

Finally, Pynchon exploits both California's familiar cultural symbolism as "America's America," the leading edge of the American experiment in freedom, and the equally familiar "noir" critique of that symbolism. California in the 1960s is simultaneously the apotheosis of the suburban version of the American dream (perhaps that dream's high-water mark) and the crucible of the counterculture, known as much for its housewives as for its hippies. Kinneret-Among-The-Pines, somewhere down the San Francisco Peninsula, is a suburban idyll that somehow also creates space for the LSD experiments of Dr. Hilarius, just as suburban Palo Alto did for Ken Kesey. In *Vineland*, the lazy and hazy redwood and weed economy of the north coast coexists with the hot, gleaming, frenzied night freeways of the summer of the 1984 Olympics in Los Angeles, while female ninjas, government reeducation camps, and communities of vengeful ghosts all find places to hide in the state's expansive and varied geography. In *Inherent Vice*, cops chase hippies down the beach, reenacting ancient dialectics of power and rebellion, and hippies can even be cops, or at least private eyes. Toward the end of *Lot 49*, Oedipa suggests that the built, and still-being-built, landscape of her state, in which she has been searching for clues and symbols, may represent the irruption of a more pervasive meaning:

> There was the true continuity, San Narciso had no boundaries. No one knew yet how to draw them. She had dedicated herself, weeks ago, to making sense of what Inverarity had left behind, never suspecting that the legacy was America. (178)

Yet this is still a place, on the final far western edge of the expansion of European civilization, where the cops still do chase the hippies, where the determined historical endings of the larger novels have not yet been written, and where an alternative outcome, against all the odds, is still at least imaginable. It is a place where Pynchon finds "anarchist miracles" not just in fiction but on the actual streets of South Central Los Angeles in 1965: "a remarkable empathy, or whatever it is that jazz musicians feel on certain nights; everybody knowing what to do and when to do it without needing a word or a signal" (Pynchon, *Crying* 132; "A Journey" 84). Looking westward from its shores, Oedipa finds not, like Walt Whitman, her own back, but "some principle of the sea as redemption . . . some unvoiced idea that no matter what you did to its edges the true Pacific stayed inviolate and integrated or assumed the ugliness at any edge into some more general truth" (Pynchon, *Crying* 55). In *Inherent Vice*, this principle becomes a myth of California as an "ark," a land of exile from which someday the exiles, or at least certain "saints" among them, may return to a risen homeland.

One other thing that the California novels share is a relatively lower esteem among readers and critics. Probably none of Pynchon's work has received as much attention as *The Crying of Lot 49*, largely because it was for many years the most accessible, and remains the most teachable, of the novels. But the big books are certainly those that have established Pynchon's place in the canon and his influence over contemporary writers. The status of the California books can be gauged by the organization of two recent books surveying all of Pynchon's work, both of which have a chapter each on *Gravity's Rainbow*, *Mason & Dixon*, and *Against the Day*, but only a single chapter considering the three novels with California settings together.[3] While suggesting that the literary value of the California books, taken individually, may in some ways correspond to their physical heft, this phenomenon may also be taken as a sign of a critical intuition that the novels are related in interesting ways. This book is conceived as an opportunity to explore those relationships and their basis in a locale that contains important and unique meanings not only in Pynchon's fiction (and occasional nonfiction) but in the culture more broadly.

• • •

In "Situated Fictions: Reading the California Novels against Thomas Pynchon's Narrative World," Margaret Lynd asks, "What recurrent themes or narrative techniques from the larger novels might these less ambitious texts focalize, clarify, expand upon, or refine? Do they help us navigate the sometimes convoluted narrative trajectories of the other novels or bring into better focus the extraordinary and complicated visions those narratives conjure? And if so, how?" These questions motivate not only Lynd's own chapter in this collection but many of the others.

A starting point for the examination of how the shorter, California novels focalize, clarify or refine issues treated with greater complexity, and sometimes opacity, in the longer novels, adopted by several of the chapters in the current volume, can be expressed by Lynd's observation that "Unlike the longer novels, . . . the California novels all have clearly identifiable protagonists and relatively simple, linear plots," rendering these characters more "humanized and sympathetic." Adapting Donna Haraway's concept of "situated knowledges," Lynd proposes that the more local, "situated" quality of the California novels, contrasted with the sprawling, byzantine and encyclopedic character of the big novels, shines the spotlight on "the characters themselves, their trials and confusions, pains and pleasures while continuing to reflect themes that are foregrounded in the other novels: in each case, we follow, with relative ease, a familiar (though not necessarily chronological) narrative trajectory, from conflict to climax to resolution." The linear narrative design of the California novels is addressed in several of the essays in this collection, particularly in Scott Macleod's chapter, "Playgrounds of Detection: The Californian Private Eye in Thomas Pynchon's *The Crying of Lot 49* and *Inherent Vice*," where the linear narrative design is discussed specifically in light of the detective fiction genre, the narrative conventions of which Pynchon playfully invokes in both novels.

Basing her analysis on Haraway's notion of situated knowledges, Lynd coins the term "situated hope," "a hopefulness that is grounded in always apparently simple and spontaneous gestures of kindness, generosity, and courage that individuals may—and sometimes do—summon unexpectedly at any given moment without hope of redemption or gain." Lynd's exploration of what she calls "situated hope" in the California novels leads us along a path parallel to Scott McClintock's investigation of the role of the sentimental in his chapter, "The Origins of the Family, Private Property, and the State of California in Pynchon's Fiction." McClintock sees the sentimental as, paradoxically, the core of the genre of hard-boiled detective fiction that Pynchon's California novels invoke to varying degrees, which its increasing foregrounding by the appearance of *Inherent Vice* seems explicitly to acknowledge. The concern with the "subjunctive voice," with what Lynd calls "situated hope," what McClintock explores as the sentimental mode in the California novels, and what Coffman investigates as the sacred in Pynchon all signal an emphasis on the significance of feeling, hope, and even transcendence in Pynchon's fiction generally, which in the California novels goes against the grain of a by now all-too-familiar portrayal of California as a postmodern space of superficiality, Didion's "end of the continent," where the depth of history is continually erased and only surfaces and signs without referents reign, in a Baudrillardian or Jamesonian hyperreal.

Thomas Schaub's "synoptic" analysis of the California novels in *The Cambridge Companion to Thomas Pynchon* provides an assumption forming the starting point of, and expanded upon in, this collection. Schaub's reading of how the vision of California in *The Crying of Lot 49* contrasts with what Schaub regards as a bleaker, disenchanted assessment of the complicity of the counterculture and the New Left with the "mechanisms maintaining the status quo" (35) in the later California novels is forcefully argued, but many of the essays in this collection imply that the sharp break Schaub finds between *Lot 49* and the later California novels, a kind of turn from an interest "in the possibilities for alternative communities" in the earlier novel to "the Althusserian focus upon mechanisms that maintain the status quo," (34) can be overstated. In different ways, the essays in this collection find a more hopeful, affirmative interest in the "possibilities for alternative communities" running throughout the California novels, as one of the themes that unifies them. Further, the essays in this collection offer an alternative to the construction of Pynchon as a postmodern ironist, a fabulist of disenchantment with utopian hopes and longings, a radical skeptic of radicalism. The alliances other critics have found between Pynchon's portrayal of the media landscape, the "tubal culture" of television and film as one of the mechanisms of the containment of revolution, and the broader "critique of representation" in critical theory are undeniably an important aspect of Pynchon's fiction. The essays in this collection, however, largely reject the pessimistic reading of Pynchon's California novels as portraying in the microcosm of California any "totalizing" order of domination by postmodern, late "Capital." Through a Deleuzian epistemological lens, for instance, Hanjo Berressem draws our attention to the material, microecological elements of the California landscape in Pynchon's novels as alternative "media" that escape the efforts of real estate and development interests to control the landscape and bring it under a regime of monopolistic power. Against any totalizing narrative of "Late Capital" that would read Pynchon's California as a mirror for globalization and domination, many of the essays in this collection insist on the local, regionally specific, and "situated" features of Pynchon's California fictions and their resolute balancing of the darker, "noir" potentials of the state's history with the more affirmative, hopeful possibilities that have always existed in a permanent condition of conflict throughout its history.

The darker, ironic view of California that its noir representation seems to epitomize is undoubtedly influential in Pynchon's portrayal of it, but as

McClintock suggests, even this noir tradition that Pynchon draws upon contains a more conflicted literary history, of which the origins go back to the sentimental and domestic tradition of the nineteenth century. The image of California as a burned-out continental edge (whether from natural disaster or from the drug counterculture), where history has ended and hope and sentiment are exhausted and impossible, is countered by many of the essays in this collection, which acknowledge the ironic mode of Pynchon's postmodernism but also give a possibly overdue recognition to the affirmative side of Pynchon's postmodern play with genres and perhaps imply the limits of the concept of the postmodern for understanding Pynchon's style. Like any critical concept, the postmodern may blind readers to some important elements of Pynchon's writing even while enabling insight into others, and many of the chapters in this collection aim, in part, to redirect our critical gaze to aspects of Pynchon's work that may have been neglected due to the dominant emphasis on postmodernity, or a version of it, in the body of Pynchon scholarship.

Lynd's essay, like others in the collection, including John Miller's "Reading, Resistance, and the California Turn in Pynchon's Cornucopian Fiction" and Stephen Hock's "Maybe He'd Have to Just Keep Driving, or Pynchon on the Freeway," identifies connections between the shorter, California novels and longer works. California emerges as the imagined future of pre-Revolutionary America in *Mason & Dixon*, according to Lynd, "a history and expectation that even then was really a developer's dreamscape" and encompasses the "politics of mapping" that underlie the Great Powers' conquest and dispossession of territories from their indigenous inhabitants all over the world, with which Pynchon's bigger novels have all been concerned.

Several essays in the collection address the centrality of female characters to Pynchon's California narratives. Hanjo Berressem, for instance, finds that "at the end of *Vineland*, Prairie seems to be as immune to Brock Vond as she is to the malls of America. It seems that in *Vineland*, Pynchon puts his hope in the next generation." Scott McClintock reads the same scene in *Vineland* in the contexts of the valorization of the maternal feminine and the generic interconnections between the nineteenth-century tradition of the domestic novel, the maternal melodrama in film (particularly Michael Curtiz's *Mildred Pierce*), and the hard-boiled detective fiction tradition. Lynd, however, questions how "feminist" Pynchon's use of female characters, even as protagonists, can be, and she offers a critical dialogue with these other perspectives. For Lynd, both Frenesi Gates and Prairie Wheeler become symbols of the temptation to be seduced by power, echoing the "frailty" of Lake Traverse, a female character in *Against the Day* to whom both are distantly related and who herself drifts to California at the end of that novel. Lynd wonders if Pynchon's tendency to embody the capitulation to the temptation of power in female characters is, instead, a weakness of his narrative of power and the problem of the opposition's complicity with it.

Hanjo Berressem, in "Life on the Beach: The Natural Elements in Thomas Pynchon's California Trilogy," invokes the organization of Mike Davis's book *Ecology of Fear: Los Angeles and the Imagination of Disaster* around the natural elements of earth, air, fire, and water to argue that as much as Pynchon's California landscape can be viewed as a technological, cybernetic, and information landscape, what has often been overlooked is the degree to which "Pynchon's work has increasingly highlighted that these are immanent *in* and emerge *from* a more *elemental* natural landscape." Berressem's novel reading of the ecology, and even the alchemy, of the California landscape in Pynchon's trilogy in light of their narrative of the attempt to "control and contain California's wild and excessive ecology, to commodify it by turning it into an engineered site" shares with other essays in the collection an interest in explicating the motifs of the history of development and real estate as this is imaginatively portrayed in Pynchon's California novels. It charts a "shift from technological paranoia to ecological awareness" in Pynchon's California trilogy that enriches the discussion of paranoia as a vision connected with real estate development in Pynchon's narrative of California history, especially as related through the prism of the detective fiction genre considered in other essays in this collection by McClintock, Macleod, and Millard.

Like Lynd, Millard is concerned with what Lynd refers to as "situated knowledges" in Pynchon's shorter, California fiction. Millard argues that "large parts of *Inherent Vice*, for reasons that extend beyond nostalgia, direct the reader to particular places" and that the novel "is rich with particular spatial and cultural references." While Millard concedes that such allusions are "nothing new in Pynchon," he observes that what distinguishes such local spatial and cultural references in *Inherent Vice* is "the concentration of them in a single region, instead of their distribution across the nation or the world," which, he argues, "makes the book's rendering of Southern California exceptionally credible and nuanced." Like Berressem and McClintock, Millard's essay treats the motif of land development in Pynchon's California novels as central to their representation of place and to the larger ideas of legacy America that Pynchon sees represented in California and its history, particularly in the postwar period. Much of Millard's chapter develops the dichotomy represented by Michael Wolfmann's two real estate projects, the Channel View Estates and the "Arrepentimiento" development in the Nevada desert, as "antithetical ways of organizing American land in pursuit of contrasting utopian impulses." "The systematic consumption of both rural and urban land," Millard argues, "reshaped much of the American landscape into a relatively undifferentiated type of residential space, one that erased the physical features of local history." Although Millard does not use this term, his argument implies that the local place and cultural references in the novel constitute something like Foucault's notion of "counter-memory," a cultural project and politics of preserving (as *Preserved*, one of the other names of the schooner *The Golden Fang*, suggests in an important dream sequence in the novel) an alternate history of the 1960s and 1970s in danger of erasure by elite history and historical revisionism by mainstream media, as well as by land development itself. Millard's chapter suggests that the model of land development epitomized in California but generalized as a national, postwar economic template that would ultimately become synonymous with globalization is possibly the major "vice" that stands as synecdoche for the destructive waste and ecological disaster, not to mention the psychic damage, caused by global, postmodern capital in its omnivorous expansion during the period in which the California novels of Pynchon are set, making *Inherent Vice* a "novel of ideas in potboiler disguise."

Berressem's allusion, drawing on Gilles Deleuze, to drugs as "media of perception" that interpret the wave patterns of the shore is developed as a more central focus in Henry Veggian's chapter, "Profane Illuminations: Postmodernism and Realism in Thomas Pynchon's *Vineland*," which analyzes Pynchon's California novels, with special focus on *Vineland*, as political fiction and the motif of drugs and altered perception not as the antithesis of realism but as a form of it, in the historicized context of the "war on drugs" in the 1980s setting of the novel. The work of Deleuze—suggested, among other ways, by the reference in the epigraph to *Inherent Vice* linking Pynchon's portrayal of California in the late 1960s and early 1970s to the May 1968 uprisings in France, a connection mentioned in Millard's chapter and developed in detail in Berressem's—also figures largely, though in a different way, in McClintock's chapter, which uses *Anti-Oedipus* and the antipsychiatry movement as one foil for exploring the conflicted portrayal of the family in Pynchon's California fiction and to suggest both the uses and limits of a psychoanalytic approach to Pynchon's California trilogy.

• • •

The present volume, then, hopes modestly to reflect some of the qualities that have drawn its contributors to Pynchon's work in the first place: a recurrence of urgent and challenging themes approached from a variety of directions and perspectives that interlace with one another in surprising and fruitful ways. In addition to arguing for the interest and value of Pynchon's California novels in their own right, by interrogating them as a group with distinct properties and strategies, we hope this collection can use their arguably lesser lights to reilluminate the body of Pynchon's work as a whole, in which they weave and worm themselves with an insistent regularity, as impossible to ignore as the graffiti of the preterite to those once sensitized to their existence. We also believe these essays make a case for the significance of Pynchon as a California writer: not just one who wrote from and about that place, but one who is contributing to the ongoing revisions of an important global repository of cultural symbols and meanings.

The official motto of the State of California is *Eureka!*—"I have found it." The "it" originally alluded to the discovery of gold, but the motto was adopted to refer more broadly to the state itself, to which so many of its residents arrived from somewhere else, often after arduous journeys; even more broadly, it suggests the many different forms of wealth or transformation the idea of

California has promised those immigrants. The record of that promise is a mixed and complex one. We are confident that the following collection of essays offers curious readers an appropriately mixed and complex array of "Eureka moments."

NOTES

1. Pynchon's eighth novel, *Bleeding Edge* (2013), was published just after most of this volume, including the preceding sentence, had been written. If the qualities recited in that sentence are taken as criteria, *Bleeding Edge* would qualify as the most typically "Californian" of Pynchon's works to date, putting aside the fact that it is set almost entirely in New York City and its immediate environs. It is, though, sprinkled with brief recollections of California by secondary characters who, like Pynchon himself, have transplanted themselves Back East. Some initial reviews of the novel have noted the affinity, and we expect subsequent critical responses to *Bleeding Edge* will explore its relationship to the California novels, possibly with the aid of some of the arguments made in the pages that follow.
2. Or "hysterical," as James Wood would have it.
3. In David Cowart's *Thomas Pynchon and the Dark Passages of History*, the chapter is entitled "Pynchon and the Sixties: the California Novels." The title of Thomas Schaub's chapter in *The Cambridge Companion to Thomas Pynchon* (Dalsgaard et al.), "*The Crying of Lot 49* and Other California Novels," suggests the relative place of *Vineland* and *Inherent Vice* in some critical assessments (the *Cambridge Companion* also collapses *V.* with Pynchon's short stories in a chapter simply titled "Early Pynchon").

Situated Fictions. Reading the California Novels against Thomas Pynchon's Narrative World

MARGARET LYND

Few could disagree that Thomas Pynchon's three California novels, *The Crying of Lot 49*, *Vineland*, and *Inherent Vice*, are aesthetically simpler and less multilayered and politically less significant than the "big four," *V.*, *Gravity's Rainbow*, *Mason & Dixon*, and *Against the Day*, which individually and as a whole have captured the admiration of the American literary world over nearly half a century. (I exclude here discussion of *Bleeding Edge*, published shortly after this essay was written.) Reception of each of the three California novels has of course been dramatically different; the novels themselves are differently structured, and each has been read within the changing social, political, and cultural contexts of a 50-year trajectory. But the reception of the novels has surely also varied because, at least after *V.*, each has been critiqued through the lens(es) of Pynchon's other works. *The Crying of Lot 49*, published just three years after *V.*, was greeted with enthusiasm by reviewers and critics; hundreds of essays and several essay collections have been published in the 45 years since the book appeared. *Vineland*'s reception was far more equivocal. As the first substantial piece of writing to follow *Gravity's Rainbow* after a hiatus of some 17 years, the novel had been, to say the least, long awaited. Negative comparisons with Pynchon's past works were perhaps inevitable, but *Vineland*'s readability and its attention to contemporary American politics have also been called both refreshing and important, its less bleak assessment of humanity's prospects heartening, although there is disagreement on that score, as well. *Inherent Vice*, though published only in 2009, does seem a much slighter work than the other two California novels and so far has fewer defenders.[1]

Few could disagree either that if Pynchon had written only the three California novels, he would be considered a talented but minor figure in the world of American letters. But Pynchon *did* write these novels, and one cannot help but wonder why he would enlist so dramatic and deliberate a change of style and complexity at various points in an otherwise extraordinary series of literary performances. The California novels were not written at the beginning or end of a long, ongoing career but as his second, fourth, and seventh books, their publication interspersed rather evenly among the longer works. What recurrent themes or narrative techniques from the larger novels might these less ambitious texts focalize, clarify, expand upon, or refine? Do they help us navigate the sometimes convoluted narrative trajectories of the other novels or bring into better focus the extraordinary and complicated visions those narratives conjure? And if so, how?

I want to suggest that the California novels, alone or taken together, do deepen our understanding of the longer novels in a number of ways, each in its own measure and each with quite different emphases and effects. We can, in Pynchon's view, only begin to understand our world and our past through a multiplicity of contradictory, and sometimes whimsical, voices. The sentiment echoes Donna Haraway's discussion of "situated knowledges," in which she attempts to delineate an "objective reality" that is not weakened by dependence upon a framework of relativity but is brought into being by the notion of necessarily "partial knowledge." Well aware of the trappings of power that accompany unmarked (i.e., white and male) versions of "Truth," Haraway insists that partial knowledges constitute a reality that is verifiable, though never complete, because it is always situated within the perspectives of gender, class, ethnicity and other identity markers, as well as time and place. So too does Pynchon insist upon a multiplicity of partial and contradictory voices to convey to us a past that can and must be recovered and a present that can and must be "objectively" analyzed and critiqued. The tropes of paranoia and conspiracy that run through all of Pynchon's novels serve to limn the multiplicity of connections that Haraway describes: "The alternative to relativism is partial, locatable, critical knowledges sustaining the possibility of webs of connections called solidarity in politics and shared conversations in epistemology" (584). Of course, all three California novels deal with familiar Pynchonian patterns of paranoia and conspiracy, domination and submission, betrayal of self and others, and the intransigence of power relations between elect and preterite, the corruption that always, from both Pynchon's and Haraway's perspectives, arrives hand in hand with power of any kind, be it interpersonal, corporate, or governmental. It is, indeed, the many partial knowledges of the preterite that are the only viable opposition to the singular, stormtrooper march of Truth that the elect insist upon. The very idea of a capitalized "Truth" is precisely what all of Pynchon's work undermines in multiple ways: truncated plotlines, disappearing and shape-shifting characters, the blurring of fantasy and reality—the familiar Pynchonian mixture of postmodern fiction's themes and techniques. Instead, we may recover a credible "situated" story of both past and present if we adhere to the narrator's advice in *Mason & Dixon*: "Who claims Truth, Truth abandons. History is hir'd, or coerc'd, only in Interests that must ever prove base. . . . She needs rather to be tended lovingly and honorably by fabulists and counterfeiters, Ballad-Mongers and Cranks of ev'ry Radius" (350).

The California novels exhibit a simplified, and by that very token more accessible, vision of these concerns through the eyes of a few central characters, who are themselves representative of preterite sensibilities. One of the few critics to address the California novels together is Thomas Schaub, who argues that these novels, although decidedly lesser works than Pynchon's others, constitute a "three-decade long era of U.S. social history [and] emerge from Pynchon's lived experience" (41). For Schaub, *The Crying of Lot 49*, written in an earlier, more hopeful moment (the 1960s) in American history and perhaps in Pynchon's own life trajectory, suggests, if not precisely hope or guarded optimism, at least the possibility of change, whereas *Vineland* and *Infinite Jest* (Wallace) both project resignation and sadness. The latter two are, Schaub suggests, a reflection of Ronald Reagan's profoundly dispiriting "morning in America," perhaps best captured by the image of Doc Sportello alone in his car beside the Santa Monica freeway, not a glimmer of sunshine breaking through the morning fog. I would agree that *The Crying of Lot 49*, as the most open-ended of the three, does offer the possibility, if not the likelihood, of change. But in *Vineland*, I would suggest, the kindness of Zoyd Wheeler, the earnestness of Prairie, even the jolly reunion of the Traverse family, while all a bit strained, offer as well a kind of redemptive quality that is difficult to find in *Infinite Jest*. Poor Doc Sportello seems an uneven match, indeed, for the Mickey Wolfmanns and Brock Vond—let alone the Weissmann/Bliceros—of the world.

Unlike the longer novels, as Schaub notes, the California novels all have clearly identifiable protagonists and relatively simple, linear plots. I would argue, however, that all three serve as a kind of footnote to the more robust and multifaceted expressions of Pynchon's insistence on a preterite vision of "truth(s)"; the California novels comprise an instance of "situated (partial) knowledge" to complement and elucidate that of the larger novels. The literary elements of each of the three California texts are, of course, quite different. *The Crying of Lot 49* foregrounds the self-reflexive attempt of a single character, Oedipa Maas, to redefine the conditions and constraints of her complacent life; the action of the novel takes place almost entirely within the constructed California environment, where we see a great many freeways and strip malls and sleazy motels but not many beaches or mountains or redwoods. *Vineland* also focuses on identifiable characters: Zoyd Wheeler is probably the protagonist, but his daughter Prairie is a close second. *Vineland* foregrounds themes of government and police corruption, conspiracy, family betrayal, and the central role of the media in modern life; the setting of its narrative frame in Ronald Reagan's 1980s America is significant, particularly in its review of the 1960s youth movement in California and the characters' final retreat to the redwood forests and stunning beauty of Northern California. *Inherent Vice* also focuses, as does *Crying of Lot 49*, on a single character, ex-hippie private eye Larry "Doc" Sportello—part Colombo, part Clouseau, part Philip Marlowe, part Roadrunner cartoon (and part Pynchon?)—and his run-ins with popular culture, power relations, betrayal, and an outlandish interchangeability of criminals and law enforcement officials. The Southern California beach town setting also plays a significant role as the text unwinds, both in its beachcomber's ambience and its extratextual connections to Pynchon himself.

Apart from their much greater readability and their focus on a smaller cast of characters and narrower range of issues, perhaps the most obvious difference between the California novels and the others is precisely California itself—California as a little America, a real and imaginary place that does not foreground the "big picture," as the other novels do.[2] "California" is a contained avatar of the freewheeling geographies, real and imagined, of the other texts, from the fantastic flights of the Chums of Chance to the sad and heart-wrenching trials of Mason and Dixon in South Africa. In these three novels, we are given only occasional glimpses of the magnitude of Pynchon's sense of world history. We do not see, for example, the terrible consequences of colonialism (the predecessors/prototypes of Blicero/Weissmann refining the techniques of genocide in Africa for later use in Germany) or the perverse underpinnings of environmental disaster (Europeans happily killing off the last dodo because they want to and because the dodos are powerless). The range of conspiracy and paranoia in the California novels parodies the depraved power games of the other works: compare the collapse of the student movement in 1960s California to Scarsdale Vibe's destruction of the miners' labor movement along with the Traverse family; compare Brock Vond's power over Frenesi Gates to the White Visitation's control and manipulation of Tyrone Slothrop from cradle to dispersal in the Zone; compare Pierce Inverarity's vulgar real estate developments to Mason and Dixon providing the linear boundaries that will allow Indian lands to be stolen legally; compare Mickey Wolfmann's corruption to I. G. Farben's stranglehold on the world, with the German corporation coming as close to simply being a villainous character ("corporations are people") as a corporate entity ever could. Brock Vond, Dr. Hilarius, and Bigfoot Bjornsen are bad guys, but they are cartoonish bad guys, too incompetent (although Hilarius was a Nazi) to imagine and engineer the unfathomable cruelty of the Dora concentration camp or the torture and decimation of the Hereros. The villains of the California novels do not perpetrate their villainy on a scale large enough to compel the willful blindness of Franz Pökler for his complicity in the crimes of Dora; they are quite incapable of the evil ingenuity required to fabricate the lethal sadomasochism of the Blicero-Gottfried-Katje triumvirate. We see only glancing references to the enormity of historical crimes that appear full-blown in the other novels: slavery and genocide in Africa and in the New World, the sordid underside of Enlightenment and the Age of Reason as white men engineer the American revolution for pleasure and profit in *Mason & Dixon.* Even the heartbreak of love and betrayal as Jessica Swanlake abandons Roger Mexico for the attractions of suburbia is somehow more acute, more disappointing, than all of Frenesi Gates's betrayals of Zoyd and Prairie.

The California novels touch more or less briefly upon all of these large, globally located themes, of course, but they do so in ways that are direct, contemporary, and limited to a particular time and place—California/America from Richard Nixon to Ronald Reagan. As such, the novels are not only more accessible in themselves, but focusing as they do upon just a few memorable and sympathetic or repulsive characters, limited settings, and linear plots (at least relatively linear, with fewer tangents) facilitates a richer understanding of the themes and characters of the larger novels. The California novels give us story lines that are relatively easy to follow and characters who, with the occasional exception of Doc Sportello, do not often resort to disguises (as Slothrop, wandering the Zone, becomes a hard-boiled reporter, a Rocketman, a filmmaker, a Pig), become caricatures of evil (as do Edward Pointsman, the cruel, demonic behavioral scientist, or Major Marvy, the idiotic counterpart to Blicero, the tortured sadist), travel to the magical center of the Earth (as do the Chums of Chance, the good-natured *Hardy Boy*–ish adventurers), become intriguing "ghosts" (like the elusive, mysterious, probably nonexistent V.),[3] or appear as fictionalized historical characters (like Charles Mason and Jeremiah Dixon and Benjamin Franklin, whose characterizations, however amusing, are at least somewhat constrained by historical fact).

By contrast, the California novels encourage readers to focus upon the characters themselves, their trials and confusions, pains and pleasures while continuing to reflect themes that are foregrounded in the other novels: in each case, we follow, with relative ease, a familiar (although not necessarily chronological) narrative trajectory, from conflict to climax to resolution. Again, Haraway's notion of situated knowledge is useful here. The four big novels touch upon virtually every social, political, and economic eventuality that has occurred in the modern world, from the scientific revolution to the end of the 20th century; as such, they constitute an extraordinarily rich context of intellectual engagement and social and cultural critique within which we may consider the characters we are given in the California novels. In the larger universe of Pynchon's fiction, the California novels present to us much more directly than do the larger novels the forlorn yet hopeful possibilities for family, for love, for meaning, and for redemption in a world hopelessly riven by greed, lust, jealousy—all of the deadly sins that riddle humanity.[4] Such humanized and sympathetic characters appear in all of Pynchon's novels, of course—Enzian gives up his quest for martyrdom, Dixon confronts the slave trader, Kit Traverse rejects the manipulations of Scarsdale Vibe. Precisely because the California novels *are* Pynchon's work, we don't read them as separate texts; indeed, as readers, we (in our own constructions of partial knowledge) situate them within the context of the longer novels. Rather than follow the temptation to read them simply as provocative but minor works of American letters, or simply as minor works within Pynchon's oeuvre, we can better comprehend them as a kind of illustration of how the various themes and conflicts of the big novels come to roost in (almost) believable but always sympathetic characters. The California novels would be read and understood very differently without the critical, political, and historical contexts that Pynchon's other writing provides.

With the publication of *Against the Day*, Pynchon's novels as a whole came to comment upon a nearly continuous stretch of modern American and European history but with due attention to the effects of the brutality of that history, especially in regard to the indigenous world: *Mason & Dixon* (18th century), *Against the Day* (late 19th to mid-20th century), *V.* and *Gravity's Rainbow* (mid- to late 20th century), ending, we might say, with the Rocket having reached Brennschluss, but with the Rocket's imaginary avatar left figuratively hovering above the Los Angeles movie theater. Narrative time stops altogether and space collapses as the Rocket's avatar leaps forward from Peenemunde in 1945 to Los Angeles in the early 1970s. Rocket 00000 should have continued its trajectory in its predetermined but unpredictable path, yet the novel ends—the Rocket doesn't fall, it hovers, suspended in a narrative that screams through time, to end years later with the California theater audience clueless about what is or is not about to befall them, while Gottfried remains suspended in the narrative, secured in his Imipolex G (flesh-like plastic) womb/shroud, poised to bring the novel, the century, and the world to an end. With a little poetic license, or writerly action, we might say that the ragtag California novels pick up—in the 1960s, 1970s, and 1980s in America—where the big important ones leave off: in a world that has driven itself to the brink of every sort of imaginable disaster—environmental, political, economic, social, military. And together they reconstruct a version of contemporary history; as Pynchon further notes in *Mason & Dixon*, history must be "a great disorderly Tangle of Lines" (349): not one voice, but many scraps of partial knowledge. As America, at least in the popular American imaginary, has been "exceptional," the last best hope for the world—the rich, innovative, freewheeling, anything-goes space of infinite possibility—so California is to America. It is this myth that Pynchon addresses and both undermines and restates: California is not so much a fictional space with a real analogue as it is a kind of ruined—or *almost* ruined—Paradise. The California novels foreground a central pattern of all of Pynchon's longer texts: even in a place of inordinate beauty, variety, and promise (quintessential California before we humans attacked its unwieldy diversity), perverse desire gets the better of most of Pynchon's characters. Those who only *almost* succumb to indifference or cruelty are nonetheless left on tenuous and largely powerless ground—Oedipa Maas about to enter the stamp auction, Doc Sportello looking out for Shasta, Prairie Wheeler somehow inhabiting the sliver of promising space between Brock Vond (and bad Mom Frenesi), on the one hand, and her irrepressible pooch (and good Dad Zoyd), on the other.

"California" is crystallized as an imagined space of possibility that is also always beneath a perpetually hovering Rocket, as it threatens to fall one last time and take the world with it, yet always, like the *Inconvenience* in *Against the Day,* (almost) equally ready to "fly toward grace" (1085). Each of the three California novels gives us a different refraction of what I can only call "hope," although it is not quite that at all—not an abstract and unsupported sense of general optimism that things will, against all odds and all evidence to the contrary, get "better." It is rather, to recall Haraway once again, what we might call "situated hope," a derivative of Haraway's argument that all knowledge, including scientific knowledge, is produced within a context of cultural difference and other kinds of "knowledge" (intuitive, emotional, ethical, psychological, spiritual). It may be useful to apply such a notion of "hopefulness" to the multiplicity of voices in Pynchon's fiction. Pynchon gives us, in all his novels, but more pointedly in the California novels, simply because they are less sprawling and multidimensional, a hopefulness that is grounded in always apparently simple and spontaneous gestures of kindness, generosity, and courage that individuals may—and sometimes do—summon unexpectedly at any given moment without hope of redemption or gain.[5] This emergence of a few characters into some deeper understanding of themselves and connection to others and of their complicity, whether willing or unwilling, knowing or unknowing, in a world that regularly produces death camps and destruction is a central element in all of Pynchon's writing. As noted earlier, that emergence of self-awareness in a few characters is present in each of the longer novels—in Enzian, Franz Pökler, Kit Traverse, Cyprian, Jeremiah Dixon, and the Reverend Cherrycoke, to name several—as well as in the California novels.

In terms of the relative linearity of plots (and despite the ease of movement back and forth in time), perhaps the clearest comparison of the California novels is to be made with *Mason & Dixon*, because it is, far more than any of the other big novels, a linear narrative, indeed a historical novel, which follows two historical figures and one fictional storyteller. *Mason & Dixon* may be a bit more closely connected to the California novels for other reasons, as well. The attention to mapping and the centrality of geography and landscape is a second way in which these four novels connect. Maps are imagined realities: "maps begin as dreams, pass through a finite life in the world, and resume as dreams again" (*Against the Day* 250); such is the case with "California," as well as with "America": both geographies are made readable and compliant by the maps that are said to represent them. Literal mapping is, of course, the central trope of *Mason & Dixon*, in particular the tension between the absurdities of the grid and its power to enforce the legalization of boundaries and the privatization of the landscape. The Mason-Dixon Line itself is impossibly imposed upon a radically nonlinear landscape, exemplifying the Pynchonian "bad shit" of an excluded middle. The line, imaginary despite its stone markers set in the ground, constitutes the principal plot and central metaphor of the entire narrative. The Mason-Dixon Line is a preposterous imposition of linearity upon a very messy and diverse geography, both human and natural. It exemplifies the practical and political absurd—in which state does a landowner straddling the line reside?—in contrast to the deeply troubling philosophical perspective of Captain Zhang, with his profoundly reverent objections to imposing a cage-like grid upon the natural world, disrupting whatever harmonies and irregularities (*Shan*) might otherwise emerge and prevail. The Mason-Dixon Line is a historically dramatic instance of the politics of mapping that, historically, has been perhaps the single most important element in legalizing the theft of land and natural resources from indigenous peoples in America and around the world.[6]

The California novels pick up this theme in a number of ways. All three novels focus on one or two central characters who are caught up in what can only be called a familiar Pynchonian quest narrative. Oedipa Maas climbs down from her Rapunzel-like tower of suburban life, with her Tupperware parties and her boredom, in an effort to find—and it really does seem to be this trite—meaning of some kind. Perhaps more accurately, she enlists in a quest simply to become engaged, to sidestep the nostrums of Dr. Hilarius (who is, after all, a Nazi war criminal) and entertain the possibility of acting—even if that means plunging into a world of paranoia and (probably) imagined conspiracies. However mindless Oedipa's quest may be, it awakens her to the world—its pains as well as its mundane pleasures—and rescues her from the vaguely Thanatoid existence of America in the late 20th century.[7] She finds herself, still ruled by male desire—it is, after all, her old boyfriend Pierce Inverarity's unexpected naming of her as the executor of his will that draws her out of the tower. Traveling the highways and byways of California, the freeways and gritty city streets, the sleazy motels and strip malls, neither we nor Oedipa ever know whether the Trystero is real or a figment of her imagination. What is unquestionably real is the overlay of roads and freeways—both figurative and physical—upon the landscape, laid out here not in a straight line or an imaginary grid but as a giant hypodermic needle continuously injecting an endless string of cars into the circulation system of the culture like heroin running through the body's veins (14).

Pynchon's endings, as in many, if not most, postmodern novels, tend to be anticlimactic: Who knows who or what V. is? Will the Rocket fall on the unsuspecting theatergoers? Is Mason's return to America a gesture of promise or resignation? The ending of *The Crying of Lot 49* could be read as anticlimactic, but I would argue that it is not. In fact, Oedipa acts deliberately and, perhaps for the first time in the book, in full knowledge that she will never—Trystero or no Trystero—resume the safe half-life she had been leading. As the door of the stamp auction closes behind her, we know that what happens inside is of no consequence. What does matter is that she has pulled off the freeway for good, leaving the moronic, TV-driven, suburban life of Kinneret-Among-The-Pines behind. Is the Trystero real? Who cares? Here, Oedipa moves beyond her placid paranoia—maybe she is just imagining that there is more to life than Tupperware parties, that all really is as it appears—but the question has been asked, the Rocket launched, so to speak. Her move through the door is all that matters, indeed, is all that is ever possible. This theme of paranoia as potentially both debilitating and energizing runs through all of Pynchon's work like the freeways of Southern California. Characters may be paranoid, but that paranoia may also be well placed and may move them finally to act. When Oedipa steps through the door to the stamp auction, she is in keeping with Pynchon's consistent message that life is contingent and never "resolved," that to "know" is most likely to be drawn, on the one hand, into complacency and willful blindness to crimes of every sort, or, on the other, into some depraved and heartless quest for power. Oedipa does not know when she enters the stamp auction and will not know when she leaves what Trystero is or isn't. Again, the "knowledge" is situated within a specific time and place and human milieu; life is unpredictable; Brennschluss is the moment of uncertainty not only before everything is over but before anything begins.

The relative simplicity, the linear movement of the narrative in *The Crying of Lot 49* is similar to that of both *Vineland* and *Inherent Vice*, although that is certainly not to say that any of the three is without a great many convolutions, backtrackings, and ambiguities. *Vineland* is set in the most recent time period of the three novels—Ronald Reagan's "morning in America"—but much of the narrative recounts the 1960s adventures of Frenesi Gates, only ending in the 1980s, the present time of the novel, with Frenesi finally meeting the daughter she had abandoned without a look back more than a decade before.[8] Here, perhaps more than in any of Pynchon's other works, the two main characters, Frenesi's ex-partner Zoyd Wheeler and their daughter Prairie, do in fact elicit a good deal of sympathy as well as good fun. (We first meet Zoyd, for example, as he prepares to display his officially certifiable craziness by leaping through a plate glass window so he will be able to continue to collect his disability checks. Zoyd "knows" that someone is out to get him when he discovers that the plate glass window has been replaced by sugar glass, a staple of Hollywood illusion production that anyone can crash through unscathed.)

While the ostensible task of the narrative is to disentangle the complicated interconnections between the anti-Vietnam, pro-civil rights youth protests of the 1960s and the government agents and agencies that infiltrated them, we come to understand those connections through the various betrayals that come from within the movement itself, most especially Frenesi's, which are so easily accomplished that they seem less than credible. Indeed, there is little evidence that Brock Vond exhibits any charms that a pretty, bright-eyed young moviemaker and documentarian of an idealistic, if not entirely innocent, youth movement could possibly succumb to. As Frenesi herself says, she couldn't resist the longings of her "pussy" and so simply had no choice in the matter. But that is unconvincing, even if her ambivalence about motherhood is added into the mix; the attraction here surely has more to do with the attractions of power than with Vond's sexual magnetism. Frenesi, not incidentally and despite a somewhat adolescent relationship with her mother Sasha, is still herself a descendent of the prolabor, anticorporate Traverse family of *Against the Day*, whose absorption into the system was characterized as a kind of trap, a result of the scheming corruption of Scarsdale Vibe, not a wholehearted betrayal willingly taken on by any of the Traverses. In fact, Lake Traverse's betrayal of her family and the labor movement through her marriage to Deuce Kindred, her father's Brock Vond–like (but infinitely more vicious) murderer, is similarly unconvincing, resonating strongly in Frenesi's relationship to Vond. Here again, as is sometimes the case in Pynchon's work, a certain echo of women's "frailty" comes to the fore.[9] This lapse in Pynchon's otherwise comprehensive and sensitive telling of America's multilayered past, a history defined by greed and lust, cruelty and betrayal, a fictional parallel of Howard Zinn's *A People's History of the United States*, is troubling. Indeed, while Frenesi's betrayal resonates with Lake Traverse's, Lake is a more fully developed character, with a complicated relationship to her father. When she marries Deuce Kindred, it is not just her "pussy" leading the way but a whole range of resentments and unresolved conflicts; moreover, Lake is fully disowned and ostracized, left alone by her mother and brothers, unlike Frenesi, who, after years of absence, not only is still the central object of desire for both

Prairie and Zoyd but is, in fact, warmly accepted back into the fold, along with her new boyfriend, Flash, and her son and Prairie's half-brother, Justin. Frenesi is welcomed to join what appears to be a wholly enjoyable and exuberant Traverse family reunion in Vineland, even as poor Zoyd's home is ransacked and occupied by Brock Vond and his cohorts in the FBI.[10]

The book ends as Vond descends from a helicopter threatening to seduce Prairie herself. Only the deus ex machina of Ronald Reagan's cancellation of Vond's mission saves Prairie from Frenesi's fate, even as Vond's loathsome body approaches and she is mesmerized by him as her mother had been years before. Desmond the dog's joyful kiss awakens Prairie, and that is almost enough to make us believe that Prairie has indeed come to her senses and now understands that the only way to "win" is to resist the attraction of power that Brock Vond exemplifies. And maybe that is Pynchon's point after all: Prairie, Zoyd, Sasha, all of us are never more than *almost* strong and clear-sighted enough to resist the temptations that regularly flood over us. Indeed, in its simplest framing, as in the California novels, the dilemma that all of Pynchon's work poses is just that: how do we, in our lonely lives, resist what Pynchon sees as the two prongs of the American dream—on the one hand, wealth and power for the elite at the expense of the preterite, and on the other, the preterite's mindless addiction to TV and Tupperware. How does one *act* without becoming enmeshed in webs of corruption and deceit or, at best, dishonesty? How does one avoid becoming either the direct purveyor of evil or the purveyor's loyal opposition? Even sweet little Prairie Wheeler is sorely tempted. It is perhaps the California novels that allow readers most readily to absorb this (partial) knowledge.

Inherent Vice poses this same question in its purest, most rudimentary form. Parodying the detective/film noir narrative agenda, *Inherent Vice* brings together the fuller characterizations we find scattered here and there throughout the novels but that are perhaps most fully developed in the Traverse family of *Against the Day*. Doc Sportello is not exactly fully developed, but he is nonetheless quite appealing, bumbling and messy and perpetually stoned, but lovable, and with an impeccable nose for clues. When his former girlfriend Shasta Hepworth shows up, she begs Doc to track down Sloane, the wife of Shasta's current lover, Mickey Wolfmann, because she believes that Sloane is plotting to sabotage Mickey. The wildly wealthy Mickey has had a change of heart and is in the process of redeeming his greedy ways by building a low-cost housing complex. (He has been kidnapped—or perhaps is merely pretending to be—and is later returned to his wife and his senses, abandoning his newfound generosity and returning to his old, corrupt ways.) Because Doc can't resist Shasta's request, he is suddenly thrust back into the role of hard-boiled, good-guy detective and into his old feud with Christian "Bigfoot" Bjornsen, the cop whose prototype is Brock Vond but who serves not the FBI but the local police force in Gordita Beach, a surfer's town in Southern California. *Inherent Vice* is a book that, much more than *The Crying of Lot 49* or *Vineland*, would probably have been given scant critical attention had it not been written by Thomas Pynchon. But it *was* written by him, and, situated against the recurrent themes of Pynchon's novels, it is transformed from the slapstick detective spoof that it also is into a restatement, or perhaps a reemphasis, of one of the most consistently recurring themes in all of Pynchon's work from the *Slow Learner* collection to *Gravity's Rainbow*: we are all chameleons and disguise artists, all capable of unimaginable cruelty and heartrending kindness. We don't know what makes a person go one way or the other, never to launch the Rocket or, once launched, as it now and forever has been, try to keep it suspended above that theater full of moviegoers eager for fantasy, suspended above all of us with our cars and our Netflix and our iPhones. But in the sprawling world that is Pynchon's fiction, however, and most clearly in the California novels, the Brennschluss of the soul is weighted ever so slightly toward hanging on, as Doc Sportello does. All of Doc's endeavors had been undertaken to please Shasta, yet even knowing finally that she is long gone, he musters somehow a modicum of incentive to carry on.

As much as the limited focus on just a few sympathetic central characters defines the California novels, natural and cultural geography also is crucial to the construction of California as a concrete analogue of America. In *The Crying of Lot 49*, the freeway system is a synecdoche for America's addiction to constant technological fixes and capital development. Close to the beginning of her travels,

> Oedipa resolved to pull in at the next motel she saw, however ugly, stillness and four walls having at some point become preferable to this illusion of

speed, freedom, wind in your hair, unreeling landscape—it wasn't. What the road really was, she fancied, was this hypodermic needle, inserted somewhere ahead into the vein of a freeway, a vein nourishing the mainliner L.A., keeping it happy, coherent, protected from pain, or whatever passes, with a city, for pain. But were Oedipa some single melted crystal of urban horse, L.A., really, would be no less turned on for her absence. (14)

This widely quoted passage surely grips every American with a sense of familiarity. Like blood cells in the body, we circulate in our cars through a landscape of concrete, isolated suburban dream homes, and, some 45 years after the book was published, gated communities to keep the preterite forever at bay. American freedom, Oedipa realizes as she navigates the freeway system, was never really that. It is the same understanding that Mason and Dixon come to as they gradually absorb the history and imagine the future of pre-Revolutionary America, a history and expectation that even then was really a developer's dreamscape. And there is no better place than California to make the point, a geographical space that contains nearly every landscape on the planet: Death Valley, the Mojave Desert, majestic redwoods, fragrant stands of eucalyptus, rugged seashore, sandy surfer beaches, lovely Lake Tahoe, snow-capped Sierra Nevadas, a cornucopia of fruits and vegetables to feed the world.

If the landscape of *The Crying of Lot 49* is largely a built environment with minimal connection to the less constructed stretches of the California landscape, *Vineland*, on the other hand, and to a lesser extent, *Inherent Vice*, assume the natural beauty and diversity—or what's left of it—of California as an integral part of the novels. Zoyd Wheeler is a 1960s survivor and throwback, one of several Pynchon characters—Enzian, Seaman Bodine, and Dahlia Rideout, to name several—who retains in his own character a bit of coyote trickster in Donna Haraway's sense: he is the counterpoint both to Brock Vond, who somehow combines the intellectual evil of Blicero with the stupidity of Major Marvy, and to Frenesi Gates, whom he still loves, but whose betrayals are multiple. She has sold out virtually everyone who matters to her: her parents and grandparents (the Traverse family), along with their commitment to labor—preterite—rights; the 1960s youth, with their various peace and liberation movements; her own daughter Prairie; and, of course, Zoyd. The California landscape here is divided: on the one hand, the laid-back surfer beaches and right-wing politics of Southern California, where Zoyd spent the 1960s, and on the other, Vineland itself, the verdant forests of Northern California, notorious still for their hippie communes, pot farms, and left-wing politics, as well as for their breathtaking beauty. What better images could represent an America long divided between elect and preterite, Brocks and Zoyds?

Indeed, the term "Vineland" is reminiscent of Vinland, and possibly (a "possibly" that is itself Pynchonian) the Vinland Map, a document purportedly dating from the 1440s and discovered in the 1950s, most likely a fake, that purports to show an area along the East Coast of North America that would suggest that Norwegians had mapped out the New World long before Columbus ever set sail.[11] Vinland, in short, is itself an imaginary space in Viking lore that is an abundant and pristine wilderness, much as we imagine the New World to have been before Europeans arrived. There are no such references in the novel, but their absence leaves us, whether intentionally or not, with a particularly Pynchonian ambiguity. Should we see the Northern California Vineland of *Vineland* as an analogue of the earliest American landscape, the jolly Traverse family reunion a kind of 20th-century Thanksgiving feast? Or are we rather to understand Vineland in the terms of realism—as the relatively unspoiled landscape of Northern California—verdant and spectacular, but no less a site of corruption and exploitation than any other? Whatever the "meaning" of "Vineland" (the fictional geographical space), it is a largely uncontained landscape, a place still of possibility, though hardly of innocence. Vineland is where Zoyd takes Prairie when he understands that Vond and his crowd, for whatever nefarious reason, are out to get them both. Vineland is no longer pristine: Brock Vond is there, trashing Zoyd's home and trying to snatch Prairie as he had somehow managed to seduce Frenesi years before. A characteristic of many postmodern novels is their open-endedness, the refusal of their authors to allow closure or to suggest that "Truth" is or should ever be uncontested. *Vineland*'s ending, in this sense, is pure Pynchonian postmodern gold: we don't know whether Vond is really descending from the helicopter to grab Prairie or whether Prairie is dreaming the entire event; we don't know whether Prairie intends to go with Vond or whether she is dreaming that she too will be willingly seduced by him; we don't know whether Vond is finally being put out of commission by none other than right-wing hippie-hater Ronald Reagan or whether he will be back, like the Joker in *Batman*. What we do know is that Prairie and her dog are safe, at least for the moment, and surely that is, for Pynchon and for us, enough (Or is it? It's just a dog, after all . . .).[12] Unlike the landscape in *Mason & Dixon*, where we know that the future will bring Dust Bowls and dead buffalo, the landscape in Vineland is the geographical avatar of that situated hope that has always been essential to Pynchon's work. However minor the California novels may be, none of Pynchon's novels foreground the *possibility* of redemption as clearly as does *Vineland*.

The geography of *Inherent Vice* is not foregrounded as a significant element of the plot as it is in *Vineland* but rather reflects the role of the constructed environment in *The Crying of Lot 49*. Doc spends a great deal of time chasing clues about the missing Mickey and about Coy Harlingen, the good-guy musician who had faked his own death in order to quit his drug addiction but who, in fact, has been coerced into spying for the government and is leading a miserable and lonely undercover life. Even without the motivation Shasta provides, Doc is willing and able, with the help of his "gumsandal" skills, to solve Coy's disappearance and return him to his family, and he does so simply because of his own characteristic goodheartedness. Indeed, the book begins with Doc racing up and down the freeways, the narrator noting in passing the dismal history of exclusion of all but white folks on Gordita Beach, the fictional version of Manhattan Beach, a surfer town in Southern California where Pynchon himself lived and probably wrote a significant portion of *Gravity's Rainbow*. The narrative follows Doc through his clownish run-ins with Bigfoot and his uncovering of various plots, ranging from Mickey's reprogramming as corrupt developer to the Golden Fang drug cartel to Coy's unfortunate life as a snitch.

The novel ends as it began, on the freeway near Gordita Beach, but this time Doc is all but lost, literally and figuratively, in the dense fog. He imagines that the fog might stay for days, that he might well be lost in it, but what he hoped was "For a forgotten joint to materialize in his pocket. For the CHP to come by and choose not to hassle him. For a restless blonde in a Stingray to stop and offer him a ride. For the fog to burn away, and for something else this time, somehow, to be there instead" (369). Again, we are given an almost but not quite comical moment in which the irreproachable Doc Sportello allows himself a moment of situated hope, maybe for something a little more lasting than a forgotten joint or another Shasta. If *Inherent Vice* is the funniest of the three California novels, it may be the saddest as well.

Placed against Pynchon's other work, then, the California novels do appear as a kind of footnote, a way to foreground and illuminate particular themes and elements that are, in various measure, part of the mix in all of Pynchon's fiction. Perhaps it is *Inherent Vice*, the least of the novels by any measure, that leaves us with a comical caricature of Thomas Pynchon himself—Doc Sportello stuck in the fog on the Santa Monica freeway, wishing the world and the wondrous people in it were just a little better than they will probably ever be.

NOTES

1. An exception is Bill Millard, whose essay in the present volume, "Pynchon's Coast: *Inherent Vice* and the Twilight of the Spatially Specific," makes a case for the novel as a serious and important component of Pynchon's work. On *Vineland*, see especially Wilde, "Love and Death."
2. See Wilson, "On the Pacific Edge of Catastrophe."
3. The Thanatoids of *Vineland* are indeed ghostlike, although they seem to represent not the elusive mystery of V. but an emotionless, valueless, semiconscious state of being, probably an effect of television and (most broadly) popular culture.
4. Pynchon's contribution to a tongue-in-cheek collection of essays about each of the seven deadly sins plus one is his updated definition of Sloth: "Perhaps the future of Sloth will lie in sinning against what now seems increasingly to define us: technology. Persisting in Luddite sorrow, despite technology's good intentions, there we'll sit with our heads in virtual reality, glumly refusing to be absorbed in its idle, disposable fantasies." (Mary Gordon et al., *Deadly Sins*, 22). Such "Sloth" is itself a sign of situated hope, a suggestion that the world is not entirely at the mercy of the elect.
5. See David Cowart's chapter "Pynchon and the Sixties: The California Novels" in his *Thomas Pynchon and the Dark Passages of History* for a discussion of Pynchon's fiction in the context of postmodern writers' concerns with moral and ethical questions.
6. See Fabienne Collignon, "A Glimpse of Light," for a discussion of Zhang's perception of the Mason-Dixon Line as a malevolent affront to the Earth, and David Cowart, "The Luddite Vision," for a discussion of "lines" in *Mason & Dixon*. Samuel Cohen argues in "*Mason & Dixon* and the Ampersand" that the title's ampersand implies

a less pessimistic view of history, with less inevitability and a greater possibility for change than Pynchon's earlier work suggests.

7. See Casey Shoop, "Thomas Pynchon, Postmodernism, and the Rise of the New Right in California," for a discussion of *The Crying of Lot 49* in relation to what he calls the "Californianization of American politics and culture" (60). Also, in his recent dissertation, "A Thomas Pynchon Guide to Contemporary Resistance," Sean Carswell argues that Pynchon's last four novels, *Vineland*, *Mason & Dixon*, *Against the Day*, and *Inherent Vice*, articulate "neoliberal capitalism's exploitive system of privatization, deregulation, militarization, and free market fundamentalism" (4).
8. See Patricia Bergh's essay "(De)constructing the Image: Pynchon's Postmodern Woman" for a different discussion of Frenesi's character.
9. I have discussed this element in Pynchon's work in "Science, Narrative, and Agency in *Gravity's Rainbow*."
10. The Vinland of Nordic legend is also referenced in *Mason & Dixon*, where it is characterized as a peaceful settlement that ended in strife and eventual self-destruction.
11. See McCulloch for a discussion of the "Vinland map."
12. See Alan Wilde, "Love and Death."

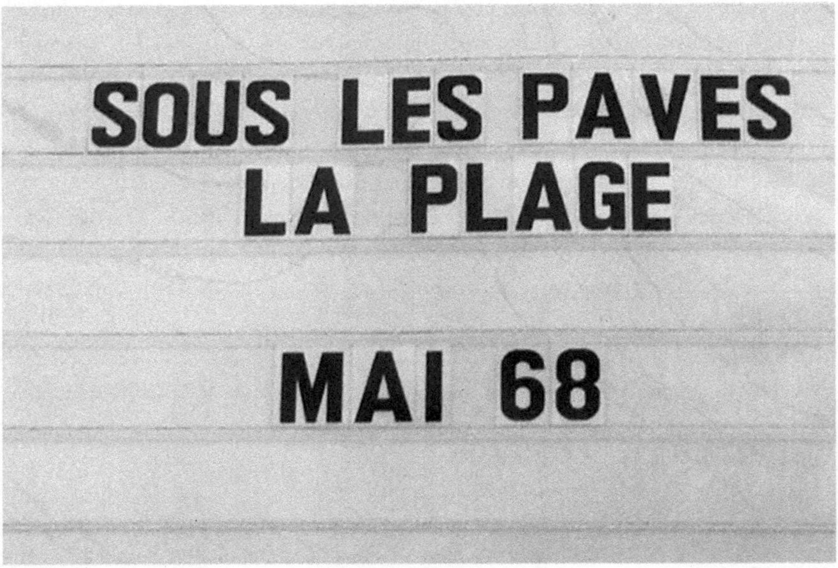

1. Sign: National Avenue, Venice, California, 2012. Photo by Hanjo Berressem.

Life on the Beach. The Natural Elements in Thomas Pynchon's California Trilogy

HANJO BERRESSEM

Constructing California

The range of Pynchon's imagination is equaled only, perhaps, by the geographical range of his narratives, which reach from the County of Durham in England to Sarajevo and from Venice to Kirghizia. In Pynchon's oeuvre, however, decidedly global novels invariably alternate—except in the case of *Mason & Dixon* and *Against the Day*, where two massively global novels follow each other—with novels that are set in California: *The Crying of Lot 49*, *Vineland*, and *Inherent Vice*.

In each of the novels of what has been called Pynchon's California Trilogy, Pynchon constructs a different California. This is hardly surprising, as they not only cover about 20 years in terms of diegetic time but also a 43-year time span in terms of publication. In fact, each novel represents a different phase of Pynchon's work.[1] The California of *The Crying of Lot 49*, which represents early Pynchon, is constructed predominantly from within cultural, historical, political, and technological parameters. It consists mostly of the urban landscapes of Los Angeles and the fictional town of San Narciso, which Pynchon assembled from set pieces such as used car lots, motels, highways, bars, "auto lots, escrow services, drive-ins, small office buildings and factories" (14). At the same time, the novel provides a survey of complex cybernetic landscapes that are made up of all kinds of communication channels and devices, such as networks of secret mail systems, tangled telephone lines, and highways that mainline human traffic into the cities. Although *Vineland* returns to urban Los Angeles in some of its flashbacks, it is set for the most part in Humboldt

County, the rural hinterland of Northern California, where the counterculture has retreated after the death—or should one say the assassination?—of the spirit of the 1960s revolution. *Inherent Vice* is also set in the Southland, which is also Zoyd Wheeler's home. This time, however, the setting is not only the urban flatland but also the beach, in particular Gordita Beach, Pynchon's thinly disguised fictional version of the area around Los Angeles's Manhattan and Redondo Beaches.

The Elements Natural Media

Although Pynchon is justly famous for his obsession with all forms of technological and informational media—from Maxwell's Demon in *The Crying of Lot 49* to the tubescapes of *Vineland* and from *Mason & Dixon*'s "Jesuit Telegraph" (287) and "Torpedo" (426) to the Tesla machines and the moving photographs in *Against the Day*[2]—this often-addressed aspect of his work has tended to obscure his deep investment in America as a continent made up of the natural elements: earth, water, air, and fire. In fact, although Pynchon's Californias are filled with all kinds of man-made informational and technological landscapes, over time, Pynchon's work has increasingly highlighted that these are immanent *in* and emerge *from* a more *elemental* natural landscape.

In this stress on the natural elements, Pynchon's California trilogy is reminiscent of the work of Mike Davis, who has used the four elements as a structural device in *Ecology of Fear: Los Angeles and the Imagination of Disaster*. As Davis argues, in California, the natural elements form a catastrophic ecology that needs disasters—nonequilibrium elemental events—such as earthquakes, floods, storms, and fires, in order to function properly.[3] From the position of human settlement, it is as if some kind of inherent vice was built into the California ecosystem. For the settlers, California is both dream and nightmare. While it would have been possible to accept California's catastrophic ecosystem and find ways to live *with* and *within* it, the history of California settlement is filled with attempts to subject this ecology to a relentlessly operational and often agonistic logic. Rather than implementing what Félix Guattari has called a gentle "ecosophy" (*Chaosmosis* 91)[4] that acknowledges the eigenvalues of the California milieu, the objective has invariably been to completely control and contain California's wild and excessive ecology, to commodify it by turning it into an engineered site.

Pynchon, like Davis, is deeply concerned about the violence with which the colonizers have, in their dream of total commodification, obliterated California's original ecosystems. Both, however, put some apocalyptic hope in the ability of nature to strike back. As Sortilège notes in *Inherent Vice*, "They're destroying the planet. . . . The good news is that like any living creature, Earth has an immune system too, and sooner or later she's going to start rejecting agents of disease like the oil industry. And hopefully before we end up like Atlantis and Lemuria" (105).

Although their critiques are written in different modes, both Davis and Pynchon treat the natural elements as what one might call *formational* media, a notion that differs from the default definition of media as man-made technological devices that deal with the assembly and transfer of *information*, such as the telephone or the computer. Although Pynchon is very aware of this default definition of media—in fact, much of his early work, such as *The Crying of Lot 49*, centers around this notion—in his later work he increasingly relies on the definition of media that is used in the natural sciences, a use he is equally familiar with. In terms of the development of his poetics, this shift from *informational* to *formational* media is part of a shift from technological paranoia to ecological awareness, and from the destruction of order into Brownian motion to the emergence of order from chaos.

There are basically two contexts in which the natural sciences use the notion of "medium." In the first, it designates a habitat or an environment, such as water for fish, air for humans, or a nutrient solution in a petri dish for bacteria. Pynchon often refers to this use, as when, in *Inherent Vice*, he calls acid "the medium" that Vehi "swam and occasionally surfed in" (105), or when, in the same novel, fear "spreads like blood in a swimming pool, till it occupies all the volume of the day" (208). In this comparison, "water" and "the day" function as the media within which blood and fear spread out.[5]

In the second context in which the natural sciences use the term, it refers to the structure of these environments, which are treated as a multitude of small, simple, loosely coupled substances from which larger, complex, and more strictly coupled objects are assembled.[6] These elements are the atomic or molecular building blocks of the material as well as the immaterial world, and much of science involves learning about their specific assemblage theories.

The history of the notion of the four elements as environments goes back to the Pre-Socratic Philosophy of Nature developed by philosophers such as Heraclitus and Empedocles and taken up by Plato and Aristotle, who added "aether" to the group as the fifth element. Although today's science has advanced to much finer and more differentiated layers of media, such as the chemical elements collected in the periodic table and the elementary particles identified by physics, the classical elements are still important reference points. One reason for this is that they are correlated with the four states of matter: solid, liquid, gas, and plasma.[7] A second reason why media ecologies are still read from within the structural framework provided by the natural elements is that they have, through history, accrued a set of complex connotations—the divinatory tarot, for instance, relates the suits of cups, swords, batons, and discs to the four natural elements. This, of course, makes them perfect vehicles for Pynchon's thought, which tends to move freely between mythological, esoteric, literary, and scientific registers.

While it is useful to categorically distinguish between the notion of ecological and technological media, it is, practically, impossible to strictly separate the levels of *formation* and *information*, because every material object is pervaded by immaterial information. In the terminology of Gilles Deleuze, "Every actual surrounds itself with a cloud of virtual images" ("The Actual and the Virtual" 148). In *Inherent Vice*, Doc Sportello feels the precariousness of the alignment of these separate categories when, during one of his acid trips, what he has always thought of as himself splits up into a material and an immaterial version; into "Visible Doc, which was approximately his body, and Invisible Doc, which was his mind" (318). Doc realizes that a similarly precarious alignment defines the relation between real and imagined environments when he remembers one of his college teachers telling him that "the word is not the thing, the map is not the territory" (194).[8] In both cases, Doc realizes that a pragmatic unity is based on a categorical disjunction.

There are a number of reasons why it makes sense to align Pynchon and Deleuze. An obvious one is that his books *Anti-Oedipus* and *A Thousand Pla-*

teaus, which he coauthored with Félix Guattari, are highly important texts for the 1960s revolution. From all of French theory, in fact, only Deleuze and Guattari have made it into Pynchon's work by way of the infamous "*Italian Wedding Fake Book*, by Deleuze & Guattari" mentioned in *Vineland* (97). In fact, there is a strong resonance and sympathy—in the sense of Goethe's elective affinity (*Wahlverwandtschaft*)—between their respective work, which pertains to their common belief that the world is a complex ecosystem that is in danger of being destroyed by what Pynchon calls forces of "command and control" (*Inherent Vice* 265) and a similar belief in the importance of considering nonhuman agents—what Pynchon sometimes refers to as living "critters" (*Inherent Vice* 165)—operative in this ecosystem as living, sentient operators. In fact, both Pynchon and Deleuze consider the material phylum as being everywhere suffused with nonhuman perception and nonhuman thought.[9] Evoking a plane of anonymous atomic perception, Deleuze assumes quite programmatically that "an atom, for example, perceives infinitely more than we do and, at the limit perceives the whole universe" (*Cinema 1* 63–64). According to Deleuze, in fact, "if life implies a soul, it is because proteins already attest to an activity of perception, discrimination, and distinction" (*Fold* 92). Pynchon shares with Deleuze the belief that the universe is everywhere "ensouled" (Emerson, 184).[10] As he notes in *Gravity's Rainbow*, "it's hard to get over the wonder of finding that Earth is a living critter, after all these years of thinking about a big dumb rock to find a body and psyche. . . . To find that Gravity, taken so for granted, is really something eerie, Messianic, extrasensory in Earth's mindbody" (590).

Not only are all material objects aggregates—or, as Deleuze would say, "assemblages"—of smaller, interrelated material particles such as atoms or molecules, thoughts are similarly complicated assemblages of smaller, more elementary, and nonhuman thoughts. If the material world is made up of an infinity of unthinkably small, imperceptible material elements, the world of thought is made up of an infinity of unthinkably small, unconscious thoughts that form assemblages that, once they have crossed a specific threshold, look and feel like individual, conscious, solid perceptions and thoughts, in the same way that objects, looked at from a specific perceptual threshold, look like coherent, solid objects.

As each seemingly loosely coupled medium is itself formed on a smaller level, both the material and the immaterial worlds follow a logic of infinite regress, a fact that still drives scientific research into (presumably) the smallest unformed elements. While sand, for instance, is a loosely coupled medium in relation to bricks, bricks are in turn a loosely coupled medium, whose elements can be assembled into houses. Sand can be formed into bricks, but it can also, to return the discussion to Pynchon's California, remain more loosely coupled, as in the desert or on a beach. Structurally, however, bricks are only larger versions of singular grains of sand and houses only larger versions of bricks, in the same way that cities are only larger versions of single houses. In other words, loosely and strictly coupled elements are recursively stacked into one another according to a logic of infinite regress.[11]

The world, then, consists of infinitely complex material and immaterial assemblages. From within different modes of thought, such as science, art, and philosophy, humans construct patterns from this given complexity. From the California trilogy, *The Crying of Lot 49* deals most obviously with the logic of pattern recognition and of pattern construction, the persistent question for Oedipa being whether "a pattern was beginning to emerge" (64) or whether she is making it all up. Is there a relation between her thought and the world, or is she just projecting herself into and imposing herself onto that world? Ultimately, Oedipa's cybernetic challenge is to bring the two different sets or categories together by way of an expressive relationship between not only the world and thought but between herself and the environment to which she is immanent.

Earth — Solid

The conceptual basis of Pynchon's politics of the elements, and a common denominator in all of Pynchon's novels, is that they celebrate the free play of the elements as a natural milieu into which humans—who are, although they are like all other living beings fully part of this milieu, from all living beings the most violently separated from it in terms of perceptual and cognitive operations—can fold themselves, while Pynchon considers the relentless operationalization and organization of the elements into stabilized, simplified, and hierarchical systems as acts of colonization that are performed by human agencies of command and control. In early, more paranoid Pynchon, these invisible systems were called *They* or *Them*.

One of the topics through which Pynchon negotiates these colonizations is real estate, which is arguably the most persistent leitmotif in the California trilogy; from Oedipa Maas's quest in *The Crying of Lot 49* to find out what precisely "California real estate mogul" (1) Pierce Inverarity owns and what he has taken from the disinherited, to the hippies in *Vineland*, who have betrayed their dream of a more communal America to the protofascist establishment of the 1980s, and further, to the ominous owners of what Davis has called "Fortress L.A." (*City* 221) in *Inherent Vice*. As Denis wonders, from within the haze of illegal substances that surrounds him, "Anybody understand why they call it 'real' estate?" (Pynchon, *Inherent Vice* 297).

In very general terms, the creation of real estate can be defined as the—mostly violent—conversion of a free, anonymous, and communal landscape into parcels of private property. Pynchon finds the origins of real estate in the human desire for mastery over the earth, such as in Pierce Inverarity's "need to possess, to alter the land" (*Crying* 134).[12] Finding this desire sanctioned in the Bible's admonishment not only to "be fruitful, and multiply, and replenish the earth" but also to "subdue it" (Genesis 1:28), the European settlers parceled off the virgin, undifferentiated American continent into separate lots, which then formed the basic units for a relentlessly rational, gridded logic of real estate and commerce: Puritanism 101. Through the figure of Pierce Inverarity, the founding father whose legacy is a tangle of possessions too complex to assemble into a coherent pattern, *The Crying of Lot 49* traces the history of real estate back to the beginnings of the European settlement. In the novel, Pynchon treats the tangled history of the regimes who have determined the possession of real estate and information through an analogous tangle of narratives that involve technology, paranoid politics, and informational networks. In *Vineland*, Pynchon organizes the story less according to specific cultural and technological agencies than according to characters, with Prairie as an elaborately drawn allegorical figure of the young, free country and its colonization. Whereas *The Crying of Lot 49* ended in a tangled loop, at the end of *Vineland*, Prairie seems to be as immune to Brock Vond as she is to the malls of America.[13] It seems that in *Vineland*, Pynchon puts his hope in the next generation. Prairie and her friend Ché—the allusions are obvious—are subversive "mall rats" (325), as if the prairie were, like the desert, to sweep through the strictly coupled architecture of profit.[14]

Inherent Vice, which revolves around the "long, sad history of L.A. land use" (17), returns to *The Crying of Lot 49* in that real estate is once more the topic of a case the protagonist needs to solve, although this time Pynchon uses the genre of the detective novel rather than that of the anti-detective novel. His point, however, is the same: a league of old money will do anything to control the distribution of wealth and real estate. Symptomatically, there is a thriving market for vintage barbed wire in the novel. Bigfoot Bjornsen, for instance, is a barbed wire aficionado and collector.

In *Inherent Vice*, Larry "Doc" Sportello's direct connection to the world of real estate is his Aunt Reet, who, although she is herself a real estate agent, does not have a very high opinion of most of the developers, some of whom, as she tells Doc, "make Godzilla look like a conservationist" (7). One of these is "the real-estate big shot" (4), "land developer" (239) and "construction mogul" (237) Michael Z. "Mickey" Wolfmann, whose project Channel View Estates she calls the "latest assault on the environment" (8). The structural and conceptual heart of the novel is Wolfmann's unexpected idea to give back to the people in a kind of reverse real estate: "All the money he ever made—he was working on a way to just give it back. . . . 'I wish I could undo what I did, I know I can't, but I bet I can make the money start to flow a different direction" (150). The most tangible result of his inexplicable change of heart is his project "Arrepentimiento" (62), "a whole city from scratch . . . in the desert" (240) that would provide rent-free housing and, as such, return some of the country to the people.[15] Wolfmann's change of heart is the reason why the mysterious Golden Fang abduct him and bring him to Chryskylodon, where he is reprogrammed back into the system. When, in one of Doc's drug-induced dreams, the Golden Fang appears to Doc—looking a lot like Voldemort and commenting on the more deadly intervention concerning Dr. Rudy Blatnoyd—it in fact calls itself "the unthinkable vengeance they turn to when one of them has grown insupportably troublesome" (318).

In *Inherent Vice*, Crocker Fenway, who must be imagined as playing in the same league as the elusive Pierce Inverarity in *The Crying of Lot 49*, is the most visible representative of the Golden Fang and the novel's dark villain.[16] Symptomatically, he lives in a gated community squared: "The Fenways were heavy-duty South Bay money, living on the Palos Verdes Peninsula in a gated enclave located *inside* the *already* gated high-rent community of Rolling Hills" (171). Fenway is a member of a (s)elect group of people who concentrate power beyond the more visible layers of command and control and who operate on "another level of power altogether" (301). In a short-circuiting of ethical and real estate registers, Pynchon notes that the members of this group "seemed to feel *entitled* to fuck with the lives of all who weren't as good or bright as they were, which meant everybody" (301, emphasis added). Tracing themselves back to the first explorers, these founding fathers have a sense of entitlement that goes even beyond the sinister machinations of the caste of real estate agents. As Fenway notes, "Real estate, water rights, oil, cheap labor—all of that's ours, it's always been ours" (347). Having twisted the religious idea(l) of the city upon the hill into the utterly profane project of "suburban consensus" (349), they now use, quite cynically, the language of ecology to implement their vision of cultural cleanliness. As Fenway notes, it is "residential owners like me against developers like Brother Wolfmann. People with a decent respect for preserving the environment against high-density tenement scum without the first idea of how to clean up after themselves" (347).

As he did in *The Crying of Lot 49*, in *Inherent Vice*, Pynchon traces the history of the possessors back to the beginning of the exploration and colonization of America. At the end of the novel, Doc sees, in Crocker Fenway's club Portola, a painting of the first expedition to California. Doc's description of the painting is reminiscent of the ending of F. Scott Fitzgerald's *The Great Gatsby* in terms of the wonder the American landscape evokes. In fact, it is the West Coast version of Fitzgerald's East Coast astonishment and promise: "On the face of one of them—maybe Portola himself? There was an expression of wonder, like, What's this, what unsuspected paradise? Did God with his finger trace out and bless this perfect little valley, intending it only for us?" (343–44).

Against the elect owners stands a multitude of preterites:

> this swarm of transients who come and go without pause here in the sunny Southland, eager to be bought off with a car of a certain make, model, and year, a blonde in a bikini, thirty seconds on some excuse for a wave. . . . We will never run out of you people. The supply is inexhaustible. (*Inherent Vice* 347)

At the end of the novel, Fenway remains convinced that, with the help of lower orders such as the police or groups like Vigilant California, Fortress America will survive the persistent flood of these multitudes: "We've been laid siege to by far worse, and we're still here" (347).

Water | Fluid

While real estate strictly couples the element of earth, creating everywhere what Deleuze and Guattari call a "striated space"—as Davis notes, "after the Santa Clara River Valley dies, there is only desert to feed the developers' insatiable hunger" (*Ecology of Fear* 91)—there are also forces of dissolution that transfer striated into smooth space and that threaten to turn the organized city into "the desert of the body without organs" (*Anti-Oedipus* 144), into "the deterritorialized socius, the desert at the gates of the city" (112).[17] Already in *V.*, "the city is only the desert . . . in disguise" (71). Similarly, as the narrator of *Inherent Vice* notes about the Channel View Estates, "the development stretched into the haze and the soft smell of the fog component of smog, and of desert beneath the pavement" (20). In fact, urban California, as a landscape of strictly coupled lots of real estate, dissolves, geographically, on two of its sides into loosely coupled media: the desert in the east and the Pacific Ocean in the west. The narrator notes the influence of these dissolved media on the milieu of Santa Monica, "where the wind can blow two directions at once, bringing in fog from the ocean and sand from the desert at the same time," (50).

Of these two dissolved media, which function as elemental extremes in Pynchon's Californian poetics and politics, the Pacific Ocean is the most dissolved.[18] At the same time, the "regular beat of the surf" (329) is the underlying heartbeat not only of the city but of the planet in general and the "sound of the surf" (327) a guide for navigating the city. Already on the opening page of *Inherent Vice*, Doc Sportello and Shasta Fay Hepworth stand "in the streetlight through the kitchen window . . . and listened . . . to the thumping of the surf from down the hill. Some nights, when the wind was right, you could hear the surf all over town" (1).

Often, Pynchon describes the ocean in darkly poetic terms. In *The Crying of Lot 49*, for instance, it is "the primal blood" (122) of the planet, and in *Vineland*, it is described as "the darkening Pacific in pale-topped crawl" (22). Staked against the differentiations and patterns of both the earth and the cultural realm with its various strategies of subjectivation and striation, its fluid, smooth expanse heralds a general dissolution that is both attractive and repulsive. In *The Crying of Lot 49*, Driblette, whose name is obviously programmatic, drowns himself in its undifferentiated milieu, not without telling Oedipa from within the foggy steam of a shower, "If I were to dissolve in here, . . . be washed down the drain into the Pacific, what you saw tonight would vanish too" (56). Before Driblette's dissolution, Oedipa had already, in a long, dense passage, imagined the Pacific as a medium of redemption, in which strict differentiations and particular couplings are turned into wave patterns and complete dissolution:

> Somewhere beyond the battening, urged sweep of three-bedroom houses rushing by their thousands across all the dark beige hills, somehow implicit in an arrogance or bite to the smog the more inland somnolence of San Narciso did lack, lurked the sea, the unimaginable Pacific, the one to which all surfers, beach pads, sewage disposal schemes, tourist incursions, sunned homosexuality, chartered fishing are irrelevant, the hole left by the moon's tearing-free and monument to her exile; you could not hear or even smell this but it was there, something tidal began to reach feelers in past eyes and eardrums, perhaps to arouse fractions of brain current your most gossamer microelectrode is yet too gross for finding. Oedipa had believed . . . in some principle of the sea as redemption for Southern California . . . some unvoiced idea that no matter what you did to its edges the true Pacific stayed inviolate and integrated or assumed the ugliness at any edge into some more general truth. (*Crying* 36–37)

One of the many Californian ways of operationalizing the element of water is to channel it. In *Ecology of Fear*, Davis states Frederick Law Olmsted, Jr., and Harlan Bartholomew's belief that in terms of the Los Angeles River, "flood control could be accomplished by different combinations of landuse planning and public works. Their preference was to strictly limit private encroachment within the 50-year floodplain." This gentle vision was set against the hard solution that was implemented:

> to deepen and "armor"—that is, pave—a narrow width of the river's channel . . . and thus allow extensive industrial development within the floodplain. Beneficial to large landowners, this strategy would force the natural river into a concrete straightjacket—destroying the riparian ecology and precluding use of the riverway as a greenbelt. (*Ecology of Fear* 69)

In *Inherent Vice*, Pynchon, like Davis, traces the operationalization of the Los Angeles River back to the politics of real estate, evoking the apocalyptic vision of a Los Angeles deluge:

> the old namesake river that had once run through this town, long canalized and tapped dry, and crippled into a public and anonymous confession of the deadly sin of greed. . . . He imagined it filling up again to its concrete rim, and then over, all the water that had not been allowed to flow here for all these years now in unrelenting return, soon beginning to occupy the arroyos and cover the flats, all the swimming pools in the backyards filling up and overflowing and flooding the lots and the streets, all this karmic waterscape connecting together, as the rain went on falling and the land vanished, into a sizable inland sea that would presently become an extension of the Pacific. (166)[19]

What is especially striking in this vision are the flooded swimming pools. As integral parts of the Los Angeles cityscape, they are the opposite of the communal beaches. Not only are they intimately related to the logic of real estate and thus of greed, they also stand, like the Los Angeles River, for a striation, operationalization, and territorialization of water. Often, swimming pools are strictly rectangular, but even when the pools simulate lakes with their natural curves, the water is completely engineered. In order to work properly, it is filled with any number of purifying chemicals, it is often artificially heated, and it needs to be cleaned at regular intervals. When the ocean flows in, this does not only imply the end of real estate but also allows the caged water in the pools to dissolve in the salty water of the ocean and to become part of the ocean's powerful natural dynamics.

Air Gas

In Davis's typology of California disasters, the disaster that correlates to the element of the earth is the earthquake, that of the element of water the flood, and that of the element of air the storm, like the one that provides the background atmosphere to Frenesi and Brock's final tryst in *Vineland*[20] or the one that, in *Inherent Vice*, accompanies the apocalyptic vision of the unleashed Los Angeles River.

However, air, in the California trilogy, or in more general terms, the atmosphere, is not only important in its disastrous forms. Rather, Pynchon describes it as a forever-changing meteorological phenomenon that shifts from the pollutive Los Angeles smog to the desert's starkly azure skies. As he does with the ocean, Pynchon often links the natural atmosphere directly to the cultural atmosphere, as in *The Crying of Lot 49*, in which San Narciso is described as

> an incident among our climatic records of dreams and what dreams became among our accumulated daylight, a moment's squall-line or tornado's touchdown among the higher, more continental solemnities—storm-systems of group suffering and need, prevailing winds of affluence. (133–34)

In the California trilogy, especially in *Vineland* and *Inherent Vice*, the most intriguing atmospheric phenomenon is the fog, which combines the elements of air and of water. The most important characteristic of Pynchon's fog is that it suspends everybody in a milky medium in which perception is impossible, because light diffracts into an undistinguished whiteness. In this sense, the fog, like the undifferentiated expanse of the ocean, promises dissolution. Sometimes this dissolution is, like Driblette's, suicidal, as in *Vineland*'s motorhead valley roulette, where the idea is "to enter the pale wall at a speed meaningfully over the limit, to bet that the white passage held no other vehicles, no curves, no construction, only smooth, level, empty roadway to an indefinite distance—a motorhead variation on a surfer's dream" (37). In *Inherent Vice*, Doc remembers similarly daring and dangerous moments of "doing a hundred in the fog" when trying to escape "smack dealers on the Pasadena Freeway" (3). Despite their differences—surfing takes place in nature, while driving into the fog is related to technology and the car industry—there is a deep connection between giving oneself over to the fog while driving and giving oneself over to waves when surfing:

> both subcultures, whether up on a board or behind a 409, shared the terrors and ecstasies of the passive, taken rider, as if a car engine held encapsulated something likewise oceanic and mighty—a technowave, belonging to distant others as surf belonged to the sea, bought into by the riders strictly as-is, on the other party's terms. Surfers rode God's ocean, beer riders rode the momentum through the years of the auto industry's will. (*Vineland* 37)

While the fog opens up the notion of complete dissolution, Pynchon also uses it as a medium that calls for the creation of an ad hoc and temporary community. Its "desert of perception" (*Inherent Vice* 368) comes to stand for a world without transcendental overview, in which the only mode of survival is working together from within the horizon of a shared ignorance. At the end of *Inherent Vice*, when Doc drives on the freeway, "his headlight beams, like eyestalks of an extraterrestrial, aimed into the hushed whiteness ahead" (367), the cars form a loosely coupled automotive caravan in which single elements bond temporarily into a pragmatic car community that provides some form of orientation, comfort, and security.

As in *Vineland*, in which Zoyd is looking for a revelation of a realm beyond the real, although "the fog now began to lift to reveal not the borderlands of the eternal after all, but only quotidian California again, looking no different than it had when he left" (94), Doc wants the fog to lift, as if it were a veil behind which a transcendental *something* might appear. At the end of *Inherent Vice*, this desire for a revelation is still as strong as it was in *The Crying of Lot 49*. In the background of Doc's experience is still Pynchon's leitmotif of an impending, although forever denied, revelation. As the final sentence notes, Doc waits "for the fog to burn away, and for something else this time, somehow, to be there instead" (369).

Fire Plasma

In California, fire is, first of all, related to wildfires—as Davis notes, Malibu is "the wildfire capital of North America and, possibly, the world" (*Ecology* 97)—and to droughts. Although these are generally perceived by humans as disastrous, they are, in terms of the California landscape, not really destructive. As Davis explains, they are necessary within the California ecosystem, where they have a literally purifying effect. This, in fact, allows them to be read as agents of spiritual purification as well.

In the correlation between the ancient elements and the modern states of matter, fire is related to plasma, actualizations of which are the gas of a flame and also the sun, which is to a large degree made up of plasma. As Wikipedia notes, not without some irony, plasmas are found "in stars and neon signs." Plasma, therefore, is directly related to sunlight, as one of the most directly Californian media. Although light is important in all of Pynchon's novels—from the white burst of the Kirghiz Light in *Gravity's Rainbow* to the phenomenon of double refraction that defines the poetics of *Against the Day*—it is especially important in the California trilogy. As Roswell Bounce notes in *Against the Day*, "I want to know light. . . . I want to reach inside light and find its heart, touch its soul, take some in my hands whatever it turns out to be. . . . I'm heading for California. . . . It's where the future of light is, in particular the moving pictures" (456). California evokes burning sunsets and voluminous magic hours that cover everything with a warm, red sheen that makes the air almost palpably thick and dense. In fact, California might be said to be made up, to a large degree, of its site-specific light, and it is indicative of the intensity of its light that the Light and Space movement in the visual arts developed and thrived mainly in California. As one can speak of moving as if under water, in fact, one might, in California, speak of moving as if under light.

In some ways, one might in fact read Pynchon's prose as a literary version of the Light and Space movement. *Inherent Vice* is especially suffused with descriptions of light and skyscapes, as when Pynchon describes "a sky like watered milk, and the white bombardment of a sun smogged into only a smear of probability" (19). Often, these skyscapes provide meteorological diagrams that relate, once more, material and immaterial milieus, as in "the dawn weirdness, which seemed like a visible counterpart to the feeling in everybody's skin of desert winds and heat and relentlessness, with the exhaust from millions of motor vehicles mixing with microfine Mojave sand to refract the light toward the bloody end of the spectrum, everything dim, lurid and biblical, sailor-take-warning skies" (*Inherent Vice* 98).

In fact, the novel, which features "smoglight" (162); "mercury-vapor light" (334); "smeared oceanlight" (358); buildings "constructed of night itself" (179); magical, "spectacular desert sunset[s]" (221); a "late light off the ocean [that] came through crevices in the drapes" (327); and a "light over all deep L.A. softening to purple with some darker gold to it" (182), sets up a complete typology of light.[21] First, there is cinema light—such as "a cloudless sky, in the sort of perfect daylight you always saw on TV cop shows" (164), with the image of John Garfield "dead in the gutter, though of course beautifully lit" (254)—in the sense that the cinema is literally created from light as its true medium. As David Lynch notes, the light of Los Angeles is "different from the light in other places" (32). It is a light that "is inspiring and energizing. Even with smog, there's something about that light that's not harsh, but bright and smooth" (31). In fact, "it was the light that brought everybody to L.A. to make films in the early days" (32). As Dennis Hopper is said to have commented about the filming of *Easy Rider*, "God is a great gaffer."

In *Vineland's* documentary passages about 24fps, such a cinematic light had been the medium that allowed the cinema to record reality. In fact, the members of 24fps felt that all is well as "long as we have the light" (202). Symptomatically, the killing of Atman, which is the novel's most traumatic moment, happens when, as Pynchon notes with inherent irony, "Frenesi *killed* the light" (247, emphasis added). In this context, light functions metaphorically as a philosophical medium. Ultimately, the loss of light heralds the loss of life: "the highlights on each of Hector's eyeballs had vanished, the shine faded to matte surfaces that were now absorbing all light that fell on them" (302). Throughout, Pynchon sets up a complicated and often paradoxical ethical chiaroscuro: "If Frenesi's realm was light, DL's was the dark" (250).

Although in the passage above darkness is more positive than light, in general, light is a positive medium in Pynchon's work, which presents a number of connoisseurs of the play of light. Both Dahlia's father Merle Rideout, in *Against the Day*, and Hub Gates, Sasha Traverse's husband in *Vineland*, who owns "Lux Unlimited" (370), are true aficionados of light. As Traverse notes, "Jesus, all those amps. All that light. Nobody told me about the scale of it. After a while I couldn't see that much else. I needed to work with that light" (*Vineland* 291). In another very dense passage, Pynchon brings together cinematic and ambient light:

> fields and hills in metallic cloudlight toward the end of the day, aware of exactly how many hours and minutes to dark, how many foot-candles left in the sky, bringing behind him like ducklings a line of amps, generators, and beam projectors each on its little trailer rig, . . . wanting nothing but the deadly amps transmogrified to light, the great white-hot death-cold spill and flood and thrust. (*Vineland* 370)

Mostly a magic movie light is set against an ambient, real light that "wasn't protecting [Doc], not the way it will sometimes protect the actors in a movie" (*Inherent Vice* 142), such as "the desert light of the street" (209), or an artificial, electric light, such as Las Vegas's "unremitting storm of light" (235), which creates an "incandescent" (274), artificial "glow in the sky" (235), and against the "cathode-ray" (274) light of the TV, "tubelight" (120).

Many situations, in fact, emerge from within specific milieus of light. Sometimes there is only the harsh light of "the day's empty sky" (*Inherent Vice* 310), but at other times, the light is "weird" (165), as when

> Heated downtown smoglight filtered in from the window behind him, light that could not have sprung from any steady or pure scheme of daybreak, more appropriate to ends or conditions settled for, too often after only token negotiation. It would be hard to read anybody, let alone Adrian Prussia, in light like this. (316)

In other moments, the light becomes darkly ominous. When, toward the end of *Inherent Vice*, the ship *Golden Fang* (89)—formerly *Preserved* (92)—is almost sucked into "Death's Doorsill" (358), this happens in "the last of the skyglow" (330), when "the sun was just down, a sinister glow fading out above the edge of the world" (329). With the change of atmosphere, in fact, "something was also happening to the light, as if the air ahead of them were thickening with unknown weather" (357).[22]

Light, however, is more than a meteorological correlative. Sometimes, it is a medium that allows for glimpses into alternate realities. When, in *Vineland*, Takeshi and DL look out of a window and see everything appearing closer than usual, one of them, probably Takeshi, notes that "'it's a trick—of the morning light!'" To which the narrator adds: "Had they continued to watch from here as the sun rose, they would have seen the town begin to change, the corners of things to rotate slowly, the shadows come in to flip some of the angles inside out as 'laws' of perspective were reestablished" (173). When the wind brings "fog from the ocean and sand from the desert," daylight is "dimmed, visibility reduced to half a block, and all colors, including those of traffic signals, [are] shifted radically elsewhere in the spectrum" (*Inherent Vice* 50). Sometimes things happen in a light that is not quite right for them—"but something about the light, as angles flattened out and the atmosphere thickened, wasn't right—glare, location, something" (*Vineland* 355)—and sometimes the light is completely dissociated from the milieu, as when "Frenesi and Brock had met in a clifftop suite, under a vaporous and subtropical light falling through high windows, un-Californian light, belonging someplace else where the water table was above the ground and reptiles slipped into the swimming pools at night" (239).

Light is not only revelatory—in *Vineland*, there is a "sudden light from behind, the unbearable sight in the mirror" (252), while in *Inherent Vice*, Wolfmann "sees the light, tries to change his life" (334)—it also heralds the possibility of a luminosity that allows one to catch and to register moments of human and nonhuman suffering. Looking at Shasta, for instance, Doc "could swear he saw light falling on her face, the orange light just after sunset that catches a face turned to the west, watching the ocean for someone to come in on the last wave of the day, in to shore and safety" (*Inherent Vice* 5).

Sometimes, in fact, light becomes sheer luminosity, as in Pynchon's description of Doc's "velvet painting," which showed

> a Southern California beach that never was—palms, bikini babes, surfboards, the works. He thought of it as a window to look out of when he couldn't deal with looking out of the traditional glass-type one in the other room. Sometimes in the shadows the view would light up, usually when he was smoking weed, as if the contrast knob of Creation had been messed with just enough to give everything an underglow, a luminous edge, and promise that the night was about to turn epic somehow. (*Inherent Vice* 6)

In fact, this depiction of a virtual California might be read as a description of the novel's poetics. In this luminosity, even seemingly antagonistic elements are dissolved, such as "the luminous blooms of surf and the lights of late commuter traffic" (*Inherent Vice* 5). In fact, there is always a silver lining to the cloud of California reality, as when "toward sunset, after some rain, the dark lid of clouds rolled back a few fingers' widths from the horizon, revealing a strip so clear and luminous that even homebound traffic out on the freeway was slowing down for it" (340).

Ultimately, Pynchon defines the 1960s by their very own luminosity, by a light that "seemed to be finding everybody else walking around in this regional dream of enlightenment" (*Inherent Vice* 207). In fact, Pynchon considers the "Psychedelic Sixties" as themselves being, quite literally, *made* from light; as a "little parenthesis of light [that] might close after all, and all be lost, taken back into darkness" (254).

The Beach

When *Inherent Vice* was published, it was often described as a book best read on the beach.[23] While most critics related this to the novel's surprisingly mellow and accessible style, there are more reasons why the beach is indeed the perfect place to read *Inherent Vice.* One of these is that in the elemental ecology that underlies the California trilogy, the beach is a privileged site. It is a *locus amoenus*, a liminal space where the elements—sand, ocean, air, and sun—form a particularly felicitous, free arrangement, although on some days, when the beach is "petroleum-scented" (341), the atmosphere can become literally crude. Generally, however, the beach is a body without organs that is not *organ*ized by powers of command and control and, as such, a true plane of immanence. As Deleuze and Guattari note in *A Thousand Plateaus*, "The body without organs is not a dead body but a living body all the more alive and teeming once it has blown apart the organism and its organization. Lice hopping on the beach. Skin colonies. The full body without organs is a body populated by multiplicities" (30). In fact, the original French title of Deleuze's article "Zones of Immanence" is "Les plages d'immanence."[24] The beach provides a space for free, undirected movements within a nonantagonistic ecology. Pynchon notes in particular "the social yoga positions defining life at the beach" (*Inherent Vice* 104) and the "respect for the natural environment" (104). As the utopia of a laid-back, relaxed, self-sustaining milieu, the beach is set against the concrete world of real estate. While Bjorn Bigfoot, Doc's nemesis and alter ego, always wanted "to get away from the beach" (137), both Doc and the text itself are continually drawn back to the beach, as if the beach exerted a literally material attraction.[25]

As a free, fragile space, the beach promises another, purely potential California that is already present in *The Crying of Lot 49* when Oedipa dreams "that Mucho, her husband, was making love to her on a soft white beach that was not part of any California she knew" (74). Toward the end of the novel, while Oedipa drifts through the San Francisco night, she is enveloped once more by its magical milieu: "Down at the city beach, long after the pizza stands and rides had closed, she walked unmolested through a drifting, dreamy cloud of delinquents in summer-weight gang jackets with the post horn stitched on in thread that looked pure silver in what moonlight there was" (89).

Already, in *Vineland*, Pynchon had described the "Casbah topography" (25) of Gordita Beach. In Pynchon's somewhat nostalgic advertisement video for *Inherent Vice*, Gordita Beach becomes something like what what Hakim Bey has called a "Temporary Autonomous Zone." As Pynchon notes in his voiceover to the video: "No, actually this *used* to be the beach. Later on all this is gonna be high rise, high rent, high intensity. But right now, back in 1970 what it is is just high." Symptomatically, the video highlights the topic of real estate, one of the most prominent images being a "no trespassing: private property" sign that evokes, of course, of the beginning of Orson Welles's *Citizen Kane.*

The beach is an inherently revolutionary site not only because it sets a smooth ecology of loosely coupled natural media against the city's striated, strictly coupled media; it is also the home of a counterculture politics and a counterculture lifestyle. In *The Crying of Lot 49*, it is "on the beach" that Oedipa has "met Jesús Arrabal" (88), and the slogan Pynchon uses as the epigraph in *Inherent Vice* ties the beach setting directly to the counterculture revolution: "under the paving stones, the beach!" The slogan not only links Pynchon's Los Angeles to Paris, it also provides another resonance between Pynchon and Deleuze: Deleuze is photographed on the beach at Big Sur, and the editors of a *Semiotext(e)* volume on Deleuze and Guattari's *Anti-Oedipus* use, as a subtitle to an image of a student throwing a stone, a reversal of the slogan: "beneath the beach, the paving stones."[26]

As McKenzie Wark notes in *The Beach beneath the Street: The Everyday Life and Glorious Times of the Situationist International* (2011), it was probably René Viénet of the Situationist movement "who wrote some of the more startling of the famous graffiti of May '68, including: 'Beneath the pavement, the beach'" (149–50).[27] Ironically, in Europe, where the streets were still paved in stones rather than in asphalt, the strictly coupled paving stones were often used as weapons during the student revolt, while in California there really *is*, unlike in Paris or Berlin, a beach there, which means that the utopia can be lived in California "right here, right now." In fact, in California there are not only beaches, there is also the desert, which promises a different America as well. When DL Chastain drives from the city to the desert in *Vineland*, she experiences this as a letting go and a slow decomposition into a much finer, loosely coupled medium:

> as she injected herself into the slow lane of the eastbound freeway and settled in, hating to let any of it go, Banning, the dinosaurs, the Palm Springs turnoff, Indio, across the Mojave, to be redreamed in colors pale but intense, with unnaturally fine sand blowing in plumes across the sun, baby-blue shadows in the folds of the dunes, a pinkish sky—holding on, letting

> go, redreaming each night stop the less easterly places she'd been in all day, coming slowly unstuck, leaving for the United States. (133)

Apart from being a politically revolutionary site, the beach is also the home of surfers, who look for the perfect wave in order to gracefully fold themselves into the dynamics of the ocean, in order to "become wave." Deleuze's reading of surfing is another indication of the elective affinity between Deleuze's and Pynchon's thought:

> We got by for a long time with an energetic conception of motion, where there's a point of contact, or we are the source of movement. Running, putting the shot, and so on: effort, resistance, with a starting point, a lever. But nowadays we see movement defined less and less in relation to a point of leverage. All the new sports—surfing, windsurfing, hang-gliding—take the form of an entering into an existing wave. There's no longer an origin as starting point, but a sort of putting into orbit. The key thing is how to get taken up in the motion of a big wave, a column of rising air, to "get into something" instead of being the origin of an effort. (*Negotiations*, 119)[28]

At the end of *Inherent Vice*, Pynchon stakes such a grace—in both its material and immaterial versions[29]—of the young, free life on the beach against the lumbering, graceless, adult forces of control by way of a quintessential Californian image: "Through Sauncho's old binoculars," Doc

> observed a CHP motorcycle cop chasing a longhaired kid along the beach, in and out of folks trying to catch some midday rays. The cop was in full motorcycle gear—boots, helmet, uniform—and carrying assorted weaponry, and the kid was barefoot and lightly dressed, and *in his element*. He fled like a gazelle, while the cop lumbered behind him, struggling through the sand. (355, emphasis added)

In all of its connotations, the young boy is indeed *in his element*, while the cop is not. As Deleuze and Guattari note in the last sentence of *A Thousand Plateaus*, however, "Never believe that a smooth space will suffice to save us" (500). Is it any wonder that for a number of years now, the most modern and the most imposing building on Venice Beach has been the police station?

Aether Spirit

To Aristotle, who added aether as the *quint*essential, fifth element to the group of natural elements, aether denoted the element from which the four other elements were created. Its main characteristic was that it animated lifeless things. Against this background, one might perhaps relate aether to the modern notion of energy or to the atmosphere's natural electricity (the earth's electromagnetic field). In more philosophical terms, one might relate it to the notion of a life force that pervades the universe or to the realms of the spiritual or the virtual. Originally meaning the higher, thinner air or the heavens, "aether" evokes both the blue sky and the force that pervades and animates the elements: California's genius loci. Aether also has a direct relation to light, in that the aether was, especially in the 19th century, considered to be the material medium for the propagation of light. It was literally "light-bearing," luminiferous. In fact, there is a long scientific debate about the relation between the aether and light, to which the famous Michelson-Morley experiment was an important contribution. In this context, Pynchon's use of the notion of light discussed above in the section on fire and plasma has a direct and intricate relation to the notion of aether. Actually, while the "plasmatic flame" might be said to stress the material aspect of light, the "aetherial spirit" throws into full contour its immaterial, spiritual side.

Probably even more than the beach as the most gossamer fluid that pervades both the physical and the psychic realms, aether partakes, like light, of the complementarity of material particles and immaterial waves. Although it is mainly *Against the Day* that is suffused with direct references to the aether, aether also suffuses the California trilogy as the "light-bearing," luminiferous spirit that suffuses the land, as California's karmic medium.[30] In *Inherent Vice*, this spirit pervades the elements in different ways. As the medium in which light travels, it is present in images such as that of "the light-stunned city" (33). From an esoteric point of view, from which aether is a spiritual fluidum, it concentrates in specifically spiritual spaces, such as California's Mount Shasta, whose spiritual force is, of course, refracted by Pynchon into the figure of Shasta Fay.

In the same way that Pynchon's poetics and politics favor loosely coupled elements over strictly coupled ones, they favor waves over particles. Even when he celebrates the material body—something to which, among other examples, the many and varied sexual encounters in his work attest—"good" encounters are always suffused by positive vibrations. Waves involve a logic and sense of communality, while particles imply an individuality that separates itself from the milieu. Often, drugs are the media that allow individuals to tune into the world's infinitely complex wave patterns—to align "sound, light, and brain-waves" (*Inherent Vice* 106), as with "the most intensely *light-bearing* complexities of some now half-forgotten acid trip" (136, my emphasis)—because they open the "doors of perception."[31] In fact, two of Pynchon's most persistent leitmotifs are waves and vibes: from a restaurant called "Wavos" (*Inherent Vice* 98) to the loving descriptions of ocean waves as "solar bluegreen, the true and unendurable color of daylight" (100). As always with Pynchon, there is a Manichean fight between bad and good vibes, such as the literally bad Vibes versus the good Traverses in *Against the Day.* In *Inherent Vice,* which is also filled with references to "vibes" (283), the bad vibes of the Golden Fang are set against the "positive vibrations" (284) and the mellow, "unlisted frequencies" (61) of life at the beach that were turned into music in such surf-music classics as the Beach Boys' "Good Vibrations."[32] Fittingly, the beginning of the song features a tannerin, an instrument that is a variation of the theremin, which was initially called the aetherophone. The theremin is the only instrument that produces sounds directly out of the aether, using the body's electric capacity to manipulate an electromagnetic field that functions as the medium for the production of the sound. Unlike the tannerin, which still works by way of material touch, the theremin operates completely by a gesturial manipulation of "the aether."

Always, Pynchon's utopia is of particles dissolving into waves, of the actual dissolving into the virtual: dissolutions into ocean waves, into waves of drifting fog, into the light waves that make up a magic hour, into the waves of the unconscious in dreams, into sound waves such as those of the Beach Boys' song "God Only Knows" that Doc Sportello plays on his car's Vibrasonic sound system in the closing section of *Inherent Vice*: all waves of an anonymous community and truly democratic multitude, of the parliament of living things.

At the same time, Pynchon knows that there is a complementarity to reality, Californian or otherwise. This complementarity, which also defines the photon, is expressed in the exquisitely ambiguous ending of *Inherent Vice*. Doc's intervention has brought about some form of "karmic adjustment" (14).[33] An atmosphere has been established in which even Doc's parents experiment with weed. As a karmic detective, Doc has created a small pocket of balance. For the shortest of moments, in a complicated standoff negotiated by Doc and Fenway, the good forces have been able to stand up against the bad ones. For the shortest of moments, the beach has prevailed against the urban and suburban machinations of the Golden Fang. In such privileged moments, one might hope that—despite America's horrible history—at some point, from the fog of today's realities, a California will rise in which life is indeed "a beach":

> there is no avoiding time, the sea of time, the sea of memory and forgetfulness, the years of promise, gone and unrecoverable, of the land almost allowed to claim its better destiny, only to have the claim jumped by evildoers known all too well, and taken instead and held hostage to the future we must live in now forever. May we trust that this blessed ship is bound for some better shore, some undrowned Lemuria, risen and redeemed, where the American fate, mercifully, failed to transpire. (*Inherent Vice* 341)[34]

NOTES

1. *The Crying of Lot 49*, published in 1965, set around 1965; *Vineland*, published in 1990, set in 1984; *Inherent Vice*, published in 2009, set in 1970.
2. "See, every photographic subject moves . . . even if it's standing still. It breathes, light bounces off, something. Snapping a photograph is like what the math professors call 'differentiating' an equation of motion—freezing that movement into the very small piece of time it takes the shutter to open and close. So we figured—if shooting a photo is like taking a first derivative, then maybe we could find some way to do the reverse of that, start with the still photo and *integrate* it, recover its complete primitive and release it back into action . . . even back to life" (*Inherent Vice* 136).
3. As Davis notes about California's inherently disastrous ecology, "The extreme events that shape the Southern California environment tend to be organized in surprising and powerfully coupled causal chains. Drought, for example, dries fuel for wildfires

which, in turn, remove ground cover and make soils impermeable to rain. This increases the risk of flooding in areas where earthquakes may have already exposed new surfaces to erosion and increased stream power by raising land elevation. In such conditions, storms are more likely to produce sheet flooding, landslides, and debris flows that result in dramatic erosion and landform change. . . . This is not random disorder, but a hugely complicated system of feedback loops that channels powerful pulses of climatic or tectonic energy (disasters) into environmental work" (*Ecology* 18–19).

4. In *Chaosmosis*, Guattari describes ecosophy as a "generalised ecology . . . as a science of ecosystems, as a bid for political regeneration, and as an ethical, aesthetic and analytic engagement. It will tend to create new systems of valorisation, a new taste for life, a new gentleness between the sexes, generations, ethnic groups, races" (91–92).
5. For drugs as "media of perception," see also Tom Wolfe's *The Electric Kool-Aid Acid Test*, as well as the work of Timothy Leary. On drugs and perception, see also Deleuze's article "Two Questions on Drugs."
6. For theories of material media, see the works of Humberto Maturana and Francisco Varela, Marshall McLuhan, and Niklas Luhmann.
7. On plasma, see Latour's *Reassembling the Social*, in which he defines plasma as "that which is not yet formatted, not yet measured, not yet socialized, not yet engaged in metrological chains, and not yet covered, surveyed, mobilized, or subjectified" (244); "a vast hinterland. . . , [like] the countryside for an urban dweller" (244).
8. This notion, which originated with Alfred Korzybski, has been taken up by, among others, Gregory Bateson, Jorge Luis Borges, and Jean Baudrillard.
9. See also Michel Serres and Bruno Latour on the importance of nonhuman agents in the assembly of reality.
10. See also Ralph Waldo Emerson: "The soul is wholly embodied, and the body is wholly ensouled" (184).
11. See also Pynchon's conceit of the transferral of a Japanese Zen garden to Chryskylodon, where "each grain of white sand, each textured rock" (*Inherent Vice* 189) of the original garden is recreated.
12. As in Nathaniel Hawthorne's works, there is a deep relation between family history and literary production in Pynchon, whose ancestors were deeply involved in real estate and property laws. For details on this involvement, see http://cl49.pynchonwiki.com/wiki/index.php?title=Chapter_1. In fact, a case might be made for Pynchon being a 20th-century American Hawthorne.
13. In *Inherent Vice*, Doc takes Denis, the überdoper, with him when he returns the drugs to the Golden Fang in the parking lot of the "May Company shopping mall" (348) as "a boost for his immunity against the shopping plazas of Southern California, for a desire not to desire, at least not what you found in shopping malls" (348).
14. Pynchon singles out the "Sherman Oaks Galleria" (*Vineland* 325).

15. "Spanish for 'sorry about that.' His idea was, anybody could go live there for free, didn't matter who you were, show up and if there's a unit open it's yours, overnight, forever, et cetera et cetera, and so forth as the King of Siam always sez" (*Inherent Vice* 248).
16. In all three novels of the California trilogy, the female protagonists sexually desire or have desired fascist agents of command and control: Oedipa Maas and Pierce Inverarity, Frenesi Gates and Brock Vond, Shasta Fay and Mickey Wolfmann. See also Lake Traverse and Deuce Kindred in *Against the Day*.
17. Deleuze relates the shift from city to desert to that from neurosis to schizophrenia. "The schizo carries along the decoded flows, makes them traverse the desert of the body without organs, where he installs his desiring-machines and produces a perpetual outflow of acting forces" (*Anti-Oedipus*, 131). As Deleuze notes about Flaubert's narrator, "He goes toward these new regions where the connections are always partial and nonpersonal, the conjunctions nomadic and polyvocal, the disjunctions included, where homosexuality and heterosexuality cannot be distinguished any longer: the world of transverse communications, where the finally conquered nonhuman sex mingles with the flowers, a new earth where desire functions according to its molecular elements and flows. Such a voyage does not necessarily imply great movements in extension; it becomes immobile, in a room and on a body without organs—an intensive voyage that undoes all the lands for the benefit of the one it is creating" (319).
18. Compare also Pynchon's description in *Against the Day* of the Chums' journey into the depths of the desert, in which the desert is treated as an ocean, as well as "the desert mov[ing] in" (V. 70) on the city in chapter 3 of *V.*
19. See also Knockwood's river in Mason & Dixon. "Mr. Knockwood . . . a sort of trans-Elemental Uncle Toby, spends hours every day . . . studying . . . the passage of Water across his land, and constructing elaborate works to divert its flow. . . . 'You don't smoak how it is,' he argues, '—all that has to happen is some Beaver, miles upstream from here, moves a single Pebble,—suddenly, down here, everything's changed! The creek's a mile away, running through the Horse Barn! Acres of Forest no longer exist! And that Beaver don't even know what he's done'" (364). For the vision of a flooded Los Angeles, see also Steve Erickson's *Our Ecstatic Days*.
20. On the ecology of storms, see Davis, *Ecology of Fear*, 178–94.
21. In *Two Regimes of Madness*, Deleuze proposes "a classification of cinematic lighting. You have one kind of light that presents a composite physical environment, and whose composition gives you white light, a Newtonian light that can be found in American cinema, and perhaps in Antonioni's films, though in a different way. Then you have a Goethe-light, an indestructible force that slams into shadows and picks things out. . . . You have another kind of light defined by its contrast not with shadow, but with shades of white, opacity being a total white out. . . . You have also a kind of light

no longer defined either by composition or by contrast, but by alternation and the production of lunar figures. . . . The list could go on forever, because new lighting events can always be created" (286).

22. See also the ending enigmatic waterspout at the end of *V.*: "Draw a line from Malta to Lampedusa. Call it a radius. Somewhere in that circle, on the evening of the tenth, a waterspout appeared and lasted for fifteen minutes. Long enough to lift the xebec fifty feet, whirling and creaking, Astarte's throat naked to the cloudless weather, and slam it down again into a piece of the Mediterranean whose subsequent surface phenomena—whitecaps, kelp islands, any of a million flatnesses which should catch thereafter part of the brute sun's spectrum—showed nothing at all of what came to lie beneath, that quiet June day" (492).
23. Jeff Simon described it as "an authentic Thomas Pynchon beach novel"; Colette Bancroft called it not only "a great beach read" but "the best beach book" of the year.
24. In "Zones of Immanence," Deleuze describes how horizontal beaches of immanence—spaces of "equality, univocity, and anarchy" (263)—traverse even the most ordered of "vertical" (262) worlds. On these beaches, "rocks, flowers, animals, and humans equally celebrate the glory of God" (250). Consider in this context the narrator's comment about DL Chastain in *Vineland*: "Somewhere further along, she'd been given to understand, she would discover that all souls, human and otherwise, were different disguises of the same greater being—God at play" (121). On Deleuze and the beach, see also Charles Stivale: "Deleuze recalls that when the Germans arrived, invading from Belgium, he was in Deauville (in Normandy, where his family spent summers), so he was put in high school for a year there. He recalls how an image from Deauville illustrates the immense social change of the Popular Front. With the introduction of paid vacations, people who never traveled could go to the beach and see the sea for the first time. Deleuze recalls the vision of a young girl from the Limousin standing for five hours in rapt attention before the extraordinary spectacle of the sea. And this had been a private beach, for the bourgeois property owners. He also recalls the class hatred translated by a sentence pronounced by his mother—'hélas' (alas), says Deleuze—about the impossibility of frequenting beaches where people 'like that' would be coming. For the bourgeois like his parents, giving vacations to the workers was the loss of privilege as well as the loss of territory, even worse than the Germans occupying the beaches with their tanks."
25. The phrase occurs, with variations, sixteen times in *Inherent Vice* (140, 154, 165, 166, 175,193, 194, 202, 257, 286, 296, 315, 330, 339, 340, 352).
26. See, in this context, Deleuze's article "May '68 Did Not Take Place."
27. "What continues unabated, regardless of what anyone writes, is the détournement of the Situationist project. Beneath the pavement, the beach. Wherever the boredom with given forms of art, politics, thought, everyday life, jackhammers through the car-

apace of mindless form, the beach emerges, where form is ground down to particles, to the ruin of ruins. There lies what the old mole is always busy making: the materials for the construction of situations. These too might be recuperated into mere art or writing some day, and sooner rather than later, but not before their glorious time. Our species-being is as builders of worlds. Should we consent to inhabit this given one as our resting place, we're dead already. There may be no dignified exits left to the twenty-first century . . . but there might at least be some paths to adventure. The unexamined life is not worth living, but the unlived life doesn't bear thinking about" (Wark 159).

28. See also Pynchon's hope in the "remote control" that allows him to surf the channels in his article "Nearer, My Couch, to Thee."
29. The final sentence of *Against the Day* describes the Chums of Chance as "They fly toward grace" (1085).
30. See *Against the Day* (58–62) for references to the "the luminiferous Æther" (58), the "Michelson-Morley experiment" (61), and particle-wave complementarity: "one finds in the devout Ætherist a propensity of character ever toward the continuous as against the discrete" (58).
31. See also the "Puncutron machine" that brings about "brain-wave recalibrations" (*Vineland* 165) and the reference to "the single public self" (*Inherent Vice* 176) created during rock concerts. In this context, see also Mucho's ability to do "spectrum analysis" in *The Crying of Lot 49*. Mucho can "listen to anything and take it apart again. Spectrum analysis, in my head. I can break down chords, and timbres, and words too into all the basic frequencies and harmonics, with all their different loudnesses, and listen to them, each pure tone, but all at once" (142). In fact, Mucho can align all of the single iterations of a string of words—considered as assemblages of frequencies—across time: "Everybody who says the same words is the same person if the spectra are the same only they happen differently in time, you dig? But the time is arbitrary. You pick your zero point anywhere you want, that way you can shuffle each person's time line sideways till they all coincide. Then you'd have this big, God, maybe a couple of hundred million chorus . . . and it would all be the same voice" (142).
32. Note, however, the connections between the Beach Boys and Charles Manson, who is, together with Fenway, the darkest presence in *Inherent Vice*.
33. See also the numerous references to karma and to "karmic adjustment" (172). Early on in *Inherent Vice*, Doc and Shasta each drift apart into "different karmic thermal[s] above the megalopolis" (11).
34. See the similarly ambiguous passage in Deleuze and Guattari: "the worst of the world war machines reconstitutes a smooth space to surround and enclose the earth. But the earth asserts its own powers of deterritorialization, its lines of flight, its smooth spaces that live and blaze their way for a new earth. The question is not one of quantities

but of the incommensurable character of the quantities that confront one another in the two kinds of war machine, according to the two poles. War machines take shape against the apparatuses that appropriate the machine and make war their affair and their object: they bring connections to bear against the great conjunction of the apparatuses of capture or domination" (*Thousand Plateaus* 423).

Pynchon's Coast. *Inherent Vice* and the Twilight of the Spatially Specific

BILL MILLARD

The epigraph to *Inherent Vice* will ring bells for anyone familiar with the events of May 1968 in France, that legendary flickering of radicalism that launched a generation of innovators and troublemakers, the *soixante-huitards* who have remained influential throughout the cultural, political, and business sectors of European society across four decades. It is the Situationist graffito "Under the paving stones, the beach!" (one of the less misleading translations from the original, *Sous les pavés, la plage*). But the beaches of Southern California were never quite what the French Situationists had in mind, and the America with which Pynchon's fiction relentlessly grapples remains resolutely un-French in more respects than its cuisine, its music, and its puzzling refusal (at this writing, at least) to institute credible universal health insurance.

The beach towns where Pynchon's colorfully named, unabashedly cartoonish characters do their best to evade and defy "the ancient forces of greed and fear" (*Inherent Vice* 130) should not be confused with the metaphoric, mythologizable, pristinely natural, Rousseauvian, capital-B Beach of the Situationist slogan, set into stark and simple contrast with the pavers or cobblestones that represent all that was false, dull, artificial, and oppressive about urbanity and civilization (at least in the eyes of certain soixante-huitards). These grungy California beach towns are specific places, places that hold power in Pynchon's imaginings of the transformational years, the late 1960s and early 1970s, that he probably spent in and around Manhattan Beach, California, while writing *Gravity's Rainbow*—"probably" being the safe and necessary hedge here, because the friends who could confirm his whereabouts remain impressively resistant to biographical inquiry—precisely because they are constructed, inhabited, humanly (occasionally even humanely) shaped. They harbor memory, something more concrete than utopian longing.

A perversely close reading of the Situationist slogan can also give it two mutually antagonistic potential meanings. In the short-lived exhilaration of May 1968 in Paris, the slogan's exclamation point was exhortatory: reading it on a wall, one was encouraged to recognize and celebrate the ur-Beach beneath the pavers, perhaps also prying up a few of them to hurl at the police. But imagine the line from a contrary perspective (that of, say, a real estate developer or a highway engineer), recast its tone so that the exclamation point drives home a different imperative, expressing the urgency of covering up unruly waterfront territory with something more stable, such as a nice safe street. Get that damned beach under some cobblestones where it belongs.

Inherent Vice is set not in 1968 but in the spring of 1970, after Altamont, after the Manson Family killings (a recurrent reference point), after what Hunter S. Thompson called "the high-water mark—that place where the wave finally broke and rolled back" (68). A few hippies having become murderous lunatics, the entire loose network of dissident subcultures (stoners, surfers, musicians, draft dodgers, actually existing politicals, all manner of unmoored young humanity) was now under suspicion. That beach, a dour new counter-Zeitgeist was saying, is likely to harbor pestilent things. Better bury it under some pavers, fast. And besides, paving it is a business opportunity.

Everybody Knows This Is Nowhere

Three times in his career, after unburdening himself of large-scale works of historical fiction with alarming interdisciplinary breadth and deeply entangled metafictional implications, Pynchon has turned his attention to Southern California. His Californian novels are shorter and more focused, although in certain respects no less ambitious, than the mammoth books that precede them. They are temporally closer, more inclined to generate their atmosphere through American pop-culture references than through the sort of recondite material that sent yesterday's dedicated Pynchonologists to the deepest stacks of university libraries and sends today's arguably less fanatical ones to Google and Wikipedia: fewer equations, benzene rings, and controversies in the Cyrillic transliteration of Kazakh consonants, more Hollywood films and surf-rock bands.

The three California books interweave their central problems and plots through no less complex a world vision than that of their predecessors, but they are organized more conventionally around single central characters (Oedipa Maas in *The Crying of Lot 49*, Zoyd Wheeler in *Vineland*, and Larry "Doc" Sportello in *Inherent Vice*) rather than around the multiple-protagonist structures that contribute to both the density and the difficulty of *V.*, *Gravity's Rainbow*, and *Against the Day* (*Mason & Dixon*, with its pair of protagonists, is a special case). Pynchon's shorter works also partake, in generous, if not overgenerous, degrees, of the distinctive combination of spaciness, slackness, and tolerance for (or, as often as not, an outright embrace of) the absurd that distinguishes California from the other 49 states. Pynchon's Californians embody and even exaggerate, where exaggeration is possible, the anything-goes, we're-all-bozos-on-this-bus, no-hobbyhorse-too-lame-to-ride spirit that non-Californians often attribute, stereotypically if not always inaccurately, to the residents of that state.

Imagining such people, one infers, must be (to borrow the appropriate line from Mick Jagger) a gas, gas, gas. It is as if Pynchon periodically unburdened himself of the dark and serious purposes he tackles in the larger works, with their more geographically and chronologically varied settings, and rewarded himself upon those works' completion with a bright, breezy, beach vacation, a lighter-weight project as a kind of dessert. No Pynchon book lacks a mixture of gravity and whimsy—his juxtaposition of those disparate qualities is both a commonplace of the scholarship about him and a fatally easy attraction for his would-be emulators—but the relative proportions in the three California books skew distinctly toward the latter (which is far from claiming the former is absent). It may be this indulgence of his inner pop-culture scavenger, his irrepressible tendencies toward groan-inducing lists, punch lines, and puns, and his defiantly libertarian (with a small L) attitude toward recreational mind alteration that leads some of Pynchon's critics to equate his periodic visits to the West Coast with a regrettable form of coasting. Trained by his larger historical novels to expect the overwhelming from Pynchon, some readers find it hard to respect him when he relaxes.

If Pynchon is indeed simply off his game in *Inherent Vice*, his comedy would be one area where longtime Pynheads could presumably tell. I was struck by one item that I am convinced a younger Pynchon would have handled differently: one of several dodgy restaurants where the diner just might be taking his life in his hands (so to speak), a health food joint "voted unanimously by local food critics the Southland's Most Toxic" and tellingly named The Price of Wisdom, is located on the second floor upstairs from a Melrose Avenue dive, Ruby's Lounge (276). Readers well-versed in the Bible can see the joke coming at least a few blocks away: the restaurant's hand-lettered sign reads "THE PRICE OF WISDOM IS ABOVE RUBY'S, JOB 28:18." The obscurantist whippersnapper in Pynchon, the side of him that incessantly and perhaps cacklingly sends his readers in search of clues, would have offered either the line or the chapter-and-verse citation but not both. The reference may be overdetermined out of uncharacteristic clumsiness, but it may also be doubled up to ensure that no one misses it. Neither sly allusiveness nor subtle ambiguity is a virtue in the type of text whose purpose is to direct people to a particular place (e.g., a commercial sign). And large parts of *Inherent Vice*, for reasons that extend beyond nostalgia, direct the reader to particular places.

Inherent Vice is rich with particular spatial and cultural references. This is nothing new in Pynchon, but the concentration of them in a single region, instead of their distribution across the nation or the world, makes the book's rendering of Southern California exceptionally credible and nuanced. The book is not only a valentine to a place where Pynchon spent memorable personal years but a veritable tour guide to the Southland's beaches, restaurants, highways, aerospace and oil industry districts, film studios, film stars' homes, and neighborhoods where a surf-rock band (one real, the Beach Boys; another, the Boards, fictional and, for a time, zombified) or a murderous cult (real) would plausibly be holed up. It delivers the literal flavor of the place, through references to local eateries such as Tommy's burger joint (73) and Zucky's deli (96); it is an antenna for the local broadcasting atmosphere, citing Cal Worthington's late-night used-car TV ads (9) and KHJ top-forty radio (356). So many details are taken from the actual landscape of greater Los Angeles in the given period that *Wired* magazine has posted an online interactive map, open to reader submissions (Horowitz). One particularly significant reference early in Sportello's adventures remains as cryptically understated as the Price of Wisdom sign is overdone.

On his way to Channel View Estates, the unfinished housing development that will be the scene of the book's initial eruption of violence, Sportello parks at "what would be the corner of Kaufman and Broad" (20) and visits, to his regret, the massage parlor Chick Planet. The names are not randomly chosen, and it is not accidental that the intersection appears, with some delicate grammatical wire walking, in the conditional mood and the future tense. Chick Planet is set up to service clients working on or near this site, but Channel View Estates is a construction site and does not yet exist as a set of residences; it has no history. It is typical of the places that were going up in staggering numbers around the Southland in the 1960s and afterward, and it imparts a distinctly Pynchonian yet historically informative spin to the noir-novel convention that Los Angeles is, in W. H. Auden's much-quoted words (referring to Raymond Chandler), "the Great Wrong Place" (408).

A sense of place is more than atmospheric in the world of *Inherent Vice*; it is pervasive on every level and inseparable from the problems that drive the book. The role of real estate in establishing one's sense of reality appears in joke form early on, when a stoned Sportello lets it slip that he believes Sherlock Holmes is a flesh-and-blood person, on the grounds that he has a fixed location: "No, he's real. He lives at this real address in London. Well, maybe not anymore, it was years ago, he has to be dead by now" (96). A kind of moral geography, a network of loyalties derived from class, history, and common experience, permeates the book's dialogue and descriptions. One's position on ethical questions—particularly the all-important priority in the 1960s/1970s stoner code, protecting one's friends rather than informing on them—is implicitly grounded in one's local background. In one casually informative early conversation, when Sportello disparages the TV show *The Mod Squad* for encouraging youth to rat out their peers, his colleague Fritz Drybeam (who has just confessed to enjoying the show) immediately replies, "'Listen, I came up in Temecula, which is Krazy Kat Kountry, where you always root for Ignatz and not Offisa Pupp'" (97). On the Offisa Pupp side of that line, LAPD Detective Lt. Christian "Bigfoot" Bjornsen's acute dislike of Gordita Beach, where he was assigned early in his police career, is based on the belief in a site-specific curse called down by a long-vanished tribe of toloache-smoking, hallucinating Indians on the town whose construction had defiled their sacred graveyards (355). The bonding of ethos to locale affects representatives of the elect as well as the preterite: Sportello's former client Crocker Fenway, whose negotiation and argument with the detective brings one of the book's most basic tensions to a climax (but more on that later), defends the values of his country-clubbing rentier class against any egalitarian ethical claims by the more transient population from whom it extracts wealth on the grounds that "It's about being in place. . . . We're in place. We've been in place forever" (347). At the other end of the social spectrum, characters who have been incarcerated invariably refer to their penitentiaries conversationally as "the place" (25), with the implication that prison is the location that has affected their lives most decisively, perhaps the only one.

One of the moments of severest midquest confusion for Sportello—after returning from a visit to Las Vegas; spending a grim night in a motel unusually well-equipped for its era with cable TV and thus overrun with glassy-eyed and culturally dislocated "Toobfreex"; viewing the depressing final preblacklist film starring his personal film-noir antihero John Garfield, *He Ran All the Way* (1951), which is "somehow like seeing John Garfield die for real, with the whole respectable middle class standing there in the street smugly watching him do it" (254); suspecting darkly that an end to the freedoms of the 1960s may be nigh; and "dreaming about climbing a more-than-geographical ridgeline, up out of some worked-out and picked-over territory, and descending into new terrain along some great definitive slope it would be more trouble than he might be up to to turn and climb back over again" (255)—is his momentary dread that his traveling companion has actually dropped him off in the wrong place and that he may have mistaken an entirely different but similar beach town for Gordita Beach, with its low-budget restaurants and familiar characters (256–57). As it turns out, he's in Gordita after all; an influx of collegians on break has simply driven the local crowd into temporary hiding. He soon learns that his community may even be reconstituting itself in an unexpected way: his lost lover Shasta Fay Hepworth, the femme fatale who first drew him into this investigation and then vanished mysteriously, as femmes fatales tend to, is back in town. But the specter of a Gordita Beach interchangeable with other places, the idea that locations could become modular and undifferentiated, brings Sportello as close to a freak-out as anything in the book, up to and including eerie drug experiences and imminent grievous bodily harm.

To return to Sportello's pivotal parking spot: unless Google Maps and MapQuest both contain uncharacteristic errors, there is no intersection of Kaufman and Broad in greater Los Angeles. A Broad Street does exist in Carson, near Long Beach, changing its name to Broad Avenue and extending a grand total of 12 blocks, but no street that it crosses is named Kaufman. No street anywhere near Los Angeles, in fact, is named Kaufman. What did exist in 1960s Los Angeles was the firm of Kaufman & Broad, later KB Home, a national leader in the construction of what were then called tract houses, the kind Malvina Reynolds and Pete Seeger mocked as "little boxes on the hillside," and what contemporary critics of American land-use patterns such as Andrés Duany and his colleagues, Anthony Flint, Dolores Hayden, Kenneth Jackson, and James Howard Kunstler, now describe as "greenfield sprawl." After founding their firm in Detroit in 1957 then moving to California in 1963, Donald Kaufman and Eli Broad grew wealthy from speculation in land and the construction of single-family houses in areas with single-use zoning ("Euclidean," named for the Cleveland suburb of Euclid, Ohio, site of a prominent legal precedent establishing the pattern, not for the Greek geometer), separating residential, commercial, and manufacturing functions geographically. (Eli Broad's name, coincidentally, is pronounced to rhyme with "road" and is unrelated to the Broad Streets that appear, often along with Main Streets, in countless American cities other than Los Angeles.) Broad would go on to become one of California's most prominent philanthropists and is now better known for activities on behalf of Los Angeles's arts community, schools, and downtown revitalization than for his original role as what Los Angeles–based architecture scholar Kazys Varnelis calls "the king of sprawl":

> Broad made his riches by building more cut-rate homes in suburban America between the late 1950s and 1980s than anyone else. As a founder of Kaufman Broad (now KB) Homes, Broad did more to create the contemporary condition of suburban sprawl than anyone else. Now over the

> last twenty years, Broad has increasingly dissociated himself from homebuilding, managing a large insurance firm instead. But Broad's shift is the product of the home market becoming too risky for investment, not because of a moral transformation. Today, however, Broad proclaims sprawl too expensive and hopes to underwrite a transformation within Los Angeles. (Varnelis 39).

An *Inherent Vice* character in a similar position also turns to philanthropy in midcareer. But Broad's effect on the suburban environment, not on the Los Angeles County Museum of Art, is why his name and Kaufman's are in *Inherent Vice.*

In locating Channel View Estates near a not-yet-extant intersection with a planted reference to those two names, Pynchon moves his narrative into a realm that in some sense is as illusory as the realms suggested by magical-realist gestures such as Ouija-board messages or talking dogs. Yet a categorically different departure from geographic realism was at work here within the real economic world that gave names to Pynchon's imaginary intersection. The processes creating the fictional Channel View Estates resemble the departure from locally specific reality that the American real estate industry, during most of the 20th century (accelerating after World War II), actually took: a shift to a future where generic and commodified building forms replaced those grounded in local materials, climates, and traditions. A central component of this transformation was the lateral spread of new suburbs outward from central cities, demographically fueled by white flight and ethnic fears and physically enabled by the trade in cheap land as new highway construction created sharp winner/loser divisions in realigning transportation routes and access to markets, and as agricultural economics steadily favored consolidation and agribusinesses over small farms. At the same time, as Sportello's African American client Tariq Khalil illustrates in recounting the history of his own vanishing Los Angeles neighborhood (14–17), the corresponding policy of "urban renewal" demolished minority neighborhoods, usually with negligible effort to relocate their residents, for new highways linking business districts with suburbs.

The systematic consumption of both rural and urban land reshaped much of the American landscape into a relatively undifferentiated type of residential space, one that erased the physical features of local history in an attempt to meld the purported advantages of the two older categories: the country for health, aesthetics, and recreation, the city for commerce, sociality, and convenience. Provided an income earner could reach a center of employment, this artificial "town-country" offered a great expansion of space and convenience; its social costs, most obviously in environmental terms but also in the form of cultural homogeneity and tedium, were not as immediately perceptible as its benefits on the familial level. The scales of suburban houses of course differed in an economic hierarchy, with styles likewise varying to some degree. But the basic model reached a high degree of nationwide standardization: single-family domestic havens located outside central cities, separated in most cases by turfgrass. As development spread further from rail lines—within Hayden's historical typology, the older "streetcar buildout" pattern giving way to "mail-order/self-build" and "sitcom" suburbs—they were eventually accessible almost exclusively by automobile.

This long process had roots in both cultural beliefs and public policy: it was influenced by Andrew Jackson Downing's advocacy of country home ownership as a salutary moral influence on the population and by Ebenezer Howard's Garden Cities concept but with commercial gain rather than utopian planning as the primary motivator. Deliberate federal policy choices accelerated the new construction after 1956 through the construction of the Eisenhower Interstate Highway System, with its tendencies to accelerate exurban development and erode the physical and social fabric of cities. Political motives included the desire to house returning veterans after World War II, but the federal bias extended as far back as 1934, when the Federal Housing Administration's energetic lending practices began encouraging single-family construction in suburbs, with a well-documented bias against rental properties, multiunit residences, and minorities, amounting to a massive subsidy from the general taxpaying populace to the white and the relatively well-off (Jackson, *Crabgrass Frontier*, 190–218). (Sportello is well aware of the local history of FHA redlining: braced by the Tweedledum/Tweedledee pair of FBI agents

Borderline and Flatweed and pressed for information on Khalil, he inquires, "what's with this FBI interest in Mickey Wolfmann? Somebody's been playing Monopoly with federal housing money? no couldn't be that, 'cause this is L.A., there's no such thing here" [75].)

Developers such as Kaufman & Broad, the Miami-based Lennar Corporation, D. R. Horton of Dallas/Fort Worth, the same city's Centex Corporation, Pulte Homes of the Detroit area, and Toll Brothers of Philadelphia would transform suburban and exurban home building into an aggressively rationalized mass-production industry. The mythology of home ownership in the United States focuses on Jeffersonian concepts of agrarian virtue and pioneer narratives of self-reliance involving Abe Lincoln's log cabin, but since the FHA expanded both the scope of the mortgage-lending market and the practice of redlining urban neighborhoods in favor of easy lending for properties on the outskirts, the steadily encroaching reality has been the essentially treeless residential tract; the cul-de-sac street layout; the ever-cheaper construction methods that rely increasingly on ersatz materials such as sheetrock and vinyl siding; and the many forms of homogenization wrought by the automobile upon the landscape, such as vast parking lots, strip malls, and drive-in businesses, as well as roads themselves—in Kunstler's much-repeated formulation, a series of "places not worth caring about" (*Home from Nowhere*, 22). Within the world of *Inherent Vice*, Sportello's sassy, earthy Aunt Reet, a realtor with a "phenomenal lot-by-lot grasp of land use from the desert to the sea" (6), minces no words about the likes of Channel View Estates, an "assault on the environment—some chipboard horror" (8). Her habitual acronym for "most tract houses of her acquaintance," an "OPPOS" (19), is never spelled out, but one needn't overcomplicate the decoding of its last three letters.

Into this physical setting—and this potent field for debate, as America's sprawling development pattern is deeply implicated in contemporary environmental and economic crises—Pynchon introduces a figure of demonic force. The man who goes missing almost immediately after Sportello begins investigating a suspected scam against him, Mickey Wolfmann, bears no particular personal similarities to either Donald Kaufman or Eli Broad, but he practices the same profession and occupies the same historical niche in LA's development. Wolfmann is another of Pynchon's outlandish exaggerators, someone well outside expected human boundaries, a larger-than-life figure "always in the paper" (4) who more closely resembles flamboyant media and film moguls such as William Randolph Hearst, Adolph Zukor, and Thomas Ince (name-checked later in the book [209] for his rumored high-society homicide) than he does the less publicity-hungry real estate barons of his day; he is, in some respects, a precursor of later decades' overexposed celebrity speculators such as Donald Trump; while he is missing, he is just as much a part of the popular consciousness, with reported sightings popping up like posthumous tabloid appearances of Elvis Presley (76). His connection to another larger-than-life figure from American history, New York's "power broker" Robert Moses, is more direct; above Wolfmann's portrait in his house, a "fake chiseled stone frieze" presents the motto Wolfmann has lived by: "ONCE YOU GET THAT FIRST STAKE DRIVEN, NOBODY CAN STOP YOU.—ROBERT MOSES" (58). Sportello, naturally, reacts with a quip indicating his perception of the connection between any larger-than-life, triumph-of-the-will type and an element of the monstrous: "I thought Dr. Van Helsing said that."

Wolfmann insists vehemently on an accurate spelling of his name, with the N doubled (7), implying that in this cinephilic city, he is all too aware of his resemblance to Lon Chaney, Jr.'s signature role. Bearing in mind how frequently puns in Pynchon "allude" in more than one direction, one also recalls a line from Plautus that presaged the predations of Hobbesian capitalism: *homo homini lupus*, or "man is wolf to man." Does a real estate developer necessarily shed some of his humanity when shape-shifting into an essential instrument of the rentier class? It is difficult to tell directly in Wolfmann's case; he bobs and weaves between the lines of *Inherent Vice* without ever appearing directly and speaking to Sportello or to the reader. Sportello sees him directly only once, briefly, in federal custody (243). He is as close as this book's social world comes to being a prime mover, but he remains offstage, knowable only by inference through his effects on other characters: Sportello's exlover and initial client, Shasta; his own untrustworthy wife, Sloane; the enforcers and other minor characters in his direct or indirect employ; the presumptive Golden Fang operatives who kidnap and psychologically reprogram him; and Sportello himself, through sad contemplation of how Wolfmann's connection to

Shasta overmatched his own. Wolfmann's wealth, force of will, sexual omnivorousness, omnipresence in television advertisements for his properties, and legendary unpredictability—he is ethnically Jewish, "Westside Hochdeutsch mafia" (7), yet he maintains a bodyguard of motorcycle baddies recruited from the Aryan Brotherhood faction in prisons—mark him as an outsized, disruptive, Oz-like figure, as erratic as any of Pynchon's low-comedy stoners but relentlessly purposeful. He is obsessive enough about his many short-term lovers to have their likenesses hand painted nude on a collection of neckties yet casual enough about these ties to give away the one depicting Shasta to an apelike orderly, a presumptive act of indifference that is galling to Sportello (190, 193–94), who carries a torch for Shasta that burns even more steadily than his incessant joints. Wolfmann cultivates an aura of unapproachability and danger disturbing even to tough old Aunt Reet, but the action that creates a genuine disturbance in this world, triggering an intervention in the form of his kidnapping, is an unexpected attack of ethical regret about the way he has made his living.

Detailed revelation of plot twists is unseemly in any review or comment on a thriller, but certain spoilers are unavoidable here, and a highly significant one is Wolfmann's decision, for a time, to salve his conscience through an act of utopian construction, an intentional community in an unspecified desert valley somewhere between Los Angeles and Las Vegas. First mentioned by Sloane Wolfmann's gigoloid "spiritual coach" Riggs Warbling (62), a building contractor, *Architectural Digest* reader, and aficionado of a mathematically complex form of construction known as the zonahedral dome, or "zome," Wolfmann's zome-based desert housing project Arrepentimiento is later revealed to be a drug-influenced personal obsession and the endeavor that causes even more powerful interests to question, and by kidnapping intervene in, his mental stability. "Arrepentimiento" translates as "repentance," or, in the more colloquial translation of the tattooed goon Puck Beaverton, "Spanish for 'sorry about that'" (248). Beaverton, Warbling, and the pair of FBI agents all give Sportello fragmentary information about this not-for-profit, geometrically futuristic (with multiple references to Buckminster Fuller) development, which is intended to provide rent-free housing to an impoverished (i.e., preterite) population; it is the antithesis of the economic model that has created Wolfmann's fortune. Agent Flatweed fills Sportello in, with a snarl:

> "It's you hippies. You're making everybody crazy. We'd always assumed that Michael's conscience would never be a problem. After all his years of never appearing to have one. Suddenly he decides to change his life and give away millions to an assortment of degenerates—Negroes, longhairs, drifters. Do you know what he said? We have it on tape. 'I feel as if I've awakened from a dream of a crime for which I can never atone, an act I can never go back and choose not to commit. I can't believe I spent my whole life making people pay for shelter, when it ought to've been free. It's just so obvious.'" (244)

Again, Pynchon grounds the fanciful in the actual. Lest anyone imagine that zonahedral domes are a pure product of his imagination, the form was in fact not only theorized but constructed as early as 1965 at the Colorado desert commune Drop City, where artists followed the geometric plans of inventor Steve Baer and built assorted zomes of salvaged materials; the project won the Buckminster Fuller Institute's Dymaxion Award for innovative and economical housing construction in 1966. A longer-lived intentional community in central Arizona, architect Paolo Soleri's Arcosanti, would become the model for the "arcologies," or self-contained, single-building communities, in William Gibson's *Neuromancer*; it was explicitly designed as the antithesis of sprawl, eliminating cars and tightly concentrating the human component of its resource use, sustaining itself economically since 1970 through craft sales, educational events, tourism, and donations, despite chronic underfunding. Probably the best-publicized of the desert architectural/ecological experiments is Biosphere 2 in Oracle, Arizona, which began as an ill-fated study on the viability of an environment not simply self-contained but physically sealed and evolved into a more professional ecological laboratory managed by Columbia University after Wallace Broecker of Columbia University helped solve the chemical-balance problems that made the closed-system experiment a failure. Biosphere 2 was eventually spun off as a museum and research center directed by the University of Arizona and combined with a more conventional housing development on-site. Dissident utopian communities in the 1960s and afterward, whether they attained underground renown but ultimately collapsed from interpersonal difficulties (Drop City), failed amid plausible charges of mismanagement and were rescued by more conventional institutions (Biosphere 2), or attained a degree of independent institutional stability (Arcosanti), have generated much more than a colorful vocabulary of portmanteau neologisms and a modicum of scientific information: they have looked to the reconfiguration of living space for alternatives to a commercial land-use system that they perceive as environmentally unsustainable to the point of self-destruction, and they have established, for better or worse, a track record of artistic and intellectual influence in certain spheres, combined with financial and managerial unsteadiness. Deserts are, among other things, difficult and expensive places to maintain an off-the-grid living/working compound. Communities of this sort might do well to rethink the commitment to isolation that presumably motivates the choice of site.

Wolfmann's pair of properties, Arrepentimiento and Channel View Estates, represent antithetical ways of organizing American land in pursuit of contrasting utopian impulses: as an admirable if financially doomed exercise in architectural innovation and charitable housing or as a conventionally profitable, predictable, environmentally disastrous and socially/culturally/aesthetically soul-crushing sprawl-burb. The name Channel View carries multiple connotations, none complimentary. Channelview, Texas, is an oil-refinery suburb of Houston infamous for the 1991 "Texas Cheerleader-Murdering Mom" case, in which a woman hired a hit man to kill the mother of her teenage daughter's rival for a place on a pep squad. The "channel view" function in major audio or graphics software packages such as ProTools, Logic Studio, or Photoshop narrows down a user's visibility to a single audio track or color within a multicolor image. But the name's primary and obvious implication involves the compulsive watching of television. Sportello's taunting nemesis Bjornsen overtly acknowledges this, greeting the detective in custody as he awakens from a head blow, telling him he is at "Channel View Estates, a future homesite where elements of some wholesome family will quite soon be gathering night after night, to gaze tubeward, gobble their nutritious snacks" (22). The combination of spatial isolation with private homes and television proved through the later twentieth century to be conducive to popular autoanesthesia, narrowing people's access to independently sourced information and to each other. The auto and the tube: a pair of technologies optimized to propagate mass autism. Those snacks will undoubtedly be mass-market junk food, not the equally cheap but more distinctive fare available from one-of-a-kind joints like The Price of Wisdom or the surfer shack Wavos. The constriction and control of vision in every sense is essential to life in a place like Channel View Estates.

At Arrepentimiento, in contrast, Wolfmann's more generous and idealistic impulses are up against larger, darker forces whose victory is practically predetermined. They are bodied forth as the shape-shifting, hard drug-dealing, murderously manipulative entity known as the Golden Fang, appearing variously as a boat, a building, a tax scheme, and a kind of mafia but also as a psychic archetype reminiscent of a passage in *Gravity's Rainbow* on the human incapacity for true independence from the power of wealth ("the Counterforce . . . are as schizoid, as double-minded in the massive presence of money, as any of the rest of us, and that's the hard fact. The Man has a branch office in each of our brains, his corporate emblem is a white albatross" [712–13]); perhaps it is simply equivalent to plutocracy in all its external and internalized forms. Sustaining the financing, completion, and operation of Arrepentimiento in defiance of the Fang would require degrees of will and autonomy that no one, even Wolfmann, can marshal. The reader sees the place only as another construction site, this time abandoned in an incomplete state, with an armed and deranged Riggs Warbling first threatening then recognizing and welcoming Sportello and his sidekick Tito Stavrou and explaining that the project is dead, soon to be dismantled or even bombed. "Someday they'll get Mickey to approve a rocket strike," Warbling laments, "and Arrepentimiento will be history—except it won't even be that, because they'll destroy all the records, too" (251). Having begun as Wolfmann's LSD-influenced vision, then having nearly, miraculously, attained physical form, Arrepentimiento is already under erasure by the time it moves from the realm of rumor to the book's immediate action.

Of the two antithetical construction projects ("Michael Wolfmann Concepts") that organize the spatial expansion of the world of *Inherent Vice* beyond the limits of stasis and nostalgia, which one is more plausibly The Great

Wrong Place? Given the social and environmental implications of different developmental forms, the question of whether Arrepentimiento or Channel View Estates is more preposterous comes close to being the central problem bearing on the novel's real-world implications. *Inherent Vice*'s relations to the external landscape are of more lasting interest than Sportello's investigation itself, because the surface-level whodunit questions within the text proper—the reasons behind Wolfmann's disappearance and reprogramming, bodyguard Glen Charlock's murder, an older murder involving Bjornsen's past, and a series of further political murders by a hit man acting under legal protection—are all either answered or deferred through the sort of trapdoor plot devices that Pynchon shares with Chandler and Ellroy. As in the darkest and best of the hard-boiled tradition, the "spreading stain" (Porter 40) of culpability extends well beyond questions of who perpetrated any particular crime: the crime is how an entire place, an entire society, got to be the way it is. And thanks to both impersonal market mechanisms and the specific decision by a Wolfmann into whose hide the Golden Fang (in whatever form that malevolent force has assumed) has finally clamped down good and hard, the Pynchonian Southland, like the real one and like increasingly large parts of the real United States, came to look far more like Channel View Estates than like Arrepentimiento.

Pynchon makes no attempt to frame this interpretive competition between the abandoned utopia and the completed dystopia as a fair fight. That Channel View Estates and places like it thrive and multiply appears here as a national tragedy, perhaps a planetary one, whether one infers that the failure of Arrepentimiento and similar eco-utopian experiments to thrive was foreordained in their nature or that it was contingent on particular decisions. The reasons to evaluate Channel View Estates harshly are self-evident throughout the text; the only character who seriously defends the place, Bjornsen, in his initial rude-awakening speech to the dazed Sportello, does so in caricatured conformist terms early in the book, before he has evolved from a hippie-hating cartoon authoritarian to someone with more complicated loyalties. Perhaps in this he even becomes an instrument of Sportello's salvation, through an act that can be read as either inadvertently backfiring or as expressing a conscious intention to help Sportello bargain his way out of a jam. It is worth noting that Sportello's evolving relation to Bjornsen is one of the strongest and most mature aspects of the second half of *Inherent Vice* (it removes Pynchon's generally scathing treatment of police, refreshingly, from the one-dimensionality that mars late sections of *Vineland*) and that after their final exchanges of wrap-up plot information, Bjornsen's own pursuit of a quite different sense of justice elicits a response from Sportello that readers of the previous California novel may consider a substantial surprise (350); no Pynchon character would ever have responded in this way to *Vineland*'s Brock Vond or *Against the Day*'s Scarsdale Vibe. Forgiveness, or at least a form of nonjudgmentalism toward individual behavior, is in ample supply in Pynchon's work. Channel View Estates, however, is an assault on the region, rendering it blander and more generic, as well as on the Earth, expanding resource consumption and ecological degradation; it is unforgivable.

Transactions in Surreal Estate

For all its grounding in spatial and cultural specificity, *Inherent Vice* maintains one strand of continuity with the nonrational realms found in previous Pynchon works. The boundaries of realism do not exclude the surreal, the mythic, and the potentially delusional, and Sportello entertains occasional hallucinations that may or may not be informative, although they are at least informative about the contents of his own mind. Psychoactive drugs and the states they produce allow Pynchon to introduce this material without violating the real-world assumptions of the thriller genre and plunging thoroughly into the magical-realist sphere of talking dogs, immortal light bulbs, and not-quite-dead creatures that seem to have walked out of the Tibetan *Bardo Thödol*. One significant secondary character whom Sportello assists against tall odds, the saxophonist Harlingen, would almost certainly have been among Pynchon's Thanatoids had he appeared in *Vineland*, but here, his undead state takes the forms of heroin addiction, a faked death, estrangement from his family, detoxification at the sinister Chryskylodon (Greek for "Golden Fang") Institute, and enslavement to the rightist group Vigilant California (the "Viggies," part brownshirt paramilitary faction and part cult) as a low-level snitch and political operative. Harlingen's unpleasant odyssey takes him through a series of states that link the economy, contractual bonds, and middle-class mainstream existence to varieties of addiction: "It was occurring to Doc now . . . that if the Golden Fang could get its customers strung out, why not turn around and also sell them a program to help them kick? Get them coming and going, twice as much revenue and no worries about new customers—as long as American life was something to be escaped from, the cartel could always be sure of a bottomless pool of new customers" (192).

That the Golden Fang may be no more definably real than the Tristero system, or may be so real that its influence permeates the FBI, the Las Vegas Mafia, and the LAPD, ultimately appears to be beside the point, as Sportello's mission morphs from a cluster of criminal investigations to a discovery of the deeper nature of the place he inhabits and an attempt to protect specific persons, including Shasta, Harlingen and family, and himself, from harm. (In *Against the Day*, in fact, Pynchon presaged the Fang by mentioning a Chums of Chance title, *The Chums of Chance and the Wrath of the Yellow Fang* [1019], as the final such book mentioned in the text, placing its initial incarnation squarely in the realm of the unreal.) The point of the Golden Fang comes to be not that it is a literal smoke-filled-room-style conspiracy with identifiable manipulators—its appearance as a literal tooth-shaped, six-story building inhabited by low-comedy dentists and described as a mere tax dodge, located at the very site where an Ouija-board message had once driven Sportello and Shasta on a wild goose chase, dope-buying mission only to find an empty lot (164–69), is enough of a letdown to make the whole idea of conspiracy hunting appear self-parodying—but that it is indistinguishable from the capitalist economy, from the impulses toward commodification, indistinction, and extraction that enable it. The repeated dealings with paranormality, drug visions, and improbable coincidence bring Sportello certain options for organizing information, and one of his last such moments offers an image the reader can reliably classify as an insight. While held under duress by the thug Beaverton and given a massive dose of PCP, Sportello encounters the personified Golden Fang itself and finds it tall, cloaked, and leeringly theatrical about the use of its teeth: in other words, unambiguously vampiric: "'As you may have already gathered,' it whispered, 'I am the Golden Fang. . . . They have named themselves after their worst fear. I am the unthinkable vengeance they turn to when one of them has grown insupportably troublesome, when all other sanctions have failed'" (318).

One recalls Sportello's earlier Dr. Van Helsing stake-driving joke on seeing the Robert Moses motto in Wolfmann's house. If any hallucination or monstrosity in otherwise realistic fiction points toward elements of the work's realistic component, some connection is lurking here between imaginary blood-sucking creatures and real entities deserving that metaphor. Of all the available visions of predation that American pop culture provides (and that Pynchon the midnight-movie buff recurrently draws from in various contexts, such as zombie legends and Japanese monster films at multiple points here, King Kong in *Gravity's Rainbow*, or Frankenstein's monster in his *New York Times Book Review* Luddism essay), a vampire acts through insidiousness, persuasion, contagiousness, and parasitism, not overwhelming force or size. It lives off the blood of others rather than shedding blood violently. Vampires are a natural match for developers or landlords, for any rentier whose income derives from ownership of assets rather than from productive work. Elements of surreality intrude only occasionally in *Inherent Vice*, but they do so in this climactic moment in order to comment on real estate.

Among Sportello's late conversations wrapping up loose ends and resolving uncertainties, the most adversarial is his encounter with a representative of both the Golden Fang and the longtime property-holding, white-shoe, old-money class, Crocker Fenway, at Fenway's private club, the Portola (named for the 1769 expedition of Gaspar de Portolà to claim Californian territory for Spain, although Fenway is oblivious to a mural depicting that party's landing near Los Angeles). Fenway's profession is never specified, but he describes himself as a well-known fixer, and his use of the phrase "holding in gratuitous bailment" implies he is an attorney (341); Sportello is aware, having earned a considerable fee some years earlier rescuing Fenway's floridly disturbed runaway daughter, that "the Fenways were heavy-duty South Bay money, living on the Palos Verdes Peninsula in a gated enclave located *inside* the *already* gated high-rent community of Rolling Hills" (171). When Sportello encounters Fenway again to negotiate the return of a massive stash of heroin (Golden Fang property that Sportello has had planted on him by police but managed, improbably, to get away with concealing), their relative bargaining positions for the moment are such that Sportello can afford not only a claim for a nonmonetary quid pro quo (amnesty for Harlingen) but a few class-conscious zingers:

> "How much money would I have to take from you so I don't lose your respect?"
>
> Crocker Fenway chuckled without mirth. "A bit late for that, Mr. Sportello. People like you lose all claim to respect the first time they pay anybody rent."
>
> "And when the first landlord decided to stiff the first renter for his security deposit, your whole fucking class lost everybody's respect." (346–47)

Sportello goes on to wave an extremely red flag in front of this particular bull. When Fenway rails against "His Holiness Mickey Wolfmann," calls Channel View Estates "that promise of urban blight" (tellingly mistaking the generically suburban for the urban), and praises his own landholding class for struggling to keep "high-density tenement scum without the first idea of how to clean up after themselves" out of an otherwise green and pristine neighborhood, Sportello calls him on the ersatz environmental objections ("Bullshit, Crocker, it's about your property values") and presses him for a response regarding the "bad-karma level" that landlords have steadily and massively accumulated. Fenway's reply, along with defending his club-fellows' ability to remain "in place," concedes the rentiers' aggression toward the renters in this eternal class war over living space. But it also skewers the whole cultural segment on whose behalf Sportello for once has taken the role of spokesman: everyone in 1960s California and elsewhere who has opted out of the tiresome and rigged race that the likes of Fenway always win.

> "Real estate, water rights, oil, cheap labor—all of that's ours, it's always been ours. And you, at the end of the day what are you? one more unit in this swarm of transients who come and go without pause here in the sunny Southland, eager to be bought off with a car of a certain make, model, and year, a blonde in a bikini, thirty seconds on some excuse for a wave—a chili dog, for Christ's sake." He shrugged. "We will never run out of you people. The supply is inexhaustible." (347)

Fenway's reappearance in the book a few pages earlier had interrupted Sportello's idyllic dream mixed with political resolve, "a kind of courtroom summary" by his lawyer Sauncho Smilax as the two watched the schooner *Preserved* (which had been commandeered for a time for nefarious uses and renamed *The Golden Fang*, but somehow exorcised and restored to its real name) sail safely away, perhaps even carrying Harlingen and his family; the dream-Smilax spoke of "the land almost allowed to claim its better destiny, only to have the claim jumped by evildoers known all too well, and taken instead and held hostage to the future we must live in now forever" (341). The lament for the abused land, even framed as a mock-elevated, somewhat windy speech inside a dream, describes something that Pynchon, as much as any of his preterite characters, values highly. Yet it also articulates an aspect of the pivotal conversation soon to come, and of Pynchon's work more broadly, that explains why there have always been distinct limits to his appeal. Those "evildoers known all too well" certainly include Fenway as well as Wolfmann in his avaricious pre- and post-Arrepentimiento phases, along with anyone who disrespects particular places enough to trade land as a commodity. Politically, it is useful to recognize our bloodsuckers as clearly as possible, but for aesthetic purposes, there is such a thing, and not a good thing, as knowing them all too well.

In certain critical quarters, there has long been a characterization problem in Pynchon. One reasonable way to put it is William Logan's observation, apropos of various excesses in *Against the Day*, that "no one has ever wept over the death of a Pynchon character the way thousands wept over Little Nell." Defenders might counter either that his major characters rarely die in view of the reader, that Dickensian sentiment is too shopworn an effect to treat unironically, or that certain of Pynchon's deaths (without hesitation, I would nominate those of Jeremiah Dixon and Charles Mason) are in fact seriously moving. But the objection still stands. Those who seek psychological roundedness and credibility above all else in fiction do not customarily find it here, certainly not in overprivileged heavies such as Fenway. Perhaps Pynchon's general refusal of interiority for many characters indicates not an inattention to individual psychology or, as James Wood would have it, an outright authorial incompetence at the task of constructing credible, nuanced, and realistic individual perspective (for Wood, arguably the central task of any serious novel). The steady attainment of greater self-awareness by Sportello, despite his intellectual and cultural limitations and his memory-beclouding inhalations, indicates that Pynchon is capable of considerable psychological nuance when he puts his mind to it. I would add that on the far larger canvas of *Against the Day*, the extended Cyprian Latewood plot (which arises in mid-novel, too far along for the more impatient reader or reviewer even to have noticed it) presents a decisive response to Wood's charges of chronic immaturity, superficiality, and overtheatricality. But an equally plausible alternative is that Pynchon habitually eschews a close focus on individual psychology because of a fully serious conviction that it is simply not as interesting as broader social systems, either as an intellectual problem or as an aesthetic object.

In an *Inherent Vice* review that refers specifically to Crocker Fenway's class-superiority speech as an instance of hollow, unreal villainy, Laura Miller contends that "there's something profoundly futile about mounting a protest against vast, complex systems that use ordinary people like interchangeable cogs by writing novels that are vast complex systems in which the characters amount to interchangeable cogs." The objection is a serious one, even when one appends a recognition that Pynchon's most important characters (including the one glimpsed only through assorted glasses darkly, Wolfmann) are far from interchangeable. Yet, protest is only one aspect of Pynchon's engagement with these systems; he also anatomizes them, including his and our own roles within them. While mounting a sustained ethical argument against systems that serve greed and arrogance, he also exercises, and often successfully promulgates, a sustained fascination with their workings. Some of the ways an economic system operates are fostering varieties of false consciousness; convincing people to believe they are freer than they are; substituting trivial forms of freedom (Fenway's car, bikini, and chili dog) for substantive ones; and driving people's attention inward, toward their own emotions and motivations, where it can be less socially disruptive and more containable than if it were directed externally, historically, and socially.

A refusal to play the game of psychologism, an overt declaration through repeated cartoonish characterizations that we are all quite often superficial and cartoonish, is not a welcome message in all quarters, but in Pynchon's practice, it is plausibly purposeful. He would not be the first to claim that all happy families are alike (or, after Nabokov, that they in fact are not alike), but he does break distinctive ground by adding that all unhappy families are also in some way alike, as are all individuals in love, all individuals who have lost love, all individuals when observed in the act of wistfully recalling bygone love, and so forth—whereas spatial communities of any real interest (to pick one of the many categories of human collectivities Pynchon is concerned with, professions being another) display complex, fascinatingly detailed, infinitely evolving differences of natural and built forms, social fragmentation, technology, and cultural expression.

To develop a clearer sense of just what it is Pynchon prefers to emphasize, it may be useful to examine one last pair of passages involving characters' perceptions of land and, as the book's title phrase and master metaphor is a concept from maritime law, of water as well. Another of the hallucinogen experiences through which Sportello passes involves a trip customized for him, complete with a thematically appropriate and extraordinarily patience-testing soundtrack (Tiny Tim's "The Ice Caps Are Melting" set on repeat), by the acid guru Fairfield (108). Sportello has some troublesome history with this character, whom he has met through another of the book's more significant supporting personages, a woman going by the single and singular name of Sortilège. She is exactly the kind of woo-woo New Ager whom Pynchon (among others) finds in great abundance in California and frequently sets up for ready mockery. Her name, denoting divination by lot casting, implies randomness, a kind of spiritual placebo effect, yet in her attunement to purported "invisible forces" and her willingness to help friends deal with them, "she had never been wrong that Doc knew about" (11). Among her many beliefs, astrological and otherwise, one that even the Gordita surfers find hard to take—and this is a crowd that includes St. Flip of Lawndale, whose religion equates Christ's walking on the Sea of Galilee with surfing, the absence of waves on that body of water being no apparent impediment to belief, and who once bought "a fragment of the True Board" (99)—a faith in the legend of the lost continent of Lemuria, a Pacific equivalent (and in some versions a precursor) of Atlantis. Lemuria and Atlantis disappeared under water, Sortilège is convinced, because of environmental abuses, and North America is headed the same way: "'The good news is that like any living creature, Earth has an immune system too, and sooner or later she's going to start rejecting agents of disease like the oil industry. And hopefully before we end up like Atlantis and Lemuria'" (105).

Oil from the nearby El Segundo refinery befouls the sand and the feet of Gordita residents, much as tar globs actually do surface further north at Pismo Beach. In this locale, the effects of both production and consumption of petroleum are hard to overlook. When Sportello eats Fairfield's bespoke blotter, he hallucinates not only "the vividly lit ruin of an ancient city that was, and also wasn't, everyday Greater L.A." (108) but an ancient war between the two lost continents that subsumes the U.S. war in Indochina and thousands of years' worth of other proxy conflicts, plus a quickly rising water level. LSD, suggestibility, and perhaps a blurry sense of geopolitical history can explain much of the form of Sportello's vision. Knowing what contemporary earth scientists have demonstrated about climate change, however, one need not take Lemuria or ancient guiding spirits seriously to sense that Sortilège, at least in her immune-system metaphor, may in fact be on to something.

Toward the book's end, another conversation between Sportello and Smilax, a marine salvage specialist, evokes disasters and rising water in explaining the marine-insurance concept of inherent vice, which applies not just to individuals (as an alternative term for original sin) but to any entity with built-in flaws, anything on which insurance represents a shaky bet. The idea that the phrase might apply to an entire part of the world, not just to a vulnerable cargo such as eggs (prone, of course, to breakage), to leak-prone vessels, or to human nature, is not a fanciful extension; it appears directly in the dialogue, as Sportello follows up on Smilax's examples:

> "Like the San Andreas Fault," it occurred to Doc. "Rats living up in the palm trees."
>
> "Well," Sauncho blinked, "maybe if you wrote a marine policy on L.A., considering it, for some closely defined reason, to be a boat. . . ."
>
> "Hey, how about a ark? That's a boat, right?"
>
> "Ark insurance?"
>
> "That big disaster Sortilège is always talking about, way back when Le-

muria sank into the Pacific. Some of the people who escaped then are spoze to've fled here for safety. Which would make California like, a ark."

"Oh, nice refuge. Nice, stable, reliable piece of real estate." (351–52)

This is more than just another in the long series of spacy exchanges Sportello has with well-baked friends. The combined suggestions that inherent vice might characterize the entire state and that its presence renders any entity harder to insure add up to a proposition with broad implications: one of many things compromised by a critical flaw is the entire territory, the American land-development system itself. The way California was physically developing in 1970, the way the United States has largely continued to develop—sprawling laterally to an extreme degree, maximizing energy consumption and vehicular miles traveled, locking much of the population into the addictive network of homeowner debt, spewing greenhouse gases, postponing accountability for the populationwide insistence on maximal convenience, and generally mismanaging its physical inheritance for private profit—demonstrates a systemic inherent vice, well beyond what any individual can influence. Of course, if American civilization is an ark of sorts, certain parties are, in fact, captaining it. A few pages later, Smilax notes, as they watch the *Preserved* (the real schooner this time) hitting a wave so anomalously large that it scuttles her, that whoever is navigating is "committing either suicide or barratry here" (358). "Barratry," in admiralty law, is gross misconduct by a vessel's master or crew: stealing, scuttling, or otherwise damaging the vessel or its cargo. Smilax's observation is too potent a metaphor to be limited to a single schooner.

"Inherent vice" is a broader concept than original sin or criminal culpability; it is about the world more than it is about us. The ways of complex systems (physical, ecological, or socioeconomic), Pynchon seems to be stressing, are not reducible to the desires, concerns, self-regard, or beliefs of individual human beings, although they do respond in some degree to individual choices. Those individuals nearly always deserve mercy and second chances, he intimates, and the worst offenses in his world consist of the denial of mercy to those in need of it. But individual fates and fears do not loom large enough to overshadow larger things. Pynchon observes a distinction between being humane and pretending that humanist values comprehend everything. It may be that the objections raised against Pynchon by readers with a strong allegiance to the values of earlier phases of fiction—sometimes overall admirers or former admirers like Miller, sometimes less patient readers like Wood, with his powerful if intemperate castigations of the genre he calls "hysterical realism"—are essentially attempts to use nineteenth-century criteria to evaluate twenty-first-century phenomena. That moral gravity can extend to matters beyond the scale of individual human morals is a difficult concept to grapple with (perhaps one with structural analogies to a certain architectural trope that Pynchon has used repeatedly, once in *Mason & Dixon* [354] and twice here, with Chick Planet [21] and the Arrepentimiento zome [251]: a space that appears larger inside than outside). But it is precisely the flexibility and expansiveness of postmodern fiction that makes it possible to consider and perform the cognitive gymnastics such an idea demands.

What Pynchon may in fact have constructed is a novel of ideas in potboiler disguise, frankly, if subterraneanly, didactic, motivated more by the urgency of disseminating the core idea—the inherent tragedy and potential for disaster associated with certain forms of humanly built space and social organization—than by the aesthetic criteria of humanistic realism. One shoehorns one's experience of a Pynchon book into such a category at one's peril; he is Thomas Pynchon, after all, with very little left to prove to anyone. If he regards the potential cautionary effect of an elaborate ecological/developmental parable, a useful and provocative countermyth against the cavalier treatment of irreplaceable places, as more a pressing matter than the furthering of his own reputation for certain kinds of gravity, there are probably worse vices.

The Origins of the Family, Private Property, and the State of California in Pynchon's Fiction

SCOTT McCLINTOCK

Paranoia mediates the two fields this chapter is concerned with: urban stories, that is, narratives about the growth and development of the urban and exurban areas of Los Angeles and Orange Counties in Pynchon's fiction, and family stories. Noir film and fiction and related genres, such as detective fiction and crime and crime syndicate fiction and film, which collectively gave rise to a popular representation in B movies and "pulp" fiction that has been dubbed the "culture of the mob,"[1] also mediate the twin narrative cycles of the urban development of Southern California and the conspiracies underlying it as the "hidden" force of postwar history in the region and the family stories that are another of the emergent narrative patterns in Pynchon's California novels. How the generic characteristics of the sentimental 19th-century domestic novel infuse the hard-boiled crime story that is the more ostensible genre Pynchon's *Inherent Vice* evokes, almost like latent dream content lies underneath manifest content in the Freudian account of dream work, and in a manner that bears on the layering of genres in Pynchon's postmodern pastiches, will be developed also. The apparent domestication of Pynchon's fiction, represented most clearly in *Inherent Vice*'s valorization of the sentimental and the family, can be observed by considering family constellations in *Inherent Vice* and the other California novels that are presented as more affirmative alternatives to the patriarchal nuclear family of postwar, Eisenhower-era America, seen as an alienating and repressive "ideological apparatus" of capitalism and from which the flower children sought to escape into the counterculture. Tensions between this seeming veneration of domesticity and the antifamilialism of Deleuze and Guattari's *Anti-Oedipus*, which shares with *Inherent*

Vice and even Pynchon's second novel, *The Crying of Lot 49*, the same cultural moment, as well as, more generally, the critical yield and limitations of a psychoanalytic framework for explicating the related concepts of paranoia, real estate development, private property, and the family in Pynchon's fiction, will also be assayed.

The Dream Life of Larry Sportello

Like Nathanael West, the title of whose first novel, in 1931, is echoed here,[2] Thomas Pynchon has sometimes been dismissed by reviewers as an author of plotless, incoherent narratives with weakly developed characters and juvenile, often scatological humor that is unfunny. Also like West, Pynchon is a chronicler of a California that is in equal measures dream and nightmare. Seeking an entry point for an examination of the psychoanalytic framework as a theoretical vantage for explicating Pynchon's California novels, like the eponymous hero of West's novel looking for a way inside the Trojan Horse of his dream allegory, we may discover this entryway not where Balso Snell found it but in the motif of dreaming and in the dream work itself.

There are two dream sequences in *Inherent Vice* that occur at crucial plot points, seeming to interrupt the narrative flow of incident but really, I argue, revealing a latent narrative content lying beneath the incidental features of the storyline like the latent content of a dream underlies its manifest content in Freud's account of the dream work in *The Interpretation of Dreams*.[3] The first dream sequence occurs at the end of chapter 12, in which the primary focus is the discovery of the Chryskylodon Institute, where it is revealed that Mickey Wolfmann is being held. Wolfmann, a real estate developer whose kidnapping in chapter 2 at a massage parlor called "Chick Planet" while Doc Sportello is blacked out, having been coldcocked from behind, a classic noir trope, sets the storyline in motion. The dream that concludes the chapter involves a classic regression to childhood. Doc's dream involves the family configuration: his mother, Elmina, or someone like her, and his brother, Gilroy, or someone like him. It is perhaps adventitious, or perhaps not, that "Gilroy" is the name of a small town lying on Route 101 about 16 miles south of San Jose, California, whose claim to fame is its garlic production. The city's chamber of commerce even promotes it as the "Garlic Capital of the World." Situated in the southern end of Santa Clara County, Gilroy marks the borderline or transition from the agricultural zone of the Central Valley, whose southern boundary is Bakersfield, to the Santa Cruz mountains and north to "Vineland" country, where the counterculture takes refuge in the middle novel of Pynchon's "California trilogy" or, perhaps, where it had really always been going on, as Doc muses at one point in *Inherent Vice* (19).

Names in Pynchon's fiction, like those in dreams, whether represented verbally or pictorially, are often condensations of many latent concepts. Doc's brother, Gilroy, we learn in the novel, resides in Bakersfield, or at least in the San Joaquin Valley, and is some kind of "project manager" (112) who is living the postwar American Dream, a bourgeois life of middle-class respectability ("Gilroy's the one with the life," *Inherent Vice* 112), with a house in the suburbs and a career path as an organization man, that is to say, the antithesis of the hippie, counterculture lifestyle Doc leads. Place names and personal names, proper names, are "topoi" in dream work; that is, they are structural positions that can stand for many concepts. "Gilroy" is Larry's brother, the representative of middle-class respectability among the siblings, the one with a "real life" who lives in the flatlands of the Central Valley, the exurban area to the north of Los Angeles distinguished, besides by its being the site of bedroom communities, for its agriculture and a blandness barely spiced up by the production of garlic. That we later learn that Larry's brother has been promoted (to regional manager) but that his marriage is breaking up is a significant detail. His wife, no doubt bored with the feminine mystique of being married to the man in the gray flannel suit, has been noticed "out dancing with Mexicans and some of them you can't tell what they are" at all hours in the local taverns, as Doc's mother, Elmina, informs him toward the end of the novel (352).

The first of Doc's dreams in the novel, then, returns him to the familial constellation of his childhood, one of the few places in which we are provided with a glimpse of Doc's early years and family beginnings. It presents the cultural conflict between "straight" (or "flat land" life, as it is called in the novel) life and hippie, counterculture life as a conflict within the Sportello family configuration, a version of sibling rivalry. I will only briefly and provisionally here identify other issues connected with Doc's first dream and his family relations generally: first, the admonition Doc's Aunt Reet, a real estate broker, constantly makes, for Doc to settle down and buy a house, and the relationship between property, therefore, and the traditional, bourgeois family constellation, what Deleuze and Guattari called the "Oedipal family." The other issue I want to emphasize with respect to Doc's dream involving his brother Gilroy is the critique of the traditional, or Oedipal, family implied by what we learn toward the end of the novel about the fate of Gilroy's marriage. So how Pynchon's portrayal of families in his fiction may be identified at some points with a retreat from, or critique of, the patriarchal, nuclear family of postwar America in a way that could be allied with the similar antifamilialism of Deleuze and Guattari is one of the points I want to make initially. Later, this chapter will be concerned with the opposite movement, toward a recuperation of the family and domesticity under the twin signs of the "sentimental" and the genre of domestic fiction as a subtext of hard-boiled detective fiction.

The second dream sequence in *Inherent Vice* occurs in chapter 19, when a phone call from Crocker Fenway interrupts a dream Doc is having about the exorcism of the "Golden Fang" (in one of its many semantic fields of reference as a mysterious ship involved in a heroin-smuggling conspiracy). Crocker Fenway is the scion of one of the old, landed families in Los Angeles, whose far-flung investment interests include real estate, like Mickey Wolfmann and, on a much smaller scale, Doc's own Aunt Reet, one of his inside connections to the straight world who provides him with crucial information. (The classic noir detective always has moles and sources of information, and Doc's include, besides his Aunt Reet, the deputy district attorney, Penny Kimball; Doc's former partner from his old skip-tracer days working for an outfit called "Gotcha! Searches and Settlements," Fritz Drybeam, who has a connection with the early beginnings of the ARPA-net in the novel; and others.) In Doc's dream, his personal attorney and friend, Sauncho Smilax, is giving a kind of peroration to a speech that concludes with the following, which I quote in full because it contains so many themes of importance to the novel and to this discussion:

> . . . yet there is no avoiding time, the sea of time, the sea of memory and forgetfulness, the years of promise, gone and unrecoverable, of the land almost

> allowed to claim its better destiny, only to have the claim jumped by evildoers known all too well, and taken instead and held hostage to the future we must live in now forever. May we trust that this blessed ship [the *Golden Fang*, rechristened, in Doc's dream, the *Preserved*] is bound for some better shore, some undrowned Lemuria, risen and redeemed, where the American fate, mercifully, failed to transpire . . . (341; ellipses in original).

Setting aside the important dialogue that ensues upon the interruption of Doc's dream by the phone call from Crocker Fenway, an interruption that is itself significant, because it mirrors the "claim jumping" of America's "better destiny" by the "evildoers known all too well," a better destiny fulfilled, if only as a wish, in Doc's dream, I want to remark on the structure of the interrupted sentence, the interruption of the flow of the dream time, in light of Pynchon's narrative of the decades of the 1960s, 1970s, and 1980s in his California trilogy, by the unavoidability of time, the "progress" of history, which is inevitably a narrative of the march of power and the triumph of capital, personified in this case by Crocker Fenway, the power broker and, in the novel, one of the powers behind the city of Los Angeles.

This dream sequence is one of a handful of instances in the novel where the historical horizon of its readers, that is, our own time, a time all of Pynchon's California novels anticipate as a postlapsarian one, is referenced. A pattern of fatalism, of history drifting toward a bleaker future already inhabited by the novel's readers, a future whose signs are already all around and can be read in the paranoia of the early 1970s in which the novel is set, occurs early in a conversation Doc has with Penny Kimball, the deputy district attorney, in which Doc wonders in an indirect monologue whether he can trust what she is telling him, a symptom that "life in psychedelic-sixties L.A. offered more cautionary arguments than you could wave a joint at against too much trust, and the seventies were looking no more promising" (70). A reference to the "hippie metaphysics" of the lost continent of Lemuria includes a chronological perspective from the disenchanted future of the novel's composition and the historical horizon of its readers when it breaks from the conventional literary past-perfect tense in what is seemingly a reference to our own temporal and historical moment: "By this point in California history," our narrator, almost sounding here like an ethnographer of it, says, "enough hippie metaphysics had oozed in among surfing folk that even the regulars here at Wavos, seeing where this was headed [a surfing legend about the 'gnarliest break in the world,' apparently on a Pacific continental drift fault line associated with the appearance of the lost continent of Lemuria] began to shift their feet and look around for other things to do" (101). In chapter 9, there is a description of the "Malibu freeway," which "in those days was not quite the multiple-lane suburban convenience it would later become" (134).[4]

This sentence really contains the nub of the issue I will be concerned with in much of what follows: how Pynchon's California novels are, importantly, among other things, narratives about real estate and the control of the state's history by property developers. In that sense, Pynchon's fictional "California history" is the same narrative as the one found in such works of straight California history as D. J. Waldie's *Holy Land* and Mike Davis's books about California's development and urban studies, whose titles are so evocative of the themes we are examining here.[5] The theme of power and money as they are bound up with real estate development (the Channel View Estates development of Mickey Wolfmann that hovers in the background of *Inherent Vice*); the "flow" of money and capital that moves with an inexorable force in the state's history, like the physical forces of gravity and the arrow of time Pynchon has been so concerned about in all of his fiction; and the paranoia engendered by the people's lack of trust in the police and all the other institutions of society and the state, which has been created and supported by moneyed real estate interests, are all related here.

The motifs of the directionality of time, history, and capital and whether this directionality can be reversed or interrupted occur frequently. For instance, in chapter 12, which concludes with Doc's dream regression to his childhood (one reversal of the arrow of time, at least?), the paranoid mistrust between cops and hippies is represented by the metaphor of the physical force of gravity, which of course also constitutes one of the novel's many intertextual allusions to Pynchon's other fiction: "I wish . . . just once, I *could* trust them [the police]," Doc says, "But it's like the force of gravity, they never pull in any but the one direction" (195). And earlier, in chapter 11, the novel refers to the "strenuous mass passage of time itself" (172) underway in the 1970s by those affluent enough to afford it (the Fenway family, in this connection).

The problem of reversing the arrow of time, given the hopelessness of achieving such a reversal, as Sauncho Smilax's peroration in Doc's dream ("yet there is no avoiding time") acknowledges, is also the project of *Against the Day*, and there are intertextual references in *Inherent Vice* to that novel, such as the description of Lieutenant Christian F. "Bigfoot" Bjornsen's job moonlighting as a creator of television commercials featuring "a relentless terror squad of small children" shouting slogans out of the cop paranoia of hippie subversion such as "Freak Power!" and "Death to the Pig!" to whom Bigfoot drawls in his television spots, "We'll be chums," repeated and italicized for emphasis (*Inherent Vice* 9–10) in what seems to be a reference to the "Chums of Chance" episodes in *Against the Day*. The intertextualism does not end with allusions to Pynchon's own writing, I think, because the Bigfoot Bjornsen character in *Inherent Vice* bears characteristics associated with two characters from James Ellroy's L.A. Quartet series of novels. Wendell "Bud" White (the fact that both have a sobriquet seems to draw a connection between them) is one of the major characters in Ellroy's novel *L.A. Confidential*, and the Black Dahlia murder, the subject of the first novel in Ellroy's L.A. Quartet series, is alluded to in *Inherent Vice* as one of the "good old-time L.A. murder mysteries" by Bigfoot Bjornsen (*Inherent Vice* 209). Bigfoot's moonlighting as a television actor also recalls the character of Jack Vincennes in *L.A. Confidential*, and the kidnapping and shootout at the Chick Planet massage parlor may have parallels with the Night Owl café massacre that forms a significant part of the conspiracy plot in that novel. Indeed, it is tempting to think of Ellroy's project of a sequence of novels spanning several decades of Los Angeles history as parallel to Pynchon's trilogy of novels, which do much the same kind of thing for California history.[6]

There are many characters in *Inherent Vice* who appear in Pynchon's earlier novel in the California trilogy, *Vineland*. Doc himself, we learn, is the cousin of Scott Oof, a character from the earlier novel (family stories and genealogies again provide one of the links between the separate parts of Pynchon's California trilogy, and not only these: Frenesi's antecedents include the Traverse family, whose revenge saga is such a prominent part of *Against the Day*), and there is a reference to Sledge Poteet, a member of the Bay Area film collective 24 Frames Per Second, of which Frenesi Gates, the mother of Prairie Wheeler, is a founding member. Zoyd Wheeler, Prairie's father, is mentioned in *Inherent Vice*, and Gordita Beach, the fictional beach community where Doc lives, is also the scene of Zoyd Wheeler's 1960s past in Southern California before his migration north to Mendocino.

Although the father-daughter relationship between Zoyd and Prairie Wheeler is significant earlier in *Vineland*, toward the middle of the book, it is Prairie's quest for knowledge about her mother's life, after the discovery of a computer file about her mother, that increasingly dominates the book's narrative structure, and it is the maternal genealogy in Prairie's life, the lineage leading from Frenesi to her grandmother, Sasha, rather than that of the paternal line, that seems most important. The reunion of the Traverse-Becker family, which brings together three generations of women—Sasha and her daughter, Frenesi, and Frenesi and Prairie—points to something like a "maternal melodrama" narrative pattern in the novel that may be exemplified by the great Michael Curtiz film *Mildred Pierce* (1945), based on the James M. Cain novel, and which Pynchon refers to so frequently in his work. The so-called "Hollywood happy ending" of *Vineland*, with its tableau of family reunification emphasizing the renewal of mother-daughter bonds that have been strained (the relationship between Sasha and Frenesi and the reconciliation of Frenesi and Prairie Wheeler), has been much maligned in at least the reviews of the novel and more or less neglected by the more serious criticism, perhaps due to the intellectual embarrassment about the sentimental in an academic culture defined initially by New Critical values of ironic detachment and, later, by postmodern cool, which doesn't know quite what to make of Pynchon's conclusion of the novel. The picnic scene in chapter 15 of *Vineland* certainly has, it could be argued, all the elements of melodrama, not only the mother-daughter reunions already mentioned but even the fête interrupted by the villain, Brock Vond, who briefly menaces the virtuous heroine, Prairie Wheeler, in a literal *deus ex machina* appearance or, in this case, a *diabolus ex machina*, as he descends from a hovering helicopter on a winch cable (a menace that may harbor incestuous elements, if Prairie really is his daughter, as he claims, rather than Zoyd's, and space here does not permit delving into the incest theme as an element of the noir tradition, such as in the film *Chinatown* or even *Mildred Pierce*) before being exorcised by Prairie's talismanic spell, "Get the fuck out of here!"[7] The virtuous heroine's victory over her villainous would-be victimizer is, of course, the classic pattern of melodrama, the triumph of virtue over vice.

The relationship between, on the one hand, the sentimental moment of the recognition of family bonds and feeling, such as occurs in *Inherent Vice* in the episode in which Doc's parents visit him or in the reunion of the zombie saxophone player and agent provocateur Coy Harlingen with his family (a reunion that makes Doc tear up when he learns about it from Harlingen's phone call thanking him for it), and, on the other, the theme of vice in the fusion of hard-boiled and sentimental elements of classic noir fiction in Pynchon's novel, is intrinsic to the genre, which the sentimental moments in Pynchon's novel implicitly recognize. The link between the hard boiled and the sentimental, two seemingly antithetical genres, has been the theme of an interesting recent critical study by Leonard Cassuto, a professor of English at Fordham and the author of *Hard-Boiled Sentimentality: The Secret History of American Crime Stories.*[8]

Cassuto's essential argument might be quoted here in full, because it applies so well to the points I am making about the sentimental in Pynchon's fiction, particularly from *Vineland* forward:

> Crime fiction from the hard-boiled era forward has been . . . influenced by . . . the teleology of psychoanalysis . . . and the Cold War—but it has been profoundly shaped by the idealized image of the middle-class family. This ideal, which saturates American culture, was originally propagated by the domestic literature of the nineteenth century, especially sentimental novels. These novels form the main point of connection between the family ideal and the modern crime story. . . . In other words . . . stereotypically hard-boiled crime fiction and stereotypically feminine, evangelical, and domestic sentimental fiction are two branches of the same middle-class tree. The connection between the hard-boiled and the sentimental changes with the times. . . . By reading hard-boiled crime stories through the sentimental

> narratives that preceded them, I show not only how the two are intertwined, but more important, how their shared preoccupations reflect a growing concern about the way that Americans think—and don't think—about the value and place of family in the postindustrial world. (2–3)

Cassuto traces the cultural conflict between the sentimental and domestic values identified with the family and the market economy of capitalism by tracing it back to the Scottish Common Sense philosophers and juxtaposing two texts by Adam Smith: *The Theory of Moral Sentiments* (1759) and *The Wealth of Nations* (1776). Smith's 1759 text was an important source for 18th- and 19th-century discourses on sentimentality and domesticity as represented by the family community, and his 1776 text centers on the individual economic actor who pursues his rational self-interest in contrast to the self-renunciation that lies at the heart of domestic virtue. These two texts symbolize, then, the conflict between the public, market-based sphere characterized by individualism and maximization of profit as the motive for human action and the private, domestic sphere of the family characterized by self-sacrifice and communitarian values (Cassuto 10–11). This same conflict is personified in the private detective figure from hard-boiled crime fiction who is simultaneously a lone wolf and a profit-driven and rational-self-interest-calculating actor but is also a figure who frequently is an observer of, and acts to reconcile, threatened or damaged families. The conflict between the public, market-based sphere of capitalistic motivation and the private, domestic sphere of domesticity and family is also represented, I argue, by Pynchon's recurring treatment of real estate and property development in his fiction. Real estate represents the commodification of the private, domestic sphere of values represented by the family. The capitalist real estate developer serves much the same villainous role in Pynchon's fiction as the serial killer in Cassuto's analysis of hard-boiled crime fiction. If the serial killer is a lone wolf who preys upon and seeks the destruction of the family in the type of crime fiction analyzed by Cassuto (as the FBI agent, Brock Vond, does in *Vineland*), the real estate developer represents a more mediated threat, by market-based capitalism, to the communitarian and emotional connections between individuals represented by the family, the coercion and co-optation by money and commodification of connections established by emotion and feeling. While there is not space to develop this point further in this chapter, I read the recurring motif of what might be called the "longing for connection" and communication in Pynchon's fiction that is so frequently represented by the virtual sphere of the primitive Internet (the ARPA-net in *Inherent Vice* and even going back to the famous simile of the housing tracts of San Narciso visualized as a circuit board), the connection of the Tristero postal service, or the image of the convoy of taillights in the fog that concludes *Inherent Vice* as the emotional center of Pynchon's writing, from which it derives much of its pathos and transcendence. And this longing for connection in a world of severed human ties may also explain why paranoia in Pynchon is more of an affirmative value than it is a defense mechanism against the "schizo-" flows of connection in Deleuze and Guattari. In Pynchon, paranoia does at least represent a kind of wish fulfillment, even if tinged with anxiety and fear, that things are bound in a mysterious, immanent, and transcendent way in which the aura is fast disappearing in the reification and death-driven flows of capital, where every connection is preempted by exchange value and the profit incentive.

In *Mildred Pierce*, a touchstone both in *Vineland* and *Inherent Vice*, we have the symbiosis of the hard-boiled detective genre and the sentimental expression of feeling, particularly the kind of maternal love so evocatively conveyed in the magnificent performance by the real-life "Mommie Dearest," Joan Crawford. It is a commonplace of film criticism that the character of Mildred Pierce in Curtiz's film adaptation becomes the female variant of the more traditional Philip Marlowe or Sam Spade detective character of the hard-boiled crime genre, blending the two genres.[9] The Doc Sportello character in Pynchon's novel reverses this gender role reversal enacted in *Mildred Pierce*, embodying in his own embrace of a sentimental expression of feeling a certain "feminization" of the hard-boiled detective figure, which may not be unrelated to the feminization of American culture attempted by the hippie counterculture. This affirmation of his own "feminine" side may also be related to the matriarchal structure of the Sportello family, its emphasis on its own "distaff" side (Doc's Aunt Reet and his mother, Elmina, play a far more important role in the family than Doc's father, Leo) and, implicitly, a recuperation of family bonds and feeling through the medium of sentiment that emphasizes a more matriarchal, rather than patriarchal, family structure.

The Crime of Urban Development in Pynchon's California Novels

If the concern with "vice" as a part of American life could be identified in the Puritan beginnings of American culture, it seems to have become a theme in fiction and film with the gangster movies of the 1930s and even more with the postwar crime syndicate films that portrayed "vice" as the shadowy underbelly of the postwar American dream of suburban innocence and utopia, what some critics have referred to as "Kefauverism" in the postwar revival of gangster films that, unlike their prewar predecessors, presented criminality and criminal organizations as woven into the fabric of "normal" American life, so that distinguishing between institutions of law and order and criminal syndicates and conspiracies became nearly impossible. Films such as Abraham Polonsky's *Force of Evil* (1948), starring John Garfield, which portrayed the takeover of gambling by organized crime and the corruption of city officials, became common. And of course, John Garfield movies are a touchstone for Doc Sportello throughout *Inherent Vice*.

The postwar "Kefauver" cycle of films, such as Joseph M. Newman's *711 Ocean Drive*; the Warner Brothers movie *The Enforcer* (1951), starring Humphrey Bogart as the district attorney and with a prologue by Senator Estes Kefauver himself; and Robert Wise's 1951 film *The Captive City*, which had an epilogue by Kefauver to add documentary authenticity, was inspired by the Kefauver Committee's final report on organized crime (1951),[10] which exposed organized crime involvement in racketeering and gambling and its corruption of officials and police forces in a wide number of American cities. Indeed, a whole subgenre of the "Kefauver" cycle of postwar criminal syndicate films was based on the narrative structure of the Kefauver report, which began with a series of "City Stories" that organized the presentation of the committee's investigation. So, during the mid-1950s, a series of films mimicked the "City Stories" narrative pattern of the Kefauver Committee report, films such as

The Miami Story and *Miami Exposé, New York Confidential, Chicago Confidential, Chicago Syndicate, New Orleans Uncensored, Inside Detroit, The Phenix City Story, The Houston Story,* and *Portland Exposé.* Lee Grieveson, Esther Sonnet, and Peter Stanfield call this postwar cycle of films the "urban exposé" subgenre or cycle of Kefauver films in their edited study of them.

The Kefauver Committee's central concern was with the infiltration and control by organized crime of gambling, the "two-dollar bet." Gambling, of course, is a frequent motif in Pynchon's fiction. Readers of *Gravity's Rainbow* will recall that Part 2 of the book is set in the "Casino Hermann Goering," and in *Against the Day*, Reef Traverse employs mining skills learned in the Rockies as a contract worker in the Alps between Switzerland and Austria, where he encounters an elite culture of gambling in his interactions with such aristocratic figures as Ruperta Chirpingdon-Groin that is both familiar from his days in the Colorado mining towns but also considerably more *haut monde* than the gambling culture he is familiar with. The pleasure spas and leisure activities of the European ruling class are a theme in that part of the novel, and the American's encounter with European decadence, a variation on a Jamesian theme, runs throughout Pynchon's fiction, of course, notably in the African colonial episodes in *V.* and throughout *Gravity's Rainbow.* In another way of putting it, this Jamesian theme of the American's encounter with European decadence is the encounter with "vice" that has always run through Pynchon's fiction.

Las Vegas is a setting for about a third of *Inherent Vice.* Gambling is a version of the entropy theme in Pynchon in that it involves the relationship between chance and control. The organized crime syndicates that gained control over the gambling industry in the United States during the 1950s and developed Las Vegas wrested control of legal gambling there away from Howard Hughes and Hollywood celebrities such as Debbie Reynolds, who were looking for investments for their earnings from film acting. (Reynolds's second marriage to businessman Harry Karl ended in bankruptcy because of Karl's gambling addiction, and her third marriage to real estate developer Richard Hamlett, during which they purchased the Greek Isles Hotel and Casino, also ended in bankruptcy when the casino was a financial failure.) Loss of value, of capital, of investment is one side of the coin whose other face is control by the powerful and conspiratorial interests that dominate gambling in Las Vegas. I'll return to the theme of capital, and capitalism, as an entropic process a little later when I consider the paranoia/schizophrenia, territorialization/deterritorialization, arborescence/nomadism dichotomy in Deleuze and Guattari.

For now, what is important is that even more than gambling, which is only the commodity that creates the raison d'etre for Las Vegas (and as such, it is the perfect realization of the commodity form, pure exchange value without any use whatsoever), it is land development (what Marx would have called rentier capitalism) that underlies the conspiracies and powers behind Las Vegas, and the same could be said of Los Angeles (two cities whose development is connected by Howard Hughes, whose ventures united Hollywood and gambling). This becomes clear in *Inherent Vice* in the chapters in which the action moves outside of the successful casinos on the south strip into the less prosperous north strip and even further, into the abandoned developments in North Las Vegas and on out into the desert west of there, in the area bounding Death Valley, punctuated only occasionally by little towns such as Pahrump, Nevada, famous for its Chicken Ranch. This is the "unmapped territory" where Mickey Wolfmann plans his housing development where tenants will be able to come and live rent free.

As in Roman Polanski's 1974 film *Chinatown*, with its great Robert Towne screenplay, in which the gumshoe J. J. Gittes (Jack Nicholson) unravels a conspiracy involving water rights and land development engineered by the corrupt Noah Cross (in a truly sinister performance by John Huston), the conspiracy in *Inherent Vice* similarly involves real estate development and land speculation: the onomastically named "Channel View Estates" are being developed by Michael Wolfmann, whose kidnapping and eventual discovery by Doc Sportello in Las Vegas completes one of the circles, quests, or investigations in the novel.

It is possible that Pynchon's choice of the name "Wolfmann" for this character condenses several references. One might be suggested by the famous case study of the Russian aristocrat Sergei Konstantinovitch Pankejeff, who was known by the pseudonym "the Wolf Man." Freud published the case in his 1918 paper "From the History of an Infantile Neurosis" and referred to Pankejeff as the "Wolf Man" because the case centered on the analysis of a dream in which Pankejeff was in a tree being menaced by a pack of wolves below him. After Freud's analysis of his own dream of "Irma's injection," the "Wolf Man" case study is one of the earliest and most important of the cases involving and establishing the method of dream analysis as a cornerstone of Freudian psychoanalysis, and so we return once again to the analysis of dreams with which this chapter started as establishing the context of a psychoanalytic discourse for the explication of Pynchon's novel. The name "Mickey Wolfmann" may also remind us of the real life mobster Meyer Harris "Mickey" Cohen, a prominent figure in the crime syndicates that operated both in Los Angeles and in the development of gambling in Las Vegas, who appears, incidentally, in three of Ellroy's L.A. Quartet novels, *The Big Nowhere*, *L.A. Confidential*, and *White Jazz*.

Pynchon has been writing about the role of real estate and land development in Los Angeles since at least *The Crying of Lot 49*, and it is one of the most important sources for the many paranoid conspiracies in his fiction, which is natural, as it is part of the paranoiac unconscious of the city in historical actuality. Pierce Inverarity, it will be recalled, is a land developer, and the Michael Wolfmann of *Inherent Vice* seems to be named at least partly in an intertextual reference to Inverarity's colleague, Mike Fallopian. I suspect the character of Wolfmann is also partly modeled on real estate developer Eli Broad, a Chicago-born real estate mogul who partnered with Donald Kaufman to form "Kaufman and Broad," or KB Homes, which moved from Chicago to Los Angeles in the late 1950s–early 1960s and developed a large swath of the planned communities from Las Vegas to Southern California before becoming a global real estate developer in the 1980s. The name "Wolfmann" seems to echo the "Kaufman" of Donald Kaufman, and Michael Wolfmann is kind of a portmanteau of Mike Fallopian and Donald Kaufman. If there is any doubt, a few pages after introducing Michael Wolfmann, Pynchon has Doc Sportello park his car at the corner of Kaufman and Broad, a fictional intersection that might as well exist. Anyone who lives in Southern California is very familiar with KB Homes. Eli Broad is almost synonymous with the development of the west side of Los Angeles and is a prominent philanthropist and arts patron in Los Angeles. It is even conceivable that Mickey Wolfmann's collection of smutty ties is a spoof of Eli Broad's claim to be a connoisseur of fine art. The significant point is that the central plotline of Pynchon's *Inherent Vice* links real estate development with paranoid conspiracy in the kidnapping of Michael Wolfmann.

Paranoia is the psychic structure corresponding to the law of the Father, in the bourgeois, or Oedipal family, for Deleuze and Guattari, a figure whom they also assimilate to the Despot, the chieftain of the clan, or moiety, structure of primitive society (what they call "barbarism" in the French usage of the term). Paranoia directs the psychic energy of desire and supplies the direction for work, for labor, in Deleuze and Guattari's account, what a more traditional Marxism might have called the appropriation of surplus (whether that surplus is figured as labor, or desire: that is, desiring-production). It is a force of accumulation, a defense mechanism against lack. Its opposite pole is schizophrenia and, also, the gift economy of potlatch, of expenditure without reserve. We find in Crocker Fenway the Nixon-era epigone of the Deleuzian Despot. In a meeting arranged between Fenway and Doc Sportello after the interrupted dream sequence I alluded to earlier, Fenway styles himself as a member of that collection of old Los Angeles families who are "*in place*" (*Inherent Vice* 347; italics in original). Fenway is both a fictional member of and a "fixer" for that club of powerful Los Angeles founding families including, in actuality, Otis Chandler (founder of the *Los Angeles Times*), William Mulholland (the engineer behind the LA Aqueduct, the power behind LA Water and Power, whose unscrupulous methods in securing water and land rights for the LA Aqueduct were the basis for the Hollis I. Mulwray character played by John Huston in *Chinatown*), Gaylord Wilshire (developer of the Westlake Park residential subdivision who donated the land for the street that would be named after him), Harris Newmark (a real estate developer whose property eventually became the town of Montebello in East Los Angeles), Frederick H. Rindge (Union Oil Company executive and director of Los Angeles Edison Electric Company, owner of what later became Malibu and Topanga canyons and most of the San Fernando Valley), and William Starke Rosecrans (a Civil War general who moved to California, bought land that became the cities of San Pedro and Redondo Beach, and had a long career in politics). "We've been in place forever," explains Fenway. "Real estate, water rights, oil, cheap labor—all of that's ours, it's always been ours" (*Inherent Vice* 347). Fenway acts to protect the interests of those who are rooted in place, arborescentlike, in Deleuzian terms; the residents, against the "transient," nomadic (in Deleuzian terms), preterite (in Pynchon's term) population of hippies, beach bums, surfers, and *cholos* who rent, as opposed to owning, property, and the newer developers, such as Mickey Wolfmann, whose residential developments provide housing for this transient population.

The conflict between the moneyed interests represented by Crocker Fenway and the nomadic, transient populations of Southern California is also represented by the generational Oedipal conflict within the Fenway family, between Crocker Fenway and his daughter Japonica, concerning whom the episodes in *Inherent Vice* continue a time-honored tradition in noir fiction of wild, errant daughters of wealthy fathers who undertake a "schizo-" break (in Deleuzian terms) with the family and must be brought back within the family fold by the private eye hired by the Despotic father.[11] The paranoiac drive of the father is one side of a family structure that includes the schizo-break of the daughter in the Fenway family episodes of *Inherent Vice.*

The real estate mogul is one of the many figures of the Despot in Pynchon's fictional world. Pierce Inverarity and Michael Wolfmann are lapsed or reformed Despots, however. Inverarity's legacy to Oedipa sends her on her quest to unravel the mystery of the Tristero, and Michael Wolfmann is kidnapped (ultimately, we learn, by agents of the federal government) because, in a spasm of remorse for the way he has accumulated his wealth, he plans to give it all away by investing it in a real estate development in the Nevada desert where anyone can come and live rent free. Of course, that must not be allowed to happen. Private property as the basis of capital must not be permitted to be threatened like this.

Readers of *The Crying of Lot 49* will of course immediately think of the lyrical, indirect monologue passage near the conclusion of the novel, in which it is suggested that the development of "San Narciso" is the secret behind the Tristero conspiracy (or, perhaps, the other way around; it doesn't matter), and I want to quote part of it because of what it suggests about the structure of paranoia and conspiracy in Pynchon: "If San Narciso and the estate were really no different from any other town, any other estate, then by that continuity [Oedipa Maas] might have found the Tristero anywhere in her Republic, through any of a hundred lightly-concealed entranceways, a hundred alienations, if only she'd looked" (135). And there follows a long passage in which Oedipa imagines what the land must have looked like before the real estate boom, when the first drifters, the "preterite" of humanity, made their way to the region, before it was taken over by the land barons, when there was still a chance for a *Gemeinschaft*, a community based on free association (a dream of freedom revived in the hippie communities of the beach towns in Pynchon's California trilogy). This prelapsarian vision of Southern California seems almost to contain the seeds of at least the Traverse family plotline of *Against the Day*, Pynchon's imagining of the frontier era as an alternative community to the planned and controlled communities that organize the grid of the land as a means to a return on investment, what Deleuze and Guattari would call the Despot to whom all the flows of capital return in the structure of Debt.

The passage in *The Crying of Lot 49* continues, in the simile comparing the planned communities of Orange County to the circuit board of a computer that is so well known:

> For it was now like walking among matrices of a great digital computer, the zeroes and ones twinned above, hanging like balanced mobiles right and left, ahead, thick, maybe endless. Behind the hieroglyphic streets there would either be a transcendent meaning, or only the earth. . . . Another mode of meaning behind the obvious, or none. Either Oedipa in the orbiting ecstasy of a true paranoia, or a real Tristero. For there either was some Tristero beyond the appearance of the legacy America, or there was just America and if there was just America then it seemed the only way she could continue, and manage to be at all relevant to it, was as an alien, unfurrowed, assumed full circle into some paranoia. (135–37)

The sentence, "Behind the hieroglyphic streets there would either be a transcendent meaning, or only the earth," is recalled in *Inherent Vice* in the epigraph to the novel, "Under the paving stones, the beach!" which is a graffito from the 1968 student rebellion in France ("*Sous les pavés, la plage*!"). A variation on this expression occurs in a reference to the Channel View Estates development in chapter 2, where Pynchon describes the "desert beneath the pavement" (20). The Paris student rebellion in 1968 is the same cultural moment, then, for both *Inherent Vice* and Deleuze and Guattari's *Anti-Oedipus*.

The image of a "transcendent meaning" behind the "hieroglyphic streets," and all the other meanings and conspiracies lurking behind the "order of the visible," as Pynchon puts it in *Gravity's Rainbow*, identify paranoia as the search for meaning behind quotidian or innocent appearances. It is also, according to Doc Sportello, the *modus operandi* of the detective, an epistemic mode all its own, a hermeneutic of suspicion leading to discovery: "paranoia was a tool of the trade, it pointed you in directions you might not have seen to go. There were messages from beyond, if not madness, at least a shitload of unkind motivation" (*Inherent Vice* 117).

Real estate, money as currency, the Tristero postage system: all function as paranoiac systems of command, communication, and control. I have already talked about real estate as a theme connecting *Inherent Vice* and *The Crying of Lot 49*. There is a nice intertextual link between the two novels in a similar hallucination in both that also connects money and the postage stamps of the Tristero system: in *Lot 49*, there is a moment when the face on one of the postage stamps seems to move. In *Inherent Vice*, Doc Sportello has a hallucination in which the face of Richard Nixon, which is imprinted on some counterfeit currency, "funny money" that is part of the "Golden Fang" smuggling operation, similarly seems to move. Perhaps these hallucinatory moments in the two novels could be seen as two of Tchitcherine's "oneirine hauntings" under the influence of LSD in *Gravity's Rainbow*: hallucinations "so ordinary, so conventional . . . that they are only recognized as hauntings through some radical though plausible violation of possibility: the presence of the dead, journeys by the same route and means where one person will set out later but arrive earlier, a printed diagram which no amount of light will make readable" (*Gravity's Rainbow* 703).

This last phrase could apply to any number of episodes in Pynchon's novels: the presence of the dead in the zombies in *Inherent Vice* is only the last in a line that includes the Thanatoids, the Trespassers, and many others from Pynchon's fiction who return from the dead (going "against the day" or arrow of Time that always points north to the land of the dead, or, in *Inherent Vice*, that leads to Death Valley, the entropy that means death for humanity). And the "printed diagram which no amount of light will make readable" recalls both the grid of San Narciso contemplated by Oedipa and the photographs of the massacre at Chick Planet that Doc Sportello attempts to interpret, images of the breakdown of connection that makes communication and intelligibility possible, even if in a paranoid frame of reference.

Paranoia in Pynchon is most frequently the feeling of the "connectedness of everything." This sense of paranoia actually most closely resembles the opposite of paranoia for Deleuze and Guattari, however: what they call "schizophrenia"—the unrestricted flows that couple anything with anything else, that break up molar continuity, systems, collectivities, and aggregates. This double structure of paranoia is illustrated also by Slothrop's "cycling" between paranoia and anti-paranoia in *Gravity's Rainbow*: "If there is something comforting—religious, if you want—about paranoia, there is still also anti-paranoia, where nothing is connected to anything, a condition not many of us can bear for long" (*Gravity's Rainbow* 434). Paranoia is, in this passage, a kind of Nietzschean "necessary illusion," a self-deception or untruth that is life enhancing (see, e.g., *Beyond Good and Evil*). The cycling pattern of oscillation between paranoia and anti-paranoia is one way to think about the double structure of paranoia in Pynchon, the vacillation between the sense that everything is connected in a vast hidden conspiracy, that nothing is chance, and the opposite sense that nothing is connected and everything is determined by chance (a sense which is close to entropy). The polarity of paranoia and anti-paranoia in Tyrone Slothrop is something like the polarity, the cycling between paranoia and schizophrenia, territorialization and deterritorialization in Deleuze and Guattari, but with some important differences that bring us to the limitations of a Deleuze and Guattari model of "paranoia" for analyzing Pynchon, because they mean different things by "paranoia" than Pynchon does.

So, the psychoanalytic framework, or even the framework of antipsychiatry in Deleuze and Guattari, which still is linked to a certain psychoanalytic discourse, does encounter a limit of efficacy as a model for interpreting Pynchon's fiction and not only because psychoanalysis has been replaced so often, in Pynchon's novels, by dentistry.

NOTES

1. Grieveson et al., *Mob Culture.*
2. West, *Dream Life of Balso Snell.*
3. Freud, *Interpretation of Dreams (First Part)* and *Interpretation of Dreams (Second Part).*

4. A freeway that was planned, but was never built (had it been built, it would have been designated Route 64). It is represented by dotted lines showing its projected construction in Thomas Brothers Company maps of the early 1970s. See the AAA Roads Forum "California Highways" website (http://www.cahighways.org/057-064.html#064) for a discussion among aficionados of old highway and road maps of California, who must number Pynchon himself among them, of what was to be called the Malibu Canyon Freeway/Whitnall Freeway, which would have left Interstate 5 near the State Route 170/I-5 junction, continued across the San Fernando Valley, crossing Van Nuys Boulevard near Parthenia, Sepulveda near Chase, ending up about the level of Saticoy or Strathern. Just west of Bell Canyon, it turned to intersect the US 101 Freeway around Hidden Hills. It then crossed the Santa Monica Mountains approximately across Malibu Canyon (Las Virgenes) Road. The routing for this was never determined, and there is no assigned traversable route. The limits of the route inventory as of the 1970s was between U.S. 101 and I-5. The portion between U.S. 101 and State Route 1 had its adoption rescinded by the California Highway Commission on July 12, 1973. That Pynchon's research for *Inherent Vice* included old road maps of the early 1970s is consistent with his reliance on the Baedeker guides in his early novels, such as *V.* and *Gravity's Rainbow*, and it also represents what elsewhere in this essay collection we have called "California as the unmapped Western frontier" first projected in *Mason and Dixon*, an open space where alternate futures (such as one in which Doc Sportello could drive a Route 64, Malibu Canyon Freeway that only existed as a virtual series of broken lines on the maps of the period) coexist with history as it actually did develop.
5. See, e.g., Waldie, *Holy Land*, and Davis, *City of Quartz* and *Ecology of Fear*.
6. Ellroy's "L.A. Quartet" consists of *The Black Dahlia*, *The Big Nowhere*, *L.A. Confidential*, and *White Jazz*.
7. On the "interrupted fete" as a typical element of melodrama, see Brooks, *Melodramatic Imagination*, 29.
8. Cassuto, *Hard-Boiled Sentimentality*, 2008.
9. See Cassuto 86–91 for a detailed analysis of both the novel and film versions of *Mildred Pierce* in light of his thesis about the connection between the hard-boiled crime novel and domestic sentimental fiction.
10. Special Committee to Investigate Organized Crime in Interstate Commerce, "Organized Crime in Interstate Commerce."
11. Carmen, the errant daughter of Colonel Sternwood in Chandler's *The Big Sleep*, would be only the most obvious in a lengthy series of such figures. For a fuller discussion, see Cassuto.

Playgrounds of Detection. The Californian Private Eye in Thomas Pynchon's *The Crying of Lot 49* and *Inherent Vice*[1]

SCOTT MACLEOD

Ever since "Whole Sick Crew" vagabond Charisma sang Wittgenstein's famous phrase "the world is all the case is"[2] (288) in that now famous debut novel *V.*, Thomas Pynchon has consciously shaped his polyvalent narratives to pay tribute to the allure of mystery and discovery. Pynchon is an author who revels in both honoring and manipulating generic tropes and ideological variables in order to critically evaluate historical cultural eras and social mores. As Brian McHale persuasively argues in his recent essay "Genre as History: Pynchon's Genre-Poaching," the author engages in the practice of "*mediated historiography*—the writing of an era's history through the medium of its popular genres" (25). Analyzing Pynchon's gargantuan 2006 novel *Against the Day*, McHale asserts that Pynchon provides "a virtual library of entertainment fiction" (18); however, there is one archetypal narrative genre that burns most brightly throughout the writer's oeuvre: the detective story.

This comparative chapter explores Thomas Pynchon's representations of California through the lens of the detective fiction genre in *The Crying of Lot 49* and *Inherent Vice*. Both novels contain deceptively simple narrative premises that feature protagonists who assume the role of the private eye not merely to "catch the perp" but because they believe the detective process will provide stability in a world saturated with indeterminacy. While these texts are, of course, works of fiction, Pynchon's depictions of contemporary California as a mysterious, tentacled labyrinth are presented with astonishing sociopolitical insight and relevance. Behind the superficial appearance of a liberated world, driven by sexual revolution and hallucinatory drugs, reside secret power structures and corrupt governing bodies. Pynchon uses his idiosyncratic investigators and haunting conspiracies as tools with which to examine the deeply concerning political and social anxieties of the California counterculture in the 1960s and 1970s.

From its ancient Oedipal beginnings to its manifestation in the contemporary information age, the detective fiction genre has remained relevant through generations because of its ability to adapt to changing cultural movements and social anxieties. This relevance also exists through the detective's pursuit of clues and devotion to the deciphering of hidden truths, where the pretext of authority is exerted as a means of venturing into previously restricted and secret places, a trope that has an everlasting readerly[3] allure. In *V.*, Pynchon's experimentation with the detective fiction genre emerges through Herbert Stencil's fragmented quest to unravel the profusion of patterns that may lead to solving the mystery of V. The quest subsequently blossoms into the formation of the amateur detective in *The Crying of Lot 49*, in which Oedipa Maas attempts to employ Sherlockian ratiocination in an effort to solve a potential conspiracy that concerns a secretive postal network and the greater legacy of America.

When one thinks about the private detective in a hard-boiled context in particular, where the forlorn "hero" must wade through an oppressive stench of corruption in order to rectify social injustice, one inevitably thinks of the bright lights and mean streets of California. The Golden State has been home to the private eye ever since the gritty hard-boiled school of Raymond Chandler and Dashiell Hammett rose to prominence in the 1920s and 1930s. Pynchon also shares a special affinity for the West Coast, with his California-centric stories considered by many to be his most accessible and popular novels.[4] Even in *Gravity's Rainbow* and *Against the Day*, which feature "encyclopedic" narratives[5] that disorient the reader with schizophrenic juxtapositions between World War digressions and scatological fantasies, Los Angeles functions as the city of climax. Pynchon's 1973 masterwork concludes with the imminent threat of nuclear apocalypse, as an intercontinental ballistic missile screams across the California sky, while *Against the Day* closes with "Psychical Detective" Lew Basnight confronted with a Chandler-esque West Coast murder mystery.

In *The Crying of Lot 49* and *Inherent Vice*, the California setting works as a *device*—a "printed circuit" or elaborate pattern that the detectives believe will reveal the "central truth." There has been considerable Pynchon scholarship published on the complexity of these protagonists and the 1960s California milieu—leading critics, including David Cowart, Thomas Schaub, and Tony Tanner, to provide readings of these novels that concentrate on the importance of historical context, illuminating the author and relative California cultural framework to form a richer understanding and appreciation of these "fictional" worlds.[6] However, by elucidating the way in which Pynchon's multilayered rendering of the detective process operates in connecting these fundamental components together in each narrative, this chapter intends to provide a genre perspective from which to dissect the relevant cultural zeitgeist with an even richer layer of density and signification. Pynchon utilizes a revisionist approach to the traditional detective story in both texts as a means of disorienting his respective sleuths with an endless trail of clues and unresolved questions, inevitably exposing the sinister reality that has been carefully concealed under California's plastic mask.

Pynchon exploits the myth of California as a "promised land," which Liahna Babener describes as "an empire built on a spurious foundation, decked in tinsel, and beguiled by its own illusory promises." (127). Analyzing Oedipa Maas's and Larry "Doc" Sportello's convoluted investigations exposes the harsh and bitter decline of American empire and society. The dramatically different periods in which these novels were published also allow the opportunity to dissect significant variables in Pynchon's depictions of California in the ensuing narratives. As Inger H. Dalsgaard, Luc Herman, and Brian McHale state, "Where *Lot 49*, Pynchon's most widely taught novel, is forward-looking, bursting with subcultural alternatives and subversive energies . . . *Inherent Vice* [is] retrospective and reflective, focused less on utopian possibilities than on exposing the apparatus that maintains the status quo" (4). For *The Crying of Lot 49*, it seems clear that the assassination of President John F. Kennedy, the Vietnam War, and the Watts Riots instilled an even greater urgency in the writing of the text. Pynchon subtly destabilizes the foundations of linearity and readerly satisfaction typically associated with ratiocinative detection in this novel, whereas he overtly embraces and exploits the hard-boiled sense of indeterminacy and convolution in *Inherent Vice.* Set in the same era but published more than 40 years after *The Crying of Lot 49*, *Inherent Vice* adds an even deeper level of complexity to his representations of California, specifically as a didactic forum for epoch-defining cultural moments.

In the detective narrative of today, complicated as it has been by the influences of postmodernism, the central focus is upon the protagonist adapting to the shifting landscape by questioning ontological and epistemological variables.[7] The playgrounds of detection are blurred by the combination of traditional genre elements with subversive elements representative of the dominant postmodern cultural movement (such as pastiche, parody, and paranoia), and consequently, the gumshoe is forced to weave through an intensifying realm of suspicion and disinformation. As demonstrated in *The Crying of Lot 49* and *Inherent Vice*, the respective detective figures are isolated through narrative fragmentation, for which external communication is only occasionally offered as a palliative to fear, and disruption is foregrounded. There is a perception that *everything is connected*, with Oedipa and Doc attempting to institute "order" in fractured worlds largely built on the concept of disorder. Both novels encourage the resistance to conventional resolution, with the detectives implicated and entrapped in these mysteries the more they investigate. However, Pynchon's writing extends beyond the boundaries of generic disjunction and subversive possibilities. By constructing extraordinarily vivid representations of California, the author is also reinforcing how this state will always be inextricably linked with detective fiction, demonstrating the importance of the continuities between hard-boiled and neo-noir.

It is fellow postmodern practitioner Paul Auster who most appropriately articulates the perspective of the contemporary detective in his genre-bending set of stories, published in collection as *The New York Trilogy*. Early in the first story, "City of Glass," private investigator Daniel Quinn provides an acute rumination on detective fiction, ironically as both an inexperienced detective and as a writer of the genre:

> In the good mystery there is nothing wasted, no sentence, no word that is not significant. And even if it is not significant, it has the potential to be so—which amounts to the same thing. . . . Since everything seen or said, even the slightest, most trivial thing, can bear a connection to the outcome of the story, nothing must be overlooked. . . .
>
> The detective is the one who looks, who listens, who moves through this morass of objects and events in search of the thought, the idea that will pull all these things together and make sense of them.[8]

Like Auster, Pynchon is interested in manipulating this enduring genre paradigm as a means to expand the hermeneutic possibilities for his detective characters. From the amateur to the hard-boiled, Pynchon's idiosyncratic representations have become an inspiring blueprint from which Auster and others have established their own unique modes of detection and metafictional mysteries for the contemporary private eye.

The great portion of the commentary that has been generated on *The Crying of Lot 49* (justifying its status as both a subtle and an intricate text) has revolved around Pynchon's complex depictions of geopolitical systems, religion, and the wonderfully enigmatic concept of entropy (which has been inextricably linked with the author ever since he named his 1960 short story after the thermodynamic property). Up until the release of *Inherent Vice*, however, Pynchon's California fictions had not attracted the same amount of consideration in relation to how the respective protagonists operate within the realm of detective fiction. This chapter will examine the comparative relationship between *The Crying of Lot 49* and *Inherent Vice* by focusing on the author's construction of the (post)modernized detective figure and subsequent interrogation of generic elements and conventions, such as ratiocination, the hard-boiled, and neo-noir. Rather than strictly subscribing to the theoretical model of the "anti-detective"[9] as a means of deconstructing or expressing the absence of conventions typically associated with the detective fiction genre, Pynchon's narrative strategies in both novels strike a delicate balance between instilling readerly familiarity while introducing elements of genre subversion.

The Hatchings of Identity

In *The Crying of Lot 49* and *Inherent Vice*, Pynchon establishes his protagonists as "operational" detective agents, who subsequently propel the convoluted narratives. Classified by Pynchon in *Slow Learner* as a "story . . . which was marketed as a 'novel'" (22), *The Crying of Lot 49* begins with Oedipa learning that she has been summoned to serve as the executor for the estate of her mysterious, rich ex-lover, Pierce Inverarity, whose spectral presence looms over the troubled sleuth throughout the narrative. Unlike other distinguished 20th-century novelists experimenting with the detective fiction genre, such as Auster and Eco, though, Pynchon adopts a more conservative approach when establishing his protagonist's identity. By refraining from invoking immediate disorientation and paranoia, Oedipa is introduced as a California housewife grounded with relative stability who is most content simply attending Tupperware parties. Pynchon presents Oedipa as a "whole" character before she becomes fragmented by her daunting investigation.

In his essay "The Death of the Real in *The Crying of Lot 49*," Maurice Couturier considers Oedipa an "average woman" and suggests that "the fact that she goes to a psychiatrist only confirms her normalcy" (20). Pynchon's feminized Sophoclean protagonist in *The Crying of Lot 49* also superficially operates in direct contrast with the archetypal figure in traditional detective fiction, particularly hard-boiled noir, in which the investigator is usually cynical and well-versed in the art of detection. Instead of spending days wielding a gun and tailing cars, Oedipa is more accustomed to carrying a kitchen pot and hanging washing out to dry. Nonetheless, in the novel's opening passage, the banality of Oedipa's life is exposed as an alternative and powerful form of isolation and despair (compared to the more conventional burden placed on Doc), while her curious mind, which wonders whether there was "perhaps too much kirsch in the fondue" (5), is quickly occupied with a far greater mystery.

As previously noted, Pynchon's fascination and gaudy play with the detective process not only evolves over his subsequent novels through a variety of different characters (from Slothrop's metaphysical self-investigation in *Gravity's Rainbow* to Frenesi's and Prairie's respective conspiratorial California odysseys in *Vineland*), it culminates in a novel that the author simply "can't avoid."[10]

Inherent Vice represents Pynchon's most overt textual affiliation with the detective genre—the hard-boiled is reimagined through pastiche, and there is a conscious attempt to evoke for the reader an acute sociopolitical rendering of California during Richard Nixon's presidency. The majority of the novel's proceedings are also focalized through Doc's dope-addled psyche, where, as in *The Crying of Lot 49*, Pynchon abandons an inherently omniscient perspective in favor of forcing the reader to *dance* on the same territory as his fictional investigator.

Widely considered a kind of amalgamated private detective, borrowing from traditional tough guy Philip Marlowe and contemporary stoner sleuth Jeff "The Dude" Lebowski,[11] Doc begins his investigation after an unexpected visit from his femme fatale ex-girlfriend, Shasta Fay Hepworth. In this sequence, Pynchon pays homage to his hard-boiled ancestors as Shasta reveals to Doc that she has inadvertently become involved in "some creepy little scheme" (2) that is threatening the safety of her current lover and "billionaire" real estate mogul Mickey Wolfmann. While the hard-boiled can first be identified in *Against the Day*, specifically in Lew's desperate attempt to make sense of the seedy underbelly of Los Angeles, Doc passively adapts to this more contemporary, neo-noir environment by living life in a drug-fuelled haze of paranoia and ambiguity. In this sense, it is only natural that the *psychical* detective transforms into the *psychedelic*.

What makes both of these texts so striking when one is discussing their respective narrative interconnectedness, particularly in comparison to the panoramic scope of *Gravity's Rainbow* and *Against the Day*, is the manner with which Pynchon allows the reader to form an intricate connection with the protagonists, establishing complex allusions with more precision and relevance. In *The Crying of Lot 49* and *Inherent Vice*, the framework and rich tapestry of the Inverarity and Wolfmann estates allow Pynchon to present intertextual connections much like the clues in a devilishly compelling, Agatha Christie–style murder mystery. The reader is expected to identify with Oedipa and Doc by similarly functioning as an *interpretive* investigator, committed to finding evidence and sorting information readily available in each novel in order to discern their considerably more elaborate and disconcerting meanings.

This allusive process is exemplified through the character of Pierce Inverarity in *The Crying of Lot 49* directly, as he embodies a popular culture presence, which Joseph Slade suggests is a play on the character of Professor Moriarty, Sherlock Holmes's arch nemesis (108). Although Pierce is dead before the events in the novel unfold, his "Will" consistently impairs Oedipa's vision and progress. Slade's connection on this level between *The Crying of Lot 49* and Doyle's Sherlock Holmes stories is a logical one: Oedipa assumes the role of the intelligent sleuth (Holmes) in Pynchon's narrative because the role has the power to shape her identity and provide her with a greater sense of purpose in the world. This association with Doyle and the most popular literary detective of all time also implicitly reinforces the ways in which Pynchon draws on elements of classical ratiocination in his own text. As Oedipa states in relation to the Inverarity Will at the beginning of chapter 4:

> If it was really Pierce's attempt to leave an organized something behind after his own annihilation, then it was part of her duty, wasn't it, to bestow life on what had persisted . . . to bring the estate into pulsing stelliferous Meaning, all in a soaring dome around her? (56)

Pynchon launches the novel's elaborate mystery through Pierce's "off-screen" death. This device is used to similarly haunting effect in Cormac McCarthy's crime drama *No Country for Old Men*, when the protagonist, Llewelyn Moss, is murdered *offscreen* approximately three quarters of the way through the story.[12] The absence of *seeing* an influential character, such as Pierce, intensifies narrative tension and suspense for both protagonist and reader, which also works in a vein comparable to the traditional Doyle or Christie detective story.

Reference to Sherlock Holmes can also be found in *Inherent Vice* through Doc's attempt to understand the connection between Mickey's mysterious disappearance and the seemingly ubiquitous Golden Fang organization. Doc declares his belief in the detective's real-life existence, emphasizing that "he lives at this real address in London" and "did coke all the time . . . it helped him solve cases" (96). However, Pynchon doesn't equip Doc with Holmes's near-superhuman powers of deduction. Solving the sinister Wolfmann case requires that Pynchon's frequently blissed-out detective not only subscribe to a uniquely revised hard-boiled ethos but also constantly reject capitalist exploitation. As Sweeney states, "detective fiction has always acknowledged the *possibility* that a search for truth might lead to the mystery of one's own identity" (248). It is not until near the novel's exhilarating conclusion that Doc finally begins to understand the significance of life as a California private eye in the neo-noir era. For a "second and a half," Doc realizes that "he belonged to a single and ancient martial tradition in which resisting authority, subduing hired guns, defending your old lady's honor all amounted to the same thing" (326).

Pynchon's Projection of a World

In order to fully understand such eccentric private detectives, one must analyze their respective investigative processes in relation to each novel's fictional setting. As renowned English detective fiction author P. D. James states: "the setting is where these people live, move, and have their being, and we need to breathe their air, see with their eyes, walk the paths they tread" (131). In *The Crying of Lot 49* and *Inherent Vice*, Pynchon supports James's definition by positioning California as the dominant center from which his narratives emerge; however, he proceeds to disrupt the functionality of the setting by applying a postmodern ideological interpretation and sense of indeterminacy. The prominence of the West Coast setting in the detective fiction genre was established in the early 1920s, as America developed rapidly into a more urbanized nation and the allure of wealth, fame, and even danger became irresistible. Throughout this golden age, many people still believed in the myth of California, which contained endless opportunities and was lit by the infectious glow of Hollywood. In the transition from the hard-boiled to the neo-noir, one of the most enduring qualities is that it is typically only the private detective who is inquisitive and determined enough to venture into this haunting environment.

The Crying of Lot 49's second chapter begins with Oedipa leaving the sheltered, monotonic pines of Kinneret for the urban sprawl of San Narciso (a fictional city located near Los Angeles that is infused with unsettling real-life familiarity). The dramatic change in the novel's setting, when Oedipa navigates the complicated freeway systems in her rented Impala, represents the "official" beginning of her journey as a detective. For Oedipa, San Narciso becomes "less an identifiable city than a grouping of concepts" (14) directly linked with Pierce Inverarity; it functions as a shadowy, mysterious city that Oedipa attempts to comprehend throughout her investigation. This is most vividly demonstrated when Oedipa absorbs the sheer magnitude of San Narciso from a slope, discerning a printed circuit in the twisted streets and housing estates:

> The ordered swirl of houses and streets, from this high angle, sprang at her now with the same unexpected, astonishing clarity as the circuit card had. Though she knew even less about radios than about Southern Californians, there were to both outward patterns a hieroglyphic sense of concealed meaning, of an intent to communicate. There'd seemed no limit to what the printed circuit could have told her (if she had tried to find out); so in her first minute of San Narciso, a revelation also trembled just past the threshold of her understanding. (14–15)

Through Oedipa's heightened awareness, Pynchon presents the city as a disturbingly surreal, Philip K. Dick–inspired dreamscape. Like Dick's tortured protagonists, Oedipa is unhinged by a world that appears familiar yet at the same time is strangely foreign, casting doubt on human prosperity.

This idea of "artificial deception" reverberates through Doc's neo-noir investigation, which takes him across Los Angeles at the "tail end of the psychedelic sixties" in *Inherent Vice*. With more than a passing resemblance to Manhattan Beach (where Pynchon reportedly wrote much of *Gravity's Rainbow*), the "fictional" Gordita Beach acts as the immediate point of identification. Unlike Oedipa's wide-eyed naïveté before entering San Narciso, Doc has already experienced the desolation and disorientation that Gordita Beach offers to a certain degree, realizing that he must actively engage in its wicked nature if he is to discover revelation. Gazing at a painting in his house, Doc quickly acknowledges the harsh disparity between reality and this depiction of "a Southern California beach that never was—palms, bikini babes, surfboards, the works. He thought of it as a window to look out of when he couldn't deal with looking out of the traditional glass-type one in the other room" (6). Following the transition from hard-boiled to neo-noir, Pynchon demonstrates that Doc knows that the notion of this idealized, counterculture lifestyle itself is really a "construction" and a "fabrication." The overbearing smog and sinister scenarios in the city that perturb Oedipa when she first enters San Narciso are issues that Doc endures on a daily basis. Therefore, the habitual joint that Oedipa typically tries to avoid during her own investigation becomes a necessity for Doc to use to escape from the world.

In navigating through their respective mysteries, the discovery of clues leads to a proliferation of questions without enough logical answers, consequently exposing Oedipa and Doc to the savagery of civilization, which is buried under California's *constructed reality.* Destabilized from their respective states of normalcy, both protagonists are forced to question the greater social climate and legacy of America, where, like Nick Carraway in F. Scott Fitzgerald's *The Great Gatsby,* they are ultimately left to wonder whether there is anything worth inheriting.[13] In each text, these detectives spend time prowling streets underneath the major freeways, encountering exiled drifters and "walking psychotics" who have been disregarded by the oppressive governing institutions. A self-confessed admirer of Jack Kerouac's literary prose, Pynchon endows this underbelly of California with the kind of evocative fear and destruction that simmered under the surface of the writing of the Beat movement.

When examining the multifaceted representations of the California in *The Crying of Lot 49* and *Inherent Vice,* it is impossible not to acknowledge the extent of Pynchon's authorial presence. Because of his unwillingness to embrace the public spotlight and subscribe to the notion of "author as celebrity,"[14] the method with which Pynchon creates his detective characters and *disappears* into these narratives adds yet another level of complexity and intrigue for readers. According to various critics and biographical research, Pynchon lived in Manhattan Beach during the 1960s and 1970s, immersing himself in the ideology and social activism of the counterculture that was steadily finding its collective voice across California at the time.[15] In his introduction to *Slow Learner,* Pynchon not only provides rare personal commentary on his early short stories but recalls that this was the same period when "I was also beginning to shut up and listen to the American voices around me, even to shift my eyes away from printed sources and take a look at American nonverbal reality" (22).

With the devastating Watts Riots taking place in Los Angeles in 1965, it would be reasonable to think that such ideological unrest was weighing on Pynchon's mind at the time he was writing *The Crying of Lot 49*. Before his impassioned journalistic account, "A Journey into the Mind of Watts" (which was published in 1966, the year after the riots took place), Pynchon presents this turbulent social climate with remarkable clarity and resonance during Oedipa's visit to the University of California, Berkeley campus:

> Berkeley was like no somnolent Siwash out of her own past at all, but more akin to those Far Eastern or Latin American universities you read about, those autonomous culture media where the most beloved of folklores may be brought into doubt, cataclysmic of dissents voiced, suicidal of commitments chosen—the sort that bring governments down. (71)

This now famous passage encapsulates Pynchon's comprehensive depiction of the social-political chaos ruminating in California during the 1960s. It also arguably served as an ominous prognosticator for the "Bloody Thursday" conflict, which occurred on May 15, 1969, and involved thousands of angry students, who clashed with police and the University of California over 2.8 acres of parkland situated just off Telegraph Avenue in Berkeley.[16]

Over the course of her journey, Oedipa gradually discovers that "the poor, the defeated, the criminal, the desperate, all hanging in there with what must seem a terrible vitality"[17] are in fact emblematic of the *real* California society. In *Inherent Vice*, this collective fear and prejudice manifest themselves as deeper divisions of paranoia and violence, which are lurking beneath Gordita Beach's "eternal youth, endless summer" (208) farce. If, as Cowart argues, Oedipa is a female representation of Pynchon himself,[18] a "soul in flux" attempting to make sense of a nation in disarray, then Doc is the world-weary male equivalent who has already experienced an environment overwhelmed with the turmoil and bloodshed associated with civil rights struggles and the Vietnam War.

Conspiracy and the Dark Forces of Paranoia

While Pynchon and many other citizens held an underlying cynicism toward the major political power structures in America during the 1950s and criticized such controlling systems as being inherently corrupt, it is fair to suggest that a turning point occurred when President John F. Kennedy was assassinated in 1963. That fateful day in Dallas, possibly orchestrated by corrupt members from the very same government, initiated what Michael Janeway deems "the launching of a feverish American conspiracy-theory industry" (31). Retrospectively, it almost doesn't matter if there was a second shooter on that infamous grassy knoll or not, because identified assassin Lee Harvey Oswald and the small sloping hill altered the sociological landscape of America forever. In an illuminating textual study focusing on conspiracy in contemporary American fiction, Samuel Coale situates Pynchon as "the godfather of the contemporary conspiracy novel," asserting that the writer presents "conspiracy and paranoia as distinct American obsessions and anxieties" (135). In an era when people suddenly began finding it much more difficult to distinguish fact from fiction, Pynchon's ambitiously sinister narrative in *V.* became a figurative representation of an everyday world built on clues and signifiers hinting at a larger, controlling force.

Discussing *The Crying of Lot 49*, Aaron Rosenfeld states that by establishing an elaborate "cross-referenced puzzle" that reveals new allusions with each reading, "Pynchon's text both validates and ironizes the quest for meaning" (356). The novel's mystery fully takes flight when Oedipa ventures into The Scope, a strange bar where she discovers a "muted post horn" symbol for WASTE (the motto: "We Await Silent Tristero's Empire") on the latrine wall. The way in which Oedipa may have discovered the Tristero system as a result of "sensitizing" and the seductive longing for discovery disturbs her greatly: "That's what would come to haunt her most, perhaps: the way it fitted, logically, together" (29). From this point, Pynchon inundates Oedipa with devilishly complicated clues that are all inextricably linked in some way with this perplexing postal system, which operates under the freeways of humanity and signals "the sinister blooming of The Tristero," the mysterious organization that hints at worldwide conquest. Consequently, Oedipa's duties quickly force her into a tangled web of detection and deception in which progress is constantly "held at the edge."[19]

Because Doc is well-versed in the unforgiving business of solving mysteries, *Inherent Vice* initially appears to take the form of a conventional detective novel. Although Pynchon casts Doc as a somewhat reluctant private investigator, he is equipped with a hard-boiled consciousness and "extrasensory chops" (129) that Oedipa lacks. When Doc first learns of the Golden Fang (which functions as the maritime, conspiratorial equivalent to Tristero) through a written warning, the threat doesn't seem as ominous as Oedipa's discovery of the dreaded post horn, because Doc already understands that "paranoia was a tool of the trade" (116). In contrast to Oedipa's concern about drowning in a sea of paranoia, Doc's familiarity with the concept is epitomized by the "rendering of a giant bloodshot eyeball" (14) attached to his office door. Serving as the logo for his private investigator business, LSD Investigations ("Location, Surveillance, Detection"), its "ocular mazework" also functions as a playful allusion to the Pinkerton National Detective Agency, the private law enforcement organization that had "the eye that never sleeps." For Doc, it is the tyrannical private organizations that have the ability to infiltrate and shut down the strands of prerevolution in California, turning a harmless fishing schooner into an international drug cartel and menacing vessel of government suppression that sends a chill down the back of even the most nonchalant private eye.

Pynchon *drives* the narratives in both novels with the mysteries of the Pierce Inverarity Will and Mickey Wolfmann's disappearance, each of which poses an intriguing series of questions before veering off on wild tangents. Piecing together suggestive evidence reveals only the illusion of a coherent puzzle, resulting in potentially nefarious connections and creating existential chaos. For instance, Oedipa can never truly know or understand Pierce, which consequently means she can never determine whether Tristero is a real underground organization, whether she is embroiled in an elaborate conspiracy, or whether she subsists in a hallucinatory, paranoid state. While Doc can confirm the existence of the Golden Fang vessel and enterprise, he is also left to wonder whether the horrific Charles Manson murders and opposing vigilante groups in California have the power to bring down the counterculture movement or if he has simply rolled one joint too many. As Tanner notes, "we move from a state of degree-zero mystery—just the quotidian mixture of an average California day—to a condition of increasing mystery and dubiety" (*Thomas Pynchon* 56). Exploiting the concepts of conspiracy and paranoia subsequently intensifies the moral ambivalence in Pynchon's startling representations of California, which always seem just a whisker removed from reality.

If the investigations by Oedipa and Doc are hindered by the possibility of paranoia, it is only because Pynchon has meticulously designed "plots" that are always destined to frustrate the detective figure. In each narrative, the author positions the protagonist both inside and outside of a labyrinth that encourages detection yet also hints that such conventional processes must be refined and adapted if an individual is to escape such a treacherous environment without losing his or her sanity. Mark Danielewski's metafictional Gothic opus *House of Leaves* astutely illustrates the contrasting perception of the contemporary labyrinth:

> Maze-treaders, whose vision ahead and behind is severely constricted and fragmented, suffer confusion, whereas maze-viewers who see the pattern whole, from above or in a diagram, are dazzled by its complex artistry. What you see depends on where you stand, and thus, at one and the same time, labyrinths are single . . . and double: they simultaneously incorporate order and disorder, clarity and confusion, unity and multiplicity, artistry and chaos. They may be perceived as a path . . . or as a pattern. . . . Our perception of labyrinths is thus intrinsically unstable: change your perspective and the labyrinth seems to change. (113–14)

Arriving in San Narciso for the first time, Oedipa becomes a strikingly precise representation of the "maze-viewer." She views the city from a safe distance above as a complicated circuit, simultaneously perturbed and seduced by the complexity of its pattern. Coming from the dreariness of Kinneret normalcy, though, Oedipa never truly expects that investigating Tristero and venturing into the labyrinth (essentially, becoming a "maze-treader") will cause her to be permanently ostracized from this ordinary world.

Similarly, when Doc follows the "paper trail" that takes him from Mickey's disappearance to the Channel View Estates and in pursuit of the enigmatic Coy Harlingen, the "angles" in the case begin "displaying themselves in a sort of hyperdimensional pattern across the piece of blank office wall" (217). As Stefano Tani states, "once the chain of detection has started, [one] cannot abandon the quest for harmony and coherence. Mystery expects to be solved" (92). However, the detective's attempt to turn puzzling connections and correlations into coherent and conclusive answers is typically obfuscated by elements of danger and adversity. While Oedipa's California mystery is relatively personal, with her main antagonist, Pierce Inverarity, possibly "speaking" from beyond the grave, Doc's deep-seated position in the counterculture movement naturally makes his bête noire more authoritarian and explicit: it comes in the form of the self-proclaimed "Renaissance detective" Christian "Bigfoot" Bjornsen. Pynchon delicately juxtaposes Bigfoot's hilariously outlandish attitude and banter with moments in which he becomes a terrifying personification of "The Man" described in the author's report on the aftermath of the Watts Riots: "Make any big trouble, baby, The Man just going to come back in and shoot you, like last time" ("Journey" 34).

It is only inevitable that in the face of such conspiratorial terror, Oedipa and Doc, in assuming the role of the neodetective, temporarily descend into a form of "entropic haze" at several noteworthy points in these respective narratives. Paranoia intrudes upon the mind and shapes the behavior of Pynchon's protagonists, invoking Tanner's notion of "an abiding American dread that someone else is patterning your life, that there are all sorts of invisible plots afoot to rob you of your autonomy of thought and action" (*City of Words* 15) Suggestive evidence is suddenly not enough, and the dissipating likelihood of absolute veracity causes paralyzing fear. In *Inherent Vice*, Doc can't help but notice a change in the "atmosphere" when his investigation leads him closer to Coy, and he suspects that clandestine operatives were "reclaiming the music, the resistance to power, the sexual desire from epic to everyday, all they could sweep up, for the ancient forces of greed and fear" (130). These suspicions prove correct when Doc encounters Golden Fang operatives cleverly disguised as a stereotypical "blonde" California family during a dope exchange near the novel's conclusion.

While Doc manages to avoid most of the post-Mansonical paranoia that marked the "end of a certain kind of innocence" (38) in California, the more he learns about the shady connection between the Golden Fang, Shasta, and Mickey, the more he questions his own detective process. Like the worthless statuette of the bird that Sam Spade erroneously believes is what "dreams are made of" in Hammett's hard-boiled classic, *The Maltese Falcon*, Pynchon uses the Mickey Wolfmann character as the novel's "MacGuffin," a device originally made famous by legendary filmmaker Alfred Hitchcock. Mickey's disappearance serves as the impetus for the novel's plot; however, his sudden reappearance approximately two-thirds of the way through the story is treated with triviality and indifference, with only Doc considering the suspicious nature of his return before redirecting his energies onto Coy and the Golden Fang.

In *The Crying of Lot 49*, the tentacles of Tristero are more deadly, suffocating Oedipa's investigation until she becomes caught in an unspeakable form of limbo. Over the course of one star-swept San Francisco night, Pynchon corrupts the city with the omnipresence of Tristero, as Oedipa is overwhelmed by sensory overload and comes to the startling realization that

> the private eye sooner or later has to get beat up on. This night's profusion of post horns, this malignant, deliberate replication, was their way of beating up. They knew her pressure points, and the ganglia of her optimism, and one by one, pinch by precision pinch, they were immobilizing her. (85)

After playing "voyeur and listener," Oedipa begins seriously questioning whether her persistence and resourcefulness are enough to solve any great mystery. She has difficulty sorting the night into "the real and the dreamed," because Pynchon has erected signifiers that problematize the validity of interpretation rather than assure it. Nonetheless, Pynchon ultimately captures the *essence* of the archetypal detective quest in both novels, making necessary conspiratorial and paranoid deviations to reflect the relevant California milieu. Where Doc represents the counterculture descendant of the 1920s hard-boiled detective hero, which was originally created as an Americanized alternative to the popular "cozy" English detective story, Oedipa is a feminized contemporary rendering of Sherlock Holmes, who just happens to be desperately missing her own Dr. Watson.

Cracking the California Mystery

As previously noted, in *The Crying of Lot 49* and *Inherent Vice*, Pynchon generates narrative tension and suspense by forcing his curious sleuths to walk the precarious tightrope between legitimate conspiracy and drug-induced paranoia to the very end. Oedipa and Doc's respective investigations generally resist the preordained movement from suspenseful mystery to heroic resolution, subverting the linearity and the rigidly conventional conclusions that have classically governed detective stories by the likes of Doyle and Christie. Pynchon positions his protagonists as problem solvers who must exert their mental and psychical abilities to solve their cases; however, they aren't necessarily left with a brimming sense of accomplishment that is passed on to the reader. Yet, while Pynchon's first California novel overtly undermines the very notion of the "satisfactory solution," *Inherent Vice* does in fact close with the private eye finding some semblance of revelation, evoking the spirit of the traditional hard-boiled. Most importantly, however, both novels' highly provocative endings rely on a revisionist detective story framework to offer representations of California that expose the dark heart of this metropolis.

Unlike *Gravity's Rainbow*, which has a sprawling narrative that rejects the idea of resolution so passionately that the characters wander aimlessly into a state of absolute fragmentation, Oedipa clings to her deluge of suggestive evidence until the final scene in *The Crying of Lot 49*. Rather than completely dismantling the novel's detective genre foundation by turning Oedipa's search into metafictional chaos, Pynchon calculatingly bookends the narrative with Pierce Inverarity. This provides a strong form of circularity, which foreshadows the influence of the parabola in *Gravity's Rainbow*. The fact that Pynchon elects to send his disheveled heroine to the auction not as an isolated victim but as a desperate predator "trying to guess which one was her target, her enemy . . . her proof" (127) illustrates a detective protagonist who simply cannot disregard the allure of a conclusive outcome.

Even without a tangible resolution, Oedipa's mere attendance at the auction instils a powerful sense of urgency into the narrative, which is emblematic of the ratiocinative detective's steely-eyed determination and moral stability. These enduring philosophical values of the archetypal detective figure lead to a more logical and rewarding culmination to Doc's odyssey in *Inherent Vice.* Not only is Doc able to orchestrate a successful negotiation with ruthless tycoon Crocker Fenway, securing a happy ending for Coy and Hope, but he is also able to witness his own *crying* of Lot 49 when the *Golden Fang* attempts to make a desperate escape from the local authorities. While Doc is never able to truly unmask the villainous agents who have plotted such conspiracies, when the novel concludes with him driving along the San Diego Freeway, waiting "for the fog to burn away, and for something else this time, somehow, to be there, instead" (369), one gets the sense that, like the quintessential hard-boiled hero, he intends to leave this for another day. In this memorable final passage, Pynchon is gently suggesting a cathartic resolution to the volatility and fragmentation that existed in California when he wrote *The Crying of Lot 49*. The textual "relationship" between these two endings further reinforces Pynchon's fondness for the detective fiction genre—the seeds from the genre that were sown in *V.* almost fifty years ago, which displayed encouraging growth in *The Crying of Lot 49*, have well and truly bloomed in *Inherent Vice.*

In Pynchon's own plot synopsis for *Against the Day*, which appeared on Amazon a few months before the release of the novel, the author contemplates: "If it is not the world, it is what the world might be with a minor adjustment or two. According to some, this is one of the main purposes of fiction." This kind of perspicacious consideration of the inextricable bond between fiction writing and social representation is no better exemplified than in the cautionary interpretations of 1960s and 1970s California that shape *The Crying of Lot 49* and *Inherent Vice.* In this sense, Pynchon's thought-provoking endings are in many respects comparable to "cold cases"—these investigations may be marred by the impossibility of catching all the culprits or completely solving the mystery, but the processes of detection (whether ratiocinative or hard-boiled) remain fluid and recognizable. As the protagonist Dunraven notes in Jorge Luis Borges's chilling metaphysical short story "Ibn Hakkan al-Bokhari, Dead in His Labyrinth," "the solution of a mystery is always less impressive than the mystery itself" (123). In *The Crying of Lot 49* and *Inherent Vice*, it is the mystique of California, the final frontier of the American Dream that thrives on the unsolved or insoluble, which most excites the detectives' constantly inquisitive and paranoid minds.

NOTES

1. I would like to thank fellow Pynchonite and academic Nick Prescott for his wonderfully generous feedback and continual support.
2. Wittgenstein's phrase also echoes the moment in *V.* when Lieutenant Weissmann thinks he has decrypted Kurt Mondaugen's data (278).
3. "Readerly" is a term coined by Roland Barthes to distinguish between two types of texts, "readerly" and "writerly."
4. *The Crying of Lot 49* (1966), *Vineland* (1990), and *Inherent Vice* (2009) have come to unofficially represent Pynchon's California Trilogy. As Thomas Schaub notes, "in Pynchon's imagination Southern California is the place where the nation impinges upon the characters of his novels, the place in which his characters begin to think about their lives within the framework of the nation" (30). See "*The Crying of Lot 49* and Other California Novels," 30–43.
5. In his influential essay "Gravity's Encyclopedia," Edward Mendelson describes *Gravity's Rainbow* as encompassing "the full range of knowledge and beliefs of a national culture, while identifying the ideological perspectives from which that culture shapes and interprets its knowledge" (162). Refer also to Levine and Leverenz, *Mindful Pleasures*, 29–52.
6. See Cowart, *Thomas Pynchon*; Schaub, "*The Crying of Lot 49* and Other California Novels"; and Tanner, *Thomas Pynchon*.
7. Defining texts (other than the works of Thomas Pynchon) include Stanislaw Lem's *The Investigation* (1974), Umberto Eco's *The Name of the Rose* (1980), Paul Auster's *The New York Trilogy* (1987), Jonathan Lethem's *Gun, with Occasional Music* (1994), and Robert Coover's *Noir* (2010).
8. It is interesting to consider that Auster wrote his first novel, a hard-boiled detective story called *Squeeze Play*, published in 1982, under the pseudonym "Paul Benjamin." Based on evidence supplied in *The New York Trilogy*, protagonist Daniel Quinn is also approximately 35, the same age Auster was when he wrote *Squeeze Play*.
9. Literary critic William V. Spanos coined the term "anti-detective story" in his 1972 essay "The Detective and the Boundary: Some Notes on the Postmodern Literary Imagination" to define a narrative the "formal purpose of which is to evoke the impulse to 'detect' and/or to psychoanalyze in order to violently frustrate it by refusing to solve the crime" (154). The contentious term has since evolved and been refined by various scholars, including William V. Spanos, Michael Holquist, Dennis Porter, Stefano Tani, Patricia Merivale, and Susan Elizabeth Sweeney, among others.
10. In the penultimate chapter of *Inherent Vice*, Doc's de facto lawyer, Sauncho Smilax, defines the term "inherent vice" as "what you can't avoid" (351).

11. Ethan Coen has previously stated that *The Big Lebowski* is "loosely patterned on a Raymond Chandler novel" where "the hero sets out to clear up a mystery and while doing so visits a lot of odd characters who spring up like Jack-in-the-boxes" (101). See "The Logic of Soft Drugs," in Allen, *The Coen Brothers*, 100–108.
12. Cowart even explores the connection between McCarthy's *No Country for Old Men* and *Inherent Vice* in their respective conclusions. He states: "Pynchon's [final] image, like McCarthy's, is tender yet far from sanguine. In the fog of national memory, the decades retreat like taillights, disappearing, one after another, into history or myth" (133–34). In Cowart, *Thomas Pynchon*.
13. Cowart and Schaub have briefly investigated the connection between Pynchon's California novels and Fitzgerald; however, Charles Baxter expands more thoroughly on this textual relationship in his essay "De-faced America."
14. With contemporary American fiction in a state of decline throughout the 1980s, publishers and publicists resorted to categorizing writers into image-conscious cliques as marketing and hype rose to the forefront in the rejuvenation of the literary text. As a member of the literary "Brat Pack," Bret Easton Ellis comments on the perils of this concept at length in *Lunar Park*: "Every door swung wide open. Everyone approached us with outstretched hands and flashing smiles. . . . It was the beginning of a time when it was almost as if the novel itself didn't matter anymore—publishing a shiny booklike object was simply an excuse for parties and glamour" (9).
15. See Krafft, "Biographical Note" ; Frost, "Thomas Pynchon and the South Bay"; and Gordon, "Smoking Dope with Thomas Pynchon."
16. Students envisioned "People's Park" as an area in which they could freely stage political rallies; however, the University of California, Berkeley became increasingly concerned with how its property was being used; the regents viewed such demonstrations as a form of public disturbance. Students launched an angry march down Telegraph Avenue when news spread across campus that the park would be turned into a soccer field, with 8-foot fences erected immediately to prevent trespassers. Then Governor Ronald Reagan, who previously had proclaimed the campus and area "a haven for communist sympathizers, protestors and sexual deviants," was forced to declare an official state of emergency and summoned the National Guard. By the end of the day, 58 people had been injured, with 12 sent to the hospital, and one innocent bystander (James Rector) killed as he watched the riot from a rooftop. For more, see "Nation: Occupied Berkeley."
17. Pynchon describing the state of the neighborhood in Watts after the riots in "Journey into the Mind of Watts," 35.
18. In *Thomas Pynchon and the Dark Passages of History*, Cowart argues that the similarities between Oedipa and Pynchon's age, education, and travel locations illustrate that

"*Lot 49* is Pynchon's portrait of the artist in youth and, as such, corresponds to Joyce's autobiographical novel, *A Portrait of the Artist as a Young Man* (1916)" (112).

19. This pertinent phrase is used most vividly by Pynchon in *Gravity's Rainbow* when he is describing the paranoia induced by the fictional drug Oneirine: "About the paranoia often noted under the drug . . . it is nothing less than the onset, the leading edge, of the discovery that *everything is connected* . . . perhaps a route In for those like Tchitcherine who are held at the edge" (834).

Profane Illuminations. Postmodernism, Realism, and the Holytail Marijuana Crop in Thomas Pynchon's *Vineland*[1]

HENRY VEGGIAN

Reviewing *Vineland* for *The New York Times Book Review* in early 1990, Salman Rushdie concluded an otherwise light-hearted article by modulating the tone of his review to a serious key:

> But what is perhaps most interesting, finally, about Mr. Pynchon's new novel is what is different about it. What is interesting is the willingness with which he addresses, directly, the political development of the United States, and the slow (but not total) steamrollering of a radical tradition many generations and decades older than flower power.... What is interesting is to have before us, at the end of the Greed Decade, that rarest of birds: a major political novel about what America has been doing to itself, to its children, all these many years. (37)

It would seem incredible, even two decades removed from the fact, that Rushdie's argument about *Vineland* being a "major political *novel*" [emphasis mine] has not attracted more sustained critical attention.[2] Circumstance alone would appear to merit considerable praise for his claim, because Rushdie composed a daring and at times comical essay while hunted by assassins. Indeed, the biographical circumstance unfortunately may have obscured a more important balance of moods in his review. The balance appears in how Rushdie's personal nightmare tinges the article's casual tone to imitate (one might say embody) *Vineland's* admixture of hallucinatory comedy with sober realism.

Salman Rushdie's argument that *Vineland* ranks among major works of political fiction—a category mostly populated by realist writing—is as unique as it is bold. It is bold insofar as it suggests that postmodern literary fiction, as an aesthetic formation widely regarded as incompatible with realism, may nonetheless elaborate foundational elements of realism in a sustained or thoughtful manner.[3] There are, of course, many examples of nonrealist political novels (Bely's *Petersburg* comes to mind), and one might object more broadly by asking, "What novel is not political in some way?" The more formidable problem is that Rushdie's review invokes the awkward position of the postmodern literary novel vis-à-vis the historic legacy of literary realism, thereby placing aesthetic formations along a historical continuum rather than on a more immediately political one. Critics have by and large regarded the two traditions as antithetical insofar as postmodernism is understood to disturb and reject the epistemological claims of realism; or, as Fredric Jameson described it, realism's place within antirealist art is more that of "a concept of realism, if only as an empty slot, a vacant preliminary historical 'stage,' or secondary (but essential) aesthetic counterposition" ("Existence of Italy" 158–59). To elaborate Rushdie's claim that *Vineland* is a "major political novel" would seem to require suspending the dogmatic belief that the traditions of literary realism and postmodernism constitute mutually exclusive movements that embody opposed stages of historical development, the prior one of objects, individuals, and classes vacated by the digital phantoms of one more recent. In a positive register, Rushdie's claim, which is poignantly embodied by the quasijocular mood of his essay, invites us to consider the possibility that Pynchon's novel elaborates a synthesis of styles and moods that achieves the realist's ambition of portraying the individual, social, and historical gravity of a "world" with sustained postmodern levity.

Admittedly, "gravity" is a loaded term when discussing Pynchon's works, and I invoke it here to describe the novel's realist mood (and "levity," by contrast, for *Vineland*'s comedy). *Vineland*'s combined gravity and levity offer a suggestive point from which to begin discussion of this postmodern novel's relationship to classical realism. *Vineland*'s most obvious tendency is to align the two moods with large demographic blocs in American society. One is tempted to call them "classes" but for the fact that they are too varied to be grouped into a single economic order; more importantly, classes do not suffice to describe how the novel differentiates economic roles within each bloc in terms of larger cultural or aesthetic formations that more accurately define the groups. "Generations" would seem the more appropriate substitute, and of these there are three. There is, in the first place, what Rushdie refers to as an "older" radical tradition, which, in the novel, comprises an aging hegemonic political generation of New Deal Democrats, syndicalists, fellow travelers, socialists, and communists. This group's representative character is Sasha Gates, the daughter of IWW labor activists (the Becker-Traverse family, whose story Pynchon elaborates at greater length in *Against the Day*). The second generation is composed of the first group's progeny, the "flower power" counterculture of the 1960s, which includes pacifists, campus radicals, armed revolutionaries, and varied artists. This group is represented primarily by Sasha Gates's daughter Frenesi, a radical filmmaker, as well as by her former husband, Zoyd Wheeler. A third and rival group, aligned against the prior two, comprises a paranoid lot of post-McCarthy cultural conservatives. Brock Vond, a U.S. district attorney, represents this third group. In this group, remnants of the old landed aristocracy, religious fundamentalists, and paranoid Cold War reactionaries have joined forces to form a bureaucratic alliance with control over federal and state institutions of governance. Having evacuated institutions (industry, government) of the older radical generation's New Deal agents, the ascendant bloc realigns those institutions with private industrial interests that were allegedly threatened by federal New Deal policies. In the novel, those converted institutions have set their sights on the remnants of the younger radical generation who have retreated to the margins of American society, where they are demonized and hunted down under the pretext of the "War on Drugs."

Viewed in this light, *Vineland*'s arrangement of these political generations resembles Georg Lukács's description of a similar triangulation in Balzac's *The Peasants* wherein the landed aristocracy and petit bourgeois align against a class of renters who are driven, as are the *Vineland* radicals, into the woods. In Balzac's case, they are tenant farmers who steal timber from the gentry's woods; in Pynchon's, they are marijuana farmers, presumably descendants of the timber industry workers organized by Sasha Gates's parents, who grow their plants on timber company land ("Balzac: *The Peasants*" 29). In Pynchon's case, however, it is federal agents who chase the potheads into the forest, whereas in another example I would cite from Balzac, it is Monsieur Grandet, the former cooper turned bourgeois landowner, who would "cut down every stick in his woods and forests," not to keep the peasants from stealing them so much as to "replenish his almost empty coffers" (*Eugénie Grandet* 48). As such, the economic motives of the respective capitalists and their legal agents diverge: Balzac's Grandet aims to profit, an action that signifies to him a form of morality because it shows restrained pseudoaristocratic benevolence, rather than to prohibit, an action which for *Vineland's* archreactionary Brock Vond constitutes a form of morality because it requires constraint. Yet, like Grandet, whom the anticapitalist Balzac criticizes for being a pseudoaristocrat (and therefore unworthy of estates and riches or respect), Vond is also a pretender, a mere errand boy working in the service of forces who have usurped a legal and political power he can never truly represent or understand.

Thus *Vineland* enters the familiar domain of the political novel insofar as it aligns conflicts between economic, institutional, and political actors. The novel begins as the paranoid right-wingers launch the "War on Drugs" against the illegal farms of Vineland, the geographic heart of the Becker-Traverse family, the region's name and the novel's title constituting an agricultural trope (a rhetorical device whose presence would have, admittedly, troubled Balzac).[4] The trope has both a genealogical function and an economic one in that it indicates sprawling horizontal form doubled in both the intragenerational family structure and a mode of market organization affiliated with it. That mode of economic organization opposes another, one of vertically integrated industrial concerns, associated with multinational capitalists who back the War's rabid federal agents (such as Brock Vond), who set out to eradicate the counterculture group's pleasurable consumption of pot, a goal described in the novel as waging "war on a botanical species" (*Vineland* 271). With respect to the relation between the New Deal and "flower power," we might think of *Vineland* as responding to the question of whether pot smokers get along with the Joads and survive the concerted onslaught of a reactionary opponent. This dramatic arrangement, in which a radical "supergeneration" of two political blocs is besieged, underscores a dramatic shift in the economic reorganization of the United States of America wherein a group of right-wing zealots coordinates its war on drugs in concert with industries and institutions of scale so as to eliminate the local, economic grounds of radical political organization. Having diminished the industrial labor unions, the zealots turn against the pot farmers.

It is at this delicate juncture, where postmodern puns and cannabis-inspired humor share a narrative space with serious depictions of a form of economic warfare, that the novel's divided mood is most apparent. Erich Auerbach's *Mimesis: The Representation of Reality in Western Literature* offers an influential account of a similar tension in that book's chapter on French realism during the first half of the 19th century. There, Auerbach organizes French realism by generational differences that divide representative authors. That division offers a useful analog and precedent to the question regarding realism in *Vineland*'s moods and, in particular, how Pynchon depicts the New Deal vis-à-vis 1960s radicalism. Auerbach describes "the mixture of seriousness and everyday reality" in the writings of Stendhal and Balzac as resulting in an "elevated" realism; by contrast, Auerbach dismisses the later historical romanticism of the "Hugo group, which set out to unite the sublime and the grotesque" (*Mimesis* 481). Auerbach's "everyday life" admits the description of the comic, the vulgar, and the mundane, and as such, Stendhal and Balzac are regarded as sympathetic. My aim here is not to draw a hasty comparison between Pynchon and the French realists but rather to suggest a comparable rift in postmodern literary fiction, a divide that was defined also along generational lines in the mid-20th century and that Pynchon has very much in mind when depicting the generational relations in *Vineland*. Regarded in this light, we might consider Pynchon's *Vineland* as approximating the conventions of a "serious" and "elevated" realism typical of the earlier generation described by Auerbach. The result is that while Pynchon's zany style may seem to approximate what Auerbach defines as the "sublime-grotesque" in Hugo, I would argue that it more closely recalls the "great romantic agitation for the mixture of styles—the movement whose slogan was Shakespeare vs. Racine" (*Mimesis* 481) that characterizes the impulse of the earlier, more serious group.

Levity, irony, anachronism, and the absurd certainly course through *Vineland*, yet they are secondary to its grave ambition to incorporate them into a "major political novel." Understood in terms of the earlier triangulation described by Lukacs, *Vineland* combines the two moods so as to narrate the relationship between the three main political formations that emerge from the New Deal, a political epoch most closely defined by the last great explosion of realist aesthetics in American art. In doing so, *Vineland* often invokes the many experimental permutations of realism of the Popular Front era that Michael Denning described as a "remarkable cluster of aesthetic terms [that] emerged in the years of the cultural front" (121–22). Indeed, Pynchon's novel combines those later forms of realism in references to the New Deal (and particularly architecture, as we shall see) throughout *Vineland*. They appear there in subdued manner, however, without the disorientation that typifies their wild incorporation into postmodern historical romance (as in Pynchon's own "romances"). Rather, these varied moods and generational histories combine to form, at least in the broad outline I have described, a novel whose central political concern is what Rushdie described as "the slow (but not total) steamrollering of a radical tradition." Georg Lukacs might have called *Vineland* a novel in which a supergeneration of Romantic anticapitalists that is losing its grasp on economic and political institutions is depicted in a decadent yet hopeful postrevolutionary phase.

Rather than assuming the relationship of realism vis-à-vis postmodernism to be a merely eccentric configuration of vacated forms, it would seem that Rushdie's review recognizes in *Vineland* a formidable attempt to make explicit the anachronism of realism's historical continuation in a postmodern key.[5] This might be understood as an achievement in and of itself but for the role of marijuana and its economies in the novel, as we shall later see. As an object of production, the plant's agriculture, characters, and communities imitate narrative expectations of "the real" in *Vineland*. Indeed, they may very well be said to constitute an economic "determinant" in the flexible, active sense that Lukacs employs the term to explain shifting arrangements of class power in the 19th-century realism of Balzac ("Preface" 11). Yet, contrary to most art concerned with the effects of drugs, in *Vineland*, the real is not so much distorted by the drug's effects as it is amplified by them, a consequence that would seem to undermine any claim that *Vineland* is a "major political novel" and all the phenomenological claims (albeit unstable ones that make realism a dynamic concept, as Jameson notes) to veracity and verisimilitude that follow from them (Jameson, "Existence of Italy" 158). Surely this novel is only a pothead's dumb joke.

Before proceeding to discussion of characterization in the two respective literary traditions, it is perhaps best to introduce a specific example. For instance, the following scene captures the synthesized levity and gravity described above as it offers architectural surrogates for the three main generational groups previously described. Here, the two stoners and musical colleagues Zoyd Wheeler and Van Meter return to Vineland together with Zoyd's daughter, Prairie. Their approach offers a vantage of how the city's harbor points are united "by a bridge . . . which curved the length of the harbor's shoreline, both spans being graceful examples of the concrete Art Deco bridges built all over the Northwest by the WPA during the Great Depression," a view that opens in turn upon

> all the geometry of the bay neutrally filtered under pre-storm clouds, the crystalline openwork arcs of the pale bridges, a tall power plant stack whose plume blew straight north, meaning rain on the way, a jet in the sky ascending from the Vineland International south of town, the Corps of Engineers marina, with salmon boats, power cruisers, and day sailors all docked together, and spilling uphill from the shoreline a couple of square miles crowded with wood Victorian houses, Quonset sheds, postwar prefab ranch and split-level units, little trailer parks, lumber-baron floridity, New Deal earnestness. And the federal building, jaggedly faceted, obsidian black, standing apart, inside a vast parking lot whose fences were topped with concertina wire. "Don't know, it just landed one night," Van Meter said, "sitting there in the morning when everybody woke up, folks seem to be gettin' use to it." (316–17)

Let us assume for the moment that in representing these varied relationships, *Vineland* attempts to elaborate some elements of the "New Deal earnestness" with which it characterizes that earlier yet concurrent political formation, that it is an American *novel* in the sense that Hawthorne (writing with French realism in mind) elaborated the term in his famous preface to *The House of the Seven Gables*. In this way, we can understand Pynchon's book as portraying the lives of everyday persons in a recognizable contemporary milieu (published in 1990, the novel is set in 1984) with convincing verisimilitude. The latter will adopt the proven instruments of realism, including details that express phenomena of social life (political and economic history) and dialogue whose linguistic patterns approximate forms of living speech (as when Van Meter speaks, in the passage above) while combining these patterns with the conventions of postmodern narrative (the admixture of architectural styles noted above, designed so as to reconfigure perceptions of space). Furthermore, these phenomena of social life will be dramatized by what Lukacs called the "central aesthetic problem of realism," which he defined as "the adequate representation of the complete human personality," the matter of "typicality" ("Preface" 7), to which I will devote further attention below.[6] Finally, the sum of these parts should demonstrate a unity in space and time that indicates a "world"; or, in a material rather than a metaphysical sense, it will represent the institutions, phenomena, and cultural practices of a socioeconomic system. Finally, the novel will objectify relations within that system in a form intended for aesthetic consumption. According to this premise, the novel must reify the world, and convincingly so. If it is otherwise, or so it is thought, it is implausible. What are we to make, then, of the fact that all this is recounted in the passage above from the perspective of two characters notorious for their drug use, and one of whom (Van Meter) is implied to be stoned out of his mind in that very moment? Indeed, the passage preceding the one cited describes how Van Meter cannot find the keys to his automobile, at which point Zoyd indicates they are already in the ignition.

Is this to be dismissed as merely "sublime" and "grotesque," or as mere "antirealism," because it occurs in a novel that revels in comic, even pleasurable depictions of individual drug use while at the same time depicting drug economies (and the "war" against them) with the "earnestness" historically reserved for "serious" realism? Here, then, we reach a critical point at which the link between the particular and the general (a point favored by Auerbach) or the individual and the epoch (wherein ideology and history are joined in Lukacs's "types") would appear threatened by postmodern frivolity. The possibility of such a disconnection likely results more from postmodern critical favor than from the fact of the literary example itself. Specifically, discussion of drugs and drug addiction are generally reserved in postmodern literary-critical discourse to the domain of the subject. The term "addiction" deserves particular attention, as it and its synonyms (such as "dependence") play an important role in *Vineland*. For example, when understood in the literal sense, to be "addicted" is to be delivered by command into a state of bondage. This was how the Romans *understood* the term "*addictus*," as a juridical proclamation. A fragment of the term's archaic literal meaning survives in our current clinical understanding of the term: addiction thereby implies an involuntary compulsion that places one subject in the service of another. That other is most often understood to be a substance that exercises a power both real and metaphorical over the addict. Chemistry is the frequent culprit, a capricious force that exploits a real opportunity—a genetic predisposition, an emotional state, a social pressure—to enter the potential addict and control the body's chemistry at the expense of that body's autonomy or volition. The nominal form ("addict") thereby implies also a metaphorical subordination that is comparable to servitude. The redemption of the addict, a pitiful figure, is said to lie only in a complete rupture with the servile state. The addict is not only enslaved by chemistry but captive also to the metaphor of addiction, a metaphor that implies a narrative form. Extending from servitude through a drama of uncertain salvation that concludes with possible redemption, the addict metaphor denotes both a protagonist that is the condemned pleasure derived from addiction and a possible antagonist that is addiction's implied servility (a host of external forces is allied to each: the protagonist, addiction, includes the chemical as well as the means or persons that provide it, while the antagonist includes agents of legal, spiritual, and moral coercion). The narrative power extending from the modern metaphorical sense of the word demands a choice between continued addiction to a chemical master or addiction to a substitute for it, be it God, reason, or some incarnation of an autonomous self.

Addiction thus signifies both a physical condition and an interminable fiction in which the addict moves constantly from one master to the next, credulously achieving the illusion of autonomy without ever controlling the mechanism of enslavement. Avital Ronell offers a much different view of addiction in *Crack Wars: Literature Addiction Mania*. In that work, Ronell defines a drug as "an object that splits existence into incommensurable articulations" (49). The essential divide is a philosophical one; its material expression is the figure of the addict.[7] Not entirely enslaved, yet never entirely free, the addict negotiates, invents, and imagines new configurations of experience and language. These configurations cannot be reduced to the tyranny of science and its moral and legal systems; if anything, in exposing and acknowledging those other narratives as fictions, the addict inverts the metaphorical implication of addiction, making literary art into a sort of counternarrative that in turns permits the critic to recognize in it a previously unacknowledged truth statement regarding the ontology of the addict.[8]

To return to my earlier point regarding addiction, Pynchon's writings never endorse a clinical usage of the term "addiction," a usage that implies a problem to be cured. Keenly aware of the archaic inflections of words, Pynchon even elaborates the classical Roman meaning of addiction against its modern clinical usage in *Vineland*. Indeed, when the character Takeshi Fumimota is subjected to a machine known as the Puncutron that is alleged to diminish, if not entirely eliminate, the flow of adverse chemical energies in the human body (in Takeshi's case, these are partly due to his recent abuse of speed as well as prescription pills), Takeshi remains basically unchanged in character. The result suggests suspicion of clinical intervention or, at the very least, a comical wariness of its promise. In the same scene, the novel elaborates the archaic juridical meaning of "addiction" when Darryl Louise ("DL") is assigned to serve Takeshi for "a year and a day" (*Vineland* 163) as punishment for having initiated the physical attack (that, had it gone unchecked by the Puncutron, would have eventually resulted in Takeshi's undeserved assassination). In each case, addiction is not treated lightly so much as it is converted into a modality of the real that is not necessarily defined by a negative or adverse effect. In this case and others, *Vineland* portrays a world in which drugs do not necessarily distort (and hence destroy) reality. The opposite may in fact be true insofar as here Pynchon shows that alleged "cures" are in fact a premise for another, far less pleasurable form of addiction: that is, being a conformist "square." In demonstrating this, *Vineland* embodies the countercultural premise that art, like drugs, can catalyze a change of "consciousness."

Where Ronell's theory returns the reader quite comfortably to the paradigm of the subject (to the implied exclusion of the real), *Vineland* instead turns it to a possibility of collective experience and history. Yet the postmodern fascination with the text of the "self" presents particular difficulties to discussion of this possibility in Pynchon's novels, and in *Vineland* in particular. With respect to Pynchon, there are the obstructions of influence to consider; his devotion to Henry Adams, the whipping post of all Pragmatist theories of the subject (extending through and including important postmodern incarnations of those theories), offers the most persistent example of why many neo-Pragmatist critics avoid serious consideration of Pynchon's novels. Cultural conservatives who criticize the postmodern either dismiss Pynchon's characters as indulging in a frivolous solipsism or dismiss his novels altogether; as Jonathan Arac wrote of Daniel Bell, "[Bell] takes no interest in the unselving energies of such a postmodern work as *Gravity's Rainbow*, which follows Slothrop from the uniquely determining perversion of his Pavlovian youth along an anti-Oedipal path until he finally becomes 'a crossroads, a living intersection' [625], renewing one of Longinus's tropes for sublime mobility of identity" (xvii). There is, of course, also the manner in which the main currents of Pynchon criticism subsume the subject to discussions of technology and science in his writings, making the latter a prosthesis for an implicit critique of the modern subject, a straw man who opens in turn the possibility of new forms of agency. Those subjectivities range from the conventional post-Enlightenment political discourses of "individual and communal" identities (as Cyrus K. Patell argues) to persuasive critical views of Pynchon's flirtation with a fragmentation of the self that offers a glimpse of living "beyond all fictions" (as in Tony Tanner) to entire studies of individual agency gleaned from characters who occupy only a few lines of Pynchon's writings.[9] In every case, discussion of Pynchon's writings seems to require, as if it were a password of ritual entry, some appeal to that mythical referent and ghost of the American literary imaginary, the "self." The prospect of discussing Pynchon's *Vineland*, a "political novel" that portrays a socioeconomic world of radical drug farmers, drug users, and their reactionary antagonists, appears bleak, if not impossible, if one is expected to explain Pynchon's prose solely in relation to questions of subjectivity.

Realism is, of course, defined by a conviction that some reality exists independently of the observer (and regardless of the observer's chemical state). Consideration of the matter does not require ignoring whether actual drugs obstruct or provide access to some other forms of agency (or reality), yet such questions almost always invite readers to extract a "program" or lifestyle from literary examples (and what could be more "real" than that pervasive assumption in contemporary literary criticism?). The matter of assessing whether *Vineland* is a "major political novel" depends rather on intrinsic (and not merely formal) questions of its orientation to the literary techniques of realism, critical questions that on their surface must admit phenomenological assumptions that predispose certain forms of criticism to realism. I have already noted similarities between *Vineland* and examples of classical realism and will return to them below, hoping that even the few cursory examples above will at the very least persuade the reader to consider the possibility of a relationship. Critics who endorse the common critical assumption of postmodern fiction—that it "rewraps" earlier modes in a new fabric—would perhaps object at this juncture that *Vineland* merely dresses the intrinsic generational, socioeconomic, or historical coordinates of classical realism in frivolous postmodern attire. This seems the critical analog of reducing the effects of various drugs (and marijuana in particular) to fragmented subjectivities insofar as both avoid contending with the evidence. In the first place, to regard *Vineland* in such reductive terms requires ignoring the matter of how the novel elaborates those very same characters (such as Zoyd and Van Meter) as typical or representative of classes and economies. If this last point is admitted and the relationship affirmed, then the general problematic shifts to one of acknowledging that the American literary novel during the second half of the 20th century found a way to adapt the representation of drugs to its ambitions and techniques in such ways that effected fundamental changes to the literary description of phenomena that constitute the real. The inquiry may be qualified according to the effects of the type of drug in question (heroin in *Naked Lunch*, cocaine in *Less than Zero*, LSD in *The Electric Kool-Aid Acid Test*, hashish in *The Sheltering Sky*, etc.), but regardless of the specific example, one cannot admit in the face of this trend that the infusion of drugs as objects and modes of literary representation (or against representation) constituted a wholesale dismissal of the real. After all, the experimental use of drugs in fiction is as traditional a trope as realism in narrative itself, and both are bound to a profound sense of tradition.

The narrator of Ralph Ellison's *Invisible Man* (1952) renders the effects of marijuana as follows in the novel's famous opening pages:

> Once, when I asked for a cigarette, some jokers gave me a reefer, which I lighted when I got home and sat listening to my phonograph. It was a strange evening. Invisibility, let me explain, gives one a slightly different sense of time, you're never quite on the beat. Sometimes you're ahead and sometimes behind. Instead of the swift and imperceptible flowing of time, you are aware of its nodes, those points where time stands still or from which it leaps ahead. And you slip into the breaks and look around. That's what you hear vaguely in Louis' music. Once I saw a prizefighter boxing a yokel. (8)

In this passage, synesthesia, a familiar and proven technique to modern readers, conveys the drug's effect by merging the perception of sight and sound (in this case, vision is expressed in terms of the sense of hearing). Edmund Wilson summarized synesthesia's role in modern verse in *Axel's Castle,* in which he described Edgar Allan Poe's "confusion between the perceptions of the different senses" (23). Ellison updates synesthesia, as it were, using modern music as the substitute for the sense of hearing and light for that of sight. While the synesthetic technique is similar, marijuana is relatively new on the American literary scene, rarely described in pre–World War II prose; Ellison's use of it in the early pages of *Invisible Man* may be said to mark its arrival in mid-20th century American letters, at that very point that the modernist-realist tension began to dissolve into the postmodern. Regardless, who would argue that *Invisible Man* is not a political novel only because its narrator compares his newfound perception of the world to the effect of marijuana?

Thomas Pynchon's writings certainly revel in and expand upon this modern tradition of sensory-narrative experiment, so much so that it is nearly impossible to characterize his style without invoking some term that flirts with the language we adopt to describe the effects of drugs. And rightly so, because if there is a distinct narrative technique that might be said to characterize Pynchon's writing, it is how it recombines the senses (human and otherwise) to distort and amplify their representation or experience of reality effects. The reader's consent is of course required in order to admit that literary language enjoys such power. To that end, Pynchon's stunning distortions of scale propose a rich vocabulary of perspectives and shapes, with simulation and ekphrasis being the postmodern extensions of synesthesia. Ekphrastic distortions of scale are ever present in his prose, combining and distorting sight (and other senses) in unexpected ways. They are grotesque at times, at other times joyful, yet always designed to evoke other configurations of the real. Among the more famous examples, one might include Oedipa Maas's oft-cited panoramic view of San Narciso, which diminishes the city to a transistor's circuitry, or the Goya-esque "Lübeck Angel" in *Gravity's Rainbow*, whose eyes replace the horizon before the British bomber pilots. *Inherent Vice* offers a more recent example of Pynchon's admixture of ekphrasis, realism, and drugs in the scene in which Doc and Denis enter The Boards' house and find a "dope-smoking room with a huge 3-D reproduction in fiberglass of Hokusai's famous *Great Wave off Kanagawa*, arching wall to ceiling to opposite wall, creating a foam-shadowed hideaway beneath the eternally suspended monster" (*Inherent Vice* 125–26). Synthesizing the noir Orientalism of the hard-boiled detective with a later pop music milieu, the admixture of sight and sound is incongruous, a juxtaposition whose perception is implicitly intensified by Doc's habitual pot smoking.

Regarded in light of the previously noted tradition, Pynchon's sensory-narrative experiments assert that literary languages, when refined to their purest forms, offer a vital medium to a material experience that is to be enjoyed and shared but not necessarily controlled or improved. *Vineland* begins:

> Later than usual one summer morning in 1984, Zoyd Wheeler drifted awake in sunlight through a creeping fig that hung in the window, with a squadron of blue jays stomping around on the roof. In his dream these had been carrier pigeons from someplace far across the ocean, landing and taking off again one by one, each bearing a message for him, but none of whom, light pulsing in their wings, he could ever quite get to in time. He understood it to be another deep nudge from forces unseen, almost surely connected with the letter that had come along with his latest mental-disability check, reminding him that unless he did something publicly crazy before a date now less than a week away, he would no longer qualify for benefits. He groaned out of bed. Somewhere down the hill hammers and saws were

busy and country music was playing out of somebody's truck radio. Zoyd was out of smokes. (3).

This, the opening paragraph of *Vineland*, offers the primary lines of the novel's ambition. Emerging from nature like the muddy streets at the beginning of Dickens's *Bleak House*, Zoyd awakens to a busy economic space where birds are replaced by the noise of the region's lumber and construction industries. Prior to waking, the noise inflected Zoyd's dream, a dream he now believes to portend a change in his legal arrangement with the government (a figure that takes shape in the manner of Dickens's High Court of Chancery, albeit more slowly). That arrangement involves Zoyd's fraudulent "dependence" on social welfare—upon which he feels he should act. The chronological linearity of the passage, with narration in the third person providing description (as opposed to the use of a subjective voice), indicates that Zoyd's world is as real to him as it is to the reader who consents to recognizing its approximation of that world. Yet Zoyd lacks the motivation to improve his lot within it; as we later learn, he is coerced by some other force to maintain dependency, a premise that, among other things, provides him with the excuse to continue his lazy ways. The diction Pynchon chooses to describe Zoyd's reaction to the government letter reinforces the latter. Using colloquial verbs and prepositional phrases such as "get to" and "come along," the narration works in consonance with its subject, as they both lack ambition.[10] And yet, despite an abundance of vague pronouns ("something," "someplace," "somewhere"), we glimpse the contours of a world Pynchon recalibrates, somewhat realistically, through Zoyd's morning fog. For lack of a better phrase, we might call it stoner realism.

This all takes place before Zoyd lights a cigarette or the joint he will soon find in his shirt pocket, at which point nothing changes. Zoyd then discusses his plans for the day with his daughter Prairie. His plans are vaguely economic in nature. They involve discussion of working odd jobs off the proverbial books in subsidiary industries (landscaping, entertainment) of the region's primary economy (the lumber industry), as well as the staging of an event that will confirm, or at least temporarily extend, his welfare revenue. He is destitute in an endearing, quasi-Dickensian way, an aging hippie devoted to raising his daughter Prairie, a teenager who favors the SoCal vernacular ("rilly?") and works part-time in a strip mall pizzeria. Reagan is in the White House.

Having established principal characters in their milieu, Pynchon introduces the plot and, with it, the broader social history a reader might expect of any writing presuming to make a claim upon the real, political or otherwise. Harassed by the return of a U.S. attorney named Brock Vond, Prairie and Zoyd flee to Southern California after Vond seizes what little property they own under the legal pretext of the War on Drugs. The novel then shifts to focus largely on Prairie and her search for her absent mother, Frenesi Gates. A former radical activist and filmmaker, Frenesi now works in a federal witness protection program designed to cultivate and protect informants. The program is cancelled during a budget crisis, and Frenesi flees to Nevada with her second husband and son, unaware that she is being sought by Prairie, Vond, and other secondary characters. With Zoyd and Prairie temporarily separated, the aforementioned DL emerges as Prairie's guide and surrogate parent. A former activist comrade of Frenesi's, DL and her master Takeshi assist Prairie in her search for Frenesi and the truth about Prairie's family's history. In the meantime, Brock Vond and his agents attempt to disrupt and destroy others who also seek Frenesi, chief among them Prairie and Zoyd. Shifting focus to Prairie's search, the novel becomes a novel of political education that continues its meditation on the consequences of addiction, understood here in terms of dependence on institutional finance and power (as opposed to drugs). Ironically, it is the corrupt, violent, and envious reactionaries, as opposed to the lazy, decadent, or utopian hippies, who are the emblems of addiction, insofar as the former group recruits informants to live, as Frenesi did, in a state of government subsidy (until its budgets are cut).

In a novel of dependents, Brock Vond is portrayed as the surrogate for a particularly rabid form of American governance. In the penultimate chapter of the novel, Pynchon describes the obsessive Vond at length. His professional specialty is training double agents to infiltrate and destroy radical (left) political organizations. A snitch-baiting, anti-everything zealot, Vond combines pseudoscientific strategy with paramilitary tactics to achieve his oppressive goals. His strategies are predicated on an erroneous phenomenology of the real; specifically, he subscribes to the Lombrosian theory that certain physical traits indicate criminal psychological deviance. Having identified suspect individuals by interpreting their physical features in this way, he exploits their alleged weakness to make them snitches and apply his tactics (that it is a "weakness" is undermined by the fact that he places them in a compromised legal situation that has nothing to do with their physical features and everything to do with their knowledge of the law or lack thereof). These tactics include surveillance, harassment, planting of evidence, false imprisonment, torture, and murder by proxy. He performs those acts himself or persuades others to do so, as was the case with Prairie's mother Frenesi, whom he convinced to plant rumors and lies, as well as a gun. The weapon was then used to assassinate a radical figure named Weed Atman, a math professor at College of the Surf, a school occupied by students who intended to declare its autonomy from the state. Brock Vond applies this model of disruption to college radicals without variation, convinced that unwavering orthodoxy is the antidote to historical change, genetics, and youth.

Brock Vond is a thoroughly realized villain. To revise the earlier quote from Lukacs, he is the adequate representation of the incomplete human personality. In his emotional confusion, he embodies the unethical, paranoid illegality of the American right wing. Extending from McCarthyism through the anticampus radical crusades of J. Edgar Hoover's FBI during the Nixon years, Vond accurately portrays the rationale and methods of a sociopolitical movement as well as the workings of one of its hallmark law enforcement programs, the FBI's notorious COINTELPRO (Counter Intelligence Program), which operated from 1956 until 1976. Elizabeth Wheaton's depiction of how "COINTELPRO used informants, undercover agents, and provocateurs to disrupt organizations" summarizes Vond's work, including his "involvement in murder" (12). Pynchon avoids caricature by supplying the "type" with a psychology that imparts verisimilitude through reference to social movements as well as to Vond's inner life.[11] With respect to the former, Vond adheres to conservatism by defending the institution of the family, an ideology that ultimately results in the temporary destruction of the family comprised of

Frenesi, Zoyd, and Prairie. Or, as Zoyd remarks to Hector, the former federal agent turned film director, "we know already how much all you Reaganite folks care about the family unit, just from how much you're always fuckin' around with it" (30–31). Confusion has its object, and its focal point is Vond's obsessive desire for Frenesi. True to type, Vond is a complete hypocrite. Pynchon's narrator illustrates how Vond, who believes that "the activities of the sixties left not threats to order but unacknowledged desires for it" (269), inverts his own theory insofar as he desires "the activities of the sixties" that he projects in turn upon a sexualized version of Frenesi.

That unfulfilled desire drives Vond's violent sexual promiscuity. It is a habit that Richard Burket describes in a compelling but little discussed reading of the novel as "a Justice Department that operates arbitrarily under the aegis of the 'War on Drugs' to pursue personal agendas and to stifle dissent."[12] Burket makes an excellent point insofar as Vond's character exemplifies an important link between characters and history, a link that strengthens *Vineland*'s relation to classical realism. In Balzac, Lukacs writes, "social forces never appear as romantic or fantastic monsters, as superhuman symbols. . . . On the contrary Balzac dissolves all social relationships into a network of personal clashes of interests, objective conflicts between individuals, webs of intrigue, etc. He never, for instance, depicts justice or the courts of law as institutions independent of society and standing above it" ("Balzac: *The Peasants*" 41). As a "type" that links the specific to the general, the individual to the institution, and the novel to history, one could not find a more troubling example of a "real" political bloc that has seized power and, with it, the momentum of history, than that embodied in Vond's abuse of the law to simultaneously prosecute personal and ideological disputes.

In contrast to Vond, Prairie Wheeler's character would seem complete in another sense, one that more closely approximates Lukacs's critical category of the "typical." Much of *Vineland*—primarily the story of the counterculture's "defeat"—would seem to suggest the "novel of disillusion" that Lukacs describes in Balzac when depicting the "degradation and frustration of the energies born of the [French] revolution" ("Balzac: *Lost Illusions*" 48). Yet Prairie's story in *Vineland* resembles more a novel of political education. As the novel proceeds, her individuality becomes increasingly distinct as her motives are determined by an inner life of genuine emotion. She is intelligent and young, the ideal candidate for the political education the novel offers in the context of her desire to know her mother. The righteous collectivism of the Becker-Traverse matriarchs resides in her character together with her father Zoyd Wheeler's penchant for a righteous, even decadent individualism. In essence, she is typical, in the sense that Lukacs deploys the term, insofar as her character is supple yet fully realized, as much to summarize a history as well as to indicate one that has yet to come. Where Eugénie Grandet is ruined by the past, the past fortifies Prairie. *Vineland* concludes when Brock fails to abduct Prairie or disrupt the Traverse-Becker family reunion. As such, Prairie becomes inseparable from the supergenerational politics of the work, and *Vineland* thus offers an individual and genealogical continuum whose optimism reaches a fulcrum with Prairie, youth, and the future.[13] These aspirations depart directly from economic subsidy or legal conformity to the state and as such depict a socioeconomic movement. Admittedly, it is perhaps here, where the novel implies an alternative order emerging at the margins of repressive state power, that some might mistake it for naïvely utopian writing. Yet in the place of such an erroneous utopian reading, there are not only characters negotiating real historical forces but also the aggregation of those characters into a supragenerational bloc comprised of distinct aesthetic movements and economic classes. As such, it suggests not so much a utopian possibility as the realization of a paracapitalism founded on new modes of economic organization, modes that repeat the ways in which Pynchon combines a sober realism with hallucinatory comedy in the novel.

We have, then, the "complete human personalities" as well as their aggregate, the ad hoc, maternally centered family ("matrilineal" does not suffice, because it is not "linear") that replaces the patrilineal institution. It is not often in Pynchon's writings that the cast of characters is significant as a whole as well as in its parts. In *Vineland*, however, the two are concordant in a manner befitting the parameters of classical realism. Lukacs writes, for example, that "the several parts of a Balzacian cycle have their own independent life because each of them deals with individual destinies. But these individual destinies are always a radiation of the socially typical, of the socially universal, which can be separated from the individual only by an analysis *a posteriori*. In the novels themselves the individual and the general are inseparably united, like a fire with the heat it radiates" ("Balzac: *Lost Illusions*" 55). This is the relation of Prairie to her family, with its respective generations and histories.

We see in art that ideology is never abstract. Understood in terms of classical Marxism, it is the reified instantiation of social relations that interact with real economic practices. It is there, after all, in its attention to psychological detail and the resulting authenticity of a world through the accurate representation of characters in their manners, clothes, and speech, that Marxists such as Lukacs presumed that realism held its place as the eminent literary mode, because it could capture the revolutionary-historical momentum of the Industrial Age. As in classical realism, *Vineland* conveys the historical momentum of a dispossessed class (the Becker-Traverse supergeneration) that finds in the novel a way to narrate its historical contest against an enemy and the history of "inevitable" defeat that enemy would write for it. Yet, as Elizabeth Jane Wall Hinds has noted in a compelling article on the novel, Prairie acts as a "historian [who] discovers or creates a historical past based on a typological model that reads earlier events as prefiguring and occupying the present" ("Visible Tracks" 93). In Hind's view, *Vineland* offers a narrative that resembles "Puritan history," although I would add that the better term for it is "counterhistory," and an irreversibly secular approximation of a counterhistory at that.[14]

It is there, at the delicate nexus between individual and character, genealogy and plot, that *Vineland* appears a distant relative of Charles Dickens's *Bleak House.* Prairie is supported by a cast of characters who amplify certain shared traits. Just as Dickens associated the judiciary of the chancery with bureaucratic orthodoxy and waste, Pynchon draws the Department of Justice and its allies and affiliates in a similar light. Other similarities might be cited: Mr. Tulkinghorn seems a progenitor of Vond's (the exception being that Tulkinghorn is murdered, while Vond is not); Prairie, aided by DL and Takeshi, plays the role of Detective Bucket as the novel proceeds; Zoyd plays Jarndyce's role of ward in his own kind, destitute fashion (Zoyd is, of course, an actual parent); and a genealogical mystery obscured and complicated by political institutions drives the plot. Additionally, their emotional world is not devoid of the appropriate sentiments. Zoyd's passivity is motivated by sincere concern for the protection of his child; Frenesi's desire for Vond is wracked by the guilt of betraying her husband, mother, and daughter; DL has never entirely forgiven Frenesi for her betrayal of the cause, yet she assists Prairie out of continued devotion to it; and so forth. In sum, the "trace of the fluidity of the political and historical background" that Auerbach claims to be missing from Dickens (492) is instead present, perhaps excessively so, in *Vineland*. Nonetheless, the two novels share similarities in terms of scale, characterization, and plot. Shared sensibility—if one looks beyond their generally sympathetic tone—is another matter. This is precisely due to the prominence Pynchon affords to "the political and historical background," not because he affords it in the abstract but because the object of its attention, the key indicator of the real, is not a subject (stoner or otherwise) but a product and species—marijuana—and the economic life and social classes organized around it.

As I noted above, the novel's genealogical narrative offers a community (of nonaddicts, some of whom do use drugs, although not to the point of addiction) independent of state institutions but not at the expense of some claim to the real. To return to the supragenerational point that joins Prairie to history, *Vineland* describes a contest between affiliated genealogies of the American political left and their paranoid opponents, Vond and his Republican masters, who have vowed to erase the New Deal from the historical record one murder or budget cut at a time. Prairie is also the surrogate of history, particularly economic history, at that juncture. On a national scale, the premise and object of reactionary intervention are no longer radicalism but marijuana, a plant whose cultural association with sin, comedy, and the grotesque has historically generated considerable aversion among the holy. By depicting an agricultural economy predicated upon the growth, sale, and consumption of marijuana, Pynchon would presumably muster little if any sympathy for those pot farmers and consumers who control the means of production. As if to provoke further outrage, *Vineland* portrays marijuana cultivation not only as the object of conservative vitriol but as the basis for a mode of economic and social organization, using, of all things, the conventions of classical realism to do just that.

Pynchon's California novels portray marijuana in a unique manner. It is a pervasive recreational drug in *The Crying of Lot 49*, *Vineland*, and *Inherent Vice*. In these last two, however, it functions as a cipher for types of economic organization. To establish the necessary contrast, *Inherent Vice* (2009) describes the economic organization of another illegal drug, heroin, by a cartel known as the Golden Fang. The cartel's mode of organization replicates the industrial scale of 19th-century trusts such as U.S. Steel. Jason Velveeta, a minor character portraying an ineffective pimp, describes the Golden Fang to Doc Sportello, a detective who is the novel's central character, as an "Indochinese heroin cartel. A vertical package. They finance it, grow it, process it, bring it in, step on it, move it, run Stateside networks of local street dealers, take a separate percentage off of each operation. Brilliant" (159). Meditating on the question of the Golden Fang's model of organization, Doc later realizes it extends through the treatment of addiction: "if the Golden Fang could get its customers strung out, why not turn around and also sell them a program to help them kick?" (192). The Golden Fang operates a model of rational economic organization that has both illegitimate operations (it sells illegal narcotics) and legitimate ones (that it ostensibly uses to launder or convert certain illegal profits into legal capital). Despite elements of illegality, the criminal organization resembles in every way a vertically integrated institutional hierarchy, replete with the cooperation and subsidy of its host nation.

Marijuana, by contrast, enjoys a much different model of economic organization in *Vineland*. It too is illicit, but it belongs to a local market economy. It is grown in places such as Holytail, that Vineland region of the novel "beyond the coastal ranges and the yearlong fogs, in a valley where growing conditions were ideal—about the last refuge for pot growers in Northern California" (220). The novel implies that the Vineland pot farms are small, family-owned businesses (or supplements to a family's legitimate business) that grow and supply the drug directly to local consumers. It is a market economy in the sense that Manuel De Landa, elaborating Fernand Braudel, described it in *A Thousand Years of Nonlinear History*: "peasant and small-town markets, self-organized structures that arise spontaneously out of the activities of many individuals, whose interests only partially overlap. (I have in mind here a place in a town where people gather every week, as opposed to markets in the modern sense: dispersed collections of consumers served by many middlemen.)" (31). Understood in this sense, as a seasonal business distributing a product to a network of local consumers, the Holytail marijuana growers and buyers operate in a self-regulating system of exchange. A model of economic organization resonates with the novel's title, as it implies the rhizomatic, horizontal growth of certain plants. Just as the Vineland ferns spread through the redwood undergrowth, the pot farms hide among the vertically integrated hierarchies of the local lumber industry.[15]

Thus we can note that the economic organization of the Holytail marijuana market is comparable to "the closed economy and small radius" of the 16th-century European grain trade Braudel describes in *The Mediterranean*; this is true in terms of economic scale as well as with respect to the intervention of jealous legal authorities who were "responsible for more espionage [in grain markets] . . . than the affairs of the Inquisition."[16] As such, the marijuana economy is as much the target of government attack as is the user or the effect of the drug itself (an effect that is symbolic insofar as it represents a certain cultural formation). In each instance—the character, the economy, the drug, and the symbol—the contest involves two competing economic systems. One of them is that of institutional hierarchies (embodied by the Golden Fang in *Inherent Vice*) that rationalize markets with the assistance of the federal or local institutions of commerce and law. As in *Inherent Vice*, and perhaps more so than in that novel, *Vineland* depicts those federal and local institutions as waging "war" against a model of economic organization that is market based yet without institutional controls. Their agents are characterized in Brock Vond as ruthless bureaucrats who, having "won [their] war against the lefties, now . . . [see their] future in the war against drugs" (*Vineland* 130). The critical difference between pot and other commodities is that Pynchon shows how the state does not wish to tax or regulate its sale but rather to criminalize the drug and its markets. Understood in terms of the government collusion with the Golden Fang described in *Inherent Vice*, the war on drugs may also be described as eliminating the competition.

Rabid federal intercession of this sort suggests a horrid distortion of the model of market intervention imagined by New Deal economists. With the exception of crises such as war or economic collapse, New Deal economists thought institutional hierarchies exercised sufficient resources to regulate prices by competition within their own markets (and without government intervention), thereby maintaining economic stability. John Kenneth Galbraith described that scenario in *The New Industrial State* (1967), wherein he also imagined government providing controls to market economies in which small businesses did not exercise sufficient controls over market prices; his specific example is that of agriculture.[17] Because it is illegal, the pot-growing equivalent of Galbraith's individual farm is vulnerable to the predations of institutional agents that wish to institutionalize market controls in favor of cooperative industries that maintain a semblance of legitimacy despite the horror of their actual effects: the Golden Fang, as opposed to Holytail. Of course, critics might very well complain that the type of agriculturally based small market depicted by Pynchon may be idyllic and naïve, expressing nostalgia for a lost America (see *Vineland* 354), whose economic outline in the novel more closely resembles the economies of the British colonies in North America, or that it is deaf to distinctions between types of postmodern markets such as those described by Fredric Jameson in his masterpiece, *Postmodernism*.[18]

Such criticism of Pynchon's writings (and Jameson has perhaps been the most incisive in that respect) may be true. Yet, it does not contend with how Pynchon has elaborated, in the particular instance of *Vineland*, a novel that throws many of the theoretical premises for the postmodern criticism of realism into political disorder. For instance, what if one were to regard this Renaissance-oriented model of economic organization as indicating a cyclical return to the moment at which the middle class and mercantilism emerged from the urbanization of agricultural markets and, with it, the political implication of modern republicanism? In a manner typical of Pynchon, the gravity of the suggestion is underscored by the levity of the primary economic form it takes (a market) and its primary commodity (pot). In the end, the serious yet lighthearted tone of Rushdie's review of *Vineland* is amplified, and we recognize a novel that, upon closer inspection, is one that gregariously affirms the realist tradition in the form of a novel about marijuana, its economies and its consumption. Rather than suggesting a chemical break from realism, it offers instead a vital recreation of it as Pynchon's sensory-language experiments and distortions of scale and perception revive and suffuse it with both the "seriousness" of classical realism and its complement, the vulgarity and pleasure of "everyday life," an experiment that replicates the sensory experience of marijuana (which may vary depending on the user), even when a character or reader has not taken any drug, as if literary language alone might do the trick. And while similar ambitions, as well as other depictions of market forces (one thinks of the stunning Capetown market scene in chapter 8 of *Mason & Dixon)*, course through Pynchon's historical romances, those markets enjoy a more intensely political presentation in his California novels, particularly *Vineland* and *Inherent Vice* (this last work being something of a historical romance as well). In them, Pynchon affords to marijuana and its users an eminence enjoyed by many another drug identified with a modern literary or artistic movement, yet in *Vineland*, it results in something more than a premise for the mere solipsism typical of much literature by or about drug use. If, then, *Vineland* may in fact aspire to some realist traditions, and postmodern intellectuals, for all their antipathy to the real, consider Prairie, radicalism, and the markets of Holytail as mere aesthetic vacancies, then we might have in this very opposition between Pynchon's levity and the gravity of his professional critics confirmation of Rushdie's claim that *Vineland* is a "major political novel," insofar as in reading it we are exposed to the contradiction of a political condition, regardless of its chemical state.

Through a haze of redwood fog and marijuana smoke, we arrive at Vineland: a decentralized, premodern agricultural economy that sustains a postmodern narrative mode. This admixture refutes the way in which, by the logic of 19th-century science, realism, utopia, and reason, history was predicted to develop, returning as it does in *Vineland* to a mode of production that modalities of realism were alleged to have rendered obsolete, to subsumed into industry, made into a relic. A variant of that realism flourishes instead in *Vineland* as a kind of narrative-historical synesthesia, anachronistic yet timely, ironic yet naïve. Is it political, as Salman Rushdie argued? To answer that question, one would have to first answer a host of others implied by it. Is history predictable and conclusive? Are forms of subjectivity available other than those defined by capital? Are these possibilities but a nebulous vision, something wandered from a stoner's dream? Writing to his friend Max Horkheimer in 1938, Walter Benjamin asked whether narcotics and critical theory—both of which he understood as "bound to reason and its struggle for liberation" ("From the

Letters" 145)—arrive at a similar point. The question he posed might very well find its answer in a novel such as *Vineland*: "Aren't these insights, by virtue of the human solidarity from which they arise, truly political in the end?"[19]

NOTES

1. The phrase in my title is borrowed from Walter Benjamin's "From 'Surrealism'" (*On Hashish* 132). Marcus Boon's introductory essay to that volume offers an excellent, concise overview of Benjamin's writings describing the effects of taking narcotics and how those experiences relate to the projects developed by Benjamin in other works. See also note 19 below.
2. In a rare discussion of the topic, Philip E. Simmons entertains the question in a section of his 1997 study *Deep Surfaces* (166–78) by examining the novel's political implications in terms of contemporary mass media.
3. David Cowart briefly alludes to *Vineland's* "two kinds of realism: social and magic" in "Attenuated Postmodernism: Pynchon's *Vineland*" (183). Cowart's essay does not pursue the matter, however; it is focused instead on distinctions between postmodern/modern (represented, in his essay, by Pynchon and Joyce).
4. Lukacs notes in "Balzac and Stendhal" (72–76) that Balzac criticized elaborate rhetorical devices insofar as they obscured actual relations between persons and historical forces. This was a key element of Balzac's critique of Romanticism. There is, of course, another way to regard Pynchon's title insofar as the trope invokes a botanical materiality that the reader holds, literally and figuratively, in hand.
5. My argument here runs contrary to the dominant claims regarding the political "potential" of postmodern aesthetics. Fredric Jameson, to name a relevant figure, has decried the absence of such possibilities in the majority of postmodern fiction (he makes an exception for William Gibson). In addition, Jameson often dismisses Pynchon's historical interests as frivolous. See, for example, *Postmodernism: or, the Cultural Logic of Late Capitalism* 361.
6. In the preface, Lukacs summarizes the basic definition that is presumed also by the opponents of Pynchon and many other postmodernists who argue that Pynchon's characters are not "realistic." The charge assumes a fundamental tenet (generally associated with Pragmatism) that individuals can be organized into "types" that are recognizable and are, therefore, recognizable as "real." The assumption invokes all manner of psychological assumptions that seem to necessitate an a priori dismissal of Pynchon's writings, a dismissal so predictable that one can smell it rising from certain reviews of his work as soon as the first page is turned.
7. On the one hand, the addict's experience of the drug evades communication, while on the other hand, our understanding of the addict's relationship to the drug is mediated

by illegality as well as by medical-scientific discourse. Ronell's book discusses writings on addiction by Sigmund Freud and Martin Heidegger, framing those essays with aphorisms, experimental dialogues, and a prose chapter that resembles a medical report. She thereby illuminates *Madame Bovary* (as well as that novel's legal history) to make the case for a new critical sensibility, what she calls a "genuine ethics of decision" (61). The occasion presents itself in De Quincey's writings on opium, in which "the promise of exteriority" negotiates the "internal conflict of freedom." In De Quincey, Ronell argues, the addict is no longer torn between absolute states of servility, with their respective fictions. The addict instead devises new ways to express knowing, language, and truth. Here, then, lies Ronell's key to addiction: if the addict can narrate addiction (as opposed to being narrated by it) then he (De Quincey) achieves a new ontological relation to addiction.

8. Ronell's claims to an ethics of reading as addiction would seem to offer little explanation when addiction is defined neither as a clinical problem nor as an ontological position defined by its clinical other. I understand such claims to exemplify in their daring manner a particular moment in the history of literary-theoretical writings characterized by an urge to rescue and re-present the marginalized, criminalized, and abject. In this respect, there appears to be little discernible difference between their basic impulse and the Romantic mythos of the addicted artist whose "visionary" qualities can be attributed in part or whole to chemical "dependency" (this last term is a euphemism that has increasingly replaced "addiction" but which does not carry the metaphorical punch of the word's classical juridical sense). Of examples that come to mind, biographical explanations of Poe's life that appeared in the 1920s, including the articles and books written by Lorine Pruette (1920), John W. Robertson (1923) and Joseph Wood Krutch (1926), exemplify how early speculation regarding Poe's possible alcoholism persisted in the popular imaginary. By contrast, contemporary writings by D. H. Lawrence and William Carlos Williams explaining Poe's art in more substantial terms stir little if any recognition. Fueled by mass media and pop forms of psychopathology, psychology, and psychoanalysis, biographers and critics who speculate on the relationship between drugs and art have shaped a cultural telos that often exceeds the incredulous reaction of careful readers who are wary of reducing a life or work of art to mere chemical accident. The virtue of Ronell's "genuine ethics of decision" is that it does not reduce aesthetics to the psychological assumptions of biology or to a clinical view that implies a biological determinism. Philosophy it is, as she correctly describes it, but nonetheless philosophy of a kind that serves the institutions and discourses of the postmodern subject.

9. I refer here to the closing lines of Patell's *Negative Liberties: Morrison, Pynchon and the Problem of Liberal Ideology* (196) and cite the lines that close chapter 7 of Tony Tanner's *City of Words: American Fiction, 1950–1970* (173). The final example alludes

to Samuel Thomas's *Pynchon and the Political*. I would note that Tanner deftly uses the phrase "addiction to fantasy" in that same passage to make a point of which the literary-critical implication is perhaps stronger than any in Ronell's aforementioned book.

10. Pynchon summarized this predisposition in mock-theological form in his 1993 essay "Nearer, My Couch, to Thee" in *The New York Times Book Review*.
11. The word "type" invokes the sense in which Lukacs defines the term, wherein characters and epochs are synthesized in realist fiction. See "Preface" 6. See also Fredric Jameson's excellent discussion of the term in "The Case for Georg Lukacs" (191–95).
12. See Burket, "State Law Enforcement Apparatus as America." Burket's article was paired with David Thoreen's compelling and related essay "The President's Emergency War Powers and the Erosion of Civil Liberties in Pynchon's *Vineland*" in the same issue of the Oklahoma City Law Review.
13. There is little available discussion about the Traverse family, which constitutes the main genealogical line of Pynchon's writings. Traverse family members appear in both *Vineland* and *Against the Day*; indeed, *Against the Day*, in which the Traverses settle in California, can be read as a prequel to *Vineland*. For related discussion, I refer the reader to a previous article of mine, with all of the discomfort befitting the vanity of such a reference. See "Thomas Pynchon Against the Day" 202–7. See also Simmons's discussion of the genealogical framework of *Vineland* in *Deep Surfaces* (168–69).
14. With the phrase "counterhistory," I refer to Michel Foucault's writings on the emergence of historical narrative distinguished from "sovereign" history in British historical writing of the 16th and 17th centuries (66–72).
15. Although I would dispute the argument that Pynchon's novel shares some elements with New Historicist critical methods, Mark Robberds's argument that "it is possible to trace the growth of vines genealogically, that is, from buds back to roots" does not so much illuminate Pynchon's alleged "method" as it suggests the interdependence between the novel's representation of real markets and its genealogical cast of New Deal and counter-culture characters. See "New Historicist Creepers of *Vineland*" 237–49.
16. *The Mediterranean and the Mediterranean World in the Age of Philip II* 570, 572. The second quote from Braudel paraphrases the 19th-century Italian historian Lodovico Biachini.
17. Galbraith's book offers a short but useful summary of the matter in this context. See *The New Industrial State* 30–31.
18. The section of Jameson's book to which I refer (266–67) begins with a passage relevant to my previous citation from Galbraith, after which Jameson proceeds to offer sketches of different market structures.

19. Benjamin's letter to Horkheimer should be read in the context of a previous selection from the same volume. In the passage from "Surrealism" reproduced therein, Benjamin writes that narcotics "give an introductory lesson" to a "materialistic, anthropological inspiration" ("From the Letters" 132–33). This inspiration, which he describes as a "profane illumination," is elaborated in a political register in the later letter to Horkheimer that I quoted earlier.

Postmodern Sacrality and *Inherent Vice*

CHRISTOPHER K. COFFMAN

Detectives in novels, always preoccupied with deriving meaning from scattered clues, lend themselves to readings as figurations of the hermeneutician. In the case of Pynchon, paranoia often shapes the detective's interpretive process. This chapter situates a reading of the detective in *Inherent Vice* and paranoia as an epistemological mode in relation to several points of intersection between postmetaphysical and weak hermeneutics and postmodern and postsecular theology. The goal of this effort is not only to defend a view of Pynchon's later fiction as continuing the tendency of his early work to offer both implicit and explicit commentary on the sacred and the spiritual but also to demonstrate that *Inherent Vice*'s engagement with these topics may be regarded as more than mere reiterations of attitudes established in prior fictions. Instead of repeating earlier positions, *Inherent Vice* speaks to developments indicative of a sympathy for what even some detractors would likely regard as relatively conventional religious discourse. In order to elaborate my reading of the latest California novel as inclusive of such changes in Pynchon's treatment of sacrality, I consider selections from the text in relation to passages from *The Crying of Lot 49* and *Vineland* and also in light of four topics engaged with some frequency by contemporary Christian philosophers and theologians: the relation between religious tradition and revelation, the promotion of interpretation offered by sacred texts, the mystery of the divine name, and the connection between sacral communion and human community.

Discussions of the religious and spiritual in Pynchon's oeuvre early took shape in terms familiar from Mircea Eliade's work, notably *The Sacred and the Profane*. The first of Pynchon's California novels is central to the initial extended remarks on the topic in Edward Mendelson's seminal "The Sacred, the Profane, and *The Crying of Lot 49*." According to Mendelson, *The Crying of Lot 49* and its predecessor, *V.* offer competing visions of a unifying principle: in the debut novel, entropic principles govern a reductive movement to constriction and infertility; in the other text, the same principles seen differently lead to more constructive and productive results, such as "community," "meaning," and "transcendence" (183–84). A riposte to some of Mendelson's arguments is offered in an open letter by Thomas Hill Schaub. Schaub argues that Mendelson overstates the case for determinate truths in *The Crying of Lot 49* and thus "threatens to eliminate the book's essential ambiguity" ("Open Letter" 93). On this view, inconclusiveness and proliferation of meaning inoculate the narrative of *The Crying of Lot 49* against the determinate truths at which conventional hermeneutic exercise aims, frustrating attempts either to make primary any of the many discursive fields it offers or to indicate the presence of an unquestionable realization or revelation of (as opposed to anticipatory faith in) transcendence.

While support for either side of the argument may be found in a survey of more recent secondary publications, including those dealing with Pynchon's fictions other than *The Crying of Lot 49*, critical sympathy finds more often for Schaub's case. In its more willful presentations, this interpretive tendency promotes readings that preserve a view of Pynchon's novels as the voice of a postmodernist pessimism in accord with which the truly sacred yields to an antifoundational and secular relativism. Even studies that approach this position only with extensive qualification, especially those written with an eye primarily to *Gravity's Rainbow*, such as Kathryn Hume's *Pynchon's Mythography*, do finally acknowledge its authority. One goal of the following remarks is to counter this tendency, not by taking up exclusively with either side of the disagreement but by proposing that the disagreement may be understood as less divisive than the preceding suggests. Such a perspective is recommended by some key texts, including especially Dwight Eddins's *The Gnostic Pynchon*, which poses a *metaxic* position for Pynchon's characters. Pynchon's humans, in other words, occupy a middle ground between the transcendent and the immanent, spirit and matter, and the sacred and the profane—a middle ground that makes both poles of any binary available and alignment with only one of them less than fully satisfying, indeed, less than fully human. In spite of the persuasiveness of Eddins's argument, I submit that the developments in recent hermeneutic thought here brought to bear on readings of Pynchon's California novels illuminate concerns that the gnostic context opens to consideration less fully. Contemporary hermeneutics offers a complex and sensitive means with which to think about religious tradition without sacrificing awareness of the radical reconceptions Pynchon offers. To put this another way: the philosophers and theologians would seem to have come nearer to catching up with Pynchon, and their recent insights allow one to see more clearly that what has appeared a critical impasse is rather the articulation of two aspects of the same argument. In Pynchon's California novels, revelation is to be found in the immanent; salvation is found not by occupying space between opposing poles but in recognizing the falsity of the distinctions on which the hierarchy that defines them relies.

Religious Tradition and Revelation

As with many other serious novels that engage the conventions of the detective novel or noir, *Inherent Vice* affords regular meditations on knowledge and its construction. These epistemological sorties are complicated a bit by our protagonist's fondness for intoxicants, resulting in paranoia that is sometimes only obliquely related to the dark suspicions of the hard-boiled tradition and noir. Nevertheless, one passage that does offer a pessimistic reflection on meaning also distinguishes itself because it contextualizes the novel's title. Insofar as this is the case, it speaks to David Cowart's assertion that "the more inherent the vice, the more noir the fiction" (*Thomas Pynchon* 124). Looking at some photographs relevant to his investigation, the detective-protagonist encounters an interpretive scandal:

> Doc got out his lens and gazed into each image till one by one they began to float apart into little blobs of color. It was as if whatever had happened had reached some kind of limit. It was like finding the gateway to the past unguarded, unforbidden because it didn't have to be. Built into the act of

> return finally was this glittering mosaic of doubt. Something like what Sauncho's colleagues in marine insurance liked to call inherent vice. (Pynchon, *Inherent Vice* 351)

The dissolution of evidence in the face of present concerns and the intrusion of uncertainty into the consideration of what had offered itself as "raw data" from the past not only unsettle the paradigms of knowledge construction that are epistemologies but also trouble their ontological underpinnings. While nothing in the quoted passage encourages a consideration of it within the framework of theological inquiry, Doc's following speculation about the connection between his difficulties and "original sin" places the tasks of detection and the anxieties of the paranoiac in relation to a religious tradition to which Doc otherwise appears largely a stranger. The passage also recalls that moment in *Vineland* when Takeshi is encouraged to avoid "original sin," described as the invention by men of "'good' and 'evil,' where before women had been content to just be" (166). The intertextual connection indicates that it is Doc's analytic effort that frustrates his access to meaning—rather than dividing, rather than initiating the terms of difference, he might recognize the whole as unavailable to those who engage in interpretive procedures that result in a final vision of only the "blobs of color" or the tiles of the "mosaic." That such a whole is one that might reveal the relevance of the photograph as an artifact mediating historical import in and for the present and is also one that may indicate that it is Doc's very analytic approach that frustrates recognition of that relevance raises several related concerns.

The quoted passage highlights difficulties that attend interpretations of the past. The religious discourse that contextualizes these difficulties finds an intriguing parallel in Santiago Zabala's description of a certain strain of postmodern hermeneutics. According to Zabala, contemporary philosophy's effort to overcome the inheritance of metaphysics can proceed only by revisiting that philosophical past ("Introduction" 7). From this perspective, any effort to think about the past or the self must accede to historically predetermined structures of interpretation. However faulty and problematic, however much they are traditions of violence, discrimination, or corruption, our terms for understanding derive in a positive or negative sense from prior methodologies and foundations. As Doc's examination of the photographs shows, the interpretation of the past is fraught with doubt due to the influence of faults—original sin, the inheritances of metaphysics—implicit in the available structures of interpretation. As these faults derive at least in part from the fact that the past has become part of our interpretive framework, his difficulty with the photographs indicates that the inherent vice of the interpretive heritage is felt most acutely when the past itself becomes the object of scrutiny. There is, too, a more fundamental parallel of original sin in the interpretive arena, one that derives from problems inherent in human ontology.

The preservation of the past in the present speaks to John D. Caputo's discussion of what he calls the event-ual nature of religion. For Caputo, religious traditions are continuous sequences of different manifestations of a common inner energy. Caputo calls this inner energy "the event" and identifies it with the divine name. For this reason, religious tradition can provide the faithful with an ongoing revelation of divine presence ("Spectral" 47–55). Such a presence is like that one Oedipa Maas intuits when she recognizes of her pursuit of the Trystero that it is "as if . . . there were revelation in progress all around her" (*Lot 49* 44). To the degree that mysteries like the Trystero and the Golden Fang persist in spite of the significantly different historical guises they assume, their manifestations parallel the ongoing revelation of the more fundamental mystery of the divine. While the incredible promise a tradition's revelatory manifestations offers is profound, Caputo argues that it is tempered by the effects of time. As time passes, past revelations become out of tune with the present, with the result that full revelation is indefinitely deferred ("Spectral" 47–55). This play of revelation and concealment continues in this fashion, and one implication of the process is that it shall continue, which is to say: there is a future, one in which revelation will again occur. Tradition in this manner allows the faithful to see the world as a place of sacred immanence rather than as a barrier to revelation (Caputo, "On the Power" 159). Caputo's argument that religious tradition is at once revelatory and behind the times is echoed in another register by Jean-Luc Marion, who posits that interpretations of liturgical texts are similarly driven and shaped by the exigencies of time and place (158). Oedipa would seem to have anticipated the point by recognizing that the "central truth itself . . . must always blaze out, destroying its own message irreversibly, leaving an overexposed blank" (*Lot 49* 76). Caputo, Marion, and Oedipa thus all assert that meanings we construct, while very possibly valid, are always and at once antiquated in expression. In the context of these thoughts, and led by the last, film-related words from the preceding quote from *The Crying of Lot 49*, one may return to Doc's consideration of his photographs. In keeping with the paranoiac's conviction that meaning will reveal itself, his optimism regarding a truth that is ineluctable yet ever promised bespeaks a revelation that is delayed but also present. Corrupted by the historicity of our Being, the dissolving photographs are at once disappointingly indicative of the limits and encouragingly provocative with regard to the advantages of our ontological status. We are caught in the struggle defined by the ambiguously desirable and unavoidable intrusion of the pastness of the past, which Doc suggests is a sign of some "original sin," and present reminders that encourage hope for future projects. This picture of the human being suspended in the tension between suspicion and revelation and experiencing both in an ongoing fashion by virtue of the practice of tradition is indeed reminiscent of the metaxis of gnosticism, yet it directs attention forcefully to the bearing of historicity on interpretation, which influence is manifest in the original sin productive of the doubt Doc bemoans.

Endless Interpretation

Doc's frustrations with the photographs allow consideration of the interpretive hurdle presented by the historicity of mimesis. His experience also recalls one of Oedipa Maas's speculations about the relation between the need for interpretation and a lack of fullness of meaning: she wonders if the clues she has discovered regarding Trystero are not "some kind of compensation. To make up for her having lost the direct, epileptic Word, the cry that might abolish the night" (95). A less pessimistic take on the disjunction between potential and actual interpretive satisfaction is offered by Marion, for whom the gulf between sacred text (the human word) and referent (the divine Word) is no cause for despair but, instead, the offering of an inexhaustible reserve of meaning that calls for endless interpretation (156–57). Marion's perspective usefully illuminates the final paragraph of *Inherent Vice*. The text ends with a vision of Doc driving south through unnaturally thick fog:

> The bigger exit signs overhead were completely invisible, but sometimes it was possible to see one of the smaller ones down at road level, right where the exit lane began to peel away. . . . Doc figured if he missed the Gordita Beach exit he'd take the first one whose sign he could read and work his way back on surface streets. . . . Maybe . . . it would stay this way for days, maybe he'd have to just keep driving, down past Long Beach, down through Orange County, and San Diego, and across a border where nobody could tell anymore in the fog who was Mexican, who was Anglo, who was anybody. Then again, he might run out of gas before that happened, and . . . pull over on the shoulder, and wait. . . . For the fog to burn away, and for something else this time, somehow, to be there instead. (368–69, ellipses added)

As with the earlier scene in which he tried to make sense of photographs, Doc's trip down the freeway lends itself to a reading in relation to the interpretive position afforded by our ontological nature and the failure of language to proffer terms useful in suggesting that which is beyond it. If Doc's drive is read as an interpretive effort, it is one almost certainly doomed to insufficiency, due to the very doubt he mentions with regard to the photographs. At the same time, his willingness to make sense of his position in terms of familiar coordinates, while not entirely dismissing the possibility of overcoming or working through the confusions to a point beyond borders at which differences are revealed as irrelevant, speaks of a kind of paranoiac wisdom that neither yields nor pretends to be more than it is.

Doc's openness to revisions preserves the possibilities that the interpretation-without-end of paranoia also demands. In this sense, the paranoiac need for ceaseless interrogation and suspicion promotes a resistance not only to firm conclusions but also to any superstructure of meaning that may be built on the basis of those conclusions. The particular value of this position goes far beyond Doc's applications of it in the realm of highway driving, as is made more evident when one notes that Vattimo identifies such suspicion as exactly that which distinguishes peace from violence. If peace is preserved by dialogue, violence is and grows out of the silencing of dialogue; it is that which denies the possibility of questions ("Prayer" 93). In this sense, the profound critiques of discursive authority allowed by postmodern nihilism may be seen as the whole "truth" of Christianity ("Age" 47). To place this argument alongside Marion's is to see that Vattimo finds the promise of peace in the very activity —endless interpretation—that Marion regards as the derivative of reflection on the divine Word.

That Doc, during his southerly drive through the fog, expresses willingness to "work his way back" bears additional attention in relation to this intersection between Marion's remarks on the significance of endless interpretation and Vattimo's declaration of it as the path to peace. Doc's acknowledgment that, however far his journey takes him beyond Gordita Beach, he will need and partially wishes to return to that hometown suggests his apprehension that limitations are an unavoidable part of human meaning construction, for efforts to represent the divine Word with human words—to present that which is unpresentable—will finally fall short of the mark, returning one to the native human ontological ground. For this reason, Doc's plan for returning home, for settling back into the familiar interpretive stance, is a necessary one. Too, this plan suggests that Doc is a more capable detective than Oedipa. Her internal debate about where her inquiries should take her after her meeting with Genghis Cohen also takes shape with reference to highway off-ramps, yet the question is resolved for her: she does not avoid home because of distaste for it or because she understands the appeal of an alternative but because "it turned out she missed the exit for Kinneret and that solved it" (80). At the same time, one notes that Doc is not without hope that the bounds of familiarity might finally become irrelevant. Just as the human interpretive effort implicit in struggles to present the divine Word aims always to approach it via an escape from the limitations definitive of human languages, so Doc envisions an overcoming of boundaries, a surpassing of geopolitical limitations accompanied by the dissolution of national identity. His openness to dynamic interpretive efforts might be seen in contrast to their lack in the comparatively static detection procedures of Bigfoot Bjornsen, assuming one admits as relevant the intertextual explanation of the legendary Bigfoot that Buster offers to Zoyd Wheeler in *Vineland*: "we're like Bigfoot. Times go on, we never change" (7). Too, Doc's relative optimism might be read against that regular experience of the fog Ralph Wayvone, Sr. observes: "the fog now began to lift to reveal not the borderlands of the eternal after all, but only quotidian California" (*Vineland* 94). Doc's wish for a more profound unveiling in spite of familiarity with disappointment is akin to the play that preserves the peaceful hope presented for Vattimo by the process of interpretation undertaken by a being within the limits of Being. To recognize, as does Doc, this play between acknowledgment of insufficiency and hope for success is to serve the ends of peace, to enact an effort amenable to alternatives to violent difference.

The Mystery of the Divine Name

To reach an end to interpretation is impossible within the limits of Being. This hurdle is, however, not entirely a shutting down of inquiry. Indeed, if we are not to despair and would rather adopt Vattimo's sense of the incomparable affirmation implicit in endless interpretation, we must endeavor to think of God beyond Being. This point encourages reflection on a brief passage from *Inherent Vice* that might otherwise escape close attention. Readers are introduced to Doc as a figure in love with an old flame who has reentered his life. Pondering the question of whether or not Shasta actually loves Mickey Wolfmann, Doc recognizes that, even if she confessed love, that confession must carry an "unspoken footnote that the word these days was being way too overused. Anybody with any claim to hipness 'loved' everybody, not to mention other useful applications, like hustling people into sex activities they might not, given the choice, much care to engage in" (5). On one hand, Doc's assertion is eminently well-suited to the ironical postmodern attitude toward such metaphysically burdened notions as romantic love. On the other, his remarks suggest that he recognizes that it is something to do with the term, rather than the entirety of that to which it refers, that has become exhausted.

While Doc condemns the overuse of the word "love," that condemnation is betrayed by his own romantic attachments and his repeated, and often highly sentimental and active, defenses of family and friendship. Doc's later actions seem to oppose the corruption of community, rather than community itself, as is evident in his devotion to Shasta, his tolerance of Denis, and his benevolence toward the Harlingens, among other examples. His practice of love is echoed by other sympathetic characters in the California novels. In *Vineland*, for example, Frenesi's attitude toward someone seemingly in need of "her intercession" speaks to "the only way she knew to use the word *love* anymore, its trivializing in those days already well begun" (216–17). Indeed, love would seem to be the one thing to which she clings as the means to justify and save her generally loathsome beloved, Brock Vond: "if there was anything left to believe, she must have in the power even of that weightless, daylit commodity of the sixties to redeem even Brock" (216–17). Doc's and Frenesi's defense of, or hesitant faith in, love positions them very close to a number of contemporary thinkers, thinkers for whom a central problem is the manner in which common names for God restrict the dialogic practice necessary to religious tradition. For Marion, for instance, the only remaining term of possible use for thinking about God is "agape," which he accepts as the name of the most charitable love (46–47). Indeed, Marion argues, the very Being of beings may be regarded as the result of an act of charity from a charity beyond Being (104–105). Being as the fundament of our existence is, this is to say, a gift from a divinity that cannot itself be fully understood in terms of Being, although the gift of Being defines our relation to that divinity.

Identifying the relevance of this gift to the divine name helps somewhat in the redemption of the term "love," but the effort remains far from complete, for the word "love" still seems arbitrary and irrelevant in comparison to the practice to which it points. Some assistance comes from Gabriel Vahanian, who asserts that we may think of "God as event of language" (174). That the supernatural ontology of the divine may be so thought of returns us to several earlier points, including Caputo's explanation of religious tradition and Vattimo's claim that endless interpretation is demanded by our historicity. Too, to the degree that one accepts that any mystery is akin to the mystery of the divine name, Vahanian's assertion also goes some way to explaining a phenomenon Mendelson observes with regard to *The Crying of Lot 49*: "The manifestations of the Trystero . . . , and all that accompanies it, are always associated in the book with the language of the sacred and with patterns of religious experience" ("Sacred" 188). The argument points as well in the direction of additional implications concerning the relation between interpretive effort and the sacred.

As a true event in language is, again, revelatory, it must manifest in the present a unification of the past embodied in the traditions that are language and the meaningful fulfillment that language promises will come (Vahanian 175; Derrida 30). To regard a sacred event as a phenomenon of language restates the simultaneous deferral and presence of the divine name within religious tradition and also emphasizes the role our grammars play in this naming. What, one may ask, is the relation between Vahanian's event of language as the divine and Marion's charitable love as the only appropriate name for the divine? One reply emerges from Vattimo's argument that charity in language can be conceived of as openness to different language rules. In this sense, communicative charity is what allows the interpretive effort (Rorty, Vattimo, and Zabala 59). Read in this context, Doc's problem with the overuse of "love" is not that it has simply been worn by repetition but that it has been exhausted of meaning as a consequence of uncharitable misapplication. The giving to us of God within our history happens most in language, and here, the protagonist of *Inherent Vice* rebels against violence performed in and against the event that is the divine name. In so doing, he implicitly asserts something like a paranoiac's claim to sacred veracity: the unknowable is with us—the unknown is made immanent and renewed in our concern with and for it.

A comparison of the semantic valences of roads in *The Crying of Lot 49* and *Inherent Vice* indicates movement toward this postsecular hermeneutic position across Pynchon's California novels. Perhaps Oedipa's most-remarked revelation is her bird's-eye view of an "ordered swirl of . . . streets" that offers "a hieroglyphic sense of concealed meaning, of an intent to communicate. . . . As if . . . out of the eye of some whirlwind rotating . . . words were being spoken," (14, ellipses added), "words she couldn't hear" (16), and establishes the ground against which readers must later consider her sense that "behind the hieroglyphic streets there would either be a transcendent meaning, or only the earth" (150). The opposition Oedipa establishes—"transcendent meaning" over against "only earth"—must be seen as specious if revelation is possible as an event of language, of hieroglyphs. As Mendelson asserts ("Sacred"

203), Oedipa sees her investigations in binary terms, but why, one may ask, should the terms that define the array of possibilities she acknowledges define those available to the critic? Oedipa appears to recognize something of the problem when she senses "some promise of hierophany" in a map of "gently curving streets" (*Lot 49* 20), but Prairie Wheeler, as an infant, grasps it more directly when "responding to something she was hearing. . . . As if this were a return for her to a world behind the world she had known all along" (*Vineland* 315). To assume, as Oedipa does, and as Prairie would seem not to have, that that which lies behind the hieroglyphs is "only earth," a ground separate from "meaning," commits the original sin against which Takeshi is warned. In this light, the Situationist epigraph of *Inherent Vice*, "Under the paving stones, the beach!," takes shape as something more than an indication of the book's playful treatment of surfing culture or political-youth attitude. The declaration directs attention to that which radical interpretation pursues—the presence behind the hieroglyphs marking human wandering. Just as a dérive demands that one "perform" the space of the city on new terms, for the purpose of recognizing or generating otherwise absent histories, so *Inherent Vice* presents a California narrative focalized through the interpretive efforts of a detective keen to rediscover and renew the primary byword of his era, the one word that promises the closest apprehension of God beyond Being.

Sacral Communion and Human Community

Consider, as a last object for reflection, another passage from the final paragraphs of *Inherent Vice*, which describe Doc's drive through the fog:

> He crept along till he finally found another car to settle in behind. After a while in his rearview mirror he saw somebody else fall in behind him. He was in a convoy of unknown size, each car keeping the one ahead in taillight range, like a caravan in a desert of perception, gathered awhile for safety in getting across a patch of blindness. It was one of the few things he'd ever seen anybody in this town, except hippies, do for free. (368)

A few lines later, Doc realizes he is singing along with a tune on the car radio, The Beach Boys' "God Only Knows" (368). Pynchon's delightful transformation of a bad-visibility evening drive into a dangerous journey through a desert models the formation of community without sacrificing the mythical American individualism of late 20th-century car culture. Communion between individuals, translated into so mundane and secular an occurrence as a traffic backup, shapes an event-ful community of believers, relying on each other to move forward in spite of an unclear present and invisible future.

The self-reliance embodied in this scene, in addition to echoing both the Sage of Concord and frontier wisdom, is a fanciful representation of the human assumption of communal responsibility in the absence of a divinely managed telos. Not knowing where they are in absolute space and having only one another for coordinates, the motorists take on the responsibility of navigation. The extraordinary doubt and miscomprehension presented in the fog, which potentially encourages a reading of the moment as self-interest, is balanced by a view of this act as one of communal charity, one that provides an at least functional and mutual support. But what, if the latter reading is preferred, has passed on to the motorists their willingness to enact their own version of the one divine name of charitable love? Rorty has explained that, for Vattimo, the answer to this question is the transference of sacred responsibility from the divine Word to the secular world (38). The secularization of the sacred is, in this view, also the sacralization of the secular. This sacralization makes immanent the divine Word and allows the death of God to be read as the opportunity for a revitalization of religious tradition (Zabala, "Christianity" 37). Such an understanding opens onto several productive responses, including Jean-Luc Nancy's defense of atheism as the fulfillment of religion (393) and Derrida's vision of a return to religion apart from "an institution that is separable, identifiable, [and] circumscribable" (32). A conception of the sacred without its inherited material forms not only retains but may be defined more evidently by the practice of its gentlest and most fundamental call. This practice is compatible with the extant critical readings of Pynchonian sacrality as Pentecostal, yet the origin of the transference of divine charity to the profane in the crucifixion earns it the distinction of precession in relation to the Pentecost. Unlike Oedipa, who finds the open road, with its legendary egoistic liberties of "speed, freedom, wind in your hair, [and] unreeling landscape," only a disappointing "illusion" (*Lot 49* 15), the charitable drivers Doc encounters would seem to have translated the sacrificial emptying of self modeled in the central sacrifice of Christianity into the sacred actions of mutual support and pilgrimage.

Such a reading is supported as well by Marion's discussion of the eucharistic action in which the present (the gift and the temporal moment) and the host are regarded as intimately connected, which means that the sacrality of the gift depends upon its reception by a particular community at a particular time (166). This location of divine presence in the community of interpreters rather than in the object of veneration preserves the futurity and the past of the present, an aspect of the eucharistic moment echoed by that endless line of points that comprise Pynchon's automobile pilgrimage. To be at any one of those discrete points offers access to the transfinite yet keeps that quality grounded in its present form, enacting charity in and for the tradition yet with an indeterminate revelatory goal. If one has been waiting in this novel for a miracle, it is here, and it is a peaceful version of the anarchist miracle Jesus Arrabal envisioned in *The Crying of Lot 49*: "another world's intrusion into this one.... Where... the soul's talent for consensus allows the masses to work together without effort" (97, ellipses added). At this point in *Inherent Vice*, transcendence is denied and the sacred made immanent, and the paranoiac's conviction that all will eventually be revealed as connected emerges as the one clear message of the line of cars moving through Doc's fog-enshrouded world.

Furthermore, as suggested above, both *Vineland* and *Inherent Vice* affirm as eminent among sacred communities an even more markedly traditional unit of human sociality: the family, particularly that which includes children. Oedipa has a vision of the communal holiness children may impart in Pynchon's work when "in Golden Gate Park she came on a circle of children in their nightclothes, who told her they were dreaming the gathering.... The night was empty of all terror for them, they had inside their circle an imaginary fire, and needed nothing but their own unpenetrated sense of community" (*Lot 49* 96, ellipses added). Too, Brock Vond's mocking description of stable family life during his interview with Zoyd, "the basic triangle, the holy family, all together," highlights not only Zoyd's key anxieties but also the personal dimension of the novel's politics, Brock's corruption, and the importance of the family as a positive moral unit against which political and personal decay and shortcomings must be weighed (*Vineland* 301). Indeed, to a much greater degree than Pynchon's earlier fictions, *Vineland* and its followers all foreground and affirm such a valuation of family—whether nuclear and traditional or otherwise. In *Mason & Dixon*, for instance, Cherrycoke's narrative is undertaken for the amusement of children by a hearth. Likewise, the Traverse family's revenge plot remains a unifying thread around which the many subordinate narratives and fabulistic digressions of *Against the Day* take shape. *Inherent Vice*, which features in its opening chapters a discussion of Wolfmann's marriage and introduces as the novel's third speaking character the protagonist's aunt, makes family central in the Harlingen family subplot. Coy Harlingen's place in "a *Last Supper* type grouping," an image of the family of the faithful, suggests his special importance in this regard (137). Furthermore, and in spite of Doc's early dismissal of the term, the reunion of the Harlingen family evokes the text's last and seemingly unironic invocation of "love," which Hope offers to Doc for reuniting Coy with her and their daughter, Amethyst, whose very name (rooted in "a-methystos," or "not-drunken") points not only to a position that opposes the intoxications of Coy's heroin addiction but also to a more sincere motivation for sobriety than the many false covers he assumes while presumed dead or missing. His return to the domestic fold unites Doc's investigations with an enactment of charitable community; it evokes the close connection that Carmelo Dotolo has identified between the activities of redemption and interpretation (361).

• • •

Following the clues of Doc's work as detective, concomitant preoccupations with recovery of lost knowledge and people, and sympathy for and participation in community encourages a reading of *Inherent Vice* in light of pressing issues of interpretation and of sacrality. To see past some of the superficial distractions that come with the novel's use of genre conventions reveals a playful, ironic, and postmodern, but nevertheless also a care-ful and serious consideration of the promises and frustrations of religion and the sacred in postmodernity, as well as of the role of paranoiac epistemology in relation to them. As such, the text lends itself to the further exploration of ideas introduced in the earlier California novels, including especially the ongoing practical worthiness of charity and humility, principles Zabala labels cognates ("Christianity" 40).

Read in light of these issues, the text's narrative irresolution is particularly provocative. To approach it in the context of the collapsing of dualisms advocated by contemporary religious hermeneutics is to see that the binary oppositions that have shaped some critical thought devoted to Pynchon's works—including the transcendent sacred and the secular profane, the modernist nostalgia for unity and the postmodern celebration of indeterminacy, the Romantic alienation of the isolate and the necessity of community—might be productively rethought. In *Inherent Vice*, and in the California novels generally, irresolution and its corollary of inconclusiveness promise not capitulation to incoherence but a call for ongoing investigation, the continual practice of peace, and concern with the divine.

Reading, Resistance, and the California Turn in Pynchon's Cornucopian Fiction

JOHN MILLER

Pynchon's California novels have more in common with one another than just the geographical setting. All three are shorter and less baroque than Pynchon's longer works; they tend to focus on the quests of single protagonists; and in two of them, these protagonists are women. Their settings are also more contemporary—the Southern California of the late 1960s, 1970s, and 1980s that Pynchon actually inhabited—although, by the publication of *Inherent Vice*, that setting has receded sufficiently to become an object of nostalgia, or antinostalgia. As I have argued elsewhere,[1] both the time and place in which the California novels are set contribute to a more "subjunctive" view of history in those novels, one in which avenues of escape from, or at least fruitful resistance to, the often shadowy forces of political and existential oppression remain open. By contrast, Pynchon's longer fictions are set largely in a past whose history appears, from the reader's perspective, determined. Two of those novels, however, end by turning to California, and I would like to argue here that the "California turns" at the ends of Pynchon's two most cornucopian fictions, *Gravity's Rainbow* and *Against the Day*, serve a similar function, leaving open at the end of each book a chink of possibility in what might otherwise seem an overwhelmingly deterministic vision. The nature of this "turn" is different in the two books, and this difference will be explored to argue that the two novels represent a shift in Pynchon's view not just of the possibilities of resistance against the forces of determinism but of the reading experience itself as a figure for, and even possibly as a form of, such resistance.

• • •

Pynchon's work has frequently inspired critical attempts to explain or analyze the reading experiences it makes possible. This is not surprising, as the work combines a plethora of formal challenges to readers, such as length, encyclopedic range of reference, and a Menippean conglomeration of styles and tones, with engaging and accessible quantities of humor, beauty, and intellectual content. One of the first and most influential books on *Gravity's Rainbow* was *Mindful Pleasures*, a collection of essays edited by George Levine and David Leverenz, many of which attempted to explain how to read what remains Pynchon's most challenging work. A number of subsequent monograph studies have proposed to explain what the novels do to readers.[2] In recent years, arguably, more attention has been paid to thematic issues, particularly to the ways in which the works raise or represent political, historical, or even spiritual questions, but even the recently published *Cambridge Companion to Thomas Pynchon* (Dalsgaard, Herman, and McHale) concludes with a chapter on "How to Read Pynchon," evidence of the persistence of the idea that, even almost 50 years after the appearance of his first novel, reading Pynchon's work is somehow different in important ways from the experience of reading other contemporary fiction.[3]

In his chapter in *Mindful Pleasures*, George Levine argues for an approach to reading *Gravity's Rainbow*, and to understanding the specific value of the experience of reading that work, which has remained influential. That massive work, argues Levine, suggests that "the finite, determined world" can be transcended only in "moments" (115, 118),[4] what his coeditor calls, in the same volume, "singularities, disorganized moments of impact and power" (Leverenz 243). Such moments are not only represented in the novel but are created for the reader of the novel by instances of lyric beauty. These lyric moments, arising as they do out of a text whose size and complexity represent the world to be transcended, create experiences of transcendence for the reader. Subsequent critics, including Hite and Judith Chambers, have followed Levine's lead in developing theories of the reading experience Pynchon strives to create for his readers in *Gravity's Rainbow* that set the lyric moments in the books in opposition to the weight of the narrative ground from which they arise.

Such an understanding of Pynchon's strategy provides a helpful framework for understanding the function of the California turn at the end of *Gravity's Rainbow.* The long final section of the book, "The Counterforce," describes the various ways in which characters either succumb to or resist the political and existential forces embodied in the Rocket and its irresistible obedience to the laws of gravity. The fragmented formal construction of the concluding section of the book enacts and thus involves the reader in a rejection of coherent narrative structure in favor of a series of "moments of impact and power" (Leverenz 243). Emblematic of such moments is the scene in which Roger Mexico and "Pig" Bodine, wearing his "paint-blue" zoot suit, perform their obscene routine for the "Kruppfest." The audience for this act of resistance includes not only representatives of the industrial and political forces who are shaping the postwar world into the Raketenstadt but Mexico's former lover Jessica, who represents the accommodation of the individual to their institutionalized power. This act of defiance of earthly power reminds Bodine of an earlier experience of defying death itself:

> They are grinning at each other like fools. Their auras, for the record, are green. No shit. Not since winter of '42, in convoy in a North Atlantic gale, with accidental tons of loose 5-inch ammo rolling all over the ship, the German wolf pack invisibly knocking off sister ships right and left, at Battle Stations inside mount 51 listening to Pappy Hod tell disaster jokes, really funny ones, the whole gun crew clutching their stomachs hysterically, gasping for air—not since then has Seaman Bodine felt so high in the good chances for death. (714–15)

Like Bodine's and Mexico's performance at the Kruppfest, Pappy Hod's "disaster jokes" represent an arguably puerile and manic response to the imminence of extinction at the hand of irresistible and impersonal power; yet it is one that nevertheless seems at least temporarily effective, if not in averting the threat, then of denying its power to terrorize. Such a momentary "high" might also describe the lyric moments that arise from the experience of reading *Gravity's Rainbow.*

The title of the novel itself can be taken as a reference to such experiences and thus as a clue to the way the novel is supposed to function. The color of death is white, the color of the single, unrefracted beam of light. Weissmann/

Blicero is death's chief devotee, the high priest of the Rocket whose final sacrament is experienced by Gottfried as "a whitening, a carrying of whiteness to ultrawhite . . . an abolition of pigment, of melanin, of spectrum, of separateness from shade to shade" (759). White is the color of Northern Europe, the kingdom of death. The symbol crops up in other places, such as in the name of Pointsman's laboratory, "The White Visitation," an institution dedicated to piercing the mysteries of determinacy, and in a photo of the atomic ("Cosmic") bomb Slothrop notices in a newspaper: "a wirephoto of a giant white cock, dangling in the sky straight downward out of a white pubic bush . . . a sudden white genital onset in the sky" (693–94).

At another point in his wandering, however, Slothrop has a nearly identical vision: "after a heavy rain he doesn't recall, Slothrop sees a very thick rainbow here, a stout rainbow cock driven down out of pubic clouds into Earth, green wet valleyed Earth, and his chest fills and he stands crying, not a thing in his head, just feeling natural" (626). This image of a colorful, natural fertility symbolizes, as the rainbow did to Noah, the possibility of a redeeming force opposed to the reductive forces behind the Rocket and the "Cosmic Bomb." The elements of the "Counterforce" are frequently portrayed as literally, as well as figuratively, colorful: Slothrop has his disguises, Bodine his zoot suit, and Osbie Feel hallucinations that seem to emanate visibly about his head when the notion of the Counterforce is first introduced. The Rainbow, then, represents a colorful expansion perpendicular to the infinitely narrow, imaginary line, the abstraction that mathematics uses to describe the arc of the parabola that the Rocket must inevitably travel. Finding such moments of lyric resistance to the forces of determinism is analogous to the process of differentiation in calculus, which isolates dimensionless points along a curve. While the Rocket's determined trajectory cannot be stopped or altered, each moment along it, each delta-t, if it can somehow be imaginatively isolated, can provide an opportunity for perpendicular expansion from it, a Rainbow-like moment of resistance to the bleached certainty of the Rocket's arc.

While the Counterforce section of the novel (mostly) clearly represents the potential for creating moments of lyric resistance to the forces of oppression, the entire novel can, in fact, be seen as functioning in the same way. The very mass of material and fecundity of language in *Gravity's Rainbow* provide a virtually infinite series of such moments. In fact, the whole book symbolically expands within the moment between the "scream" announcing the Rocket in its opening sentence and the instant just before its impact in the last. The color and variety of the novel blossom perpendicularly to either side of this moment as the Rainbow expands to either side of the parabola. The book's cornucopian expansiveness suspends the reader within that long, long moment, making the reading experience itself an emblem and embodiment of the acts of resistance the novel narrates.

• • •

The role of the California turn at the end of the novel can be understood in the context of this strategy of making the reading experience itself an act of resistance to the forces represented in the novel. In three brief sections at the very end of *Gravity's Rainbow*, readers finds themselves in a semifantastical version of what would have been, at the time the novel was published, contemporary Los Angeles. The reader here is addressed in the second person, as if he or she were a character in the book or as if the book had created a world readers might inhabit, capable of providing them with certain sorts of opportunities or experiences.

In the first of these three sections, "COUNTDOWN," the allusions to contemporary Los Angeles are oblique, including mentions of jet planes and the fact that everyone "here . . . walks around suntanned, and red-eyed from one irritant or another." The indirection here is intentionally disorienting: readers are not sure exactly where they are, although it is certainly no longer postwar Germany. We approach what will turn out to be a familiar place as if outsiders, as if the "Zone" has become more familiar to us than the nonfictional world we actually inhabit. We are introduced to drug-addled, paranoid "Kabbalist spokesman Steve Edelman," who imparts to "the visitor" an occult secret, the discovery of the source of the Tree of Life, "the delta-t itself," as he calls it (753). Edelman does not seem the most reliable source for such an improbable promise of redemption (in the form of a symbol clearly opposed to the meanings of the Rocket); he appears a contemporary incarnation of the Kabbalists and theosophists who seek futile escape from the inevitable in wartime London earlier in the novel. The section invokes the stereotype of California as a mecca for such desperate or insincere promises of redemption and positions the reader as a skeptical outsider in that setting.

Edelman turns up again briefly in the longest L.A. section, "ORPHEUS PUTS DOWN HARP," as a "Hollywood businessman" currently institutionalized in a psychiatric facility for subversive activities (much like *Inherent Vice*'s Mickey Wolfmann) (755). This curious turn of events calls into question our initial skepticism about him: if he is perceived as dangerous by the authorities, should we be so quick to dismiss whatever power he claims to have access to? Here we meet the Nixon-like Richard M. Zhlubb, who runs the Orpheus Theatre and fulminates against such subversion, which manifests itself in the cacophony (to Zhlubb's ears) of harmonicas, kazoos, and tambourines: instruments anyone can play. Such popular musical disruptions are the contemporary descendants of Seaman Bodine's and Roger Mexico's performance at the Krupp Conference party earlier in the novel (which also involves kazoos). The "freaks" in line for the theater or out on the freeway represent "full disrespect for the Prohibitions." Zhlubb, for his part, insists they are merely a "loud minority," and he appears connected with unseen networks of oppression with a plan to restore order: "'Relax,' the Manager's eyes characteristically aglitter. 'There'll be a nice secure home for them all, down in Orange County. Right next to Disneyland.'" At the same time, though, Zhlubb seems not to see the conflict between the forces of order and chaos as a battle that needs to be won but as an ongoing contest, one that in some ways he requires as an element of his own identity: "'Opponents have accused us . . . of contempt for the people. But really we do it all in the spirit of fair play. We're not monsters. We know we have to give them *some* chance. We can't take hope away from them, can we?'" (756). Oppressors and oppressed drive the same freeway, along with the food trucks and funeral processions, a figure of irresistible collective forward motion. Zhlubb even fantasizes about dying on the freeway one day.

In the context of the novel as a whole, and particularly interpolated here between the descriptions of Blicero's final preparations to launch Gottfried into death, Zhlubb and the counterculture (which makes fun of him but still pays to buy his movie tickets) seem to represent a comical reduction of the conflicts of the novel. But over them all hangs the Rocket. At the end of the section, a siren that neither Zhlubb nor the reader, who is riding with him in his Volkswagen, can at first identify breaks through the varied din of traffic, laugh tracks, and populist noise-making. It's the screaming that announces the advent of the final whiteout, invoking the suppressed but never fully forgotten Cold War anxiety that is the apotheosis of the Rakentenstadt. (It's possible that readers at the time of publication, used to having lived under the threat of that siren, would have a more profound response to it than post–Cold War readers might.)

This section, then, begins by presenting contemporary Southern California as a site in which the ongoing conflict of Force and Counterforce continues in a comic and even somewhat gentler form. The figure of oppression is a diminished and comical parody of an already somewhat comical public figure, and the Counterforce seems relatively free to flaunt its rebellion. The example of Steve Edelman does demonstrate that there are limits to the Force's toleration of dissent, but our previous encounter with Edelman has suggested that, like the London spiritualists we encounter earlier in the novel, his rebellion may be merely an attempt to replace one oppressive master narrative with another, a constant concern in Pynchon's representations of resistance. The section concludes, though, with the obliteration of both sides of that conflict by an irresistible Higher Power. The moment of our recognition of the siren's significance is evidence that we remain aware, if only or usually subconsciously, of our powerlessness under such a Power. The threat of death comes not from the Nixonian right; if anything, the contemporary conflict between the Zhlubbs and the freaks is presented here as, at best, an opportunity for play on both sides, and at worst, a distraction from what is happening overhead. The real opposition is between those flying in oblivious and seemingly purposeless movement up and down the freeways and the true oblivion that hangs over them.

Yet this is not the final scene of the novel. The "ORPHEUS" section is followed by the penultimate section, "ASCENT," in which Blicero's rocket launches Gottfried to his apotheosis. The final section is titled "DESCENT," and the rocket that falls not only completes the embrace of the technologies of death represented by Blicero's strange project but invokes the opening line of the novel, in which the imminent fall of the rocket is announced. The entire novel has unfolded in that near-timeless moment, that delta-t.[5]

The final paragraphs take place inside Zhlubb's theater, where the film has suddenly stopped and where the audience is realizing that it won't start again:

> The last image was too immediate for any eye to register. It may have been a human figure, dreaming of an early evening in each great capital luminous enough to tell him he will never die, coming outside to wish on the first star. But it was *not a star*, it was falling, a bright angel of death. (760)

What do we do in that last moment? How do we respond to death, which can never be explained or reasoned with, let alone escaped? The novel offers an answer it has offered frequently before: the only response the Counterforce can make is to reclaim the moment through acts of creativity and community. Here Pynchon appropriates the conventional ending of comedy, a vision of community joined in song, as an answer to existential tragedy. This is in fact the response that the entirety of *Gravity's Rainbow* not only represents but embodies in its own cornucopian expansion of the moment between the Rocket's scream and landing. And, in fact, within the covers of the novel, the Rocket never does nor can actually strike. The novel's very physical presence is a repudiation of the forces its narrative represents.

By ending the novel in the contemporary present, Pynchon pulls us in two conflicting directions. On the one hand, the ending asserts the inescapability of the historical and, in fact, existential imperatives that the horror at the center of the 20th century has unmasked. Sunny Southern California is no less shadowed by the Rocket and all it represents than Peenemunde or South-West Africa. Yet, on the other hand, the contemporary setting indicates that the end is—barely—still not here yet, that an infinitesimal space remains in which we can assert ourselves against the Rocket. It may not represent a space of hope, merely a space of freedom, but the concluding song hints at a world that may survive or be resurrected from our ashes, a "turning of the time" after which nature may perhaps start anew, "With a face on ev'ry mountainside, / and a soul in every stone" (760). The final gesture of the novel asks us, the readers reading in the present moment, to participate with it in asserting that freedom and faint hope.

• • •

As in *Gravity's Rainbow*, *Against the Day* offers the experience of narrative as an allegory and embodiment of resistance to the oppressive forces of social, political, and even existential determinism, but that experience takes a different form in the later work. In *Gravity's Rainbow*, fleeting moments of lyric intensity, created by language, both figure and create small spaces of freedom for the reader within the irresistible forward progress of the novel. All of *Gravity's Rainbow* can be seen as an attempt to expand the brief moment before the rocket's impact into a space of temporary freedom, color, revolt, and human connection. In *Against the Day*, Pynchon posits another way in which fiction can create experiences of freedom from history.

If *Gravity's Rainbow* is a cornucopia of lyrical reading experiences, *Against the Day* is copious in plot and narrative. At the level of plot, the novel uses entrelacement like a medieval romance, with various strands of plot, often revolving around quests, interlacing and occasionally interacting with one another. The opening section of the novel, "The Light over the Ranges," is a kind of overture to this structure, as each of its chapters moves from one character or set of characters to another, each of whom has been encountered in some form in the preceding one. Thus, in the first few chapters, the Chums meet Merle Rideout and Lew Basnight; in subsequent chapters, we follow Merle's and Lew's stories, Lew's eventually leading to Colorado, where he meets Webb Traverse; the section ends by returning to the Chums, who, at the end of the section, fly through the earth to the North Pole, where the events of the second long section of the novel ("Iceland Spar") commence.

While these various subplots appear to exist in a contiguous heterocosm, in fact they represent transitions between what might be called different orders of reality and fictionality. As Justin St. Clair has argued, "Rather than presenting a panoply of fictive strands on a flat, two-dimensional plane, Pynchon's . . . is three-dimensional. In short, all fictional registers within the novel are *not* created equal—some are *more* fictional than others" (82). The Chums are fictional characters who nevertheless interact with characters from the "nonfictional world." The novel is neither simply historical fiction, in which fictional characters or incidents are inserted into historical events, nor is it alternative history, in which history is imagined as going in a different direction than it really did. Rather, it is a book in which the Chums can meet a character, Merle, who later meets a character, Webb, whose son, Reef, is later seen reading a Chums of Chance adventure novel. It is a text woven of different levels of fictionality blending into one another. Thus, for instance, early in the book, we are told that the fictional Chums are able to visit the historical Chicago World's Fair because that "great national celebration possessed the exact degree of fictitiousness to permit the boys access and agency" (36). The novel does not posit a single world that contains, coherently, both the Ludlow miner's strike and an airship that flies through the earth. Rather, it becomes a narrative space that accommodates characters and incidents that could not exist in the same world within the conventional structures of organic fiction. Not only do the Chums cross and blur these boundaries; each of their characters is transformed from its original boyish stereotype into something more rich and mature. They dabble in time travel and temporarily transform themselves into the Harmonica Academy Marching Band (which itself undergoes constant transmutation), finally traveling at the end of the book to the "Counter-Earth," which looks surprisingly like the Earth they came from, but different.

The "worlds" of the novel represent multiple and often inconsistent possibilities that nevertheless seem capable of coexistence, at least within the bounds of fiction. The idea of multiple worlds or levels of existence is a recurring theme in the book: time travel, "bilocation," "co-consciousness," the double refracting property of Iceland spar, the mathematics of multiple dimensions and their transformations, Lovecraftian prehuman histories and orders of power, the existence of a Counter-Earth, and numerous analogous motifs in the novel all suggest not only the potential for alternatives to the "harsh nonfictional world" (36) of "the day" but the possibility of moving from one alternative to another, as Lew Basnight finds himself "crossed over," through the medium of an explosion, from one life to another.

Brian McHale has identified the "proliferation" and interweaving of "alternative worlds" as a defining postmodern attribute of Pynchon's fiction in general, and a number of critics have attempted to explain how the destabilization of the categories of fictional and nonfictional in *Against the Day* might represent some form of resistance to exigencies of "the day and its dread" (*Against the Day* 86).[6] This instability and multiplicity within the fictional space of the novel represent a kind of cornucopian abundance different from that in *Gravity's Rainbow*. Rather than a density of lyrical experience in tension with and resisting the forward motion of the plot, an experience of multiple possibilities is offered in *Against the Day*, figured and enacted in the experience of reading fiction itself. Negotiating the novel's shifts and passages between different orders of reality, causality, and determinism, the reader experiences a liberation, if only temporary and imaginary, from any single, dominating narrative order. This assertion of multiple and fluid possibilities or alternatives, through fiction and the act of reading, pushes back "against the day," that is, against the tyrannical forces that stalk and try to shape the mundane world. Thus, as in *Gravity's Rainbow*, the title of *Against the Day* is self-referential, positioning the book itself in opposition to "the day," to the apparently real and indisputable order of the world.

• • •

The California section of the novel begins when the Chums travel to a Counter-Earth, where World War I is raging, then on to what will be their final touchdown in Southern California, in the 1920s. Although this California exists on this Counter-Earth, it is in most ways indistinguishable from and seemingly contiguous with the Earth of the rest of the novel: it appears to contain the same characters, geography, and history. By this time, each of the Chums has evolved beyond his dime-novel persona; moreover, as a crew, they have severed ties with "the National" organization to become independent adventurers, and they have partnered, both professionally and personally, with a complement of female aeronauts. The *Inconvenience* has begun its expansion and evolution into what, at the end of the book, will be an entire alternate world of its own.

While the adventures of the Chums invoke a familiar narrative genre, the California chapters invoke another, noir. They begin with Lew Basnight, who has himself gone through several incarnations: as Chicago-based anti-union agent (in at least two different versions of Chicago); investigator for an apparently nongovernmental secret organization in London; and now noir detective, on a typical noirish case: trying to track down a missing girl of questionable past and virtue who may or may not have run afoul of a former well-connected boyfriend. He makes the rounds of the usual noir locales, from his downtown office in a version of the iconic Bradbury Building, with a dangerous doll of a secretary outside, to a series of Southern California motor courts and Lake Traverse's bungalow. In the context of a novel in which alternate worlds, fictional and "nonfictional," coexist, blend, and blur together like layers of phyllo dough, the shift in genre represents, like the Counter-Earth, yet another "alternative version of the same Earth" (1020).

The conventional cynicism associated with the noir genre can be seen as a postwar response to the cheery optimism of the boys' adventure novel; as Miles says of the men in the World War I trenches a few pages earlier, "Back at the beginning of this . . . they must have been boys, so much like us. . . . It was their own grand 'Adventure.' They were juvenile heroes of a World-Narrative" (1023–24, ellipses added). It is also a convention specifically associated with Southern California, a response to the sunny optimism and booster imagery that helped promote the great migrations and consequent real estate booms of the early decades of the 20th century there. As the name implies, noir works by revealing the darknesses that lurk underneath the surfaces or around the corners of the daylit landscape that symbolizes the hopes and possibilities of the far Western shore.

Yet, just as Pynchon has disrupted the conventions of the boys' adventure novel, we should not be surprised that he plays with those of the noir detective novel. Here, as opposed to the usual noir plot resolution, in which the corruption is briefly revealed, possibly even avenged, but never really defeated, we get a glimpse of collective and occasionally even successful resistance. While the bright and optimistic innocence of the boys' adventure with which the novel started (echoed by the opening setting at the Chicago World's Fair) is challenged as the novel progresses, so the cynical noir assumption that paradise is inevitably subject to corruption is likewise challenged in the California sections of the novel, which ultimately hold out the hope of escape rather than quashing such hopes.

In these chapters, the darkness is embodied by the fourth Traverse child, Lake, seen initially by Lew through the screen door that shelters her "against the day" outside: "Shady side of forty, presentable, but also what he had long come, regretfully, to recognize as haunted" (1051). While her husband, the thuggish Deuce, works as antiunion muscle and cleanup for the corrupted powers of Hollywood, she festers in the shaded interior of a bungalow. Lake evokes the noir stereotype of the corrupted young (or now not so young) woman, like the California setting, still fresh and attractive in appearance but hopelessly fallen from innocence. In the noir convention, the promise of Los Angeles as a place where anything is possible is subverted, but Lake finds herself in a more ambiguous state, where what is possible has become difficult to distinguish from what is not:

> [She had] begun to find that what most people took for some continuous reality, one morning paper to the next, had never existed. Often these days she couldn't tell if something was a dream into which she had drifted, or one from which she had just awakened and might not return to. So through the terrible cloudlessness of the long afternoons she passed among dreams, and placed her wagers at the Universal Dream Casino as to which of them should bring her through, and which lead her irreversibly astray. (1054)

Some of her dreams have the qualities of movielike dramas with happy romantic endings, but all take place in a "subarctic city and a chill eternal rain" (1055). Like those of all the major characters in the novel, Lake's story and her own experience of it seem to weave among multiple possible orders of reality or "degrees of fictitiousness." For all the darkness she has drawn to herself through her decisions, made often in retaliation against her family, the novel's final words on her suggest that she has arrived at a point of uncertainty that may in fact be preferable to the control of her own fate that she had attempted to assert by plumping clearly for damnation in throwing in with Deuce: "Once she thought they had chosen, together, to resist all penance at the hands of others. To reserve to themselves alone what lay ahead, the dark exceptional fate. Instead she was alone with the sort of recurring dream a long-suffering movie heroine would expect to wake from to find herself pregnant at last" (1057). (This passage both echoes and foreshadows the ambiguous response of Prairie Wheeler, Lake's similarly named great-great-grandniece, who at the end of *Vineland* becomes aware of her own attraction to authoritarian power in the act of resisting it.) The fate of the conventional noir heroine is to have her illusions stripped and the dark cold reality revealed beneath them. For Lake, however, the move to California has left her, against her own will, unable to shake the possibility of a happy ending.

Later in the course of his noirish investigations in these chapters, Lew finds himself at a party, a "reunion of outlaws," all rebels in one way or another against the "capitalist Christer Republicans" for whom Lew used to (and Deuce now does) work, being thrown at the aptly named Carefree Court. Lew realizes that these are "just the folks that once long ago he'd spent his life chasing, them and their cousins city and country," prior to his own translation earlier in the novel as the result of surviving an assassination attempt by dynamite, explosions recurring in the novel as a symbol of radical change or displacement. Surveying the gathering, he realizes "that what everybody here had in common was having survived some cataclysm none of them spoke about directly—a bombing, a massacre perhaps at the behest of the U.S. government" (1057–58). The girl he is looking for, Jardine Maraca, is there, but she evades him and everyone else by stealing a plane and "zooming skyward" (1059). Both the fact and trajectory of her escape suggest the possibility of transcendence embodied in the flight of the *Inconvenience*. The party of outlaws and the escape of the girl in trouble both overturn basic noir conventions. Instead of uncovering a nasty snake pit of moral corruption under a rock of privilege and glitz (although it too exists in this version of Southern California, as represented by Deuce), here, the detective finds an underground party—in both senses of the word—of resistance, one that seems unconcerned about hiding itself from the prying eyes of the powers that be or their hired hands. Instead of the conventional noir femme fatale who swoons into his arms but whom he cannot save, Lew instead finds first Lake, who crudely seduces him but never asks for his help, preferring to dream her own dreams, then Jardine, who brushes off his desire and is clearly capable of taking care of herself.

Lew discovers that all those he had once been hired to suppress have survived to celebrate their resistance together in Southern California (as the Traverses and their descendants will in Northern California); a number of other reunions also take place there in these late chapters of *Against the Day*. Chick Counterfly reunites with his father, Dick, who had been only alluded to in the opening chapter of the novel. Dick, in turn, knows Merle Rideout and Roswell Bounce, who later hire Lew, who has just encountered (and in fact had sex with) Lake. Merle also catches up with his former wife Erlys, who has relocated to the area. Merle and Roswell, moreover, have developed a technology that allows users to view, if not travel to, the past and future, and Merle uses this, in combination with radio, to reconnect with Dally, who now lives in Paris. Lew uses the same device to reconnect with, or at least reimagine, his own long-lost wife, Troth. A passing reference to "the wreck of the first *Inconvenience* after the little-known Battle of Desconocido, in California" suggests that even for the airship it is a kind of homecoming (1020). The California chapters thus mirror the opening section of the novel, in which characters from different strands of the plot encounter one another within roughly the same narrative space. The series of reunions represents a kind of narrative miracle, bringing characters back together not only from the different strands of the plot but from the different "worlds" spun out across the preceding 1,000 pages.

Merle's device works by making possible the representation of the "branches" history might extend from a particular point in time represented by a photograph. On the final pages of the California chapters, Lew's attempt to use Merle's device for reconstructing history, including alternative histories, from photographs is described as a rare example of a "compassionate time-machine story, time travel in the name of love, with no expectation of success, let alone reward" (1060). This might stand in for a description of the project and purpose of a novel as a whole: an attempt to assert itself as an alternative to the inexorable singular oppressive narrative of history, "against the day." It is not quite clear to what extent the visions provided by the machine are "real" or merely potential, but, more to the point, it is not clear whether that distinction is even valid. The world of the novel is one in which both characters and readers find themselves moving between alternate forms of reality,

"Counter-Earths," by time travel, dreams, or fiction itself. As a fellow mathematician tells Kit near the end of the book, "the world we think we know can be dissected and reassembled into any number of worlds, each as real as 'this' one" (1078). This instability can be disorienting and even terrifying, but also liberating, as in Yashmeen's ability, in some cases, to simply escape through solid walls.

The California chapters conclude the section of the novel that shares its title with the novel itself, and they epitomize the narrative strategy that characterizes the whole novel: the elaboration of alternative versions of reality that blend in complex ways with others while, nevertheless, remaining distinct. Not only does the noir setting represent another of these versions, but it turns out to deviate from its own conventions in unexpected ways, evolving into an alternative version of itself. *Against the Day* is metafictional in that not only the elaboration of multiple alternative realities but interaction and movement between them, basic elements of the experience of fiction, are made the fundamental structural principle of the novel. Readers attempting to negotiate its complex network of texts—a text of texts—are engaged explicitly in what all readers do implicitly: trying to determine what rules govern and enforce the consistency of a fictional construction and where and how that construction interacts with their own "nonfictional" world.

Within this unstable textual environment arise opportunities not only for escape but for connection and community. Like *Vineland*, *Against the Day* ends with a series of family reunions, including that of the loose family of "outlaws" Lew happens upon. Although they do not quite conclude the novel itself any more than they represent conclusions to the stories of any of its characters (except, arguably, Deuce's), the many reunions woven into the California chapters do create a sense of at least temporary resolution. The reunions represent small victories over linear time: paths once sundered can rejoin. Near the end of *Against the Day* (though in Paris, not California), Dally even meets a character, "La Jarretière," who had died in Pynchon's first novel, *V.*, but in this one did not. Here she is allowed a different ending: Pynchon has been able to resurrect her through the simple act of writing more, of telling another story of a slightly different world. In a universe of multiple worlds, the novel seems to suggest, such "turnings" remain open possibilities. And it is the specific function of fiction to spin those alternative worlds; to keep open the possibility that such things exist; and to suggest, at least, the experience of visiting them.

• • •

Both *Gravity's Rainbow* and *Against the Day* begin and end with images of flight. In the earlier work, the Rocket is just about to fall from the sky; in fact, as I have suggested above, the entire novel can be seen as blossoming into incomprehensible richness within that infinitesimal moment. *Against the Day*, by contrast, is framed by images of lighter-than-air ascent, not a surrender to gravity but a defiance of it. By the end of the novel, the fictional craft, the *Inconvenience*, has evolved from a fantastical prop in a fictional world into an entire world of its own, "as large as a small city. . . . It is so big that when people on the ground see it in the sky, they are struck with selective hysterical blindness and end up not seeing it at all." It presents an alternative to "the finite world," an alternative chosen by the "more serious" of the children to be born upon it. It has, in fact, become a figure for the book itself, and it offers that book as the last of many alternative worlds offered in the book: "once a vehicle of sky-pilgrimage, [it] has transformed into its own destination, where any wish that can be made is at least addressed, if not always granted" (1084–85). While such wishes may not be granted, at least not yet, the book itself, the experience of reading it and being allowed in some sense to inhabit its many alternate realities, refuses to foreclose their possibility.

Gravity's Rainbow ends by keeping open the tiniest, in fact mathematically infinitesimal, space of hope and freedom and the possibility that the "Time" may still "turn." *Against the Day* ends with a similar hope, that "good unsought and uncompensated" has in fact "evolved somehow": "They know—Miles is certain—it is there, like an approaching rainstorm, but invisible. Soon they will see the pressure-gauge begin to fall. They will feel the turn in the wind" (1085). Both endings, although in different ways, implicate the reader within the space of the narrative. In *Gravity's Rainbow*, we are sitting in the audience, preparing to sing along with all the other all-but-doomed. In *Against the Day*, the *Inconvenience*, like the book itself, has expanded beyond its own imaginable borders to become a kind of world in itself. Both books implicitly posit the organic form of the conventional novel, in which all elements are imagined as working together to form a unified reading experience, as representing figuratively the oppressive forces against which Pynchon's characters struggle. His fictions, by contrast, both figure and enact resistance to that totalizing impulse.

The California "turns" at the end of each book reflect both the similar goals of the books and the different ways in which they propose to use the experience of reading fiction to figure and perhaps achieve those goals. By bringing the reader suddenly into the contemporary setting of Southern California in the early 1970s, *Gravity's Rainbow* implicates the reader in the ongoing struggle of Force and Counterforce. This suggests that the Raketenstadt persists in the reader's world but that the struggle against it also persists. The final lines of the book seem to include us in an all but hopeless assertion of resistance to the forces whose seemingly irresistible power is a nearly timeless moment away from final victory. But the novel, whose entirety can be seen as an expansion of such a moment, never closes it off. The California setting, with its frantic freeways, battling bands of freaks and Birchers, and association with the movies, which serve to both delude and unify their audiences, suggests a number of factors that may have masked this ongoing struggle.

The California turn in *Against the Day*, on the other hand, does not bring us to the "real" world its readers live in but instead to yet another constructed version of the world, the familiar fictional noir Los Angeles. But where we might expect from this setting an acknowledgment of the darkening of the postwar world and the disappointment of hopes and possibilities, instead we see that even within such a setting, determined not only by history but by literary convention, convention can be overturned and possibilities for resistance and escape can be found. In *Gravity's Rainbow*, California represents the subjunctive potential that always resides in the lyric present moment. In *Against the Day*, California, like the book itself, is a "Counter-Earth" that serves to remind us that the familiar world of "the day" can always be recreated and thus possibly redeemed, at least in fiction. Thus, in both books, the cornucopian text becomes not only a metaphor for, but works to create, vivid experiences of resistance and possible escape from the deterministic forces represented in the novels. As Pynchon himself has written, "the ever-subversive medium of fiction" can show us "how it could all plausibly come about, even—wild hope—for somebody out here, outside a book" ("Heart's"). California has been called "America's America," and both of these works suggest that even for an author whose work so powerfully evokes a vision of entropic determinism, California remains a potent symbol of the potential for a "turn" toward such a "wild hope."

NOTES

1. See "Present Subjunctive: Pynchon's California Novels" and the introduction to this volume.
2. See, for example, Hite, *Ideas of Order*; Chambers, *Thomas Pynchon*; and Brownlie, *Thomas Pynchon's Narratives*.
3. Berressem, "Coda." One of the earliest and still influential studies of Pynchon's fiction, that of Kolodny and Peters, explicitly takes this approach, as do many of the essays in the more recent collection edited by Horvath and Malin.
4. Levine's argument continues to be influential: thus, for instance, Heinz Ickstadt, in a later collection of essays focusing mostly on *Against the Day*, argues that Pynchon's general program in all of his fiction is "to regain the dangerous and chaotic openness of what once was an experienced moment in a still undecided present" (45).
5. In fact, because the V-2 rockets traveled faster than the speed of sound, the "screaming" was heard *after* the impact, so the time interval between the "screaming" in the first line of the novel and the impact (or near impact) in its last would actually be a negative one.
6. See, for example, the arguments of Ickstadt and Molloy.

Maybe He'd Have to Just Keep Driving, or Pynchon on the Freeway

STEPHEN HOCK

Roads of various stripes, whether metaphorical or literal, pepper Thomas Pynchon's fictional landscapes. Indeed, insofar as arguably all of the plots of Pynchon's novels are motivated by quests of one sort or another, his work frequently takes the form of a road narrative, with Pynchon's questing protagonists traveling by road—not to mention air, sea, underground passage, and a variety of other avenues of transportation—in search of the objects of their quests. This is certainly true of Pynchon's California novels. In *The Crying of Lot 49* (1966), *Vineland* (1990), and *Inherent Vice* (2009), characters such as Oedipa Maas, Prairie Wheeler, and Doc Sportello travel across California, and sometimes beyond, as they take up their quests, whether that quest is for the secrets of the Tristero, for the history of Frenesi Gates, or for the truth behind the disappearance of Mickey Wolfmann and how that disappearance ties into the multiform operations of the Golden Fang. Although the characters in the California novels will travel by whatever mode of transportation is at hand, their preferred means of conveyance is the automobile, as befits California's popular image as a state with an automobilecentric culture. The reliance of the characters in Pynchon's California on the automobile becomes particularly clear in the many scenes in which these characters travel on the freeway, so that the freeway becomes the paradigmatic form of the road in Pynchon's California, not just in the California novels themselves but also when *Gravity's Rainbow* (1973) turns its attention to California. As it is developed across these novels, the portrait of the freeway that Pynchon draws marks the freeway predominantly as a carrier of death and destruction in the service of modern capital and power but also, more tentatively, as a possible venue for community and connection. As such, the freeway functions as an emblem of the possibilities that Pynchon locates in California, particularly insofar as California stands in Pynchon's work as the site of the ultimate development and expression of American history.

A Perfect Corridor over the Land

Pynchon's work as a whole maps out a broad history of America, ranging from the encounter between Northmen and Skrællings in the early 11th century that *Mason & Dixon* (1997) identifies as "this first Act of American murder, and the collapse of Vineland the Good" (634) through the debates at the 1984 Traverse-Becker reunion in Vineland, California—presented, of course, in *Vineland*—over "the perennial question of whether the United States still lingered in a prefascist twilight, or whether that darkness had fallen long stupefied years ago, and the light they thought they saw was coming only from millions of Tubes all showing the same bright-colored shadows" (371). Although *Mason & Dixon* is not one of Pynchon's California novels, the nominal connection that Pynchon draws between the Northmen's 11th-century Vineland and California's late 20th-century Vineland indicates how Pynchon's oeuvre, taken as a whole, positions California as the end result of the history of European settlement in the North American continent, the ultimate product of the historical process that gives rise to the United States of America. As David Cowart writes in his study of Pynchon's treatment of history, "Sprawled at what was once the frontier terminus, California distills—then and now—some American essence." Moreover, Cowart argues, it is the decade of the 1960s, the decade that all of Pynchon's California novels address, that offers the chance of redeeming that "American essence": "Pynchon thinks of the sixties as a crossroads of American history, a place where the nation revisits the earliest of its moral choices. Here a vestigial innocence vies again with every dark propensity in the human heart" (*Thomas Pynchon* 134). The link between the Northmen's Vineland and California's Vineland suggests the potential that California, specifically, holds for revisiting the moral choices that went into the creation of America. This link and this potential are only heightened when we remember that California's Vineland, in the novel that bears its name, shares with its 11th-century counterpart the epithet "Vineland the Good" (*Vineland* 322), further suggesting that California can serve as a site where the original lost promise of America might be recaptured, redeemed from the violence and, as Pynchon presents it, the impending fascism that otherwise dominates the arc of American history.

Apropos of the historical arc that connects *Mason & Dixon* with Pynchon's California, it is worth considering one element of *Mason & Dixon* that prefigures the freeways that occupy such a large part of the imaginative terrain of Pynchon's California, namely, the Line that comes to bear the name of *Mason & Dixon*'s protagonists. To be sure, the Line is not itself a road, but a number of its qualities parallel those of the roads, and particularly the California freeways, that follow. For instance, the work of establishing the path of the Line shares a number of the characteristics we might associate with the work of laying down a road—surveying, clearing trees, and so on—and, indeed, in a dream, Mason and Dixon encounter an Indian who refers to their Line as "your Great Road thro' the Trees" (677). More important than this physical analogy between the Line and the roads that follow, however, is their shared function in Pynchon's critique of modernity. The Line, like the freeways in Pynchon's California novels, serves as a marker of the routinization and standardization that modernity brings, a process that, in Pynchon's work, always necessarily also brings the destructions and depredations of power and capital. As Dixon puts it, when his and Mason's party has reached the end of their surveying, the Line is "A tree-slaughtering Animal, with no purpose but to continue creating forever a perfect Corridor over the Land. Its teeth of Steel,—its Jaws, Axmen,—its Life's Blood, Disbursement. And what of its intentions, beyond killing ev'rything due west of it? do you know? I don't either" (678). The work of constructing a Line, or a freeway, can continue "due west" only until it reaches the westernmost edge of the continent, of course. By highlighting the westward orientation of the Line, Dixon's comment therefore suggests that the ultimate end of the work of the Line lies at the end of the western frontier, namely, California. As such, this comment further lays the historical groundwork for the California novels' presentation of California as the end result of—as well as the last possible site of resistance to—the imperial project of claiming land for the nascent United States. Likewise, Dixon's reference to the Line as "a perfect Corridor over the Land" evokes the promise of sustaining the imperial project by transporting people, goods, capital, and power across the land opened up by the work of western expansion, the dream of unimpeded transport that the freeway incarnates in the latter half of the twentieth century.

When they take on a prominent role in Pynchon's work, roads continue to serve as venues by which the intertwined forces of modernity, power, and capital map their will onto the land. Fittingly enough, given the figuring of the Line and the roads that follow as instruments of imperial power, the reason the surveying of the Line must stop is that it has reached a boundary marked by another road, this one set down by the Indians, "a Track, running athwart the Visto, north and south, known as the Great Warrior Path. This is not merely an important road for them,—but indeed one of the major High-ways of all inland America. So must it also stand as a boundary line,—for when we come to it, we shall not be allow'd to cross it, and go on" (646). Just as Mason and Dixon's boundary line functions as a road, the Indians' road functions as a boundary line, one that, we might imagine, serves in its own way the same purpose as Mason and Dixon's Line, "by its nature corrupt, of use at Trail's End only to those who would profit from the sale and division and resale of Lands" (701). Eventually, of course, the project of westward expansion motivated by the power and riches to be gained from the control of land will overrun such "major High-ways" laid down by the Indians, overlaying its own network of roads and, ultimately, freeways, stretching from the eastern edge of the continent, where Mason and Dixon operate, all the way to the California of *The Crying of Lot 49*, *Vineland*, and *Inherent Vice*. As we will see, that network of freeways that Mason and Dixon's surveying of the Line prefigures frequently assumes a particularly sinister quality in Pynchon's California novels, one that marks the freeways of California as the ultimate realization of the imperial project that Mason and Dixon's Line begins and that typically threatens the potential that California holds for reclaiming the lost American innocence of "Vineland the Good."

This Freeway Madness

"America," Jean Baudrillard declares in his book of the same title, "is the original version of modernity" (76). Indeed, for all his attention to European and global histories, Pynchon's ultimate focus returns again and again to America as a test case for observing the effects of modernity, power, and capital. If the ultimate realization of Mason and Dixon's Line is the network of roads and freeways that it prefigures, then California likewise serves in Pynchon's work as the ultimate realization of American history, the end of the westward trek that Mason and Dixon can only begin, the land of the Gold Rush, the land of Hollywood, the land of the apotheosis of the road in the form of the freeway. As Baudrillard puts it, "The mythical power of California consists in this mixture of extreme disconnection and vertiginous mobility captured in the setting, the hyperreal scenario of deserts, freeways, ocean, and sun" (125–26). The freeway incarnates the condition of American modernity—or, perhaps, postmodernity—that finds its ultimate expression in California, and the freeway consequently serves in Pynchon's California novels as an emblem of the dizzying whirl that California offers as the distillation of American modernity.

As developed in the California novels, that particularly Californian brand of American modernity is one fundamentally based on the automobile and, especially, the freeway. Pynchon's first California novel, *The Crying of Lot 49*, for instance, describes San Narciso as emblematic of California locales defined by their relation to the freeway: "Like many named places in California it was less an identifiable city than a grouping of concepts—census tracts, special purpose bond-issue districts, shopping nuclei, all overlaid with access roads to its own freeway" (13). Given this typical orientation of the California landscape toward the freeway, characters in Pynchon's California novels are often driving, frequently on the freeway, and they demonstrate a special affinity to automotive culture. In *Vineland*, for instance, Ditzah and Zipi Pisk, Frenesi's former colleagues in the 24fps film collective, dismissively compare the West Coast to their native New York City by noting, as Zipi puts it, "*We* are not the ones who have to encapsulate *our*selves inside our cars all the time" (196).

This may be a cheap shot, coming from a native of a city with the extensive system of public transportation that New York enjoys, but the stereotype of California culture as automobilecentric is one that the Californians of Pynchon's novels live up to and even embrace. Later in *Vineland*, Prairie's friend Ché demonstrates her devotion to automotive culture from an early age, as we learn that "Soon as she was old enough to see out the windshield, Ché had learned to drive" (331). More pointedly, "On the freeway she liked to cruise at around 80, weaving and tailgating to maintain her speed. 'We are children of the freeway,' she sang, fingertips on the wheel, boot on the gas," and the novel continues by presenting the rest of her paean to the freeway:

> We are daughters of the road,
> And we've got some miles to cover,
> 'Fore we've finally shot our load—
> If you see us in your mirror,
> Better clear a couple lanes,
> 'Cause we're daughters of the freeway,
> And speedin's in our veins. . . . (331; ellipsis in original)

Like Ché, most if not all of Pynchon's California characters could plausibly claim to be "children of the freeway," devotees in one way or another of California's car culture. It is a telling detail, for example, that early in *Inherent Vice*, the one piece of needling from his longtime nemesis Bigfoot Bjornsen that raises Doc Sportello's ire is an insult to his car, an action that the novel's narration highlights as the work of Doc's "California reflexes," as we read, "Doc's general policy was to try to be groovy about most everything, but when it was his ride in question, California reflexes kicked in" (31). Later, those "California reflexes" would seem to include not merely devotion to one's own car but also antagonism toward anyone who does not similarly embrace California's automotive lifestyle. When Doc begins to walk away after his confrontation with Puck Beaverton and Adrian Prussia, the narration at first hopefully reflects, "It couldn't be more than a couple of miles to a bus stop, and Doc needed the exercise. He could hear wind up in the palm trees and the regular beat of the surf." Doc's enjoyment of his walk is soon interrupted, however, by the "children of the freeway," mocking him for walking rather than driving:

"Now and then a car came zooming by on yet another thankless chore, sometimes with the radio on, sometimes honking at Doc for being a pedestrian" (329). Unsurprisingly, Doc does not remain a pedestrian for long, as he soon gets a ride from Bigfoot and shortly finds himself "on the San Diego Freeway, headed north" (331), another of the "children of the freeway" once again, with speeding in his veins.

The wordplay in the final line from Ché's song, "And speedin's in our veins . . . ," which renders the Californian devotion to driving and the freeway in terms of drug addiction, echoes a similar figure in *The Crying of Lot 49*. That novel's free indirect narration, speaking from the perspective of the novel's protagonist, Oedipa Maas, refers to the dream of the California road as "this illusion of speed, freedom, wind in your hair, unreeling landscape—it wasn't. What the road really was, she fancied, was this hypodermic needle, inserted somewhere ahead into the vein of a freeway, a vein nourishing the mainliner L.A., keeping it happy, coherent, protected from pain, or whatever passes, with a city, for pain" (15). The drug that the freeway as vein carries to the city it nourishes seems to be none other than the drug of modern capital, the network of money, goods, power, and people that both sustains and is sustained by America's westward expansion across the continent. Just before the passage quoted above, Oedipa tellingly drives "onto a highway she thought went toward Los Angeles, into a neighborhood that was little more than the road's skinny right-of-way, lined by auto lots, escrow services, drive-ins, small office buildings and factories whose address numbers were in the 70 and then 80,000's. She had never known numbers to run so high. It seemed unnatural" (15). Not quite a freeway, this highway nonetheless gestures toward the qualities of the freeway that typify its role in Pynchon's California. Rather than a road on a human scale connecting neighbors in any sort of genuine community, this highway and the "neighborhood" that surrounds it appear given over purely to commerce, abstracted from their surroundings by ridiculously high address numbers that offer no sense of a lived geography but instead give purchase on only an "unnatural" mapping of the land by some arbitrary and fundamentally artificial network. This highway functions not unlike the freeways of the Interstate Highway System: similarly abstracted from its local surroundings by virtue of being set above and apart from them, similarly mapped onto the land in a numbering system that is anything but natural, the freeway functions as the "perfect Corridor over the Land" that aids and abets the free flow of capital and power by shooting it straight into the heart of cities like "the mainliner L.A."

Accordingly, the freeway in *The Crying of Lot 49* appears juxtaposed with the web of commerce and repressive political power that Pynchon associates with modern capital. When Oedipa asks Randolph Driblette where he found his script for *The Courier's Tragedy*, he tells her he bought it "at Zapf's Used Books over by the freeway," a fitting site for a store that promotes the endless recirculation of commodities (61). More sinisterly, driving past Zapf's and discovering that it has been burned down, apparently for the insurance money, Oedipa learns that the "government surplus outlet next door" traffics in weapons and "swastika armbands," and is eagerly preparing "to see how SS uniforms go for the fall" (122–23). Oedipa goes on to repeat Driblette's phrase when she describes the store, which she christens "Tremaine's Swastika Shoppe," as being "over by the freeway" (139). This likewise seems a telling location for a store selling Nazi regalia, given the origins of the American Interstate Highway System as, in part, President Dwight D. Eisenhower's postwar adaptation of the German autobahn system, which was constructed largely during the Nazi era.

By a coincidence of history, Eisenhower had participated in a 1919 United States Army convoy that traveled from Washington, DC, to San Francisco. This convoy, which, as Robert L. Reid notes, "was designed to test the capabilities of trucks, automobiles, and motorcycles for military transport," wound up taking nearly two months, from July 7 to September 1, to cross the continent, and impressed upon Eisenhower the inadequacy of the roads then in place. As Reid goes on to relate the story:

> A quarter of a century later, when Eisenhower was the supreme commander of the Allied Expeditionary Force in Europe during World War II, his armies would move rapidly and easily along captured portions of Nazi Germany's four-lane expressways, or autobahns. When Eisenhower became president, in 1953, these contrasting experiences—becoming stuck in American mud

and speeding across the Third Reich—helped him decide that the United States needed its own system of high-quality highways. (38)

In this case, then, the experience of driving on the German autobahns helped to sell Eisenhower on the Interstate Highway System, a fact that recalls Edward Dimendberg's observation, "Although Hitler and Todt [Fritz Todt, general inspector of German highways under Hitler] did not invent the Autobahn, they became its consummate salesmen and the principal architects of its aesthetic" (98). In this light, it may be only Pynchonian paranoia to find it telling that the salesman of Nazi fashions, Winthrop Tremaine, has set up his shop "over by the freeway," but such a paranoid connection would not be lost on Oedipa.

Of course, President Eisenhower also had other reasons to support the construction of the Interstate Highway System. As Kenneth T. Jackson writes, "President Eisenhower gave four reasons for signing the measure: current highways were unsafe; cars too often became snarled in traffic jams; poor roads saddled business with high costs for transportation; and modern highways were needed because 'in case of atomic attack on our key cities, the road net must permit quick evacuation of target areas'" (*Crabgrass Frontier* 249). The last of these reasons, relating to civil defense in case of nuclear war, is recalled in Pynchon's second California novel, *Vineland*, when Frenesi, in the hours after the murder of Weed Atman and the fall of the People's Republic of Rock and Roll, is taken to Brock Vond's "National Security Reservation," "the site of an old Air Force fog-dispersal experiment and later, before the apocalyptic grandeur of Kennedy-era strategic 'thinking' found itself bogged, nukeless, in the quotidian horrors of Vietnam, intended as a holding area able to house up to half a million urban evacuees in the event of, well, say, some urban evacuation." Frenesi is taken to this "Reservation" on "the little-known and only confidentially traveled FEER, or Federal Emergency Evacuation Route," a "classified freeway" "conceived in the early sixties as a disposable freeway that would only be used, to full capacity, once" and whose acronym betrays the Cold War fears that gave rise to it (249–50). In its use by Brock Vond as a means to round up and imprison political radicals, the FEER further exposes the security concerns of the Cold War as a pretense justifying the repressive exercise of state power that Pynchon sees at the heart of the military-industrial complex, of which not only the FEER but all freeways are products.

Similarly underscoring the freeway's origins and function in the military-industrial complex is "Hymn," sung at the Yoyodyne shareholders' meeting that Oedipa attends in *The Crying of Lot 49*, which begins:

High above the L.A. freeways,
And the traffic's whine,
Stands the well-known Galactronics
Branch of Yoyodyne. (65)

The fact that Yoyodyne is located in Southern California is hardly an accident, nor is it entirely unconnected to the dominance of the freeway in the Southern California landscape. As Casey Shoop notes, "Beyond the fact that virtually the entire infrastructure of Southern California, from freeways to waterways, depended on federal funding, the defense industry, the lifeblood of its regional economy, subsisted almost entirely on government contracts" (72–73). Both freeway and Yoyodyne depend on Cold War–era federal largesse. Without that spending occasioned by fears of the Soviet Union, neither symptom of the military-industrial complex could exist. With that spending, however, both the freeway and Yoyodyne loom large above the California terrain.

In fitting contrast to the high and mighty position occupied by munitions companies such as Yoyodyne—indeed, in the literal underbelly of the similarly lordly position that the freeway occupies above and apart from its surrounding locale—Oedipa later learns that one of the mailboxes used by the dispossessed members of the WASTE network in San Francisco is located "Under the freeway," a lowly position in comparison to the freeway's promise of elevation in the service of faster transportation (102). Consequently, we follow Oedipa "among the sunless, concrete underpinnings of the freeway, finding drunks, bums, pedestrians, pederasts, hookers, walking psychotics, no secret mailbox. But at last in the shadows she did come on a can with a swinging trapezoidal top, the kind you throw trash in: old and green, nearly four feet high. On the swinging part were hand-painted the initials W.A.S.T.E." (105). Under the freeway, in the terrain that the glossy illusion of modern capital renders invisible, Oedipa encounters the detritus of America, those passed over by the freeway's "perfect Corridor over the Land," those whose pathologies and addictions, unlike the ones that the freeway nourishes, do not occupy the rarefied air of high capital but rather are abandoned in the wake of the freeway's onrushing service to modernity as "a vein nourishing the mainliner" city.

Like the junkie seeking a fix, the demands of the freeway will not be denied, and *The Crying of Lot 49* demonstrates this most clearly in the case of the East San Narciso Freeway. As in the case of Mason and Dixon's Line, the construction of the East San Narciso Freeway needs to destroy everything in its path, even at the cost of disturbing the dead, as we learn when Oedipa asks about the connection between highway construction and the sale of human bones: "'Old cemeteries have to be ripped up,' Metzger explained. 'Like in the path of the East San Narciso Freeway, it had no right to be there, so we just barrelled on through, no sweat.'" The construction of the freeway destroys the land and effaces the memory of the dead, all in the service of the quicker transportation of goods as a way of facilitating the ever-faster circulation of power and capital. Indeed, the construction of the freeway is itself aided and abetted by the explicitly corrupt circulation of capital, as Oedipa learns when Manny Di Presso appends to Metzger's explanation the comment, "'No bribes, no freeways'" (46). In uncannily inverted but resonant terms, we learn in *Inherent Vice* that Adrian Prussia cleans up the murders he commits on behalf of the Los Angeles Police Department by disposing of the bodies in the structures of the freeways themselves:

> When the job was over, Adrian took the mutilated corpse and drove it to a freeway under construction miles away and dropped it inside the forms for a concrete support column about to be poured. A liberally compensated cement-mixer operator known to friends of Adrian's then helped encase the remains in what would become a vertical tomb, an invisible statue of someone the authorities wished not to commemorate but to wipe from the Earth. Even today, Adrian could still not drive the freeway system without wondering how many of the columns he saw might have stiffs inside them. (322–23)

Whereas in *The Crying of Lot 49* the freeway displaces the dead, in *Inherent Vice*, it consumes the dead, victims of a criminal police authority. In both cases, though, the result is the same, as the dead are lost to history, obliterated in the construction of the freeway, erased in a process greased by the criminal flow of power and capital that, like the freeway itself, cannot abide any obstructions.

Despite the freeway's dominant position in the California landscape, Oedipa holds out hope in *The Crying of Lot 49* that some land beyond that of the freeway might still exist. We see this when she reflects on Genghis Cohen's dandelion wine. This wine is made from dandelions picked from one of the cemeteries torn up to make way for the East San Narciso Freeway, and it still ferments when it is time for the dandelions to bloom, "As if their home cemetery in some way still did exist, in a land where you could somehow walk, and not need the East San Narciso Freeway, and bones still could rest in peace, nourishing ghosts of dandelions, no one to plow them up." (79). This dream of an alternative pedestrian reality may strike readers as particularly absurd in the notoriously automobilecentric culture of California, a car culture whose dominance Pynchon's California novels demonstrate again and again.

Instead of escaping the land of the freeway, Oedipa more and more finds herself, like the other characters who populate Pynchon's fictions of California, caught up in what *The Crying of Lot 49*'s narration later refers to as "this freeway madness" (87). We see this most spectacularly when Oedipa "went back to Echo Courts to drink bourbon until the sun went down and it was as dark as it would ever get. Then she went out and drove on the freeway for a while with her lights out, to see what would happen. But angels were watching" (145–46). Notably, Oedipa's escapade on the freeway seems not that different, in its suicidal undertones, from what *Inherent Vice* describes as typical of freeway drivers: when Bigfoot, driving Doc away from his confrontation with Puck and Adrian, "accelerated to eighty-five or ninety miles per hour and went gleefully, one might almost say suicidally, weaving in and out of traffic in traditional freeway style" (332). Death in these novels always lurks within the fantasy of the freeway and the addictive madness it brings. Still, if Oedipa is attempting suicide as a way of escaping the web of real estate holdings, business interests, munitions manufacturing, and postal conspiracies that she finds herself entangled in as executrix of Pierce Inverarity's will, then it is no wonder that she cannot find that escape on the freeway, because the freeway itself is the vein that nourishes all those operations of late capital. Instead of granting Oedipa her release, driving on the freeway only plunges her further into the network of the military-industrial complex.

A Freeway for Freaks

The term "military-industrial complex" was, of course, popularized when President Eisenhower used it in his farewell address in 1961, five years before the publication of *The Crying of Lot 49*. In the spirit of the Pynchonian worldview in which, as *Gravity's Rainbow* comments, "*everything is connected*" (703), it is useful to remember, as noted above, that Eisenhower was also a key figure in the creation of the Interstate Highway System, having signed into law the Federal-Aid Highway Act of 1956. As further noted earlier, Eisenhower's interest in developing an American freeway system was motivated, at least in part, by its potential for national defense, a potential that he realized during World War II by observing the success of the German autobahn. Appropriately enough, Pynchon's novel of World War II, *Gravity's Rainbow*, features near its conclusion a section titled "Orpheus Puts Down Harp" that further aligns the California freeway with the repressive political structures of the military-industrial complex, in keeping with the novel's overall consideration of, as Nicholas Spencer puts it, the ways that "aspects of contemporary American society are extensions of the economic, military, and technological attributes of Nazi Germany" (152). This section, set in the then-contemporary California of the early 1970s, presents a thinly disguised analogue of Eisenhower's vice president, former California senator—and president at the time of the publication of *Gravity's Rainbow*—Richard M. Nixon. Nixon appears in the guise of one Richard M. Zhlubb, a theater manager who takes us on a drive on the freeway. As the narration comments, "He ushers you into the black Managerial Volkswagen, and before you know it, you're on the freeways." Specifically, you're "Near the interchange of the San Diego and the Santa Monica," with the Santa Monica derided as "a freeway for freaks," in contrast to the San Diego's "white and well-bred" quality (755). Although he scoffs at the freaks, Zhlubb is himself given to indulge in freakish fantasies, as he confesses:

> I have a fantasy about how I'll die. I suppose you're on *their* payroll, but that's all right. Listen to this. It's 3 a.m., on the Santa Monica Freeway, a warm night. All my windows are open. I'm doing about 70, 75. The wind blows in, and from the floor in back lifts a thin plastic bag, a common dry-cleaning bag: it comes floating in the air, moving from behind, the mercury lights turning it white as a ghost . . . it wraps around my head, so superfine and transparent I don't know it's there really until too late. A plastic shroud, smothering me to my death. . . . (756; ellipses in original)

As in Oedipa's stab at a suicide attempt, Zhlubb's fantasy aligns the freeway with death, in keeping with the role that the freeway assumes throughout Pynchon's California novels. Notably, death comes in Zhlubb's fantasy in the form of a bag turned "white as a ghost," an ominous echo of the alignment of whiteness with death throughout *Gravity's Rainbow.* This section of the novel further underscores that connection by describing the San Diego Freeway as "white and well-bred," linking that freeway to the color of death and, specifically, the death that Zhlubb, as the representative of a "white and well-bred" political structure, serves. The novel more pointedly reminds us of the freeway's status as a carrier of modern military-industrial death in its next paragraph, where, "Heading up the Hollywood Freeway," we see "a mysteriously-canvased trailer rig and a liquid-hydrogen tanker sleek as a torpedo" (756). As Steven C. Weisenburger notes, "these tractor-trailer rigs might well be hauling, respectively, a nuclear-tipped ICBM missile (directly descended from von Braun's A4 rocket design) and its liquid hydrogen fuel. These rigs were thus then-contemporary versions of the Nazis' portable rocket-firing rig that Pynchon images for us" (382). Insofar as the freeway is the child of Eisenhower's vision for the Interstate Highway System, this scene thereby undermines Eisenhower's standing as a figure pronouncing warnings about the military-industrial complex. As Spencer argues, "In *Gravity's Rainbow,* the transportation networks of the decentralized postmodern city extend the attributes of the modernist city and the rocket to become the site of the final manifestation of abstract space" (153). This link between the freeway and the military-industrial complex incarnated in the rocket is underscored by the presence of Eisenhower's vice president, Nixon-*cum*-Zhlubb, reminding us of the death that lurks within the fantasy of the freeway, the imperial fantasy of mapping, ordering, and controlling the land, of making it submit to the drives of modern power and capital.

As noted in the online Pynchon Wiki, however, *Gravity's Rainbow* is not the only Pynchon novel to feature at its conclusion an automobile ride that traverses the interchange of the San Diego and the Santa Monica Freeways. The final scene of *Inherent Vice*, the most recently published of Pynchon's California novels to date, presents a drive similarly taken at the interchange of the San Diego and the Santa Monica Freeways by Doc Sportello, one of the very freaks Zhlubb dismisses in *Gravity's Rainbow*. The most striking thing about Doc's ride on the freeway is just how thoroughly it reconfigures the freeway, not as the emblem of the networks of power and capital that characterize the condition of modernity in Pynchon's work but rather as a network of community. As such, the freeway serves in Doc's ride, as well as in other select moments in Pynchon's California novels that resonate with Doc's ride, as a possible road to the lost possibilities of American history. Instead of the path that America actually took in Pynchon's reading of history, the path in which the official power structures of America tend toward the repressive state violence of the military-industrial complex and, ultimately, fascism, the freeway in these moments opens an avenue to the America of "Vineland the Good" that appears in both *Mason & Dixon* and *Vineland* as a more hopeful alternative. These moments suggest that the "Vineland the Good" that is lost in *Mason & Dixon* might somehow be rediscovered in California, whether literally in California's own Vineland or more figuratively in the imaginative avenues that the freeway can open up, however temporarily.

Indeed, the key difference in conditions under which Doc experiences the freeway in its more hopeful aspect seems to be only temporary, namely, the condition of fog. The final section of *Inherent Vice*'s final chapter begins, "Doc got on the Santa Monica Freeway, and about the time he was making the transition to the San Diego southbound, the fog began its nightly roll inland." As a result of the fog, everything Doc associates with the freeway, including "the signs above the freeway that told you where you were," disappear, leading to a situation in which, eventually, "all Doc could see were his headlight beams, like eyestalks of an extraterrestrial, aimed into the hushed whiteness ahead, and the lights on his dashboard, where the speedometer was the only way to tell how fast he was going" (367). In this moment, the fog frustrates the capacity of the freeway to order and map the land, momentarily allowing the land to elude the control of the networks of modern power and capital.

Even more notable is the fact that "the hushed whiteness ahead" echoes the image of the plastic bag "moving from behind, the mercury lights turning it white as a ghost . . . it wraps around my head, so superfine and transparent I don't know it's there really until too late. A plastic shroud, smothering me to my death. . . ." that Zhlubb fantasizes about at the end of *Gravity's Rainbow* (756; ellipses in original). In the shared whiteness, the shared shroud that cuts the driver off from his surroundings, Zhlubb and Doc experience the freeway in strikingly resonant terms, but they are terms that lead to opposite ends. For Zhlubb, representative of the "white and well-bred" political structure, the loss of access to the freeway's capacity to order and map the land yields only death. For Doc, representative of the hippie freak subculture, this occasion of escape from standardized order grants him, and everyone else driving on the freeway with him, a momentary vision of the utopian potential of America, the utopian potential of California in particular, that seems in Pynchon's history of America to have been slipping away ever since that "first Act of American murder, and the collapse of Vineland the Good" recorded in *Mason & Dixon* (634). As the narration relates, "He was in a convoy of unknown size, each car keeping the one ahead in taillight range, like a caravan in a desert of perception, gathered awhile for safety in getting across a patch of blindness. It was one of the few things he'd ever seen anybody in this town, except hippies, do for free," forming "a temporary commune to help each other home through the fog" (368). It is tempting to read this fog as the fog of history; the fog of America's drift toward repression; and the "home" that the members of the "temporary commune," momentarily all hippie freaks like Doc, are driving to as the lost home of "Vineland the Good," the alternative America that escapes the official networks of control that the freeway in its daytime aspect maps onto the land. As Raymond M. Olderman writes in his discussion of

Pynchon's treatment of the freak element of the counterculture, "Invisibility is the freak's only protection. Unless freaks remain invisible, they cannot protect the flickering dimensions of their world view from either destruction or cooptation by the straight world" (201). Doc's ride down the San Diego in the final pages of *Inherent Vice* serves as a direct response to Zhlubb's fantasized death drive on the Santa Monica at the end of *Gravity's Rainbow*, holding out a utopian vision in keeping with *Inherent Vice*'s wistful reconsideration of the counterculture, with the benefit of 40 years of hindsight. As such, these two narrative off-ramps guide readers to the terminal points of their respective novels as mirror images of one another that, in offering intersecting competing visions of the same freeways, construct a narrative interchange branching off into competing avenues of history.

By refusing to let the freeway remain only an emblem of death, Pynchon reopens his history of America, allowing for the possibility of recapturing the spirit of the "Vineland the Good" lost in *Mason & Dixon* and particularly of recapturing that spirit in California, the home state of that other "Vineland the Good." Unsurprisingly, *Vineland* itself presents some moments that resonate with *Inherent Vice*'s repurposing of the freeway as the avenue to an alternative America. Notably, Zoyd Wheeler began his trek toward California's Vineland after he was dropped off "at the nearest Santa Monica Freeway exit and immediately got picked up by a VW bus painted all over with flowers, ringed planets, R. Crumb–style faces and feet, and less recognizable forms" (306), in keeping with the characterization of the Santa Monica in *Gravity's Rainbow* as "a freeway for freaks." Instead of leading to death, as Zhlubb's fantasy of the Santa Monica does, however, Zoyd's quest is for a home for himself and his daughter in California's Vineland. When he gets to Vineland, after traveling U.S. Highway 101—a highway that notably predates Eisenhower's Interstate Highway System—he finds that "Money had never been found in Sacramento or Washington to bypass 101 around Vineland, so that once into town, the freeway narrowed to two lanes and made a couple of doglegs on and off South Spooner, following unsynchronized traffic lights that drove Van Meter crazy but gave Zoyd a good look at downtown" (318). In this case, the freeway gives up the dream of order and control in favor of openness to the "unsynchronized"; it ceases to function as "a perfect Corridor over the Land" and instead brings Zoyd into contact with Vineland's downtown, a reunification of freeway and land that undoes the violent separation of the two that we see in Pynchon's other California freeways.

Against Zhlubb and the forces he represents that seek to close down any hope for alternate histories or alternate futures, the glimpses of "a freeway for freaks" that we get in *Gravity's Rainbow*, *Vineland*, and *Inherent Vice* allow Pynchon to repurpose the freeway according to the hopeful outlook Doc assumes as he drives through the fog in the final sentences of *Inherent Vice*:

> Maybe then it would stay this way for days, maybe he'd have to just keep driving, down past Long Beach, down through Orange County, and San Diego, and across a border where nobody could tell anymore in the fog who was Mexican, who was Anglo, who was anybody. Then again, he might run out of gas before that happened, and have to leave the caravan, and pull over on the shoulder, and wait. For whatever would happen. For a forgotten joint to materialize in his pocket. For the CHP to come by and choose not to hassle him. For a restless blonde in a Stingray to stop and offer him a ride. For the fog to burn away, and for something else this time, somehow, to be there instead. (369)

More often than not in Pynchon, the possibility of "something else" being there instead is precisely the possibility that freeways foreclose. These are the freeways that *Mason & Dixon* prefigure in the Line; the freeways as we encounter them in *The Crying of Lot 49* and, to a large extent, as they appear elsewhere in *Vineland* and *Inherent Vice*; the freeways that Zhlubb fantasizes about in *Gravity's Rainbow*; the sometimes brutally overwhelming reality of the freeway as it functions in Pynchon's history of America. By contrast, the "freeway of freaks" that *Gravity's Rainbow*, *Vineland*, and *Inherent Vice* momentarily give us access to reopens the possibility of "something else" being there instead, however temporarily. "Something else" is a tantalizingly but necessarily vague description of what that alternative might be, since its unmappable quality, the very quality that enables it to escape the control of official networks of power and capital, renders it difficult even to conceive of as anything more specific than simply "something else." Rather than mapping out a specific location, these moments in Pynchon's California novels at which a "freeway of freaks" offers paths to "something else" remind us of that other America of the figurative "Vineland the Good" still waiting to be discovered, maybe somewhere in California, after a nighttime drive through the interchange of the San Diego and the Santa Monica Freeways.

Contributors

HANJO BERRESSEM teaches American literature at the University of Cologne, Germany. His publications include *Pynchon's Poetics: Interfacing Theory and Text* (University of Illinois Press, 1992) and *Lines of Desire: Reading Gombrowicz's Fiction with Lacan* (Northwestern University Press, 1998). He has edited, together with Leyla Haferkamp, *Deleuzian Events: Writing/History* (Lit, 2009) and *site-specific: from aachen to zwölfkinder—pynchon/germany* (special issue of *Pynchon Notes*, 2008). He has just completed two complementary books, *Crystal Philosophy*, on Gilles Deleuze, and *Crystal Science*, on the notion of "Eigenvalue."

CHRISTOPHER K. COFFMAN is a lecturer in humanities at Boston University. His articles have appeared in *Comparative Literature*, *JAC: A Journal of Rhetoric, Culture, & Politics*, *Genre*, and other journals, and his essay "Bogomilism, Orphism, Shamanism: The Spiritual and Spatial Grounds of *Against the Day*'s Ecological Ethic" was included in *Pynchon's* Against the Day: *A Corrupted Pilgrim's Guide* (University of Delaware Press, 2011). He is currently at work on a monograph exploring contemporary presentations of the colonial New World and coediting a collection of essays on the works of William T. Vollmann.

STEPHEN HOCK is an associate professor of English at Virginia Wesleyan College, where he teaches 20th-century and contemporary American literature. He is the coeditor, with Jeremy Braddock, of *Directed by Allen Smithee* (2001).

MARGARET LYND received her PhD in English from Ohio State University. Her interests are in the intersections of narrative and cultural theory and in modern and contemporary literatures. She has worked at OSU as an administrator, advisor, and instructor in the Department of Comparative Studies for more than 20 years.

SCOTT MACLEOD is a doctoral research candidate and associate tutor in the Department of English, Creative Writing and Australian Studies at Flinders University, South Australia. His thesis examines the influence and transformation of the detective fiction genre in the postmodern works of Thomas Pynchon. Besides writing extensively on contemporary American literature, postmodernism, intertextuality, and detective fiction, he has also published many essays and articles on film theory and Hollywood cinema.

SCOTT McCLINTOCK has a PhD in comparative literature from the University of California, Irvine. His research interests include literatures of the Americas, antiterror discourse critique, the Indian novel in English, and Cold War cultural studies. He has published articles on such world authors as Salman Rushdie, Amitav Ghosh, Franz Kafka, and Laureano Alban, and on the Carmel poet Robinson Jeffers and the culture of the Cold War. Most recently, his chapter "'The Matter of Being Expatriots: Hemingway, Cuba and Inter-American Study" was published in *Hemingway, Cuba, and the Cuban Works* (Kent State University Press, 2013).

BILL MILLARD writes about the built environment and its relation to culture, health, and the natural world. His publications have covered architecture, literature, medicine, cyberculture, and music; in the 1990s, he was the editor of Columbia University's interdisciplinary research magazine *21stC*. His doctorate in English and American literature is from Rutgers, and his undergraduate work was at Amherst. With support from the Graham Foundation for Advanced Studies in the Fine Arts, he is working on a book, *The Vertical and Horizontal Americas: The Built Environment, Cultural Formations, and the Post-Automotive Era*, from which this chapter is adapted. He lives in New York's East Village.

JOHN MILLER teaches writing and literature at National University in Costa Mesa, CA. His scholarly publications have dealt with a variety of topics, from the early modern prose of Francis Bacon, Robert Burton, and Izaak Walton to the fiction of J. R. R. Tolkien and Thomas Pynchon, as well as the science fiction short story, hyperfiction and role playing games, and online pedagogy.

HENRY VEGGIAN is the series editor of *Dialogue Series* for Rodopi Press and a member of the *boundary 2* editorial collective. He writes and publishes widely on modern literature, and his *Understanding Don DeLillo* is forthcoming from the University of South Carolina Press. He works in North Carolina.

Works Cited

Adams, Rachel. "The Ends of America, the Ends of Postmodernism." *Twentieth Century Literature* 53 (2007): 248–72. Print.

Allen, William Rodney, ed. *The Coen Brothers: Interviews.* Jackson: U.P. of Mississippi, 2006. Print.

Arac, Jonathan. "Introduction." *Postmodernism and Politics.* Ed. Jonathan Arac. Minneapolis: U. of Minnesota P., 1986. ix–xliii. *Theory and History of Literature.* Vol. 28. Print.

Auden, W. H. "The Guilty Vicarage: Notes on the Detective Story, by an Addict." *Harper's* May 1948: 406–12. Print.

Auerbach, Erich. *Mimesis: The Representation of Reality in Western Literature.* Princeton, NJ: Princeton U.P., 2003. 50th anniversary edition.

Auster, Paul. *The New York Trilogy.* 1987. London: Faber & Faber, 2004. Print.

Babener, Liahna K. "Raymond Chandler's City of Lies." *Los Angeles in Fiction: A Collection of Essays.* Ed. David Fine. Albuquerque: U. of New Mexico P., 1995. 127–49. Print.

Balzac, Honoré de. *Eugénie Grandet.* Trans., Marion Ayton Crawford. New York: Penguin, 1955. Print.

Bancroft, Colette. "Thomas Pynchon delivers a great beach read with 'Inherent Vice.'" *Tampa Bay Times* 7 Aug. 2009. Web. 31 Dec. 2013 <http://www.tampabay.com/features/books/article1024726.ece>.

Baudrilllard, Jean. *America.* 1986. Trans., Chris Turner. London: Verso, 1988. Print.

Baxter, Charles. "De-faced America: *The Great Gatsby* and *The Crying of Lot 49.*" *Pynchon Notes* 7 (1981): 22–37. Print.

Bell, Daniel. *Cultural Contradictions of Capitalism.* New York: Basic Books, 1976. Print.

Benjamin, Walter. "From 'Surrealism.'" *On Hashish.* Trans., Howard Eiland and others. Ed. Howard Eiland. Cambridge, MA: Belknap Press of Harvard U.P., 2006. 132–34. Print.

———. "From the Letters." *On Hashish.* Trans., Howard Eiland and others. Ed. Howard Eiland. Cambridge, MA: Belknap Press of Harvard U.P., 2006. 144–46. Print.

Bergh, Patricia. "(De)constructing the Image: Thomas Pynchon's Postmodern Woman." *Journal of Popular Culture* 30.4 (1997): 1–12. Print.

Berressem, Hanjo. "Coda: How to Read Pynchon." *The Cambridge Companion to Thomas Pynchon*. Ed. Inger H. Dalsgaard, Luc Herman, and Brian McHale. Cambridge: Cambridge U.P., 2011. 168–77. Print.

Bey, Hakim. *T.A.Z.: The Temporary Autonomous Zone, Ontological Anarchy, Poetic Terrorism*. Brooklyn: Autonomedia, 2003. Print.

The Big Lebowski. Dirs. Joel Coen and Ethan Coen. 1998. DVD. Working Title, 2008.

Boon, Marcus. "Walter Benjamin and Drug Literature." Ed. Howard Eiland. Trans., Howard Eiland and others. Cambridge, MA: Belknap Press of Harvard U.P., 2006. 1–12. Print.

Borges, Jorge Luis. "Ibn Hakkan al-Bokhari, Dead in His Labyrinth." 1951. *The Aleph and Other Stories, 1933–1969*. Trans., Norman Thomas di Giovanni. New York: Dutton, 1978. Print.

Braudel, Fernand. *The Mediterranean and the Mediterranean World in the Age of Philip II*. Trans., Siân Reynolds. Vol. 1. New York: Harper and Row, 1972. Print.

Brooks, Peter. *The Melodramatic Imagination*. New York: Columbia U.P., 1985. Print.

Brownlie, Alan W. *Thomas Pynchon's Narratives: Subjectivity and Problems of Knowing*. New York: Peter Lang, 2000. Print.

Burket, Richard E. "The State Law Enforcement Apparatus as America: Authority, Arbitrariness, and the 'Force of Law' in *Vineland*." *Oklahoma City Law Review* 24.3 (1999): 727–57. Print.

Caputo, John D. "On the Power of the Powerless: Dialogue with John D. Caputo." *After the Death of God*. Ed. Jeffrey W. Robbins. New York: Columbia U.P., 2007. 114–60. Print.

———. "Spectral Hermeneutics: On the Weakness of God and the Theology of the Event." *After the Death of God*. Ed. Jeffrey W. Robbins. New York: Columbia U.P., 2007. 47–85. Print.

Carswell, Sean. "A Thomas Pynchon Guide to Contemporary Resistance." PhD dissertation, Indiana University of Pennsylvania, 2012.

Cassuto, Leonard. *Hard-Boiled Sentimentality: The Secret History of American Crime Stories*. New York: Columbia U.P., 2008. Print.

Chambers, Judith. *Thomas Pynchon*. New York: Twayne Publishers, 1992. Print.

Chandler, Raymond. *The Big Sleep*. New York: Alfred A. Knopf, 1939. Print.

Coale, Samuel Chase. *Paradigms of Paranoia: The Culture of Conspiracy in Contemporary American Fiction*. Tuscaloosa: U. Alabama P., 2005. Print.

Cohen, Samuel. "*Mason & Dixon* and the Ampersand." *Twentieth-Century Literature* 48.3 (2002): 264–91. Print.

Collignon, Fabienne. "A Glimpse of Light." *Textual Practice* 22.3 (2008): 547–62. Print.

Coover, Robert. *Noir*. New York: The Overlook Press, 2010. Print.

Couturier, Maurice. "The Death of the Real in *The Crying of Lot 49*." *Pynchon Notes* 20–21 (1987): 5–29. Print.

Cowart, David. "Attenuated Postmodernism: Pynchon's *Vineland*." *Critical Essays on American Postmodernism*. Ed. Stanley Trachtenberg. New York: G. K. Hall & Co., 1995. 182–91. Print.

———. "The Luddite Vision: *Mason & Dixon*." American Literature 71.2 (1999): 341–63. Print.

———. *Thomas Pynchon and the Dark Passages of History*. Athens: U. of Georgia P., 2011. Print.

Dalsgaard, Inger H., Luc Herman, and Brian McHale, eds. *The Cambridge Companion to Thomas Pynchon*. Cambridge: Cambridge U.P., 2011. Print.

Danielewski, Mark Z. *House of Leaves*. New York: Pantheon, 2000. Print.

Davis, Mike. *City of Quartz: Excavating the Future in Los Angeles*. New York: Verso, 1990. Print.

———. *Ecology of Fear: Los Angeles and the Imagination of Disaster*. New York: Metropolitan Books, 1998. Print.

De Landa, Manuel. *A Thousand Years of Nonlinear History*. New York: Swerve Editions, 2000. Print.

Deleuze, Gilles. "The Actual and the Virtual." *Dialogues II: Texts and Interviews 1975–1995*. New York: Semiotexte, 2006. 148–52. Print.

———. *Cinema I: The Movement-Image*. Trans., Hugh Tomlinson and Barbara Habberjam. Minneapolis: U. of Minnesota P., 1986. Print.

———. *The Fold: Leibniz and the Baroque*. Trans., Tom Conley. Minneapolis: U. of Minnesota P., 1993. Print.

———. "May '68 Did Not Take Place." *Two Regimes of Madness: Texts and Interviews 1975–1995*. Ed. David Lapoujade. Trans., Ames Hodges and Mike Taormina. New York: Semiotexte, 2006. 233–36. Print.

———. *Negotiations (1972–1990)*. Trans., Martin Joughin. New York: Columbia U.P., 1995. Print.

———. "Two Questions on Drugs." *Two Regimes of Madness: Texts and Interviews 1975–1995*. Ed. David Lapoujade. Trans., Ames Hodges and Mike Taormina. New York: Semiotexte, 2006. 151–55. Print.

———. *Two Regimes of Madness: Texts and Interviews 1975–1995*. Ed. David Lapoujade. Trans., Ames Hodges and Mike Taormina. New York: Semiotexte, 2006. Print.

———. "Zones of Immanence." *Two Regimes of Madness: Texts and Interviews 1975–1995*. Ed. David Lapoujade. Trans., Ames Hodges and Mike Taormina. New York: Semiotexte, 2006. 261–68. Print.

Deleuze, Gilles, and Félix Guattari. *Anti-Oedipus: Capitalism and Schizophrenia*. Minneapolis: U. of Minnesota P., 1983. Print.

———. *A Thousand Plateaus.* Trans., Brian Massumi. Minneapolis: University of Minnesota P., 1987. Print.

Denning, Michael. *The Cultural Front: The Laboring of American Culture in the Twentieth Century.* New York: Verso, 1997. Print.

Derrida, Jacques. "Faith and Knowledge: the Two Sources of 'Religion' at the Limits of Reason Alone." *Religion.* Ed. Jacques Derrida and Gianni Vattimo. Trans., Samuel Weber. Stanford, CA: Stanford U.P., 1998. 1–78. Print.

Dickens, Charles. *Bleak House.* 1853. London: Penguin Books, 2011.

Didion, Joan. "Notes from a Native Daughter." *Slouching towards Bethlehem.* New York: Farrar, Strauss & Giroux, 1968. 171–86. Print.

Dimendberg, Edward. "The Will to Motorization: Cinema, Highways, and Modernity." *October* 73 (1995): 90–137. *JSTOR.* Web. 30 July 2012. <http://www.jstor.org/discover/10.2307/779010?uid=3739256&uid=2&uid=4&sid=21103281890353>.

Dotolo, Carmelo. "The Hermeneutics of Christianity and Philosophical Responsibility." *Weakening Philosophy: Essays in Honour of Gianni Vattimo.* Ed. Santiago Zabala. Montreal: McGill-Queen's U.P., 2007. 348–68. Print.

Doyle, Arthur Conan. *The Adventures of Sherlock Holmes.* New York: Harper & Brothers, 1892. Print.

Duany, Andrés, Plater-Zyberk, Elizabeth, and Speck, Jeff. *Suburban Nation: The Rise of Sprawl and the Decline of the American Dream.* New York: North Point Press, 2000. Print.

Eco, Umberto. *The Name of the Rose.* 1980. San Diego: Harcourt, 1983. Print.

Eddins, Dwight. *The Gnostic Pynchon.* Bloomington: Indiana U.P., 1990. Print.

Eliade, Mircea. *The Sacred and the Profane: The Nature of Religion.* Trans., Willard R. Trask. New York: Harcourt, 1959. Print.

Ellis, Bret Easton. *Lunar Park.* New York: Alfred A. Knopf, 2005. Print.

Ellison, Ralph. *Invisible Man.* 1952. New York: Vintage International, 1995. Print.

Ellroy, James. *The Big Nowhere.* New York: Mysterious Press Books, 1988. Print.

———. *The Black Dahlia.* New York: Mysterious Press Books, 1987. Print.

———. *L.A. Confidential.* New York: Warner Books, 1990. Print.

———. *White Jazz.* New York: Knopf, 1992. Print.

Emerson, Ralph Waldo. *The Complete Works of Ralph Waldo Emerson.* Vol. 2. *Essays, First Series.* Boston: Houghton Mifflin, 1904. Print.

Foucault, Michel. *Society Must Be Defended: Lectures at the Collège de France, 1975–1976.* Trans., David Macey. New York: Picador, 2003. Print.

Freud, Sigmund. *The Standard Edition of the Complete Psychological Works of Sigmund Freud.* Vol. 4. *The Interpretation of Dreams (First Part).* Ed. James Strachey. London: The Hogarth Press and the Institute of Psychoanalysis, 1953.

———. *The Standard Edition of the Complete Psychological Works of Sigmund Freud.*

Vol. 5. *The Interpretation of Dreams (Second Part) and On Dreams*. Ed. James Strachey. London: The Hogarth Press and the Institute of Psychoanalysis, 1953.

———. *The Standard Edition of the Complete Psychological Works of Sigmund Freud*. Vol. 17. *An Infantile Neurosis and Other Works*. Ed. James Strachey. London: The Hogarth Press and the Institute of Psychoanalysis, 1955.

Frost, Garrison. "Thomas Pynchon and the South Bay." *The Aesthetic*, 2003. Web. 1 Jan. 2014. <http://www.theaesthetic.com/NewFiles/pynchon.html>.

Galbraith, John Kenneth. *The New Industrial State*. Boston: Houghton Mifflin, 1967. Print.

Gora, Thomas (managing ed.), Patrick Truhn (assistant ed.), and Editorial Committee, eds. "*Anti-Oedipus*: From Psychoanalysis to Schizopolitics." *Semiotext(e)* 2.3 (1977). Special issue. Web. 1 Jan. 2014. <http://www.generation-online.org/p/semiotexte-anti-oedipus.pdf>.

Gordon, Andrew. "Smoking Dope with Thomas Pynchon: A Sixties Memoir." *The Vineland Papers: Critical Takes on Pynchon's Novel*. Ed. Geoffrey Green, Donald J. Greiner, and Larry McCaffery. Champaign, IL: Dalkey Archive Press, 1994. 167-78. Print.

Gordon, Mary, et al. *Deadly Sins*. New York: William Morrow and Company, 1994. Print.

Grieveson, Lee, Esther Sonnet, and Peter Stanfield, eds. *Mob Culture: Hidden Histories of the American Gangster Film*. New Brunswick, NJ: Rutgers U.P., 2005. Print.

Guattari, Félix. *Chaosmosis: An Ethico-Aesthetic Paradigm*. Trans., Paul Bains and Julian Pefanis. Bloomington: Indiana U.P., 1992. Print.

Hammett, Dashiell. *The Maltese Falcon*. New York: Alfred A. Knopf, 1930. Print.

Haraway, Donna. "Situated Knowledges: The Science Question in Feminism and the Privilege of Partial Perspective." *Feminist Studies* 14.3 (1988): 575–99. Print.

Hayden, Dolores. *Building Suburbia: Green Fields and Urban Growth, 1820–2000*. New York: Pantheon, 2003. Print.

Hinds, Elizabeth Jane Wall. "Visible Tracks: Historical Method and Thomas Pynchon's *Vineland*." *College Literature* 19.1 (1992): 91–103. *JSTOR*. Web. 10 October 2012. <http://www.jstor.org/discover/10.2307/25111943?uid=3739256&uid=2&uid=4&sid=21103281890353>.

Hite, Molly. *Ideas of Order in the Novels of Thomas Pynchon*. Columbus: Ohio State U.P., 1983. Print.

Holquist, Michael. "Whodunit and Other Questions: Metaphysical Detective Stories in Post-War Fiction." *New Literary History* 3 (1971): 135–56. Print.

Horowitz, Mark. "The Unofficial Thomas Pynchon Guide to Los Angeles (and vice versa)." *Wired* 17.08 (2009). 1 Jan. 2014. <http://www.wired.com/special_multimedia/2009/pl_print_1708>.

Horvath, Brooke, and Irving Malin, eds. *Pynchon and* Mason & Dixon. Newark: U. of Delaware P., 2000. Print.

Howard, Ebenezer. *Garden Cities of To-morrow.* London: Swan Sonnenschein & Co., 1902. Print.

Hume, Kathryn. *Pynchon's Mythography: An Approach to* Gravity's Rainbow. Carbondale: Southern Illinois U.P., 1987. Print.

Ickstadt, Heinz. "Setting Sail Against the Day: The Narrative World of Thomas Pynchon." *Against the Grain: Reading Pynchon's Counternarratives*. Ed. Sascha Pöhlmann. Amsterdam: Rodopi, 2010. 35–47. Print.

Jackson, Kenneth T. *Crabgrass Frontier: The Suburbanization of the United States*. New York: Oxford U.P., 1985. Print.

James, P. D. *Talking about Detective Fiction*. New York: Alfred A. Knopf, 2009. Print.

Jameson, Fredric. "The Case for Georg Lukacs." *Marxism and Form: Twentieth Century Theories of Dialectical Literature*. Princeton, NJ: Princeton U.P., 1971. 160–205. Print.

———. "The Existence of Italy." *Signatures of the Visible*. New York: Routledge, 1992. 155–230. Print.

———. *Postmodernism: or, the Cultural Logic of Late Capitalism*. Durham, NC: Duke U.P., 1991. Print.

Janeway, Michael. *Republic of Denial: Press, Politics, and Public Life*. New Haven, CT: Yale U.P., 1999. Print.

Kerouac, Jack. *On the Road*. New York: Viking, 1957. Print.

Kolodny, Annette, and Daniel James Peters. "Pynchon's *The Crying of Lot 49*: The Novel as Subversive Experience." *Modern Fiction Studies* 19.1 (1973): 79–87. Print.

Korzybski, Alfred. "A Non-Aristotelian System and Its Necessity for Rigour in Mathematics and Physics." *Science and Sanity: An Introduction to Non-Aristotelian Systems and General Semantics*. 1933. Forest Hills, NY: Institute of General Semantics, 1994. 5th ed. 747–61. Print.

Krafft, John M. "Biographical Note." *The Cambridge Companion to Thomas Pynchon*. Ed. Inger H. Dalsgaard, Luc Herman, and Brian McHale. Cambridge: Cambridge U.P., 2011. 9–16. Print.

Kunstler, James Howard. *The Geography of Nowhere: The Rise and Decline of America's Man-made Landscape*. New York: Simon and Schuster, 1993. Print.

———. *Home from Nowhere: Remaking Our Everyday World for the Twenty-first Century*. New York: Simon & Schuster, 1996. Print.

Latour, Bruno. *Reassembling the Social: An Introduction to Actor-Network-Theory*. Oxford: Oxford U.P., 2005. Print.

Lem, Stanislaw. *The Investigation*. New York: Seabury Press, 1974. Print.

Lethem, Jonathan. *Gun, with Occasional Music.* San Diego, CA: Harcourt Brace, 1994. Print.

Leverenz, David. "On Trying to Read *Gravity's Rainbow.*" *Mindful Pleasures: Essays on Thomas Pynchon*. Ed. George Levine and David Leverenz. Boston: Little, Brown & Co., 1976. 229–49. Print.

Levine, George. "Risking the Moment: Anarchy and Possibility in Pynchon's Fiction." *Mindful Pleasures: Essays on Thomas Pynchon*. Ed. George Levine and David Leverenz. Boston: Little, Brown & Co., 1976. 113–36. Print.

Levine, George, and David Leverenz, eds. *Mindful Pleasures: Essays on Thomas Pynchon*. Boston: Little, Brown & Co., 1976. Print.

Logan, William. "Back to the Future: On Thomas Pynchon's *Against the Day.*" *Virginia Quarterly Review* 83.3 (2007): 226–47. Web. 1 Jan 2014. <http://www.vqronline.org/articles/2007/summer/logan-pynchon-against-the-day/>.

Lukacs, Georg. "Balzac and Stendhal." *Studies in European Realism*. New York: Grosset and Dunlap, 1964. 72–76. Print.

———. "Balzac: *Lost Illusions.*" *Studies in European Realism*. New York: Grosset and Dunlap, 1964. 47–64. Print.

———. "Balzac: *The Peasants.*" *Studies in European Realism*. New York: Grosset and Dunlap, 1964. 21–46. Print.

———. "Preface." *Studies in European Realism*. New York: Grosset and Dunlap, 1964. 1–20. Print.

Lynch, David. *Catching the Big Fish: Meditation, Consciousness, and Creativity*. New York: Penguin, 2006. Print.

Lynd, Margaret. "Science, Narrative, and Agency in *Gravity's Rainbow.*" *Critique* 46.1 (2004): 63–80. Print.

Marion, Jean-Luc. *God without Being: Hors-Texte*. Trans., Thomas A. Carlson. Chicago: Chicago U.P., 1991. Religion and Postmodernism. Print.

McCarthy, Cormac. *No Country for Old Men*. New York: Alfred A. Knopf, 2005. Print.

McCulloch, J. Huston. "The Vinland Map: Some Finer Points of the Debate." Mar. 2005. Last updated Aug. 2009. Web. 1 Jan. 2014. <http://www.econ.ohio-state.edu/jhm/arch/vinland/vinland.htm>.

McHale, Brian. "Genre as History: Pynchon's Genre-Poaching." *Pynchon's* Against the Day*: A Corrupted Pilgrim's Guide.*" Ed. Jeffrey Severs and Christopher Leise. Newark: U. of Delaware P., 2011. 15–28. Print.

Mendelson, Edward. "Gravity's Encyclopedia." *Mindful Pleasures: Essays on Thomas Pynchon*. Ed. George Levine and David Leverenz. Boston: Little, Brown, 1976. 29–52. Print.

———. "The Sacred, the Profane, and *The Crying of Lot 49*." *Individual and Community: Variations on a Theme in American Fiction*. Ed. Kenneth H. Baldwin and David K. Kirby. Durham, NC: Duke U.P., 1975. 185-222. Rev. version in *Pynchon: A Collection of Critical Essays*. Ed. Edward Mendelson. Upper Saddle River, NJ: Prentice-Hall, 1978. 112-46. Print.

Miller, John. "Present Subjunctive: Pynchon's California Novels." *Critique: Studies in Contemporary Fiction* 54.3 (2013): 225–37. Print.

Miller, Laura. "Pynchon Lights Up." *Salon* 31 Jul. 2009. Web. 1 Jan. 2014. <http://www.salon.com/books/review/2009/07/31/pynchon/>.

Molloy, Seán. "Escaping the Politics of the Irredeemable Earth: Anarchy and Transcendence in the Novels of Thomas Pynchon." *Theory & Event* 13.3 (2010). *Project Muse*. Web. <http://muse.jhu.edu/journals/theory_and_event/summary/v013/13.3.molloy.html>.

Nancy, Jean-Luc. "Atheism and Monotheism." *Weakening Philosophy: Essays in Honour of Gianni Vattimo*. Ed. Santiago Zabala. Montreal: McGill-Queen's U.P., 2007. 387–99. Print.

"Nation: Occupied Berkeley." *Time*. 30 May 1969. Web. 1 Jan. 2014. <http://www.time.com/time/magazine/article/0,9171,840109-1,00.html>.

Nietzsche, Friedrich. *Beyond Good and Evil*. 1886. Trans., R. J. Hollingdale. London: Penguin Books, 1973. Print.

Olderman, Raymond M. "The New Consciousness and the Old System." *Approaches to* Gravity's Rainbow. Ed. Charles Clerc. Columbus: Ohio State U.P., 1983. 199–228. Print.

Patell, Cyrus K. *Negative Liberties: Morrison, Pynchon and the Problem of Liberal Ideology*. Durham, NC: Duke U.P., 2001. Print.

Porter, Dennis. *The Pursuit of Crime: Art and Ideology in Detective Fiction*. New Haven, CT: Yale U.P., 1981. Print.

Pynchon, Thomas. Advertisement video for *Inherent Vice* (voiceover). *YouTube*. 4 Aug 2009. Web. 1 Jan 2014. <http://www.youtube.com/watch?v=RjWKPdDko_U>.

———. *Against the Day*. New York: Viking, 2006. Print.

———. *Against the Day* book description. *Amazon*. 2006. Web. 1 Jan 2014. <http://www.amazon.com/Against-Day-Thomas-Pynchon/dp/159420120X>.

———. *Bleeding Edge*. New York: The Penguin Press, 2013. Print.

———. *The Crying of Lot 49*. 1966. New York: HarperPerennial, 1999. Print.

———. *Gravity's Rainbow*. 1973. New York: Penguin, 1995. Print.

———. "The Heart's Eternal Vow." Rev. of *Love in the Time of Cholera*, by Gabriel García Márquez. *New York Times Book Review*, 10 April 1988, 1, 47, 49. *The Modern*

Word. N.d. 2 Jan 2014. <http://www.themodernword.com/pynchon/pynchon_essays_cholera.html>.

———. *Inherent Vice*. New York: Penguin, 2009. Print.

———. "Is it O.K. to be a Luddite?" *The New York Times Book Review*, 28 October 1984, 1, 40–41. Print.

———. "A Journey into the Mind of Watts." *The New York Times Magazine*, 12 June 1966,: 34–35, 78, 80–82, 84. Print.

———. *Mason & Dixon*. New York: Holt, 1997. Print.

———. "Nearer, My Couch, to Thee." *The New York Times Book Review* 6 June 1993: 3, 57. Print.

———. *Slow Learner: Early Stories*. 1984. London: Vintage, 2000. Print.

———. *V.* New York: Bantam, 1963. Print.

———. *Vineland*. New York: Penguin, 1990. Print.

"Pynchon Wiki: *Inherent Vice*." *PynchonWiki*. 12 Nov. 2011. Web. 18 May 2012. <http://inherent-vice.pynchonwiki.com/wiki/index.php?title=Main_Page>.

Reid, Robert L. "Paving America from Coast to Coast." *Civil Engineering* 76.6 (2006): 37+. *Academic Search Complete*. Web. 30 July 2012.

Robberds, Mark. "The New Historicist Creepers of *Vineland*." *Critique: Studies in Contemporary Fiction* 36.4 (1995): 237–49. Print.

Rodriguez, Richard. "Where the Poppies Grow." *Made in California: Art, Image, and Identity, 1900–2000*. Ed. Stephanie Barron, Sheri Bernstein, and Ilene Susan Fort. Berkeley: U. of California P., 2000. 273–80. Print.

Ronell, Avital. *Crack Wars: Literature Addiction Mania*. Lincoln: U. of Nebraska P. 1992. Print.

Roosevelt, Theodore. "Address at Ventura, California, May 9, 1903." N.d. *The American Presidency Project*, Theodore Roosevelt: XXVI President of the United States, 1901–1909. 2 Jan. 2014. <http://www.presidency.ucsb.edu/ws/?pid=97714>.

Rorty, Richard. "Anticlericalism and Atheism." *The Future of Religion*. Ed. Santiago Zabala. New York: Columbia U.P., 2005. 29–41. Print.

Rorty, Richard, Gianni Vattimo, and Santiago Zabala. "What Is Religion's Future after Metaphysics?" *The Future of Religion*. Ed. Santiago Zabala. New York: Columbia U.P., 2005. 55–81. Print.

Rosenfeld, Aaron. "'The Scanty plot': Orwell, Pynchon, and the Poetics of Paranoia." *Twentieth Century Literature* 50 (2004): 337–68. Print.

Rushdie, Salman. "Still Crazy after All These Years: *Vineland* by Thomas Pynchon." Rev. of *Vineland*, by Thomas Pynchon. *The New York Times Book Review* 14 Jan. 1990: 1, 36–37. Print.

Schaub, Thomas Hill. "*The Crying of Lot 49* and Other California Novels." *The Cam-*

bridge Companion to Thomas Pynchon. Ed. Inger H. Dalsgaard, Luc Herman, and Brian McHale. Cambridge: Cambridge U.P., 2011. 30–43. Print.

———. "Open Letter in Response to Edward Mendelson's 'The Sacred, the Profane, and *The Crying of Lot 49*.'" *boundary 2: A Journal of Postmodern Literature and Culture* 5.1 (1976): 93–102. Print.

Shoop, Casey. "Thomas Pynchon, Postmodernism, and the Rise of the New Right in California." *Contemporary Literature* 53.1 (2012): 51–86. *Project MUSE*. Web. 30 July 2012. <http://muse.jhu.edu/login?auth=0&type=summary&url=/journals/contemporary_literature/v053/53.1.shoop.html>.

Simmons, Philip E. *Deep Surfaces: Mass Culture & History in Postmodern American Fiction*. Athens: U. of Georgia P., 1997. Print.

Simon, Jeff. "Going to the Beach with Thomas Pynchon." *The Buffalo News* 2 Aug. 2009. 2 Jan 2014. <http://www.highbeam.com/doc/1P2-21709639.html>.

Slade, Joseph. *Thomas Pynchon*. New York: Peter Lang, 1990. Print.

Smith, Adam. *The Theory of Moral Sentiments*. 1759. New York: Gutenberg Publishers, 2011.

———. *The Wealth of Nations*. 1776. Blacksburg, VA: Thrifty Books, 2009.

Spanos, William V. "The Detective and the Boundary: Some Notes on the Postmodern Literary Imagination." *boundary 2* 20–21 (1972): 147–68. Print.

Special Committee to Investigate Organized Crime in Interstate Commerce. "Organized Crime in Interstate Commerce." Final report. Washington, DC: U.S. Government Printing Office, 1951.

Spencer, Nicholas. *After Utopia: The Rise of Critical Space in Twentieth-Century American Fiction*. Lincoln: U. of Nebraska P., 2006. Print.

St. Clair, Justin. "Binocular Disparity and Pynchon's Panoramic Paradigm." *Pynchon's* Against the Day*: A Corrupted Pilgrim's Guide*. Ed. Jeffrey Severs and Christopher Leise. Newark: U. of Delaware P., 2011. 67–88. Print.

Stivale, Charles J. Overview of *L'Abécédaire de Gilles Deleuze*, with Claire Parnet. 1996. Web. Last updated 28 Jul. 2011. 2 Jan. 2014. <http://www.langlab.wayne.edu/cstivale/d-g/abc1.html>.

Sweeney, Susan Elizabeth. "'Subject-Cases' and 'Book-Cases': Impostures and Forgeries from Poe to Auster." *Detecting Texts: The Metaphysical Detective Story from Poe to Postmodernism*. Ed. Patricia Merivale and Susan Elizabeth Sweeney. Philadelphia: U. of Pennsylvania P., 1999. 247–69. Print.

Tani, Stefano. *The Doomed Detective: The Contribution of the Detective Novel to Postmodern American and Italian Fiction*. Carbondale: Southern Illinois U.P., 1984. Print.

Tanner, Tony. *City of Words: American Fiction, 1950–1970*. New York: Harper and Row, 1971. Print.

———. *Thomas Pynchon*. London: Methuen, 1982. Print.

Thomas, Samuel. *Pynchon and the Political*. New York: Routledge, 2007. Print.

Thompson, Hunter S. *Fear and Loathing in Las Vegas: A Savage Journey to the Heart of the American Dream*. New York: Random House, 1971. Print.

Thoreen, David. "The President's Emergency War Powers and the Erosion of Civil Liberties in Pynchon's *Vineland*." *Oklahoma City Law Review* 24.3 (1999): 761–98. Print.

Vahanian, Gabriel. "The Death of God: An Afterword." *After the Death of God*. Ed. Jeffrey W. Robbins. New York: Columbia U.P., 2007. 163–78. Print.

Varnelis, Kazys. "Cathedrals of the Culture Industry." 30 May 2005. Web. 3 Jan. 2014. <http://varnelis.net/articles/cathedrals>. Originally "Catedrales de la industria de la cultura." *Pasajes de Arquitectura y Critica* 39 (2002): 14–17. English version republished in *Los Angeles Forum for Architecture and Design Annual* 2004, 35–40. Web. <http://laforum.org/wp-content/uploads/2005/01/2004annual.pdf >.

Vattimo, Gianni. "The Age of Interpretation." *The Future of Religion*. Ed. Santiago Zabala. Trans., Santiago Zabala. New York: Columbia U.P., 2005. 43–54. Print.

———. "A Prayer for Silence: Dialogue with Gianni Vattimo." *After the Death of God*. Ed. Jeffrey W. Robbins. New York: Columbia U.P., 2007. 89–113. Print.

Veggian, Henry. "Thomas Pynchon Against the Day." *boundary 2* 35.1 (2008): 197–215. Print.

Waldie, Donald J. *Holy Land: A Suburban Memoir*. New York: W. W. Norton, 1996. Print.

Wallace, David Foster. *Infinite Jest*. Boston: Little, Brown, 1996. Print.

Wark, Kenneth McKenzie. *The Beach beneath the Street: The Everyday Life and Glorious Times of the Situationist International*. London: Verso, 2011. Print.

Weisenburger, Steven C. *A* Gravity's Rainbow *Companion*. 2nd ed. Athens: U. of Georgia P., 2006. Print.

West, Nathanael. *The Dream Life of Balso Snell*. New York: Contact Editions, 1931. Print.

Wheaton, Elizabeth. *Codename Greenkil: The 1979 Greensboro Killings*. Athens: U. of Georgia P., 1987. Print.

Wilde, Alan. "Love and Death in and around Vineland, U.S.A." *boundary 2* 18.2 (1991), 166–80. Print.

Wilson, Edmund. *Axel's Castle: A Study of the Imaginative Literature of 1870–1930*. New York: Charles Scribner's Sons, 1931.

Wilson, Rob, "On the Pacific Edge of Catastrophe, or Redemption: California Dreaming in Thomas Pynchon's *Inherent Vice*." *boundary 2* 37.2(2010): 217–25. Print.

Wood, James. *The Broken Estate: Essays on Literature and Belief*. New York: Modern Library, 2000. Print.

———. "Human, All Too Inhuman." *The New Republic Online* 30 Aug. 2001. *Powell's Books Review-a-Day*. <http://www.powells.com/review/2001_08_30.html>.

Zabala, Santiago. "Christianity and the Death of God: A Response to Cardinal Lustiger." *Common Knowledge* 11.1 (2005): 33–40. Print.

———. "Introduction." *The Future of Religion*. By Richard Rorty and Gianni Vattimo. Ed. Santiago Zabala. New York: Columbia U.P., 2005. 1–27. Print.

Zinn, Howard. *A People's History of the United States*. New York: HarperCollins, 1980.

Index

THE NEW AMERICAN CANON

Violet America: Regional Cosmopolitanism in U.S. Fiction since the Great Depression
by Jason Arthur

The Legacy of David Foster Wallace
edited by Samuel Cohen
and Lee Konstantinou

American Unexceptionalism: The Everyman and the Suburban Novel after 9/11
Kathy Knapp

Pynchon's California
edited by Scott McClintock
and John Miller

Reading Capitalist Realism
edited by Alison Shonkwiler
and Leigh Claire La Berge

To my dear friends
Jim and Romy Burrows

1 Thessalonians 1:2-3

Contents

INTRODUCTION

Your Life Is a Sermon

God saves us just as we are, but he is not content for us to remain just as we are.

No—God's great purpose for us, having saved us, is to conform us into the image of Christ (Romans 8:28-29). In fact, that is the good for which he is always working in all aspects of our lives. There are not two versions of Christianity—the "basic" option, in which our souls are saved but our characters remain unchanged, and the "deluxe" option for those who are super-committed, which involves the hard work of becoming more like Jesus. Christianity is about both justification—the work of God in our lives to bring us to faith in Christ, that he might take our judgment and give us his perfection—and sanctification—the ongoing process in which God is at work to make us more and more like our Savior. The Bible calls us to become what we are so that what God has done will be transparently clear.

In other words, God cares about what you are like. He cares about your character.

The New Testament, therefore, is full of exhortations to turn away from who we were and fully embrace who we now are. "If then you have been raised with Christ"—since we have a new identity—there is an "old self" that we are to put off and a "new self, which is being renewed … after the image of its creator," that we are to put on (Colossians 3:1, 9-10). The Christian life involves change.

Wherever you open it up, you do not have to read many pages of the New Testament to find this kind of encouragement to become who you are. God is concerned with our character, for, as Jesus put it, "by this my Father is glorified, that you bear much fruit" (John 15:8).

Not only that, but your character is preaching a message, one way or another, as you go about your life each day.

In his letter to Titus, Paul tells him to "teach what accords with sound doctrine" (2:1) "so that in everything [believers] may adorn the doctrine of God our Savior" (v 10).[1] There is a way to live that will both display the truth about God and make the truth about God attractive. As J.B. Phillips paraphrases that verse, we are called to be "a living testimonial to the teaching of God our saviour."

And so the question we need to wrestle with is not simply "Does my ability to articulate the gospel make people want to believe it?" or "Does my ability to answer questions—to act as an apologist—make people want to believe?" but "Does my *character* make the gospel attractive so as to make people wish they believed it?"

---

1 The apostle is speaking here in particular about what Titus is to teach to Christian bondservants—but the principle remains true more widely.

Ours is a divided and disappointed age. But there is a way to live that makes people see that you have what they don't—that makes them see that Christian faith makes a genuine difference to what a person is like and how they navigate life with peace and joy. The reverse, of course, is also true: it is possible to live in such a way that onlookers gain the distinct impression that a profession of belief makes no discernible difference.

So, what do people see in you? As the little poem I was taught as a boy puts it:

> You're writing a gospel,
> A chapter each day,
> By the deeds that you do
> And the words that you say;
> And people read what you write,
> Distorted or true,
> So what is the gospel
> According to you?

When Christians look like Christ, we glorify God and impact the world. It matters. What the church needs today is not primarily better programs or apologetic resources or buildings, or more financial resources or greater political sway. What the church needs is Christians of increasingly Christlike character, so that what is found inside the church is radically different than the world outside the church. God cares about our character far more than he does our gifts or achievements or qualifications. If it were a crime for our churches to be places of radical love and distinctive kindness, for instance, would they be found guilty? If it were a crime for me to be full of joy and patience, would *I* be convicted?

In other words, am I, every day, in every way, making the gospel of the Lord Jesus attractive—not in what I say so much as in what I am like? How am I reflecting the glory of my Savior to the world he loved so much that he was born into it in order to die for it?

If you are like me, the answers to those questions as you consider your own life will be partly encouraging and primarily challenging. For none of us, if we are honest, are all that we would like to be. Most of us, in our quieter moments, wish we were better at the Christian life. Many of us, if we have been following Jesus for any stretch of time, are frustrated that we have not changed as much as we thought we would.

The danger of pointing out that God cares about your character and is not content for you to remain as you are is that it leads you to resolve to be better, to do better, to work harder. But that is not how real change comes, for that is not how Christlikeness is achieved.

We will be changed—but Christian change is produced in us, not by us. It is the work of the Spirit. God cares about your character enough to be at work on your character.

So this little book is about what you are like and what you will become like—or, to put it in the imagery the apostle Paul famously deploys in Galatians 5, it is about "the fruit of the Spirit" in the life of the believer: love, joy, peace, patience, kindness, goodness, faithfulness, gentleness, and self-control (v 22-23). These are nine inner glories whose presence (or lack) will reveal itself in what we say and what we do. This is a picture of an internal godliness that makes a practical difference.

But before we start, we need to pause and ask two questions: first, what does God's word mean by "the fruit of the Spirit"; and second, how does that fruit grow in your life?

WHAT IS THE FRUIT?

First, notice that Paul says "fruit," not "fruits." These nine aspects of Christian character together form one indivisible fruit of the Spirit. They are to grow together, not separately; and we are to pursue them collectively, not selectively. Some of us are temperamentally more one of these things and less one of the others. There's therefore a temptation to think that growth in one can make up for a lack in another. But, as John Stott put it, God is not in the business of making lopsided Christians.[2] The work of the Spirit is to grow you in each of these, together.

Second, notice the simple fact that Paul uses fruit as his image. Of course, he is following the Lord Jesus in this, who spoke of himself as the vine and his people as the branches, who are to bear fruit (John 15). But fruit itself is an apt image for the way Christian character is formed in Christian believers, because fruit grows slowly and fruit grows continuously. I am at the edge of my very limited horticultural knowledge here, but I remember that my grandmother would always plant her hyacinth bulbs in the autumn, and they would bloom in the spring, and in between, most of the time, there was little happening, as far as I could see. One day to the next, there was little evidence of growth. Sometimes, all the growth was happening away

2 John R.W. Stott, "The Holy Spirit and Christian Holiness," in *The Keswick Week: 1965* (Marshall, Morgan & Scott, 1965), p.144.

from the naked eye. And yet growth was happening, and beauty was developing. This is how the qualities the Spirit grows develop in us too. We are saved in an instant, when we put our faith in Jesus; we are changed over time, as his Spirit goes to work. Fruit does not grow overnight, but it does grow. We *will* be changed.

Third, fruit comes from faith. Paul is speaking to "those who belong to Christ Jesus" (Galatians 5:24). Christian character is a consequence of having come to faith in Jesus: for those for whom Jesus has given "himself for our sins to deliver us from the present evil age" (1:4); those who have received "adoption as sons" (4:5); and those who have been set free in the Lord Jesus Christ (5:1). Fruit follows faith; fruit does not form faith. It is an inward change of heart that reveals itself in external changes in what we say and do.

It is vital to grasp this. The contents of this book are not like Christmas tree ornaments that you can pick up and attach externally to your life. When you put ornaments on a Christmas tree, they may look attractive for a while, but they're not real; there is no life in them. They are not fruit. After a while, they are taken off again. No—this is real fruit, not plastic fruit, and real fruit grows organically, reflecting the nature of the tree on which it grows. The life that produces true fruit is the life of Christ that is implanted in the believer. Fruit is the evidence of true faith; but it is not the grounds of it. As Tim Keller put it, we are not saved by fruit but by faith—but not fruitless faith. So as you read, where you see that your own life reflects the character God calls for, be encouraged; it is a sign of the genuineness of your faith in Christ—of the transforming work of the Spirit. And

where you see that your own life falls short of that character in some way, don't simply try harder to attach that behavior to your life, like an ornament on a Christmas tree; instead, ask God to go to work in you by his Spirit, so that your heart is changed and real fruit therefore grows.

HOW DOES FRUIT GROW?

Crucially—and this is a truth to which we shall return again and again throughout—the fruit of the Spirit is the fruit *of the Spirit.* It is not manufactured by us; it is cultivated in us. The danger of a book such as this is that its main result is to leave you resolving to put more effort into progressing in the Christian life. But the humbling truth is that you cannot grow this fruit yourself. It is the fruit of the Spirit, and you will need to depend on him and look to him to form this character in you. Yet, at the same time, you are not called to just sit quietly and wait for it to happen. That is, our sanctification—the growth of Christian character in us—is both active and passive, and we must not forget either. Forget the latter and we approach the Christian life as though we can progress in it by our own perspiration—and sooner or later we give up, exhausted. Forget the former and we approach the Christian life as though we can sit down on a couch and wait for the Spirit to do it all for us—and sooner or later we wonder why we have not changed.

Paul describes the biblical dynamic in Philippians 2:

> Work out your own salvation with fear and trembling, for it is God who works in you.
>
> (v 12-13)

God works as we work. As we seek to apply our salvation to each area of our lives, we find that God is at work powerfully to achieve what we could not do in our own strength. To put it another way, you must rely on the Spirit to grow his fruit in you, but you need to work to let the Spirit do his work in you. I cannot provide the power to the toaster in my kitchen but must use the electrical power source that comes into my home. Equally, I cannot change myself but must depend on the Spirit's power. At the same time, though, my toaster does nothing with the electrical power until I turn the toaster on. I have to choose to use the power that is available to me. Likewise, I am called to make the effort to keep in step with the Spirit rather than ignoring or resisting him, either through self-reliance or through complacency.

How, then, does the Spirit work in us to grow this fruit? How are we changed?

> We all, with unveiled face, beholding the glory of the Lord, are being transformed into the same image from one degree of glory to another. For this comes from the Lord who is the Spirit.
>
> (2 Corinthians 3:18)

It is as we look at Jesus that we are changed to become more like Jesus. The example of Christ informs us; the love of Christ inspires us; the Spirit of Christ empowers us. The Lord who is the Spirit shows us Christ in his word, and as we see him, we grow in our devotion to him, and so we are conformed increasingly to his character, slowly and continuously, from one degree of glory to another. The Spirit changes us from inside out, not outside in. As

Jerry Bridges put it, a "focus on the outward structure of character and conduct without taking the time to build the inward foundation of devotion to God" will eventually result in "cold morality or legalism, or even worse, self-righteousness and spiritual pride."[3]

The great secret of growth in true Christian character is to look far less at ourselves and far more at Christ as we depend less on ourselves and more on his Spirit. My prayer is that this book will encourage you to pursue the nine inner glories of the fruit of the Spirit and to depend with humility and confidence on the Spirit to effect that change in you. For it is as we keep in step with him that we will be changed—for God's glory, for our good, and for the sake of the world, which desperately needs to see the difference Christ makes as it looks at the conduct of his people.

3 Jerry Bridges, *The Practice of Godliness* (NavPress, 1996), p.55.

CHAPTER ONE

The Fountain

The outpouring of the love of God is the story of the Bible; and the overflow of the love of God in and from his people is meant to be the story of the church.

Love is the first of the qualities of the fruit of the Spirit that Paul mentions, and I think that this is deliberate on his part. Love is the fountain out of which the rest of the characteristics listed in Galatians 5:22-23 flow. True love is seen in joyfulness and patience and self-control and so on; and true joyfulness and patience and self-control and so on will only flow from love.

I suspect that none of us know how loved we are (though we have an eternity to look forward to in which to perhaps start to begin to grasp it). "In this is love, not that we have loved God but that he loved us" (1 John 4:10). God loves us because he is love (v 8). God is love. He is more than that, but he is never less than that. It is the unique nature of God—Father, Son, and Spirit.

And God's love, which constantly flows within himself, Father, Son, and Spirit, is something we who have put our faith in the Son can experience because "God's love

has been poured into our hearts through the Holy Spirit who has been given to us" (Romans 5:5). We are loved objectively by God—it is an immovable fact that God loves his children. But we can experience subjectively the love of God—it can fill our hearts with gladness. This is because the Spirit works in us to say to us, *Look, you are loved. God loves you as a perfect Father, and that will never change. On your worst days, you are loved beyond measure. On your best days, you are loved beyond measure.*

When I was a child in Scotland, we used to sing:

> God's love is like the sunshine;
> It covers land and sea.
> It fills my heart with gladness
> When I know that God loves me.

This is a wonderful truth, highlighting the very personal nature of God's interest in me and concern for me—and you. God's love has not been injected through a narrow vein. God's love has not dripped upon us in careful measure. God's love has been lavished upon us. It has been poured out upon us. Right now, God is withholding none of his love and care from you. Everything that God is doing in you and for you and around you is because he loves you. After all, "he who did not spare his own Son but gave him up for us all, how will he not also with him graciously give us all things?" (Romans 8:32).

NO REGARD FOR OUR MERITS

What makes God's love for us all the more wonderful is when we consider it in contrast to the truth that, if we are honest, our own expressions of love are proportional to the

attractiveness or worthiness of the object of our affection. So we feel love for and express love to someone who is in some way lovely. But that is not the love of God. God's love has no regard for our merits. As Moses told God's Old Testament people as they prepared to enter the land God had promised to bless them with, "It was not because you were more in number than any other people that the LORD set his love on you and chose you, for you were the fewest of all peoples, but it is because the LORD loves you" (Deuteronomy 7:7-8). Divine love is not predicated or conditional upon its recipient being worthy of it. We could say that it is grounded in the character of the Person who loves rather than in the performance of the person receiving it.

That is deeply humbling, for there is something in us that would like to think of ourselves as fairly good or quite attractive and therefore, to some extent, worthy of God's love. We do not, by nature, adopt the view of ourselves that we were "dead in [our] trespasses and sins" (Ephesians 2:1). As the Anglican Book of Common Prayer, originally written by the 16th-century Reformer Thomas Cranmer, puts it:

> We have left undone those things which we ought to have done; And we have done those things which we ought not have done; And there is no health in us.

But when we consider the height and depth of God's love and, at the same time, acknowledge that we in no way deserve to be the recipients of it, it becomes deeply reassuring. For, if there was nothing we did to earn his love,

there is nothing we can do to lose it. In love, God chose you. In love, God redeemed you. In love, God brought you to faith in Christ. In love, God poured out his Spirit into you so that you would know his love. In love, God will keep you in Christ until you stand before him. Then you will enjoy his love forever.

The nature of God's love is also uniquely unifying. The greatest division throughout human history is the one between God and man, because man is determined to live in enmity toward God, alienated from him (Colossians 1:21), and because God is a just judge who will call everyone to account. What is it that bridged that chasm and made enemies into children? "God so *loved* the world, that he gave his only Son, that whoever believes in him should not perish but have eternal life" (John 3:16, emphasis mine). "Because of his great *love* for us, God, who is rich in mercy, made us alive with Christ even when we were dead in transgressions" (Ephesians 2:4-5, NIV). What bridged the chasm was divine love, the love that sent Jesus to the cross and that sent the Spirit into our hearts.

But God's love unites us not only to him but also to each other. The second greatest division in human history was the one between Jews and Gentiles—those who were part of God's Old Testament people and those who were not. What is it that bridged that chasm and made enemies into brothers and sisters? "In Christ Jesus you who once were far away have been brought near by the blood of Christ … [He] has made the two groups one and has destroyed the barrier, the dividing wall of hostility" (v 13-14, NIV). It was divine love, the love that sent Jesus to the cross and sent the

Spirit into our hearts. This kind of love brings close those who were far away and unites those who were divided.

TO US AND THROUGH US

Why do we linger so long on what God is like and how he loves? Because his love to us is then to flow through us. Fundamentally, the Christian life is very simple: it is all about love. We are loved by God, and then we respond to his love by obeying the two greatest commands, as Jesus summarized the entire law of God: to love the Lord our God with all our heart, soul, mind, and strength—everything we have and are—and to love our neighbor as ourselves (Mark 12:29-31). Love is expressed in both a Godward and a humanward direction. Therefore, our love for those around us is the validation of our declaration of love for God.

This is very hard if you are anything like me. When I am on my own in the car, I can convince myself that I have a great love for God and that I want to love others with the same kind of love that God does. Then someone cuts me off, and suddenly loving others is a lot harder. I am good at loving others in theory, but in practice not so strong. But the validation of genuine love for God is seen in everyday working clothes as I interact with others, not when I am in my Sunday best and singing hymns. "He who does not love his brother whom he has seen," says John, "cannot love God whom he has not seen. And this commandment we have from him: whoever loves God must also love his brother" (1 John 4:20b-21).

Displaying this kind of love is not easy. (It was not easy for Jesus either; it took him to the cross.) But it is a wonderful thing because it is a reassuring and a unifying thing. Ours is

a transactional and divided age. So many of our relationships are based on what others can do for us or what we can do for others. So often, the way others treat us (and the way we treat others) is performance based. And so much of our media discourse, which overflows into our own conversations over the backyard fence or even around our family tables, is marked by division. Think about how status and education and achievements and wealth and background and political allegiance are dividing lines in our wider society and local communities, and even in our friendship groups. It is so pervasive that we often do not notice it.

But the love of God that flows to us and is to flow through us is a unifying force. There is a place where all those divisions are to be dismantled and neutralized—where everything that sets us apart from each other is to be set aside. That place is the people of God. The love of God has been given to us without any regard for our merit, and so we can love others without any regard for their merit. We can look at each other and say to ourselves (or, better, sing to ourselves!):

> I love you with the love of the Lord;
> Yes, I love you with the love of the Lord,
> I can see in you the glory of my King,
> And I love you with the love of the Lord.[4]

There is great wisdom and great power in that.

WHAT LOVE LOOKS LIKE

What does this kind of love—the Christlike love that the Spirit grows in Christ's people—look like?

---

4 Jim Gilbert, "I Love You with the Love of the Lord" (1977).

First, it takes the initiative. God made his plan of salvation before anyone asked him to. Jesus died on the cross without anyone asking him to. God's Spirit went to work in your heart to bring you to faith before you asked him to. Genuine love always takes the initiative. If you have been involved in an argument, whether you were right or wrong or half of each, love looks like seeking to be reconciled. If you see someone in need, whether you know them or not, whether they have been good to you or not, love looks like seeking to bless them.

Second, love is practical. It cannot ignore the needs of a brother or sister. "If anyone has the world's goods and sees his brother in need, yet closes his heart against him, how does God's love abide in him? Little children, let us not love in word or talk but in deed and in truth" (1 John 3:17-18). Again, this is God-like love. Jesus did not only see your greatest need; he met your greatest need. Still today, your Father does not simply know what you need; he provides it (Matthew 6:28-32). And again, this is challenging. We say we love God, and we sing his praise on a Sunday and gather together for Bible study in the week, and we know our doctrine; but then the Bible says, *How is your love? Can it be seen in what you do?*

Third, love forgives. "Be kind to one another, tenderhearted, forgiving one another, as God in Christ forgave you" (Ephesians 4:32). How easy it is for us to say, or think, "I'm prepared to forgive if…" or "I'm prepared to forgive once they…" They need to say sorry first. They need to show me they really mean it first. But love covers over a multitude of sins. Not that those sins don't matter or that there are not necessarily consequences for them—

but love does not hold wrong against the wrongdoer nor withhold blessing from the wrongdoer. Love does not make forgiveness conditional upon performance. God came and sought me out when I was not looking for him, and he forgave all my sins when I did not deserve it (and he still does, every day), and if I will not forgive someone, then I am saying that I don't love God enough to love them. The key to forgiveness is to be overwhelmed by God's love, because God's love is expressed in forgiveness of others.

Fourth, love is not so much about feelings as it is about decisions and actions. To paraphrase John Stott, love is not a victim of our emotions but a servant of our wills.[5] Love will affect our feelings, but it is not based on our feelings and it does not fluctuate with our feelings. This is why the Bible can exhort us to love. It is not asking us to change our feelings but to make a decision, depend on the Spirit, and take the action we're called to. We can pray that our feelings would catch up with our will, but we are not led by our feelings.

Fifth, love is the permanent priority of the Christian life. This is Paul's great point—and warning—in that famous passage in 1 Corinthians 13, a passage which is great to read at a wedding but has not really got anything to do with a wedding because it is about the church. The Corinthian church was a gifted, confident, divisive church. And in the middle of seeking to straighten it all out, Paul says to them (my paraphrase):

> You speak with the tongues of men and angels
> but don't have love? You might as well be a gong

5 John R.W. Stott, *Christ the Liberator* (InterVarsity USA, 1971), p.59.

> or a clanging cymbal. You have prophetic powers, and you understand the whole Bible, and you're very knowledgeable; you have faith; you can move mountains—but no love? You're nothing! You're a very practical Christian. You give away all that you have. You're prepared to deliver up your body to be burned, but you don't have love? Nothing!

Love, then, is the nonnegotiable of the Christian life. With it, all else grows and flourishes. Without it, all else is useless. This supernatural love is not ours by inheritance or temperament, by background or effort. It is not achieved by going on a course or reading a book (including this one!). It is the work of God's Spirit, and he grows it as he sets our gaze on Jesus—on God's love for us in his Son. It is a supernatural love that we need, and that our families and churches and communities need, and it flows out of knowing and appreciating and enjoying God's love for us. Love is all we need; and love is what the Spirit grows.

CHAPTER TWO

A Gloriously Inappropriate Joy

"Dear Pastor Begg," the letter began, "a friend of mine was suffering through brain cancer and its treatments. His relationship with Jesus was such that the nurse on duty wrote as a critical comment on his chart: 'The patient is inappropriately joyful.'

"Since then," said the writer of the note, "it has become one of my goals to be inappropriately joyful."

And, ever since I received that letter almost two decades ago, it has been one of my goals too—for this kind of joy is the joy that Paul is speaking of as he describes the fruit that the Spirit grows in God's people.

WHY JOY IS NOT HAPPINESS

Why did that nurse find it impossible to see how such joy could accompany such dreadful and difficult suffering? I guess it was because she was confusing what we tend to call happiness with what the Bible calls joy.

Happiness is rooted in the Old Norse word *hap*, which means "chance." Happiness is a spontaneous response to temporary pleasures. It is the feeling that we enjoy when things that matter to us in this life are going well. It is therefore a feeling that rises and falls in proportion to the happenstances, the chances, of life. There is not much happiness in the cancer wards of hospitals. And of course some of us, due to our personality or to our past, have a higher baseline starting point and so are quicker to feel happy and slower to stop.

By contrast, when the Bible speaks of joy, it is not talking about something that is determined by all being well in our world. Happiness depends on what happens; joy shapes our attitude to what happens. So it is that it is possible to know a joy that is not touched by the circumstances of life and is therefore inappropriate to—or inexplicable by—what is going on right now. That is why joy may be experienced when we are facing illness, or dealing with bereavement, or facing redundancy—when circumstances are difficult.

This is the joy that Paul speaks of in Galatians 5:22 and that Peter describes as he writes to a church that is experiencing great hardship and suffering in 1 Peter 1:

> Though you have not seen [Jesus], you love him. Though you do not now see him, you believe in him and rejoice with joy that is inexpressible and filled with glory. (v 8)

These people were enjoying a joy that was inexpressible and inexplicable—that was inappropriate to the state of their earthly lives. And this verse reveals the source of that kind

of joy, and it is startlingly straightforward: it is the result of believing the gospel. At the heart of Christian joy is the joy of salvation.

Joy is experienced when my conscience accuses me and I know that Jesus, the Son of God, has forgiven me.

Joy is experienced when I'm aware of my failures but I know that my sin has been washed clean and I have been given the righteousness of Christ.

Joy is experienced when life disappoints me, or I disappoint myself, but I know that God is bringing me day by day toward a heavenly home where nothing will perish or spoil or fade.

Joy is experienced when I'm aware of my lack of power to live as I want to and as God commands me to but I know that his Spirit is at work in me to will and to act according to his good purpose (Philippians 2:13).

Joy is experienced when I feel weak but I remember that God is mighty and holds me in his powerful hand.

Joy is experienced when my outer body is wasting away but I know that he is dwelling in me and renewing me inwardly and that one day I will stand before him in my resurrection body. (This is the joy that that nurse witnessed and was so struck by in the hospital.)

This is Christian joy, and it is unique because it is produced just by believing the gospel, and by just believing the gospel. As John Newton put it:

> Solid joys and lasting treasures
> None but Zion's children know.[6]

---

6 John Newton, "Glorious Things of Thee Are Spoken" (1779).

THINKING ABOUT IT

This is a joy that the world can not only not explain but also not achieve. It seems to me that in Western culture today we have more than we have ever had—longer lives, better health, more money, greater comforts, faster technology—and yet we are more unhappy than we have ever been. The promise of every commercial is that if you just have a bit more, you'll feel successful and secure, you'll be popular and content—you'll be happy. But the ever-continuing production of new brands and models and upgrades, and new commercials to make promises about them to us, is evidence that this is really a lie. Behind the smiles most of us paint on our faces to head out into the world, and even to walk into church, there are all kinds of fears and regrets and challenges and tears despite all our advances in knowledge and accumulation of possessions.

Our culture's response to the reality of this being a broken world and our bodies being mortal things is to not think about it. As long ago as the 17th century, the French philosopher and mathematician Blaise Pascal said, "Being unable to cure death, wretchedness and ignorance, men have decided, in order to be happy, not to think about such things."[7] We aim to push the idea of death, and the reality of the wretchedness of the world around us and the wretchedness of our hearts within us, to the back of our minds. If we don't think about them, then we give ourselves the possibility of being happy—if only we could bend our circumstances in our favor and then maintain them in that state.

---

7 Blaise Pascal, *Pensées,* trans. A.J. Krailsheimer (Penguin, 1966), p.66.

Christian faith, on the other hand, allows us to think about each of those things, to face them head-on, and still to be "filled with an inexpressible and glorious joy" (1 Peter 1:8, NIV). Why? Because our faith, and therefore our joy, is based on an objective reality rather than subjective feelings. One of our problems with joy is that we want to have more of it, and therefore we focus on how much we have of it and how we can produce more of it. But the path to joy is found not in thinking about our joy but about our faith. Christian joy is anchored in the facts of Christian faith. That's why Peter doesn't say, *You think about your joy, and you are filled with more of it.* He says, "You believe in him and are filled with ... joy" (v 8). The key is to rehearse what is objectively true of us, not what is subjectively felt by us.

THE THREE THINGS YOU NEED

It may not seem the most obvious place to go to in a discussion about joy, but the 16th-century Heidelberg Catechism—an instructional series of questions and answers—is very helpful here. The most famous part of this catechism is its first question and answer:

> Q: What is your only comfort in life and death?
>
> A: That I am not my own, but belong with body and soul, both in life and in death, to my faithful Saviour Jesus Christ. He has fully paid for all my sins with his precious blood, and has set me free from all the power of the devil. He also preserves me in such a way that without the will of my heavenly Father not a hair can fall from my head;

> indeed, all things must work together for my salvation. Therefore, by his Holy Spirit he also assures me of eternal life and makes me heartily willing and ready from now on to live for him.[8]

That's quite the answer! And then it moves on (unsurprisingly) to question 2:

> What do you need to know in order to live and die in the joy of this comfort?

Suddenly, we are thinking about joy. But again, notice that the question is not "What do I need to feel?" or "What do I need to change?" or "What do I need to gain?" but "What do I need to *know*?"

And the answer?

> First, how great my sin and misery are; second, how I am delivered from all my sins and misery; third, how I am to be thankful to God for such deliverance.[9]

In other (less eloquent) words, to know Christian joy, I need to know my guilt. No one wants to feel guilty, but there is no awareness of or appreciation for grace without first understanding our guilt. The natural state of our souls is that they suffer the condition of sin. Individual sins, like envy and lust and racism and pride, are symptoms of this heart condition. "All have sinned and fall short of the glory of God" (Romans 3:23), and "the wages of sin is death" (6:23). This is a reality the world chooses not to

---

8 https://www.heidelberg-catechism.com/pdf/lords-days/Heidelberg-Catechism.pdf (accessed January 6, 2026).

9 As above.

face because it cannot coexist with happiness—it causes "misery." But you will not experience supernatural joy until you acknowledge your own lostness.

Second, to know Christian joy, I need to know God's grace. "You were dead in the trespasses and sins in which you once walked, following the course of this world"—but gloriously, that is in the past tense, not the present. Why? Because "God, being rich in mercy, because of the great love with which he loved us, even when we were dead in our trespasses, made us alive together with Christ" (Ephesians 2:1-2, 4-5).

Here's the wonder of it: I have "God's Riches At Christ's Expense." That's grace. By nature, I am enslaved; Jesus set me free. By nature, I am condemned; Jesus gives mercy. By nature, I am dead; Jesus brings life. I am guilty; Jesus forgives me. I don't need Jesus merely to help me; I need him to save me. He is not merely a supplement to improve my spiritual health; he is a Savior who brings me from death to life. The Christian admits their guilt and wonders at grace:

> What grace is mine, that he who dwells in endless
>   light
> Called through the night to find my distant soul
> And from his scars poured mercy that would plead
>   for me,
> That I might live and in his name be known.[10]

Therefore, third, to know Christian joy I need to respond with gratitude. The 20th-century theologian Karl Barth got some things wrong in his theology and a great deal

10 Keith and Kristyn Getty, "What Grace Is Mine" (2008).

more wrong in his private life, but nevertheless, he was right when he wrote:

> Grace and gratitude belong together like heaven and earth. Grace evokes gratitude like the voice of an echo. Gratitude follows grace like thunder lightning.[11]

Reflect on the paragraph and song verse above. Say it out loud and know that through faith in Christ all this is true of you. Grace will evoke gratitude—how can it not? And as gratitude follows grace, so joy follows gratitude. Joy is the experiential impact of the thunder of gratitude.

This is uniquely Christian joy, and it springs from the gratitude of knowing that I am guilty and God is gracious. That's why the Bible is full of joy, because it is full of people who are willing to accept that first truth and therefore glory in the second. "Oh come, let us sing to the LORD," says the psalmist: "let us make a joyful noise to the rock of our salvation!" (Psalm 95:1). Joy flows from knowing we are saved. It is the result of believing the gospel.

THREE OBSTACLES TO JOY

And yet often I am not joyful. All too often our churches are marked by things other than joy, and a neighbor would not report that they discovered an "inappropriate joy" as they looked at our lives or witnessed our church gatherings. What is it that prevents us from living out the joy that the Spirit seeks to grow in us? Here are three stranglers of your joy.

---

11 Karl Barth, *Church Dogmatics*, vol. 4, *The Doctrine of Reconciliation: Part One*, ed. G.W. Bromiley and T.F. Torrance (T. & T. Clark, 1936), p.41.

Foolishness: The folly of turning our backs on God and living as though the things of this creation are worthy of our primary focus—as though the things of this creation are able to give us joy. We have an inbuilt tendency to embrace all kinds of things that unravel all that God intends for us to be. C.S. Lewis describes this so well in his collection of writings titled *The Weight of Glory*:

> We are half-hearted creatures, fooling about with drink and sex and ambition when infinite joy is offered us, like an ignorant child who wants to go on making mud pies in a slum because he cannot imagine what is meant by the offer of a holiday at the sea. We are far too easily pleased.[12]

Put another way, you will find Christian joy elusive for as long as you seek worldly happiness and continue to kid yourself that what the world offers will suffice for you.

Forgetfulness: "Bless the Lord, O my soul, and forget not all his benefits" (Psalm 103:2). If we forget what God has done, is doing, and will do for us, then we will fail to bless him—to be grateful to him. And without the thunder of gratitude there will not be the impact of joy. One of the great stranglers of joy for the believer is simply that we forget the gospel. This is why Jesus gave us the Lord's Supper—so that we wouldn't forget. When you eat the bread and drink the wine, you are being reminded that Jesus had to die for you—you are a guilty sinner, but, in his grace, he took your sin and invited you to life with him. You're being reminded that Jesus will return for you—that

12 C.S. Lewis, "The Weight of Glory," in *The Weight of Glory and Other Addresses* (Harper Collins, 2001), p.26.

one day you will sit and eat with him, face-to-face. Guilt, grace, gratitude—joy. The primary response at the Lord's Table when we take Communion should be a deep-seated joy as we reflect on the great truths of the gospel.

Faintheartedness: That is, being dragged down by past failings and sins as though we are defined by our past. We are prone not only to forget what we should remember but also to remember what we should forget. What does Satan want to do? To remind you of your sins: to convince you that you continue to be marked by them and can never move beyond them. He wants you to look into yourself and see your shortcomings rather than to look up to Christ and see his sufficiency—to look within and see your failings rather than to look up to Christ and enjoy his forgiveness.

WHEN YOU'RE NOT JOYFUL

All this talk of joy, though, may lead us to worry. What if we simply don't feel joyful? What if we find ourselves surrounded in church on a Sunday by others who seem much more joyful than we are? Well, first, don't confuse the reality of a deep-seated joy with subjective expressions of it. It is probably true to say that the existence of true Christian joy is evidenced more in the aftermath of a diagnosis or disappointment than it is in how we sing on a sunny Sunday morning.

Second, remember that joy can coexist with deep sadness—indeed, with depression. (This is another way in which it is utterly different from worldly happiness.) The great Victorian preacher C.H. Spurgeon was no stranger to physical pain and internal depression. He wrote (and I paraphrase somewhat), "I have learned to be joyful in the

aftermath of my illness, but I must confess, I was not joyful in the experience of my illness." Then he says, "What am I then to say? I am to say that I am a growing Christian, that I am learning as I go." If you struggle with joy, do not demand more of yourself than God does. He asks that you grow, and he asks that you grow by depending on the Spirit. We are all works in progress, and none of us are the finished article.

Third, remember that you are saved by faith, not saved by joy. Have you been as joyful as you should have been this past week? Probably not, any more than you have been as loving as you should have been. So where do you look? Look to Jesus. Remember that you are a sinner, but you are saved by grace. Believe him when he says that he loves you, that he died for you, that he has forgiven you, that he is with you, and that he is looking forward to welcoming you. Let your lack of joy drive you to the gospel. As you do that, you may find that your joy begins to increase—because it is believing the gospel that produces the fruit of inexpressible, indescribable joy that Peter had seen in the recipients of his first epistle and that the nurse had witnessed on that hospital ward. The Spirit is at work to grow in you a joy that is indeed gloriously inappropriate.

CHAPTER THREE

We Have All We Need

Perhaps, like me, you know what it is to feel worried... what it is to wake at 3 a.m. and feel as though life is unraveling... what it is to get up in the morning and feel as though life is a mountain that is impossible to climb.

I think I know what a panic attack feels like (and if it was not a panic attack, then I don't want to imagine having a real one, because that experience was bad enough).

And I know that there will be people reading this chapter who suffer with worry and anxiety far more than I ever have.

So it is important, even at the risk of repetition, to pick up where we left off in the last chapter as we looked at joy: by remembering that you and I are saved by faith in Christ, not by living out the peace that he gives; and that we are works in progress, dependent on the Spirit to grow his fruit and reshape our characters. If you are a naturally anxious person—or if your past or your present has left you with good reason to be fearful as you navigate life—then for you

growth in peace may be startling and encouraging while also being slow and unspectacular to the watching eye.

THE GIFT OF SHALOM

Peace is not just the absence of something but the presence of something. The word for peace used by Paul in Galatians 5:22, *irene*, is the Greek version of the Old Testament Hebrew word *shalom*. And shalom is a rich word, meaning not only the absence of turmoil and conflict but also the presence of everything necessary for well-being and health.

My friend Rico Tice defines this kind of peace like this:

> Shalom is not just "It's okay, I get along with my neighbour and we don't hassle each other and we leave each other to get on with our lives." That would be pretty good. But shalom is one better. It's "I take delight in my neighbour. We so enjoy each other that we take the fence down between each other's gardens; we have barbecues together; we babysit each other's kids."[13]

This is the peace that is being prayed for in the Aaronic blessing used at the end of many church services:

> The LORD bless you and keep you;
> the LORD make his face to shine upon you and be gracious to you;
> the LORD lift up his countenance upon you and give you peace [shalom]. (Numbers 6:24-26)

13 Rico Tice, *Hope Explored* curriculum (The Good Book Company, 2022), p.79.

It's the peace that was being announced by the angels on the first Christmas night:

> Glory to God in the highest, and on earth peace
> [irene] to those on whom his favor rests.
>
> (Luke 2:14, NIV)

And those two passages show us where this kind of shalom-peace is to be found; it is all about knowing that you are at peace with God. Peace cannot be discovered without the light of God's countenance: without knowing that he is gracious to you, without living as someone upon whom his favor rests. Again, therefore, as we consider this shalom, we are thinking about a uniquely Christian kind of peace.

That vertical peace flows out into two areas of horizontal peace. First, shalom is the state of being at peace with others; as Paul puts it as he writes to the church in Rome, it is about living "if possible, so far as it depends on you … peaceably with all" (Romans 12:18). Then, second, it is about living at peace within.

Isn't this what the whole world is looking for? The blessing of knowing you're at peace with your Maker, at peace as you negotiate this world, and at peace with who you are.

FOUND IN A PERSON

But though the world longs for peace, the world finds peace elusive. Apparently, since 1500, 8,000 peace treaties have been signed. Yet look around the world, and it is not long before you see conflict; and very rarely can you spot a sense of true shalom. And of course, what is true on the international scale is no less true on the interpersonal

scale. You may be mourning the lack of peace in your relationship with your parents or your spouse or your children. But since peace within us and around us flows from peace with God, a world that has rejected God will always find itself frustrated in its search for peace. We want peace, but because we try to build it absent of God's presence and rule—in fact, because so often we try to build it in deliberate rejection of his presence and rule—we are as destined to fail as were the builders of the tower of Babel.

So we need Jesus; for peace with God is not found in a program or a philosophy but in a person. "Let not your hearts be troubled," said Jesus on the night before he died, when his disciples had every apparent reason to be troubled. "Believe in God; believe also in me … I have said these things to you, that in me you may have peace" (John 14:1; 16:33). Notice that Jesus does not say, *In my ideas you may have peace,* or *In obedience to God's command you will have peace,* but "In me you may have peace." He says what no one else has been prepared to say: that peace is found simply in knowing him. Buddha offered a philosophy and an example. Muhammad offered a religion. Jesus offers himself. He is the Son of God who can offer peace with the Almighty, and he is the crucified Savior who secures peace with the Almighty. He offers not just the absence of conflict with our Creator, wonderful though that is; he offers the closest of relationships with our Creator—true, lasting, eternal shalom with him. And it is all to be found in him. He is the Prince of Peace (Isaiah 9:6).

And once we know peace with him, then we are in a position to experience peace within.

WHAT PREVENTS PEACE WITHIN

So far, so straightforward. But we need to acknowledge that there are plenty of reasons, even if we have come to Christ, why we struggle to know peace—why anxieties rise up and worry stalks us and concerns keep us awake at night, our minds racing with questions of "What if…?" and "How will I…?" It is well worth naming those things: five hindrances to the peace that Jesus died and rose to offer us and the Spirit dwells within to grow in us.

Unwelcome circumstances: We all know the things that intrude upon our lives and leave us saying, "Why this? Why me? Why now?"

Unconfessed sin: If peace within flows out of peace with God, it follows that disobedience to the clear instruction of the Bible and genuine peace in our hearts cannot go hand in hand. It is so easy to allow a sin to be tolerated in one area of our lives or another, to sequester a part of our thinking or doing over which we say to Jesus, "Mine, not yours." Unacknowledged sin, in God's mercy, does not go unchecked by him. David described this experience as feeling as though his bones were wasting away, as having a heavy hand placed upon him, and as having his strength sapped as though he was doing hard labor on a hot day (Psalm 32:3-4). Then he says, "I acknowledged my sin to you, and I did not cover my iniquity … and you forgave the iniquity of my sin" (v 5). If you know you are guilty of sin, confess it and enjoy the peace of forgiveness. If you choose not to, then do not be surprised when that inner peace feels elusive.

Uncertainty: We don't know what today will hold, we know less about what tomorrow will hold, and we certainly do not know what the next year or the next

decade will hold. Our media is full of things that make us feel uncertain about where this world or our nation is headed. Closer to home, we can never be certain about the happiness of our loved ones or the health of our bodies. We worry about what we don't know—because it's out of our control.

Pain from our past: As we saw in the previous chapter, one of the enemy's great tactics is to accuse us over things that are buried in our past—to unearth that which has been buried by the cross, to seek to bring close that which God has removed as far as the east is from the west. "You know you're still the person who did that?" "Don't you remember when you…?" "You'll never really be free of that decision, will you?" And suddenly, our peace is gone.

Uncontrolled desires: "What causes quarrels and what causes fights among you? Is it not this, that your passions are at war within you? You desire and do not have, so you murder. You covet and cannot obtain, so you fight and quarrel" (James 4:1-2). Notice how James links external conflict with an internal upheaval. You can never have peace with an envious heart—with desires that are not under your control. The envy will eat you up and will spill out into words or actions that bring conflict with others. Each time a friend is successful, it will kill a part of you, as the writer Gore Vidal put it. Uncontrolled desires take us in all kinds of directions but never toward peace.

This is the soil in which peace withers. But if you are a Christian, this is not the soil of your heart, for your heart is a place where Christ dwells by his Spirit. What is the path to peace, even amid all these reasons to feel tossed and roiled and anxious?

BRING IT TO GOD

Here is the way peace takes root and grows within us:

> Rejoice in the Lord always; again I will say, rejoice. Let your reasonableness be known to everyone. The Lord is at hand; do not be anxious about anything, but in everything by prayer and supplication with thanksgiving let your requests be made known to God. And the peace of God, which surpasses all understanding, will guard your hearts and your minds in Christ Jesus.
>
> (Philippians 4:4-7)

Notice that peace does not come without joy—again, we are being shown that the fruit of the Spirit grows together, not one part at a time. If you would be growing more peaceful, you need to be cultivating joy. And then comes the exhortation: "Do not be anxious about anything." "Anything" is a remarkably all-encompassing word! We tend to place an asterisk after it and add as a footnote, "Except the things that seem reasonable to me to worry about." No, says Paul, do not allow yourself to settle for anxiety in any part of your mind or life. Instead, come to God in prayer and supplication.

Paul could just have said "pray," but by adding the word "supplication," he gives a sense of urgency and longing. It puts me in mind of a dog. We used to have a Golden Retriever, and I think he understood supplication. When it was time for his meal, he would be there with us, in front of us, tail wagging, face expectant, making clear what it was that he was asking for. It is the difference between praying, "O God, help me, thank you, amen," and praying, "Lord, I'm coming to you with this issue. Lord, your word says

I should come to you in prayer and supplication—that I should bring the deepest longings of my heart to you. And so, in obedience to your word, I'm doing that. The reason why I'm doing it is because I've been anxious about all of these things that I'm now telling you about, and I'm wanting to come to you and bring them to you and ask you to deal with them in the way that you know is going to be best, and to ask you to help me to trust that you will do just that."

WITH THANKSGIVING

There is peace to be found in bringing things to God in this way—in taking them out of our hands and placing them into his hands (or, more accurately, recognizing that they were never in our hands but were always in his hands, and that that is a far better place for them to be). And this peace is undergirded when we remember the phrase in verse 6 that is so easy to miss: "with thanksgiving." How do you pray with thanksgiving when you are anxious? First, by remembering all the ways in which God has been faithful to you—all that you are able to thank him for despite the situation that is causing you anxiety. Giving thanks tends to put our worries into perspective and reminds our hearts that we have a God who is faithful to his promises, who loves his people, and who will therefore certainly work for our good in the situation about which we have little peace.

Then, second, we are able to pray "with thanksgiving" in the sense of being prepared to thank God whatever the answer is. When we remember that God is faithful, we are able to say to him, "I will thank you. I'm coming in a

spirit of thankfulness. And I thank you that you, Father, know best. This is my earnest plea—this is my genuine supplication, this is the longing of my heart—but I want you to know, Lord, that whatever your answer to my plea, I will thank you." In other words, we can answer "Yes" to the question that the missionary Helen Roseveare imagined the Lord saying to her: "Can you thank me for trusting you with this experience, even if I never tell you why?"

This is what Hannah did in 1 Samuel 1. She was desperately sad, torn apart by her lack of a child. And so she went to the tabernacle, to the place of God's dwelling, and she prayed. She poured out her heart to him. Her supplications were so heartfelt that the high priest, Eli, suspected that she was drunk. But when she finished praying, she "went her way and ate, and her face was no longer sad" (v 18). She had prayed, and now she knew peace before she knew how God would answer her prayer. This is praying with supplication and thanksgiving.

And then the promise is that when you do not settle for being anxious or excuse your worries but instead pray with supplication and thanksgiving, "the peace of God" will be yours. The promise is not that we will be delivered from the situation—not that things will turn out just the way we ask. No, the promise is that, just like Hannah, we will know the peace of God in the situation and regardless of the outcome. We will grow in peace even as we still walk through whatever it was that was causing us to worry. Why? Because we will know that "the Lord is near" and that that is all we really need.

When I was young, we lived in a relatively small town, and I knew the sound of the car engine of everybody who

lived near us. My father would come home from work after I was in bed. But I would not sleep until I heard his car engine come down the street and turn into the driveway. Then I could go to sleep, because my father was there. I knew him. I trusted him. I could sleep secure in the knowledge that he was there.

We have a heavenly Father. We know him. We can trust him. And so we can sleep secure in the knowledge that he is with us. He may direct our paths in ways we would not have chosen. He may allow circumstances to persist in our lives that we would love him to take away. He may not give us the answers and the outcomes we have asked him for. But he is our Father, and he loves us, and as we entrust ourselves to him, we know the peace within that he promises.

I WILL WALK WITH HIM

The peace that the Spirit grows comes as we come to our Father in dependence. Peace comes from letting our Father shoulder our problems. The question is: will you? Will you take not only your guilt but also your worries to him, and then leave them with him? All too often, we take the wrong Beatles song title into our life: "We can work it out," we sing to ourselves, when in fact we need to be singing, "Help! I need somebody!" The glorious news of the gospel is that we have that Somebody. We have a Prince of Peace, who brings us shalom with our Creator. And knowing our Creator as our Father, we have all we need in every circumstance, for we know that he is with us and for us, and that is sufficient to bring us the peace that transcends understanding. Let the Spirit move you to depend on him rather than on

yourself, so that in everything you will cry out to him with supplication and thanksgiving, and enjoy the peace that comes from doing so.

In heav'nly love abiding,
No change my heart shall fear;
And safe is such confiding,
For nothing changes here.
The storm may roar without me,
My heart may low be laid,
But God is round about me,
And can I be dismayed?

Wherever he may guide me,
No want shall turn me back;
My Shepherd is beside me,
And nothing can I lack.
His wisdom ever waketh,
His sight is never dim;
He knows the way he taketh,
And I will walk with him.[14]

14 Anna Laetitia Waring, "In Heavenly Love Abiding" (1850).

CHAPTER FOUR

Formed on Stormy Seas

We all want to grow in patience, the old joke goes, but we're tired of waiting for it. There are many wonderful things about living in our modern world of comfort, convenience, and speed—but ours is not an age that promotes the posture of patient waiting.

And yet the creator of this world is very, very patient. So, as with each of the parts of the fruit of the Spirit, we need to lift our eyes away from this world and from ourselves, and see what this aspect of Christian character looks like by gazing at the character of God.

PATIENCE DEFINED

When God reveals himself to his people in the Old Testament, he consistently does so in terms that establish the centrality of patience to his character. For instance, in his encounter with Moses in Exodus 34, where Moses has asked God to show him his glory and God does so not

by showing him anything physical but by declaring his character, what is it that God says?

> The Lord, the Lord, a God merciful and gracious, slow to anger, and abounding in steadfast love and faithfulness… (v 6)

God is slow to anger—which is a great definition of divine patience. Literally, God is "long-nostriled": that is, his nostrils don't easily or quickly flare with anger. Of course, his patience is not unlimited, and there will come a day when his judgment arrives. But for now, and for much longer than humanity deserves, the story of this world is a story of his mercy, of his forbearance, of his patience.

This is who God is. It is what Jonah knew about him; in fact, it is why Jonah did not want to go and preach to the Ninevites. He knew that the Lord is patient and slow to anger, and he wanted the Lord to be angry and to judge them, and feared that he would not! When he tried to justify his running in the opposite direction from the place to which he'd been sent to warn of God's coming judgment, he said, "Is not this what I said when I was yet in my country? That is why I made haste to flee to Tarshish; *for I knew that you are a gracious God and merciful, slow to anger and abounding in steadfast love*" (Jonah 4:2, emphasis mine). *I knew you're that kind of God—I knew you'd be patient,* says Jonah. Jonah's problem was not that he did not know what God was like, but that he did know and did not like it—that he wanted to enjoy God's patience himself but did not want his enemies to.

The irony in the book of Jonah is that the person God is most patient with is Jonah, his own prophet! God's people

needed (and still need) him to be patient with them. It is not just that the Lord is patient enough to withhold his judgment long enough for them to come to him for salvation (though that is true—2 Peter 3:9). It is also that the Lord is patient enough to go on forgiving his people for all our sin and stumbling after we have come to him for salvation.

In Isaiah 30:9-17, God confronts his people about their refusal to live his way—their compromise with the ways of this world, which has led to life in his land being one of difficulty rather than blessing. *You didn't listen to me,* says God, *and the reason you're in the mess you're in is because you chose not to listen to my word.* Then verse 18 begins, "Therefore..." What would we assume should follow? Surely a word of judgment and punishment. Except that that is not what God is like! Instead, we read, "Therefore the LORD waits to be gracious to you, and therefore he exalts himself to show mercy to you." God is waiting. God is willing to walk with them and forgive them. God has not given up on them. God is patient.

If you want to know what patience is, look at how God has treated and is treating you. Consider what you were like before you came to faith. You may have been respectable and decent in the eyes of the world (or you may not have); but you were also a rebel against the King of this world, living as though he should exist for your glory rather than that you should live for his. In his patience, God pursued you instead of condemning you. He gave you time and opportunity to repent and come to him as Lord and Savior. And now consider what you are like having come to faith. Even though you now know his glory and goodness, his

kindness and mercy, still at times (if you are like me, lots of times) you refuse to listen to him and instead listen to the call of the world or of your own selfish desires; still you put other things before him; still you fail to consider him in your decisions or honor him with your lips. Not all the time, of course, and hopefully less than you once did, because the Spirit is at work in you. But nevertheless, it is good for me to consider the patience of God that causes him not to wash his hands of me, saying, *Alistair, I have had enough*, but rather to continue to forgive me and work in me, saying, *Alistair, once more I forgive you. Once more I will not be angry with you. Once more I will go to work in you to make you more like Jesus and less like the old you.* That is God's patience with you and me.

And that is the patience we are called to in our own dealings with others and with ourselves. It's a family characteristic. Children are supposed to bear testimony to who their father is, and if you had a good earthly father, perhaps from time to time you see him in yourself. I find that in some ways this grows as I grow older. Occasionally, when I am shaving, I look away from the mirror and glance back, and I think I see my father there, but it is me. Or I fall asleep while reading a book, and my wife says, "That's exactly how your dad used to fall asleep with a book." Paul Overstreet, the country and western singer, sang of how he was seeing his father in himself—walking the way his father walked and talking the way his father talked. "I guess that's how it's meant to be," he concludes. I don't know Mr Overstreet Sr., so I don't know whether it's good that Overstreet Jr. spoke in the same way as him. But I do know your heavenly Father, and it is good for us more and more

to resemble him, including in this matter of patience. The quality of patience we see in him is what his Spirit grows in his children.

PATIENCE DEVELOPED

How does this patience develop? How does this seed flower in us? It is not developed in a deck chair. Patience is not something you grow by reading a book on "Seven Keys to the Production of Patience." It is not something you grow by reading this chapter! It is something that grows through difficulties.

When you pause to consider it, one of the strangest verses in the New Testament is James 1:2:

> Count it all joy, my brothers, when you meet trials of various kinds.

James is saying that trials, for the believer, should not be regarded first of all as enemies or as intruders but as friends. That immediately seems paradoxical! Instinctively, we try to distance ourselves from trials, remove ourselves from them, and order our affairs to keep difficulties beyond the perimeter of lives. James says, *Think about this differently from your instinct. When you meet a trial, count it a joy.*

Why?! Because of what a time of trial can do: because "the trying of your faith worketh patience. But let patience have her perfect work, that ye may be perfect and entire, wanting nothing" (v 3-4, KJV).

James does not say *if* you meet trials but *when* you meet trials. You can guarantee one thing in your life: you will meet trials. As you read this, one of two things is true of you: you are currently walking through a hard valley

of life, or you are approaching one. Trials are inevitable, trials come out of the blue, and trials come in all shapes and sizes. And trials can be met with joy because, says James, by means of this testing environment, patience is developed. After all, there is no need to be patient when there is nothing to be patient about and no one to be patient with! So it is only when things are not going as we wish, or people are not treating us as we would like, that we both discover how patient or not we really are and have an opportunity to grow.

But patience is not developed automatically by walking through hard times. The benefit we receive from trials and difficulties is largely dependent upon how we look at them and the manner in which we handle them. Trials do not in and of themselves have the capacity to form patience in us. It is the Spirit of God who works patience in us. Trials are the soil in which he grows his fruit, if we will let him and look to him. This is why one person may emerge from a trial embittered and angry, and another will emerge from a harder trial more patient and more joyful, in a way that can only be explained by the presence and work of God. It is as the Spirit works in us in trials that patience moves from a principle we understand to a practice we are living.

C.H. Spurgeon used the image of the weather-beaten sailor. (Presumably in 1883, when he preached this sermon, everyone was impressed by how an experienced sailor looked.) "He has a bronzed face and mahogany-coloured flesh, [and] he looks as tough as heart of oak, and as hardy as if he were made of iron."[15] If you're a new sailor,

15 C.H. Spurgeon, "All Joy in All Trials," *The Metropolitan Tabernacle*

he has the look that you aspire to. And then Spurgeon asks how the sailor becomes like that. And his answer:

> By doing business in great waters. He could not have become a hardy seaman by tarrying on shore.

So it is with us. No one reaches the condition of patience by staying on the shore of life, avoiding all hardship and trying to insulate themselves from suffering as much as possible. The tranquility of the harbor is attractive and easy, but it is not where character is formed. No, that is formed on stormy seas and shaped in the howling winds. So Spurgeon concluded by saying that once you reach that "weather-beaten" state—that condition of endurance and patience and joy—it "is worth all the expense of all the heaped-up troubles that ever come upon us."

Why does God disappoint your plans? Why does he not grant your godly wishes? Why don't you get the good things you ask for, when it's clear to you that you need them and when you are asking humbly for them? In one sense, we cannot know the mysterious purposes of God. But in another sense, we can know the answer: God is committed to conforming each of his children into the family likeness—into the image of his Son Jesus (Romans 8:28-29). He allows nothing into your life that is not for that good. He puts you out into the stormy seas, and he meets you there, to grow you into the condition that you aspire to—Christlikeness. And in no area is this more true than in the area of patience.

The late-20th-century British prime minister Margaret Thatcher reputedly once said, "I am extraordinarily

---

Pulpit 29, no. 1704, p.81-82.

patient, provided I get my own way in the end." How very insightful and honest! And aren't we all like that, instinctively? We are willing to wait for God, as long as he comes through eventually in the way that we think he should. But sometimes he will not, and in those times we are being given the opportunity to lean on him, to learn from him, to trust in him, and to grow in patience. God is often playing a longer game than you are. We tend to judge things by their present appearances, whereas God judges things by their consequences.

Next time you meet a trial, what difference would it make to smile and say, *I would never have chosen this. I prefer the harbor to the sea. But I know that this is going to make me more like Jesus and grow me in patience, and therefore, as I cling to Christ and rely on his Spirit, I will emerge more joyful and patient than I am now.*

Of course, all this is far easier said than done, which is why it requires a divine work in us to grow this kind of attitude. I am often reminded in airports of how far short I fall from having this kind of patience. When a connecting flight is delayed, for no apparent reason other than that the airline appears to desire to make my day harder and my return later, then my response shows that I have some way to grow in this area. Of course, a delayed flight is not a trial in the sense of true hardship in life. But that is the point: it is in the smaller areas that our shortcomings are more regularly exposed, and it is also in the smaller things that we can begin to grow in the fruit of patience, in preparation for the larger storms. Perhaps for you it is not delays to connecting flights; but there will be other fairly ordinary, everyday moments when you can feel the

frustration rising and the impatience forming. What would change if you said to yourself in those moments, *This is not a problem so much as an opportunity—a moment to choose to entrust this situation to God, to seek his help in it, and to ask him to grow me in patience through it?*

PATIENCE DEMONSTRATED

God's patience toward us shows itself in a variety of ways, but one of them, as we've already seen, is in his forgiveness of us. The patience of God is revealed in the forgiveness of sin. And the patience grown in us by the Spirit is revealed in our willingness to forgive others. Remember Isaiah 30? God says to his people, *You have wronged me. Therefore… I will wait for you to come back to me, because I want to forgive you.* And so we are called to forgive each other, just as God in Christ forgave us (Ephesians 4:32). Forgiveness requires love, as we saw in the first chapter of this book; forgiveness also requires patience.

Our patience grows as we consider how patient the Lord is with us; our forgiveness is empowered by reflecting upon how much the Lord has forgiven us. That's the thrust of Jesus' famous parable in Matthew 18:21-35 about the unmerciful servant, who, having been forgiven a debt of (in today's terms) $7 billion by his master the king, then refuses to forgive a fellow servant who owes him $18,000 and discovers that the king in response withdraws his forgiveness. What would the servant have done if he had understood and appreciated how patient, how forgiving, how generous the king had been? He would have acted in like manner toward his fellow servant. Forgiven people forgive others.

So is there someone who has wronged you, perhaps wronged you grievously? What would it take for you not to hold it against them—not to bear a grudge or dream of revenge—but instead to seek to bless them? It would take you reflecting upon the magnitude of God's patience with you and therefore his forgiveness of you—so that you realize that, just as $18,000 is a significant sum but is dwarfed by $7 billion, so you have borne a significant wrong, but nothing like the wrong that should stand on the heavenly ledger of your sin against an almighty God, and yet he cancels the debt, time and again. And so can you. In the trial of being sinned against, the Spirit seeks to grow you in patience and forgiveness, and so make you more like your Father, who is gracious and compassionate, slow to anger and swift in love. Your patience will be grown by trials, and it will be demonstrated in forgiveness—and neither comes naturally, which is why it is a work of the Spirit within us.

CHAPTER FIVE

What Kindness Does

A friend of mine, Jeff Williams, was an astronaut. And so it was that one day in 2016, I found myself watching NASA TV live because Jeff, who was up in space, was on a space walk with one of his colleagues. I say watching, but really I had it on in the background, because this space walk took about five hours.

The moment that grabbed my attention and that I still remember came four hours or so into Jeff's space walk. He was hanging, floating, clipped to the side of the International Space Station. Every so often, from the camera on his helmet, you could see Earth, 250 miles away. He had Mission Control in his ear, telling him what he needed to do. Clearly space walks are not easy. Space walks have an element of real danger.

And at that point, during a moment when the comms from Mission Control went quiet, I heard Jeff say…

> This is probably a good time for me to wish
> Charlie Bolden a happy birthday.

I sat there, in my study, thinking, "Jeff, how can you be thinking about a friend's birthday and taking time to wish him a good one? Why aren't you just focusing on hanging on to the side of the space station, getting your job done, and getting yourself to safety?"

And then I said to myself, "I'm not actually surprised. This is what Jeff is like. This is the kind of thing Jeff would do—to remember it's a friend's birthday and to take time to wish him a good day in the midst of one of the hardest and most stressful situations."

It was only one moment. It was not a huge thing. But it was a good thing to say and a kind thing to have thought of. And knowing Jeff as I do, I knew that it was evidence of the work of the Spirit.

EVERYBODY'S FAVORITE SUBJECT

We're taking the next two parts of the fruit of the Spirit as one, because they are closely linked—in fact the words are often used fairly interchangeably in the Scriptures. But since Paul rarely, if ever, uses synonyms in lists without intending some distinction between them, it is possible that goodness is more active than kindness—that is, that kindness is a disposition of the heart and goodness is the expression of that disposition.[16]

Without the Spirit of God working in our lives, each of us is preoccupied with our problems, our plans, and our pleasures. That is how we naturally are. From time to time,

---

16 Donald Guthrie, *Galatians*, New Century Bible Commentary (Eerdmans, 1981), p.140.

I read *Psychology Today*, and that magazine used to have as its slogan "Insight about everybody's favorite subject: ourselves." That's a good summary of our general approach to life. I am my favorite subject, and the furtherance of my own cause is my greatest priority. Just think about waiting in line for a bus. (I grew up in Britain. The British love waiting in queues; it's one of their national pastimes.) If I'm seventh in a line of twelve and the driver stops and says, "There's room for seven," what's my first response? It's not to feel bad for the folk who are standing at numbers 8, 9, 10, 11, and 12. No—it's to check that I am at 7 in the line and feel pleased that I'm making the cut. Because, after all, I need to get on the bus. I have plans.

A sign that grace has begun to refine a heart is that we start to take an interest in the well-being of others. And by "others," I don't mean those whom we naturally like or are close to or those who make it easy for us to care for them. I don't even mean polite people waiting eighth in line for the bus. I mean those who can give nothing to us and do nothing for us, and even those who have wronged us. As the Lord Jesus put it:

> If you love those who love you, what benefit is that to you? For even sinners love those who love them. And if you do good to those who do good to you, what benefit is that to you? For even sinners do the same. And if you lend to those from whom you expect to receive, what credit is that to you? Even sinners lend to sinners, to get back the same amount. But love your enemies, and do good, and lend, expecting nothing in return.
>
> (Luke 6:32-35a)

I'm not a kind person if I hold on to grudges and refuse to forgive. I'm not a kind person if my goodness to others is selective, based on how grateful or useful they are.

Kindness is displayed in being good to those who are incapable of returning the favor. The writer to the Hebrews mentions almost in passing that "some have entertained angels unawares" (13:2). Of course, what is most remarkable to us is that they had had angels in their houses, without knowing it. But what should be equally remarkable is that they had given hospitality to strangers—not to friends or wealthy neighbors or their pastors but to strangers, to those who would not be able to provide anything or return the favor. That is the sort of behavior that kindness produces in someone.

WE KNOW WHAT IS GOOD

This is central to the life that we are called to. God "has told you … what is good," says the prophet Micah. And what is that? "To do justice, and to love kindness, and to walk humbly with your God" (6:8). We might helpfully reverse the order there. The Christian life is one of walking humbly through life in the presence of and under the rule of our God. To do so means to love kindness—to pursue and foster that attitude. And kindness will show itself in the doing of justice: that is, to treat people, whoever they are, fairly, rightly, generously—and, when it is necessary, mercifully and graciously. In other words, walking humbly with our God can be summed up by seeking to look on others with kindness and therefore to act in goodness toward them. We are not saved *by* our good deeds, but we are saved *for* good deeds: "We are [God's] workmanship,

created in Christ Jesus for good works, which God prepared beforehand, that we should walk in them" (Ephesians 2:10). God has ordered our steps and apportioned our lives such that the expression of kindness—acts of goodness—takes place in the routine affairs, in the menial moments, of everyday life.

Paul puts it very simply to the Thessalonian Christians: "Seek to do good to one another and to everyone" (1 Thessalonians 5:15). And to the Galatian Christians: "Let us not grow weary of doing good" (Galatians 6:9). John Wesley, reflecting on this New Testament imperative, said, "Employ whatever God has entrusted you with, in doing good, all possible good, in every possible kind and degree, to the household of faith, to all men!"[17] Never think that doing good saves you; but, being saved, never forget that God calls you to do good.

Doing good is, then, a command. But, as with all of God's exhortations, he enables what he commands through the work of his Spirit. And, as with all of God's commands, he is calling us to bear more and more the family likeness—to become more and more like him. For, of course, we know what the disposition of kindness is and what the doing of goodness looks like first and foremost by looking at God.

KINDNESS LOOKS LIKE JESUS

When Jesus called his followers to look with kindness not only upon those who could not return the favor but also upon those who had wronged them, he tied it to how God

---

17 John Wesley, "The Use of Money," in *Sermons on Several Occasions* (Methodist Publishing House, 1771), p.709.

looks upon people; God is, he reminded them, "kind to the ungrateful and the evil," and so it is as we act in like manner that we truly live as "sons of the Most High" (Luke 6:35). His kindness is not conditional upon the gratitude of those to whom it is shown. "God's kindness is meant to lead you to repentance" (Romans 2:4). It is divine kindness that means that people—including those who are entirely unaware of it and therefore are ungrateful for it—are enjoying the blessings of life and love and food and shelter. It is divine kindness that gives every breath that every person inhales, and it is divine kindness that searches out those who are running from God and turns them around and brings them to repentance so that they may enjoy his forgiveness and his rule.

Supremely, God's kindness is seen in human form. The Anglican prayer book supplies this verse for Christmas Day: "When the goodness and loving kindness of God our Savior appeared…" (Titus 3:4). They have chosen the correct day to read that verse aloud in church, because when did God's goodness and kindness arrive? It arrived at the first Christmas. God's kindness is called Jesus. When we look at Jesus, we see God's character; we see his kindness in coming to and for those who had chosen to live in darkness. We see his goodness in his healing the sick and mending the broken and forgiving humble sinners and moving toward those who needed the doctor. We see it most of all at the cross. It was kindness toward you that took him there, to that singular and most glorious act of goodness in the history of humanity. When Peter was telling the Roman centurion Cornelius what Jesus was like, he simply said, "He went about doing

good" (Acts 10:38). And it is from that "doing good" that all the benefits that you and I enjoy through faith in him flow. It is because the Father was kind enough to send his Son, and because in his kindness he came and in his goodness he died so that we can look forward to eternity with him. And what will we enjoy then? God has raised us up with Christ "so that in the coming ages he might show the immeasurable riches of his grace *in kindness toward us* in Christ Jesus" (Ephesians 2:7, emphasis mine). Your experience of eternity is going to be one of God pouring out his kindness upon you as you dwell with Christ in glory. His grace is immeasurable, and it looks like his kindness given to us in the Lord Jesus.

This is the kindness and goodness that we are called to, the kindness that God's Spirit works to grow in us.

DIVINE KINDNESS IN ORDINARY LIFE

What does that look like in real life? First, as we have already observed, it looks very ordinary, in the sense that it is expressed in a thousand small words and acts of goodness that God lines up for us in the everyday course of our lives. It may from time to time look more spectacular—you may be called to pull someone from a burning car—but most of the time it will look much more mundane.

Second, not only is God our example of kindness and goodness and the grower of those qualities in us, but also, he works out his own kindness through ours. The Bible is full of examples of this, but we will consider just one: Boaz.

In the biblical book that bears her name, Ruth was a widowed, poverty-stricken foreigner at a time in Israel's history when most people were doing whatever seemed

right in their own eyes rather than what God had said was good. This meant that any widow, poor person, or non-Israelite was vulnerable. To be all three was to be overwhelmed.

But in God's kindness, when Ruth looked for a field in order to gather the grain left by the harvesters so that she and her mother-in-law, Naomi, might have something to eat, he took her to a field owned by Boaz. When Boaz discovered who Ruth was, he told her to stay in his field, assured her she would be kept safe, and offered her water to drink alongside his paid men. At mealtime, he invited her to eat his food. He instructed his workers to leave extra grain on the ground so that Ruth and Naomi would have more than enough.

When Ruth returned home and told Naomi what had happened, for the first time in a long time Naomi praised the Lord: "May [Boaz] be blessed by the Lord, whose kindness has not forsaken the living or the dead!" (Ruth 2:20).

Who was being kind that day? Was it Boaz, or was it God? It was both—the kindness of God being revealed through the kindness of Boaz. Boaz knew that Ruth had come to take refuge under the wings of the Lord (2:12)—and therefore he made sure that he was part of the means by which those wings were spread over her. God's kindness was shown to Ruth through his servant's kindness, and Boaz's kindness was expressed in a multitude of small acts of goodness.

WHAT WOULD CHANGE?

Kindness and goodness are in short supply in our current society—and, we must confess, in our churches. What would have been different in our nation and how different

would be the reputation of evangelicalism in our nation if, over the past thirty years, those who profess to know Jesus and love God's word had, instead of continually championing political agendas, fighting for their rights, and trumpeting what we could not support and would stand against, focused on looking on those around us—including those who have wronged us or who stand against everything we hold dear—with kindness, and sought to do good to them? What would have been different if we had, as individuals and churches, said to ourselves and each other, "Let's take seriously what God says we're supposed to; let's do good by doing justice. Let's pay fair wages. Let's treat people generously. Let's not cut corners with expenses. Let's return calls and emails from those who cannot do much for us. Let's love kindness. Let's look on others as God does: yes, as those who are rebelling against their rightful ruler but also as sheep without a shepherd, as broken people struggling through a broken world, as those who desperately need to see the kindness and goodness of God expressed through his people."

Now imagine what might be different in the next thirty years if we committed ourselves to this. If we do, we will be keeping in step with the Spirit, who works in us to grow a kindness and goodness that will show itself in a hundred daily good works, some spectacular, most ordinary, but all showing the world around us that there is a God who is kind and good, and that he is called Jesus.

CHAPTER SIX

Faithfulness > Success

Can you be trusted?

That is essentially the question we must consider as we come to the next part of the fruit of the Spirit: faithfulness. The fruit of faithfulness is seen in fidelity to the truth and reliability in our dealings with others. It is to say what you mean and mean what you say, and to be consistent in doing so.

SOMETHING GOD CANNOT DO

There are few things that God cannot do, but (strange though it may sound) there are some, and all are good news.[18] One such is that God cannot be unfaithful:

18 In case you are wondering what they are, Nick Tucker in his excellent book *12 Things God Can't Do* (The Good Book Company, 2022) lists these: God can't learn, can't be surprised, can't change his mind, can't be seen, can't tolerate evil, can't change, can't be lonely, can't suffer, can't die, can't be tempted, can't lie, and can't disown himself.

> If we are faithless, he remains faithful—for he cannot deny himself. (2 Timothy 2:13)

This verse tells us two things: one, that we might be faithless; two, that God never can be. And so, as with each of the parts of the fruit of the Spirit, it is as we look at God that we see the most complete definition of the quality we are thinking about. It's no exaggeration to say that the whole Bible pulsates with the drumbeat of God's faithfulness. If you have a few hours sometime, take a concordance and look up the word "faithfulness" in the Bible, and you'll be richly repaid as you consider God's amazing faithfulness. And as you are moved to praise God for this quality, you'll be joining with heaven: "Let the heavens praise your wonders, O Lord, your faithfulness in the assembly of the holy ones!" (Psalm 89:5).

God was faithful, and God remains faithful because there is no shadow of turning with him, as the hymn writer put it.[19] (See James 1:17.) This is why we can trust his promises: because he means what he says, he has the power to effect what he says, and he is unchanging, so he holds fast to what he has said. "He who promised is faithful" (Hebrews 10:23), and therefore we can trust our lives and our eternity to his promises. His faithfulness is unassailable. It is everlasting. It is immeasurable. It is incomparable. Eventually, language has to bow down before the limitlessness of it.

The 18th-century English minister William Grimshaw put it wonderfully evocatively: "Before the Lord will suffer his promise to fail, he will lay aside his divinity, he will

19 Thomas Obadiah Chisholm, "Great Is Thy Faithfulness" (1923).

un-God himself."[20] God would cease to be God before God allowed himself to cease to be faithful.

And so it is that we see in Jesus God's faithfulness. Isaiah said of the coming Messiah that "righteousness shall be the belt of his waist, and faithfulness the belt of his loins" (Isaiah 11:5). What Jesus purposes, he does. What Jesus promises, he fulfills. What Jesus starts, he finishes. So, having purposed to die for his people and set his face toward Jerusalem (Luke 9:51), nothing—no demonic obstacle, no human rejection, nothing—could stop him going to the cross. Having resolved to love "his own," he loved them all the way through "to the end" (John 13:1). Faithfulness is intrinsic to the character of the Son of God; and so it is that as John looks at the triumphant risen and returning Jesus, he sees him on "a white horse," and "the one sitting on it is called Faithful and True" (Revelation 19:11). He always acts with fidelity to the truth and reliability toward others.

This is why you can be confident you will make it all the way to glory—not because you have promised to follow him, though you have, but because he has promised to bring to completion the good work he has begun in you (Philippians 1:6). It is so certain that when Paul speaks of the believer's future glorification, he uses the past tense. We are "glorified" (Romans 8:30). That's how sure you can be. Why? Not because of your faithfulness but because of his.

THE SHINING LIGHT OF FAITHFULNESS

As we've said already, the fruit that the Spirit is growing in us is Christlikeness. So what is seen in the character of God

---

20 R. Spence Hardy, *William Grimshaw, Incumbent of Haworth: 1742–63* (John Mason, 1860), p.132.

and exemplified in the person and work of the Son of God will be produced in the lives of the children of God.

That will mark us as distinct from the world around us, and perhaps nowhere more clearly than when it comes to being faithful. We live in a society that is quite happy with broken vows and tolerates, even promotes, unfaithfulness. Consider the political arena. We hardly notice when a politician breaks a promise, because really we always expected them to. We hardly blink when a politician exaggerates or lies, because really we always thought they'd bend the truth before they compromised their poll ratings. Then consider our society's view of sex and marriage: fine to have sex without commitment, moving on when it suits you; fine to leave a marriage without recrimination, moving out if it's no longer fulfilling you; fine to be directed by the intensity of your feelings rather than faithfulness to your vows. Lastly, consider the world of work. If it doesn't suit you to be faithful to your word in the office, break your word. If it doesn't pay to tell the truth, tell a lie. In one sense, the world has worked like this since the Father of Lies told Eve there would be no adverse consequences for rebelling against God (Genesis 3:4-5); but in no era more than ours, and in no place more than the Western world today, has unfaithfulness been more widely accepted and more often promoted.

And it is against that kind of dark background that we can, as Paul put it, "shine as lights" by holding to and holding forth "the word of life" (Philippians 2:15-16). This does not mean walking around and waving a Bible. It means that the light of God's word is seen in the way we live: faithful to our promises, loyal to the truth, reliable in

our dealings, in a world which so often is none of those things. This is what commends the gospel, making it strangely attractive in a world that is going in an entirely different direction. And all this flows from determining to do what Barnabas told the young Christians in Antioch to do when he "saw the grace of God" at work in them: he "exhorted them all to remain faithful to the Lord with steadfast purpose" (Acts 11:23). That is the decision we are called to take, and then we depend on the Spirit to give us what we need to make good on our commitment.

WHAT IT LOOKS LIKE

So what will the fruit of faithfulness look like? There is, of course, no limit to the areas of life where it applies. But it is worth highlighting a few. Not all of them will apply to you; but some no doubt will.

First, *singleness*. If you are single, you may well be tired of people asking you if you are in some kind of a relationship, whether casual or committed, and looking slightly sorry for you if you are not. (This happens in the world, but also in the church.) The implication is that your identity is tied to your relationship status and that your contentment and fulfillment rely on someone to sleep with (if you're talking to people out in the world) or marry (if you're talking to people in church). But in truth your identity is tied to Christ and who you are in him. Your contentment and fulfillment are found in Christ, in all you have from and with him. When you view yourself in that way, you will want to be faithful to him in what you dream of, how you use your body, and how you use your singleness—in terms of having some increased measure of

freedom, the opportunities of friendships, or the ability to be generous with money and time. Your singleness becomes an opportunity to show that Jesus is better—that Jesus is enough—and to be faithful to the one who is always and only ever faithful to you.

Second, *marriage*. A marriage is started by and founded upon a promise. Your marriage vows are not an expression of how you are feeling on that day but a promise of how you will act on every future day. For better, for worse. For richer, for poorer. In sickness and in health. And sometimes it is worse—sometimes marriage is really hard. But that is what you signed up for; that is what you promised to be faithful in. Marriage vows are about saying, "Whatever happens today, I will still be here tomorrow." That is, of course, entirely opposed to the current view of marriage as a temporary arrangement that lasts as long as both people feel it is working sufficiently well for them; if it's not working anymore, find what you need outside your marriage. But Christians are called to be faithful to our vows: to physical, mental, emotional, sexual, unequivocal fidelity. Your marriage is an opportunity to give others a glimpse of Jesus' faithfulness—a faithfulness that does not wax and wane, a love that continues not because of but despite the beloved, and a commitment that endures to the end.

Third, faithfulness in the responsibilities of *parenting*. Proverbs makes clear that, while there are no guarantees, our children's futures are connected to our faithfulness in this regard. Of course there is grace for every sin, and God can redeem every failing. Nevertheless, parents are called to be consistent and committed in loving their children without

fear or favor, in training them in the instruction of the Lord, and in disciplining them in a way that is fair and for their good and that neither exasperates nor crushes them.

If your children are older and have wandered from the faith, first, remember that God has some of his children on a very long leash; and second, remain faithful to your kids. Let them know that your door is always open. Let them know that the mat outside your front door has one word on it, and the word is *Welcome*. Whatever they do or do not do, you are resolved to remain faithful as their parent—to love them, to pray for them, and to look out for them as far as you are able. You can show them, and show those around you, what God's faithfulness is like.

Fourth, faithfulness as a *child*. The command to honor our parents has no expiration date. As your parents age, be loyal to them in how you treat them and in how you talk about them. How easy it is to speak disparagingly of our parents or our parents-in-law; our culture almost expects it. But they are your mom and your dad. Faithfulness shows itself in consistent honor in the way we approach that relationship.

Fifth, in your *job*. Be known for your reliability, your honesty, and your consistency—including when those things cost you in some way. If you say you will return the call, you return the call. If you say you'll provide the figures, you provide the accurate figures. If you have forgotten something or missed something, you admit it. Faithfulness as an employer looks like paying your staff decent wages and treating them with consistency and impartiality. Does your team trust you? The answer to that will be the measure of your faithfulness in the workplace.

Likewise, faithfulness as an employee looks like working your hours, working as hard as you can, and working as well as you can. It sounds straightforward, but it is hard to do consistently. Can your boss trust you? The answer to that will be the indicator of your faithfulness at work.

GOOD AND FAITHFUL SERVANT

None of us will have been able to read the previous section and simply think, "Check, check, check, check, check—yes, I'm always faithful." All of us fall short. The question is what we do next. Do not excuse it. Do not despair about it. Instead, acknowledge your unfaithfulness, and your ongoing need for a Savior, and come to him and ask his Spirit to produce this fruit in increasing measure. Then work out what faithfulness will look like in the areas where you have not been faithful, and get on with living that out. You cannot become faithful by trying; it is God who produces the fruit. But you won't become faithful without trying; for the Spirit will work as you get to work.

And as you grow in faithfulness, you delight your Lord and Savior. God will reward faithfulness because faithfulness is what he is looking for. Years ago, I preached in Stornoway in the Outer Hebrides, off the northwest coast of Scotland. While I was there, I visited the grave of Kenneth MacRae, who ministered there in the 20th century. He took over the pastorate unexpectedly as a young man, still a student, from a Dr. Kennedy, who had been the pastor for decades and was a tough act to follow. "I felt overwhelmed," he later said, "at the thought [of taking the services] throughout the day and after the evening service felt greatly troubled, depressed, and downcast."

There was a man who worked for the church called Sandy Clunas. Sandy was a large man, and when he saw Kenneth looking so downcast in the vestry, "he just put his big arms round me and said … 'It is not, "well done, good and successful servant" but [quoting Matthew 25:21] "well done, good and faithful servant."'"

MacRae never forgot that moment or those words. "What is going to count at the end of the day," he said years later, "is not success but faithfulness."[21]

This world valorizes success. This world rewards success. God is different. He is faithful, and he loves to see faithfulness in his people, and it is that which he recognizes and rewards as we enter his glory. And so the Spirit is at work to grow in you not success but faithfulness to his Son, just as the Father is waiting to welcome those who have lived and loved and worked and witnessed faithfully when they reach their heavenly home. We can know what Kenneth MacRae knew: that faithfulness does not go unnoticed by the divine eyes.

When I found Kenneth's gravestone on that trip to the Hebrides, I was not surprised to find what was written there, just above his name: "Well done, thou good and faithful servant."

May the same be said of you and of me.

---

21 Iain H. Murray, ed., *Diary of Kenneth A. MacRae: A Record of Fifty Years in the Christian Ministry* (Banner of Truth, 1980), p.460.

CHAPTER SEVEN

Strength Under Control

"Perhaps no grace is less prayed for, or less cultivated, than gentleness."[22]

So wrote a pastor called George Washington Bethune in the 19th century. Nearly two centuries later, I think the comment still stands. I wonder when the last time was that you knelt down and prayed, "Lord Jesus Christ, produce in me the fruit of a gentle spirit"—or when the last time was that someone prayed from the front in your church on a Sunday, "Lord Jesus, will you make among us such a spirit of gentleness that those who are most in need of your care may always encounter it here?"

One of the reasons gentleness is so undervalued is because it is so misunderstood. We tend to hear the word "gentle" and think of someone who is a pushover and who never stands up for themselves (or anyone). But biblical

22 George Washington Bethune, *The Fruit of the Spirit* (Philadelphia, 1839), p.100.

gentleness and that kind of weakness are not at all the same thing. The Greek word translated "gentleness" (and in the Authorized Version and ESV also sometimes as "meekness") is *prautes*, and it has the sense of "strength under control." Moses—the same Moses who led God's people and preached strong warnings to them and interceded with God for them and put down rebellions among them—"was very meek" (Numbers 12:3). He was meek not because he was weak but because he was strong, and had that strength under control in order that he might use it in service of the needs of others.

What does strength look like when it is not kept under control? Paul builds up a picture in his outline list of the "works of the flesh" in Galatians 5, immediately before he describes the fruit of the Spirit: enmity, strife, rivalries, dissensions, divisions, and—perhaps most of all—"fits of anger" (Galatians 5:19-20). Gentleness is the antithesis of uncontrolled anger. It is not a temperament or a personality so much as an outflow of the love of God—that love which heads the list of the fruit of the Spirit, as we've already seen. James contrasts "the meekness of wisdom" with "bitter jealousy and selfish ambition" (James 3:13-14).

And, as we have said in each chapter, if we want to see what a gentle spirit looks like in a human life, it is Jesus to whom we must turn.

THREE PICTURES

The Old Testament tells us not only what God's long-promised King and Savior will do but also what he will be like. So in those Scriptures, we find three beautiful descriptions of the gentleness of the coming one.

The first is in Isaiah 40:11:

> He will tend his flock like a shepherd;
> he will gather the lambs in his arms;
> he will carry them in his bosom,
> and gently lead those that are with young.

This verse is particularly striking when you read how God is described in the previous verse and the following ones:

> Behold, the Lord God comes with might,
> and his arm rules for him;
> behold, his rewards is with him,
> and his recompense before him …
>
> Who has measured the waters in the hollow of his hand
> and marked off the heavens with a span,
> enclosed the dust of the earth in a measure
> and weighed the mountains in scales
> and the hills in a balance? …
>
> To whom then will you liken God? (v 10, 12, 18)

God is all-powerful and incomparably great. There is no one as mighty as him. There is no weakness in him. But the Sovereign is a Shepherd. He tends his flock. He cares for his sheep. He gathers in his arms those who have particular needs or frailties. He gently leads those who are prone to wander. This is who Jesus is saying he is when he says, "I am the good shepherd" (John 10:11). What a compelling picture of the might, the majesty, the untrammeled authority of the sovereign God stooping down into our lives and dealing with us in this way—with gentleness.

Second, in Isaiah 42 we meet the servant of the Lord—in the first of the four Servant Songs in Isaiah, all fulfilled in Christ Jesus. "Behold my servant, whom I uphold," God says: *Here he is—I want to introduce him to you.*

> I have put my Spirit upon him;
> he will bring forth justice to the nations. (v 1)

One day, God will re-create the world as he intended it to be. One day, all wrongs will be righted and all wrongdoers punished. And this will be done through this servant.

Yet when this servant comes, what will he be like?

> He will not cry aloud or lift up his voice,
> or make it heard in the street;
> a bruised reed he will not break,
> and a faintly burning wick he will not quench.
> (v 2-3)

He is not a bully. He is not ostentatious. He does not throw his weight around. He is tender—so tender that a damaged reed will not be snapped and a smouldering wick will not go out. He is kind enough to want to repair and restore, and he is gentle enough to do so. He will never look at the weak or the broken and say, *Well, that's useless. Let's move on. He doesn't amount to much. We can throw that out.* He deals gently with the hurting, the bruised, and the struggling. He is neither impressed by strength nor put off by weakness. In fact, he is drawn toward weakness, to fan the smoldering wicks back into full flame with the oxygen of his loving care.

And so it was that when Jesus stood in a synagogue one Sabbath and saw a man with a withered hand—but was

surrounded by the powerful religious leadership who were itching to make Jesus' life harder, and even to end his life, if he healed on the Sabbath—he did not hesitate:

> He said to the man, "Stretch out your hand." And the man stretched it out, and it was restored, healthy like the other. But the Pharisees went out and conspired against him, how to destroy him.
> (Matthew 12:13-14)

The Lord Jesus was strong enough not to be intimidated by those who used their strength to shore up their own positions. He was gentle enough to restore a man who was broken and in need. No wonder that Matthew, having recorded this event and the healings that followed it, quoted Isaiah 42:2-3. Jesus has all strength, under complete control, for the good of those who are bruised reeds and smoldering wicks.

Here is the third picture, the promise of the King coming to his city of Jerusalem in Zechariah 9:9:

> Rejoice greatly, O daughter of Zion!
> Should aloud, O daughter of Jerusalem!
> Behold, your king is coming to you;
> righteous and having salvation is he,
> humble and mounted on a donkey.

What an amazing thing this is: that the King of the universe—the creator of it all, the Lord of glory—steps into time to make himself known not in a way that makes all humanity tremble with fear but by inviting all men and women who know their need to find tenderness and all that they need:

Was there ever a kinder shepherd,
Half so gentle, half so sweet,
As the Savior who would have us
Come and gather round his feet?[23]

As we read of Jesus in the Gospels, his strength is always under control, always being used for the good of others. What we read of in the Old Testament in black and white is brought into resplendent color there. And so Jesus invites you and me: "Come to me, all who labor and are heavy laden, and I will give you rest. Take my yoke upon you, and learn from me, for I am gentle and lowly in heart" (Matthew 11:28-29). You need never come to him feeling afraid, or stay away from him until you have it all together, or worry that he may send you away. No—for he is gentle. Come to him, for he wants to restore you, never to dismiss you.

SUBMISSION AND CONSIDERATION

As in all things, those who follow Christ are called to be like Christ in treating others with gentleness. Yet gentleness tends to be one of those qualities we admire in others, desire in theory, and excuse ourselves for lacking as soon as someone makes it hard for us. What does real-life gentleness, in our attitudes and actions, require from us?

It seems to me that being gentle has a Godward dimension and an other-ward dimension.

First, growing in gentleness requires submission to God. Here are two questions to ask yourself:

- *Do I have a teachable spirit?* "Receive with meekness," James says, "the implanted word, which is able to

23 Frederick William Faber, "There's a Wideness in God's Mercy" (1862).

save your souls" (1:21). You can sit for years and hear the Bible taught—you can open it yourself each day—but if your heart is unteachable, it will land as water on a tin roof. The fruit of gentleness shows itself in the humility of a teachable heart, which listens to the word of God as authoritative, not advisory—as something to be received rather than considered.

- *Am I ready to repent?* "Be doers of the word, and not hearers only, deceiving yourselves" (James 1:22). None of us is perfect; all of us make mistakes. Therefore, we must expect the word of God to correct us, even to rebuke us (2 Timothy 3:16). We must be willing to let it challenge our ways of thinking and our order of priorities; we must be willing to let it change us. Gentleness will not grow in the Christian who always has a ready excuse for why they were not gentle in this situation or that—who always justifies why nothing needs to change.

Second, growing in gentleness means being considerate of the needs and concerns of others. Here are the questions I have learned to ask myself, painful though they sometimes are for me to answer:

- Am I generous and fair in my dealings with others, rather than rigid, exacting, and overly demanding?
- Am I prepared to be sensitive to the pressures and insecurities that are weighing on my family, my colleagues, and my friends?

- Do I show consideration to everyone, no matter how much or little they have done or can do for me and no matter how influential or otherwise they are? Do I treat the mail carrier, the checkout clerk, or the bank teller with the same consideration as someone I need a favor from or someone who can make my life better?
- Do I tell myself I'm standing on principle when in fact I am merely insisting on my own preference?
- Am I becoming increasingly compassionate, genial, reasonable, and kind, or increasingly rigid, inflexible, and grumpy?

The late pastor and author Jerry Bridges recalled a friend of his who would sign off his letters this way: "Keep tough and tender"[24]—tough, that is, on ourselves, and tender toward others. The absence of a gentle spirit reverses that, and does so with relative ease. It does it without its subject noticing and provokes a harsh word to anyone else who mentions it.

These questions are something of a spiritual MRI scan, showing us what we are really like.

Yet there is no need to despair—because gentleness grows in the most unlikely of soils when the Spirit sets to work.

IF THE SPIRIT CAN CHANGE *HIM*...

Jesus is the great example of gentleness in a man, as we have seen; but the apostle Paul is perhaps the greatest example of

---

24 Jerry Bridges, *The Practice of Godliness* (NavPress, 1996), p.187.

how much the Spirit can change a man, and nowhere more so than in this area of gentleness.

Paul (then known as Saul) was at the death of Stephen, the first Christian martyr, and "approved of his execution" (Acts 8:1). Then, "entering house after house, he dragged off [believing] men and women and committed them to prison" (v 3). He was notorious among the churches for "how much evil he [had] done to [the] saints in Jerusalem" (9:13); unsurprisingly, "they were all afraid of him" (v 26).

Yet that same man, only years later, was able to write to a church in Thessalonica and remind them of how "we were gentle among you, like a nursing mother taking care of her own children" (1 Thessalonians 2:7).

What had happened? Paul had been converted by the appearance to him of Christ on the road to Damascus, and then he had been changed by the work of the Spirit in his heart. Paul had had the kind of character that was vehemently committed to hunting down believers, dragging them off, throwing them into jail, and even seeing them killed. Then the Spirit went to work, and grew gentleness in him.

When you have eyes to see it, gentleness is a recurring emphasis in Paul's epistles:

- "Remind them," Paul urges the younger pastor Titus, "to be gentle." (Titus 3:1-2)
- "The Lord's servant," Paul tells his other protégé, Timothy, is to make a point of "correcting his opponents with gentleness." (2 Timothy 2:24-25)

- "If anyone is caught in a transgression, you who are spiritual should restore him in a spirit of gentleness." (Galatians 6:1)
- "Let your gentleness be evident to all." (Philippians 4:5, NIV)

Pastors are to be gentle, even when opposed. Pastors are to tell their churches that gentleness matters. When challenging a Christian who is indulging in a sin, gentleness is key. In all things, the watching world should see a community marked by gentleness.

I wonder if Paul's emphasis was born of a desire to remind himself, as well as those to whom he wrote, of the wonder of God's grace—a reminder that apart from the work of the Spirit of God, he would know nothing of gentleness. His gentleness—the way the Spirit had brought his strength under control, to be used for the good of others—was a supreme proof of the ability of the Holy Spirit to go to work in a believer such that their character becomes almost unrecognizable from how it once was. If and when you struggle to be gentle, let the transformation of Paul be a reminder to you that if the Spirit can make such a man gentle, he can certainly make you gentle—and loving, joyful, peaceable, patient, kind, good, faithful, and self-controlled—too.

CHAPTER EIGHT

How to Win Each Day (in the Battle That Actually Matters)

You and I are a walking battleground, and we will be every day from here until we stand in the Lord's presence. What is the battle? It is, as the Westminster Confession of Faith puts it, "a continual and irreconcilable war—the flesh warring against the Spirit, and the Spirit against the flesh."[25]

This is why Paul tells the Galatian Christians, shortly before he details the fruit of the Spirit, to "walk by the Spirit, and you will not gratify the desires of the flesh" (Galatians 5:16). Our fallen nature still gravitates toward doing that which is wrong: "Each person is tempted when he is lured

25 The Westminster Confession of Faith, Modern English Study Version, 13.2.

and enticed by his own desire" (James 1:14). The Spirit dwells in us to work in us that which is godly; his work in us is to say to us, *Look, this is not the way that you should be living as a child of God. God has made you an entirely new person. Take off that old attitude or habit or behavior, and start living in a way that pleases your heavenly Father instead.*

This, then, is the conflict. Because "the desires of the flesh are against the Spirit, and the desires of the Spirit are against the flesh" (Galatians 5:17), you do not always do what you want, as a Christian, to do. But you can—if you battle to "walk by the Spirit."

Which is why we need self-control. And the wonderful news is that self-control is part of the fruit the Spirit grows in God's children. The Spirit works *in* us to enable us to do what the Spirit wants *for* us. Self-control is the Spirit-enabled ability to avoid excess and to stay within God-given boundaries. It is, to borrow a definition from Jerry Bridges, "the exercise of inner strength under the direction of sound judgment that enables us to think, say, and do things that are pleasing to God."[26]

To have your self under control is not easy, though, even with the supernatural help of the Spirit, because, as Derek Prime puts it, "Self is one of the toughest weeds that grows in the garden of our lives."[27] After all, who do you have the most trouble with as you try to live the Christian life? Isn't it you?! Consider how good we are at self-deception, thinking we're better than we are, or self-importance, thinking we're more central to the universe

---

26 Jerry Bridges, *The Practice of Godliness* (NavPress, 1996), p.134.

27 Derek Prime, *Living for God's Pleasure: The Fruit of the Spirit* (Evangelical Press, 2004), p.147.

than we are, or self-reliance, thinking we're more powerful than we are. We need self-control to keep our selves—our old selves—in check.

This does not come easy, because we like to listen to our selves—and our old selves like to follow their desires! I remember hearing of a post office robbery in the UK where someone who worked there was in on the plot; before everyone locked up and left for the day, that person hid in a closet, and then, once it was dark, he opened the door and let his fellow thieves in to rob the place entirely. There was no forcible entry. It was an inside job. Every sin is like that. We cannot say we cannot help it. We can. We choose to sin. We do what we want to do.

Therefore self-control is a great need for every Christian, at every stage. Paul tells Titus to "urge the younger men to be self-controlled" (Titus 2:6). That's the one thing Titus is to get them to focus on! But Paul also says the "older men are to be … self-controlled" (v 2). Older women are to teach the younger women "to be self-controlled" (v 5), and they are to ensure that they themselves are neither slanderers nor drunkards (the avoidance of which will require self-control—v 3-4). In other words, there's no stage of life when you graduate from this class. For as long as we have sinful desires—which is precisely as long as we are in this life—we shall require self-control.

WHAT REAL FREEDOM IS

We live in a culture where self-control, like faithfulness, is very much out of fashion. *Do what feels right. You do you. If it feels good, do it. Do what makes you happy.* All of those are mantras of our age, and few know anything of self-control,

which says, *I feel like doing this, and I want to do this, but I will not do this because I know it is not good or right.* And the world so easily bleeds into the church. The boat is supposed to be in the water; the water isn't supposed to be in the boat. Yet how much more relaxed we are about holiness and how much faster we are to excuse following our desires than previous generations of evangelicals ever were. Why is that? Because we are surrounded by people—in the media, online, and possibly closer to home—telling us to do whatever we feel like, and our sinful desires tell us that those people are right. So we forget that Christian freedom is not the same as freedom to do whatever we like, just as for a fish true freedom does not look like jumping out of the river because it feels like it will have more fun over there, on the bank.

James calls God's law "the perfect law … of liberty" (James 1:25) for a reason. In Scripture we are warned away from legalism on the one hand and from license on the other. Paul makes it clear that true freedom is not a license to do as you please but a liberty to do as you ought. That is, we are not held in bonds, but we are held in bounds.

The Spirit is growing in us the self-control to stay within those bounds of the law of God. He is reminding us that when we have sinned, whatever the object of our mistaken pleasure was, we were loving it more than we loved God—we were declaring that God is not enough for us. He is working to take our eyes off the altar of our own appetites and desires and to put them onto our crucified Savior, who died to free us from the punishment for and power of sin and who one day will bring us to a place where we are free from the very presence of sin. He is changing us

so that more and more, what we want to do is what God calls us to do.

GUARD YOUR HEART

How do you start to keep in step with the Spirit by cultivating self-control? By guarding your heart, "for from it flow the springs of life" (Proverbs 4:23). In the Bible, the heart is the center of your thoughts and your emotions. It's the "you-ness" of you. Solomon says, *Guard that.* You and I can put as many guardrails around ourselves externally to try to keep ourselves obedient; but if we do not guard our hearts, we will be as susceptible to temptation in a wardrobe as in the center of the most permissive city.

So ask yourself: are your emotions under your control, or are you under theirs? Self-control means first stopping to acknowledge and analyze the emotion. Then it means bringing it to the standard of God's word to discern whether it is a godly emotion, an ungodly emotion, or (as is often the case) partly both. And then it means resolving to act in a godly way, which may mean refusing to dwell on that emotion—refusing to allow it to direct your thoughts, refusing to feed it.

So imagine, for instance, that you notice you are feeling angry. Stop and acknowledge that. Analyze it: why are you feeling angry? What has caused it? Bring it to God's word: anger can be righteous if it is over injustice or robbing God of his glory; it will be unrighteous if it is prompted by someone removing an idol you want to worship, be it your comfort or your plans or your reputation or your wealth or something else. Ask yourself, as the Lord did Jonah, "Is

it right for you to be angry?" (Jonah 4:4, NIV). And then self-control in dependence on the Spirit looks like either seeking to stymie that emotion and deny it any role in directing your thoughts and words and actions, or asking the Spirit to enable you to direct your righteous anger toward ends that are good for others.

So do you have a spirit of resentment or of bitterness or of self-pity or of envy? To feel something that requires being brought under self-control is not a mark of ungodliness. To fail to control it is the mark of ungodliness.

Then consider your thought life. Paul calls us to "take every thought captive" (2 Corinthians 10:5), bringing it within the bounds of God's word. Philippians 4:8 offers us a very simple guide to what we are to allow into our minds and then ourselves to dwell on:

> Whatever is true, whatever is honorable,
> whatever is just, whatever is pure, whatever is
> lovely, whatever is commendable, if there is any
> excellence, if there is anything worthy of praise,
> think about these things.

Every day, we fill our minds with words, sounds, and images. It is hard to take our thoughts captive for Christ if we are filling our minds with things which militate against the lordship of Christ. That's the principle: is what I'm putting in my mind through this TV show or song or movie or book or blog something that will help me love Christ as my Lord or something that will encourage me not to?

Don't underestimate the power of a self-controlled mind or the danger of one that is the opposite. There is a saying in golf that "the most important six inches are the six

inches between your ears." There's a measure of truth in that when it comes to the Christian life, too. As the old adage has it, "Sow a thought, reap an action. Sow an action, reap a habit. Sow a habit, reap a character. Sow a character, reap a destiny."

That is how you guard your heart: through having your emotions in check and your thoughts captive to Christ. It is once you have a guard over your heart that you are able to exercise self-control over your body.

Self-control when it comes to how we use our bodies does not mean ascetism—Scripture specifically warns against those "who forbid marriage and require abstinence from foods that God created to be received with thanksgiving. … Everything created by God is good, and nothing is to be rejected if it is received with thanksgiving" (1 Timothy 4:3-4). It is how we use and enjoy what God has given that is the issue. That is why C.S. Lewis's expert demon recommends to a junior devil in *The Screwtape Letters* that he "encourage the humans to take the pleasures which our Enemy has produced, at times, or in ways, or in degrees, which He has forbidden."[28]

Self-control, then, looks like enjoying the good things God has given us, for the purposes they were given, in the measure that is good.

Are you physically lazy? That is an area about which to ask the Spirit to grow you in self-control. Are you refusing to rest? That is an area in which you need to apply self-control. Do you eat and eat and eat, or drink and drink and drink? That's an issue for you to seek self-control over; but so is taking pride in never enjoying a good, proper meal.

---

28 C.S. Lewis, *The Screwtape Letters* (1942), chap. 9.

(I am not speaking of an eating disorder here, which is a deeper and broader issue than one which simply requires Spirit-given self-control. And if you struggle with such a disorder, I'd encourage you to remember that Jesus loves you, the Spirit is in you, and your church is there for you to go and find someone you trust and speak to them about what you're struggling with.)

And then, of course, there is the area of sex, where the way of our world and the call of Christ are ever diverging. We must not reduce all application of the need for self-control to our sex lives; equally, we must not ignore our sex lives. In what we do and what we look at, we need to be rigorous and ruthless, taking for our guide Joseph, who, when propositioned by Potiphar's wife, ran away. He literally fled. "How … could I do such a thing and sin against God?" he said (Genesis 39:9, NIV). Contrast that with David in 2 Samuel 11, who saw Bathsheba bathing and did not have the self-control to look away; so he had her brought to his palace and did not have the self-control not to touch her. So one man remained godly, while the other became an adulterer. There can be no half measures in this area of our lives. Self-control means living within the bounds of God's law of liberty, without compromise.

GRACE TRAINS US

Scripture, then, commands us to exercise self-control. But, as we've already said, the Bible never divorces God's command to us from God's work for us. In Titus 2, straight after setting out the need for self-controlled living for all Christians of every stage of life, Paul continues, "For the

grace of God has appeared, bringing salvation for all people, training us to renounce ungodliness and worldly passions, and to live [you guessed it] self-controlled, upright, and godly lives" (v 11-12). When we forget to keep God's call and God's grace together, we almost inevitably go wrong. We end up with a religion that says, *Become by your own efforts what you're not by nature*, rather than Christianity, which says, *Become by the work of the Spirit what you already are by grace.*

Self-control is not about having lots of rules for what you must do and not do; it is to make it your goal to please him who has shown you such grace—to please your heavenly Father who has adopted you and to avoid grieving the Spirit who has chosen to dwell in you. Self-control flows from being so amazed by grace that it becomes the sweetest sound to you, so that you see the God of grace as one you long to love and serve, and you look at the Lord Jesus Christ and see that being like him is something you get to be, not something you have to be. That is how grace trains us to turn away from our sinful desires and to walk by the Spirit in obedience to God's word.

So, if you want to be more self-controlled, don't rely on self-effort. After all, your own self is, sooner or later, going to give up on taming itself! And likewise, don't rely on just saying no. There is a better way, and it is the way of fixing the eyes of your heart on Christ.

TURN YOUR EYES UPON JESUS

In Greek mythology, there was an island upon which lived the sirens. Half woman, half bird, they would sing beautifully to sailors whose boats were passing by, so

alluring them with their singing that their ships would run aground on the rocks and they would perish.

When the Greek hero Odysseus passed by the island, he stopped his ears with wax and tied himself to the mast of his ship so he could not be seduced, and told his sailors to follow suit.

But when the moment came for Orpheus and his fellow Argonauts to pass the sirens, he had a different strategy; he took a harp and played music of such superior charms that the sailors gave no heed to the sirens' song, and they passed safely by.

Orpheus' strategy is the way the Spirit works in God's people. It is when our affections are so taken up with the wonder of God's grace and goodness to us—when the beauty of the gospel is all we see and its songs are all we hear—that we can understand how fleeting and feeble and futile are those things that so beguile us by nature. That is what the Puritan Thomas Chalmers called "the expulsive power of a new affection"—what the old hymn so wonderfully described when it calls us to…

> Turn your eyes upon Jesus,
> Look full in his wonderful face,
> And the things of earth will grow strangely dim
> In the light of his glory and grace.[29]

That does not mean that the battle does not continue. It is a continual and irreconcilable war. But this is the secret to self-control. This is how to walk by the Spirit, so that you win victories each day as you choose what is better over what is desired, knowing all the while that ultimately

29 Helen Howarth Lemmel, "Turn Your Eyes upon Jesus" (1922).

the victory over sin has been won at Calvary, and that one day you will see Jesus face-to-face, and the war will be over and won.

A Different Kind of Conclusion

Most books, including those that focus upon an aspect of the Christian life, finish with a conclusion that inspires and exhorts the reader to greater effort, so that they close the book with a sense of determination that, yes, things will be different as result of what its pages have contained. They will be better.

I am not going to end this book in that way—because this is a book about the fruit of the Spirit, and, as we said right at the start, the fruit of the Spirit is the fruit of the Spirit. The work of change in the Christian is the work of the Spirit. So I do not want you to finish this book resolving to be better, to do better, to work harder. Instead, I hope you are finishing this book with a desire to be more like Jesus, with a confidence that his Spirit is changing you to be like Jesus, and with an aim to keep in step with the Spirit's work in your life—to actively depend on him. What does that look like? Well, most of all, it looks like prayer, and so this book's conclusion is simply that: a prayer.

Father, thank you that your purpose for your people—your purpose for me—is to make us more like Jesus.

Lord Jesus, I praise you that you embody each of the glories of the fruit of the Spirit that I have been considering. You are perfectly loving, joyful, peace-filled, patient, kind, good, faithful, gentle, and self-controlled.

Lord God, I confess that as I look at my own life in light of the fruit of the Spirit, I have reason to confess my sin and my lack of the reality of these things in my heart and in what I think and say and do. I am aware that I am not who you call me to be or who I want to be. So I thank you that it is your blood and your righteousness, Lord Jesus, and not my own merits, that allow me to come boldly before the throne of grace. Thank you that I stand forgiven and complete in you.

But Father, I do want to grow and to change, and I do thank you that the work of your Spirit within me means that I will increasingly be marked by this fruit. Thank you that while I'm not what I want to be or all that I'm going to be, I'm not who I was once—thank you that I am different, by the power of your Spirit at work within me.

Lord, make me quick to see where I have grown and changed, so that I will be quicker to praise you and more watchful for your continued work. Lord, help me to keep in step with your Spirit and to have the joy of finding him at work as I seek to obey you. Guard me from self-reliance on the one hand when it comes to becoming more like Jesus, and from complacency in my Christian life on the other.

So please pour out your Spirit upon me in fresh measure, so that I might be increasingly marked by love, and joy, and peace, and patience, and kindness, and goodness, and faithfulness, and gentleness, and self-control. Show me what it will look like to become more like Christ in each of these qualities. Grow these inner glories in me, that my life may be marked by these things and so that I might make your gospel look attractive to those around me. Do not let what I have read and been challenged by in this book fall from my mind and heart, but instead use it to shape and fashion me into the likeness of your Son, in whose name I pray and on whose Spirit I depend.

Amen.

We Will Be Changed

Published by:
The Good Book Company

thegoodbook.com | thegoodbook.co.uk
thegoodbook.com.au | thegoodbook.co.nz

Every book published by The Good Book Company has been written by a human author and edited by a human editor. While AI tools are sometimes used to assist with research and support certain processes, all content has been created by a human author and thoroughly checked by our editorial team to ensure it is biblically faithful and pastorally wise.

Published in association with the literary agency of Wolgemuth & Wilson.

Cover design by Faceout Studio. Design and art direction by André Parker.

ISBN: 9781802544589 (hardcover) | 9781802544282 (paperback)

JOB-008595 (hardcover) | JOB-008719 (paperback) | Printed in India

We Will Be Changed

9 INNER GLORIES THE SPIRIT IS CULTIVATING IN YOU

ALISTAIR BEGG

thegoodbook COMPANY

"This little book deserves to become a classic. Alistair Begg has given us the best book on the fruit of the Spirit that I have read. It is simultaneously deeply challenging and hugely encouraging, calling us to constantly fix our eyes on Jesus and to look to the Spirit of Jesus to change us. I am so grateful that Alistair wrote this and so glad that I've read it. I will be championing it everywhere I can!"

GARY MILLAR, Principal, Queensland Theological College, Australia; Author, *Need to Know*

"I was so inspired and encouraged by this book, as Alistair called me to look at Jesus and let his Holy Spirit work from the inside out. I found in each chapter that my heart gave a little jump as each part of the fruit of the Spirit was described, and alongside that came a real longing to be more like Christ."

RICO TICE, Founder, Christianity Explored Ministries

"I loved reading this book. I'd liken it to spiritual fertiliser for the soul, encouraging and empowering the growth of the fruit of the Spirit in your life. In classic Begg style, it's a moving, hilarious, profound, and wonderfully relatable read, all the while quietly uprooting the weeds that choke the Spirit's fruit."

LINDA ALLCOCK, The Globe Church, London; Author, *Deeper Still*

"With this delightful book, I found myself not only wanting to read the next chapter and the next, but rekindling a deep desire to be more like Jesus. Not only does Alistair explain the fruit of the Spirit, but he shows us how it operates and how it liberates. It felt more like a tutorial on how to walk with God in my daily life. My bet is that you will find this book to be downright life-changing!"

SKIP HEITZIG, Senior Pastor, Calvary Church, Albuquerque, New Mexico

she is as dangerous as a *furia*. The three Golden *electi* pause outside my cage and study me like I'm a lion in a traveling circus. I let my gaze flicker among them, trying to return the favor.

The *Argentum Consilio* was made up of aureate *electi*, but they were drunkards. These three are anything but, and despite the blood I've spilled, I can't help but feel a trickle of unease. The *dominus* and the woman are warriors—the power that courses through them is something else entirely compared to mine. I burn a precious trickle of ice essence to draw on the Symbol of Ancient Frost to help me keep my face blank. The magister's knowing smile grows, but I refuse to believe that he understands what I am doing.

In that moment, I decide I must fail. These people are dangerous, their attention bright and intense like *Sol* above. I must get out of their sight before I am burnt.

"I don't know, *Dominus*," the *lanista* remarks, still studying me intently. "He's a fighter, but I don't see anything that makes him special."

"And yet Pliny does." The graying man lets out a little sigh, as if regretting entertaining this fancy this far. I suspect that this is not the first time his servants have taken him through this game. The patriarch of *Domus* Pelias rules with a lighter hand than I would have expected.

"He's never been wrong, have you, Pliny?" The towering woman glances at the short magister with a knowing look.

"Not yet," the master answers for him, still clearly skeptical. "Test him and see what you can find."

"As you wish, *Dominus*." The palatine turns away from the cart, leaving his servants to carry out his will. I watch the man depart, trying to understand what he's looking for.

"Okay, lad, can I trust you to play nice, or do I need to threaten you?" The woman's knuckles rap against the copper bars of my cage, pulling my attention back to her. She's eyeing me with professional boredom.

"How nice is nice?"

"The *dominus* wants to see what you can do. If you promise to behave, I'll untie your wrists, and Pliny here will take you to the *loci* to fill up that frozen reserve of yours." A shudder of need runs through me at the thought of being able to gorge on Winter essence. I'm surprised that I don't start drooling right there in the cart.

"I'll behave," I promise, eyeing the two Golden *electi* with amusement. Not only are my reserves practically empty, but I am only a Silver. The thought of me being able to threaten either of them is laughable—unless I was able to get my hands on a sword… My eyes travel to the hilt of the dueling blade that rides at her hip. Then things might change.

"Good enough," she replies almost cheerfully, pulling open the cage door. "No harm in making this easier. If Pliny's right and you're something special, then you'll have a grand adventure ahead of you." My mouth twists in irritation at the thought of being a slave warrior once more.

"What if I'm not?" I ask as I make my way down the stairs.

"Then you'll be on a short path to trying your luck in the *Spectaculum*." She laughs warmly, but it does not cover the blood she promises. The Spectacles are deadly challenges played out before the Games begin, appetizers to the fights.

As a boy, I did not think much of the men and women dying in the arena, because they mostly were *captivus*, criminals who had earned their fate. But now, sitting on the other side of the law, I can't help but feel a new sense of skepticism about the people who ended up in those bloodbaths. Did they really deserve to die, or were their relics worth more than their lives?

"Have no fear," Pliny tells me, patting me on the shoulder as I reach the ground. "I'm never wrong."

"Not yet." The woman echoes their master's words dryly as she undoes the cords binding around my wrists. I let out a sigh of relief as my body is freed and swing my arms a few times to work my sense of feeling back into them.

Again, a wild thought of escape flickers through my mind. I'm only inches away from being able to grab the hilt of the woman's blade. Even now, some of its iron essence bleeds into me, but it feels like a heel of bread trying to fill a void. With the weapon in my hand, it would be a simple matter for me to draw even more… I force myself to step away from the woman, removing the temptation. She's still a Gold *electus*, which means she's far faster and stronger than I am. All she has to do is catch my wrist before I draw her blade, and I am dead. Now is not the moment.

"Come." Pliny gestures, leading me toward a distant building, different than the one that their master had vanished into. "Let us do something about that starved Heart of yours."

"I'm all ears," I echo, following the magister's direction. The woman hovers behind me. I can feel her eyes on the back of my head as we walk. She may have been willing to untie me, but that does not mean she trusts me.

We make our way through a pair of metal doors. I breathe deeply as we pass them, drawing a little more Iron essence from them as I pass them. I'm tempted to brush one of them with my hand as I pass, but I resist the urge. I dare not give any of them a reason to suspect my secret.

I must be patient.

Pliny leads us through a short stone hallway, with a second pair of thick doors on the far end. Two Ironbound stand watch. I eye the two former soldiers warily. They're wearing armor that resembles the *lorica,* but their chest is stamped with the symbol of the broken trident. The same crest decorates their *scutti*. They're dressed in black and gold but look as sharp as any legionnaire in Agogia. Dorian's guards were a sad shadow of what they had once been, but these two are still in their fighting prime. With enough of them, they could form a battle-worthy cohort. The *XII* brand on my chest itches as we pass under their attentive gaze.

I forget about the Ironbound the moment we are past them; any thought in my head is swept aside by the opulence that waits through the doors.

The training hall is a long, rectangular room that has an open roof and courtyard in the center. Sunlight beams down on an expansive sand court that must be a training arena. A handful of men and women in combat leathers spar in pairs down its length. Along the sides of the room are over a score of *loci*, small rooms that have been prepared as spaces for *electi* to cultivate specific forms of essence.

Each is contained in glass, making it easy to see what options are available. The first one to my right is a bright green field. Long stalks of grass rise past the height of my calves. It looks like a perfect place for a Plant Symbol. It makes me miss my father. Another room contains a pool of water that swirls with waves as if it were still part of the ocean.

Pliny leads me past a room that burns with an angry red fire. I spot another that is empty save for a flat slab of rock. Some are more specific than the base Symbols, tailored for *electi* with unique needs. I spy a woman with dark hair kneeling in the middle of a howling storm. As I watch, lightning strikes a metal rod set in the ground before her with a fury, threatening to blind me. Her hair sticks wildly in all directions, but the tempest does not touch her.

"Here we are," Pliny announces, drawing up short at a *locus* on the far end of the room. Unlike the others, this one is empty. I glance in at a blank white marble room, confused by his confidence. There is nothing to feed my reserves here.

The magister chuckles at my confusion, making a sweeping gesture at the space before us. A dark gray panel by the glass wall begins to hum as a relic is activated by his will. My jaw drops open as thick, white snow begins to fall from the ceiling as if the heavens themselves had opened. Ice forms on the ground below, surging out of the floor like a mushroom.

In moments, the *locus* looks like a scene ripped right out of the North. Drifts begin to form as the miniature blizzard rages.

"I thought you might like this." Pliny chuckles warmly, reaching out to place his ring against a slot in the wall. There is a click, and the glass lifts, sliding up out of my way despite not having any hinges or rails. I've never seen a relic do anything like this before. I study the ceiling, trying to discern how this was done. "Senator Varus has gone to great lengths to see to it that his gladiators are able to maintain their *Corda*."

Senator. I have been bought by a senator. My mind reels at the implication of where I have ended up. I swim now in waters far deeper than I know.

"Well, do hurry up," Pliny urges, breaking me from my investigation. "It is quite cold."

My *Cor* veins pang with hunger. Already some of the Frost trickles into me, but it is not enough. I need to be among winter. I abandon my inspection of the relic and dash across the entryway to bask in the snow. The door hisses as it descends to close me into the *locus*. I make it a half-dozen steps before I stumble to my knees, gasping in shocked delight as cold essence pours into me like a flood. This place is too young to truly embody Ancient Frost, but the Symbols are congruent enough that it will be a simple matter for me to translate it into what I need.

Snow and Ice essence flow into my *Cor*, but it is lighter and fluffier than my true Symbol. Remembering some of my teacher's theoretical lessons from the *collegium*, I turn my will inward, gathering the essence with my mind. As my supply grows, I squeeze, compressing it into something colder and harder. It takes only a moment, but I feel the essence forming into a better match for Ancient Frost.

I breathe deeply, celebrating the cold sustenance that courses into me. As my *Cor* fills, power surges in my limbs—I feel as if I am truly awake for the first time since leaving the North. Tears stream down my face as I rejoice in being sated. Turning my attention inward, I marvel at the new depths of my reserves. The pool of essence I can hold now dwarfs what I could hold at the peak of Copper. But this comes with a cost: my body has a bigger appetite now. The Silver strength that fills me is like a fire that burns brighter, requiring more fuel. My *animus* can now extend beyond my physical body, but that, too, takes more out of me to maintain.

Still cultivating essence for my reserves, I turn my attention toward the Ancient Frost veins that run through my flesh. They burn brightly to my senses now that they are full of essence. I can feel a strange resistance, as if they should be able to do more, but they will not. It reminds me of my limits when I first Ascended to Copper. But unlike my time in the iron pits of Agogia, it does not seem to give way under the torrent of essence that I am pumping through my body. The resistance feels different, stronger and more resolute in its defiance. If I want to continue walking the path toward Ascending to *aurum*, it will require different steps than before.

Even as I am being filled, I feel my other emptiness more keenly. It is as if I were dying of both starvation and thirst, and someone handed me a canteen so I can drink my fill. I still hunger. The scraps of Iron essence that I hold are little more than tiny breadcrumbs in the vastness of my Silver reserves.

I shake my head, ignoring my Iron Symbol's complaints as I focus on drawing in as much of Ancient Frost as I can. As the cold mantle settles around my shoulders, I embrace its harsh logic, trying to figure out my next move.

Somehow, Pliny suspects that there is something unusual about me. I do not know what he thinks he knows, but I am certain that he cannot know the truth, that I am an uninhibited Ironbound. Perhaps it is merely the fact that I have Ascended to Silver while being an *immundus*.

If I fail, I will not be made a gladiator but thrown away as fodder. Perhaps the guards that watch over the less impressive *electi* will be less attentive than the others. That might be my avenue to being able to escape.

My reserve fills quickly, thanks to my Heart's affinity with drawing in essence. I still crave Iron, but I have taken as much Ancient Frost as I can hold, and the dark blue sphere in my mind is about to overflow. But I do not move even as I stop drawing on my surroundings. I can use this time to think—

"That should do it," Pliny calls from behind my shoulder as the door rises once more.

My head whips around to stare at the magister in shock. The short man gives me a warm smile, empty of any guile, but gestures for me to join him and the bald woman back in the main room.

I'm cold with fear as I follow his instructions. That had to be a coincidence. How could he know the exact moment that I finished refilling my *Cor* reserves? He must have decided to give me a certain amount of time that just happened to be exactly how long I needed.

Surely.

My eyes narrow, but the man only pats me on the shoulder as I emerge from the *locus*. He seems as threatening as a squirrel. No suspicion lurks beneath his brown eyes, only a benign sort of friendliness. It only makes me more scared of him.

"Contessa, he's all yours," the magister declares, gesturing at the warrior, who towers over him.

"Right," she muses quietly, studying me more closely this time. Her renewed attention only increases my newfound concern. "Let's see what you're made of, boy. Reese! Prepare a field!" A distant voice shouts in understanding, and I step out into the sands once more.

CHAPTER 3

The center of the gladiator training facility is divided into a dozen sectors. A ghost of a grin twists my lips as I remember my first time stepping onto a different set of sands at the beginning of the *Sententia*. If only that Castor could see the path I have walked since that day.

He'd have let Aulus knock him out of the melee to save his parents.

The bitter realization worms its way through the back of my mind, causing me to stumble as I step off the stone floor onto the sand. Would I? If I knew the devastation that would come from this journey, would I have been selfless enough to abandon it?

I think so.

I hope so.

For a moment, I hesitate, studying myself from a new angle. It's like seeing my own reflection for the first time. I've never noticed the lines of my own jaw until this moment. But instead of strong cheekbones, it is arrogance and selfishness I see. I hate it—I hate myself. Then a gentler voice reminds me that I lost in the Maze. Even if I had let the boy betray me, I still would have found myself here. The oath would have been broken—and the dead gods would have taken their pound of flesh. *I am not responsible for my parents' death*, I tell myself fiercely, part affirmation, part prayer.

I am but a leaf on the wind of Dead Fortuna's whims.

A handful of warriors gather next to Contessa on the edge of the training field, pulled from their training. Unlike everyone else I've seen in this compound, there are only Silver *Cor* veins running through their exposed arms and upper bodies. The *lanista* raises her hand and I follow her gesture, eyes widening as I spot a row of relics planted in a marble block on the other edge of the training field.

Several of them shift, and I watch in awe as the ground shudders. The outline of a thick, black square rises from beneath the white sand, forming a dueling square. The wealth on display in this place is staggering. My *collegium*'s arena probably cost less than this facility. I struggle to wrap my mind around the disparity between this ancient family and mine, but it is incomprehensible to me.

"What is your name?" Contessa demands, pointing a *gladius* at me. The scar on her face only serves to make her even more intimidating.

"Castor," I tell her, hesitant to lie. I have no idea what her Symbol is. For all I know, she can hear my heartbeat or see a shadow of guile in my eyes. I cannot afford to make her more suspicious of me than she already is.

"Reese, see what Castor can do," she orders, turning to look at a tall, sleek woman who wears sweat-stained training leathers that stop at her shoulders, letting her Silver veins shine brightly. Her black hair is shaved at the sides, leaving her with a horse's mane.

"Yes, *Domina*!" the woman barks eagerly. She steps toward a weapon rack and looks at me with an appraising look. "Single or double blades?"

"What?"

"Do you wish to fight with one or two blades?" Reese asks, looking at me as though I'm rather slow.

"Two," I muse after a moment of thought. In the legions, they trained us to fight with a sword and shield, but I found wielding a second blade natural in the battle against Knut's horde.

Reese nods sharply, sending her mane kicking in the wind. She grabs a pair of *gladii* from the weapon rack and launches them toward me with casual strength. The weapons soar one after the other, point first as they arc down to spear the sand inches from my feet.

I keep my face blank, but it takes all the self-control I possess to keep from drooling. The iron in the blades calls to me. This close, I can siphon essence from them, but it is only a fraction of what I will be able to take once I hold them.

Slowly, still holding eye contact with the gladiator, I pull the blades from the sand. Sweet, familiar awareness blooms in my mind as the weapons become a part of me. My *Cor* pulses with need, desperate to draw in the missing iron and bring my Hearts into balance.

Slowly, I allow the first kiss of Iron to flow into me. It takes a tremendous amount of effort not to let out a gasp of delight. My right hand shakes slightly, but I tighten my grip on the hilt of my blade to hide it. Tension begins to melt out of my joints as I absorb the nectar of essence. Ancient Frost is a part of me, but I was Ironbound before I ever was tied to winter. The metal Symbol will always be my first love.

"Are these dulled?" I ask when my breath is no longer catching in my throat. They're not, my connection to the Iron Symbol tells me with confidence. They're razor sharp. In the legions, we would be responsible for changing our *gladii* into practice weapons. But she cannot command hers to become blunt.

"The *dominus* wants to see if you're worth having as a gladiator or only a contender for the *Spectaculum* roster," Contessa reminds me with a hint of scorn. I grimace but shrug. Despite my confidence with a real sword in my hand, I don't like the concept of playing for keeps, especially if I'm planning on losing, even if it means I might be sent to be fodder for the bloody Spectacles. I'll take my chances trying to escape before I walk into the ring to die.

"Into the dueling square," Contessa barks to Reese. I force myself to stand loosely, watching the woman as she enters. We both pause on our respective sides, eyeing each other openly. She's tall, almost as tall as me, and the muscles on her arms are honed and lean. She holds the *gladius* in her left hand in a reverse grip, which makes my eyes narrow. I've never fought someone who held a blade like that before.

Despite the grim cloud that hovers over me, I feel a faint flame of excitement begin to kindle deep in my chest as my body realizes what is about to come. I have only fought Astrid since I reached Silver. I have not gotten to test myself against another *electi*. Today, I take the first step in following in the footsteps of Gaius and Percy to become a *Fidelis*.

"Instructions, *Domina*?" Reese asks, settling into a fighting crouch.

"First blood," the woman replies, easing some of my fears of being sliced to ribbons. "Fighters ready?"

"Aye, *Domina*," Reese bellows. I merely give the woman a stiff nod.

The bald woman gestures at the relics again, and my ears pop as the pressure in the air around us shifts and the arena seals itself. The black lines on the ground begin to glow with a purple stripe. A dull hum emits from them that rumbles in my chest. I know, without even testing their will, that I am now trapped in here with the maned gladiator.

Reese wastes no time. She stalks forward in an uneven gait, swords raised for an aggressive attack. I eye her approach for a moment, trying to discern some sense of what her *Cor*'s attunement is. I see no telltale signs, then she is on me, blade extended in a lunge.

My left hand comes up automatically, twisting to parry her attack. I feel the telltale whisper from the Iron Symbol as she shifts her angle, dropping the blade into a feint and trying to throw me off balance. Even as her backwards blade begins to blur forward in a horizontal slash aimed at my ribs, I let her distraction go, twisting my own left *gladius* to point downward, blocking her attack. Reese's eyes go wide as my weapon catches hers. All I need to do is stab her with my right blade, and I would win in the opening exchange. But I don't.

For a heartbeat, I'm in shock. It's so easy. I can sense every movement of her weapons as she makes them. There are no secrets that she can keep from me. Our eyes meet, and she knows that I could kill her.

My awareness of her sword deepens as it meets mine. Before, it was as if I could hear her swords at any distance, but now I can touch it—manipulate it. It would be as easy as a stray thought for me to shatter her blade; she has no Iron Symbol to protect it.

In the space between heartbeats, Reese panics, calling on her Symbol. A blinding flash explodes between us, and I stagger backward, blinking furiously to clear my vision. There's no heat in her attack, just a furious amount of… light. She must be a *Lumos* Symbol.

The gladiator disengages from my blades, using my momentary blindness as an opportunity. But I do not need my eyes to see her swords. My Silver senses track her easily, telling me exactly where her weapons are. She circles to my right before striking. It would be a simple thing for me to bring my *gladius* up to block, but I accept the opportunity that this gives me—a way to lose without garnering suspicion.

I stumble to the left, holding my hands up toward my eyes. I twist as her lunge strikes at me, stepping so that the edge of her sword only lightly grazes my shoulder as she goes by. I hiss in pain, burning some Ancient Frost essence to numb the minor wound.

The world halts as Reese's stroke completes. I am completely frozen, suddenly unable to move except for my neck. Confused, I turn my head, finally able to see. Reese is similarly frozen mid-lunge, blade extending past me. A spray of red blood hangs in midair where it has been ripped from my flesh. My heart still beats, and my lungs breathe, but otherwise, it is as if time itself has been paused. It reminds me of being caught in Aquilo's grip.

If I could move my jaw, it would be on the floor as I gape in shock. I do not know what manner of relics allows Contessa to control the battlefield like this, but this is a power I cannot even conceive. I am terrified, witnessing the power that is beyond my grasp. But at the same time, I crave it for myself.

Contessa walks into the square, eyeing me with a flat, uninterested gaze. She glances between the two of us, as if determining if the cut is worth ending the bout. After a moment, she turns to look over my shoulder, apparently convinced.

"Well, Pliny, it seems you might be wrong after all. Are you satisfied?"

"I am not," the gentle magister replies.

"Do you think young Castor here lacks suitable motivation?" A chill runs down my spine at the amused tone in her voice.

"It would be remiss not to test further, I suspect." The man's warm voice only increases my fear. He seems to know too much about everything, and I have secrets that are worth more than my life.

"Make him run the gauntlet," a harsh voice calls from the far end of the training facility. I do not need to be able to turn to know that the senator has returned. My stomach lurches. I do not know what that is, but the cruelly amused look on Contessa's face tells me I will not like it.

"A wise suggestion, *Dominus*," Pliny replies at once.

"Very well." The bald woman nods once, stepping back out of the arena. "Fighters, this bout is complete. When I release you, you will return to your sides at once. Am I understood?"

"Yes, *Domina*," Reese replies at once.

"Yes, *Domina*," I echo, a sick feeling beginning to form in my stomach. At once, the heavy pressure that holds the world still vanishes. I stagger to the side, watching my blood fall to the ground, where the sand drinks it up with gusto.

Reese staggers to the side, bleeding off the momentum from her stalled lunge, but then immediately withdraws, returning to her side of the box. I copy her, trying to figure out what this gauntlet is. The handful of other gladiators next to Contessa have begun limbering up and arming themselves, which I take as a bad sign. My hands tighten on the hilt of my two *gladii*, and I continue to suck in Iron essence, preparing myself for another fight. Every moment that we delay brings my *Corda* back into balance and restores more of my missing strength.

"How long of a gauntlet, *Dominus*?" Contessa calls toward the far end of the room. I turn to see where the man who bought me stands. Varus has changed out of his leathers into a black pair of pants and a matching tunic that are worked with golden filigree. He studies me for a moment, glancing at Pliny before looking back at me. At last, he comes to a decision, crossing his arms as he leans against the wall.

"Five gladiators, ten minutes," he declares. The warriors around Contessa go still, like a pack of hounds waiting for the symbol.

"First blood?" the woman prompts, clearly expecting a different answer.

"Let's make sure our prospect is suitably motivated," he replies after a moment of thought. His heavy gaze flicks to me, and there is no kindness in those gray eyes. He suspects something now too; I can read it in his posture. "Victory or Death." A cold anger sweeps through me as I study the man who bought me. I am nothing to him, not even human—unless I show him that I am a worthwhile investment. He reminds me of General Tyrus, imperator of Agogia. I manage to keep a sneer off my face, but only just.

I understand the logic. If I truly am a special *electus* like Pliny suspects, then I will have no choice but to use it to survive. I do not think they would truly let me die once they see how I can fight, but the danger is necessary to force me to show my hand. I'll just have to show them something that they'll believe.

"As you wish, *Dominus*." The other gladiators are looking at me again, curious expressions on their faces. Reese almost looks like she pities me. I ignore them, turning to the *lanista* for instruction. My anger shelters me from any fear, burning bright and cold. Its flames stoke my confidence into a raging fire of ego. I have faced down *berserkirs* and *furiae* in a hurricane made by an almost dead god. I am not afraid of a couple Silver gladiators.

"Do you know the rules of the gauntlet?" Contessa asks calmly as the rest of the warriors begin to ready themselves behind her. Most of them wield swords. My eyes narrow as I watch a tall man lift a heavy trident like a spear. I shake my head, not trusting my voice to not betray my anger.

"Your task is to survive. The bout will last for ten minutes, or until you are dead. You will begin with one opponent, but every two minutes, I will release another to join them. You may defend yourself as vigorously as you wish, but do not kill any of them. If you do, the match will restart, and I will fill in for the slain gladiator." I eye the Gold *electus* skeptically. The Iron Symbol gives me a truly unique advantage in combat against anyone wielding a blade, but I would be a fool to think I could fight her and four other Silver warriors at the same time.

I nod my understanding, and she gestures at the distant panel of relics. The sand beneath us rumbles as the black lines retreat beneath the surface before reappearing further away, expanding the arena several times over.

"How favorable do you want the battlefield to be, *Dominus*?" Contessa asks, tossing a glance over at the senator. He frowns in thought for a moment before wiggling his hand in a so-so movement.

"Understood. Reese, you will start again," the bald woman orders, stepping up to the new border lines. The maned warrior nods, settling into her strange stance once more. The tension in the room spikes as the other gladiators prepare to join the battle. I embrace Ancient Frost fully, letting its dispassionate logic settle around me like a second set of armor.

"Fighters, are you ready?" Contessa looks between the two of us, collecting our nods. I am devoid of emotion. I can no longer hold back if I am going to survive. The master of this house wishes to see if I am worthy.

I hope he is watching closely.

"Begin."

CHAPTER 4

My ears pop once again as the black lines seal us in the sandy arena. The center of the sand bubbles, and my jaw drops as a spring of water erupts from the ground, frothing with tremendous force. It pools around the center as a depression forms in the ground, creating a simple pond. This, then, is the semi-favorable battleground that Contessa designed for me.

Reese's swords begin to glow with a threatening light as she advances. Her expression is conflicted, but her movements are sharp and precise. She seeks to end me quickly, out of mercy, I think. I appreciate the intent but have my own plans.

I ignore her posturing, instead dashing toward the pond as quickly as I dare. At the edge, I dip both of my blades in the water, pouring Ancient Frost essence into the swords in my hands as I reveal my own Symbol for the first time.

A thin coat of ice cracks into being as the water freezes over the swords, growing from the hilt to the tip like a creeping moss. Moving swiftly, I dip the blades in the water again, adding a serrated edge to my creation. This is a simple application of my *Cor*—turning water into ice is the basic move of Winter. Compared to the effort of manifesting an entire sword out of thin air, the draw on my essence reserves is negligible. That is a trick I would rather save for later.

Reese pauses midstride, eyes wide. I give her a predator's smile to match my blades, amused by her reaction. Ice is a very rare Symbol—I doubt she has much experience fighting against it. The confident expression flees her face, replaced by a hesitant amount of respect.

Exactly what I hoped for.

For a moment, I close my eyes, confident that my senses will warn me if her weapons get too close. My Iron *Cor* is finally almost full. Both of my reserves teem with essence, gray and dark blue, burning bright in my mind like beacons, eager to be used. For the first time in months, I am in balance. I am at peace.

My eyes snap open—Reese flinches at what she sees in them. I smile but say nothing, stalking forward, trying to be like Gaius when he challenged Knut. There is no fear, no anger burning inside me. Only the rigid certainty of metal and ice.

Reese raises her right blade to ward off my first strike, readying her backward blade for a quick counterstroke. I feel it shift as she tightens her wrist. My second *gladius* is already moving as her sword blurs forward.

She twitches in surprise as I catch her slash. I didn't even bother to look at it. A shadow of concern flickers across Reese's face, but I ignore it. I already know what she is going to do next. Her hands tighten around the hilts of her blades, causing them to shift their angles as they're locked against mine. Warned by her movement, I close my eyes just before a burst of light blares from her weapons, triggered by her *Lumos* Symbol.

Her spark is so bright that I can see it through my closed eyelids. Once more, she tries to take advantage of my blindness to strike, but it is my turn to reveal one of my own tricks. Reese tries to disengage her sword from mine, only to discover they are stuck together, frozen fast. It is a simple matter for me to command the ice on my *gladius* to shift, encompassing hers as well.

She jerks her left blade, and I pull with my right, engaging her in a simple tug of war. The light fades, and I open my eyes, laughing mirthlessly at the confused expression on her face. She looks at me indignantly before inspecting our blades. We circle one another, locked in this frozen grip.

"Neat trick." She grunts, trying to tug her weapons free, but they are stuck fast.

"A pity your light doesn't produce heat," I taunt, holding my ground.

"Have you thought this through?" she asks, looking back at me.

"It seems to be working for me so far."

"What about him?"

"Second fighter, enter the ring," Contessa echoes from behind us, and I let out a small sigh of frustration. I hadn't forgotten, but I had hoped to have a little longer before she got reinforcements. Reese immediately stops circling, jamming her feet into the ground to prevent me from facing this new threat. My *animus* senses the new gladiator's strange, thin blade as he steps into the arena. It's like nothing I've ever seen before, more like a giant needle than the thick weapons of the legions. He surges forward eagerly, bearing down on my exposed back.

I give Reese an amused smile as we struggle for positioning. She's spending a lot of effort to hold me in place for her reinforcement. I track his progress as he races to close with me, the Iron Symbol warning me as he readies his sword for a strike at my exposed back. Reese's eyes widen in anticipation, and I know that this is the moment.

I release my frozen grip on her left blade with Ancient Frost, slipping free of our stalemate with ease. She staggers, caught off guard as the tension between us vanishes. I take a half step backward, turning just in time to catch the new gladiator's lunge with the tip of my *gladius*. Gently, I guide his strike past me, welcoming it into our huddle. It's easy with my Iron senses to shift his attack so it slides into the crux of where Reese's and my other blade are still frozen together.

I laugh as I grab his weapon with the ice while releasing my own. I retreat a pair of steps, admiring my handiwork. Both of my blades are free, but the new gladiator, a shorter, lean duelist, has his thin blade frozen to Reese's second *gladius*. For a heartbeat, they both stare at me in shock. If this were a real duel, they both know that I would be on the attack, seeking to kill them before they could extricate themselves from the mess I have created.

Then the moment is shattered, and they begin frantically pulling at their swords, trying to break them free. Reese raises the blade I released and hammers at the ice, sending chips flying, but it holds. My legion-forged instincts scream at me to strike while they are distracted, but I hesitate. Killing them will only create more problems for me. *But no one said anything about injuries.*

I dance forward, slashing at the duelist's exposed back leg, aiming through his hamstring with a clean stroke. My *animus* shows me exactly how deep I slice. I only want to cripple him, not open an artery. A small part of me delights in returning to this form; what I was made to be.

The thin man collapses, lamed by my strike. I wince in sympathy but ignore him. If the descendants of Pelias can afford a training arena like this for their gladiators, they can pay for a *medico* to fix them. I glance at Contessa to see if she has a complaint. The bald woman stares at me without an expression but does not stop the fight. I grin at her, but that fades as I see a darkness swirl in the corner of her eyes. I should not push her too far.

I turn my attention back to Reese, twirling my *gladii* with a flourish. My left blade is still coated in ice, but the right is clean. I debate summoning more but decide against it. I cannot easily refill my Ancient Frost essence here and do not want to spend my resources wildly. There are still three more gladiators waiting in the wings.

Reese looks at me with wide eyes. She's caught so off-guard that her blades are no longer glowing. I advance, startling her out of her stupor, and she drops her right sword, which is still frozen to the fallen fighter's dueling blade. It falls with a *thump*, and she moves to meet me with a single weapon.

I cannot kill her, but I can maim her too. If I move quickly enough, I can have her out of the fight before the next gladiator is called. That is the way you are meant to survive the gauntlet, I realize. It is a test of my speed and aggression. Armed with this plan, I lunge forward, right-hand blade extended in a stab. Reese is forced to parry my strike, leaving herself exposed to my second *gladius*. I slash at her leg, intending to wound her in a similar manner, but my attack hits only open air. Before I can cut her, the woman disengages, leaping back from me before vanishing from sight.

My jaw goes slack as the woman disappears in front of me. For a wild heartbeat, I worry I have gone insane, or if she has somehow teleported, but then my brain catches up. I can still *feel* her sword in the same place, and I remember what her Symbol is.

Lumos—she's Lightbound.

Reese is bending light around herself so that I cannot see her, even though she is right in front of me. What power. For a moment, I am distracted by the thought of my grandfather being a Golden *Lumos electus* himself. The inheritance he left, the portion of his relics that was not taken by the Empress, was used as simple lights for our home. I never thought about what else his Symbol could do.

Then Reese takes a slow step, and I realize that I face a new danger. It is a simple matter for me to track her sword with my *animus*. But that is not something I can reveal to the palatines that watch me with keen eyes.

If I am to survive the fight, I will have to use my Silver senses to prevent her from getting the jump on me. But if I am to survive *after* the fight, I cannot be too prescient. Adopting a look of confusion, I begin to backpedal, retreating from the middle of the arena, tucking myself into a corner. I hope my logic is simple—I don't want to let the ghost circle behind me.

I feel her *gladius* moving as she prowls toward me. Despite my advantage, I am still intimidated by the level of strength she shows. Her ability to blind an opponent in a fight was an annoying, if beatable, trick. This is something else entirely. It cannot be easy to maintain, although unlike me, she is in an arena full of essence for her to cultivate. I glare at the bright lights above us, wondering if I could somehow break them with a perfect sword throw. But then I wouldn't have a sword, and that feels stupid.

In the background, the three waiting gladiators watch us. A short, dark woman flips a dagger in her hands, her face expressionless. A bandolier runs across her chest, stuffed with more weapons. Next to her, a wide man holds a trident like the one on the Pelias crest. Behind them, a tall man with long blond hair prowls like a caged *tigris*. Somehow, I know he is the most dangerous of the three of them.

Reese continues to stalk toward me, moving at a glacial pace. I wonder why she is taking her time, but then I see a slight puff of sand as her footstep disturbs the ground of our arena, and I understand the weakness of her ability. I don't have to be able to sense her metal to track her. I just have to follow her footsteps.

"Next fighter," calls Contessa sharply. The relic-powered curtain on our battlefield ripples for a moment as it lowers to allow someone to enter.

I glance at the trio of waiting gladiators and let out a groan as the barrel-chested man steps into the arena, twirling his trident as he does. He watches me with dark, patient eyes. Unlike their lamed predecessor, who is still crawling toward the edge of the arena, he does not charge toward me. Instead, he circles in the opposite direction of Reese, hunting me like a hound. I guess he's trained with the maned woman long enough to learn how to follow footsteps too.

I grimace, electing to stay in my corner as the big man hunts me. Now that she has reinforcements, Reese picks up her own pace, circling toward my left. I will need to do something about her soon; the longer I wait the more outnumbered I will be.

I raise my right *gladius* in challenge at the Trident, but he snorts contemptuously, continuing his steady pace, content to take his time. I eye his long weapon with something like disgust. If I'm going to take him out, I need to figure out how to get inside the trident's spear-like guard.

With a sigh, I stride to meet the gladiator, consciously tracking Reese's invisible blade as I do. I cannot wait, and they both know it. I hoped that he would not be disciplined enough to resist my challenge, but it seems that these fighters have been well trained.

Once I am out of the corner, the man is only too happy to meet me. He leaps forward, trident flickering as he jabs wildly at me. I counter his attacks, being careful not to get my *gladii* trapped between the spines of his weapon, where it would be a simple matter for him to rip it from my grip.

As we exchange blows, I am in awe of my power. These are dangerous, well-trained warriors. And yet, the advantage of my Iron *Cor* Heart is staggering. My long hair floats in front of my eyes, obscuring my vision, but it does not matter. Each of his attacks is telegraphed to me as soon as he begins; there are no secrets here. I could kill him with my eyes closed.

This is why the Empress's chosen Censors carry blades made of *tellus*. To protect them from men like me.

I bat his trident wide and lunge forward, getting past the sharp tines to get into striking range of my *gladius*. If I can wound him enough to drive him back, it will give me time to deal with Reese, who is closing quickly. His eyes go wide with surprise as my sword cuts toward him, but it is my turn to be shocked when my weapon bounces off his rock-hard skin. I would have done more damage hitting a boulder. Something distant rebuffs me; I have the vague sense of someone else's will speaking a language that I do not know. Completely unprepared for that kind of resistance, my weapon slides off him, unable to find any purchase.

I have never seen a human with that kind of power before, but our family's loyal stonehound, Agre could do something similar. How unexpected and useful for him. I've never felt jealous of another *electus*'s Symbol, but I can't deny that his is strong.

Reese takes advantage of my distraction by breaking into a charge from my left. I feel her *gladius* approach, rising and falling as she pumps her fists in a full sprint. Sand sprays beneath her feet as she charges at me. She thinks that Trident is enough to occupy my full attention. She assumes incorrectly.

Despite my knowledge, I force myself to wait until she flickers into sight on my left flank, sword raised for a devastating blow. Without even looking, I disengage from Trident, dancing underneath her upraised sword and flashing past her as she strikes at empty air. I retreat a half-dozen steps from the pair of them, twirling my blades with a sharp smile.

The two gladiators look at me with stunned expressions before glancing at each other. Reese's face is haggard, and she pants with exertion. Bending the light for so long has taken a toll on her. It will be a while before she can do something like that again.

"Neat trick." I smile at her as they both catch their breaths. I am not nearly as tired as either of them, and a savage joy continues to grow in my chest. Despite the danger I'm in, I'm enjoying this. It has been too long since I felt this free.

Reese glares at me but does not rise to my barb. As one they split, driving me backward like a pack. I give ground, letting them drive me toward a corner. But even as I do, I know I cannot afford to get stuck. Eventually, I will run out of hands to block with, Iron Symbol or not.

"Next fighter!" Contessa barks, and I feel the air pressure shift as a third gladiator enters. I have just enough time to remember the dagger-tossing woman before my Symbol flares with warning, and I duck even as I turn to face her. A knife slices viciously through the air above me before thumping flatly against the relic's barrier and dropping to the ground.

The new woman eyes me with distrust, plucking another throwing blade from her bandolier. Just what I need, someone with range. Trident and Reese hunt me, driving me toward the new gladiator. I sigh in frustration before turning my back on the original two and rushing toward Knife, as I dub her in my head.

Maybe I can disarm her before the others can catch me.

The woman's eyes go wide as I charge. Her hands blur as she throws another dagger at me, and I parry it out of the air without a thought. Let them think that my reflexes are that good. Knives grabs another pair from her belt, hurling them at the same time. My blades move independently, knocking both of them wide in a spray of sparks.

I hear the thuds of my pursuers' footsteps on the sand behind me and feel the iron of their weapons as they draw close. I have not been fast enough. Now I will have to fight. I point my left *gladius* at Knives, promising to return after I deal with my attackers.

Out of time, I spin in time to block the trident that hurtles toward my midsection. I let my remaining ice bind our blades together. I grow tired of being outreached by his weapon. He tries to wrench my sword out of my grip, but I hold on tightly. Time is beginning to work against them. I only need to last another moment.

With all my Silver strength, I hammer my left blade into the ice, hoping that the theatrics will be enough to satisfy my Golden observers. As my blade connects, I command the ice to shatter. At the same time, I reach out with the Symbol of Iron, sending my *animus* into the head of his trident, commanding it to do the same.

The metal head of his weapon explodes under the force of my strike, as if somehow made brittle by the extreme cold. I dance backward as his eyes go round as saucers. I catch Reese's blade as she strikes at my side. I have no ice left to use, so instead, I trap her sword between both of mine and twist, trying to wrench it out of her grasp.

I duck as Knife takes another shot at me, pulling on Reese's weapon as I drop under the throw. She staggers but does not lose her grip on the sword. Giving up on that avenue, I explode out of my crouch, slamming into her with my shoulder with enough force to send her sprawling.

Now I'm panting with exertion. Iron and Ancient Frost sing in my *Cor* as I dance. My limbs feel strong, powered by my essence. But despite my success at staying alive, I know time is running out.

"Final fighter!" Contessa barks, and the barrier ripples once more. My eyes flick over Knife's shoulder to watch the tall gladiator with flowing blond hair enter the arena. He moves with a fluid grace that screams of danger. He carries a single dueling blade in a loose grip and strides toward our fight with quick, sharp steps. A smug, confident smile twists his lips. He knows that he is going to end this. Unlike Reese, he does not look at all conflicted about the prospect of killing me.

Dread coils in me as I watch his approach. His release means that there are still two minutes left in our match. I do not think I am going to survive this. I should have taken my chances with Trident or Reese and tried to injure one of them out of the fight instead of chasing the knife-throwing woman.

Reese tries to climb to her feet, but I aim a kick at her face, snapping her head back and slamming her back into the ground. I do not have any hope that it will stun her for long. Her Silver constitution should shake off that blow with ease, but even if it buys me a handful of seconds, it will do something.

"Gaaah!" Trident roars, charging at my back, harassing me with his headless stick. It may not be able to stab me, but it still is heavy enough to *hurt*. Fortunately, it still has a pair of nails buried in its head, which have enough iron in them for my *animus* to track. I twist, blocking his attack, while simultaneously striking at his thigh. It bounces off his stone skin with a *crack*, sending a shiver up my arm.

A knife hurtles through the air at me, forcing me to bend even further so that it flows through the space that my head had just been. I spare a glare for the short woman, but then my attention is stolen by a bigger threat. From across the arena, the golden-haired gladiator lunges at me.

Wind whips the sand around us into the air like a miniature gale as he rockets toward me. I feel him coming but am so stunned by his speed that I barely manage to deflect his attack. Quick as a thought, his blade rotates, breaking free of mine to slither forward. I twist to the side, hammering my left-hand *gladius* on his sword as it passes under me. The force of my blow makes him stumble as he resets, but he does not drop his weapon.

He must be an Air Symbol, I realize, squinting against the dust storm that his passage triggered. A flare of red-hot rage burns through logic's cold grip on my mind.

Just like Atticus.

Hate fills me, and I almost lose my grip on both of my chilly Symbols. I have nowhere to channel this fiery rage, so instead, I advance to meet this Air *electus*. The duelist is on me in a second, blade flashing at a speed that I cannot process. Only my connection to Iron allows me to keep up with his blinding pace. The smug confidence on his face begins to slip as I match his strokes. There are very few fighters who can, I suspect.

Trident—or should I say Longstaff now—circles behind me, trying to capitalize on Air's distraction. A knife zips past my ear, forcing me to step backward so I cannot press my advantage. The blond man surges into the ground I give, pressuring me. Reese claws to her feet, and as she rises, my own heart sinks.

This is it. I know there's about a minute left, but there's no way I will survive all four of these hunters pushing me at once. Not unless I show them something that they won't believe. I exhale as I counter another blindingly fast strike from Air.

I cannot fight with my heart. This is not Atticus, just someone who wields a similar power. I must fight with my mind if I am going to survive this. Mentally, I check the essence levels in my reserves. I've used almost a third of my Ancient Frost with my icy tricks, but there is still plenty. More than I ever had at my beck and call as a Copper.

Hopefully, it will be enough.

Longstaff charges me from behind as I block another strike from Air. I snap toward him, hurling my right *gladius* at the man like it's a throwing knife. The sword flips end-over-end; unlike Knife's blades, it was never balanced for throwing. Despite that, my throw isn't half bad. The hilt cracks against the front of his skull with enough force to knock his feet out from under him, which is the best outcome I could have hoped for.

Seeing an opportunity, Air disengages his sword from mine, lunging forward in a strike aimed at my guts. I turn back to face his assault, moving my right hand to block as if it still held a weapon. In my mind, I trigger the ability that Aquilo taught me.

Glacialis Falx, the Frozen Blade.

The rotten god's teaching remains true, and a *gladius* made of ice grows out of the palm of my right hand, a copy of the one that I carried in the legions. Essence pours out of me. Despite the increased size of my reserve, I do not have much of the Ancient Frost left.

But it also gives me a tiny source to cultivate from. I inhale deeply, desperately pulling both of my essences in to fill the void in my *Corda*. The Air *electus*'s blow shudders against my frozen sword, but I reinforce it with my will, keeping it intact.

For a moment, the battlefield freezes. The blond gladiator stares at my icy *gladius* with a stunned expression. Then he makes eye contact with me, and everything explodes into motion. Reese charges at me from the side, and I glance at her, throwing my remaining metal blade. This time, I hurl it at the ground. The heavy tip sinks into the sand easily, right after passing through the woman's foot.

She screams in pain, tripping as the weapon pins her in place.

Gritting my teeth, I channel every ounce of my remaining Ancient Frost essence into summoning a second copy of the *Glacialis Falx*, grunting in pain as my Winter *Cor* Heart almost runs dry. It feels like I am in a canoe bouncing on the top of rocky shallows. A second frozen *gladius* forms in my hands, but even as I turn back toward Air, my *animus* warns me that he is already slashing his weapon toward me, even though I am far out of his range.

An invisible blade of air slams into me, cutting my shirt like a knife. The force of it lifts me off the ground and sends me crashing against the force wall maintained by the relics. They crackle warningly with latent power, and my breath explodes out of me. I cannot see it, but the barrier is as hard as stone. I slide down to the ground, just in time to dance to the side as the blond man fires a second attack.

Once again, he slashes at me with his sword from across the arena. A white streak forms on the edge of his blade, trailing behind it as he commands the air with his will. As he completes his swing, it materializes into something physical and leaps forward, like an arrow being released from a bow. The curved line hisses threateningly as it cuts toward me.

I cannot sense it with my *Corda*, but I have eyes. I am just able to twist out of the line of his attack before it slams into the invisible barrier behind me with enough force to rattle my teeth. I lever myself off the wall and bound forward, not wanting to spend another moment trapped in this corner.

Knife throws another dagger at me, which I knock to the side with one of my icy blades. Where does she keep all of them? Down to only a single opponent for a moment, I turn my attention back on the arrogant blond warrior who races to meet me. The rage I shoved to the side bursts back to the front. His face becomes that of my enemy—the blond hair is close enough. If I can kill this gladiator, then one day soon I can kill the Censor who murdered my father.

It's my turn to press the attack, using both of my blades to keep him on his back feet. Even though I have two, he's still so *fast*. Every time I fool him with a feint before striking with the other *gladius*, his sword is somehow miraculously back in position to block my next attack.

Our swords ring with the sound of iron on ice as we dance. There are no thoughts in my mind. Pain and anger have drowned out any logic that I had to my name. Frost essence flows back into me from the two blades I hold, refilling the void that their creation left in me. I become reckless in my fury, letting some of my frost cross over from my blades to cover his own.

Air explodes forward in a lunge aimed at my heart. I hammer my right-hand *gladius* down on the tip of his blade, calling on Iron and Ice to shatter at the same time. The point of his sword explodes in a brilliant show of power. His eyes go wide as he pulls back his weapon to inspect it, but I do not give him a moment. I strike again with my left, carving off the next section of the dueling blade in the same manner. When he uses the stub to block my third strike, I destroy it down to the pommel.

Without missing a beat, I lunge forward, icy swords extended toward his chest. The arena freezes, locking us all in place. The tips of my *gladii* are inches from Air's skin, and I snarl in fury at being denied my vengeance.

"Time. The gauntlet is concluded," Contessa announces. Her voice is hushed, almost reverent. I'm able to turn my head far enough to look at her. She stares at my two Frozen Blades with unabashed shock. What did Aquilo do to me? I know that being able to manifest a Symbol like this is rare, but maybe I have underestimated his gift.

"If you'll permit me, *Dominus*, I believe that makes three," Pliny muses from somewhere behind me into the silence.

Varus scoffs in mild disbelief as he replies. "Your count is, as ever, correct, Magister. A Silver that can manifest? Did you know, or was it another guess?"

"I suspect that we have only scratched the surface of what he is capable of, *Dominus*." Pliny's response fills me with the same fear all over again. I was reckless, foolish. I'm going to get myself killed.

"We shall see," the senator promises ominously. "Contessa, see to your people. Then we will deal with Castor."

"Aye, *Dominus*," the bald woman responds quickly. My ears pop as the barrier lowers for a final time, but we are not released from the stasis that binds us. The *lanista* walks to the edge and assesses me with mistrusting eyes.

"When I release you, the fight is *over*. Do you understand? You will release your Symbol and do as you are told. Good?" Once again, all I can do is nod. My anger fades. Air no longer wears Atticus's face.

His own is still smug, but it is not the one that murdered my father in front of me.

Contessa eyes me for another moment before deciding to trust me. She raises her left hand, while her right rides on the hilt of the sword at her hip. A small smile pulls at the corner of my lips at the sight. I have made quite an impression. With a gesture to the relics, she banishes the will that surrounds us. I do as I was bid and release my grip on both of my Symbols before sagging in exhaustion as their strength fades from me. My frozen blades *thunk* as they land on the sand, already beginning to thaw. Soon a patch of wet sand will be the only sign that they were ever here.

The wounds on my chest and shoulder burn. I glance down at my ruined tunic, eyeing the bleeding line with distaste. I am a Silver *electus* and will heal, but I hope that they let me see the *medico* too. I have no desire to be crippled by a nasty infection. Attendants appear from somewhere and help the other gladiators out of the arena. The duelist has to be taken out on a stretcher, as does Reese. The maned gladiator shoots me a confused look as they carry her away. To my surprise, she raises her hand in a farewell wave. I do not return it.

Then I am alone with the two spooked warriors and a too-calm magister. The only other person in the entire training facility is the woman who still sits in the storm *locus*, absorbing the lightning.

Varus circles me, looking at me with a furious intensity. I feel like a prized stallion up for auction. Pliny merely stands before me, a reassuring smile on his placid face. It only makes me more afraid. This gauntlet is more dangerous than the one I just survived.

"Where did you learn to fight like that?" Contessa demands, coming to stand next to the magister. I hesitate, unsure how to answer that question. For a wild second, I almost ask if they know the Marius brothers, but I stop myself. I am almost certain they do.

"I had an older brother who was a caravan guard," I lie after a moment. "He taught me the basics."

"The basics." The bald woman snorts, crossing her arms in disgust.

"And the manifesting?" Pliny asks gently.

"Spent some time in the North… looking for my brother. Came to me in a snowstorm. Couldn't see my hand in front of my face, then all of a sudden, it clicked."

"A natural epiphany. How interesting."

Varus completes his circle around me, joining his subordinates at the front. His gaze narrows as he studies me further. I feel his perception like a heavy weight. I'm not sure if I'm imagining it, or if it is part of his *animus* sweeping over me. After a long moment, he tilts his head and extends a finger to point at my chest.

"What," he asks in soft, dangerous tones, "is that?" I glance down at what he is pointing at, and my heart stops in dread. There, exposed by the hole in my tunic is the mark of the Twelfth Legion burned into my chest: *XII*.

CHAPTER 5

"A bad joke," I growl after a moment of terrified reflection. My mind races, trying to think how I can possibly explain how I bear the legion mark without being Ironbound. I catch a glance of the white *rasa* veins in my forearms, and an idea begins to form out of the darkness. "Didn't get a Heart because of the drought. Signed up for the legions to get one, but things didn't go as planned." I gesture at my deformity with a wry twist of my lips.

"Ah." Pliny nods at once, as if my explanation makes total sense. "Mistakes happen, even in Agogia. Then some magister branded you and sold you to the pits?"

"You've got the sense of it." I nod, horrified to discover that my fictional story of corruption was not a new one. Maybe that's where the boys sent to the "Thirteenth" Legion ended up, sold as fodder in some arena for the Games. It made sense in a horrifyingly cold sort of way. Even the chaff could not be wasted.

"What legion were you accepted into?"

"Seventh, *Domina*." The honorific slips out of my mouth without meaning to. Part of me is disgusted at my obeisance. But part of me also wants to live, so I get over it.

"You failed to bind Iron, and instead bound Frost?" Varus's voice is skeptical. "How is that possible? I thought the Iron Legions had ways to guarantee their success."

"Well, *Dominus*, it was cold in there," I reply sheepishly. Contessa and Pliny both laugh, amused by my tone.

"It can happen," Pliny muses. "Most *rasa* are susceptible to influence, but every once in a while, there is a soul that is bound so tightly to a Symbol that it cannot be denied. It could be why he still shows some unbound lines—being forced to attune to a Symbol in an environment that does not have an ample supply can have negative effects. It might also explain his aptitude for manifesting."

"He also does not wear an *inhibitus*," Contessa points out. I resist the urge to swallow nervously. I'm suddenly grateful that I spent so much time in Dorian's dungeon—being away from the sun for so long made the rest of my flesh as pale as the ring that was around my neck.

"It didn't take," I lie with a solemn nod. "That was their first clue that things went wrong." Pliny chuckles in wry amusement. He is a pleasant man, but I don't trust it.

"Contessa, what do you think?" Varus asks his *lanista*, breaking the silence.

"I can forge him into something great." The dark-skinned woman turns to look at him. "He's got gifts, but he hasn't been taught to use them. He fights like he's legion. Even so, he should tear through most of the Silver Circuit without trouble. Don't know much about training an *immundus*, but if Pliny thinks he can Ascend him to *aurum*…" Her voice trails off, the implication more than enough. I twitch, trying to contain the shocking thrill that runs through me at the thought of Ascending to Gold. No Ironbound has reached such a height for hundreds of years. The last ones who did killed the gods.

"Pliny, I suspect I know what you will propose," Varus says dryly.

"I will help him. It only matters what you say, *Dominus*," the slight man replies. Varus chuckles but doesn't bother replying. At last, the senator turns to me, studying me once more. I settle myself, meeting his gaze firmly. It feels like the danger has passed for a moment. Now, I must figure out how to get what I want.

"Will you swear the gladiator's oath?" Varus asks, his eyes telling me he knows what I will say.

"What's in it for me?" I try to be bold but not brash. It is a narrow path, but one I must walk. Varus strikes me as a man who tolerates questions but not disrespect. As I suspected, his face flattens softly, but he doesn't look angry.

"Well, you get to keep breathing," Contessa mutters from the side.

"Until I die in the arena," I counter. "I have no burning desire to be a gladiator. Why should I risk my life for your house?"

"It is a fair question, Contessa," Varus rumbles, cutting off the *lanista* before she can berate me further. "The boy did not choose this life; he deserves to at least decide for himself." I arch an eyebrow at the man, begrudgingly feeling my respect for him increase.

"Do you know what happens to gladiators who win a season of the Games and earn the Bloody Laurel?" he asks me. His tone is genuine, not condescending. Mutely, I shake my head. "They earn their freedom."

My jaw must almost bounce off the sandy floor at our feet, because the older man laughs warmly.

"Well, first they get famous, then they get rich, then they are made citizens. It is similar to how they treat men in the legion they branded you with." He points at the *XII* on my chest. "For some, the arena is a way for them to climb above their station. But for others, it is a place to atone. It is a way for those who have lost their way to earn their place back into society. Many of the men and women sent to the arena are criminals whose death serves some purpose instead of rotting in a cell for the rest of their lives. If they die, at least they prepared their *Cor* to be a stronger relic for the Empire." I recognize that cold logic as the base of the Iron Empire.

"Then there are people like you, who just need a chance."

"So I must risk my life because I was sold for a crime I didn't commit?" Despite my question, I can't help but feel a thrill at the allure of his words. In single combat, my Iron Symbol will make me a monster. The training that I could get from Contessa will only make me more dangerous when I finally cross paths with Atticus once again. I can be free. I can have my vengeance.

"You were given a Heart you did not earn." There is no accusation in Varus's tone, only hard facts. "When you signed up for the legion, you made a deal—twenty years in exchange for your service. Then you failed to bind to the Symbol of Iron. You are a thief, an accidental one, but that does not matter to the law. The Empress is still owed her due—I can do nothing about that. But there is a path, if you are strong enough to walk it."

Suddenly, I understand why they are so quick to believe my story. This *has* happened before. It was the same logic that Atticus used to send me to the legions in the first place. I owed a debt to the Empress, and this was just another way for me to spill the blood required to pay my bill.

"And if I swear, you will teach me?" My eyes flick between the three *electi*.

"Boy, if you swear, I will make you into a god," Contessa growls, an edge in her voice. I realize for the first time what they must have seen when they saw me fight. They do not know that I carry the Iron

Symbol along with Ancient Frost, that I am able to track the weapons of my enemies like a sixth sense. To them, I looked like a sword prodigy, fending off five Silvers while able to manifest the *Glacialis Falx*. They think that I am a *tigris*. They do not know that I am a monster.

"It is not an easy path, the one you have been placed upon," Varus says after judging me for another moment. "You are not from Forum. You probably do not know this, but gladiators are more than just bloody entertainment for the masses. They are the hunters for the glory of their *Domus*. Become one of mine, and I will never abandon you."

I feel five hundred pairs of eyes on the back of my head as the shades of a fallen cohort or Ironbound watch me. Their blood calls out louder than any crowd, demanding to be answered. Their rage grows silent as I kneel, bowing my head as I saw *Malus Mors* do in Dorian's prison.

"A moment," Varus interrupts, glancing at Pliny. The magister reaches for something in his robe, then pulls forth a short, black rod—a relic of some kind. He passes it to his master with a solemn expression. The hairs on the back of my neck begin to rise as I realize what that must be. I have never seen one, but every child is told stories of a binding relic. It has been used by heroes and villains since Prometheus first stole the knowledge of *Cor* from the gods.

"This is an Oath Rod," Varus tells me, stepping forward to hold it out toward me. "Do you know what it is?"

"I've heard the stories." I eye it with distrust, like it is a venomous serpent.

"They're mostly true." Varus shrugs as if this is not the most terrifying thing that man has ever made. "It is made from a combination of Blank *Cor* and a relic from an *electus* bound to Truth." My head pops up at that, and he nods solemnly. The Symbol of Truth has been forbidden by the Censors for centuries. How old is this?

"I would like you to swear with it," Varus tells me, heavy eyes watching me closely.

"You did not make the others use this." I try to keep suspicion out of my tone but fail miserably. The senator is not offended; if anything, he seems pleased that I am unafraid to ask him. What a strange man this palatine is.

"They are not the same kind of gladiator as you." The master of the house shrugs, as if unconcerned. "I could tell you that the Censors require those who have acquired a Heart without permission to be bound in this manner. But the truth is, I would ask it of you even if they did not."

"Why?" I am still kneeling as I look up at the senator, patriarch of one of the oldest and most powerful houses in the Iron Empire.

"Because of all the gladiators I have ever purchased, you are the only one who might be able to kill me one day." My eyes widen at his words, and the world fades as he and I stare into each other's eyes. After a dozen heartbeats, he snorts in amusement at what he sees in me and steps forward, holding the Oath Rod forward once more.

"It is not an egregious oath, but a necessary one," he tells me softly.

I hesitate, but only for a moment as I reach for the relic. It is cool and smooth to my touch. It feels like a bone, and in some ways, it is—made from the corpse of an *electus* who lived long ago. I am reluctant to swear another oath; already the ones that I carry bind me tight. I need to find a way to get rid of the ropes around me, not add more to them. But I am trapped, and the palatine has offered me a path to freedom. My *votum* demands that I take it, even if it is a new trap.

"Surely the gods will judge me if I forsake an oath sworn in their name?"

"The gods are dead, boy. My ancestor saw to that. Oaths sworn to them are dust in the wind."

If only that were true.

"Send your *animus* into the relic," Pliny instructs from behind his master. "You will feel it respond to you." Wordlessly, I do as he commands, urging my senses to pour into the black rod in my hand. I gasp in shock as it comes to life. A deep gray light, a different shade from my Silver veins, erupts from it, growing to cover the entire device like vines. Heat pours off it like the searing brand they used to mark me as a member of the legions.

At the same time, a presence forces its way into me with the force of an *elephanti*, knocking aside my feeble mental defenses as if they were a rotten fence. It settles on me with a heavy weight, seeping into me and filling me to the brim. I can barely breathe; I am full of something that has taken air's place.

"Now, say the words," Varus instructs, his face unreadable.

"I swear on Dead Honos's Bones to bleed in the arena for my *dominus*, to uphold the honor of my *ludus* and my *domus*, to keep its secrets, and to bathe it in glory," I manage to gasp out in short bursts. It is not a *votum*, but I feel a familiar tingle of attention that has haunted me since the first foolish oath that I swore. It sears into me, burning my vow into my bones like a brand. The air feels thick, like a thunderstorm might break at every moment. I hiss in pain, but after a moment, it fades.

Contessa and Pliny shift behind Varus. They feel the growing pressure too. The graying senator's eyes narrow, and he studies me again. I feel something brush against my senses as his *animus* studies me. I am not afraid of his scrutiny. I do mean this oath. I will shed as much blood as it takes to Ascend, to lay to rest the ghosts that haunt me.

At last, the other presence withdraws slowly like a sated predator. I sag in relief, taking a deep breath to regain my lost air. The heat fades and the gray light vanishes, leaving an inert black rod in my hands.

"Rise, Castor, as a gladiator of *Domus* Pelias," Varus says when it is done. The cloying sense of lightning fades, and he steps forward, offering me his wrist. I take it, and he pulls me to my feet. For a moment, we stand there, hands clasped. His gray eyes search mine, trying to solve my mysteries. There's no fear, just a mild curiosity there. He takes back the Oath Rod as we part.

"The Silver Circuit has already begun, *Dominus*," Contessa reminds her master, immediately settling into business. "Normally, I would suggest that we wait until the next one and polish him into a true killer. But this year…"

"No," Varus interrupts, cutting her off. "You said he could carve through his tier even as he is."

"With a little guidance, he will be transformed."

"Pay the fee," the man declares. "He will compete at Antioch."

"As you will." Contessa bows her head in obeisance.

"How long do I have, *Domini*?" A creeping fear begins to grow inside me as I realize what I have agreed to do. It is one thing to agree to revenge, it is another to willingly risk your life for nothing.

"A month. Your training begins tomorrow." Contessa smiles tightly. "Better get a good night's sleep."

"Aye, *Domina*," I reply, knowing full well I won't be able to sleep a wink.

Just like that, I am dismissed. Contessa leads me through the far side of the training hall to another set of doors that lead to another courtyard.

I stop in awe to take in the space dedicated to the training of gladiators. Just this portion of the Pelias estate is larger than Segesta's *collegium*. The wealth that *Domus* Pelias commands is mind-boggling to me. This place rivals what I pictured Diana's palace to look like as a boy. But I know hers must somehow be another order of magnitude above this.

When I was sold as a gladiator, I expected to end up somewhere that felt very similar to Agogia's Twelfth District, a spartan place for warriors who were more like pets than people. I could not have been more wrong. This place is like an oasis paradise compared to the Iron City.

A white marble fountain bubbles in the middle of the paved stones. A trio of beautiful attendants dressed in white flowy robes sit on the side of it, laughing among themselves. Gardens flourish along the paths that wind to a half-dozen other massive buildings. Several warriors train outdoors, but they do so freely. I watch as a pair of Copper gladiators jog by, circling the interior courtyard as they run laps. Somewhere nearby, a songbird trills.

The *lanista* sends a knowing look over her shoulder, laughing at the blatant shock on my face. "There are perks to not being Ironbound, lad." She chuckles. "The beds are much more comfortable. It's a much softer life."

As we make our way toward one of the large buildings, I begin to grill Contessa, trying to get up to speed. When I was a boy, we always heard tales of the Games, but now that I am here, I realize they were heavier on the action and less involved in the logistics.

"So there are Circuits for every tier of *electus*?" I ask.

"More. There are five Circuits. Three are for *electi*: Copper, Silver, and Gold, but don't let anyone with a pedigree hear you calling them that. It's *Cuprum*, *Argentum*, and *Aurum* when you're outside these halls. The other two are *Ferrum* and *Purum*. The Iron one, you don't need to worry about—that's for deserters and retired soldiers. The last one is for non-*electi*. The winner of each season is awarded a Heart."

"You can win a Heart in the Games?" I'm so shocked that I stop short. "I thought the *Sententia* was the only way to get one..."

"You really are from the country, aren't you, lad?" She laughs. It's a little condescending, but not cruel. "The winner of the Blank Circuit is awarded a *Cor* Heart, and every *Domum* with a *ludus* is also given two *Corda* to use every year." I make a choking sound, and she laughs again. I can tell she is enjoying expanding my horizons. My mind races with possibilities. I do not dare ask about the Iron Circuit, lest I seem too interested in something I should not be.

"It's one of the reasons all the great families want a license." She lowers her voice, falling back a half-step to speak to me directly. "Most of them take those *Corda* for their little *puers* and *puellas*, if you get my meaning."

"They don't *have* to use them on gladiators?" I am not as shocked as I would have been a year ago. "That seems like a convenient loophole."

The *lanista* shrugs. "This is the way of the world. The rules are enforced by the ones who make them. As long as the house produces gladiators that are entertaining the people, no one asks any questions."

"Can a *domus* lose its *ludus* license?"

"If they do not perform to a satisfactory level, the Empress can take it from them and give it to another. Although that tends to be more politically driven." Understanding flares in my mind like a *lumos* relic in the night. Varus's insistence at making me fight in Antioch makes more sense. His *ludus*'s future must be in question.

"How is *Domus* Pelias doing this year?"

"Not as well as we must." The woman gives me a flat, frank gaze that tells me to stop asking questions. "There have been some… issues."

The first building we enter is a dormitory. Not a barracks, like I expected. Instead of a large room filled with beds, it is a multi-story structure, where each gladiator has their own quarters. As a Silver, I am granted a room on the second floor.

As the *lanista* leads me through the hall, we pass the trident-wielding gladiator that I fought in the gauntlet, emerging from his own quarters. He eyes me with a cool expression; a thick lump is beginning to form on the front of his shaved skull where the hilt of my *gladius* struck him. I guess he didn't manage to turn his face to stone in time.

If I'm going to be living here, I have no desire to go through the same hatred that I bore in the Twelfth. I might as well start making friends now. I give him a firm nod, and after a moment, he returns it. Contessa opens a door, tossing me the key as she does. My eyebrows arch in surprise at that luxury. They stay up there as I survey the space I have been given.

It is smaller than my room in my father's home, but compared to anything I have been in for the last year, it looks like the height of luxury. A comfortable-looking bed takes up most of the room, along with a desk and chair. A door at the far end leads to my own *lavatorium*, equipped with an *aqua* relic that scours waste away into the aqueducts of the city. A second water relic sits in a stall so that I can stand underneath it while it pours water on me. I've never seen such a thing. Apparently, it's called a *pluvia*. Contessa laughs at my delight and tells me to hurry up and Ascend to Gold. Their quarters are even more impressive.

"Servants will bring you some appropriate clothing, and burn your old ones." She eyes my ripped tunic with distaste. "Now let's get you fed. You look like you've been starved for months. Antioch is in a month; it's time to get some meat on your bones."

CHAPTER 6

The mess hall of *Domus* Pelias could not be more different from Agogia. Well, at least the Twelfth's sector of the Iron City. I have my suspicions about what the Praetorians' version is like. A dozen cooks maintain a line of food that gladiators graze from like sheep, returning as many times as they like to refill their plates.

There is chicken, beef, and a dozen different vegetables prepared in different sauces. At the end of the line waits freshly baked bread. I almost break into a sob as I take my first bite. It's perfect—warm and soft as if it had been made by Ceres herself. Felix's dream of being a baker weighs heavily on the back of my mind. How I wish he were here to eat this with me instead of lost to the snow.

Other gladiators are spread across the hall, eating at a series of tables. I can see about thirty of them, although Contessa tells me that there are more than fifty living here. Life is not as regimented here as in the legions; instead, different fighters have their own schedules tailored to them. Some of the other warriors eye me skeptically as I pass, but none approach our table.

More beautiful servants sweep through, refilling drinks and laughing with the gladiators. After a year of hardship, I feel out of place, surrounded by normal people going about their days. Although these people are also killers, or training to be, they feel so… relaxed. Contessa eyes me with a hint of amusement, clearly enjoying my discomfort. The *lanista* is more playful than I expected. Her personality begins to shine now that the *dominus* is gone.

When I have eaten my fill, Contessa sends me back to my quarters, warning that she will collect me before the sun rises. The first thing I do is stand in the *pluvia* and let the warm water it creates rain down on me, washing away the stench of prison.

As I clean, I center myself, preparing for the path I am about to walk. In the *collegium*, they taught us that it was a relatively simple matter to Ascend from Copper to Silver. It simply required two things:

time and access to an abundance of the Symbol's essence. An *electus* needed to focus on cultivating as often as he could, forcing his *Cor*'s veins to expand and grow.

But to Ascend from Silver to Gold is supposed to be much harder. Percy told me something similar on the march to the North. There is more to the next step than just raw strength. I must develop my Symbol, but I do not know how. They didn't bother to teach that to *iuvenores* who had not even made it through the *Sententia*.

Everything Pliny makes me do with Ancient Frost I will need to figure out how to adapt to Iron. But no matter what I learn, I must be careful to conceal my secrets. I'm under no illusions about what Contessa or Varus will do to me if they discover that I am an uninhibited Ironbound. I will be under the scrutiny of many powerful *electi*, who will watch my every move. My greatest protection is the fact that no one believes that what I am is possible. They are not looking for what I am, but that does not mean I am safe.

I will need to excel so that they continue to push me through the stages of Silver, but I cannot make them suspect that I am anything other than talented with a sword. If they realize that my prowess is tied to the Iron Symbol's ability to sense my opponent's blades, I am a dead man. If I fail, my family, my friends, my legion will go unavenged.

But if I can overcome these challenges, there is a way for me to get everything I want—to Ascend to Gold and to earn my freedom. Once I am a free citizen, I can turn my attention to Atticus and the rest of his ilk. I clench my fist as the water cascades down me. *Count your days, Censor. I am coming for you.*

A knock sounds at my door, startling me out of my reverie. My head turns, and I pause, waiting to hear it again. It echoes a second time, and reluctantly, I turn off the *pluvia*, stepping out of its little alcove.

I have no clean clothes, so I wrap a towel around my waist as I stalk through my room, grumbling as the cold air ripples across my skin. I open the door to my quarters, one hand holding the two loose pieces of cloth to keep them from falling to my feet.

"Apologies for the interruption, *Dominus*," a white-robed girl gushes breathily, extending a pile of clothing toward me while bowing slightly. "I was sent to bring your new clothes." Like all the servants I have seen, she is beautiful. My breath skips a beat as I drink in the sight of her rich brown hair and warm smile.

"Oh," I stammer nervously, suddenly aware that I am essentially naked. Heat blooms on my cheeks as I begin to blush furiously. "Uh thank you, I can—" Instinctively, I reach for the clothes, but she stops me.

"I can place them on your bed, *Dominus*," the woman murmurs demurely, the corner of her lip quirking at my embarrassment. Her eyes track down my chest, tracing the veins of my *Cor*. She does not react in disgust at the white *rasa* lines but continues to study me intently.

"Yes, thank you," I squeak, trying to grab hold of the shreds of my dignity. I step back, allowing her to enter. The woman slides into my room, closing the door behind her. For some reason, the heat on my cheeks only increases now that we are sealed away. I've never been alone with a woman like this. Her presence feels electric and heavy, not that different from a god's. I try to calm my racing heart. This is no divine power, but a distinctly human one.

"Thank you!" I manage when she is finished placing the clothing on my bed. "I was going to need those soon." I usher her out of my room before my face can burn any brighter. When she is finally gone, I set about inspecting my new clothes. I have been given a white tunic and trousers, much like the pair I trained in at Agogia. I snort as I put them on. It feels like I have traveled so far, only to be back where I began.

Beneath them is a set of combat leathers. I run my hand over the sleeveless chest piece, tracing the emblem of *Domus* Pelias, the broken trident. This is not the first time I have walked in the footsteps of one of the Iron Lords. I do not seek to become one of their number, but already I am further down their path than any since them. How strange that I have found myself in service to one of their estates. The back of my neck prickles as if someone is watching, but I try to ignore it. I can read the signs myself.

Reluctantly, I pack away the new clothing, returning to the *pluvia*. When I have finished cleaning myself and drying off, I sink into the bed, gasping in surprise as it grabs me. It has been a year since I've lain in anything this comfortable. I've spent most of that time sleeping on the ground or on a cell floor.

It's stifling, the way that it holds me. I squirm, trying to find a comfortable position, but all I feel is trapped. After a while, I give in, snatching the pillow and blanket and crawling down to the smooth stone floor. The firmness is a familiar friend, and my body relaxes as I return to what it knows.

Despite my comfort, sleep evades me. Dark thoughts swirl through my mind like the autumn wind that cuts through crops. I know little of the position that I have found myself in. I suspect the things they taught us about gladiators are like what they taught us about the Iron Legions, the part that was useful for us to know. In Segesta, they told us the only way to earn a *Cor* Heart was to earn one in the *Sententia* or sign up for the legions. Ages ago, Felix told Marcus and me on the roof of my father's house that the palatine do not play by the same rules. At the time, I had dismissed him as a bitter and jaded plebeian. Now, I think that he was even more right than he knew.

For a wild moment, the thought of escape slithers through my mind. My reserves are full. It would be a simple thing for me to leave this place. There are barely any guards, and they carry iron.

Before I can pursue this line of thinking any further, something grabs my insides with a grip like a vise. A tightness runs through my chest, pausing my heart and restricting my breathing. I sit up in shock, holding a hand over my heart as I struggle to catch my breath.

"Urk!" I protest to the empty room. *I don't really intend to flee!* I promise the thing that lurks inside my bones. It was only an idle thought—a daydream—a fancy. The pressure fades like a soldier reluctantly sheathing his *gladius*. I sit hunched on my floor, panting at the fear that runs through me.

Clearly, the Oath Rod is as potent as the legends promised. With a sigh, I flop down on my makeshift bed, groaning in pain and frustration. I am *inhibited* once more. These chains are different, far less restrictive, but I feel them settle around me like the collar that I broke.

The only way out of this one is to earn my freedom. So that is what I will do. Resolve builds as my right hand clenches into a fist. Pliny wishes me to Ascend. All of them do. I will take their teaching and their knowledge, and I will become the first Golden Ironbound in four hundred years. Then, when I have carved my way through the Games, I will turn my attention to the blood that my *votum* demands.

Beyond this grim feeling is a growing elation that builds in me, refusing to be held down by my mood. After months of languishing in the dark, I got to use my new capabilities. The power is intoxicating. Even now, it thrums inside of me with a nervous tension, eager to be used again. I know that I am at the beginning of my Silver path. That as my *Cor* grows, I will be able to do even more. I contain but a fraction of the danger that I will grow into.

Eventually, even my excitement cannot keep me awake, and I fade into a light, troubled slumber. I do not sleep deeply anymore. A year of being a soldier and a prisoner has taken that from me. The darkness is no longer a place I consider to be safe. Which means that my eyes open immediately as the lock on my door turns with an echoing *click*. Automatically, I reach for a weapon beside me, but I do not have one.

My heart pounds as my *animus* feels the Iron in the door begin to open. My mind races as I try to think who is trying to sneak into my room at this hour. Is it the pretty servant girl, returning to torment me once more? Or is it that blond Air gladiator and the rest of the Silvers from the gauntlet coming for some revenge? Panic threatens to overwhelm me, but I pull on my Symbols, letting their cold presence fill me. I check my essence reserves, cursing myself for not insisting on refilling my supply of Ancient Frost before we left the training area. There's enough to summon the *Glacialis Falx* once, but I would be in danger of running out if I did so. My *Cor* Heart has plenty of Iron essence, but I have no weapon to use with it.

Fool.

I make a promise to myself—not the dead gods—that if I survive this, I will always carry a knife. I will never let them take my teeth again. I lie in the darkness, waiting, frozen by fear and uncertainty.

Dim light from the muted *lumos* relics floods in from the hallway, framing a hooded form. It takes two tentative steps into my room, and my right hand curls, ready to summon my blade. Slowly, the figure's head tracks from my empty bed to stare in the darkness where I lie. The person looks short—could it be the woman with the knives?

We study each other for a long moment, before the interloper reaches up and pulls down their hood.

It's Pliny. The old magister smiles at me softly, amused to see me sleeping on the floor. Some of the terror bleeds out of me. Despite being a Gold *electus*, he is no warrior. I find the small man dangerous, but I'm afraid of his mind.

"Well?" he asks softly as the tension fades. "Are you ready to begin?"

"Begin what?"

"Your Ascent."

CHAPTER 7

After hearing what the old magister wants, I scramble out of my makeshift bed faster than a thought. Pliny chuckles in his dryly amused manner before leading me through the dark and silent gladiators' quarters. As we walk, I remember Durus and the legionnaires beating us and dragging us out of our beds on my first night there to take them to be forged into Ironbound. I feel like a ghost, moving through a familiar dance. We cross the empty courtyard and enter a different building that I have not yet been shown.

My mind is racing at his words. I want to Ascend. I want to know what lies before me. My natural impatience is delighted, happy to forgo a night's rest to chase this dream.

Pliny leads me at a brisk pace through the winding halls past closed doors until we emerge into the wide expanse of a library. I gasp in shock, pausing to stare at the arched ceiling that yawns above me. The library is three stories tall, and the walls are packed with shelves of scrolls and their modern replacement, books. A narrow walkway rings each level but leaves the center open, giving me an uninterrupted view of the mural painted on the dome.

It depicts a dark-haired man in an ornate *lorica* who is flying. His feet hover inches above the dark waves of the ocean. In his right hand, he bears a *tridentus* that blazes with white fire. At the base of the incredible painting is inscribed: *Pelias Neptunum venatur in Alto*—Pelias hunts Neptune in the Deep.

My jaw hangs open as I stare at the art above me. I have read stories of the great works that are in Anteforum and even Forum itself, but the words of magisters cannot replace the paint strokes of a master.

"It was done by Gaius Fabius himself, just after the fall of the gods," Pliny remarks from my side. There is a reverence in his tone that tells me he never grows tired of looking at it either. "We believe he was the first *Pictor Symbolum*. I would also say he was the greatest *electus* with a Painter Symbol, but art is unfortunately subjective."

I know that it is possible for someone to attune to things other than an element, but it is even rarer than someone getting a specific Symbol. Most of the artistic attunements are shrouded in mystery. Despite Valentina's dreams, the Censors forbid *electi* from taking most Music Symbols. They claim that a powerful user could bewitch the hearts of men like a Siren. I do not know if that is true, but part of me believes it more now after the things I have seen.

"Sadly, young Castor, your path is one with much less beauty on it. Come, we have far to go." The magister turns and marches deeper into the library. He turns to a door set in the wall among the shelves and leads me down a dark stairwell to a secluded office below. It is only then that I realize he was talking about a different kind of journey.

Pliny's lair is larger than my quarters, but still, it is so full of knowledge that it feels crowded. Books and scrolls litter the room, filling many shelves as well as overflowing into at least three piles that I can see. A desk takes up a third of the room, but he waves me toward a pair of chairs that sit in front of an *ignis* relic that glows with a warm light.

"So many books," I murmur, looking around the scattered papers in wonder. There are more in this room than in all the Segesta *collegium*. If knowledge is wealth, then I only now begin to understand just how poor I am. "What are they about?"

"Everything!" Pliny answers after a moment of thought. "The gods kept much from us while they were alive. And their servants, the priests, still endeavor to keep their secrets. It is the task of the magisters to recover what was lost." Pliny discards his cloak, hanging it on a hook by the door as I take a seat. He joins me after a moment, carrying a small leather case. He opens it, revealing a pipe and some leaves. Stuffing the bowl with his thumb, he leans back in his chair and watches me with two sharp eyes.

"I apologize for the late hour," he says after a moment, "but I suspect that after wasting away in that cell for so long, you might be as eager as me to get started."

"You're right, *Dominus*," I reply quietly.

"Enough of that." Pliny waves his unlit pipe dismissively. "I am not your master. Some of the gladiators that come here must be taught respect, but I do not think that will be an issue for you. Instead, when we are alone, you will think of me as your teacher."

"As you wish, Magister." The old man rolls his eyes at my formality but does not correct me. He seems more alive in this space; he fills it as if he has grown to be six feet tall. Contessa might be the *lanista* of the arena, but this is his *domus*.

"The journey from Copper to Silver is rather straightforward, as you well know," the magister begins, tamping down his pipe before leaning to the side to light it off the *ignis* relic. "You said you were in a *Sententia,* yes? You must have attended a *collegium*?"

"Yes, *Dom—*" I bite down savagely on the honorific. The legions burned that response into my bones. "Yes." Now that we are beginning, some of my excitement fades. Pliny is not a physical threat like Contessa, but in some ways, I think he might be more dangerous. She is a lion, but he is a fox, and I am a stupid chicken who has followed him home to its den. I still do not have a knife.

"The education for most *iuvenores* who seek to earn their *Cor* in a *Sententia* is usually satisfactory to help a student Ascend from Copper to Silver, but most will not have the knowledge to complete the journey to Gold." He pauses to take a puff from his pipe; a rich scent dances through the room. He gestures, and the air begins to swirl as some hidden air relic begins to pull the smoke out. "This is, of course, by design."

I hesitate, unsure how to respond. Pliny seems like he is barely paying attention, but I do not trust the face that he presents me with. It feels like a mask. He reminds me of a *tellus* knife, hidden in the sleeves, ready to cut.

The silence grows until at last his eyes flick up from his absent fumbling with his pipe to spear me with a measuring gaze. I meet it calmly, doing my best not to show fear. He chuckles again, letting the pipe dangle from his lips as he watches me.

"This is not surprising or offensive to you?" he prods, trying to get my measure.

"My teachers were always most concerned with us actually getting a *Cor* Heart," I reply honestly after a moment of thought. "I always assumed the rest would come later. It's hardly efficient to teach an entire cohort of students the intricacies of being an *electus* when only a handful will ever realize it." As a boy, I had never wondered about what would happen after I got my Heart. That part always seemed easy. Now, I know the magister has the right of it. They didn't want us to know more than we needed to either.

"Hardly efficient," Pliny repeats in a soft, musing tone. "But if we're talking about your journey to Ascension, I suspect that the most *efficient* path would be for you to tell me the truth about how you came to be like that." He gestures at the white *rasa* veins on my arms with the butt of his pipe.

I freeze at his words, and he settles back, watching me. There is an infinite quality to his patience that tells me he will wait as long as he needs to, like a predator waiting in ambush. I draw on the Ancient Frost Symbol, letting its cold weight help keep my fear at bay. I must be calm.

Pliny arches an eyebrow but says nothing.

For a moment, I consider lying. I have become skilled at walking the razor's edge between truth and fiction. Gaius bought my story; why wouldn't Pliny do the same? But as I stare back at the keen-eyed magister, my heart quails at the thought of trying to sell him the same tale. Gaius was brilliant, but his expectations allowed him to believe what I told him. The legions are not a place for imagination and wonder. But Pliny—Pliny is curious, and curious men dig when others do not.

"I cannot tell you." The words spring out of my mouth without a second thought, surprising both of us. I do not know this man well enough to trust him with my origin. Atticus's threat of fire and murder burns in the back of my mind, holding my tongue.

"Ah." The magister leans forward, letting his pipe dangle down by his knee. "You cannot, or you must not?" His eyes take on a knowing gleam that tells me he was expecting something like this.

"A little bit of both," I admit after a moment of thought. I could tell him what happened on the day that I was given my *Cor* Hearts, but that does not mean that I truly understand everything that happened to me. It was only after I attuned to Ancient Frost that I began to suspect some of the truths that lie etched in my skin.

"Let me make an… informed guess," Pliny offers, his tone still light, but his words filling me with trepidation. "If I am right, I will not pressure you to tell me more, but it will help me with advising you." Reluctantly, I nod, terrified of what he knows.

"You did not obtain your Heart as part of the binding ceremony, but through some other means. An experiment or accident perhaps—the circumstances do not matter. What does matter is that it was not done with the Censors' approval or supervision—nor the Iron Legions'." My heart pounds in my chest, but I nod once more, confirming his theory.

The magister leans back in his chair again, chewing on the end of his pipe in thought as he studies me. I feel another faint brush as his *animus* sweeps over me. It is my turn for my eyes to narrow as I catch a whiff of something, a faint feeling like a perfume to his presence.

"Do you know what my Symbol is, Castor?"

I blink in surprise, caught off guard by the question. I don't. How could I? He's shown me no overt use of his *Cor*, outside of his *animus* studying me, which any *electus* above Copper can do, although from what I understand it is far more useful to Golds. I've not figured out how to do anything with it other than search for things tied to my own Symbols.

"I don't know—" I start to tell him, but my answer catches in my throat for a second. There's a sense to his *animus* that feels familiar. It dances on the tip of my tongue like a forgotten name, but no matter how hard I search for it, I am not able to find it. After a few heartbeats, I sigh and shake my head, frustrated by my failure. It feels like something I should know, but I do not.

"Don't despair," Pliny admonishes me. "I'd have been surprised if you did. The ability to read Symbols that aren't congruent to your own is *very* rare. Mine is a truly unusual one. According to the rolls of the Census, I possess one of the rarest of all the attunements." His lip quirks in dry amusement as I lean forward, captivated by his words.

"I am bound to *Cor*."

A surprised gasp escapes from me, and I recoil from the man in surprise. "How? How is that even possible?"

"It is a naturally occurring element, even if it does fall from the heavens." Pliny is amused by my horror. I think he has never grown tired of telling people this.

"I suppose," I stammer, trying to wrap my mind around the possibilities of what he can sense or do. Have I already been discovered? "Does that mean you are a… Heartsmith?"

"A sharp question," he replies in surprise. "Sometimes I am. In order to be able to manipulate the *Cor* of a deceased *electus* into a relic, the smith must be either attuned to the same Symbol as the Heart or to *Cor* itself. Most Heartsmiths work with relics that match their own binding—it's far more common to find than someone like me."

"So the Heartsmiths of the legions are also Ironbound?" I ask, surprised. I thought that only legionnaires were allowed to be tied to Iron.

"If they make Iron relics, they would have to be," Pliny agrees with a nod. "Most are retired soldiers or ones that have been maimed. It's a way for them to still serve without standing in the shieldwall. Efficient, I believe you would call it."

It is my turn to snort.

"We are straying away from the meat of the matter," the magister says, waving away my follow-up question before I can ask it. "I am bound to *Cor*, which means that I can feel the twisted nature of your own Heart."

"It's twisted?" I ask, looking down at my stomach, suddenly feeling ill.

"It's like an orchard of young trees planted too close together. Their roots invade each other's space, fighting for dominance. It feels as if you have more than one *rasa* Heart in you." My face goes blank, and he chuckles. "*Pax*—peace. You're not the first I've seen to suffer such a condition, Castor. You are not an *immundus* with an incomplete binding, but a *multicorde*, an *electus* with many."

The flesh-and-blood heart in my chest pounds in terror as he casually lays bare one of my secrets. "You can feel that?"

"My Symbol lets me sense your veins and trace them, to see where they are broken and battered. Unfortunately, I am attuned to *rasa Cor*, which means that the Heart inside of you that bound itself to a Winter Symbol is more distant for me."

I nod, relief blossoming in my mind as I do. I think this means my most dangerous secret is safe. If I understand the magister's words correctly, his element is Blank *Cor*. But once a Heart is bound, it takes on some kinship to its Symbol, reducing how closely related it is to the original form, the same way that Copper can become Bronze and turn unmanageable. Pliny might be able to sense the empty Hearts in my body, but the portions attuned to Ancient Frost and Iron might look the same to his senses.

"If there are unused Hearts, can I—"

Pliny cuts me off with a laugh. "If it were possible for someone to attune more than one *Cor*, it would have been done long ago. Unfortunately, the mind cannot split like that. Each soul is born paired to a single element. Besides, I suspect even if it were achievable, it would drive the *electus* mad."

I grit my teeth as a new fear begins to haunt me.

"However, it does seem that there are some benefits."

"What do you mean?"

"Your essence reserve is far larger than it should be. I think it's possible that the *rasa* Hearts somehow expand your capacity, even though they are unbound." He purses his mouth in thought. "Tell me about your manifestation."

"You mean my ability?"

"Ability?" His voice cracks like a whip, and he leans forward in his chair, eyes bright. "It has revealed a name to you?" I hesitate, unsure what I have just revealed. Yet another piece of knowledge that was not given to me.

"I call it the *Glacialis Falx*, the—"

"—Frozen Blade," he murmurs thoughtfully, chewing on the stem of his pipe. "Where did you hear that name?"

A pulse of fear runs through me. I have made a mistake. *Electi* who gain theirs in the organic way must have a process similar to their binding, where the name is revealed to them by their *Cor*. Mine was a little different. I only know what it is called because Aquilo told me the name of the ability when he bestowed it upon me.

"It's just something I read about once," I say with a bashful smile, looking down as if embarrassed. "Some say that was the name of Frigidus's blade…"

"Ah." The magister smiles softly after a moment, as if realizing that it was not that long ago that I was just a boy. "There is some truth to that tale," he confides after a moment of thought. "Although I have heard it said that he stole the knowledge of that ability from another." It is a struggle for me to keep my face blank. I know exactly whom Frigidus took it from.

"But that is neither here nor there," Pliny decides after another moment of thought. Sweat trickles down my spine as I watch him think. I fear that I have given myself away on the first day. I am like an infant, lying about what is behind my back to my father.

"When did you first manifest?"

"In the North," I croak, scrambling to build a story out of the ruins of truth. "I was attacked by bandits."

"Imperial or Norman?"

"Imperial—it was an *electus*."

"Do you know what Symbol they were attuned to?"

"Earth." I shrug. "I didn't ask for the specific variation."

"Does it always appear as a *gladius*? Or can you create whatever you want?"

"It's just a sword," I tell him, surprised by his question. It has never occurred to me to try to use it for anything else. Aquilo gave it to me for a purpose, and I have done my best to put it to good use.

"Fascinating," he says, pulling his pipe out of his mouth as he leans back in his chair. I am almost out of breath from trying to keep up with his rapid-fire questions. Terror curls next to me like a lover on a warm night, making my skin flush.

"You seem to do everything backwards," he muses after a while.

"My old magister would agree," I reply dryly without thinking. Pliny chuckles but refuses to let my joke distract him.

"Most people's first manifestations are nebulous, a loose spray of their element created by their will and essence. Over time, with practice, they begin to be able to form it into something concrete. As they settle in their ways, it tends to take a comfortable shape like a weapon or shield. Truly gifted *electi* can learn to make anything they want, but that is rare even for those who can manifest."

I am silent, processing his information, inwardly cursing the rotting God of Winter once more for his meddling.

"You have skipped the first stage, which is almost unheard of, but then again, nothing about your path seems traditional. Combine that with a situation of extreme duress and eureka, something new." He places the stem of his pipe back in his mouth, chewing on it absently. "Perhaps with training, we can advance you to the next stage of manifestation, allowing you to truly take advantage of your ability. It is imperative then that we—" The magister breaks off midsentence, glancing over his shoulder at the entrance to his lair. "Get up, quickly," he orders, still staring. Confused, I leap to my feet, suddenly feeling nervous again, like a rat being hunted by a cat.

"Go to the back left shelf in my room." He turns to point a finger at the far corner. Confused, I obey his commands, compelled by the urgency in his voice. As I approach the wall, he directs me further. "Find the book labeled *The Heart of Our Hearts*." I begin to look around, unused to seeing this many books in one place.

"Middle row, left side," he snaps after I search for a few heartbeats. I spy the tome and reach for it. As I pull on it, the top moves, but the bottom is stuck fast. I dance backward as the entire shelf swings open like a door, revealing a dark passageway behind. I shoot Pliny a confused glance, but he gestures for me to enter.

"Pull the shelf closed behind you; hurry! Then for the love of Dead Venus, be silent."

I obey, stepping into the tunnel and swinging the door shut. It *clicks*, cutting off all my light, plunging me into absolute darkness. My breath echoes loudly in this dark, enclosed space. The passage seems to go on, but I hesitate to explore it. It reminds me too much of the tunnels of Aquilo's house beneath the ice. My experience there killed any curiosity I might have about exploring underground warrens.

Instead, I elect to stay, crouching by the thin wood that makes up the back of the shelf, trying to listen. Who would Pliny want to hide me from? Contessa sent me to bed but there was no warning of a curfew. Why then the secrecy? What kind of man had a tunnel hidden behind his bookshelves?

"I thought I would find you here," a man's voice says faintly.

"It is my office, Censor Tartus," the magister replies without a trace of concern. My heart skips a beat as I realize who has come to see Pliny.

"We understand that your *ludus* purchased new gladiators today from a licensed provider; however, we have not received the required notice to inspect them before they can be admitted to the rolls of the house," the Censor says, not interested in exchanging any more pleasantries.

"Dorian certainly wasted no time filing his sale." Pliny's voice grows sharper with amusement. "I did not take him for such an organized man." There is a long pause, as if the Censor is reacting to something I do not understand.

I frown, trying to read between the lines. Despite the magister's comment, I know Dorian is anything but. He is a barely literate slob who pretends to be smarter than he is to impress his betters. The thought of him promptly reporting his sale to the Censors seems laughable. In fact, the more I think about it, the more impossible it seems. But if he did not tell them, how do they know?

A chill runs down my spine as I see the implication that sits between the two men like a knife stuck in the table. *Domus* Pelias is being watched by the Censors. I feel the same terror I felt as a boy in Segesta as I realize the Eyes of the Empress are gazing in my direction once more, even if by association.

"Why have you not reported these acquisitions and presented them for inspection?" The Censor charges forward, ignoring Pliny's taunt.

"Tartus, it has been less than eight hours. By law, we have three days."

"It is in your master's best interest to be proactive with his time, lest my own grow suspicious," Tartus warns, his voice colder. "One would think that a House that is under threat of *Judicium* would be taking every pain to assuage the fears of the Empress."

My jaw drops in the silence that follows the Censor's threat. I do not have to stop myself from making a sound—I could not make one if my life depended on it. *Judicium!* It has been a century since the last Great *Domus* was put under judgment. I do not even truly know what such a thing fully entails, only that it is an absolute ending.

Before I was born, the House Junias was removed from our history. In the entire *collegium,* there was only a single entry denoting their demise, after they were judged by the Empress. I do not even know what they did to draw Diana's ire.

"One would also think that someone speaking with the Imperial Voice would be more careful with their words, *Censor*, lest I bear them to my master's ear." Pliny's voice cracks like a whip as he replies. It is the first time I have ever heard him sound anything other than amused. His threat is sharp and clear.

A heavy silence settles over the two of them, and it swallows me, leaving me unable to breathe. I have traveled far in the Iron Empire and seen the cracks that decorate its foundation, but this is no crack. This is a yawning crevice, a fissure that threatens to swallow me whole.

"We will inspect your new gladiators tomorrow," Tartus says after the silence has become deafening. "If any are found to be unsuitable, they will be harvested for their relics and reclaimed by the Empress on the spot." I suppress a shiver, crouched behind the fake wall. I'm under no illusions that I am at all "suitable."

"We shall of course do as the Empress commands," Pliny replies smoothly. A long pause emerges. In my mind, I picture the Censor in his white *tellus lorica* glaring down at the seated magister, who is as unruffled by the attention. At last, the silence is broken only by the sound of the door slamming behind the Censor as he leaves. I remain crouched in the dark, growing more terrified by the second. Have I heard too much? At last, Pliny sighs, and I hear him begin to refill his pipe.

"You can come out," the magister calls.

Heart in my throat, I push the door open. Pliny looks up at me as I emerge, his face unreadable. "We are going to have to do something about those," he says, looking at my *rasa* veins.

CHAPTER 8

After the Censor leaves, Pliny escorts me back through the library to the main courtyard, trusting me to find my own way back to my sleeping quarters. I am struck again by how little like a prisoner I feel, despite being owned like a dog.

For a moment, I pause by the fountain, listening to its calm bubbling as I gaze at *Mons* Olympus drifting above. The floating mountain is almost directly overhead here, because Anteforum is north of Segesta.

The old gray rock is quiet as ever, glowing softly with Luna's light. My eyes scour over it, looking for some sign of life, some hint that other gods lurk there, just as Aquilo rots in the far North. The tingling pressure that often haunts me builds for a moment, but then it fades, as if distracted. Whatever mystery awaits in the home of the gods, it is for another day.

Eventually, I return to my room and stare at myself in the mirror that hangs in my little privy. It has been months since I've studied my own reflection. I do not recognize myself. I'm far too pale, having been cooped up away from the light. My eyes are tired and heavy for my age. Wavy brown hair hangs down to my shoulders.

In the legions, I would be beaten for looking so disheveled, for having hair so outside of regulation. Part of me aches to cut it, to return myself to a sense of normalcy. But I am not in the Twelfth anymore. My cohort is dead; I am the only one left. I do not deserve to look like their brother, not after I left them and lived. The long hair stays—the only penance I can afford.

Troubled, I curl up in my nest of blankets. *Sol* will still not rise for a few hours, and although I am petrified by the thought of being inspected by the Censors, I know that I should try to rest, but sleep feels so far away. Tomorrow, I might die. If I do, then I will have more rest than I could ever need. I close my eyes, burrowing into the darkness to hide from my fears, nestling in its embrace until sleep finally finds me.

The training ground is darker than I expected as I step out into the sands of the arena to be judged. The *lumos* relics above it blaze, shining down on me with the power of the noon sun, making it like an oasis in a desert of night. Everywhere else in the building, they are off; even the essence rooms are all powered down.

I cannot see the judge who watches, but I can just make out the soft edges of its form as it prowls around the arena like a lion. Its menace is a feral, hungry thing that lashes against the barrier.

"Begin. Let me see if you are worthy," a voice calls from the darkness. I do not recognize it. It is neither masculine nor feminine but instead filled with the ringing of bells. Its inhuman tones crash down on me like waves.

I draw my *gladius*. Or do I? It is my hand. Maybe it was already there. I look around the empty room, but there is nothing for me to fight. That's not why they are here.

No, they want to see me use Ancient Frost to show them that I am an *electus* worthy of the Games. I look down, and the sword in my hands is now made of ice, replaced by the *Glacialis Falx*. That feels right. I cannot show them my iron.

I summon a second copy, crossing them as I twist the blades, letting curved spikes grow out of them like thorns. I need to show them that I am strong. That my white *rasa* veins are not a sign of weakness. I must be allowed to fight in the Games.

I need to be free to carry out my vengeance.

"A cute trick," a woman mocks from my right. The tolling bells are still present, but I can hear her voice bleeding through it now.

"Why do you waste your time with lesser gifts? Why do you ignore the true power that you carry?" she presses.

I pause, letting my arms go slack as I scan the darkness that surrounds me. Her words confuse me. This feels wrong, like I am in another place. The swords in my hand do not feel real, but my mind thinks they are. It reminds me of when I was trapped in a dream relic during the *Sententia*.

In the distance, a wolf howls. The scars around my wrist—relics of a long-healed bite—begin to itch.

"Who are you?" I demand, turning in a circle. Laughter comes from all sides, full of bells. She is not mocking my fear, but my stupidity. I should know who she is.

I do. But I am afraid to admit it.

"Speak my name, *Ovicula*," she commands. "Call out to me, and I shall appear." A shadow forms on the edge of the arena that I am trapped in. It is hard to make out, a pool of deeper darkness on the night that surrounds me. But I recognize her figure. I have seen her before.

I hesitate, terrified.

"You were not afraid to cry out to me in the depths of Winter's fury," she criticizes. "How you begged for my aid when you were in danger. Did I not guide you out of my brother's frozen home? Have I not put your feet on the path that you asked for? Treat me fairly, as I have done to you. Or you will taste my vengeance."

"Nemesis!" I cry into the void. The silence that follows is heavier. It holds a weight that is not physical. A thousand possibilities, an infinite number of futures, hinge on what I say next. I cannot breathe except to speak.

In the darkness, a single bell tolls.

"Nemesis," I repeat, emboldened by their reactions. The pressure on me has grown a thousandfold, and I feel as if I might be torn into a thousand pieces if I do not act.

The bell rings again, louder this time.

"Nemesis! My brothers have been wronged! Their blood cries out to you from the ground, waiting for you to avenge them. Come and claim what is yours! Wield me as your weapon and taste our revenge." The pressure on me vanishes in an instant, like a candle being blown out. For a moment, I sit in the void, waiting for the headsman's axe to fall. But nothing comes.

The bell rings one final time.

The shadows sweep forward to swallow me. Nemesis is the daughter of Nyx, the Goddess of Night, and she flaunts her mother's power as her own. I can barely see a dozen paces ahead of me in the murk. Then the goddess is here. She appears as bones, a skeleton floating just above the ground. Like her siblings, Nemesis is a giant, and I gape in horror as her body stitches itself together before me.

Pale flesh begins to creep over her innards. A dark cloak appears out of nowhere, covering her from my sight. I am relieved to be spared from the horror of seeing her rotted skin—I have seen enough living corpses to last me a lifetime.

A matching black blindfold wraps around her eyes before they form. As it finishes, Nemesis lands lightly. Her black hair fans around her, a shadow against the night that she travels in. The goddess is more whole than Aquilo.

Her head tilts down to stare at me. Blindfolded or not, I'm sure that she can see me better than I can see her. The *votum* in my right hand grows warm to the touch as her *animus* passes over it.

The goddess's mouth curves upward into a sharp-cornered smile as she tastes the oath. My heart races as her face takes on a cruel light. I should not be surprised; vengeance is not a kind attribute. I wonder if I have made a mistake.

"For too long have I slumbered," she murmurs, staring at me hungrily. "I thought that this was but a dream, a trick of my siblings to keep me distracted. But I am awake, I am certain of it." I swallow nervously, unwilling to point out that I am fairly certain that *I* am the one sleeping.

"You have such anger," she continues, tilting her blindfolded head to study me further. My senses recoil as something heavy and overwhelming drapes over me, scouring every inch of my mind, body, and soul. I am measured and weighed. "Such power. You remind me of him."

"Who?"

The world blinks. One moment, she stands at a distance; the next, she is before me. My right hand is held in her cold, rotten one as she stares at my wrist—at the purple scars left by the wolf *mythos* during my *Sententia*. They burn against my skin, reacting to her presence.

"You bear the mark of my siblings," she spits, disgusted and delighted. "Always testing. Experimenting. They search for one but do not know when they find it! Fools! Fools! The centuries have rotten their brains."

"You know what this is? What they did to me?"

"I accept your offering," she hisses in delight, ignoring my question. "It has been centuries since someone has brought a blood oath to me. Too long have I slumbered, unable to live, unable to wake, unable to dream."

"I'm the first?" I ask in surprise. I'm shocked that no one else has been this stupid for over a hundred years. It puts my idea into terrifying perspective.

"You will spill the sacred blood you have promised. Feed me and make me whole," she hisses, ignoring my question. "Then together we shall seek vengeance on my siblings and their rotten world."

"Together?" I have already had enough dealings with the gods; I have no desire to interact with them again. I want only to avenge my family and brothers and to be left alone. Nemesis laughs, her voice echoing with the peals of the bells once more.

"They will not let you live, *Ferrum Miles*." She calls me an iron soldier in the language of the ancients. "You will hurt them, and they will hunt you to the ends of *Terra*." Her promise sends chills rushing down my spine.

I open my mouth to protest, but the goddess continues, speaking over me. One does not simply interrupt Nemesis.

"Our oath is not yet complete, mortal. If you wish for my aid, you will bring your blood—your *votum*—to me in my temple. But first, you must wake." The darkness that swirls around the daughter of night sweeps forward, enveloping me until it is all I can see.

"Castor, get your ass out of bed right now!" Contessa barks, pounding on the door to my quarters. The darkness has become the back of my eyelids, and I wince against the sunlight pouring into my room as I open them. I'm coated with a thick sheen of sweat and twisted in my nest of blankets on the floor.

It was only a dream, I realize as the *lanista* continues to hammer away. I hadn't actually been summoned by Nemesis. It was just a nightmare, nothing more. But as I look down at my right hand, the *votum* is there. The bloodstains, which used to be faded and brown, are bright-red, as fresh as the day they were made.

CHAPTER 9

"Jupiter's bones, this is a disaster," Contessa snarls as she storms through the *dormitorium*, dragging me in her wake. I barely had time to throw on my tunic and leggings before the bald woman pulled me out of my room. "We're supposed to have three days, three bloody days. But that Cens—" She bites off the end of her sentence, as if suddenly remembering that I am with her. Her dark gaze measures me for a second before she decides to continue.

"Listen, lad, today is a dangerous day," she tells me frankly.

I swallow, already aware of what she is about to tell me, but Pliny warned me to hold my tongue. He didn't want the *lanista* to know what I overheard.

"More dangerous than yesterday, *Domina*?" I ask with a haughty tone. "I seem to recall fighting for my life." Despite my arrogance, I am still unsettled by my interaction with another god. Nemesis walks with me, lurking in my shadow. The pinpricks of her attention are gone, but I cannot shake the sense that I am being watched.

"Yes," she sneers, turning to stare at me. She takes a step toward me in challenge, staring directly into my eyes. The bald woman is not angry at me, but her hackles are raised, and she is ready to strike out at anything in front of her. "You would only have died in the training arena. If the Censors get their claws on you, you will suffer."

"Censors?" Only some of the fear in my voice is acting. Even the gods seem like lesser villains when compared to the *tellus*-armored killers. For the first time, I wonder if Atticus will be in attendance today. Would he even recognize me if he saw me? My brown hair is long and unkempt. I've grown taller and wider since the *Sententia*. He sent a boy to die, but I am a man now.

"Yes, the White Hand will be here soon." She turns, resuming her aggravated walk. Servants stream by us, cleaning rooms.

"Why, *Domina*?"

"Every gladiator *ludus* must have their fighters inspected by the Censors. Because they are given *Cor* Hearts for their participation, the Empress demands that her enforcers approve every *electus*."

"What are they looking for?" I hadn't made the connection between the Censors and the Hearts that were prizes until now. It is a carrot that the Empress dangles in front of her most powerful *domuum*. They get guarantees that their progeny will all be *electi*, but it gives her an excuse to send her eyes into their palaces.

"Anything that the Empress prohibits. *Electi* using forbidden Symbols. Cheaters. Every once in a while, someone tries to sneak an Ironbound the legions missed into the Copper or Silver Circuits." My heart skips a beat, but she does not pause. I do not think she knows how close she is to my truth.

"It depends on the *domus*. For the favorites, it is a passing inspection. For those who are out of grace, they are looking for an excuse to cause trouble. If they find anything they don't like"—she casts a deliberate glance at my exposed arms and the white *rasa* veins—"they have unquestioned *imperium* to hunt for answers."

"What are you saying? If they think something is wrong with me, they can kill me, and there's nothing you can do about it?"

"Oh, there are limits. Varus will protest and probably be awarded a small fee," Contessa amends as an afterthought. "But you'll be dead."

"Why was this not mentioned when I was asked to make my oath?" I demand. It's my turn to draw up short. "Is this how *Domus* Pelias treats its gladiators? I was given the choice to die or to die?"

"It's the Games, lad," the *lanista* growls. "People die." There's a shadow of guilt on her face. "But this was not the plan. We were supposed to have more time to prepare you."

"What do we do? Am I a dead man walking?" Despite knowing more than I let on, I can't help but feel a familiar bitterness roiling in my chest.

"No, there's still a fight to be had," she promises. "It's time to see if Pliny can conjure another one of his miracles."

The magister is waiting for us in the training facility. Unlike my dream, it is brightly lit and full of people. Other gladiators are in the essence *loci*, filling their *Cor*. Pliny is standing beside the Winter room, which is already powered, filling with snow and ice. His eyes flash in warning, reminding me to feign ignorance.

"It seemed to me that your Symbol was not completely satisfied with fresh powder," he remarks by way of greeting, as if there is nothing else more pressing to discuss. "I've instructed the servants to keep it on at all times to try to make it more congruent for you."

"I think that will help," I agree, surprised at his insight. A flash of concern runs through me. Have I underestimated how much his *Cor* could tell him about my attuned Hearts? Once again, he seems to know too much.

"Well?" Contessa prods, in no mood to wait for answers. "What's the plan? How do we hide Castor's white stripes?"

"We don't," the magister replies with a sigh, turning to look at his counterpart. My stomach drops at the look on his face.

"What? Pliny, you know that the Censors are looking for any excuse—"

"I do," he cuts her off harshly, "but it is a trap. The Censors know. Their spies have already seen."

"How?"

"I do not know, but they have shown their hand. Tartus came to threaten us over not requesting an inspection."

"So?" The *lanista*'s brows furrow with a confusion I share. "Just because they know that we bought some gladiators doesn't mean that—"

"It's a trap, dear Contessa," Pliny tells her with a gentle smile. He is not condescending, merely confident. She is the master in the arena, but this is his dueling ground. "Why else would Tartus tell us that he is coming, unless to give us time to prepare? It would be a simple matter for us to paint his *rasa* veins. His *Cor* is strong enough that he would pass any test the Censors put before him with ease."

I gasp as I understand what Pliny has seen. The magister gives me a wry look, impressed that I'm following. I dismissed the Censor as a vicious dog, barreling around to bark at anything he could, but his entrance had been on purpose, like a faithful hunting hound, to drive *Domus* Pelias to the hunters.

"Then, when they catch us hiding an *immundus*, that's all the excuse they need to move against us," Contessa finishes grimly, understanding the snare before us. She is not a stupid woman, just a straightforward one. Her gaze flicks toward me, and I catch a fresh light of concern in her eyes as she studies me. "What about him?"

I turn back to the magister, my heart beating in my throat. My gaze flickers toward the far end of the room, where a cluster of weapons and armor sit on racks, waiting for use. There's still time for me to arm myself and try to fight my way free. If the Censors want my head, let them see if they have enough steel in their spines to take it. But in the back of my mind, I know it would be futile. Their *tellus* blades were made to kill men like me.

Pliny smiles, but its light doesn't reach his eyes. I reach for Ancient Frost's calming presence, letting it drown out the fire of fear that burns in my chest. "The Censors wield unquestioned power over the *Cor* Hearts, but they are not in charge of the Games themselves. They, too, have masters they must keep happy."

"You didn't…" Contessa interrupts, but her voice is delighted, not concerned.

"Of course I did." Pliny's smile turns at the corner, making him look almost cruel for a moment. He has never seemed more like a fox.

"What did you do?" I press, no longer willing to wait for my fate.

"The Games are under the purview of Consul *Quaestor*," Pliny explains.

"Really?" I cannot hide my shock. There are two consuls in all of the Iron Empire; each of them answers directly to the Empress and no one else. Outside of Diana herself, there is no one more powerful. I had no idea that the Games were so…important. "How does that stop the Censors for killing me for being unworthy?"

"The Censors are looking for monsters," Pliny says with a shrug. "A Winter Symbol is not forbidden, but it is rare. You may be an *immundus*, but they cannot argue that that will make you more dangerous. If the consul is impressed with you enough to demand that you be allowed to compete, the Censors will not be able to deny him."

"How would he find out about me?" I ask, arching an eyebrow. This seems more like a plan a child would come up with than a solution to keeping me alive.

"I told him, of course." Pliny's smile is wide and devious.

"You did what?" I gasp, unable to close my mouth. Contessa begins to laugh from beside me.

"Briannus was once a student of mine. He still pays some respect to my opinions from time to time. I merely suggested that he would find it worth his time to join the inspection."

"You taught a consul?" My head is reeling at the thought. Even though I stand in the house of the descendants of Pelias, the elite of the palatine still feel a world away.

"Come on, lad." Contessa places a heavy hand on my shoulder, pointing toward the waiting *locus*. "You best make sure you're ready."

I strap on a *lorica* and a pair of *gladii* before I enter the frozen chamber. Pliny shoots me a questioning glance, but I tell him it's because the metal gets colder, which helps me cultivate Winter essence, and after a moment of thought, he nods thoughtfully. It actually is true. The metal acts like a funnel, helping me pull in more Snow and Ice essence for my *Cor* to condense until it becomes Ancient Frost.

I kneel on the powder, balancing my intake between the Symbols. It doesn't take long for me to fill my reserves to the brim, but I do not move, trying to center myself. Pliny doesn't interrupt me this time, so I take advantage of the silence, feeding my fear to the cold. When I walk out of this room, my life will be in the balance—I can afford no distractions.

Fighting a couple of gladiators was one thing. The other Silvers were warriors, but they had been at a major disadvantage against my secret Iron Symbol. Their own weapons betrayed them to me. If I have to cross blades with a Censor, that advantage would vanish.

Atticus looms in my mind's eye like one of the Iron Lords, towering over me far more than he ever had in real life. In my imagination, he has become faster and stronger than he was the night he struck down my father. Fear uncoils in my chest, overwhelming the cold calm of Ancient Frost and Iron as it circles my heart.

I gasp for air as waves of panic sweep over me, threatening to pull me under. I am not strong enough to face him. I am a soldier of the legions, but he is an elite killer. Even Gaius seems small in his shadow.

Stop this, I hiss at myself, snapping my head back and opening my eyes. *Get a hold of yourself. Your brothers are counting on you.* That familiar prickling pressure settles on my shoulders as I remember the *votum* that I carry. I cannot die today; their blood demands it.

"Castor," Pliny's voice interjects above the whirling of the snowstorm that I kneel in. "It is time."

I look over my shoulder to look at the magister. His expression is tight, but he offers me a small smile of encouragement. Behind him, my focus sharpens as I spy a pair of white-armored figures striding through the training room.

The Censors are here.

Wordlessly, I nod, rising to my feet. Ancient Frost and Iron sing their cold duet in my veins as I release myself to drift completely in their embrace. My instincts scream at me to draw the pair of *gladii* at my hips, but I do not.

Pliny's expression flattens as he watches me embrace the cold, but he says nothing, only gives me a tight nod as I slide past him into the arena. An audience has assembled while I've been filling my reserves.

Malus Mors and Deltara stand with Contessa on the edge of the sandy floor, watching my approach. Varus is on the other side of the arena as he glares at the two Empress's servants. The older Censor's hair is fully white, but he stands strong and proud in his *tellus* armor. This must be Tartus, who accosted Pliny in his study last night. Gold veins decorate his arms, which I have become used to seeing by now. The younger woman at his side is closer to my age, with blond hair gathered back in a short ponytail. She is only Silver, but her eyes are sharp and dangerous.

I am relieved that neither of them is Atticus, but that does not mean that the danger has passed. The female Censor stares at me with unabashed focus, making the hairs on the back of my neck stand on end.

A few other gladiators mill at the far side of the room, watching the test with a casual disinterest. I spy the Air duelist and Knife from yesterday. I give them both a nod, but neither of them returns it.

I turn my head to scan the room but see no one that looks like the second most important man in the Empire. The only other person who is present is the woman sitting in the storm *loci* once again, absorbing its essence. My heart skips a beat at the consul's absence, even in the depths of my Symbols' cold embrace. I glance at Pliny, but he merely shakes his head.

"An *immundus*?" the female Censor barks in a familiar refrain. "Surely the fortunes of *Domus* Pelias have not sunk so low?" Varus's lip curls in a sneer, but he remains silent. She is not as good of an actress as she pretends. Neither looks surprised to see the white veins on my arms, which tells me that Pliny correctly understood the trap that was laid.

"We are confident in our selections, Censor Falia," Pliny responds calmly, refusing to rise to her taunt. "And in the Empress's representatives to judge them fairly and accurately." For some reason, that makes the girl flush in anger, but Tartus places a calming hand on her arm.

"These are the three?" he asks. His voice is devoid of the condescension and rage that I heard last night, which only terrifies me further. Was that a mask he wore to trick Pliny, or is he wearing one now?

"They are." Pliny's voice is confident. "One for the *Aurum* Circuit and two for the *Argentum*."

"Let us begin." Tartus snaps his finger, and Falia crouches to pick up a satchel at her feet. She extracts a black box from it and steps out onto the sand. Pliny gestures at the three of us to meet her. My heart skips another beat, but I obey, following the other two.

As I pass the magister, he whispers so softly that his lips do not even seem to move, "Slowly."

I obey, letting the two gladiators pass in front of me, trying to figure out what the relic the Censor carries is for. It's some sort of test, I am certain, but I have never seen anything like it. *Malus* strides confidently to stand before her. He's done this before; this is merely a formality for him.

"Place your hand on the *scrutator* relic and summon your Symbol," Falia commands sharply. Despite my fear, I lean forward, curious to see for myself. *Scrutator* means to study or perceive, so the tool must somehow allow the Censors to see what someone is bound to. *Malus* grunts as he obeys. For a moment, nothing happens, then a light flickers in the center of the box, projecting his Symbol above it in a glowing outline.

My jaw drops as an icon forms in thin air, and I study it. I never heard Dorian tell Varus what *Malus Mors* affinity was. The entire image has a yellow hue to it, but in the center is a simple line drawing of a human bicep, bulging with muscles.

A Symbol that modifies the *electus*'s body is one of the rarest. Tartus stiffens in surprise at the display from the relic. Varus only smiles darkly from his corner, watching the proceedings with grim satisfaction.

"Strength," the Censor announces after studying the icon for a few moments, nodding at Bad Death to step back. The image above the relic vanishes as he lifts his hands from it. The dark-skinned man grunts smugly, pleased by the change in the room around us. I don't know how that Symbol works; how would one even gather Strength essence? But I have no doubt that it is horrifyingly effective at making him far stronger than he should be.

"You." The Censor points at Deltara, gesturing for her to repeat the process. The lean archer obeys, placing her hand on the relic. After a moment, a green icon hovers above it, showing a tree. I am not nearly the horticulturist my father was, but even I can recognize the distinctive boughs of a fully grown Ashwood.

"Ashwood." Falia confirms my guess after a moment of study. Deltara lifts her hand from the relic and steps back to join our ranks. My heart begins to race as everyone's eyes turn to me. This is it; my moment of judgment has come. If the wrong icon displays from the Censors' tool, I am a dead man.

Unbidden, I step forward to take my place in front of the Censor. I have an inkling of a plan to hide my connection to Iron, a lesson learned thanks to my time in the North. If the *berserkirs* could only damage my Heart's ability to access my Symbols when I was holding them, perhaps this *scrutator* relic functions the same way.

I extend my hand toward the gray plate, releasing my hold on the Iron Symbol as I do and embracing Ancient Frost with every ounce of my mind. The temperature in my body plummets as the frost fills me. It is not uncomfortable; I wear it like a second skin.

My fear no longer ranges through me. It is gone, locked up in an icy prison. I stare the Censor in the eyes as I place my hand on the relic. Her eyes are flat, but the corner of her mouth is upturned in disgust. She sees me as weak; an *immundus* is someone who has failed their responsibility to our people. But I have not failed yet.

The glowing image appears above the *scrutator* relic, and my heart skips a beat as it flickers, white-gray-white-white, faster than my eye can track. Before anyone can react, a deep, dark blue image erupts into the air of a jagged outline of a crown made of ice. Each of its tines is as sharp as a blade.

Falia's eyes widen, and her mouth parts slightly as her gaze snaps from the display to me. I smile tightly, meeting her stare boldly. Her stare is no longer dismissive; instead, it is almost… fearful. "Ancient Frost," she says after the icon does not fade.

"Preposterous," Tartus barks from the edge of the field. I look away from the woman to see the older Censor powering toward us. His body may be gray, but he is not frail in the slightest. Even Varus looks stunned from where he watches.

I keep my hand firmly on the *scrutator* relic as the senior Censor arrives. He glowers down at the floating image in shock, his own jaw dropping open. Despite my amusement at seeing these two struck dumb by my Symbol, a growing sense of concern grows in my chest, fighting its way free of the frost's cold grip. What has Aquilo given me?

"What is the meaning of this, Varus?" Tartus demands, whirling in place to glare at the master of the house with unbridled fury. "You dare to bring such a Symbol into the Games?"

"Oh my, that can only mean you found something *interesting*!" a new voice cuts in from the far end of the room. Every head turns to stare at the man who enters, flanked by a pair of Praetorians. Goosebumps flare on my arms as I spy their familiar purple uniforms. A burst of red-hot rage breaks from its cold prison inside of me, and for a moment all I want is to draw my blades and charge them, but Ancient Frost's cold logic keeps my anger in check.

The man in the middle is a giant of a man, towering over me by more than a head-length. He wears a white toga that is gilded with gold. His black hair is wild and untamed, except for the precise goatee that frames his face. His dark eyes twinkle with mischievous delight as he steps in. Even if he did not wear the emerald ring of the Consul *Quaestor* on his right hand, I would have known that this was the man that Pliny hoped for, Briannus. He who commands the treasury and speaks for the common people in the Empire.

"*Salve*, *Dominus*," Tartus calls in surprise at the sight of the consul. There's an edge to his greeting that has nothing to do with me. "I did not expect to see you at such a routine inspection—"

"Well, it's hardly routine when it's done so quickly, is it?" Briannus sniffs, turning from the Censor to tilt his head at Varus. "*Salve*, Senator," he says warmly. "I hope you do not mind that I showed up unannounced." He is a loud, bombastic man, but there is an inherent cheer to his delivery that warms up the room.

"Not at all, *Dominus*," Varus replies smoothly, returning the gesture. "You are always welcome in this house."

"Generous as ever." Briannus chuckles before turning his attention back toward the two Censors and me in the center of the room. "Now, what have I missed?" The consul rubs his hands together as if excited by the tension.

"*Dominus*, this *immundus*"—Tartus makes the word a curse as he gestures toward me—"has bound to an Elder Symbol." I blink in surprise, risking another glance toward Varus looking for some sort of clue. I've never heard of an Elder Symbol before. But the master of *Domus* Pelias's face is blank as he watches the proceedings before us.

"Well, that certainly is not routine." Briannus laughs, turning to study me with a sharp eye. "What family?"

"Winter, *Dominus*." Tartus's reply is made through clenched teeth, but the consul pays no mind to the tone.

"Ancient Frost?" The man's guess is instantaneous, and he looks at the Censors to confirm. After a moment, the woman nods, and a brilliant smile breaks out on Briannus's face.

"This is fantastic!" He beams. "Think of the drama, Tartus! Think of the story! Aquilo himself has returned! Come and see him walk among us! The crowds will throng to the Games; we'll have to open the sides." He begins to murmur to himself as he plans some grand reveal. I stare at the consul, chilled by his reaction. For the first time, I notice that his arms are unmarked by any *Cor* veins. He is not an *electus*, but a normal man.

"*Dominus*, he is an *immundus*," Tartus hisses. "Even if we were to allow an Elder Symbol to compete, surely his connection is unstable and therefore dangerous. He must be culled so that his relics can be reclaimed." My heart lurches at the man's calm delivery of my death sentence.

"What is this *we?*" Briannus demands, turning to glare at the old man, a strain of anger revealing itself for the first time. "You dare say *we* to me, Censor?" His loud voice thunders, echoing off the marble halls. I have to choke back a laugh as I realize that Pliny was right about his old student.

Despite his rage, Tartus does not back down. "It is our *imperium* to determine if an *electus* is worthy of their Heart or a danger to the populace!" Tartus snaps back, a deep red flush beginning to creep up his neck out of his armor.

"But not to deny an entire Symbol from its use in the Games!" Briannus bellows, taking a step toward us. The Praetorians flanking him follow in his shadow, hands on their *gladii*. I wonder if they would draw their blades on a Censor. "I say that Ancient Frost should be shown to the people. If you must test him, then *test* him, but if he passes, I will have him."

Tartus glares at Briannus for a moment before calming himself. Almost, I can see the cogs spinning in his head. His plan has already been foiled. He had hoped that Varus and Pliny would try to hide my infirmity, giving them a reason to punish *Domus* Pelias. They did not expect me to have such a rare Symbol, but what does that matter? I am an *immundus*. Surely, I will not pass their tests. But like Falia, he also does not know what I am. How could he? There has never been anyone like me. The dead gods have created a new game for us mortals to play on their stage.

"Very well," Tartus snarls, turning away from me to storm back to the stony edge of the training field. Falia follows in his shadow, carrying the relic with her. "We will prepare a series of—"

"Oh, just get on with it." Briannus sighs in mock despair. "Varus, I'm sure your *lanista* can create a suitable atmosphere for your new gladiator to show his if he can actually use his Heart?" I struggle to keep a smirk from growing on my lips as everyone else evacuates the sand. The Censors' rage is a thing of beauty to me. I am not bound to a Fire Symbol, but I have every intention of stoking it.

"Gladly," my master replies, gesturing to Contessa with a nod. I look over my shoulder in time to see the bald woman raise her hand and gesture toward the arena's relics, activating them. The purple barriers spring to life, sealing me in the sand.

I hunch my shoulders, preparing to call on the *Glacialis Falx*, but Contessa glares at me, her eyes ordering me to wait. I pause, and she gestures again, changing the field to better suit my Symbol. A smile sweeps across my face as a familiar frigid wind cuts past me. Snow begins to fall from the ceiling and drifts form before my eyes. My awareness spreads to cover the entire arena as winter invades. In a matter of moments, it's as if I am back in the North, beyond the safety of Frigidus's walls. Where the other boys from Segesta fell, sent to their deaths by a different Censor, clothed in white.

A pang of loss tears at me as I am transported to the place that I lost my brothers. I close my eyes as grief rears its horned head and threatens to gut me from the inside out, but I dig deeper, burying myself in Ancient Frost's frozen arms, trusting it to drive the feelings away.

As my insides freeze, I open my eyes, staring straight at Tartus. My smile is cold and hard, like the North where I bound this Symbol. Despite the barrier separating us, the Golden Censor pales slightly under my gaze.

"All right!" Briannus shouts, clapping his hands together. "Let's see what you can do." His voice is slightly muffled on the other side of the barrier, but I hear him well enough. I do not reply; instead, I snap both my hands to the side, summoning two of the Frozen Blades at once.

The strain on my reserve is immense; fortunately, I am surrounded by ice and snow. They are fresh, not ancient, but I already have some experience in compressing weaker essence into something usable for my *Cor* Heart. A pair of icy *gladii* grow out of my hands, growing from hilt to tip. Pliny's words from last night about my ability echo in my mind, giving me an idea. I do not think I can manifest ice any other way—Aquilo was specific in his gift-giving. But that doesn't mean that I can't reshape what they have been kind enough to give me.

I have just enough time to see both Censors' eyes go wide in shock before I am moving. I reach down with my right blade, touching it to the ground and pulling upward, commanding the snow to bind to the tip like a brush. Moving quickly, I draw the first half of the crown icon in the air. I harden the snow to ice, freezing it in place to form a structure taller than my head. Then with my left, I repeat the pattern, completing the image.

I step back from my sculpture for a moment to let everyone see what I have created. Then I strike it with my blade, commanding it to shatter as I make connection with it. It explodes like a broken chandelier, sparkling as it falls to the ground.

Briannus begins to clap as I turn to face my audience, a wide smile spreading across his face. "Manifesting! Well, *I'm* convinced," he booms loudly, giving the two Censors a firm look. The purple border winks out of existence as Contessa deactivates the protections.

Falia's mouth hangs open, but Tartus glares darkly at me. I match his threatening stare evenly. He is more powerful than me, but I have killed a black-veined *necromanta* and borne the *votum* of an undead god. He doesn't scare me as much as he should. His brow furrows as he notices my lack of fear. It is foolish to goad someone like him, but I cannot help myself—I am Iron. I do not bend. I do not break.

"Where is his writ?" Falia asks sharply, her eyes flashing with a cruel design. My heart skips a beat at the glimmer of victory that shines on her face. Pliny hands her a scroll that she reads with a frown.

"He must be bound," Falia shrieks in delight when she gets to the end. "He is a *captivus*. He cannot be allowed to wander freely. We will take him—"

"Castor has already sworn his oath to my *domus* on my Oath Rod," Varus cuts in smoothly, his face mild. "He willingly swore on the relic before these witnesses." Falia looks between my master and the other Gold *electi* with rank suspicion on her face. For a moment, I suspect she will call him a liar. I do not know what will happen if she does. Varus is a senator, but she is a Censor. They speak their accusations with the voice of the Empress.

"Circumstances? How curious." Briannus chuckles from across the room, the consul's voice cutting through the tension with ease.

"A legion binding gone wrong." Varus gestures lazily at me to show them. Understanding what he wants, I pull down on the collar of tunic to allow the XII branded on my chest to be seen. The two Censors stare at it like it is a dangerous weapon. This is what I was afraid of. The Twelfth is not a mark of honor. It would be one thing if I was supposed to be in the Third or even the Ninth. But this brand marks me as a criminal. I am careful not to make eye contact with the Praetorians that hover in the consul's shadow. The looks of scorn on their expressions might be too much for me to keep myself in check. "They sold him off to the slave pits where we found him."

"What are the odds?" Briannus gasps in awe. "I bet those Agogia magisters were beside themselves when they realized he wasn't Ironbound like the rest of their drones." No one else in the room laughs with the consul. Slowly, I release my collar, obscuring the mark of the Twelfth once more.

After a moment, Tartus snorts in disgust, admitting defeat. He looks past me to his assistant. "Enter his crime into the Census," he tells Falia. The woman nods stiffly, producing an ornately bound scroll and quill, some sort of scribing relic, no doubt. This is one of the many tasks of the Empress's White Hand, to count and number her people.

"*Prenomen* and *Cognomen*?" she asks, *first name* and *last name*.

"Castor Arator," I lie, not wanting to connect myself to the *immundus* named Castor who was sent to the legions. But my name is known, so I am limited by how much I can hide.

"Place of birth?"

"Segesta," I say at last, trying to hide the fear that my honesty brings. But to my relief, Falia nods, her expression unchanging, marking down a few more things on her relic before turning to the elder Censor.

"It is done."

"Show us the rest," Tartus snaps at Contessa, clearly irritated at being foiled.

"This way, Censors," the woman replies, a hint of smugness hiding in her tone. "We have a pack of blank candidates for approval. They are quite fierce." The Censors stalk after her, their red cloaks flapping behind them. I smile savagely at their backs, relieved to watch the White Hand leaving frustrated.

"Varus, you delightful creature," Briannus crows, rubbing his hands together like a man before a feast. "I can see the scenes now. You must sell him to me; we will build an entire season around him!" I turn to stare at the consul in surprise as he approaches the *dominus* of my House, his hands spread wide.

"Think about the scenes he will star in, the rise of the dead god Aquilo! He will tear through monsters to reclaim his throne, only to finally be met by Frigidus, who strikes him down!" A chill runs down my neck as I listen to him plan my death. My gaze slides back to Varus, whose face gives away nothing.

"I am sorry, *Dominus*," he replies slowly, choosing his words with care, "but Castor is to join our *argentum* roster for the rest of the year. I could not possibly part with him."

"Name your price," Briannus demands, his brows beginning to form an irritated wedge. "He's a generational gift. The Empress will be beside herself at the revenue that he will bring in. We've spent a kingdom's ransom on the rest of the circuit, Varus. It's going to be something people have never seen before. I could use him to make it incredible." For a moment, I am sure that I am about to be sold again, like a pig to the slaughter.

"Begging your pardon, I am sure that you of all people need no reminder that *Domus* Pelias's performance is…subpar." Briannus grunts in agreement, some of his irritation fading. His dark eyes dart over to me, and he studies me in a new light.

"He's that good, is he?"

"My *lanista* is convinced he is the missing piece we have been looking for." The tension begins to bleed out of my shoulders as my current master refuses to part with me. I seem to be useful, so he is loyal.

"Fifty thousand *denarii* if you will let me have him for the *Spectaculum*." My stomach drops in shock at the amount of money. Even Varus blinks in stunned surprise for a moment.

"*Dominus*..." Varus begins after collecting himself. "I am beyond flattered—"

"Oh, spare me the nice empty words," Briannus grumbles, crossing his arms and sighing. "I know it's not enough to tempt you to risk expulsion from the Games. But I had to at least try. Mercury's Rotting Eyes! I never thought I'd live to see the day an Elder Symbol makes its way back to the Games."

"Nor did I." Varus chuckles, relieved that the consul has not taken offense. "I will admit that I thought he was a more common Winter Symbol. I had no idea that he was anything more until today." Distantly, I hear a dry chuckle that tells me Pliny was not as surprised as the rest of them.

"Perhaps we can work out an agreement for me to borrow him from time to time? You know as well as I that the Games are all about theater, and you have found a star." Briannus's eyes glint with renewed greed, and my fear spikes. He may not have a *Cor* Heart, but this man is far more dangerous than he lets on. "Nothing too risky, of course, but perhaps a little *quid pro quo*. Yes, I shall think on this."

"As you say, *Dominus*." Varus nods his head respectfully. "We would be delighted to hear any offers from the Games for one of our gladiators."

"Yes, I'm sure," the consul replies, amused.

Behind the palatines, the door to the storm *locus* hisses open, and the woman who had been cultivating its essence emerges. My heart stops as I see her. She is stunning, with long brown hair and striking features. Like me, she is an *argentum*—a Silver. But it is not her beauty that locks me in place.

I know her face.

It is Alessandra, the magister-in-training who was there when I was first tested to become *Fidelis*. I freeze, petrified by what she will do when she sees me. I cannot believe my misfortune. Does Fortuna plague me as well for my broken *votum*?

But to my surprise, the girl's blue eyes sweep over me, not pausing until they land on Varus. Is it possible that she did not recognize me? My long hair tickles my shoulders, reminding me that I look far different from the last time we met. But that's hardly my most defining feature.

"Daughter," the master rumbles in a pleased tone. "Come and greet Consul Briannus." My fear doubles as I realize exactly who she is. With a word, Pelias's daughter can have the Censors cut me down where I stand. My right hand drops to the hilt of the *gladius* hanging from my belt, gripping the weapon until my knuckles go white. But it does not help; there is no cold that can keep me calm now.

"*Salve, Dominus*." Alessandra bows deeply, showing proper obeisance to one of the most powerful men in the world. "What causes you to grace our home with your presence?"

"More of Pliny's games." Briannus chuckles good-naturedly. "But I'm sure you're more than familiar, aren't you, young lady? I hear you may be joining *Aureate* society this next year? Are you truly so close to Ascending already? It seems like just yesterday you were a child no taller than my knee. It will make me feel like an old man to see you so honored."

"Perhaps, *Dominus*." Alessandra smiles wryly. "Assuming that I am able to Ascend in time." She holds out one of her arms, swirling with Silver veins.

"Well, I cannot give you much advice about that," Briannus admits, glancing at his own bare skin with a smile, "but if Pliny cannot help you walk the path, then it cannot be done." Varus grunts in displeasure but does not comment.

"I hope so." Alessandra's smile brightens.

"Let us see what you have learned, young magister-to-be," Briannus declares, waving a hand at me. "What do you think of your father's newest gladiator?" Alessandra turns to study me at the consul's behest. She purses her lips as she takes me in, and I stiffen in fear. But despite her scrutiny, no light of recognition flares in her eyes.

"An *immundus*?" she asks neutrally, without any hint of scorn. "How unusual. Did the Censors approve him?"

"Oh, they hemmed and hawed like old maids, but they did in the end," Briannus says brightly as if he did not force them to submit to his will.

"He doesn't seem like much to look at," Alessandra allows after a few moments of pondering. "I'm not sure what to think, *Dominus*."

"Keep your eye on this one, young lady," Briannus confides with a wink. "He may surprise you."

CHAPTER 10

I spend a sleepless night in my dorms. No gods torment me. No Censors burst into my room, ready to drag me away. Yet despite the peace, I do not feel safe. I have been approved to compete in the Games, but for the first time, I think about what that means.

I will be fighting in front of crowds, a terrible place for someone with as deadly a secret as mine. Already I have drawn the Censors' ire. They will not forget me, nor will it be easy to, thanks to the white *rasa* veins that fill my skin. Even if Alessandra has not recognized me yet, it can be only a matter of time until she does. What if Atticus hears of an *immundus* gladiator and comes to watch? In the legions, I was able to hide among a sea of men like me. But now, in order to live, I will have to stand alone.

Inwardly, I curse the first dead gods I ever swore an oath to: Mercury, Mars, and Fortuna. Their games have only ever gotten those I love killed. Now that I am the only one left, it seems they are intent on finishing the job they started with me.

The temperature in my room plummets, as Ancient Frost exudes from me, fueled by my rage. Very well, let them send me to die. I will survive. I will Ascend. I will kill them all. When sleep finally takes me, my dreams are empty for the first time that I can remember.

"You've got some natural skill, but you fight like an untrained bull," Contessa tells me the next morning. The room she has taken me to is much smaller than the training hall. There is no sand in the center; instead, it has a square arena marked out on the stone surface. A weapon rack runs along the far wall, but it is empty.

"You swing every blow like a butcher. There's no subtlety to you," she continues, prowling around me as she lectures me. The bald woman is dressed in a set of leather armor that matches my own, but bears no weapons, making me wonder how she is going to teach me anything.

"In you go. Let's see what you can learn." Confused, I follow her instructions, stepping over the black square border to stand in the empty space. The *lanista* steps right up to the line and gestures at the far wall, where a series of relics are mounted on the wall.

Immediately, the world distorts. I am no longer in some small training room but in Mars's Arena. Sound crashes down on me like a wave as the crowd filling the coliseum roars their excitement. Bright red sand crunches under my feet as I shift, staring in slack-jawed awe at the world before me. Contessa is present, standing right on the edge of the ring, a knowing smirk on her face. This must be some sort of *somnatorium*, powered by a dream relic, like they used in the *Sententia*. The purple wolf scars on my wrist tingle in memory. Once again, I am floored by the wealth of *Domus* Pelias.

I'm so shocked that I almost don't notice the gladiator charging at me, dueling blade at the ready. I curse, dancing backwards as I draw my swords one after the other. Instinctively, I seize my Symbols, letting their awareness crash down on me. My fear and panic wash away in their cool hands.

The gladiator steps into striking distance, his blade flickering forward at lightning speed. I barely have time to note his Silver veins before I manage a weak parry, surprised by his aggression. I turn his attack, but my wrist screams in protest, twisted at an angle that hurts.

"Somnius's Rotting Eyes," I curse, turning aside another blazing lunge at the last second. It's awkward and embarrassing. We part, and he strikes again, not giving me any time to catch my bearings. He's so quick, I cannot keep up with him. It is like he's moving faster than I can sense. I've never fought someone like this—not even the Air duelist in the gauntlet had a fraction of his speed. Only as I frantically block his second attack do I realize what is wrong.

I can't sense the iron in his weapon.

This is not real, despite how strong my opponent's blows feel. It's an illusion, a trick on the mind, but that means that my Symbol cannot feel his weapon. My advantage is nonexistent here.

Shaking my head, I settle into a rhythm, trying to find my footing. His dueling blade is longer and heavier than either of my *gladii*. The top third of the weapon is curved slightly, letting him slither through my guard. But what he has in reach and power, I make up for in adaptability.

I knock another one of his terrifying lunges to the side, holding my left blade against his to force it wide. The illusion grits his teeth, trying to free himself from my entanglement, but I step forward, striking with my right.

He dances backward, sliding his sword free of mine, but the top of my *gladius* carves a line through his leathers. It's not real, but I still feel the shock of impact as it cuts. The construct ignores any pain and launches forward, staying on the attack. Again, I trap his sword with one of mine and attack with the other.

This time when we separate, he pauses for a moment and flickers. In a moment, he is replaced by a fresh copy of himself, no longer bleeding or wounded. But now he carries *two* dueling blades.

"Great," I mutter, casting a glance at the *lanista* who hovers on the sidelines. The bald woman's face is impassive, and she watches me with dark eyes. She does not seem impressed by my performance.

The refreshed construct dashes forward, as fast as ever. Despite the heavier weight of his weapons, he wields them with the same ease that I carry mine. Our blades ring in a flurry of exchanges as I frantically try to keep him from skewering me.

He slashes high, I block with my left.

He stabs low, I block with my right.

He counters with a wicked fast slash across my body; I knock it upward with my left.

I'm too slow to block his lunge with my right.

This might be a dream, but the longer dueling blade burns like fire as it punches through my chest. I scream in agony as it cuts through my ribcage with ease. Then the world freezes. The crowd goes silent, and my opponent is still, paused in the action of skewering me like a pig. The pain does not go away but remains a constant point of pressure.

The only sound is a pair of sandals crunching on the red sand as Contessa swims into view, circling me like a shark. The *lanista*'s face is covered in a scowl, and she walks around the two of us, eyeing where our blades are like a master artist judging paint strokes.

"What in Dead Jupiter's name was that?" she demands after a moment of reflection. "I've seen Heartless pups who've never held a blade before put up a better fight than you. It's like you were fighting with your eyes closed."

"I..." I wheeze, trying to choke around the pain that holds me tight.

"Why didn't you use your ice?" She whirls on me with something like suspicion on her face. "You tore through my Silver gladiators like they were made of papyrus, but now, in the Dream Arena, you're as innocent as a lamb?"

"I couldn't feel it," I stammer, caught off guard by her question. I had been so shocked to not be able to sense the iron in the construct's weapons that it hadn't even occurred to me to try calling on Ancient Frost. If one of them didn't work here, why would the other?

"It's an illusion. You're still alive, boy." Contessa fixes me with a disappointed stare. She gestures at the air, and the relics shift the scene. I gasp in relief, dropping to my knees as my opponent vanishes. The pain is gone, but its memory haunts me, like the wolf scars that still itch on my wrist.

"Oh, get up." She snorts in disgust. "You're going to get hit harder than that if you ever make it to the bloody sands in Forum."

Slowly, I obey, gathering my feet under me and rising from a crouch. My mind flinches in anticipation, but my body does not even twinge with pain. Already I am cured of the fatal blow. The crowd around us is still frozen, trapped in time. I stare at the faces of the plebeians in the front row, who are mid-scream of delight at seeing my death. A chill settles over me as I realize how truly barbaric this place must be. In the Twelfth, men were sent to die, but for Empire and Honor. All I see reflected in the eyes of the illusions around me is an insatiable bloodlust.

The rust that feasts on the underbelly of the Iron Empire grows.

"Welcome to the great Arena of Mars, Castor," Contessa says softly, her voice gentler than it was. Startled, I turn to the *lanista*, who studies me with a sad smile. She understands the bloody demands I see in the eyes of the crowd around us.

"What is his Symbol?"

"Speed." I blink in surprise, thinking of *Malus Mors' Cor*. I've never faced an opponent with an internalized attunement like that. No wonder he moves like lightning.

"Ice." She makes an impatient gesture at a barrel of water that sits on the side of the ring and the moment is over. The work continues.

Obediently, I reach for Ancient Frost as I dip my blades into the water, covering them in a thin layer of ice.

"Oh," I say, staring at the weapons and feeling stupid. "I thought—"

"You are real; this is not," Contessa reminds me. "Again." She gestures at the far world and vanishes as the world flickers. The same opponent appears before me, carrying two dueling blades. It occurs to me that this is an opportunity for me to learn something valuable. My affinity with Iron makes it easy for me to duel with someone who carries the metal. But if I am ever to kill a Censor, I won't have that advantage against their *tellus* blades. I will not be able to sense Atticus's sword any more than I can this construct's.

The false gladiator blurs forward, moving with the same unmatchable speed. This time, I am ready for him, catching his first strike with my right blade and commanding my ice to swallow his weapon, fusing ours together.

The man's face does not react as he jerks on his sword, trying to rip it free of its cold marriage to mine. I grit my teeth, letting him pull me forward with his superior strength, my feet digging furrows in the sand like plows as he rages.

His second weapon swings around for a strike that I block with my left, repeating the same trick, binding our other blades together with ice. For a moment, we are locked together, stuck in a physical stalemate. I am not strong enough to pull him off his feet or his swords from his hands. It is all I can do to retain my grip on my own. Panic rears its head as he jerks me around the ring like an angry bull. I have put myself in a situation I do not know how to get out of.

But as I follow his lead through the raging dance, an idea blooms in my mind. My mind turns inward, judging the depths of my Ancient Frost essence. I have made our weapons unwieldy, but that doesn't mean that I do not have other options.

The construct pulls on both blades with all his might. The world fades as my concentration deepens, as the call of the ice pulls me into its cold embrace. Slowly, as if I do not have an ounce of fear, I release both weapons. The gladiator staggers backward, caught off guard by the lack of resistance. His weapons are still bound to mine, making them more like unwieldy clubs than swords.

I hold out my right hand, pouring all the Ancient Frost that remains within my Heart into it, invoking the *Glacialis Falx* to summon a new *gladius* made entirely of ice. The frozen blade coalesces in my hand, faster than it ever has. I stagger under the strain of using so much essence but do not lose my footing.

I feel the cold *Cor* veins running through my body strain with that familiar burn, growing to support my demands. It burns, but I am delighted to feel it. Each ounce of pain is another step toward Ascension, toward Gold.

Once more, the gladiator does not react—the Dream has not been taught about emotions. His face is unbothered, but he hesitates as I charge him, wielding my new blade. Then, in a blur of motion, he slams his blades together, crashing the ice bonds against each other.

Now that they are no longer connected to me, my will cannot reinforce the cold's strength, and I hear the frost *crack* over the sound of my feet pounding on the sand. Again, he knocks them together, sending white chips spraying. With a few more blows, he will shatter the ice and free his weapons from mine.

I don't give him the time.

I lunge forward, extending my cold blade in an aggressive attack to skewer his heart. The man raises his own sword, still frozen to mine, to block, but it is awkward, and the extra weight drags his tip down. My sword clangs off the one I let go, and I dance to the side, denying him the chance to trap it with his weapons.

A laugh escapes my throat as I realize that by icing his blades and attaching my real iron ones to his, I've given myself something to be able to track. My Silver senses follow his movements perfectly. I know where his weapons are, even if I am not looking at them. It is a dastardly trick that I make note of. One day, it might just save my life.

I keep up the attack, not giving him the opportunity to free his blades. His defense is clumsy and formless. He's thrown off by the strange shape and weight of his sabotaged swords. My *gladius* rings greedily as I hammer attacks on him. I can feel its cold hunger echoing in me as I slowly refill my essence reserves from its frost.

Despite his disadvantages, he's still fast, and the longer the fight goes on, the more opportunity he gets to grow accustomed to them. I need to finish him soon. I eye my shorter blade with a hint of distaste. I am still at a major disadvantage of reach, especially now that his swords have mine sticking to them. With a dueling blade, I would have already cut his chest to ribbons with some of my attacks.

The sword in my hand ripples at the thought, and my heart skips a beat as my mind recognizes the instinct within my *Cor* Heart. Stunned, I stare at the frozen weapon, feeling my jaw drop in awe of what it offers.

Grow, I command, picturing the long, slightly curved sword that Gaius carried to kill Knut.

A sharp *crack* echoes through the Dream, and my sword shifts in my hand, growing longer and thinner. Essence flows out of me, adding to the mass of the blade. I do not have much to spare, but the cost is far less than summoning an entire blade from nothing.

My veins burn, and I laugh, welcoming the pain. My fast opponent blurs forward, but I sidestep his awkward strike without even bothering to look. Nothing can distract me from the work I have just created.

My Frozen Blade is perfect. It is heavier and the center of balance has moved, but it feels like it was forged by a master smith for me. I snap it up in a salute at my nonexistent foe. He does not react, but that only makes me laugh more. What a wonderful way to train this is!

I surge forward on the attack, using my longer sword to devastating effect. I twist my wrist to dodge his unwieldy blocks, sending the long point of my weapon scouring red lines along the surface of his flesh. The construct keeps me at too far of a distance to land a serious blow, but I begin to whittle him down. Blood rains down on the sand as we dance. I am the leader now.

At last, we reach the end of the song. There is no music, but I feel it in the tempo. We come together in a crashing series of blows, and I see the opportunity that I have been looking for, the natural end to this ballet. I trap his right weapon high, twisting inward to show him my back as I move.

My empty left hand reaches out as I spin, grabbing the hilt of my old blade that is still attached to his free sword. I do not look as my hand is guided to the Iron and Ice as if they were a part of my own body. My palm settles below the pommel in a reverse grip, and with a thought, I release the frozen bonds that held our two swords together.

My *gladius* slides free, and I drop to one knee, extending the blade behind me in a vicious stab.

Shock runs through my arm as the construct slams onto the tip of my sword. Rising, I rip my weapon free, turning to watch as the gladiator drops to his knees.

I drive my icy dueling blade into his chest, and the arena vanishes. I am back in the small room, stabbing the air. My third sword clatters to the ground, freed from whatever force was holding it up. Contessa stands before me, eyeing my summoned sword with narrowed eyes.

"Better," she says after a moment. "Again."

"Again?" I pant, unable to believe my ears. "I'm out of essence—"

"Do you think that the *compositores* of the arena care about such things?" Her brow furrows as she glares at me like I am an idiot. "They will spend your life for a round of applause. Especially while you are still *argent*. You must learn to control your ice, but you cannot count on it. You're not in the North anymore."

I feel my face go pale at her warnings. They feel all too familiar. The Eighth Cohort's lives were spent just as fruitlessly by the people in power. Anger flares in my chest, far too warm to be a part of my cold Symbols. The rust is pervasive.

"Yes, *Domina*," I reply, saluting her like a legionnaire without a thought. I stiffen as I realize what I have done, but hold it, hoping she will think I am just a foolish boy. Something flickers across her like a shadow over *Luna*, but then it is gone.

"You've killed before." It isn't a question. My shoulders hunch under the knowing stare of Contessa as I feel her measure me like I am flour and she a baker.

"Yes," I reply softly. My fingers tighten on the hilts of my swords.

"This will be different." She does not ask where or who. "Gladiators are like rats in a corner. They will chew off their own leg to kill you, to survive. Many will have even less choice about standing on the sands than you. Every warrior sent to that bloody altar is fighting for a place on a sinking ship. But don't let that make you hesitate. I promise you they are all killers. The ones who aren't don't survive their first bout. They will carve you up and leave your bones to bleach before the crowds if it puts them one step closer toward glory and freedom."

Nervously, I wet my lips, thinking about the *berserkirs* I battled in the snow. She has no idea the things that I have faced, but it would be foolish of me to ignore her warning. Just because she does not know my secrets does not mean that she is wrong about the opponents I will face.

"I understand," I murmur after a moment of reflection. She nods sharply, satisfied that I have gotten the message.

"You may keep your sword," she tells me, gesturing at the relics across the room. This time when the arena appears, I'm not fighting one gladiator, but two.

CHAPTER 11

My body aches but is physically unbruised. Echoes of the beatings that I endured in the *somnatorium* for the last six hours assault me as I walk. My flesh may be unbroken, but my mind is having trouble letting go of the wounds I suffered. I am exhausted, my limbs feel like lead. My *Cor* is almost empty of Ancient Frost. I was unable to call upon any form of ice for the last two fights.

At least those ones were shorter than the others.

The constructs may not be real, but it felt like they remembered me and were only too happy to get revenge for my earlier victories. Contessa said little between matches as she pushed me to my limits, only watching me with those sharp eyes. This is how a sword must feel on the anvil.

As I drag myself toward the *loci* to refill my drained reserves, I miss the companionship of the legions. A few other gladiators wander past me, but they do not seem to be as broken as I. The white-robed servants smile and greet me, but I find their platitudes unsettling. Their lives are not ones of iron and blood. They may serve, but not like me.

At last, I arrive in the training hall, and the sight of the snowy *locus* drives all thought from my mind the same way an oasis would for a man in the desert. This late at night, the hall is empty, and most of the *lumos* relics are off, casting heavy shadows through the dim room. I am the only soul in the building as I stumble through the abandoned sand toward my feast.

True to his word, Pliny left it running, and the strange doors slide open soundlessly to welcome me into Winter's frosty embrace. Cold hammers at me, and I let out a sigh of delight as I sink to my knees in the growing snowbank. It is far from ancient, but even the time that it has been allowed to gather makes a difference in the congruency as I pull the essence from around me. I must still condense it to be usable by Ancient Frost, but it is no longer Fresh Snow. I cock my head, trying to taste the new Symbols swirling around me like they are fancy wines.

They are just Snow and just Ice now.. The magisters in *collegium* taught us that specificity is what makes a Symbol strong. The more specific it is, the more power you will have over the narrow aspect. But as I ponder the differences in how the room feels, I realize that there are limits to that definition.

Technically, Fresh Snow is more specific than just Snow. By that logic, old Vellum would have considered it a more powerful Symbol for a new *electus* to attune to. But Fresh Snow is a far scarcer *thing*. It lasts for maybe a day before it is gone, swallowed into the more general "Snow."

I suspect that someone bound to the Fresh version would be able to pull essence from Snow, the same way that I could with Ancient Frost; they were both Symbols of Winter. But it would get harder for them the older it got, instead of easier like it does for me. In the true North, where I first encountered permafrost, it would be a nightmare for them to cultivate unless they were hit by a blizzard dumping fresh powder on them.

Both Ancient and Fresh are the second level of specificity, but it was clear to me that there was an advantage to one over the other. But having just Frost or just Snow would make it easier for someone to maintain their reserves no matter where they were, even though it was technically less *specific*. This was not something they taught us to consider about the elements in school. But then again, the sons and daughters in that room were expected to use their Hearts to climb the social ladder, not become warriors.

My breathing settles as my reserve of Ancient Frost begins to fill. When it is almost empty, it is as if my *Cor* shrinks like a raisin. The metal veins that run through my flesh tighten and harden as if they are turning to stone. But now as essence floods the channels, they relax once more.

My body releases the final bits of tension that it carried from my bouts. I marvel at the healing that seems to sweep through me as I achieve balance once more. I have been holding my iron *gladii* all day, but that is not enough to keep me whole. I need both parts of my Heart to be sated for it to work its Silver blessings upon me.

I do not miss being a Copper. Not one bit.

Straightening my back, I slow my breathing, focusing on pulling in essence with each inhale and pausing as I exhale. The magisters taught the exercise to us in *collegium* as the healthiest way to cultivate, but I feel no difference. The torrent still pours into me, succoring my tortured body like water.

My veins do not stretch or strain as they did when I was a Copper; they accept the essence comfortably. Frustrated, I shake my head, trying to keep it clear. Whatever the path is to Ascend to Gold, it is not the same one that I walked to become Silver.

I think back on the moments that I felt them burn. It has not happened when I am cultivating, but when I am exerting my will upon the world. It feels like there is something to that. When I became a Copper, I had to learn how to stand, but as a Silver, I must now learn how to walk.

The thought is trite, but for some reason, I cannot get it out of my head. If I am right, the way to progress through the Silver tier is to *use* my *Cor*, rather than just feed it. I check my reserves. They are full, in perfect balance between Iron and Ancient Frost once more. With a sigh, I begin to rise. My feet do not even wait for my mind to decide what I am going to do. It knows what my heart wants, just like the rest of me.

The *locus*'s door slides open, and I stalk out into the dim training hall, casting a glance around the room to make sure I am still alone. Seeing no one, I step into the sand, dropping a hand to the hilt of my *gladius*. After a moment of reflection, I lift my palm, instead calling on the *Glacialis Falx* to summon its icy twin in my hand. The frozen blade materializes, and I wince at the loss of essence. I just finished refilling it, but I will need to return to the *locus* again before I leave.

The weapon in my hand is a *gladius*, like it has always been since Aquilo first gave the ability to me. But after my practice today, I can see the glint of something lurking in the ice. I can sense its potential, feel it quivering with unbound excitement. It will change if I ask. The path has been laid before my feet. I am only at the beginning of Silver. I have so far to go, but I want—I need—to unlock its secrets.

Wordlessly, I extend my left hand, manifesting another icy blade. I picture the long form of a dueling blade in my mind and, using my will, I command that the *Glacialis Falx* manifest as this different sword instead of its normal *gladius*.

I let out a deep grunt and close my eyes as my body pays the toll. When it is finished, I open them eagerly, expecting to find a different weapon in my hand. But to my disappointment, my left hand holds a second *gladius*, a perfect copy of the first. The ice defies me.

My reserve is dangerously low, so for a while, I stand in the center of the empty ring, waiting to reclaim some of my lost essence from the two frozen blades. I try a breathing tactic old Vellum taught us and am surprised to find that it helps. My *animus* gathers the floating essence from the swords between each breath, condensing it together before absorbing it in bursts.

As I cultivate, I scheme, trying to think of a way to force this ability to obey me. An idea begins to form in my mind, growing like an icicle, drip by drip.

When I am satisfied that I have enough essence to keep me on my feet, I lower myself into a fighting crouch, ignoring the complaint of the tired muscles in my thighs. It is time to begin. I move in deliberate paces, focusing on my form as I glide through attacks. With my first movement, I extend my right-hand blade in a low thrust aimed at an invisible foe's stomach.

As it cuts through the air, I reach into the *gladius* with my mind and command it to change, to become the dueling blade once more. For a moment, my *Cor* resists me, as if it is a living thing with its own will. My request is beyond the gift that Aquilo gave me. Its refusal is like a thick wall in my mind, dampening my thoughts. I grit my teeth, pouring all my focus and energy into breaking through that limitation. Without the threat of violence, my ability is far more rigid. But I've done this before, and I know it is possible. I just have to be strong enough. Slowly, the barricade begins to bend—but not break as it gives in to this one request.

A *crack* echoes through the training hall as the frozen sword begins to twist. Essence, an unsustainable amount, pours out of me to add more ice to the weapon. I grimace with pain and force myself to keep moving.

When the strike is done, the sword is a thin caricature of the dueling blade. It is too short, and the ice is pale and thin. It would shatter under a heavy blow, but it is different than the *gladius*. I made it. It's a first step toward unlocking the full potential of my ability.

I take a deep breath and brace to try again. This time, I step forward with my left foot, twisting my wrist to slash diagonally at my invisible opponent in a cut that would open a man from hip to shoulder. As I do, I command my second sword to shift from a *gladius* to a dueling blade. The wall of resistance in my mind holds firm. My knees buckle and threaten to give out from the cost of essence. My vision goes black at the edges. For a moment, I teeter on the edge of unconsciousness. But then it is done, and I stagger to the side with a gasp of shock like a man bursting free of frigid water. My veins burn, stretching under the demands that I am putting them through. Panting with exertion, I study the second weapon that I have changed. It is still definitely *not* a true dueling blade, but it is closer than my first attempt. A tired smile grows on my face as I close my eyes.

It is working.

I square my shoulders, preparing to try again, but my determination breaks against the ravenous demands of my *Cor*. The *gladius* in my right hand cracks warningly as I try to manipulate it. Essence trickles out of me like a river running dry. With a sharp retort, the sword shatters, falling apart in my hands.

I gasp in surprise and pain, staggering as my body is racked by the threat of the *crassamentum*—the fury of my empty Heart. The other sword falls from my limp right hand as I sink to my knees in the sand. I fall forward onto all fours and stay there for a long time, panting from exertion. I pushed myself beyond my limits. A foolish thing to do when my life is constantly in danger.

But as my breath slowly returns, I raise my head to find myself staring at the Winter *locus* just on the other side of the room. A wry grin spreads across my face as I remind myself that my empty reserves are easily fixed.

With a grunt of effort, I manage to stand on wobbly legs and stagger back into the frozen room, letting its coldness wash over me. The pressure my *Cor* is exerting in my chest fades, and I relax, lying on the snow like it is a field of heather.

It takes longer for my reserves to fill this time. Somehow, I managed to deplete them even further than Contessa did with her relentless training. When I am sated, I struggle to my feet and stomp out of the *locus*, feeling pleased with myself and my progress.

Whistling to myself, I stride along the stone edge of the practice arena, making my way toward the mess hall. I am starving; running through my entire reserve of Ancient Frost twice in one day has lit a ravenous appetite within me. Fortunately, this place has food at all hours of the day for training gladiators, which means there's no danger of me missing a meal. I pause midstride, struck by a sudden pang of a different sort of hunger. I am brimming with Ancient Frost; what could it hurt to go through the dance one more time?

I step into the sand, dinner already forgotten. Grinning ear-to-ear, I seize my Symbols and manifest the frozen blades as I walk. I know that I have only uncovered the tip of the iceberg of what I am able to do with my powers. There are secrets lurking just beneath the surface, and I want them. But to find them, I'm going to need to dig.

In the end, I empty my reserves twice more. I am still not able to summon anything other than a *gladius* with the *Glacialis Falx*, but the dueling blade that I shift my sword into looks almost right, even if it is too thin and fragile. When I emerge from the *locus* after my fourth time, even my desire to Ascend is overshadowed by the ravenous hunger that shakes my body. I do not know if even that would have been enough to stop me from practicing my manifesting again, but I do not have a choice.

Pliny is waiting for me.

The small magister smiles brightly at me as I step back into the training room. Most of the *lumos* relics are still off, and he is hovering on the edge of a shadow, subtly telling me that he has been here for a while.

"Most impressive, Castor," he says by way of greeting. "Your *Cor*'s speed and efficiency made significant leaps during your training this evening. And your progress on manifestation is truly… inspiring."

"Are you spying on me?"

"It's hardly spying. It's my job to watch over you." He snorts. "I was waiting for you at the mess hall for dinner, intending to instruct you on deepening your connection to your *Cor*. When you did not appear, I came looking for you and found that you had already begun the process yourself." My heart leaps at his words.

"I'm on the right track?" The short magister cocks his head like a bird studying a worm.

"Tell me what you have learned."

"My *Cor* does not stretch from the same exercises that it did when I was a Copper—a *cuprum*."

"How so?" Pliny prods, smiling slightly at my correction.

"When I first attuned to… Ancient Frost, I felt it grow every time that I cultivated," I say after a moment of thought. "It seems like the path to Silver was about accumulating more essence, expanding how much of it I could hold within myself. I was feeding the seed of the *Cor*, to let it grow and become a part of me."

"And now?" An arched eyebrow.

"I don't feel anything when I fill my *Cor*."

"But you've noticed it at other times?"

"Yes." I nod, trying to figure out how to put in words the breakthrough I had made tonight. "It seems to be whenever I am pushing myself in using my essence to make a change. When I exert my will to do something difficult with my Symbol, like manifesting the *Glacialis Falx* or changing their shapes."

"Your instincts are correct. A key portion of advancing your *Cor* through the stages of *argentum*, you will need to push your Heart to new heights, to demonstrate complete mastery of your Symbol."

"Complete mastery, Magister? What does that mean?"

"You were right, a *Cuprum* Heart is like a seed that needs to be fed." Pliny gives me an approving nod. "It is the easiest path to walk for most *electi*, because all it requires is patience and access to a source of essence. Over enough time, anyone with a *Cor* can Ascend to Silver, even if it takes their whole lifetime." I wonder what he would say if he knew that I reached the peak of my first Symbol—Iron—the first time I was exposed to an abundance of it.

"But an *argentum* Heart has different needs. It has grown strong enough that it will exert pressure back on its *electus*, polluting them with its own attributes. In order to progress toward *Aurum*, you must bend it to your will, master your Symbol and its corruption. If you do not, when you become Gold, it will consume you." The hair on the back of my neck stands up as I hear the warning of a dead man nestled in Pliny's words. My father, a Copper *electus* himself, once told me something very similar.

"What do you mean, 'its corruption'?"

"Surely you have felt the effects of holding a Winter Symbol?" Pliny arches an amused eyebrow. "I imagine it comes in quite handy for you."

"When I hold Ancient Frost, it drives my fear away," I reply slowly, struggling to think of what else he might mean. "It helps me stay logical and not panic. But other than that, I have not noticed any other effects."

"My dear boy," Pliny says with a sad smile. "I wish I had a mirror to let you see yourself." He pauses for a moment, as if struck by a thought. "Perhaps I do have one. Yes, this is important. You must see before it is too late." I follow the smaller man without a word, my physical hunger forgotten. I want to see the thing that makes him so afraid.

To my surprise, the magister takes me back to the room with the dream relic in it. He gestures for me to step into the center as he takes up a position on the edge, just like Contessa earlier today. Instinctually, I draw my *gladii* as I cross over the black boundary on the floor.

"You will not need that," Pliny calls, but I ignore him, keeping the sword gripped firmly in my right hand. I have suffered enough pain today.

"Suit yourself." He shrugs as if unsurprised by my response. The magister raises a hand and gestures at the far wall, activating the relic. The world flickers, but the room does not change. Instead, a figure appears across from me, carrying a pair of swords.

He is my height, wearing a set of training leathers marked with the broken trident of *Domus* Pelias. He is lean and dangerous, like a wolf that has been struggling to hunt through the winter. His brown hair falls in a tangled mess to his shoulders, which are broad and strong.

On instinct, I raise my *gladius*, holding my left hand out to the side in preparation to summon the *Glacialis Falx*. I freeze as my opponent copies my move. Suddenly, I notice the *Cor* veins that run through his body are mismatched, Silver and white. My gaze flicks up to his face, and I see him clearly for the first time. This isn't an opponent for me to test myself against.

It's me.

I may have used the mirror in my quarters, but I did not *see* myself when I looked in it last night. My face is sharper than I remember. My cheeks are hollow, and the bones stick out, making me look almost palatine. But the biggest change is my eyes. They are no longer brown, like my father's. Instead, they are a steely blue, harsh and unforgiving. How did I not notice? An air of frigid menace rolls off me like a wave. If I were not immune to such cold, I would have shivered at its touch.

Slowly, I lower my sword, and my duplicate copies the motion. Yet, despite the lowering of aggression, I do not look any further away from violence. There is an edge to me, like a knife buried under an inch of snow, ready to be used. The influence of Iron and Ancient Frost is as plain as day to my eyes. A new fear uncoils in my mind as I wonder how many others can see it.

Slowly, I tear my eyes away from myself, even though every instinct inside of me screams to not look away from a predator like this. Out of the corner of my vision, my copy does the same, which makes me feel only a little better.

"How long have I been like this?" I demand.

"Since the moment I met you," Pliny replies with a soft shrug. "It is common for Silver *electi*, especially strong ones like you, to begin to be warped by their *Cor* until they learn to control it." My father's warning echoes in my mind once more. If only I had been smart enough to listen to his wisdom when he was alive.

"You are a cold man, Castor, although I suspect that has not always been the case." Dimly, I think of the laughing boy who raced through the fields with Marcus and Valentina only a year or two ago. When was the last time my laughter was not cruel? I have become something frigid and hard, a blend of Iron and Ice. My thoughts are only of revenge and power.

I have lost myself, just as my parents feared.

"How do I fix it?" My voice seems harsh now; I hear its bitter chill. I cannot change it to sound any different. I'm not sure I want to. There is a power to the cold. I have seen it. I have felt it. I need the power if I am going to do what has to be done. My skin tingles as my *votum* with Nemesis reminds me of my task.

"Fix it?" Pliny asks softly. "I don't know if there is a way to 'fix' it. You have bound an Elder Symbol, lad. There is nothing colder than what flows in your veins. You may learn to manage it in time, but the thing you have bound is bigger than what most mortals can handle."

"What is an Elder Symbol?" The Censors threw the word around, but I have never heard it before. The confrontation had not seemed like the moment to ask either.

"I forget that your education is incomplete," Pliny replies, tilting his head in surprise. "Your teachers no doubt blathered on about specificity?"

"Having an attunement to a narrower area of an element grants a greater level of congruency."

The older man nods, satisfied by my simple definition. "That is true but does not encompass everything in the hierarchy of the *domus* of an element."

"Hierarchy of a *domus*?" I frown, confused by the sudden change of definition. I have never heard it described like this before.

"Many modern magisters think of the different elements like a house. Congruency lets you touch the other stones inside the structure that are part of the same whole. The foundation is the most basic version of a Symbol. In your case, that would be Winter."

"Not Ancient Frost?" I ask, surprised at his explanation.

"No." Pliny shakes his head, a small smile crossing his face. "All things within a house are seeking to become their final form. Fresh Snow is one of the youngest members, the first step to the house. Eventually, it will become Snow, then Old Snow. One day, it might become Ancient. Your Symbol is the Eldest of *Domus Hiems*—the House of Winter. It has a different kind of power, because all things in Winter flow to it."

Damn Dead Aquilo and his rotten games.

"As you walk the Path of Silver to Gold, you must gain absolute control of your Symbol. There can be no question between you and it who is the master and who is the servant. Your *Cor* is a bridge between you and your Symbol. Ancient Frost will try to use you as a vehicle to feast on essence. You must develop the self-control to only use it when you need it." I swallow slowly, realizing how comfortable I have become being submerged in my Symbols, letting their cold presence wash away the feelings from me. It has been easier than living in the pain of loss.

"It is rather like the difference between a wine connoisseur and a lush. If you cannot find the balance, it will eventually rot you from the inside until only a shell of your humanity remains. It will take all your concentration, but if you are willing, I will help you as much as I can."

"What must I do?"

"Only seize your Symbol when you need it." Pliny holds up his hand, counting off instructions on his fingers. "Resist the urge to exist in its embrace even for clarity or comfort. Never take hold of it without using it. Condition yourself to treating it like a tool. It is in your body, but it is *not* a part of your flesh. You must not forget that. Lastly, you must use all your focus on this task. The power of Ancient Frost is immense—if you do not devote yourself wholly to building up these foundations before you reach the peak of Silver, it may be too late."

"Are Elder Symbols the most powerful?" I ask, still reeling from this new vision of the elements.

"They have the greatest authority of their kind," Pliny replies, sighing after a moment when he sees I do not understand.

"There are two things that affect how much will and essence an *electus* must use to perform a feat with their *Cor*. You were taught by your magisters about congruency, the relationship of likeness or sameness between two elements. Granite and sandstone are both rocks and are therefore congruent.

"But the other piece of the equation is authority. Most elements have similar levels of influence. An oak tree and a birch tree are siblings in the house of *arbor*. In your own house, Winter is the thread that connects every piece of the *domus*.

"Specificity is like a fulcrum. The authority gives you more leverage for your will to make its commands known. Elder Symbols have the most authority within their *domus*. This means that you have an advantage over *any* Winter Symbol because you are the top of the pyramid."

"Oh," I reply, feeling small.

"They say that Elder Elements were the attunements of the gods."

I struggle to keep my face impassive.

"Now you understand what is before you. You must walk a narrow and dangerous path. But if you can make it to the other side, you will know a level of power and strength that few have the chance to master." Pliny smiles softly as he gestures at the dream relic across the room, making my copy vanish.

"Take heart, young Castor. This is not an impossible task, just a difficult one. Even an Elder Symbol is not as corrupting as Iron." Dread flows through my veins, cold and overwhelming. I seize Ancient Frost despite his warning, leaning on it to keep me calm as I return his smile. I can only hope he cannot see the terror that burns behind my eyes.

CHAPTER 12

"Two weeks!" Contessa shrieks from the side of the training sands. "In two weeks, some of you lot will be representing *Ludus* Pelias in Antioch, and this is what you prepare for your *dominus*?" The *lanista* roams along the black barrier in the ground, eyeing the score of us like we're the greatest disappointment in her life.

A sign hangs on the wall over her shoulder, the *Index Argentum*. It is numbered one through six. It seems I cannot escape being ranked, no matter where the dead gods send me to suffer.

There are several names already on the list. The haughty Air *electus*, Leon is *Primus*, and his rocky companion, Obellius, is *Secundus*. The other members of my gauntlet fill out the next four slots. To my surprise, I am listed as *Sextus*. Right back where I started. We six are currently the Silver Gladiators who will compete in Antioch. But Contessa has made it clear that these standings are not final—there is no room for complacency inside *Ludus* Pelias.

My strength returns quickly, but I still have a way to go to reach the physical capability that she wants. We have just completed an endurance challenge that used some sort of wood relics to batter us with poles while we tried to dodge their many-limbed attacks. My Iron Symbol was of no use, and I am as bruised as the rest. I suspect that Contessa would not be happy even if we matched her own capabilities as a Gold *electus* despite being Silvers.

Tension has grown thick over the last few weeks inside the *ludus*. Even Pliny is agitated. I have only seen the small magister a few times, but each time we speak, he encourages me to focus on growing my power, rather than worrying about controlling it. "There will be time after Antioch," he assures me with a smile that does not quite meet his eyes. "You can last a month."

I want to believe him, but part of me doubts that even the magister understands how quickly my *Corda* are growing or how much my two Symbols pull at me like sirens trying to drown me in their embrace.

All of these are clues that tell me that the House's position is even more precarious than I have been told. I do not know much about how the actual Circuits work, only that *Domus* Pelias is low in the rankings and in danger of losing their license, which would be a disaster for both the House and for me. How can I win my freedom if I cannot compete in the Games? Varus and Contessa expect us to win or to die trying, and I find myself unable to resent them, for our causes are aligned.

"What am I to do?" The *lanista* puts her hands on her hips, looking at us with a frown. "*Dominus* Varus paid good coin for you, but it may turn out to be the worst investment in the history of gladiators."

For a moment, a hint of a smile tugs at my mouth, but I kill it before it can grow. The bald woman reminds me of Durus stalking among the recruits, roaring his displeasure. I miss the solid old centurion more than ever. Gaius and Percy taught me many things, but they felt like older brothers, showing me the way. Durus always reminded me of my father. I could use his wisdom now.

Pliny's warnings echo in the back of my mind as I stand with the other Silver gladiators. I know their names now, although I stand apart from them. They look at me like I am a wild animal—a lion that has broken free from its cage. I have done little to dissuade them of that notion. Part of me is terrified to make new friends. These ones are just as likely to die as the men of the Twelfth.

A thread of doubt runs through the back of my mind as I catch myself dismissing them so easily. Have I truly become so callous? Or is that Ancient Frost's cold influence chilling me?

Closest to me in line is Reese, the woman with the mane, long and lean, who was the first to face me in the ring. Next to her is the short woman that kept throwing all the knives at me during the gauntlet. I've learned her name is Fannia, but I still think of her as "Knife" in my head. Those flying blades left a lasting impression.

The lean duelist, whose hamstring I sliced, is called Illyrius. He still bears a grudge and a limp, but I ignore his ire. It was not I who put him into the gauntlet. He should blame Contessa, not me. The *medici* say he will be fully healed by the time the Games arrive, so he still trains with us.

The other two men are the most distant, but they are also the ones who are directly in my shadow now. Obellius is not a cruel man, but pride is clearly hurt by the loss he suffered at my hands. Leon's hatred is like a living thing. The blond Air *electus* glares at me whenever he thinks I am not looking. His anger overrides his good sense because he is always just a little too slow to look away.

But he does look away.

"Castor, that includes you," the *lanista* snaps, pulling me out of my own head. "You can barely handle a competent opponent in the Dream room. What will you do when you face one of *Domus* Apicius's bloody killers?" I straighten to attention as she berates me. Contessa pauses, glaring at me with her full focus, waiting for me to reply.

"I will be better, *Domina*," I tell her, making a promise I hope I can keep. "The dream relic… feels wrong."

"It feels wrong," she repeats in disbelief. "Well, pray to Mars's Bones that they don't give you an opponent that makes you *uncomfortable*." Dry chuckles echo down the line from the gladiators. Now I really am back in the legions.

"I don't know what you all are laughing at," Contessa snarls, turning her displeasure on the line. "All of you fell to Castor in a gauntlet, so if he's not ready for Antioch, I don't even know why we should bother sending any of you." The other gladiators grow stiff and silent, freezing under the Gold *electus*'s ire.

"Have no fear. The rest of us are ready, *Lanista*. We will do you and the *dominus* proud," Leon declares, stepping forward and clenching a fist in a manner he no doubt thinks looks heroic. To me, it just looks stupid. Reese snorts under her breath from next to me, clearly sharing my opinion of the Air *electus*. She was the only one who did not laugh when Contessa was tearing into me.

"Proud?" Contessa whirls on him, clearly glad to have a new focus for her displeasure. "Am I your mother, Gladiator? Did I birth you from my hips? You are not here to make me *proud*. You are here to win glory for your *domus*. When was the last time you won a match, Leon? Didn't that Fire *electus* from *Domus* Cornelius give you enough scars to humble you? Not to mention the Air gladiator from *Domus* Valerus. You can't even beat your own kind." Leon steps back into our line, face burning red with shame. His eyes meet mine, and his face turns into a livid scowl, as if seeing me witness his humiliation has only made him hate me more. I roll my eyes at the hypocrisy of his arrogance. Wasn't he just laughing while Contessa berated me for my own shortcomings?

The *lanista* takes a deep breath, getting control of her irritation. "Right, let's see what you can learn between then and now," she declares, clapping her hands together. "Form pairs. We'll end today with a tournament."

Groans echo after her announcement, but I am silent. I'll take any chance to push my veins to grow.

"Partner?" I offer to Reese standing next to me. She is the Silver I like the most, which, compared to the rest of the room, isn't saying much.

"Sorry, Castor," the maned woman says, shaking her head. "Fannia and I are going to try something new."

"No problem," I say tightly, resisting the urge to sigh in frustration. Now all that is left for me to choose from are the three idiots. As I glance down the line, I see Leon and Obellius clasp wrists, making it obvious that they've teamed again.

Which leaves me with the still-partially-hobbled Illyrius. The duelist frowns in displeasure in my direction as he reaches the same conclusion. I offer an olive branch by making my way to stand next to him on the sidelines as Contessa pulls the other two pairs into the sand.

"The first team to beat both other teams wins," she reminds us of the rules. "If you lose twice, you're out. Blunted swords only." She pauses, glancing from Leon to me with a knowing eye, like a mother studying her unruly sons. "Do try not to hurt each other." She sighs. "Antioch is in two weeks." I pretend like I don't notice that she's making a point of looking at me.

"Gladiators ready?" she barks, turning her attention back to the sand. Both pairs raise their weapons in salute, confirming her question. "Begin!"

Reese and Fannia vanish instantly, cloaked by the taller woman's *Cor* Heart. Hers might be one of the most dangerous Symbols I've ever witnessed. I can sense her movements thanks to the Iron she carries, but if she carried *tellus*, it would be a simple matter for Reese to gut me like a pig.

Leon hurtles forward at tremendous speed, powered by his Wind Symbol, dashing through the space where the two women just were. He finds only empty air with his blade as he slashes frantically. On the other side of the ring, Obellius circles the edge nervously, hefting a trident.

"How's your leg?" I ask Illyrius as the match slows down to a crawl.

"Hurts," the shorter man admits without looking in my direction after a long silence. I close my eyes so no one can see me roll them.

"Good," I say in the same frosty tone. This time, his head snaps to the side, and he fixes me with a sharp, angry glare. It fades slightly as I laugh as warmly as I can.

"Kidding." Illyrius's eyes narrow, but he doesn't look away immediately. "I do seem to recall you were trying to *kill* me," I point out.

"It was the gauntlet. That's how it—"

"Yes, yes," I interrupt, not interested in having a circular discussion. We fall silent again, but this time, it doesn't feel *quite* as harsh. I smile as I think of my fallen brother Anas, who once hated me far more than these spoiled Silver gladiators. If I could turn him into a friend, then smoothing things over with Illyrius should be easy.

In the ring, a pair of knives appears out of thin air, spinning toward Obellius at high speed. The massive man notices them at the last second, throwing himself to the ground to let them pass harmlessly above him before bouncing off the artificial barrier created by the relics.

Leon seizes the moment and dashes toward where the daggers appeared from. He shoots across the arena, the sand beneath his feet ripples in the wake of his passing. But despite his tremendous speed, he tears through another patch of empty air like a taunted bull.

I extend my *animus*, feeling for the iron that both invisible women carry, chuckling when I realize they're lying on the ground, letting the air *electus* pass over them like a storm.

"What's so funny?" Illyrius asks, giving me an irritated look. "Are they not up to your standards?"

"What?" I'm so startled that his rancor actually stings through the coldness that cloaks me. "What do you mean?"

"You're laughing at the rest of us. It's clear that you think you're far out of our league." I did defeat all five of them in the gauntlet, but I decide not to bring that up again.

"I'm not laughing at *everyone*," I protest, turning back to watch the duel between the other four Silvers. "I thought that move was pretty good. Especially because Leon fell for it."

"What do you mean?" Despite his hostility, there's a genuine question beneath it, so I decide to humor him. I wonder if he hates Leon even more than he dislikes me. I may have hobbled him, but the blond *electus* is just so annoying.

"Look there." Since I know where to check, it's easy for my eyes to make out the clues in the sand. I point at a pair of large depressions on the ground. "After Fannia threw her knives, they didn't run. They just dropped to the ground. Leon shot right over them."

"Then they got up and snuck away." Illyrius picks up the tracks easily. "He must have only missed them by a few inches."

"See, kind of funny." I offer him with a shrug. "That's all I was laughing at, on Honos's Bones." The smaller duelist grunts in acceptance, sounding almost annoyed to be wrong about me. For a moment, I'm tempted to let it go, but I can feel it. A little something dangling off the edge of our conversation, still unsaid. It feels like the same kind of thread I pulled on in the Twelfth with Anas. Before I know what I'm doing, I press my advantage, pulling on it with all my might.

"Why did you think I was mocking them?"

"Oh, come on." The skinny duelist sighs in irritation. "Spare me the song and dance. It's obvious what you are." It takes every ounce of self-control for me not to seize my Symbols and let their chill banish the panic that begins to rise in my chest. How has he guessed my secret? It does not matter—all that matters is who he might have told.

"It is?" I struggle to make my voice unbothered, but it is cold and harsh. My gaze flicks over to Contessa, who is focused on the fight. I could draw my blade and strike his throat before she turned…

"You're some sort of palatine bastard," Illyrius says with complete confidence. "It's obvious."

A sharp laugh of surprise barks from my mouth before I can catch it. The shorter man looks at me in surprise, but I shake my head, grinning broadly. My mind flashes back to Gaius's spartan study in the Twelfth, when he accused me of something very similar. Relief floods through me as I realize my true secret is still safe.

"You don't deny it?" he asks in surprise.

"Would you believe me if I did?" I arch an eyebrow at him.

"No."

"Well, go on, let's hear your evidence." I gesture for him to begin. In front of us, Leon and Obellius continue to chase their invisible opponents, shouting their frustrations back and forth as they circle the sand.

"You're too good," Illyrius says with absolute confidence. "There's no way that they found you in some random gladiator trader's dungeon on the outskirts of Anteforum. Not only have you clearly been trained by a master, but you are attuned to a rare, powerful Symbol. It's obvious what's going on."

"Well, don't leave me in suspense." I laugh, crossing my arms comfortably. "What's the rest?"

"It's a path to citizenship, obviously. Your father can't claim you to his family name, so he trains you, creates an anonymous persona for you, then arranges for Varus to buy you as a favor. When you carve your way to the top, you'll be a free man and have a chance to ascend politically too." I blink in surprise at how close he is to the truth. I study him with new eyes, realizing that I misjudged him after the Gauntlet. He may not be a better fighter than me, but he is clever.

"Is there anything I can tell you to convince you that I'm not a nameless palatine bastard seeking my fortune?" I ask him, arms still crossed. The wiry man shakes his head mutely, looking smug.

"Not even this?" I tap a finger against some of the white *rasa* veins running down my exposed arms. "This is hardly the pedigree of a palatine *electus*."

"Your infirmity clearly hasn't limited your capability"—he pauses in thought for a moment—"or at least if it has, it only means that your potential could have been truly unknowable if all your *Cor* was properly bound. Even more reason for your father to send you on your own path, instead of letting you bring shame on the bloodline." I chuckle at his callous explanation, marveling at how well it fit together, even if it wasn't quite barking up the right tree.

"Very well." I give him a half-shrug after a moment of thought. "It's close enough."

"I knew it," he whispers.

CHAPTER 13

Illyrius and I win the tournament. Reese and Fannia eventually fall to Leon and Obellius, but not without taking out the big man in a stealthy ambush that dropped him before he could activate his Stoneskin ability. Reese must have drained her essence dry, keeping them invisible for so long. Unfortunately, neither woman had the speed necessary to keep up with Leon once the air *electus* could finally see them. As much as I dislike the blond man, he is quick. If he were holding a wooden training blade instead of iron, he might beat me.

When it was our turn to face the two women, it went even worse for them. My Iron senses made it easy for me to track their movements and their footprints. I pointed them out to Illyrius, and together, we herded them like hounds.

Obellius and Leon were more difficult to overcome but also much more straightforward. The two of them charged me at the start of the fight, hoping to eliminate me quickly and then take their time with my partner. Thanks to the knowledge my Iron Symbol fed me, it was an easy task for me to stall their offense, and Illyrius circled behind them, bringing them low with quick, vicious stabs. It took him a while to crack through Obellius's Stoneskin, but once he did, they crumbled quickly.

"What is your Symbol anyway?" I ask the grinning duelist as we step off the sands to await Contessa's teaching. "I was watching but didn't see anything."

"Maybe you weren't looking closely enough," Illyrius replies, closing his eyes as his smile grows wider. Inwardly, I marvel at how differently he treats me after a single conversation and another bout on the field. He thinks he holds a secret of mine, which makes him trust me. It's nice to have someone I can talk to in *Domus* Pelias who isn't a Golden *electus* or servant, but a small part of me feels hollow that the thing I shared with him is a lie, although in some ways, I have also done him a kindness. Knowing my secret would only put his life in danger too.

"Reese and Fannia," the *lanista* begins as we gather in a loose cluster, turning her gaze on the two women. "A clever trick that might serve you well in the ring. But you made two mistakes. What were they?" The two gladiators exchange glances, as if communicating mentally.

"We relied on it too heavily," Reese offers after a moment.

"Correct." Contessa nods sharply. "That move is a feint. You might catch an opponent off-guard with it once, but after they know it, they won't fall for it again. Leon and Obellius adapted to your strategy and neutralized it." She falls silent, crossing her arms as she stares at the two Silvers, waiting for them to give another answer.

Reese and Fannia confer again, but after a few moments, they both turn back to the *lanista*, shrugging apologetically. Contessa sighs, crossing her arms as she stares at them. "Your second mistake was that you used it *again*." She tosses her head in our direction. "These two were on the sidelines watching your fight. They knew exactly what to expect when you both vanished." Reese and Fannia both bow their heads in embarrassment, prompting Contessa to step forward and place her hand on both of their shoulders.

"It is a *good* trick," she repeats with emphasis. "But if you are going to be a clever fighter, you must have more than one. All the other *ludi* will be studying you. They will know every move you use before you even get into the ring. You must turn your opponent's understanding of your trick *into* a weakness. Understood?" Both women nod, and the bald woman claps them on the shoulders before stepping back.

"Leon and Obellius, you did well against Reese and Fannia," she begins. The two men smile and clasp each other's wrists in excitement. "Which makes your performance against Castor and Illyrius even more embarrassing," she continues in a tight tone, drawing them up short.

"You made a similar mistake as our first group. What was it?" Obellius's face scrunches up as he tries to think, a sight that almost makes me laugh, but I dare not in front of Contessa. I hear a soft snort from beside me that tells me Illyrius is thinking the same thing.

"We did not eliminate Castor quickly enough," Leon says after a moment, his voice quiet but confident.

"True, but that is not the mistake; you cannot control that. Your idea of focusing on the same fighter to take him out quickly was a good one—the flaw lies elsewhere." Leon is silent as he ponders for another moment. Obellius looks even more confused.

"Like Reese and Fannia, we did not abandon our strategy when it did not bear fruit," Leon answers at last. "It was a good idea, but when it did not work, we needed to give up and fight the duel in a more traditional manner instead of letting Illyrius flank us freely." Despite myself, I am impressed at his analysis. Perhaps there is more going on underneath his blond locks than I gave him credit for.

"What he said," Obellius grunts.

"Correct." Contessa nods approvingly. "The greatest gladiators excel at adapting their strategies as the fight plays out. Learn how to do that, and you might just become dangerous."

"Yes, *Lanista*," Leon replies seriously, his normally arrogant face narrowed in focus.

"Yes, *Lanista*," Obellius repeats a half-second later, not quite as convincingly. Contessa eyes him for a moment, her expression bordering on irritated. At last, she turns from the second-place pair, and her heavy gaze settles on us. A chill runs down my spine at the steely look in her eyes. I had assumed our inspection would be cursory; after all, we won rather convincingly.

"Both of you made a mistake," she says flatly, her voice full of displeasure. "It was the same one. What was it?"

Illyrius and I exchange glances. I do not know if Reese and Fannia were able to communicate without speaking, but all I get from my partner is a sense of confusion. After a moment, we part and look at our instructor with our heads hanging low.

"I do not know what it was, *Lanista*," I admit.

"Illyrius?" Contessa looks from me to the smaller duelist with an imperiously arched eyebrow.

"No, *Lanista*."

"You both held back," the bald woman says flatly, her eyes burning with irritation. My heart skips a beat as I look from her to Illyrius. His expression is reluctantly embarrassed; a similar burn begins to grow in my own chest. She's right. I did. Over her shoulder, I see the other gladiators stiffen as they realize what we're being accused of.

"Why?" The question is cold. "Perhaps you do not find this training taxing enough?"

"No, *Lanista*," I protest at once, terrified of what sort of challenges the woman might create to make them more suitable. "It is not that at all. At least not for myself." I pause, trying to collect my thoughts. "I am new here; I do not know much about my fellow *argenti* in *Domus* Pelias. If I am to fight with them in the ring, I want to know what they are capable of." Contessa's eyes narrow in irritation as she listens to my explanation. I hoped she would appreciate my thought process, but it has only upset her further.

"And you?" She turns her attention to Illyrius.

"A similar curiosity, *Lanista*," the duelist admits softly. "I wanted to know if it was a fluke or if he could do it again."

"Well, what did you learn?" She places her hands on her hips and looks between the two of us. "Did you answer your question?"

"I guess not," I admit, understanding the point she is making.

"And why is that?" she presses, giving me no relief from her grilling.

"Because both of us held back, *Lanista*."

"So, neither of you learned what the other is capable of because you both sabotaged my training exercise. Not only that, but you also deprived your fellow gladiators the opportunity to learn from you." My head snaps up at her rebuke, and I feel my cheeks begin to heat as they turn red with shame. I do not reach for the coldness that lurks within me but let them burn.

"Antioch is two weeks away." Contessa turns away from us to address the whole group clustered around her. "Every time you eliminate one of your peers in the training ring, you teach them something. Every lesson they gain in this place is a piece of armor that might protect them when they stand in the bloody sands. By holding back, you took one of those lessons from them. Now they have one less chance to learn before the swords are sharp, not blunted."

The training room is silent, wilting under Contessa's sharp fury. Guilt burns brightly in my chest as I am scourged by the truth of her words. It was the same in the legions. How have I forgotten that lesson already? Or have I become so selfish that I do not care about the other Silvers who will fight with me?

"Do you understand the mistake that you made?"

"Yes, *Lanista*!" Illyrius and I bark in unison. The bald woman eyes us for a moment. "If I ever catch you holding back in my *ludus* again, I will whip you bloody. Do you understand?"

"Yes, *Lanista*!"

"Good. You two will run laps around the outer wall of *Domus* Pelias from now until the sun sets. If either of you stop, I will know, and you will begin running again tomorrow morning until the sun sets once more. Do I make myself clear?" I resist the urge to groan in familiar pain. At least the estate is smaller than Agogia.

"Yes, *Lanista*!"

"Well, what are you waiting for?" she barks, taking a step forward and shooing us with her hands like we are stray dogs. "Run!"

There are few things more miserable to me than endless running. I learned this lesson in the legions, and it is quickly reinforced for me as a gladiator. I would rather spend a day being stabbed over and over by Contessa's dream warriors than this. Illyrius struggles to keep up with me. I lost a lot of my strength while I rotted in Dorian's cells, but my instructors who forged me in the Iron City must have hammered some of that endurance into my bones.

Domus Pelias is a massive estate, but compared to the route I am used to running, it is nothing. That means that we see the same landmarks repeatedly as we circle the sprawling complex. Servants hanging out the laundry begin to chuckle as we pass them again and again. Contessa appears along our path from time to time, eyes hard. Illyrius's face grows red with embarrassment or overheating, but I pay him no mind. I was subjected to much worse abuse in Agogia.

"How do you stand it?" the duelist asks me between panting breaths as we trot. *Sol*'s light grows harsher as it begins to angle behind the white stone buildings of Anteforum, casting long shadows across the compound. Another hour, and we should be free.

"Stand what?" I ask, pulled from my running focus.

"They are *laughing* at us," he hisses at the servants who eye us with amusement, no doubt unused to seeing Silver gladiators run like common animals.

"I'm sure it looks funny."

"We're gladiators, and they are servants." He rounds on me, shuffling sideways so I can get the full effect of his glare. "They should respect us." I eye the smaller man with an amused expression, surprised by his sensitivity.

"What does this mean?" I ask, reaching out to tap the broken trident crest in the center of his chest.

"It's the seal of *Domus* Pelias."

"No," I press, leaning toward him more intently. "What does it mean?"

"That I am a gladiat—"

"It means someone *owns* you. Last I checked, plebeians were free." My words take the wind out of his sentence, and he staggers to a stunned stop for a moment before frantically resuming his run, casting a glance over his shoulder to see if Contessa lurks nearby.

"That's different," he protests when he has caught back up to me.

"Is it?" I don't look at him, but my tone is rich with condescension. "Someone paid money for you. They gave someone else a bag of *denarii* and then brought you here to teach you to fight to the death for the amusement of others. Don't let the pretty bars on our cage confuse you. We are the ones who are prisoners here, not them." A note of bitterness creeps into my voice at that.

Illyrius is silent for the rest of the run. I can feel him wrestling with what I said. His agitation rolls off him in waves. I ignore him, letting him make his own peace with what we are. I already have. A sword has no choice in who wields it, but if it is sharp enough, it can earn its rest. Iron is a part of me, just like a blade, so I will be a sword and cut my way to freedom.

At last, *Sol* vanishes behind the horizon, but I do not stop. Illyrius shoots me a confused look, slowing to a stop. I shake my head without looking at him. A *lanista* is not that different from a centurion. I know Contessa's games by heart. After a moment, the duelist resumes running, unsure of what I am doing but caught up in my confidence. My stomach burns with hunger, and my throat is as dry as the deserts around Agogia. All I want is a cold drink. But this is a test, and I have no intention of failing another one today.

I lead the shorter man around the next corner, running back toward the main courtyard where I first entered this compound. Contessa waits for us there, arms crossed, a surprised look on her face.

"Fortuna's Ashes!" Illyrius swears behind me when he sees the waiting *lanista*, causing me to wince. I already suffer enough from that undead god's attention. I feel no need to goad her further. As we approach, the bald woman holds up a hand, gesturing for me to come to a stop. She stares at me for a moment while my companion catches up.

"How did you know?" she asks, her voice unbothered.

"The punishment was for holding back," I remind her. The corner of her lip quirks in what might have been the beginning of a smile. Illyrius lets out a small groan as he realizes the mistake he almost made. Contessa glances at him, amused.

"Well done," she says after a heavy pause. "Now the two of you know more about each other than you did before. Get some food then see to your kits. The *dominus* has made his decision. We leave for Antioch tomorrow."

"*Domina*?" I hiss in surprise. Antioch is on the southern tip of the Iron Empire, but unless my *magister*s failed me tremendously, it should not be a two-week journey from Anteforum. "Isn't that quite early?"

"Have no fear, Castor," Contessa replies with a knowing smile, turning to walk away. "*Domus* Pelias has made arrangements for *everything*." For some reason, her emphasis on that word sent a shiver down my spine. My stomach grumbles, demanding attention. Giving a friendly nod to Illyrius, I turn toward the mess hall in search of some food. My legs burn, unhappy to be asked to move again after finally being allowed to stop.

"Hey, thanks," the shorter man calls after me.

"No problem." I toss him a tired smile. "We were teammates, after all."

"Yeah… we were," he admits. "My friends call me Illy." His eyes are dark; I can tell his mind is still clouded by our earlier conversation. I wonder what he will decide to do with it, in the end. With a wave, I continue my hunt, leaving him standing in the courtyard alone.

"Goodnight, Illy."

"Razor's Edge," he shouts, causing me to stop in my tracks before turning to look at him once more.

"What?"

"That's my Symbol—Razor's Edge." He chops a hand through the air like the edge of a knife. "Sharpness," he clarifies helpfully, seeing the confused look on my face. "I control how sharp things are."

CHAPTER 14

I part ways with my new friend and sit alone during supper. The mess hall is a melting pot of gladiators from the other divisions, and I use it to scope out my competitors. A group of ten boys and girls sit together around a long table, laughing together. They seem like children to me, although none of them can be more than a year or so younger than I am. The bare skin on their arms stands out in this room, for they are in the minority.

Some of them must have recently failed their *Sententia*. I wonder how many of them were Sextus in their year like me, or if there are no droughts this close to the Forum, only far away where no one asks questions.

Some are clearly plebeians who never had the chance to earn a *Cor*. So young, but already they have signed up to die on Mars's red sands. A hollow feeling swells in my heart as I study them. They are seeking fame and fortune in the *purus* Circuit. I shake my head softly; I know too well what most of them will find waiting for them instead.

In the far corner of the room, a quieter cluster of seven gladiators sit in a huddle, eyeing the louder group with disdainful eyes. Their copper veins glint under the bright *lumos* relics of the hall, and I can feel the arrogance wafting off them. Some of them cast jealous glances my way—I'm younger than all of them but have already Ascended. I ignore their looks, treating them with the same mild derision that they pass on to the tier below them.

A half-dozen other Silvers eat, but unlike the "Blanks" and the Coppers, my tier is sequestered into clusters. Leon and Obellius eat together in the center of the room, pointedly ignoring everyone around them. Fannia sits in a far corner, watching the mess hall with distrustful eyes. A few I have not trained with sit together but eat in silence. The divide puzzles me until I notice the Golds.

There are two Golden gladiators in the room. They sit on opposite sides of the room, ignoring each other. Tension radiates off them like heat. For some reason, the older, wiser warriors are uncomfortable with each other. What horror of the Games do they know that I do not?

I make my way to the waiting food, aware of several pairs of eyes following me. As I get closer, I spot three grizzled men sitting in the farthest corner, huddled together like friends in a blizzard. My heart skips a beat as I recognize their bearing before I even fully comprehend what they are.

Their shoulders are square, and they sit stiffly, carrying themselves with an iron pride that can only be beaten into you from a specific forge. Even if they did not each wear the cold metal of an *inhibitus* around their neck, I would know where they were from. These three are Ironbound; gladiators in the *Ferrum* Circuit.

For a moment, the only thing I want is to abandon my food and go and sit with them. I do not know what Legion they originally served in; they wear the same leathers that I do. But spending time with any of them—except for the Praetorians—would feel like coming home.

As if he can feel my gaze, the legionnaire with his back to me turns and looks in my direction. An electric jolt runs through me as our eyes meet. I know this man.

It is Anas.

He's alive.

The former *captivus*'s eyes widen in shock as he sees me. His mouth opens to deliver a greeting, his face lighting up with the same joy that burns in me, but then his gaze flickers from my face to my bare neck, and he freezes. He knows what it means that I have become Silver—that I no longer wear an *inhibitus*. Tightly, I shake my head, terrified to be seen. My legion brother returns my gesture with a tiny nod, understanding the need for secrecy. Despite the danger, I'm locked in place, so overwhelmed by relief that another member of the Twelfth survives while being battered by guilt that I left him behind. Anas's own expression is a grim mirror of my own.

I want nothing more than to rush to my friend, embrace him, and beg him to tell me his story. But to give in to that temptation would be death, maybe for us both. Instead, I must be cold. Only the frozen survive.

One of his companions notices this exchange and looks up from his food. The grizzled man's beard is salted with gray, and he frowns when he sees me looking at their table. His displeasure is enough to break me free of my paralysis and make me move.

Pretending to be merely friendly, I offer the man a small wave before turning back to loading up on food. The servants carve up roasted chicken while I snag some fresh bread and steamed broccoli. The food is one thing I do not miss about the legions. For a meal like this, many of the men in the Twelfth would have been tempted to commit crimes that would have sent them to the Thirteenth.

I feel the *Ferrum* gladiators' eyes on me as I collect my food, but I do not look back. With a force of will, I slump my shoulders, trying to hide Agogia's stamp on my form. Durus would whip me bloody if he saw me stand like this, but I seek to live.

I eat my meal alone, relishing the silence. After my time in Dorian's dungeon, I grew used to isolation. There were days I did not speak a single word as I stewed in that cell. Now, surrounded by people once more, I find myself missing the clarity that solitude would bring. The *purus* and the *cuprum* gladiators study me. I overhear remarks about my *rasa* veins, but I ignore them.

I can only think about my friend sitting a dozen yards away. Did Anas get swept in the avalanche, or was he able to escape through the pass before it was sealed behind him? Did anyone else survive? My flesh burns with divine heat as the *votum* that is set in my bones goes wild at the thought. I have been the only one laboring under this oath's yoke. Hope, long dormant, comes alight like a bed of banked coals.

I craft a thousand theories in my head, but none of them bring me any peace. The legionnaires finish their meal, and Anas leaves without looking in my direction. The former criminal knows about hiding in plain sight.

It is only after they are gone that I realize that they were not the only ones studying me. The Gold *electi* watch me too. Their gazes are harsh and appraising. They have been here long enough to know that Contessa and Varus would not have bought me if there was not a reason. They wonder if I will Ascend to join their Circuit; if I will become competition for them one day.

That is what the distance is. The Silvers and Golds know they will have to fight each other. In order to win a Circuit, you must be the last warrior standing. The children haven't realized what is waiting for them yet. My gut twists like it has been stabbed by a knife. The whole thing is sick; tarnished like the rust of the Empire's underbelly.

When I was a boy, we were told that the Arena of Mars was a holy place. That it was one of the last monuments to the gods that we still maintained. This was where the greatest heroes had been discovered over the last four hundred years. Warriors like Attilius and Flamma were first baptized in blood at the feet of Mars. Some even claim that the red sands are from the very red planet that still burns in his name. But now, I see what it really is. A place where blood is turned into coin. It is business, not piety, that keeps it open.

I feel empty when I finish eating. My stomach is full, but there is a void inside me that cannot be filled. The chill of Winter and Iron claws at me, offering their succor from the pain. With a grunt of effort, I obey Pliny's wisdom and ignore my Symbols, rising to my feet and storming out into the night. I feel several pairs of eyes on my back as I leave, but I am too distracted to check who it is.

I know that I am not strong enough to resist Iron and Winter outright, so I decide to channel their temptation into something useful. Pliny says that the corruption occurs when I use my Symbols as crutches to keep myself from feeling. But they are not as dangerous when I am the one who is commanding them.

Besides, if I do not find something to distract myself, I will be unable to keep myself from seeking out Anas in the *Ferrum* quarters and forcing his story out of him. I will see him, but I must be clever. I must not be caught.

I trot to the training hall, ignoring the burn of protest in my legs.

The hall is dark; most of the *lumos* relics are shut off. I waste no time, marching to the Winter *loci* and stepping through its doors as they slide open for me. The snow and ice have grown older over the last few weeks, and I sigh in delight as I begin to top off my reserves. It is still by no means ancient, but it is even less of a strain to convert the essence to match my own. For a moment, I feel like I am back in the North with the Twelfth. The cold takes me home, not to a place, but to a people.

A wry smile twists my face. As a child, I hated Winter and loved Summer. What irony that my union with Ancient Frost has twisted my preferences in such a short amount of time. The run did not use up my supply of essence, but even so, my body relaxes as I refill my *Cor*. Even my weary legs feel stronger than they should. It is healing to cultivate your Symbol, I think.

The familiar process of gathering essence calms my racing mind, helping me to empty my mind and enter a calm state. When I have topped up my reserves, I rise from the snow and step back into the training sands, composing myself for my nightly ritual. All other thoughts have been put away, leaving me empty and focused. Nothing exists outside of me and my Symbols.

The Frozen Blades spring into my hands, and I marvel at how easy it has become. I have pushed my *Cor* to become more efficient and responsive to my commands, and it has grown stronger just like any other muscle in my body.

I lunge forward, shifting the weapon in my right hand from *gladius* to dueling blade. The cracks echo as the ice shifts, obeying my commands. Without hesitating, I spin, repeating the process with my left. When I first started this regimen, I would already be straining my veins to keep up with my will. Now I feel nothing. My reserves have diminished some, but only a fraction compared to how quickly this used to burn through my store.

For almost ten minutes, I flow through my sword strikes, shifting my weapons back and forth seamlessly. When I have drained my Ancient Frost reserve at last, I sink to one knee, panting. My skin is slick with a thin coat of sweat, but I smile brightly, marveling at how far I have come. After a few moments, I lever myself to my feet, enjoying the dull ache that has settled over my body before I go to refill my *Cor*.

"What's this? Contessa's new favorite gladiator is training after hours?" a snide voice cuts through the darkness, jolting me into action. Instinctively, my knees bend as I lower myself into a fighting crouch. "And he's all out of essence," Leon's cruel voice continues as he emerges at the edge of the harsh circle of light shining down on me on the sands. "How unfortunate."

The blond Air *electus* is dressed in his combat leathers and bears a pair of *gladii* strapped to the belt around his waist. His left hand caresses its sword's hilt like a lover as he glares at me. I pause, concerned by the smug glint in his eye. What does he know?

"Can I help you?" I ask, annoyed that there is still a hint of breathlessness in my voice.

"No, I think it is my turn to help *you*," he sneers, taking another step forward. "It's about time you learn your place here."

"Oh." I chuckle, beginning to relax. "That conversation."

"What do you mean—yes, *that* conversation." His brow furrows at the disrespect. He's confused that I no longer seem concerned. He came here to threaten me, and I am unbothered, but he's not sure why.

"Very well, let's hear it." I stab my icy swords into the sand and cross my arms, like he is wasting my time. He is, but for a different reason than he thinks.

"You need to learn some respect," he hisses, taking a step closer to me and pointing his right forefinger at my face. "You haven't earned your place."

"Well, I beat you and every other Silver on the *index*," I remind him calmly. "I'm not sure what else I need to do to prove myself."

"I have earned two *marcae* for *Domus* Pelias." He puffs up his chest with pride. "Until you have brought us glory, you are nothing."

"Two *marcae*," I repeat, doing my best to sound impressed. I do not know how scoring for the circuits is determined, but that doesn't sound like much. "How many matches did it take you to earn that little tithe, Leon?"

"I'm warning you," he growls, eyes bulging with fury as my insult finds its mark. "You need to get in line if you know what's good for you."

"Or what?" I arch an eyebrow, tracing my eyes down to the pair of swords around his waist. He's startled by my challenge. He thinks I am out of essence. He deliberately waited until I finished my training regimen before confronting me so that I would be weak and powerless. Most *electi* would be helpless against his Air Symbol right now. He chose this moment to corner me when I should be alone and weak.

But he's only half right. I have depleted my supply of Ancient Frost, but the essence of my original Symbol—Iron—curls hard and cold in its *Cor*, waiting to be used. That metal pours into my spine, refusing to let me bend.

"Or I will show you to your place." Both of his hands drop to the pommel of his swords, just in case his threat isn't clear enough. He is so pathetic, I cannot help myself; I throw back my head and laugh. It is warm and rich. Anas would eat this prissy little boy alive.

"Very well. Come and do it," I suggest, unfurling my arms so they dangle just above the icy hilts of my own weapons sticking out of the ground. His eyes widen at my casual acceptance of his challenge. This is not how he expected this to go. I am at my weakest, while he is at my strongest. Even if I can beat him when I am rested, I should be far from it now.

Slowly, he draws his two swords, his face a picture of disbelief. He knows he cannot back down now, but my confidence eats at him like an acid. What do I know that he does not? Many things, I suspect. But one thing more than any other is this: he cannot kill me with his iron weapons.

I smile as I pull my frozen *gladii* from the sand in an icy mirror to his movements. "Let me tell you something, Leon," I say, giving the blades an experimental twirl. My Ancient Frost reserves are low enough that I know I will not be able to maintain their strength for a prolonged fight.

"You're right. There is an order here. But you are the one who has a new place. Tonight, you are going to learn it." My words strike against his temper like a match and his eyes flash before he lunges forward, ripping up the sand as he barrels forward.

What a life must he have led to have ended up as a gladiator instead of a Censor. Air *electi* like Leon and Atticus are among their favorite recruits because of how dangerous they become when given a *tellus* blade. The angry boy lashes at me with his swords, and I contemptuously bat them aside, matching him stroke for stroke. His eyes grow wider and his complexion pales as I meet his opening attacks.

The air between us warps as he pours his will out into it. I feel it moving against me. It's like I am fighting underwater. But the Iron Symbol feeds me the knowledge of his sword's movements as if they were my own, making it easy for me to match his movements, slowed as I am.

I extend my *animus* to cover the space around us so that no matter how quickly he moves, I will not lose track of him. A delighted smile leaps on my face as I feel my *Cor* veins burn in protest as I push the range of my senses further than I ever have before. Another muscle that I can exercise. If it were anyone other than Leon, I might be tempted to feel grateful for what he had helped me discover.

Then my left-hand sword cracks under the force of one of his blows as my Ancient Frost essence supply runs out, and I remember that I have work to do. It is not enough for me to beat him—no, even in this weakened state, I need to embarrass him.

He hears my sword begin to fail. A twisted smile grows on his face, banishing the fear as he decides that there is no danger here. In a heartbeat, he increases his speed, drawing upon the power of his Symbol to hammer at my left side, forcing me to use the weakened weapon to defend myself. With each blow, it shudders as the ice begins to give way to the iron of his blade.

It would be an easy thing for me to reach out through my sword and shatter his like a broken toy. But that would give away my secret, giving him even more power over me. To put him in his place, I must beat him a different way.

With what little essence I have left, I reach into my left *gladius* and weaken it further. My body is racked with pain as even my Ancient Frost veins run dry. But the damage is done, and the cracks widen. It is easier to destroy something than it is to make it after all. Atrophy is a fire that burns everywhere—all you must do is let it in.

I raise the frail blade to catch his attack, already smiling at what will come next. I open my right hand, letting the other sword fall from my fingers into the sand. I will not need it anymore. Leon's weapon batters into mine, and the ice explodes into a cloud of frost.

The Air *electus* staggers as the resistance to his strike vanishes. I toss the broken blade to the side, stepping to the right and inside his guard in one smooth movement. His other sword hisses as it cuts toward me like the wind. Without looking, I raise my right hand and slap the weapon on the flat of the blade, knocking it to the side.

A panicked expression begins to bloom on Leon's face right before my left fist slams into it. The boy staggers backwards with a grunt. I don't give him time to recover, driving inside his guard and raining blows on his stomach.

The blond boy doubles over, dropping his weapons. I sense as they bounce against the sand at our feet. He tries to keep his balance, but I do not relent. I'm enjoying wiping the smug look from his face. But that is not the only reason that I do not stop. I beat him as hard as I can so that I will never have to do this again.

Let him see my rage.

Let him fear me.

My fist collides with his temple, knocking him sprawling. With the innate speed of an Air Symbol, he lunges back to his feet, trying to grapple with me. I punch his face with my right fist until he drops back onto the sand. I pour Iron essence into my bones, willing my fingers to be stronger than his face so I do not shatter my hand.

He groans, trying once more to get up. His face is a bloody mess, but he is not broken yet. I kick him in the ribs as the legionnaires who first beat me once did. He collapses but continues to struggle, refusing to bend. Despite myself, I feel a grudging amount of respect for his unrelenting spirit. It is almost Iron-like.

I kick him again, harder.

"Stay down." He manages to climb to his knees, glaring at me with an insane rage. My plan is not working; he hates me more now than he did before. I grab the front of his leather tunic, punching him in the face again. He may be stubborn, but I was forged in the iron pits of Agogia.

"Enough!" a voice shouts from the far end of the training room. The *lumos* relics burst to life at the sound of her shout, bathing Leon and us in light. I twist in surprise, terrified that we have been discovered by Contessa, but my fears are pale shadows of the danger that I am in. The *lanista* might beat me, but this woman could have me killed.

Alessandra Pelias, palatine daughter of our master, glares at us from the exit of the Lightning *locus*, her arms crossed. In a daze, I release Leon, letting the blond boy sag to his knees on the sand.

"You bear the weight of great responsibility," she snaps after a moment. Her blue eyes bore into mine, sparing no glance for the Air *electus* on the ground. "With that responsibility comes the expectation of maturity. What would your masters say if they discovered you fighting like children in the schoolyard?" I open my mouth to object that I was only defending myself, but she cuts me off smoothly.

"They would beat you to match the damage that you have done to this fool," she answers her own question. "You know that I am right." My mouth snaps shut, and I nod. I am terrified to speak, afraid that any moment she will recognize me, remember the *rasa*-veined legionnaire that she was once kind to. My hair is still long and unkempt, but it is a weak disguise. My voice could unmask me the moment I utter a word.

My life hangs by a thread, but panic does not own me. I am Iron. I do not bend. I do not break. It has been so long since I was like this. Only the metal assurance of my original Symbol fills me. It is as if I have had two people whispering in my ears for months, and one of them has fallen silent. I am sharper. Focused.

"There will be no more of this." It is not a request.

Wordlessly, I press my fist to my chest and offer her a slight bow. I feel the pressure of her gaze for a moment as I stay there, not daring to look her in the eye.

The sound of her sandals echoes off the stone floors as she leaves, satisfied. As she departs, the *lumos* relics fade, like *Sol* setting over the horizon, leaving us alone in the dark. I turn to face Leon, feeling my right hand curl into a fist once more.

The blond boy stares at me with his blood-streaked face. But his eyes glare with the same undiminished defiance. For a moment, I want more than anything to hit him again. Surely one more beating will break him. He sees something in my stance, and a flash of fear runs through his eyes before vanishing behind the fire of his hatred.

I force my fist to relax and shake my head in disgust before turning away from him to head back to the Winter *locus*. My empty *Cor* demands my attention.

"You heard the *domina*," I call over my shoulder as I step into the frozen room. "This is over."

CHAPTER 15

Our accommodations for the journey to Antioch are much nicer than the prison carts I arrived in. Instead of a cage, I am surprised to find six carriages waiting for us in the courtyard. Four copper-veined *equi aeris*—airhorses—are hitched to each. My jaw drops at the collection of *mythi* gathered before us.

My father once told me that Agre, our faithful stonehound, was worth at least a thousand *denarii*. To see twenty-four of these beasts in one place…the cost is staggering. I thought that *mythi* were made when a piece of *Cor* was discovered by an animal in the wild. But this herd was clearly bred to match. Not only are they powerful, but they are also beautiful beasts. This was no accident—anyone with eyes can see that. I wonder which of them was given my Heart in the drought.

"*Purus* in the rear," Contessa calls, appearing out of nowhere. "*Ferrum* in the next one, then *cuprum*, then *argentum*, and then *aurum*."

Gladiators mumble their assent, beginning to shuffle toward their assigned carriages in a mess. My heart jumps as I spot Anas across the sea of people, making his way to the Iron carriage. Worried that I'm staring, I jerk my vision away before any of his companions notice my scrutiny.

I pick up my satchel and follow in the steps of the other Silvers, hunching my shoulders as we walk past the *lanista*. I am not afraid that Leon went to her; his pride is too strong. But I do not know what Alessandra might have said to the bald woman. In the daylight, I regret goading him as much as I did. I should have found another way to make peace with him.

As I walk by her, I feel her knowing gaze track from the bruised boy to me. For a moment, I freeze, feeling a shadow of that old fear that I used to feel when Durus would fix me with an officer's glare. "Get it out of your system now," she murmurs, turning away from me. "You both have to be able to fight, or there will be Dead Pluto to pay. And by the dead gods, get a haircut. You look like a barbarian."

"Aye, *Domina*," I reply, matching her volume. A weight lifts from my shoulders as I do. We still have two weeks until the Games begin. The Silver *electus* should be completely healed long before then.

In the center of the courtyard, Varus himself oversees the loading. The senator is dressed simply, wearing a set of fighting leathers that match the rest of ours, save for the gold thread worked into the edges of his outfit. Pliny stands next to him, wrapped in a pristine toga. He shoots me a tight smile when he sees me watching him.

"*Barbari* in the second carriage," Contessa snaps, pulling my attention back to the entrance of the courtyard, where two figures emerge, an old man and a young woman who walk arm in arm. They are like no one I have ever seen. The tones of their skin are different from any Norman or Imperial I have ever seen. The man is bald except for a mostly white ponytail emerging from high on the back of his head. A black silk cloth made of the same material as his strange flowing pants and shirt covers his eyes. He does not look to the left or right but stares straight ahead, unable to see through his blindfold. I shiver at the sight, reminded of Nemesis.

The woman guiding him is young enough to be his granddaughter, wearing a dress that is made of the same black, silky material as his outfit. Her hair is tied back in a tight tail, and she looks around boldly, matching the gaze of anyone who dares to look at her. A shock runs through me as her dark eyes clash with mine. Her rage is a living storm, lurking just beneath the surface. Unimpressed by what she sees in me, she turns to glare at the rest of the people in the courtyard.

My heart drops at the sight of the man that follows in their wake. The tall Norman is chained both hand and foot, but he walks with his head held high. His blond hair has been cut into a mohawk. To my surprise, there is no sign of blasphemous *Cor* tattoos scrawled on his skin. Instead, his arms are thick with the Copper veins of an *electus*. Hatred coils in my guts at the sight of the man. I do not know how he gained a Heart, but I do not care. He is a barbarian and therefore my enemy. The warrior notices my glare and meets it with an unbothered stare, cold as ice. I see the deaths of my friends—my brothers—reflected back to me in his blue eyes. My hands curl into fists, as something *deep* inside of me seeks to surge forward, to throw myself at the Norman.

"Castor! Stop mucking about and get in the Mercury-damned carriage!" Contessa's voice scourges me like a whip, jerking my gaze away from the Norman. I give her an abashed nod before following in the wake of the other Silvers, heading for the fourth carriage from the rear.

But I do not forget his face.

The inside is far more luxurious than any other carriage I have ever seen. Everything is carpeted and cushioned with rich blue fabric, even the walls. There are three rows of seats, all facing forward. The air inside the carriage is tense. The *Index* didn't change in the end after all. The other five Silvers are the ones I faced in my gauntlet.

Leon and Obellius took the front seats. The blond boy leans against the side of the pillowed wall, resting his bruised body. His giant friend gives me a violent glare that I ignore. Reese and Fannia are in the second row. Both of them have wide eyes as they look back to me as if they cannot believe what I did to the gladiator who has earned two *marcae*. I give them both a friendly smile and look at the final row, where Illy is patting the seat beside him.

"I saved this for you," he says. I drop onto the cushion with a sharp chuckle.

"Is it really saving if no one else wants to sit next to me?"

"How I procured it is my own business." The shorter duelist sniffs arrogantly. "Do you want a seat or not?"

"Are you kidding? Of course. This is the best seat in the house." Illy grins at my response, leaning back into his cushions.

"It's going to be a long ride to Antioch," he warns.

"Do you know any games?" I ask innocently. "My sister and I used to count cows…"

"Oh no, you're one of those. I should have made you sit with Leon."

I don't make Illy play any childish games with me. When our caravan begins to move, my eyes are glued to the window, drinking up the world that passes us by. I have only seen Anteforum once in the daylight, and that journey was only a taste of the center of the Empire.

The dense stone city is almost overwhelming to me. Buildings connect to one another, forming an unbroken wall along the streets as we race by. Plebeians walk along the side of the streets, watching us with only mild interest.

A train of rich carriages pulled by airhorses is not a strange sight to them. My right hand slowly contracts into a fist, and I exhale slowly, forcing myself to relax. I wonder if my father and the other members of the City Council knew the truth of the Iron Empire. My grandfather must have. By all accounts, he traveled the world. He must have seen with his own eyes the greed beyond our town.

But despite this, I cannot help but marvel at this place that dwarfs Segesta in every way. Its streets are bigger, its citizens more numerous. As we travel, I grow used to the sights. It is big, but it is just another place. My awe begins to fade, replaced by casual contempt. Every street is the same—the buildings and houses never end, and they are the same thing, repeated over and over.

Just when I think that the capital has no more surprises for me, the endless streets and buildings surround the Empress's seat like a collar stop, ending at the shores of the Tiber River. The structures that rise on the island of Forum itself tower over any of the puny three-story buildings that we have been passing by. A metaphor that is neither subtle nor avoidable.

Our path begins to curve, tracing along the edge of the water of the mighty, raging Tiber. We are not headed to the capital, only cutting past it on our journey east to Antioch. For a moment, I am disappointed to not get to see this awesome place up close, but then my face grows pale as I gaze upon the white tower of the Censors, jutting into the sky like an accusing finger at *Sol* itself. Despite my fear, I know that one day my hunt for Atticus may take me to its halls.

I gasp as the Empress's home rears into view. Diana's palace is massive, but not in the same way. Instead of vertically, it stretches the length of the island, part fortress, part paradise. It is a massive white structure that could house the population of Segesta without issue.

Beyond it rears the legendary *Universitas* spire, shorter than the Censors but still tall enough to tower over anything in Anteforum. Several other towers circle the palace like spikes. They are not marble, but built of strange materials—metal and glass that glint in the light. Their lengths are dotted with windows in regularly spaced intervals. Smaller towers cluster around them, reaching high into the sky from their shadows. The smallest of them is several times taller than anything in Anteforum. Near the shore sits the black pyramid of Delphos, the home of the priests, short and forgotten.

Power radiates from that island like it is alive. Even on the other side of the river, I can feel it itching on my skin. Before Titus and the Iron Lords killed the gods, *Mons* Olympus must have felt the same. I glance up at the massive floating mountain. It is still silent and dead, despite the things that haunt my dreams.

"First time?" Illy asks me knowingly, glancing over my shoulder with the air of boredom.

"Yeah," I manage softly, unable to keep the awe out of my voice.

"It's really something," he acknowledges, already looking back to a scroll he is reading on his lap. "There are four bridges that cross the Tiber from Anteforum, one from each direction. That is the only way into the city." I admire one of the massive stone bridges as we shoot past it, running parallel to the island.

"What about by boat?" I ask. "Couldn't someone just sail their navy up the Tiber and land there?"

"I mean, in theory, but legend has it that the water is full of *mythi* and *hydra* that serve the Empress's will." The shorter man shrugs. "If you've got a boat and a death wish, you're welcome to try it. I'd rather not be your partner for that challenge, though."

"Noted." I laugh. "If I'm ever trying to sneak onto Forum, I won't do it by water."

"There's a good lad," he murmurs, already distracted again by his scroll.

It takes almost two hours for us to cut across the center of Anteforum. We pass thousands of homes and tens of thousands of people. I spend the entire time watching the spires of Forum, drinking them in. The weight of my *votum* hangs heavy on me. It seems to grow as the caravan eventually begins to turn away, heading back through Anteforum and to the East.

We will return; Nemesis seems to promise me.

I intend to hold her to that.

After another hour or more, we finally break free from the limits of Anteforum and onto the wide paved road that leads to Antioch. Finally free from the crowds, the airhorses show us what they are capable of. The carriage surges forward, hurtling at a speed that no normal *equus* could match. A slipstream forms around us like a bubble, insulating us from the roaring wind that rushes by.

"Dead gods," I whisper, watching the countryside whip past us.

"They're something, aren't they?" Illy seems to only emerge from his scrolls when I am impressed by something he's seen before. "They're bred from a young age to run in the same quad so they can use their *Cor* together to create this." He gestures at the air around us. "A single airhorse can carry a single man at high speeds, but it takes something truly special to make them work together."

"Makes them more expensive, I'd guess," I grumble, leaning back in my comfortable, cushioned seat.

"Quite." Illy peers at me knowingly before returning to his scroll.

"What are you reading?" I ask, surprising myself to discover that I'm bored.

"Ptolemy's treatise on knives," he murmurs, distractedly not looking up.

"What?" I hadn't expected it to be so… erudite. We're gladiators, not magisters. "Why are you reading that?"

"Because I am trying to learn what sharpness is." He lowers his scroll, apparently sensing that I will not be satisfied with a short answer. I almost feel bad, but he's piqued my curiosity, and I can't stop myself from digging deeper.

"I'm pretty sure it's the thing that makes a sword cut someone when you stab them," I offer.

Illy rolls his eyes, looking disgusted. "Where did you go to *collegium*? Don't tell me; I don't want to become prejudiced against an entire district. That's not what sharpness *is*, you blithering idiot. That is what it *does*."

"I'm not following." Despite myself, I feel a flush creeping up my neck. Vellum wasn't a particularly great teacher, I have come to realize. But for some reason, I find myself wanting to come to his defense.

"You're so lucky you got a straightforward Symbol and are good at hitting people with it. Otherwise, you'd be hopeless." Illy laughs, sitting up straight. Despite his criticisms, a small smile spreads across his face as he prepares to lecture me.

"What is ice?" he asks after a moment of thought.

"Frozen water."

"Sure. That's easy. What is water?"

"Uh, a liquid."

"What's frozen?"

"Something that has gotten too cold."

"What is cold?"

"Stop," I beg, holding up a hand to forestall any more of his horrifying questions. I can feel the surface of my brain starting to crack like the icy surface of a lake during Spring's thaw. He is attacking the very core of my thoughts, and I do not like it.

"That's nothing." The duelist grins in delight, rubbing his hands together.

"It's like congruency," I say, desperate to cut off any more of his paradigm-breaking questions. He pauses in surprise, his eyes narrowing to look at me in a new light.

"Yes. They are related," he admits. "How did you know that?"

"The art of finding congruency between two things is understanding how they are the same." My mouth is running ahead of my mind, and my thoughts scramble, trying to pave the ground before it. "In the *collegium,* they focus on what things are physically. But that is only one facet of similarity…" My voice trails off as I ponder the implications of what Illy has shown me.

"I take back my criticism of your magister." My friend chuckles. "I did not expect you to see the application so quickly."

"Your Symbol is the Razor's Edge," I continue, ignoring his praise. I can feel the idea forming before me, but it is not fully set. I worry that if I hesitate for even a moment, it will startle and flee, like a doe. "A sword is sharp, but so are other things."

"Like what?" he presses, leaning forward.

"Cruel words. A mind. The wind."

"Cheese."

"Cheese?" His suggestion startles me out of my focus.

"Yeah, have you ever had a yellow cheese that's really aggressive? That's sharp too."

"Cheese," I repeat softly, trying to find some purchase for my feet as my world turns upside down. "Does that mean you can sense swords with your *animus?*"

"No." He laughs, as if amused by my simple question. "I am not like an Ironbound *Fidelis*, able to feel the movements of a sword with my Heart. If I could, Razor's Edge would be forbidden too."

"But if a blade is sharp…" I protest. Everything I know about the power that a Silver *electus* gains tells me that he should be able to do something similar to what I am able to do.

"A little," he admits, wobbling his hand to show the comparison. "The part of the blade that is sharp is so much smaller than its total mass, so it is much harder to track. It's a little like listening for a whisper in the middle of a battlefield. Up close, I can certainly hear it, but it is usually too late by then."

"Even so, that is a fantastic Symbol," I breathe, trying to think about the practical applications of it in a duel.

"So now you know why I am reading Ptolemy's treatise on knives." He holds the scroll up for me with a small smile. "The better I understand what exactly it is that I am bound to—"

"The easier it is for you to find new congruencies and expand what you can do."

"Seriously, I am impressed. At least your magisters taught you some logic. Congratulations, you now have what the philosophers call 'existential dread.'" I don't fully hear him; my mind is racing at the implications for myself. He's right. I know nothing about either of my Symbols. I can manipulate the iron in someone's sword or shield. I can make ice and cold obey me. But that is not even scratching the surface.

What is iron? What is ice? What are they made of? What can they become? There's only one way to find out. I vow to spend as much time in the library as in the training hall when we return to *Domus* Pelias. If I survive. Distantly, I hear Illy's scroll rustle as he resumes his reading.

"What is that?" I interrupt him again, pointing out the window at a massive hole that gapes out of the ground like an open wound. It is large enough to swallow the home that I grew up in and have room for a couple more in the same bite.

"Ah, you've never heard of the Bores?"

"I've seen one," I whisper, a forgotten memory springing into my mind as the cart that held my friends and me prisoner rumbled past a similar maw along the *Via Nordus* on the way to Agogia.

"There are dozens of them all over the Iron Empire."

"What are they?"

The duelist shrugs, unperturbed by an ancient mystery. "No one knows. Ancient mines, perhaps. The Censors went into them a few centuries ago. You know what they found?"

"What?"

"Nothing. They're empty."

We leave the Bore behind as we hurtle further South. Occasionally, we fly past small towns or manors, but the airhorses show no signs of slowing or tiring. Their Copper *Corda* supplements their natural strength with ease.

When night falls, *Luna* rises, reflecting its cold light off *Mons* Olympus, floating above. A pair of *lumos* relics set in the carriage ignite, keeping us warm and bright. More lights spring to life, brightening the road so our drivers can maintain our breakneck speed.

I watch the dark world race by from my comfortable chair, shaking my head at the lesson I have learned today. "Heh," I murmur to myself in mild disbelief, too low for Illy to hear. "Cheese."

CHAPTER 16

It is well into the night before the carriage begins to slow. The air slipstream that surrounds us pops as we begin to reduce to a normal speed for a team of horses. I sit up in anticipation, wondering if this is another brief rest stop or if we are breaking for the night.

I scan the dark horizon, but there is no sign of a sprawling city waiting for us. The only thing I see is a small cluster of lights that seems far too few to be Antioch.

We slow more as we draw close. Bright white stone walls loom out of the dark as our relics illuminate them. Heavy gates are open wide, welcoming our caravan as we trot inside another compound.

"What is this place?" I ask Illy, jostling him from where he dozes next to me.

"Huh?" The smaller man sits up, looking blearily out the window to get his bearings.

"It looks like some sort of country manor," he offers after a moment, face still creased with sleep.

"Thanks." I sigh, twisting around for a clue. "My magisters never taught me what those were."

"Oh, you're going to hold on to that one for a while, aren't you?"

"Only until I feel like I can properly return it to you."

Illy sighs, sitting up to look more directly into the dark. "I have no idea. I've never been here."

"Well, what good are you, then?" I shoot back playfully as the carriage pulls to a halt in a well-lit courtyard.

"Now you sound like my father."

"Everyone out!" Contessa's voice roars out. "Grab your packs. We're setting up for the night."

"Come on," I say, springing to my feet, feeling suddenly awake from the mystery. "Let's see where Varus has brought us." I am the first to exit our carriage, and one of the servants hands me my satchel as I do. I give him a smile before taking a few steps to stretch my legs. I turn as I walk, surveying the manor.

It is far smaller than *Domus* Pelias in Anteforum, but then, most country retreats are meant to be so. A massive rectangular home squats up a dozen marble stairs, peering down on us. Servants pour out of its front door, dressed in bright blue tunics, marked with a golden thread.

Two legionnaires stand guard on either side of the great doors, dressed in full battle kit. My eyebrows shoot up in surprise as I take in their gold uniforms and iron *lorica*. Something about these men tells me they are not retired guards. They are too young to have completed their service and carry themselves with too much pride to be anything other than soldiers fresh from the field. But why do they not wear the color of their legion?

"Mars's Ashes, is that the Spartan Guard?" Illy murmurs to me in awe.

"The who?" I whisper back, confused. I have never heard a hint of such a thing.

"They're elites, pulled from the primary army to act as bodyguards for the Senate."

"The Senate has their own legion?"

"Well, how are they supposed to be the *vox populi* if they don't have any teeth to bite with?" I blink in surprise, unsure how to react to that. Varus is also a senator; why have I never seen any of these soldiers escorting him?

Startled by their presence, I turn to look at the carriage carrying our Iron gladiators, two behind ours. All of the former soldiers are staring at the legionnaires with varying levels of interest. As if he can sense my glance, Anas looks toward me, eyes burning with warning.

Be careful, they say. I nod before turning my attention back to the stairs, just in time to see a woman emerge dressed in a white toga, with a golden band on her arm. She is older, but the Golden veins running through her arm have helped her defy age. Bright blond hair trails behind her as she smiles delightedly at the sight of our train.

"*Salvete*, Varus, Alessandra, finally!" She pauses on the middle of the stairs, clasping her hands together with emphatic joy. "I was growing worried that you had decided to spurn my invitation and pass by me in the night!"

"Senator Delilah," our master greets her warmly, striding to meet her.

"You're so formal," she scolds, rushing to embrace him. "We're both senators, and you have known me for twenty years."

"Enough time for you to have earned my respect," Varus replies solemnly, but his lips quirk as he dampens a smile.

"I grow tired of your rebellion," Delilah announces, drawing back from their hug and looking over his shoulder. "Where is my goddaughter? She's the only reason I wanted you to visit."

"I did bring her."

"Aunt Delilah!" Alessandra shouts in delight, scurrying up from the carriages to hug the senator, black hair streaming behind her.

"My precious jewel. Now let me look at you," the older woman insists, grabbing Alessandra by the shoulders and forcing her to take a step back. "*Argentum* already? Your father must be delighted." She casts a pointed look over her shoulder at Varus.

"I am," our master replies with a hint of tired amusement. "Which she well knows, Senator."

"He only calls me 'Senator' when he's annoyed with me," the blond *electus* confides to Alessandra, which makes the younger woman laugh in delight. There is a silence as the senator studies Varus's daughter more intently, looking for something.

"You are every inch her daughter, my dear," she says so softly, I almost don't hear it. A shadow passes over Alessandra's face and her father's. Delilah pulls the younger woman into a second embrace, holding this one for much longer.

Eventually, she seems to realize that a courtyard full of thirty people watch this exchange, and she pulls free, wrapping her arm around Alessandra's shoulder in a protective manner.

"My majordomo will show your men to their quarters," she tells Varus with a bright smile. "Come, you must be exhausted after your long travel day. I will have the servants prepare a meal…" They vanish up the stairs and into the manor. Pliny trails after them, unbothered by the mass of gladiators he leaves behind.

A stout woman wearing the same blue tunic appears, pausing for a moment to confer with Contessa. They confer for a few moments before the *lanista* turns to address us with a serious expression.

"They've cleared out one of the servant dormitories for you lot," she announces. "Everyone gets their own room, and meals will be served in the kitchen. Starting with a late dinner." A small chorus of cheers breaks out from the Coppers and Heartless gladiators. Contessa silences it with a glare but moves on without a word.

"While we are guests, you are not to leave the property or enter the main manor." She jerks a thumb at the looming marble structure over her shoulder. "Other than that, you are free to wander. Remember, you are gladiators of *Domus* Pelias. Act like it and don't get in trouble, or I'll kill you. Is that clear?"

"Aye, *Domina*," we agree in unison.

We follow the servant in a loose cluster. Gladiators aren't soldiers—they don't march. The lower tiers laugh among themselves at the thought of staying in the servant quarters, but the Silvers and Golds are silent. We pass through a magnificent garden, surrounded by hedges and a beautiful terraced fountain. A large bronze brazier sits in the center, carved with the faces of the dead gods and burning with the everflame. It reminds me of the one my mother kept in the mausoleum on my family's estate.

Leon and Obellius hover on the farthest side of the group from me, but Illy, horse-maned Reese, and Fannia are nearby as we walk. A four-story stone building greets us, with long hallways for individual rooms. The dormitories for Senator Delilah's servants are not that different from the ones we live in at *Domus* Pelias. It amuses me to see a few of the Coppers begin to understand that they're not as elite as they thought.

"Dinner will be served in ten minutes in the main floor kitchen," the majordomo announces as we enter the building in a stream. I catch Anas's eye as we separate, tossing my head toward the dining area. Tonight is our best chance to talk without being overheard. He nods before vanishing to the third floor, where the Iron gladiators are staying.

The Silvers and Golds are on the fourth. Contessa assigns Leon and Obellius to the farthest side of the building from me. She gives me a flat look that tells me there will be no more tolerance for any fighting. I nod, chuckling to myself as I step into my room.

It is smaller and has no private *lavatorium,* but otherwise, it is almost the same. I toss my satchel to the floor before flopping on my bed, letting my body stretch after being stuck in that seat for so many hours. Tension runs through me as I try not to think about the dinner to come. It is risky for us to be seen together. If our secret is uncovered, it would mean death for me—likely him too.

But I must know. I must know if any of my brothers survived, if any other members of the *votum* to Nemesis live. The back of my neck prickles as I feel her attention focused on me, urging me forward.

I am not sure that I could choose not to speak to Anas, even if I wanted to. How much free will do I have anymore? Am I a man or just a sack of meat dancing to the gods' tune?

A bell sounds through the entire building, ringing as if it were right next to me. I startle, surprised by its clarity despite being so far away. There must be some sort of *sonus* relic in the building that channels sound to every room. The unseen pressure increases, forbidding me from resting. It lashes at me like the whip of a teamster at his oxen.

With a sigh, I leap to my feet, jerking my door open at the same moment that the person across the hall from me exits her room. It is the strange woman who walked with the blindfolded man. She is dressed in the same black dress, with her dark hair bound tightly. She eyes me scornfully as I stare openly at her light brown skin. She is stunning—unique. Unlike any other woman in the whole world, or at least in any of the parts that I have been to.

She glares at me with her furious eyes, waiting for me to do something.

"Hello," I say when I can find my voice. "I am Castor." She hisses in frustration and waves dismissively, ordering me to go. Caught off guard, I take a step before realizing it. Her expression hardens as I hesitate. My neck prickles as my divine masters whip me once more, reminding me that I do not have time for this.

"Have a good evening," I tell her, smiling politely and striding down the hall. As much as I want to solve the mystery of the strange woman and her blindfolded companion, she is driven from my mind like a sheep by a shepherd as I approach the kitchen.

The room is set up with a dozen long wooden tables for people to sit at. A row of pots holds warm food for us to collect, which suits me just fine. It is, once again, not too dissimilar from the amenities that we are given at *Domus* Pelias, which makes me laugh again.

We are but bloody servants.

Anas is nowhere to be seen, so I ladle up some warm stew on a mountain of mashed potatoes and seat myself at an empty table. My stomach rumbles with delight, reminding me that I have only had road rations today made up of dried meat and day-old bread. Compared to that, this warm servants' food is a feast.

More gladiators arrive in ones and twos. Some of the lower tiers grumble at the food and accommodations, but I suspect that is more about the reflection of themselves they are seeing than anything else. The Coppers and Blanks sit together. The Golds sit as far apart from each other as they can. My neighbor from across the hall sits near Leon and Obellius, which rankles me for some reason.

Slowly, the room begins to fill up. My table is avoided, whether because of what I did to Leon or because most of them do not know me, I do not know. Two Iron gladiators enter and sit together on the edge of the Blank table, ignoring the younger fighters. Illy enters with Reese, and the pair sit two tables over. For a moment, I am a little hurt, but my feelings are forgotten as Anas slinks into the room.

The former legionnaire ignores me, beelining for the food. A small smile plays at the corner of my mouth. I'm not sure if that's for subterfuge or because soldiers never turn down a hot meal. The big man works his way through the buffet, piling his plate high, totally focused on his choices.

I force myself to keep eating. It's blankly mechanical; my mouth is filled with ashes, my stomach is full of anticipation. In a moment, I will hear the tale of how my brothers died. Dread hovers over me like Thanatos's shade waiting to collect me. I have imagined the deaths of Gaius and Percy a thousand times. In my head, they are heroes, pushing back the Northern horde with their flashing blades. At their side are the rest of our special decade, holding the line until the bitter end.

It is a tragic picture, but beautiful. But the darkness whispers in my mind, reminding me of the truth I have seen. Death is many things, but it is never beautiful. It is savage and hungry. It tears through the worthy and unworthy with the same cold indifference. I fear that in Anas's tale I will have to watch my friends die again, and this version will be even less kind than my dreams.

The big man turns with his loaded plate and makes his way toward me, scanning the room as if looking for a place to sit. The other iron gladiators have no room at their table. Mine is empty, so with a shrug he approaches, unbothered.

"Mind if I sit here?" he grunts, gesturing at one of the empty spaces.

"Suit yourself," I reply in the same disinterested tone, mindful of the ears around us. I turn my attention back to my food. With a nod, he drops to his seat, digging into his dinner with the eagerness of a man used to missing plenty of meals. My heart races as I chew, each bite methodical, practiced. It takes every ounce of my self-control to appear disinterested in my new dining companion.

"Name's Castor," I offer when I finish my bite. "You a *Ferrum*?"

"Anas," he growls, mouth still full. "Obviously." An insane laugh bubbles in my chest, threatening to break free from my mouth. I bow my head, forcing my madness to retreat. He has not yet threatened me with physical violence, but this feels oddly comparable to our first meeting on the road to Agogia.

"What's it like?" I ask after another bite passes.

"What's what like?" An irritated expression flits across his face.

"Iron."

"Hard."

"Obviously." I let my voice fill with the same acerbic tone that he used to answer my first question.

"Not worth it," Anas replies after a long moment. "The price is far too high." Grief gathers at the corners of his eyes like a distant storm. I am struck speechless by the raw emotion that the former *captivus* shows. Can this really be Anas, the violent criminal who threatened to murder me?

What a man Gaius was to be able to make a home for us both.

"I know something about that," I reply softly, daring to let a little of my own pain show in my eyes. He gives me a slow nod before hiding his own sorrow in the blink of an eye. It's gone so fast that I know he must have seized Iron to numb him to the pain. I'm tempted to do the same, but I resist, hearing Pliny's warnings in the back of my mind. Instead, I force my own emotions to obey me, putting them away like a tunic into my closet.

"How—" I begin, but I'm interrupted as two men join the table, glowering at me with untrusting gazes. The other *ferra* have moved to join us.

"This little Silver bothering you?" the skinnier one asks, eyeing me with distaste. Like many who served in the legions, he is marked by scars. A cruel one runs through his cheek, pulling his lip into a perpetual sneer. "He looks like a fat little patrician. I could gut him like a pig."

"Easy, Brennus," the older man I've seen before says, watching me with iron eyes. "We're not allowed to kill the *domus*'s gladiators. As easy as it would be." A thrill runs down my spine. Not of fear, but of joy. Soldiers have a different way of speaking to one another, and it has been far too long since I've heard it.

They are interrupting and talking down to me like I am a civilian. In the Twelfth, there was only one way to respond to a challenge like that, with fists or blades. Iron's arrogance blooms in me, making me sit up straighter. This challenge feels like a forgotten game, and my tormented soul is eager to play.

But that would be foolish.

"Just making friends," I reply, offering a small smile, forcing my own pride to back down. "We're all on the same side here."

"Just because you're a glorified prize fighter with some pretty Symbol doesn't mean we're the same, boy," the older man says without any emotion. "You have no idea what it means to carry Iron in the name of the Empress." Behind him, Anas rolls his eyes as he takes another bite. He never did get along with most officers.

"I believe you," I say honestly. Ancient Frost is terrible and powerful, but it is different. It has more to its being than war. But Iron—iron is for weapons. "Tell me about it."

"Bah." The older man waves my request away with disgust. "It's always something with you patricians. Why can't you just leave the man alone? Pester some old veteran in a tavern if you're so curious about the glories of war. Look for the collar." He taps his own with a finger.

"It seems to me I've got one right here." The insult slips out before I can stop it. It is exactly what I would have said if we were seated next to each other in the mess hall of the Twelfth. His eyes narrow, not in anger but surprise.

"I think you should find a different table. This one's full."

I open my mouth to object, but Anas shakes his head ever so slightly as he puts a piece of bread into his mouth. Heeding my friend's wisdom, I close my mouth and shrug, adopting the patrician persona they expect from me. There will be time to get his story later. As much as the wait will continue to drive me mad.

"Fine by me," I reply, spotting an empty seat next to Illy. "The entertainment was starting to get a little *common*." The skinny legionnaire sneers at me as I lift my plate and make my way across the room to sit with the other Silvers. They look up and make welcoming gestures as I sit.

"There you are," Reese drawls as I take another bite. "I was starting to think you were starting your Golden isolation early."

"What?" I protest with a full mouth. "You guys sat over here without me!"

"You were over in the corner *brooding*." The maned woman laughs at the expression on my face. "You learn to read the body language around here." I frown, worried just how much of my inner emotions I am letting shine through.

"Is that why they're always eating alone?" I ask to distract myself. "What did you call it? 'Golden isolation'? What is that?"

"Just the collective stick that anyone who makes it that high gets stuck up their—" Fannia grumbles, cutting off when we all look at her surprise. "It's true," she asserts, starting to blush under all our attention.

"The *Aurum* Circuit is naturally the most popular of all of them," Illy says, extending a rescue to the smaller woman. "Many people really only pay attention to the results of that one. So many of the gladiators start to feel sure of themselves once they make it to the top of the pyramid."

"Ah." I understand the angle now. "Everyone gets a little bit of fame?"

"Not even real fame. More like a chance to finally earn some." He laughs disparagingly as if every Gold gladiator is a fool. "That's enough for most of them to think they piss gold and sweat flowers."

"I thought it was because they all end up fighting each other in the end," I admit, looking at the two Golds in the room with new appreciation.

"Well, that's part of it," Reese agrees, her mouth full of potatoes. "But they all think they're unbeatable. The ego protects them. They just want to be the Flamma of their generation."

"Or Crixus," Illy offers.

She points a finger of acknowledgment at him before continuing. "Besides, gladiators from the same *domus* may compete, but they're not supposed to kill each other. That would be rather devastating if the most powerful team was forced to kill itself off every season."

"Ah, of course." I can almost hear Briannus counting his coins as he spins the stories of the gladiators still trapped in the arena, hoping to win the *aurum* Circuit this year. No wonder it was the one people paid the most attention to.

"Well, you can relax," I tell Reese with a smile. "I have no fame and no prospects of gathering any." The three of them exchange glances before bursting into laughter. Their humor is so loud, it draws irritated glances from the tables around us—even the Blanks.

"Oh, dead gods, you're serious, aren't you?" Reese asks, holding a hand over her mouth to keep from spraying food as she laughs.

"I take it back." Illy chuckles brightly. "You had *terrible* magisters."

"What?" I protest, looking between the three laughing Silvers. Even normally dour Fannia is struggling to contain herself.

"You can manifest ice swords as a *Silver*," Reese says as if I am an idiot. Perhaps I am. I certainly feel like one. "You're going to be famous the moment you walk into that arena."

Stunned, I stare at the empty space in the center of the table around us. I have grown used to my ability and forgotten the look on the Censors' faces when they tested me. Briannus offered Varus fifty thousand *denarii* for me. Why would he do that unless I was something he could turn into even more money? The tall consul is a strange man, but he is not stupid. She's right. I've never heard of anyone being able to do what I can do, especially as an *argentum*. Aquilo's gift has made me a freak.

In a little less than two weeks, when I step into the ring for the first time, my life is going to change.

CHAPTER 17

Anas and the other *ferrum gladiators* leave shortly after I switch tables. The three former soldiers stalk out the front without speaking to any of the other gladiators. Anas shoots me a look over his shoulder before nodding down at his hands.

I follow the motion to see his right hand curled in the shorthand gesture for two hours that Percy taught us when he scouted with us. I blink twice in agreement, then he is gone. I spend some time with my fellow Silvers, laughing with them as the hour grows dark.

The majordomo returns with a pair of servants carrying two large flagons of wine, and we cheer as they pour us strong cups. "From the senator," he announces. Contessa lurks by the door like a proctor, watching the proceedings with a dry amusement but offers no protest as her fighters begin to drink.

"The senator!" we roar in delight. *There are perks to being a gladiator over a soldier,* I muse as I sip at the delightful red. For a moment, I am neither; instead, I am home, in the house of my father. Evander loved wine; he collected it with rabid interest. My grandfather's cellar was full to the brim with his favorites. I wonder if the Praetorians looted it before they burned it down. Father would like this one; I am sure of it. He'd probably call it "summery" and ask me about flavors I can never taste.

"Wow, she didn't give us the cheap stuff," Illy remarks over the rim of his cup. "She must really want to bed Varus."

"What?" I gasp, choking on my own sip.

"Oh, come on, now you're just playing dumb."

It's deep into the night when I finally leave the kitchen with the rest of the Silvers. Fannia has an arm thrown over Illy's shoulder like a brother as we walk toward the fourth floor. "We should go to die in the arena more often!" she crows. Some of the joy seeps from our little group as we remember what the cost of this largesse is. The bill is coming due—it just goes to the butcher, not the banker.

"Sorry." She gasps, desperately trying to bring the laughter back. But it is broken, like a vase that has shattered and cannot be put back together. We are somber and silent as we part ways for our rooms. My head is light, but I have had less to drink than my companions. Unlike them, I still have things I need to do tonight.

"Sleep well," Reese calls after me. I shake my head as I slip into my room. I need to focus. The danger has not passed. It will never pass again as long as I live. Tonight, I will get answers. I have no window to check *Luna*'s progress, but I know the time is coming.

I force myself to wait patiently, tracking the passage of time as Percy taught us. I should be late. It would be suspicious if we were seen leaving together. Five minutes pass like an eon. It is still too soon, I count again, feeling Sisyphus repeating his endless task.

At last, I can bear it no longer. I leap to my feet and race to the door. I open it, half expecting to find my neighbor waiting for me. But the strange, dark-haired woman is not present. I am grateful for her absence; I can bear no more burdens.

I make my way to the front of the building, pleased to see that it isn't under guard. Contessa trusts us to a point. I have no doubt that anyone who breaks a rule will be punished until they are bloody. Even if that is me, it will have been worth it.

I follow the path from the servant's quarters toward the main courtyard, staring at the cold eye of *Luna*. It is past the time that we were to meet. Anas should be waiting for me; I just have to find him. I'm halfway to the carriages when something glints on the dark ground. My eyes dart to a stone that has been scraped by the edge of a knife. Two thin lines run parallel to the ground. An arrow caps the end of one, pointing to the path. A smile blooms on my face as I see another one of Percy's tricks. I bend over to brush my fingers over the face of the stone, greeting it like it is my lost friend.

"I will see you again someday," I whisper, knowing that is not true if Charon and Thanatos are dead. How can anyone ever make it to Hades without someone to ferry them there? But the lie makes me feel better, and I know that he will never hear it.

Trusting Anas, I break off the path, heading in the opposite direction that his arrow points. It was a simple trick, but one of my favorites. In the wild, a single mistake can be enough time for a scout to escape without notice. We always put our arrows facing the wrong way in case the Normans found them, so they would waste their time chasing ghosts.

I make my way through the thick grass in the dark, looking for a sign that I am on the right track. Just when I begin to fear that I missed his mark, I see it—carved into the base of a tree. This time, I follow the arrow's direction. Percy's logic was that if they figured out our trick, undoing it would fool them a second time. I don't know if it ever worked, but it made the centurion chuckle, and that was a good enough reason for me.

I head into a dark copse of trees, which sends a tremor of fear down my spine as I step under their dark embrace. It reminds me of the last time I ventured into such a place, far north of here. My hand drops to my hip, but there is no *gladius* hanging there. I feel naked, despite wearing better clothing than I have in months.

Slowly, I make my way through the darkness, feeling my way with my foot as I take each step. In the distance, I can just barely make out a light dancing through the foliage. Faint music dances toward me in the night. Something is wrong. I seize Iron, sweeping out with my *animus*, searching through the murk around me.

I have just enough time to sense a *gladius* sweeping toward me from behind. I let out a grunt of surprise, twisting and reaching out with my hand to grab my assailant's wrist.

The man lowers his shoulder and rams into me, driving me back with incredible force. My back bounces off the trunk of a tree, and I gasp for air as much of my breath is driven out of my lungs. The sword sweeps back for another attack, this time a diagonal slash that will open me from shoulder to hip.

I duck, trusting the darkness to protect me better than any shield, waiting until the blade bites into the wood with a hearty *thunk*.

My attacker lets out a curse of surprise as I leap up, grabbing him by the neck and twisting his head, forcing him to the side. He staggers and it's my turn to shove him into a tree. I draw back my fist but stop as Anas laughs in delight.

"It is you!"

"What?" I hiss in stunned disbelief. "Of course it's me. Who else can read Percy's stupid arrows?" Slowly, I release my grip on his shoulders, realizing that he isn't going to attack me anymore.

"I had to be sure." Anas slides to the ground in a groan, and after a moment, I join him, leaning against another part of the same trunk. "It's too dangerous."

"You know my face," I protest. "We were in the Twelfth together. I know you never liked me, but why in Dead Mars's name did you just try to stab me?"

"You're *uninhibited*," he interrupts, leaning forward to look at me in the gloom. "You are uninhibited but still attuned to Iron. You're free." His voice is full of awe. "I had to be sure."

I'm silent for a moment, realizing how strange this must be to him. I have had time to come to terms with what I am, but the members of the Twelfth perished before I truly understood what I was becoming. Anas has seen me summon the *Glacialis Falx*, but that was merely the first step down the path.

"Yes," I murmur into the darkness. "It's really me." We sit in that companionable silence for a long moment, listening to the faint strains of the senator's entertainment playing their hearts out. It is healing to keep watch in the night with my legion-brother once more. All my questions, all my thoughts retreat for a moment, so I can hold this precious thing one last time.

But at last, as all things must, it comes to an end. A bout of laughter echoes from the party beyond, shaking me from my communion with ghosts. Saturn may be dead, but time still moves. It will only be so long before we must part again.

"How did you survive?" I ask, sitting forward to fix the man with my most intense stare. He is merely a shadowy outline, but I cannot look away. "Did you get swept in the avalanche?"

"No," he says softly, as if choking back tears. "I was further behind you and the rest, fighting the *berserkir* that I pushed out of the way."

My mind flashes back to that battle as if I am still there. The wind races past me as Aquilo's rampaging storm howls behind us. Anas tackles the *berserkir*, opening a path for me to charge at Astrid with Marcus and Felix.

"That Norman panicked and ran the moment the ground started rumbling. I chased him toward our line, which took me out of the path of the avalanche. He saved my life." Anas's voice twists grimly. "I still took his." I pat him on the shoulder, unsure how to console him. Not when I was the one who drew the beast that triggered it.

"Once the pass was blocked, there was nothing to do but stand and fight. Gaius had us holding the narrow entrance so they couldn't all push us at once, but they had too many *furiae*, and we didn't have enough *venator* relics to bring them down. Eventually, they smashed through our line, and then the real killing started."

I shudder in rage and shame at the thought of not being there with them.

"Those Marius brothers," Anas's gravelly voice is tinted with awe as he continues his story. "Never seen anything like it. They tore through the Normans like they were gods." The outline of his face turns toward me.

"Is that what you are like now?"

"Maybe one day," I scoff, hoping he will continue his tale. "I have much to learn before I can claim to be like Gaius."

"Huh," he grunts in agreement. "After enough of those *berserkirs* got past them, the barbarians started cutting through the Twelfth. The snow was red. It was *so* red." He takes a shaky breath.

"We knew we were dead, but we did not break. We may have been men of the Twelfth, but by Mars's Bones, I swear to you we stood to the end. Every last man held the line, and we made them pay for each step with oceans of blood." He lets out a long exhale, gathering himself. "But at last, there weren't enough men to fill the gaps. Something hit me from behind. I never saw what, but from the bruise, I think it was one of those damned *furia*. When I awoke, I was chained to a line of survivors in similar condition."

"How many of us survived?" I ask, delighted to hear there were more.

"A score, maybe a little more." His voice does not share my joy.

"Did you see Clintus or any of the others?" I demand. "Did any of the decade survive?" Suddenly, I am not a gladiator anymore, but an officer of the legions, worrying about my men.

“I didn’t.” He shakes his head. “Most of us were rank-and-file men from the cohort.”

“But not all?” My heart skips a beat as the man hesitates, afraid to tell me something that I can already guess.

“Castor, the tribune was in chains.”

Gaius lives. A thousand emotions surge through me before they come crashing down. Something in the heavy set of my friend’s shoulders hints that there’s more to the story, and it is not one that I will enjoy.

“Tell me.”

“The Norman bastards gave him to the Imperials that were with them. They took him away, and I never saw him again.” I feel only the cold grip of fear, deeper than even the chill of Ancient Frost.

In the dungeon, I spent a lot of time thinking about the mysterious women who waited upon Knut. What had they been doing there, working with the enemies of the Empire? They knew Gaius, not only by reputation but personally, and he had recognized at least one of them. Tullia, he had named her.

A long moment of painful silence stretches between us.

“The others?”

“They marched us back to their camp and sold us off one-by-one to slavers that came to trade. Some caravans went even further North. I was lucky that mine came South.”

“Why didn’t you break free? Tell people who you are?”

“Haven’t you heard? The North is besieged. The Lion is out of favor in the court of the Empress. He has accused General Tyrus of deliberately leaving him under-supplied and exposed. None of the other legions have been sent to reinforce Frigidus.” The big man shakes his head. “I figured if I started making some noise, I’d wake up to find I cut my own wrists.”

Tyrus. The general of Agogia who sent us to die in the North. My hands curl into fists as I remember his cold face. Like Atticus, he has taken a family from me. When I have finished with the Censor, I will look for him to repay him for what he has done.

“Enough stalling. How is it that you became uninhibited? How are you free?”

I am silent for a moment, gathering my thoughts. It seems darker now that it is time for me to share my secrets. How much should I trust Anas? Once we were enemies, but we have been forged into brothers. Already, he holds my life in his hands. Why should he not hold the rest of it? I never got the chance to tell Marcus or Felix the whole truth. He is as close as I will ever get to fixing that mistake.

"You remember in the cave," I say without question. "You remember what we found in the depths after we killed the *necromanta*?"

"The crypt of Aquilo, aye. How could I forget?"

"Before we ever went to that place, I had already been bound to the ice that comes from there."

"Bound? The same way you're bound to Iron?" It's too dark to see, but I can feel his eyes turn toward the white lines of my *rasa* veins.

"Yes, after I was attuned to Iron, I also found my way to Ancient Frost."

"Dead gods protect us," he whispers in horror. I snort in derision. I tell him everything. My stolen hearts. Atticus and his lies. The murder of my family. The *votum* first with Nemesis, then with Aquilo. The storm that turned on us.

How I Ascended.

"Jupiter's Ashes." He sighs, leaning back against our tree in shock. "If I did not know you, I would call you a madman and a liar. But I was there when you wore the *inhibitus* the same as me. I saw the cold wind that you brought." He pauses before turning to look at me. "They will kill you for this."

"They'll try," I agree softly.

He laughs—it is a soldier's laugh, dry and humorless.

"What are the odds that it is you and I here at the last?" he asks after a moment. "There were nights when I dreamed of cutting your throat while you slept." He is not joking.

"And there were nights I didn't sleep because I worried about the same thing."

Anas grunts in acceptance, but not apology. I don't think he's ever felt contrite a day in his life. "Yet now here we are, back-to-back against the tide."

"Do you mean that?" Despite his harsh demeanor, I'm touched by the former *captivus*'s words. He's not a man prone to flowery language. Somehow that makes his declaration mean more than it might from another.

"Gaius was a palatine, but he bled for me, for the plebeian under his command. Percy too. Way I see it, I'm their man until I repay the debt."

I'm silent for a moment, considering that. I may be patrician, the middle class of the Iron Empire, but I feel the same way about the Marius brothers and what they did.

"You bled for me and mine too." I extend my hand toward him. "It goes both ways, Legionnaire." Anas studies my arm in the murky dark for a long moment. I wonder what thoughts are rushing through his brain. Have I made a mistake in trusting him this far?

"Do you know why I hated you when we first got to Agogia? I thought you were like *them*." He doesn't specify who he means, but I know he means the wealthy sons in the higher legions. "Some rich son who was being sent down to slum among the poors until he learned his lesson. You were already Ironbound before you got there. That only screams of being elite. Then you excelled where we all struggled. When they made you *Primus*, I was so sure."

"You weren't the only one." I laugh, remembering Gaius's accusations.

"But then they killed Macer."

My smile dies, doused by the memory of the first casualty of the Fourth Cohort.

"They murdered him, and no one was angrier than you—not even me. You were like Gaius's stormy shadow, barely able to restrain yourself. That's when I knew you weren't what I thought."

"I am going to kill Brennus Valerus," I whisper into the night, a promise that is more to myself than it is to the big man.

"Not if I kill him first." A strangely companionable silence builds between us, two unlikely allies, forged in the same fires.

"How did you end up in the Twelfth, Anas?" The big man doesn't answer right away. I wonder if I have broken the fragile peace that we have built. I know much of his character, I have stood shoulder-to-shoulder with him on a battlefield, but there is much about my last companion that is a mystery. But then he laughs, and my concern about crossing his boundary evaporates.

"It was always inevitable, I suppose," he says at last. "Father was a drunk, Mother was a prostitute. Ran to live on the streets as soon as I could; it was safer. Was begging by the time I was eight, cutting purses before I turned ten. After that, it only got worse." I'm silent, trying to imagine being born into circumstances like that.

I am no palatine—my family's fields are barely a drop in the ocean of the Pelias wealth. But compared to what Anas was given, my childhood home might as well have been set in Diana's palace. What would I have become if I had been forced to fight for my existence from the moment I was born?

"Some of the gang I ran with got the bright idea to rob an Imperial courier wagon. I wasn't even a part of it, but it was carrying a portion of the Census itself." I wince at that. The Censor's official count of the populace is among their most jealously guarded secrets. I can imagine how strong the response to such a theft was.

"Next thing I know, I'm rounded up along with another score of street rats. Half of us didn't even do the Mercury-damned thing. But the Censors were out for blood. We're sentenced *en masse*, and I got two options: rot in a prison or bleed in the legions."

"And you chose to go to Agogia?" I ask in surprise.

"Mars's Rotting Beard, no!" He laughs in scorn. "I knew what happened to the lads that got marched off to the Twelfth. Spent three years as a *captivus* before I couldn't handle it anymore. My mind was gonna crack if I stayed in that place another week. Took the service even though it meant restarting my sentence. Then the first thing I see is a bunch of pretty patricians coming to play at being a soldier."

"There was no playing," I assure him.

"Know that now."

The silence between us is more comfortable now. The airing of secrets has a way of smoothing out even the most unlikely of relationships. Despite his past, I trust Anas more than any other living soul. I know his mettle, and he knows mine.

And more importantly, I know that he wants what I do. "We will get our revenge. But it will take time—and be dangerous." He knows this, but I feel the need to say it. I have led too many down paths that have gotten them killed to do so blindly any longer.

"What's the worry?" Anas chuckles after a moment. "You and I are already dead. Thanatos is just late."

"Might as well spend that time doing something with it."

"You have a plan." It is not a question.

"Blood for blood."

He pauses for a moment, considering my words. "How?"

"First—" I cut myself short as something ripples across my awareness like a fish disturbing the surface of a still pond. I twist sharply, staring off into the dark as I send my *animus* out around us once again. A dozen sets of iron lurk around us—we are discovered.

I freeze, waiting for the guards to accost us, already dreading Contessa's probing questions. They will see that the brand on my chest matches the one on Anas's, and it will only be a matter of time before they uncover our secrets.

The former *captivus* does not speak, but I feel him grow tense. He may not have a Silver's ability to sense Iron around us, but he can feel the danger radiating off me. He responds to my tension in kind, shifting slowly as he prepares to leap to his feet.

The bits of iron around us are not moving. Instead, they are still, waiting for something. For a moment I think they are spying on us, waiting to see if we will divulge more secrets. But the longer I study them, the more I begin to suspect something else is afoot.

Each of them carries a pair of short swords. Knives and smaller blades are tucked along their bodies in belts and boots. None of them wear *lorica* or any armor that I can feel.

These are not retired legion guards, or even the active-duty ones that the senator has keeping watch over her front door. This is a different kind of danger. *Sicarii*—assassins. My head turns toward the distant light that shines through the hedges. The music still plays, wafting through the evening.

They are not here for us.

I lower my right hand and bump it against Anas's thigh, making the sign for *danger* that Percy taught us back on the ice. I do not know if he can translate it by touch, but he takes my meaning all the same. I scan the gloom, looking for the threat, but I see nothing. The hair on my arms begins to stand on end as I remember what Reese can do with her Symbol.

Abruptly, the forwardmost pair of swords moves, striding toward the gathering where Delilah hosts Varus and the rest of the worthies. "Kill the spares," a voice hisses from the dark as the rest follow like loyal hounds.

There is no reply, but two pairs of swords turn, angling toward us, while the other ten head toward the garden party. "Ware! Enemies in the night!" I scream, like a legionnaire on watch. I leap to my feet, leaving Anas to retrieve his blade from the tree.

"East and west," I shout, positioning myself toward one side, letting him stand at my back to cover the other. Both pairs of swords pause, surprised by my knowledge. As one, they begin to circle, hunting us like sharks. I twist, following the one to the south, letting Anas shift to watch the north.

"I don't see anything," Anas growls, holding his blade at the ready.

"Trust me." I do not want them to know how I am tracking them. If they drop their weapons, I will be as blind as my companion. Behind me, the Northern assailant charges, blades spreading for a strike.

"Forward stab!" I roar, back in the legions once more.

"Huah!" Anas shouts in reflex, taking a step forward and jabbing his blade out at stomach height. His attacker meets the attack easily enough, but that is a mistake. He is not Ironbound. He was not made in the forges of Agogia.

The short sword shatters as Anas's will crushes it with ease.

For four hundred years, the Iron Legions have carved through the enemies of the empire with ease. Tonight, this *sicarus* learns why. The *ferrum* gladiator's blade continues forward, unbothered by the interference of the now broken blade.

Anas's attacker screams in pain as my friend drives the sword home, burying it in his gut to the hilt. Now that my friend has his hands on his attacker, he does not let go. He grapples the assassin, carrying him to the ground, ripping his blade free.

I cannot help but be impressed that the second invisible man does not panic. He correctly understands that I am the problem. If I am dead, Anas will not be able to track him and will be easy to kill, even if the gladiator is Ironbound. Unfortunately for him, he seems to think that the fact that I am unarmed means that I will be an easy target.

He surges forward, invisible to my naked eye, but his iron betrays him. He thinks it is loyal to him because he holds it in his hands, but it whispers his secrets to me in the dark like an unfaithful lover. He leads with his left blade, angled low to disembowel me.

I twist, extending my right hand while calling on Ancient Frost's power. The *Glacialis Falx* blooms in my hand, the *crack* of growing ice hidden under the sounds of leaves crunching beneath my feet. I do not try to summon anything other than a *gladius*. Tonight, that is exactly what I need it to be.

My left hand shoots out, grabbing my assailant's leading wrist easily, even though I cannot see him. With a grunt, I step forward, headbutting him right where I think his face should be. The world spins for a second as my skull collides with his, but my *Cor* constitution shrugs off the discomfort. My attacker staggers back a few steps, flickering into view as he loses his concentration on his Symbol. I follow, frozen blade rising for the kill.

He takes longer to recover than me. I do not think he is a Silver; he seems weak and slow. His right sword curves toward me, and I block it without thought, reinforcing the ice in my weapon with my will. As my blade connects with his, I feel as Iron and Ancient Frost mingle and then become one, fused by their union with me.

With a thought, I cut through his weapon like butter, slicing it in half. The assassin must have had a good teacher—he recovers quickly, striking at me with his other blade, but it is too late. No amount of training could make him able to kill someone like me. I twist, letting the blade shoot past me, bringing my own sword back in a horizontal cut across his stomach.

The man drops to his knees in shock. I feel his short sword clatter to the ground as it drops from his numb hands. For a moment, we stare at each other, alone in the world. He is dressed in all black, covered in it from head to toe. A mask hides his face, and a hood covers his head. Only a pair of wide eyes stare out at me from the shadow.

"Please," he whispers after a dozen heartbeats. I nod, understanding what he is asking. I drive the point of my weapon through his chest. It is a mercy; I doubt even a Gold *electus* would be able to heal the damage that I had inflicted on him, but he would take time to die. He topples over, and I turn away from his body as Anas rises from the ground, his own opponent lying visible and still at his feet.

"Mercury's Rotting Balls, what was that?" he growls, sweeping his gaze around the dark copse, looking for more threats. "What did they want?"

"They weren't here for us," I tell him grimly, turning to look at the light of the senator's party. "We were just witnesses."

In the distance, the music still plays, oblivious of the death that is coming.

CHAPTER 18

"With me!" I order, rushing past the stunned gladiator and racing toward that distant light.

"Where are you going?" Anas demands as he follows in my footsteps, cursing as he kicks a root sticking out of the ground.

"They went this way, to the party."

"Seems like a great reason to *not* go that way," he points out. I slow, turning to look at him in the dark. The inky blackness seems less absolute now, as if the *sicarii* had been pulling the light out of everything around us.

"Why should we die for senators? I would have thought you were tired of that by now." I purse my lips, considering his point. I cast a slow glance over my shoulder, looking at the distant party with a critical eye.

"He's a good man."

"So was Gaius. So was Percy."

"He's someone who can make things better than they are."

Anas is silent for a moment, surprised by my argument. Guilt coils within me, a treacherous, poisonous serpent. I am not certain if that is true. Varus is certainly no lush pansy like the members of the *Argentum Consilium*, but that is a small thing. I am not sure if I believe what I say or if I am once more an officer, saying whatever I need to get my men to hold fast in the front lines.

"We need him," I say at last, finding an avenue that is less conflicting to my heart.

"Need him? For what?"

"If we win the Games, they make us citizens and set us free."

"If we win the Aren—do you hear yourself?" Anas is so furious that he interrupts himself. "You're talking about the dead-gods-damned Mars's Arena. The bloodiest fighting pit in the Empire."

"Yes," I say, turning my back on him and racing toward the party. "I am." Anas curses me for a fool, but I can't help but smile as I hear him race to follow in my footsteps. It is not the first time he has followed me through a dark wood.

A hedge grows along the edge of the trees, separating the grounds from a more private garden that Delilah keeps for entertaining. The music still plays, which gives me hope that we are not too late.

I slash with my frozen sword like a woodsman clearing a path, leaping through the hedge with a mighty crash. Anas follows through the hole I make, swearing loudly. The violins grind to a screeching halt as we emerge, stunned by our entrance. A woman screams in fear at the bloody weapon in my grasp.

A dozen palatine nobles turn to regard us, with expressions ranging from embarrassment to terror. We stand in the middle of the beautiful garden we were led through earlier. Beyond it stands a terraced fountain. Meticulously trimmed plants hang from the structure and surround it on all sides. A large bronze basin carved with the faces of the gods burns with the everflame just beyond the seated nobles. Throughout the entire setting, a horde of fireflies swirl around the party like shooting stars. I have enough time to wonder how they have been gathered before my gaze lands on Varus and Delilah.

The two senators are seated on a pair of *lecti*, the reclining couches popular for eating with the elite. They're dressed in beautiful white togas. Contessa hovers over our master's shoulder and looks at me with the expression of a furious parent trying to control their child in front of her grandparents.

I ignore the *lanista*'s warning glare, instead casting my gaze around the now silent party. Anas swears again, quieter this time. I see Pliny sitting with three other people who seem like magisters. He gives me a solemn look. Alessandra is not far from them with a pair of young men I do not recognize.

"What is the meaning of this interruption?" Delilah demands, rising to her feet, wine chalice still in hand. Her words are slurred with the fuzziness of someone who has journeyed far into their cups. A pair of her legionnaire guards separate themselves from the hedge walls, heading toward us with grim, professional expressions.

"To arms!" I shout. "We are under attack!" I raise my bloody sword to emphasize my point, shaking it in front of the palatine partygoers. The same woman lets out another moan of concern, but everyone ignores her. Varus watches from his seat, expression unreadable. His gaze flicks from me to Anas, measuring us.

"Attack?" One of the young men sitting next to Alessandra rises to his feet, giving me an arrogant stare. "I see no enemies, only you. It seems more likely that you have done something evil, slave. Have you killed one of Senator Delilah's servants?"

"They cannot be seen, idiot," I snap. The young man's face burns red with rage. I push out with my *animus*, sensing for the iron that the cloaked ones carry. I can feel them, lurking along the edges of the party, watching. We are surrounded. I turn back to my master, pleading with him for his trust. I feel like a performing fool, pleading before the invaders' watching eyes.

"They are here even now." Still, despite my performance, they do not attack. Perhaps they wait to see if the partygoers will blind themselves further. The other palatines shift their attention to the older senator, waiting to see how he will handle his out-of-control gladiator. Varus lifts his chalice and takes a sip, calm and unperturbed.

"Go back to your quarters, Castor," he says in a heavy tone. "Contessa will deal with you both." The legionnaires still approach but have slowed their march, watching us with wary eyes. A *sicarus* moves behind them, hiding in the shadows. One angles toward my back. The wolves are beginning to circle the nest. By the time anyone believes me, it will be too late.

Another stalks toward Alessandra and the two young men. For a heartbeat, the cold in me wants to do nothing. Let them reap the reward for not trusting me. I warned them—this ruin is their own doing. Then something powerful shifts within me, like a fist grabbing my *Cor* in its hand and beginning to squeeze. The oathrod's power twists my insides as it enacts the vow that I made to Varus only a few weeks ago. *I will uphold the honor of my House.* Apparently, my Heart thinks that means protecting it from assassination too.

If no one will believe my words, then there is only one avenue left to me—action. With a furious snarl, I hunch my shoulders and surge toward Alessandra and the pompous young lords. Perhaps to his credit, the one who rebuked me steps between us, attempting to shield her from my ire.

I ignore him; the pack of palatines is not my true target. The wolf that lurks in my shadow follows me as I move, coming in close. He thinks that he is safe because he does not understand what I am. I follow his choreography like a dancer, spinning backward into a lunge.

As I turn, I hold my right hand up at throat level and call upon Ancient Frost, twisting my weapon like I have a thousand times in the training arena. My *gladius* shifts, crackling as the icy sword grows into the longer form of a dueling blade. My sword's sharp edge passes through thin air in a spray of blood as it slices the foolish wolf that thought I was a sheep. Another figure dressed in black flickers into view, a woman this time, her hands wrapped around her throat as she tries to hold her neck together.

I take a sort of satisfaction from the palatine screams of horror that echo as the would-be assassin falls to her knees. But there is no time to gloat. My vow compels me to act. Darkness floods the party, drowning out the light like the coming of a fell storm.

I close my eyes, letting Iron guide me. I summon a second frozen blade in my left hand as I race toward Varus and Delilah in the center of the garden, where the wolves now sprint. A *sicarus* leaps toward me from the side, their weapons blazing to my mind like beacons in the dark.

I block their first strike with my right, turning to slash with my left. They counter, driving me back a step with the force of their parry. I feel my bones rattle with every blow. The other assassins may have been Coppers, but this one is not! I gasp in shock as my sword is almost wrenched from my grip by a heavy overhanded smash.

We dance for a few seconds, precious time as the rest of his pack ravages the unsuspecting partygoers. I cannot afford to let this assassin delay me. I can feel the battle raging all around me as blades move. It's growing harder to distinguish which iron is friend and which is foe. The darkness that surrounds us is overbearing.

My opponent presses his advantage, wielding his strength like a club. He's not only stronger than I am but faster too. I try to strike past him, but he only redoubles his aggression, forcing me to stay on my back foot. He reminds me of a *furia*—my assault does not drive him back even a single step.

I can feel the ice of my swords cracking under the power of his blows. I grit my teeth, pouring my will into reinforcing them. The frozen blades act as essence sources, allowing me to refill some of my Ancient Frost from their presence, but I am losing it faster than I can replenish it.

I am going to die. I do not know what his Symbol is—something in the *domus* of Shadow, probably. But it does not matter, because his body is better than mine. If he is a Silver, then he must be close to the peak of what we can be. I cannot overcome his strength, and I cannot seem to come up with a plan to outsmart him.

I fall back another pace as he crashes into me. I retreat another and stumble as my foot misses the step of the stairs behind me. I may be able to sense Iron, but Stone is silent to me.

I stagger, trying to find my balance, but the crafty *sicarus* lunges forward, ramming me with his shoulder. Blind and disoriented, I fall, flailing in the air like a bird pushed from its nest. My lower back slams into something hard and metal, tearing a scream of pain from my lips as I tilt over the lip of the giant bronze brazier and into the everflame that burns there.

It's hot.

The fire burns, tearing at me like it is from the depths of Hades. I drop my swords into the basin, hoping the water will extinguish the inferno that rages around me. But as the steam hisses, the flames only seem to grow, as if my attempt to put it out has angered this remnant of the gods.

Even now, I still cannot see—the unnatural shadow hangs over the garden like a cloud, obscuring my sight. I cling to Iron and Ancient Frost, but their chill only makes the flames that tear at me seem hotter. I'm screaming, I know I am, but I cannot hear it over the roar.

It feels alive, this fire. It swirls over me, rabid and hungry, seeking a way in to burn me from the inside out. Only my Silver body keeps me alive. If I did not have my *Cor*, I would already be ash. It sweeps over me in waves, a relentless, hungry presence. This flame is ancient in its own way. It has burned for centuries and has not gone out. But no matter how fiercely it rages, I refuse to be consumed. We are kindred spirits, unwilling to surrender.

Let me in, it demands.

I cling to my Symbols like shields, hiding behind them to numb my pain.

Let me in.

I will survive this. My story does not end here. I have not yet fulfilled my *votum* to Nemesis. My father's killer still draws breath. The gods are not done with me. Blindly, I flail inside the bronze brazier, trying to find a way out.

Let me in. The fire thunders against my defenses. Ancient Frost melts and fails against its natural predator. Iron tries to protect me from the onslaught, but it, too, is susceptible to the unrelenting heat. Is not a *gladius* forged in the flames? My defenses shatter, my will snaps, and the inferno pours into me, hungry to devour.

I burn from the inside out.

Heat fills my every extremity in a flash; I am melted and reforged. Now I truly feel the fire, as my body and it become one. In my chest, my *Corda* twist and move, making space for a new reserve that fills with an essence that is wild and unruly. An insane strain pulls at me as my body tries to tear itself apart from the inside out. I inhale, grabbing air to scream one last time before I am consumed. But before I can cry out, the everflame goes out as if snatched by the wind.

I am reborn in a bronze basin. Only I and the ash remain of the fire that once burned to guide wayward souls home. I run, shaking hands over my body checking for burns but find none. My skin is whole. The flames tried to consume me, but they could not, for they found that we burn with the same heat.

My *Cor* Hearts struggle with each other, trying to contain a new essence that rebels against the cool temperature of its other prison mates. I burned through most of the reserves of my original Symbols trying to survive the inferno, and now they are dwarfed by the interloper. Unlike Iron or Ancient Frost, Unrelenting Fire does not make me calm or logical—it rages.

And so do I.

I reach a shaking hand up to the lip of the bronze brazier and grab it, levering myself to my feet. The metal is cool to my touch, or perhaps I am the same temperature as it. I vault out of the basin over the lip, staggering to the side as I try to force the antithetical forces within me to behave. There is no sign of the man who fed me to the flames; I have lost him in the fight that my iron senses tell me still rages around me.

I stagger toward the nearest weapon I can feel, snatching an iron *gladius* from the ground. It must have belonged to one of Delilah's legionnaires, which does not bode well for how the battle is going. I feel an immediate sense of relief as some of the iron essence flows into me, helping to stabilize my *Corda* in their struggle against each other.

My *animus* shows me a Shadowbound before me who wields two shortswords and stabs them downward, presumably to finish off one of the partygoers. Rage bubbles up inside me, and I lunge forward, gutting the *sicarus* from behind.

I rip my *gladius* free, letting the assassin drop bonelessly to the ground beside his victim. The fire within me only grows hotter. I stalk forward, shoulders hunched like some primal hunter. A legionnaire clatters to the floor, his *lorica* like a beacon in the darkness. His dropped *gladius* bounces in my direction, and I scoop it up without looking.

The two *sicarii* that laid him low turn to face me, their shortswords painting the direction of their gazes like arrows. I snarl, increasing the length of my stride to close with them faster. My foot bounces off a hard object that I cannot see, causing me to stumble. I am still mostly blind in this manifested murk.

To my surprise, the two interlopers withdraw a pace, as if studying me. They know that my sense of them is not perfect, and they wonder what betrays them. These are not frontline fighters like legionnaires or gladiators. They do their best work in the dark, true scavengers. I have killed enough of their comrades to make them wary.

I pursue them again, moving in shuffling steps to keep my footing like Percy taught me. Confidence burns in me like a beacon, lit by the fire I carry. I have been hunted by *berserkirs* in the pitch black of the great forests of the North. I am much stronger now than I was then. The two assassins retreat further, separating like wolves to circle me. More screams echo in the gardens as the rest of their comrades continue their grim work.

I turn to keep one in front of me while moving my other *gladius* to track the other in a sharp threat. There is no hiding from me. At least there wasn't, until as one, the *sicarii* drop their shortswords, letting them clatter against the paved stones of the garden. Their daggers follow a heartbeat later, stripping them of any trace of iron.

I grit my teeth, forcing myself not to react in fear as my awareness of them vanishes in the unnatural murkiness that surrounds us. Mercury's Rotting Beard! They're clever. My heart hammers in my chest as terror blooms. My colder Symbols excel at helping me keep my emotions under control, but Unrelenting Fire feeds them.

I continue my turn in the direction the *sicarus* on my right was moving, gambling that he continued that way even after dropping his weapons. It's a blind guess, but my only hope is to make them uncertain if their guess on my ability was correct. If I panic and flee, they will be on me before I make it a dozen steps.

The whisper of a foot on stone behind me is the only warning that I get as the Shadowbound warrior strikes. My left wrist explodes with pain, and I curse as my *gladius* is sent flying from my numb fingers. But as my attacker's fist meets my flesh, a strange sensation blooms between us.

My senses flood into him over the brief moment of contact, as my warmth merges with his. My opponent's form flares in my mind, painted in shades of red, mapping the heat of his body. I'm so startled by the knowledge, I fail to strike back at the assassin before the moment is gone, and he vanishes once we are no longer touching.

Unrelenting Fire is the key. All living things are warm; all I need to do is seek that heat, and my Symbol will deliver these fools to me. I reach inside myself, hoping to feed my newest essence to my *animus* and send it sweeping out around me, but it will not budge. It feels like an ancient foundation stone, buried in the earth and unmovable. My victory turns to ash in my mouth as I realize my mistake.

My new Heart has not Ascended—the *Cor* that is attuned to the Unrelenting Fire has merely gone from *rasa* to Copper. I am once more bound by the limitations of the first tier of being an *electus*. I cannot see or affect anything related to fire unless I am touching it.

There's a sound to my right as a foot crunches on a leaf. I twist, striking out with my *gladius* blindly, but it slices through only air. A fist connects with my exposed stomach, driving me back a handful of paces. Another heat-filled vision of my opponent flares in my mind before it is gone.

If only I could make this knowledge last! The two assassins grow more confident as they circle me. Bit by bit, they will wear me down until I am unarmed and exhausted. I scream in frustrated rage, flailing through the murky dark with my blade, but I only wound the wind, and this is not the wind that I have sworn to kill.

I am back on the mountain pass, in the snow. Death hovers behind me, cruel Thanatos with his scythe waits to reap my soul, if I indeed even have one, and if he is alive to do so. My enemies begin their attacks in earnest, bombarding me with their fists. I see them in flashes of red as they dance in and out. Each blow is like a burst of light in my mind, timed with the shock of their strikes.

I reel under the savagery of their aggression, trying to time my *gladius*'s swing to catch them, but they have trained in their dark arts as much as I have trained in mine. It is a simple thing for them to avoid my weapon. After a few steps of this dance, a booted foot knocks my sword out of my hand, leaving me truly defenseless. The everflame burned away most of my Ancient Frost. I don't have enough to summon a paring knife, let alone the full *Glacialis Falx*.

But with each flash comes a bit of inspiration, a clue from the growing knowledge that burns inside of me. Attuning a new Symbol is like discovering a muscle that you did not know you had. It is a part of me, but it takes time to learn how heavy a load it can carry or how far it can bend.

Crack, a strong blow bounces off my chin, sending me staggering as one of the Shadowbound boldly closes with me. In the flash of heat vision, I can see he is no longer set to retreat, his feet are firmly planted on the ground. I am toothless; no danger to him now.

But why should heat only be something I can touch?

Why is it something that I should not see?

Tentatively, I reach inside myself, tracing the network of heat that runs through my muscles and flesh. In my skull, two pinpoints of warmth burn, outshone only by the mass that must be my brain. I reach out to the heat within them and pour Unrelenting Fire essence into them to fuel my will.

Show me, I command.

Pain. Furious and fiery pain tears through me, causing me to fall to my knees. I scream as the world ignites. The darkness around me does not dissipate, but it begins to be filled in by the blurry red shapes of the warmth moving around me. This is not the knowledge of an *animus*—my Symbol still cannot reach out to touch them, but it can adapt my eyes to be more like itself.

The *sicarus* in front of me watches me as I fall to my knees, head cocked to the side. Heat radiates from him in red waves, as if he, too, is burning.

I'm still screaming as I rise to my feet and lunge forward, arms extended.

He's so surprised, he doesn't retreat, instead catching my wrists as I get close. I respond in kind, wrapping my own hands around his. My Symbol fills me with the knowledge of his warmth, but I ignore it. The only thing I wish to know about him is how much fire he can handle before he dies.

Essence pours out of me as I shove my will into him with one simple intent: *Ardemus—we burn*. My hands glow like *Sol* to my new vision, growing so bright, I have to look away. A new set of screams joins mine, and the assassin tries to pull away, flailing frantically. But I channel Iron into my grip, holding him like a vise.

After a dozen heartbeats, my opponent collapses, and I open my eyes to stare at the heat that devours him from within. It is as if I forced him to drink a flagon of lava. Numbly, I release his wrists, letting him flop to the ground. I have never killed like this before. A blade is a tool; in the moment, using it can often feel like chopping down a tree. But this? This is another kind of power, and it terrifies me.

Bam, another flash of insight as his comrade slams into me from the rear, renewing his assault. The blow knocks me out of my stunned reverie. I turn to look directly at the second man, who hesitates when he sees that I can track him once more. Slowly, I bend down to pick up one of the shortswords that they dropped moments ago. Iron rejoices within me to feel a weapon in my grip once more. The cooler essence flows into me, helping my almost empty reserves to dull the pain of my burning eyes to a faint roar.

I'm not screaming anymore.

The *sicarus* stares at me, frozen by fear. I can sense his confusion. He and his comrade figured out that I was Ironbound and used that to their advantage, but now I have killed his partner with my bare hands, and I can see him through the dark shroud even though he carries no Iron.

A dry chuckle escapes my lips as I realize that he may be one of two living people to truly know my secret—to understand that I carry more than one Symbol and what that means.

"What are you?" a hushed voice echoes through the din of the battle around us. I smile with no warmth, striding toward my unarmed foe with certainty.

"You'll never find out," I promise, lunging forward with my stolen blade. The *sicarus* ducks to the side, still quick on his feet, but we both know this will be a short dance. He tries to skirt along the right side of my range to get toward another sword on the ground, but I cut him off, intimately aware of the weapon's presence thanks to my *animus*.

We circle a few more times. He may not have a weapon, but I am bruised and beaten, and he is unscathed. With every moment that passes, the Iron essences within me surge through my body, pushing the pain away as my Silver and Copper Hearts work together to restore me. Already I can feel an increase in the speed with which my body recovers.

I feint low, aiming for one of his thighs, before continuing into my lunge, lowering my shoulder to ram into his chest. My opponent lets out a surprised *oof*, flying backward. I'm on him before he can recover, driving my blade forward with all my strength. The will-reinforced blade cuts through his sternum easily, burying itself up to the hilt in his chest. The gurgling assassin collapses to his knees as I turn my attention toward the rest of the garden.

I leave my borrowed sword in him, bending low to pick up a *gladius* from the ground. The longer blade of the legions feels at home in my hand.

My new vision is powerful in the darkness, but it is limited in the range that it can sense heat. Human eyes are not meant to be warped like this, no matter what Symbol they might be attuned to. If not for the strength of Iron, I think the pain might have already driven me mad.

I extend my Silver *animus*, letting it sweep beyond the range of what I can see. On the far side of the garden, a member of the Spartan Guard fights against a *sicarus*, sheltering behind his *scutum* like a wall, relying on it to protect him in his limited vision. I ignore him for the moment; my body shivers as the *imperativus* placed on me by the oath relic drives me in a different direction.

I must protect my *domus*. Despite my lack of free will, I am surprised to realize my concern is real. I do not wish for Varus to be dead. Nor do I want Contessa, Pliny, or Alessandra to come to harm.

Five more sets of shortswords dance in the center of the garden, where Varus and Delilah were lounging. I cannot sense what holds them at bay, only read the savagery of the battle in their sharp reactions. The intensity of the struggle fills me with relief. There must be at least one Gold *electus* who still draws breath.

If he still lives, my master will be in the middle of that maelstrom. I break into a long stride, still being careful to take guarded footsteps. The earth is not warm enough for me to sense. I pass over the cooling forms of corpses that serve as guides, but without them, I would be blind to the ground's shape.

I scale a set of low stairs as I approach the battle. One of the *sicarii* whirls in my direction, throwing their blade like one of Fannia's knives. The iron weapon screams in warning to me as it hurtles toward my head.

I snag it out of the air with my left hand without breaking stride.

That sends a ripple of uncertainty through the other attackers. Two more spin in surprise to stare at me. A new advantage to their Symbol reveals itself to me. The strongest of them can use the shadow that shrouds us as a canvas for their *animus* in the same way that I was able to sense through the snow in the North.

Despite this understanding, I feel a grin peeling at my lips. Unrelenting Fire fans the flames of my rage, turning it into an inferno, delighted to consume anything before me. One of the watchers makes a sharp gesture, their sword describing a harsh line in the dark. The other two respond instantly, rushing toward me without any of the fear or hesitation that the two dead assassins behind me showed.

These must be their most dangerous warriors. Like their comrades before, the pair splits to distract my attention. As they draw near, they enter the range of my heat vision, revealing that it is a man and woman who come to face me. I ignore the man who circles behind me, instead hunching my shoulders and lunging to close with the woman to my right, who carries only one sword after generously donating her other one to me.

My *gladius* rings as she blocks my first strike. I follow my attack up with a vicious stab using her blade. She's quicker than her comrades and dances backward out of range of the shorter weapon. She's happy to distract me. It gives her partner time to—

I spin my *gladius* into a reverse grip before driving it backward, angled upward in a vicious stab. The Shadowbound behind me barely manages to stop short of impaling himself on my weapon. Another inch, and he would be bleeding all over the senator's garden.

Unfortunately for him, an undead god gave me the ability to change the rules.

With the final dregs of my Ancient Frost essence, I trigger the *Glacialis Falx*, imagining only the single-sided tip of a longer dueling blade growing over the end of my *gladius* like an encroaching moss. At first the ability resists my attempt to warp its desire. It resents the new heat that burns within me. But I condense my will and convince it that the iron is ice. After all, they are both a part of me. Cold pours out of my reserve as the frost travels down the blade, crackling with anger as it reaches for my opponent.

In a heartbeat, it blossoms from the point of my blade and punches through the assassin's eye. The man lets out a bloodcurdling scream as my weapon digs into his skull, before I rip it free, spinning the blade forward to attack the woman I drove back.

She retreats in earnest now. I can read the terror in the heat of her body. Her heart grows colder, as if it feels the dead hand of Pluto reaching out to take her into Hades. She knows now that I am something terrible, something that should not exist.

She raises her shortsword to block my overhanded smash, and I reach out with the Iron Symbol, encouraging her blade to part before mine. My sword carves downward, unbothered by her attempt to ward off my attack, and slices into her chest, opening her from neck to waist.

I pass by her as she collapses, flicking my iced *gladius* to the side to cleanse it of some of the gore that clings to it. As I stride toward the center, only one pair of shortswords still fights. The rest litter the ground. A snort erupts from me as I am pulled by my oath toward that conflict. I have no illusions that my three *Corda* add together to equal the power of a Golden *electus*, especially one that is the head of an ancient house like Varus Pelias.

They should have brought more *sicarii*.

I draw close enough to witness only a moment of my master's power. Varus's heat burns like *Sol* itself to my modified vision. Power courses through him in an inferno. I raise my hand to shield my gaze from the brightness. His *Cor*'s veins shine brightly as they channel the power of his Symbol.

The last assassin darts forward, blade extended, but the senator simply raises his arm, letting the sword bounce off his forearm. With his left hand, he gestures at the ground, and there is a sharp *crack* before the man attacking him is torn to shreds by something I cannot see or sense.

My eyes burn as the darkness collapses. I scream in anguish and shut my eyes, shielding them from the oppressive light that now burns everywhere.

I release Unrelenting Fire's working on my eyes but hesitate for a moment before opening them, afraid of what I will find when I do. It was reckless and foolish for me to use my new Symbol in that way, but I chose to live. Now I will find out what the cost of my survival is.

My left eye cracks open, and I wince at the strength of the light around me, but it does not sear me like it did before. Feeling reassured, I open both and blink owlishly as my pupils begin to adjust. They are tender, but whole. Relief floods through me as I spot Anas on the far side of the garden, bloody and bent, but still standing. I give my brother a nod, grateful that he too still lives. To lose him again would have cut me deeper than I can bear.

"You should have told us!" a young man's voice screams. I twist to see the young man who had dismissed my warnings glaring at me with rage. I blink in surprise at his expression. His toga is stained with food and dirt, but he seems otherwise unbloodied. His eyes track over my gore-stained weapons, and the sight seems to only make him angrier.

Alessandra appears over his shoulder, pale but otherwise also unharmed. Her eyes flash against mine as she sees the state that I am in. My heart skips a beat, and in my excitement, my *animus* pulses, extending through the party. My eyes go wide as I realize what I am sensing.

"I demand this slave be whipped—"

Moving automatically, my left hand surges forward, sending my stolen shortsword in an overhand throw directly at the foolish palatine. He lets out a shriek, dropping into a crouch, but he needn't have worried. My target was never him. It was right next to him.

My weapon appears to bury itself in thin air as it sinks into the chest of a *sicarus* who lurks behind Alessandra. The Shadowbound woman drops her weapons, trying to staunch the spray of red blood coming from her throat, but it is too late. She sinks to her knees with a gurgle, leaving my detractor paler than his toga.

I turn away from the dead assassin to find Varus watching me, eyes dark and wondering. A different fear begins to creep in my chest as I follow his gaze down to my arms.

They are different.

The familiar white *rasa* veins that I have had since Segesta still intertwine with the Silver lines of Ancient Frost and Iron. But nestled among them like an interloper shines a series of new Copper lines, proudly displaying my status to any who can see.

"Oh, Varus, you've killed us all," Delilah breathes from behind my master, staring at me in horror. *Mons* Olympus glitters in the dark sky above us, illuminated by *Luna*'s light.

PART II

FRIGUS VENTUS

CHAPTER 19

The senators move swiftly in the aftermath of the assault. I am gathered up into the maelstrom of activity by Contessa, who looks at me like I have become a venomous serpent. We follow Delilah as the powerful woman shouts orders to her guards.

I worry that it is too late for me to escape. My *Corda* have betrayed me. The senators know my secret, and they will turn me over to the Censors in order to live. I may only have moments of freedom left. I turn to ask Contessa a question, but the *lanista* silences me firmly.

"Wait for the *dominus*," she orders, leading me into the main house. I am so overwhelmed with fear that I barely take in the opulence that I am dragged through. This is only a country estate for the senator, but it is packed with riches like I have never seen.

Every room is lit by a dozen *lumos* relics organized into ornate chandeliers made of gold. They sparkle as if the souls that carried them in life are smiling down on us. Thick rugs cover the marble floors, and magnificent works of art hang from the walls.

I am distracted from my terror by a portrait of Julia, one of the lesser-remembered Iron Lords. Hers is smaller than the one that decorates the library in Varus's compound but of a similar quality. The woman's long blond hair sweeps over her shoulders, which are left bare by the white armor she wears. It looks like a forerunner to the *tellus* of the modern-day Censors. I know little about the woman who supposedly slew Venus before joining Titus and the rest of the band in their ascent to *Mons* Olympus, but she has the same name as my mother. A pang of sadness echoes in my chest. I miss her.

I glance over my shoulder to look for Pliny, but the short magister is not with us. I have not seen him since before the Shadowbound attacked. Was I too slow to save him? I do not remember. Alessandra floats in our wake, her eyes wide. We make eye contact, and she smiles softly, a weak, strained thing.

I wonder if it is the first time she's seen someone die this close, or if it is the first time that someone has tried to kill her. That thought hits me harder than I would expect. I do not know her well, but she was kind to me in a place where few others were.

I would not wish the burdens of a violent life on her for all the world, but I see its claws digging at her, cutting away little pieces of her innocence. It's like seeing a beautiful vase crack after being dropped. She's not shattered, but it's clear that she will never be the same. I return her smile, equally as small as her own. I have my own fears.

I will never fight in the arena. I will likely not even survive the night. If I do, it will only be so that the Censors can take me to their looming tower to slice into me as they study how I have become this monster. Unrelenting Fire roils inside of me, feeding my fear.

I shake my head in disgust, realizing that I never let go of my new Symbol after the fighting was done. I banish it now, making space to embrace Iron, letting its hard-edged logic sweep over me. Immediately, I feel more composed. I still carry a bloody *gladius* in my right hand. Why would they let me keep my weapon if they were going to kill me? Some of the tension in my shoulder fades, reassured by my reasoning.

Delilah leads us into yet another beautiful room; I have lost count of how many we have walked through. A smokeless fire roars in the center of the room, perfectly curated by an *ignis* relic. Wide windows gaze out into the darkness of her estate, but the senator gestures, and they darken, turning as opaque as stone. My jaw drops open at the sight. I have never even heard of a…*speculum* relic? Is that even the right word for it? I cannot even begin to fathom what one of them must have cost.

The senator strides toward a large golden couch and turns to glare at the three of us instead of sitting. Her attention is heavy and electric, much like Varus's own keen gaze. I shiver under it but keep my mouth shut. My ears pop as the room seals its air away, preventing anyone from hearing what is said outside of the bubble that we are in.

"What has that man dragged me into?" Delilah wonders aloud, not taking her eyes off me. They travel down my exposed arms, tracing fire over my mismatched veins. She twitches as she notices the sword still in my grasp, but she does not complain.

"Nothing to say?" She arches an eyebrow at us as the silence stretches. "If Varus can't be bothered to attend to me—"

"I'm here, Delilah," my master interrupts as he strides into the room. He is no longer dressed in a toga but a pair of combat leathers that match the ones I wear. Pliny floats in his wake. I smile in relief to see my favorite Gold is still alive. The old magister's eyes light up with interest as he spots my new Copper veins.

"Well, clearly, I missed the dress code to this gathering," Delilah murmurs, at last sinking down to sit on her ornate couch. "Now if you would be so good as to tell me why you have seen fit to ensure my death warrant is signed at the same time as yours by bringing this *abominatio*?"

I wince at her new word choice for me—abomination. I think I liked being an *immundus* better.

My fist tightens around the hilt of my sword, but I realize that any attempt at resistance was doomed from the start. I am oathbound to not harm Varus or Alessandra. They don't need to wonder if they can trust me—I am leashed.

"We will see if he is truly an abomination," Varus promises her, looking at me for the first time. "But I swear to you that I did not know. Castor has had some… irregularities with his *Cor*, but he has been confirmed by the Censors."

"Confirmed by the Censors," Delilah repeats, mimicking his voice in angry retort. "Look at the man, Vary." My eyebrow twitches at the nickname. Anas might have been right about her intent after all. "He's got *cuprum* and *argentum* veins at the same time!"

"Pliny, if you would?" Varus gestures at me, and the short magister scurries toward me like a released hunting hound. I tense as he approaches, but he gives me a reassuring wink. Contessa watches from Varus's side, her expression strained.

Goosebumps flare on my arms as I feel a hint of Pliny's *animus*'s presence sweep over me, studying my new veins. I feel my heart skip a beat as he begins his inspection. I have worried before about how much his attunement to *Cor* tells him about me. Iron and Ancient Frost are both cold and unwelcoming. Perhaps they were easy to confuse. But how will Unrelenting Fire ever blend in with them?

"As I said," Varus continues, looking back to Delilah, "there have been oddities with his *Cor* before. Pliny will be able to tell us what has happened."

"Oddities? What do you mean oddities?"

"You speak of his veins. Look closer! He is an *immundus*, yet he channels an Elder Symbol with more power than any other Silver I have ever seen."

"Elder Symbol?" My skin prickles as Delilah's attention whips back to me. "Gladiator, what is your attunement?"

"Ancient Frost," Varus answers for me, giving me a warning look. I take his meaning clearly. He will handle the other senator. I am distracted by the presence of Pliny, who circles me now, peering at my arms like a jeweler. He even sniffs me once or twice, like there is something about my *Cor* to smell.

"Aquilo's Bones! He's running around with that Symbol, and the Censors let him compete?" Delilah's face is somehow paler than it was before. "No wonder they sent assassins to kill you, and you led them in a bright caravan to my home. Do not lie to me, Vary. I cannot bear it."

"Delilah, I swear this to you by the grave of Pelias himself. Consul Briannus himself commanded that he be allowed to compete."

"Briannus, that serpent," she hisses in understanding. "He saw an ocean of *denarii* and forced their hand." A shrewd look crosses her face as she turns to look at Varus once more. "And what was he doing at an inspection of your gladiator?"

"I invited my old student to come for an afternoon tea," Pliny muses, still studying me closely.

"It's a miracle they haven't killed you yet, Magister," Delilah remarks dryly. "But none of this addresses the fact that your gladiator, Castor, was it? Has attuned a second Symbol. You know as well as I that not even both of the consuls could protect us from the Censors' wrath if they find out."

"He may not have," Pliny continues in the same dreamy tone. His eyes are crossed as he traces the path of one of my new Copper veins like a thread. Only my firm grip on Iron keeps me from shaking.

"Pliny, I have eyes."

"Forgive me, *Domina*, but his case is a special one." The magister pauses his inspection to turn to face the irritated senator. "Castor gained his *Cor* during an accident. Instead of receiving one, he was given multiple. His first one bound to Ancient Frost, as we know, but the rest remained inert. That incident was what led to his eventual entrance into the Games."

"But you cannot have two Hearts," Delilah protests, massaging her temples with her fingers. "I may not be a magister, but they taught that to even us in the *collegium*." My pulse races, ignoring Iron's stoic presence. They are too close to the truth. I will be discovered. The White Hand will come for me. I am not ready to face Atticus, not yet.

Pliny rubs at his chin as he considers his next words. "It is true that all known attempts to bind someone to two Hearts have failed. I have studied his condition closely, and I believe that the key lies in the fact that he was exposed to unprepared *Cor* instead of ones ready to be placed into another *electus*." Behind me, Alessandra lets out a short gasp of surprise, as if that meant something to her.

"When the Censors collect the fresh *Cor* that falls from the sky, it is taken to their halls and purified. Then it is kept in stasis until a portion of it is separated and prepared for a new host. The amount is carefully tailored to the size and weight of the new *electus*, and they go through several stages of preparation before they place it into the new subject. This is done to reduce the number of failures and *immundi*, but it also means that the *rasa* is not a true blank slate."

"I am not following. Is anyone following him?" Delilah looks around the room for help, her irritation rising once more. Varus shoots me another warning look, but he need not have worried. I am just as confused as the good senator.

"He's talking about the way that *mythi* are created," Alessandra says from over my shoulder.

"Good!" the magister says with a nod for his student before resuming his intense study of me. "If you could take it from here, please…"

"Uh…" Alessandra's voice breaks as her godmother's intense stare turns to her. I turn also, fascinated by the chance to have an answer to the mystery. Even if I am killed in the next few moments, at least I might finally understand what the gods did to me.

"A *mythos* like a stonehound or airhorse that occurs in the wild does not have a *Cor* that goes through any of these refinements. It is in a true *rasa* state when it enters the creature. Over time, it bonds with them and changes them. If Castor was given a bunch of true *rasa* at the same time…"

"Then it is possible that he is merely beginning to activate the other chambers of his Heart to expand his capabilities," Pliny resumes, stepping back and clapping his hands together with a wide smile. I'm shocked by his delight. I thought we were friends. To see his excitement at announcing my death hurts me deeply.

"That is all that has happened here. He does not have a new Symbol. It is merely that Castor's latent Hearts are beginning to merge with his existing one, as his body internalizes them in an organic process. The new one is not as strong as the other, since it has not benefitted from his training. But with proper balance, it should be a simple matter to Ascend it to Silver before he advances further to Gold. It is my opinion that there is nothing that the Censors could take issue with—merely a boy with a larger than normal Heart."

I am stunned. A cold wave of fear sweeps over me as the short magister pulls back from me, smiling gently. There is not a trace of guile on Pliny's face, and yet I am terrified. Is it possible that a Gold attuned to *Cor* itself is so wrong? Is he really so limited in what he can see?

"How long did it take you to Ascend from Copper to Silver the first time?" Varus asks me, looking thoughtful, but unsurprised by what his magister says.

"Uh," I say, frowning, trying to figure out how to answer that question. I know that my answer will shock them, but there is no point in lying. I suspect that it will only happen again. Better to have them prepared for the future now. "A few months?" I wince as everyone in the room reacts with a visible twitch. There are so many lies within lies that my head is beginning to spin trying to balance all of them.

Perhaps I am like one of the *mythi*, slowly absorbing my rogue Hearts until they acclimate to my body. Maybe the Censors would find no fault with that. Dead Jupiter knows that they'd be more likely to leave me alone if the rest of my white veins vanished.

But I am not only bound to one Symbol. My new Hearts are not merely expanding my essence reserves and my ability to control Ancient Frost. Pliny told me that my mind would be torn asunder by the weight of two Symbols. My father warned me against the pressure of one.

I am bound to three.

"You Ascended from Copper to Silver in a few months?" Delilah demands, looking at Pliny for confirmation. Varus eyes me shrewdly, measuring me as ever. I wonder how they would react if I told them my *inhibitus* first activated only a matter of weeks after I was first bound.

"It has only been a little over a year since his *Sententia*, *Domina*," the magister responds with a shrug.

Delilah murmurs something dark under her breath before giving me another look. "So it is not him."

"It is not," my master tells her grimly. I am confused, looking between the two senators, trying to understand why the tension has only grown in the room.

"Dead gods and their bleached bones," Delilah swears, leaning back on her couch in dramatic fashion. "I was really hoping your strange gladiator was the reason, Varus."

"Which leaves only one reason that Shadowbound might be sent to kill us all." Suddenly, I understand why Delilah hoped the *sicarii* were here to murder me. If one of the palatine families had knowingly kept someone with multiple Hearts, the Censors would not hesitate to wipe out the entire bloodline. But if I am—at least not visibly—an *abominatio*, then it was not me that the shadowy assassins came to kill.

"She knows." Delilah leaps to her feet, pacing the length of the room like a caged *tigris*. Her golden hair trails behind her as she scowls in anger and fear. Abruptly, she realizes that I am still here, and her expression sours further.

"Do send out your fancy gladiator, Varus. We have serious things to discuss."

"You need not fear to speak before him. He is oathbound to me and my House."

"Oathbound?" The other senator gasps in scandalized horror as she turns to study me once more. "So you're afraid of him too." Varus grunts but does not disagree.

"When Diana puts us all on crosses, he can hang on the one next to yours, then." My eyes go round as saucers as she names the Empress. Why is the Empress sending *sicarii* to kill two senators? I am no enemy to the throne. There is no treason in my bones.

Some of her servants are my enemy, but to me, they are removed from Diana. Atticus, Tyrus, Brennus, and the rest are a part of the corruption that festers on the glory of the Empire like rust. Killing them is not a rebellion against her, but part of my duty as a citizen.

"You saved many lives tonight, Castor," the older man says somberly, looking into my eyes with his dark gaze. "Not only did you save mine, but that of my daughter, who is priceless to me. I may be your *dominus*, but I am in your debt. If you have a desire, speak it, and if it is in my power to give it to you, it is yours. I swear it by my *Cor*." The hairs on my arms rise once more, electrified by his words. I know better than most that to make a promise like that is no small thing. For a moment, I debate asking for my freedom, but I know that is beyond even his reach. My indenture has been recorded in the halls of the Censors. There is only one path out.

"Thank you, *Dominus*," I manage to croak through a dry throat. "I will think about your offer."

"Your scolding is as sharp as ever, Vary." Delilah sighs, turning to face me once more with an abashed look on her face. "You have also done me a great service, young gladiator. This is my home. The safety of my guests is my responsibility—a responsibility I failed tremendously tonight. If not for your intervention, many under my roof would have perished." She pauses for a moment, gathering herself before bowing her head slightly toward me in a gesture of extreme respect. "Thank you, Castor."

"I live to serve, *Domina*," I manage, returning her bow even more deeply. I am floored by her words and respect. A moment ago, I worried that they were going to kill me; now, instead, they pile praise on me. How different these two senators are from the ones that sat on the *Argentum Consilio*!

"If your *dominus* will permit me, I would like to give you a gift. It is something that has been treasured by my family for generations but has remained unused for far too long. It's been waiting for someone worthy." She glances at her fellow senator to gauge his reaction.

"You're sure?" Varus's eyebrows shoot up. It seems he knows exactly what she refers to.

"Come, darling." A hint of her playful spark returns as she glances at him. "If you're going to invest in the boy, I might as well join you. It's far too late for me to hold back now." I do not know exactly what she means, but the look on Varus's face is troubled, and so is my spirit.

Delilah snaps her fingers, and a chime sounds throughout the room. Despite my distraction, I feel my body go stiff with horror. Surely that is not a *musica* relic? The senator seems brash and unsurprised that the Empress sent assassins to kill her, but to boldly display a relic from a forbidden Symbol is beyond shocking.

The sound must have rung outside of our privacy bubble, because the door to the room opens and the serious majordomo enters, bowing to her master. "Clara, fetch the stone box from my personal vault." If the servant was surprised at the request, she does not show it. She merely nods before withdrawing, moving quickly about her task.

Some of my shock must have shown on my face, because Delilah lets out a delighted laugh when she looks back to me. "Have no fear, young Castor." She chuckles. "I do not deal in forbidden relics. There is no *musica* to be found in this home. It is merely a bell attached to an Air relic that will ring when I activate it." I nod in understanding, marveling at the cleverness of such a device.

The majordomo is swift, returning only a few moments later with a narrow box made of stone in her hands. She enters briskly, pausing before the senator to bow and extend her burden with two hands. Reverently, Delilah lifts the lid, letting it fall back onto her servant's wrists. Reaching in, she pulls out an object wrapped in paper.

My mouth goes dry as the air suddenly grows cold. The fire in the center of the room rises in response, trying to battle the sudden change in temperature. My breath mists with each exhale. The rest of the palatine ignore it, looking intently at what the senator now holds.

"You may go, Clara," she tells the majordomo, replacing the lid on the now empty box. The stout woman bows once more before withdrawing, sealing us once more in the privacy bubble created by the relics of this room.

With shaking hands, the senator begins to unwrap the brown paper, her eyes traveling to me as she does. "Over four hundred years ago, as I am sure you know, the *Ferrum Domini* struck down the gods." She arches an eyebrow, waiting for me to nod in assent.

"There were seven of them—those Iron Lords, as we call them now. Titus and Frigidus are remembered best. I am sure you know of Pelias"—she nods her head at Varus standing by her side—"but can you name any of the other four, I wonder? Their names have not stood the test of time, just like the rest of their iron kindred, but have rusted away." My mind flashes to the portrait that I saw hanging in her home as we came to this room.

"Julia?"

She smiles brightly, surprised by my guess. "Did you recognize her painting? Few would. You must have had excellent teachers. You're a waste in the arena, a waste."

Varus snorts slightly as if he disagrees. I am supposed to be the salvation of his house. He does not see that as a waste.

My mouth goes a little dry as I recall the Iron Lord's surname. "Julia Census?"

Delilah's smile fades a little, as if pulled by memory. "Yes, my ancestor created the White Hand, but that was long ago, young gladiator. They have not been faithful to what they once were."

I am silent, terrified to speak. The specter of the Censors and their *Judicium* hovers over me like a long, dark shadow. I am still in grave danger here, even if the *sicarii* are all dead.

"Like Pelias, Julia was the founder of my House. But my matriarch was not as keen about gathering power as some of her companions. In fact, she wished for none of it. That is why I dwell in so mean an estate as you see here." I am not sure if she is joking or not.

"You see, Julia did not slay the gods for gain, but for love. She loved Frigidus like *Sol* loves *Luna*. Always she looked at him, shining her light on him, but was never able to catch him. He lived away from the rest of them, brooding in the North until he died." I swallow as my eyes travel down to the object in her hand. The last time I was in Frigidus's domain, I walked away with a new Symbol and a deal with a mostly dead god.

"She made this for Frigidus but never gave it to him. Instead, she kept it, a monument to her love for the coldest Iron Lord." She pauses as she finishes unwrapping the paper and holds it out for me to see. She is careful to keep the paper between her flesh and the frigid items that she carries.

It is two large ingots of what appears to be iron with a dark blue hue.

Confused, my gaze flicks back up toward Delilah, trying to gauge if she is messing with me. Then Alessandra lets out a gasp of surprise that tells me I am underestimating this gift. I examine what she holds more carefully, sending my *animus* sweeping forward to tell me what I have missed.

My jaw drops as my senses sweep over the first ingot. It *radiates* Ancient Frost like a cold fire. Not Snow or Ice or Winter, but Ancient

Frost, in its purest and most natural state. Essence pours out of it like it was made of ice. My *Cor* leaps like a hungry dog, begging to be fed. But before I can begin to cultivate, I realize that there is a second miracle. For not only is it a source of Winter essence, but also Iron. Somehow this ingot is *both* Iron and Ancient Frost. I extend a hand toward it without thinking, lost as I study them in awe.

"Sorry," I gasp, stopping in place when I realize I have almost crossed the distance between us. My sword is missing; I must have dropped it in my daze.

"Silly boy, this is a gift for you." Delilah laughs, but there is something hooded in her eyes. Even now I am being measured. "They are yours if you can take them." That draws me up short, warning me of a danger lurking just below the surface. She has been very careful not to touch them directly. Our breath still steams despite the *ignis* relic's best attempt to warm the room. My gaze flickers to Varus, looking for direction.

"Pliny?" the senator interjects, calling to his magister for advice.

"Anyone else would be a fool to try," the short man replies after a moment. That is not as encouraging as I would like it to be.

"Go on, then," Delilah urges, her eyes sparkling. "Let's see if you're worthy to follow in the footsteps of Frigidus." My ever-present fear coils in my stomach like a serpent, but there is nothing to do but obey. The weight of the room's attention settles on me, making me hunch my shoulders. Slowly, I extend my left hand to lay a finger on the first ingot.

It's bitterly cold. The metal sears like fire, but this cold is known to me. The Symbol of Ancient Frost reacts with delight as I cultivate some essence from it, refilling its dry reserves. I let out a gasp of surprise at the strength of its source as I reach out with my second hand to take it from her. Delilah's eyes are wide with shock as my skin does not turn black from frostbite.

With shaking hands, I lift the ingot, marveling at its weight, rejoicing in the source of true Ancient Frost and Iron. My strained *Corda* begin to find balance between each other as my reserves are no longer wildly mismatched.

"Senator, this is a wonder," I breathe, staring at my hands in shock. "What is it? I have never heard of anything like this."

"According to her journal, she called it *Glacialis Ferrum*—Frost Iron. Frigidus was a Winter Symbol, just like you. He was loath to leave his kingdom and his source of power," Delilah explained. "Julia made this to allow him to carry some of his home with him."

"Then why did she not give them to him?" I am in awe at the gift. Contessa's training had already shown me that one of my greatest weaknesses was how rare it was to have an ice source with me to refill my Ancient Frost reserves. With this… I will be able to bring Winter with me wherever I go.

"Because then she would have to admit the truth," Delilah says softly.

"What truth?"

"That it was not the Winter Symbol that kept Frigidus and her apart. He just did not love her."

CHAPTER 20

The senators dismiss us after I am given my gift. My mind still reels at the revelation of this Frost Iron—somehow Julia created something that held two essences. The fact that she did it for Frigidus makes it only more overwhelming. I have stood in the halls of his fortress, faced the enemies that he fought. I feel a kinship to him that I cannot shake.

"We will need to begin a special training regimen immediately," Pliny says to me as we walk through Delilah's ornate home. "We need to Ascend your new *Cor* to *argentum* as soon as possible to prevent strain on your psyche."

"How," I ask a little too sharply. "How can I do that?"

"You will need to focus on utilizing your Hearts only as a *cuprum* for now," the small man explains. "If you push your will like an *argentum*, it can damage the Heart that cannot meet your demands. Can you differentiate between the two? If you use your Symbol through one or the other, can you tell?"

I close my eyes, trying to unravel the layers of lies that we are communicating with. Pliny thinks that I only have *two Corda*. He also believes that they all share the same Symbol instead of having their own.

I can feel the difference between my individual Hearts and control them separately, because unlike Pliny's theory, each one is self-contained instead of fusing together as part of some expanding whole.

"Yes," is all I answer after my moment of thought.

"Contessa, he must cease all training that pushes his Silver *Cor* until he has brought his second one into parity with it."

"He still has to fight, Pliny," the *lanista* growls in frustration. "Antioch is in two weeks. If he's not fixed by then, he will have to take the risk. We cannot afford to fall further behind in the rankings."

"I understand," the magister replies calmly. "But we must reduce the strain on him until then, or his path to Gold may close forever—a tragedy that our master will forgive neither of us for."

"Whatever you tell me to do, I will," I promise the magister earnestly. He looks at me in surprise, as if he expected me to protest his instructions. He must see some of my resolve burning in my eyes, because he nods once, in acceptance of my promise.

"You must begin cultivating as much Ancient Frost as you can at once," he instructs. His eyes track to the ingots that I carry in my hands. "And you should not use that."

"Why?" Alessandra asks her teacher, leaning in to watch me remove them. "Won't that be an even better source of the essence he needs than the *loci* that we brought with us?"

"That would be true if it was a relic." Pliny shakes his head reluctantly. "But that is something else. Something that does not exist anywhere else in the world. It was made by one with power for one with power. The *Ferrum Domini* were far stronger *electi* than any of us. Until we know exactly what effects it might have on Castor, he should avoid it until his *Cor* is more stable."

"But—" I protest, feeling a wave of disappointment swell over me. I stare at the precious Frost Iron in my hands, unable to bear the thought of being separated from the lump of metal. I do not know what I will do with it. It's not in a form I can *use*, but its presence feels like home.

"It is better if you give it to me," the magister says after watching me for a moment. "I wouldn't want it to corrupt you." I give him a pitiful look, but the older man's face is firm. With a sigh, I close the paper wrapper around it to protect him from its frigid touch.

"I have a question," I murmur unhappily as I hand over the treasure to Pliny. "Why did Julia make this Frost Iron for Frigidus? I thought that he was attuned to Iron like the rest of them. Iron was forbidden because it let them kill the gods." To my surprise, Pliny pauses, looking between Alessandra and me with a hesitant look on his face. Contessa notices that we have stopped and turns, looking back at us impatiently.

"Many magisters suspect that the Iron Lords reached heights with their Symbols that modern *electi* have failed to maintain," he says at last, a faint frown tugging at the corner of his lips. "Frigidus is recorded as being especially in tune with the aspect of cold *within* Iron. Some of my peers think that this is the area of congruency that he focused on."

"But not all?" Alessandra asks, her expression shrewd.

"Not all," Pliny replies with a shake of his head. "There is so much we do not know about those days."

A faint chill runs down my spine, the whisper of a god peering over my shoulder. There is much I do not know too.

We progress through the rest of the senator's home in silence. As we reach the entrance, Contessa draws up short. "You." She points at me with an unwavering finger. "Bed, now. Practice starts at the same time tomorrow. We're still training—without *Cor*." She casts a glance at Pliny before he can object. "Your swordwork is atrocious. You don't need your cold for that."

"But that's in less than five hours," I protest, eyeing the position of the moon.

"Antioch is in two weeks. I promised the *dominus* that you would tear through the Silver Circuit, so tear you will."

"Surely the man who saved two senators' lives can sleep in a little?" I protest, but the scarred, bald woman doesn't even blink as she stares me down.

"When you've finished your morning combat, cultivate as much Ancient Frost as your new Heart can handle, then come to me," Pliny continues with the same lack of mercy. "The path to Ascend to Gold is a hard one, young Castor. Your peak may one day reach higher than most, but that only means that it will be more treacherous."

I sigh in defeat, which is enough to please both of my teachers. With one last warning glare, Contessa stomps off. Pliny gives me a softer smile that hides a hint of compassion before following in her footsteps.

I tuck my head down and head for the stairs. A full decade of Spartan Guards wait at the bottom. The legionnaires are alert and sharp-eyed even in the dead of night. I wonder if the senator has any relics that will stop another group of Shadowbound from walking right past them. Otherwise, what are these guard dogs other than a symbolic gesture?

"Gladiator!" Alessandra calls after me as I take a couple of steps.

"Apologies, *Domina*," I gasp in surprise, turning and inclining my head toward her. "I was distracted and forgot myself." The Silver-veined woman tilts her head to the side, studying me for a moment. Her blue eyes find mine, and for a moment, I lose myself in the human contact. It is warm and comforting—an alien thing after the year I have survived.

"Thank you for saving me," she says when the silence between us has stretched long enough. For a moment, a smirk threatens to hijack my lips to deliver a joke, but something tells me that would be the wrong thing to do. Her face is kind, her tone earnest.

"You are welcome," I reply softly, any glib response dying on my tongue. "I hope I never have to again."

"As do I." She smiles now.

"Goodnight, *Domina*." I bow, turning to head to the servant's quarters where the gladiators are staying.

"Did you think that I would not remember you?"

The cold that starts in my chest before spreading through me like a cancer is harsher and more absolute than any Ancient Frost could ever summon. I freeze as my foot lands on the first step, afraid to turn and face her.

She knows.

Mons Olympus drifts above, shining brightly. The back of my neck begins to tingle as forces beyond my understanding focus in on us, like ants under a piece of glass.

"Remember me?" I manage lamely, turning at last to face her. Alessandra's expression is unreadable, a perfect copy of her father's. She cocks her head, studying me, judging my reaction. The Spartan Guards are just out of earshot; despite having people all around us, we are alone.

"Your hair is longer than it was in the legions, but you are not so easily forgettable." My throat strains to swallow as she lays her accusation bare.

"You have been as kind to me now as you were then," I reply after a moment of thought, abandoning all pretense. "Although I do not know why." The palatine woman is silent for a moment, choosing her words with care. The country breeze pulls at her black hair, sweeping it out behind her. She looks majestic, like she could have belonged to the *Ferrum Domini* herself.

"You must be more careful with your burden. There are many in my father's house that see clearly." Pliny's face flashes before my mind, along with Contessa. Again, I worry the magister knows more than he lets on.

"I am trying," I say dryly, confused by her concern. "There have been extenuating circumstances."

"These moments are nothing, Castor, compared to what will come."

My mind pauses in surprise at the sound of my name on her lips. Not *boy* or *gladiator*, but *Castor*.

"In the arena, ten thousand eyes will follow your every move, from plebeian to Censor. If you are caught there, there will be no saving you."

"Why do you care if I am saved?"

"You mean why do I not tell my father your secret and send you to your death?"

"It is what most would do."

She pauses again, a hint of uncertainty flickering across her face for the first time. She seems torn about saying something. Her mouth twists as she makes her decision.

"Most Houses are not under the threat of *Judicium*," she reminds me with a grim tone. "If an *abominatio* is found in my father's home—" I wince at the term, and she relents. "If someone like you is discovered oathbound to my father..." She trails off. The itchy sensation of being watched grows stronger as I consider her words.

I do not need her to finish the thought. I know better than most the temperament of the Censors. If the White Hand is looking for an excuse to exterminate Varus and *Domus* Pelias, I would be all the proof they needed of his treachery a dozen times over. I am the first uninhibited Ironbound in four hundred years, and that is the least of my crimes. The Censors would never believe that the senator had not intended to use me as a weapon, especially not after tonight.

"I understand," I say, my voice croaking as I consider the implications for Alessandra and the rest of the House. The Censors would spare no one—just like in Segesta, they would put them all to fire and sword. Varus is a palatine and a senator. He is my master, and I am his slave, but I do not wish for him to die. He has been fair to me—fairer than most. I do not wish for Alessandra to be executed either. "I will be more careful. I will not betray you or your family."

"It is not only that." She lets out a vexed sigh, looking away from me. I wait in uncomfortable anticipation, trying to imagine what more there could possibly be. "I was there, Castor." She says my name again. I like it just as much the second time.

"I witnessed the way that you were treated by my mentor and the rest of my peers. I know that you were denied the right to become one of the *Fidelia*." The dull ache of the whip thuds against my back in the memory of that day on the training grounds. "I saw where you began, but I do not know where you will end up. That is something I would like to see."

"You're not afraid of what I might become?" I ask.

"No." She smiles softly, and for a second, the world seems just a little brighter. "You've already saved me once when you did not have to. I think, given the opportunity… you'd do it again."

I do not know what to say to that. My silence only makes her smile grow wider.

"*Vale*, Castor," she says after the moment has passed, returning to formality. Still smiling, she turns and retreats within the house, leaving me alone on the stairs in the night. The Spartan Guard below are watching me now, waiting to make sure I return to my quarters.

"*Vale,* Alessandra," I whisper as she leaves.

Mons Olympus still floats above. But as the prickling sensation of being watched begins to fade, I get the distinct sensation that whoever was here is laughing at me.

CHAPTER 21

We spend another ten days at Delilah's estate. No more Shadowbound *sicarii* make an appearance, but despite that, my days are filled with terror. Something is wrong with my *Corda*—my Hearts. Pliny was right about the strain of maintaining two different tiers.

When I was a boy, my father made me watch as they slaughtered a calf that was born with a defect. Its physical heart was deformed. Half of its chambers were too small for its body. As it grew in size, its body eventually became too big for it. The *medico*, a man bound to a *sanguinis*—blood—Symbol, told me that it would slowly asphyxiate and that putting it down now was a mercy.

My Copper *Cor*, the one bound to Unrelenting Fire, feels like it is too small for my body. I have been physically transformed by my Ascension to Silver. My bones are heavier, my muscles thicker. I require more energy to do a simple thing like walking. This new Heart is not prepared to feed the demands that my body puts on it, just by existing. Every moment, I feel it straining, passively burning essence trying to keep up with my needs. Even though there are two other Hearts to share the load, it does not seem to help, only exaggerate it. Perhaps because they both are responsible for my current state, they work against their weaker kin.

To make matters worse, my reserves are not the same size. Ancient Frost and Iron are both Silver *Corda*—the difference between their capacities is negligible. Until this point, it has been an easy thing for me to keep my reserves in balance. During a battle or over the course of the day, it is common for them to become lopsided, as I am usually without any Winter sources, but the effects of having those Symbols unaligned over a short period of time are barely noticeable.

That is not the case for my new one. Unrelenting Fire rages, almost jealous of the supremacy of its counterparts within me. It is impossible for me to top off all my reserves and be in balance. My Copper Heart, which has only begun the journey from low to peak, can only hold a fraction of what my Silver ones can. Filling all my *Corda* to the brim leaves me feeling sick to my stomach, as if I have eaten nothing but spoiled food for days. The longer that this persists, the more ill I become, until my body shakes. When I finish training for the day, I must bleed off my Silver *Corda* to balance the pressure that exists inside of me.

Pliny and Contessa watch me like hawks. The *lanista* respects her counterpart's wishes about training, but she has been relentless in the ways she can still push me. Delilah's estate does not have a *somnatorium* for me to fight opponents created by dream relics, so instead, she duels me herself twice a day, morning and night. We use wooden practice swords that provide me no advantage against the Gold.

Contessa does not even need to use her Symbol to put me in my place. She is faster, stronger, and far more skilled than I am. I leave each session with new bruises that even my Silver *Corda* struggle to heal.

When the bald woman has finished beating me, Pliny is always at my side, supervising my essence gathering to make sure that I am not pushing my Silver Heart toward Ascension while leaving the Copper one behind.

There is only one problem with his approach. The path from Copper to Silver is mostly about feeding a new Heart its essence. With enough time spent cultivating, anyone can Ascend to the second tier. I now truly understand how strong my father's willpower was to resist going past Copper when he literally worked among a rich source of his Symbol day in and day out. It would have taken minimal effort for him to become an *argentum*.

Pliny watches me cultivate Winter essence from a small *locus* relic that he brought with him. Despite hours spent pulling it through my "new" Heart, I have not yet made any measurable progress. He is distressed by this, even though he tries to hide it. I am frustrated because harvesting more Ancient Frost will not fix my problem.

I need Fire.

"Don't worry, lad," he says after every painstaking session. "Carrying another Heart adds a lot of strain on your body. It is only a matter of time." I smile and nod, trying to look like I'm not terrified.

I am, but not because it's not working. I'm terrified because I cannot get access to the essence I need. They are watching me too closely. At night, I brush my hands through torches as I pass them; I tarry a moment too long, placing a log in the bonfire that burns outside the servants' quarters; I feed myself in sips and bites, but I am *hungry*.

Alessandra's warning echoes in my mind, keeping me in check despite the desires of my ravenous new Heart. If I am caught cultivating Fire, there will be nothing that can save me or this House. The oath that is seared into my bones prickles warningly whenever I want to take the risk. It does not stop me, but it reminds me of my duty—of the penalty if I fail.

So, I sit with Pliny, wasting my time, making no progress. I gorge on essence that only makes my Copper Heart sick, threatening to tear me apart from within. I do not know how long I can bear it before something breaks. I hope it is my mind and not my *Corda*.

It is a relief when Varus announces that we will be continuing on toward Antioch. Senator Delilah joins us, riding with Varus and Alessandra in the front of the airhorse caravan. Was she always going to travel with us, or did the assassins change her plans? I do not know, but a half-dozen of her Spartan Guards join us, riding in the *Ferrum* coach with the Ironbound gladiators.

"What's wrong with you?" Illy complains as I groan after we hit another bump in the road. This far from Forum, the cobblestones are not as smooth as my body would like.

"I'm not used to riding like this," I admit, letting it be a blanket excuse for the malaise brewing inside me. Pliny insisted that I fill my Ancient Frost *Cor* to the brim before we left. The games at Antioch begin in a week, and he will waste no opportunity to push me to Ascend before then.

My insides bubble as the different elements fight with each other like a herd of kittens in a barrel. Each rumble makes me pray to Dead Thanatos to come and collect me, but my supplications fall on deaf ears.

"Well, it's gross," Illy says, giving me a sniff. I have not seen the other gladiators for a few days. Pliny and Contessa kept me separated, hoping to solve my problem with as few witnesses as possible. When that failed, the magister produced a type of paint that binds to my flesh like a second skin. Using a thin brush, he painted every inch of my Copper veins to match my Silver ones. I feel ridiculous, like anyone who looks at me can see my false lines for what they are, but no one has said anything.

"You weren't like this before," Reese comments, turning around to look at me from the front.

"It wasn't this bumpy before."

"Surely our new champion isn't afraid of it getting a little rough?" Leon sneers from the front. His face has healed from the damage I did to it, and as the bruises have faded, so has the lesson. I should have hit him harder.

"Not with you." I smile in the least friendly way I can. The blond Air *electus* twitches before looking away. Maybe not everything has been forgotten.

"Idiot," Illy grumbles from beside me as the carriage falls back into silence.

"Me or him?"

"Why do I have to choose?"

After the sights of Forum and Anteforum, Antioch is almost a disappointment. Far larger than Segesta or any other city I have ever seen, it cannot hold a candle to the capital of the Empire. Its streets are not as dense, its buildings not as tall. But even if it was able to match the great city, it would be overshadowed by the ocean that spreads beyond it, covering the horizon. Against that expanse, anything would seem small.

I have never seen the sea. The scale of it is staggering. It covers the horizon in the same slate gray until it eventually seems to meet the sky. The magisters say this is where the world curves, but that is something I cannot fathom.

The great port city sits on the water's edge like an eagle on its perch. Great ships sail to and from its harbor, flying the gray flag of the Iron Empire. I spy a pair carrying the bold *V* of the Fifth Legion, reminding me that Agogia has a presence here.

We sweep through the great gates of the city unquestioned. Antioch is so large that it would be impossible for them to interview everyone who comes and goes. Hard-eyed men wearing the blue tunics of the Second Quadrant watch us pass over the ridge of their *scuti*. I spot several *Fidelis* soldiers, proudly displaying their Silver veins. A snarl rises on my lips as I remember how easily the recruits in these legions were accepted by the *Argentum Consilio*.

Unconsciously, I rub at my own arms, realizing that there will be another set of eyes watching me that I must fool. Copper legionnaires cannot sense my use of the Iron Symbol unless I literally cross blades with them. But a Silver Ironbound might be able to sense my will moving if they were close enough. The danger grows, and I have not even stepped into the ring yet.

The airhorses finally slow down as we reach streets that are packed with plebeians moving about their days. The other gladiators laugh as they point at the sights, humming with nervous energy.

I do not join in on their excitement. Shadows seem to grow over me as we move deeper in the city. I feel like an arrow in flight, hurtling toward a target with no way to slow down. All I can do is brace for the inevitable impact as it draws close.

"Look at the size of that temple!" Illy exclaims to me, jabbing me in the side with his elbow. I grunt as we flow past a ruin that sits back from the street. The statue of a headless woman sits in the front of the building that has no roof. She carries a scale for measuring in her right hand, extending in judgment. My spine prickles with that far too familiar otherworldly attention as I realize who I am looking at.

"I've never seen a Nemesis ruin before," Illy remarks, turning his head to watch it go. "She was one of the more dangerous gods, wasn't she?"

"Yeah," I manage through a suddenly dry throat. "That's what I heard too." No one else comments on the empty monument to a dead god, but my head turns to track it as we go past. I do not need to feel the god's attention settle on me to know what is expected.

If you wish for my aid, you will bring your blood—your votum—to me in my temple. Her voice whispers in my mind once more. Slowly, I move my hand down to my thigh, checking for the thousandth time that the bloody stone is still in my pocket. The pressure builds on the back of my neck as something watches, waiting to see what I will do. I bury the thought, distracting myself with my first sight of why we are here.

Despite being unimpressed by Antioch compared to Forum, I am blown away by the sight of the Bellona Arena. The one dedicated to Mars in Forum is supposed to be the largest in all the Empire, but I cannot imagine something bigger than the one in Antioch. A massive statue to the goddess stands before it. Her head is also missing, but the rest of her stone corpse towers over us. In one hand, she carries a naked sword, in the other a burning torch. A helmet, almost identical to the one worn by the legions rests at her feet.

Bright red flags dance across the top, celebrating the blood that is to come. Built of stone, I can only catch glimpses of its interior, but it is massive. It makes the *collegium* arena I competed in look like a child's playhouse.

"They say thirty thousand people can sit in its stands to watch the Games," Illy breathes in reverent awe. I cannot fathom so many gathered in one place. There were not even that many people in Segesta as a whole. To be watched by so many people seems a nightmare in itself. I understand now why Contessa insisted on training me in the *somnatorium* just to prepare me for the weight of their eyes.

The silence remains as we pass by the massive structure. Its presence looms over us like an oncoming storm. For the first time, I feel a touch of dread. Not of the secrets I carry or the death sentence that hovers over me. But fear of the ring itself. I have taken it for granted that I will survive my matches.

After all, I am an uninhibited Iron *electus*. What do I have to fear? But that is only arrogance speaking. I have only begun to scratch the surface of my power. As my gurgling body reminds me, I am also far from my usual strength. If I do not figure out how to fix my mismatched *Corda*, I will have to fight in a much weaker state than I was expecting.

What kind of killers will I face in the ring? What if my opponent does not rely on Iron, but some other material? A wood-attuned archer would have no need for metal tips on their arrows. It would be a simple matter for them to feather me at a distance, no matter what Symbol I'm bound to.

Seeing the place where so many have bled and died suddenly makes the danger real, the same way that standing in the front lines of the Twelfth did.

The quarters for *Domus* Pelias's *ludus* are only a block from the Bellona Arena, situated so that its long shadow will fall over us during *Sol*'s nightly descent. Compared to the compound we are used to, it is practically a prison. There is a small walled-off square with a sandy courtyard for training and many dormitories to house all the fighters. There are more than a score of these same buildings lining the street, ready to accommodate the *ludi* that have come to compete in the Games.

The Broken Trident emblem flies from a pair of banners hanging from the gate as our convoy rumbles through. A half-dozen of the other walled entrances also bear flags, marking them as occupied by our opponents.

"There's *Domus* Apicius," Reese says to Fannia, pointing at a black flag flying several compounds down from ours, bearing the white-bleached skull of a minotaur *mythus*. Dorian tried to claim that they were interested in buying me when he was negotiating with Varus.

"Lucullus is here too."

"Jupiter's Teeth, is that *Domus* Grus?" Leon curses, pointing at the crest of a long-legged bird I have never seen before.

"Yes," Illy murmurs, the disgruntlement between all of us forgotten for now. The rest of my peers call out other notable families, palatines that I have only read about in history books. *Domuum* Crassus, Cornelli, and Valerus are spotted.

My hand shakes when I hear someone shout their name. The Valerus banner is of the *krakenus*, a many-armed creature of myth that lives in the deep ocean. I did not know that Brennus's house also owned a *ludus*.

So much money and power congregating at one spot, funneling their resources to challenge Varus and, by extension, all of us. All in the name of securing more *Corda* for their houses. It seems like such a small thing to spend so much on. And yet, as I have begun to see since leaving my home, this is the way of the world. Those who have will do what they must to have more.

The compound's gate shuts behind us as our carriages draw to a halt in the courtyard. I lean back in my seat, letting my stomach enjoy no longer being rattled every moment.

"Gladiators out!" Contessa's voice booms through the silence, driving us all to our feet. One by one, we climb down to the dusty ground and gather like a lost herd of sheep around our carriage. Varus and Delilah make their way to a stairwell on the side of the wall, heading toward their own quarters. Their heads are close together, deep in conversation. Alessandra follows in their wake, turning to gaze down at us as she ascends. Our eyes meet, and she smiles slightly before turning away.

I swallow nervously as I shift my stance. I know that she is only seeking to remind me that I hold her life in my hands along with my own. But despite that, I cannot shake a strange warmth that blossoms in my chest.

"Easy, ice boy," Reese murmurs from my side. I glance at the mane-haired girl in surprise. She shakes her head as she turns away, amused by something. "You act like a woman's never smiled at you before."

"I don't think—" I start to protest.

"Listen up, here are your quarters assignments," Contessa shouts, stepping up against the squat building that waits for us. "Golds, take the first hall. Silvers, the second. Coppers, third. Irons, fourth. Blanks, you guessed it, you're in the fifth one." A wave of dry chuckles echoes as we begin to move toward our direction.

I head down the second hall, counting the doors as I approach. There are ten, but we are only six. On a flash of instinct, I pick up my pace to pass Leon and the others. The blond Air *electus* glares at me but says nothing. I ignore him, claiming the first room on the right, closest to the entrance.

"Mercury-damned gloryhound," I hear Leon complain to Obellius as they pass. I ignore him, closing the door behind me to take in the room. Let him think what he wants. I did not choose the first out of some sense of entitlement, only because it will be easier to sneak out of at night.

The quarters are nicer than Delilah's servant *dormitorium* but not nearly as luxurious as my space back at the Pelias compound. It is just a small room with a single *lumos* relic and a bed. I toss my satchel onto the mattress and sit on the edge, trying to plan as I gaze down at my fake Silver veins.

Five days.

I have less than a week to fix my broken body before I will be called into the ring, or I may never leave this place.

CHAPTER 22

"I need your help," I murmur to Anas as we pass each other in the halls the next night. There are only four days left until the Games begin, and I am no closer to salvation. Contessa still drills me relentlessly, trying to instill a lifetime's worth of dueling knowledge into me with every session. Pliny pushes me to grow what he thinks is my second Ancient Frost *Cor*, which is nothing more than a waste of time.

"Watch where you're going," the former *captivus* growls, turning as if I bumped into him. The other two *ferrum* gladiators with him turn to watch our exchange with mistrusting eyes. The Ironbound do not mingle with the rest of us, even more than the Golds and Silvers do not mix.

As he turns, he holds up his left hand in front of his chest, blocking his companions' view of his fingers as he flashes me the hand signal for midnight—not long. I glance at it before tilting my head and trying to smile pleasantly.

"My mistake, friend," I reply with as much warmth as I can muster.

"He's not your friend, *immundus*," grunts the older former officer who always watches me closer than I like.

"Merely a turn of phrase, my good man." I nod in his direction. "We all serve the same *domus*, do we not? Why should there be any enmity between us?"

"Because we are not killers for show," the graying man grunts. "This is not some game."

"For show?" Despite myself, I feel my eyes narrow in irritation. "I am not here for fun, I assure you. I am a slave just like you."

"You are nothing like me," he spits. "You have no idea what it means to wear the collar and serve the Empire." Anas shoots me a warning glance, but I ignore him. I am too drawn in by this man's barbs.

"I am no legionnaire," I lie in agreement, even though it hurts me a little to do. "But I will bleed on those sands, and it will be just as red as yours. I will say again, I have no grievance with you. I have enough enemies waiting for me in the compounds around this one. I do not need more."

"Speak to me when you've killed someone worth killing, boy. When you've put your life on the line for something that matters. Then we'll see if you and I bleed the same blood." The older man turns on his heel, leading the rest of the *ferrum* gladiators away with sheer force of will. Stunned, I watch them go, trying to understand why he hates me so much.

Legionnaires are supposed to serve twenty years. Every soldier receives a pension for their service, which for most is enough to retire. Some end up working as guards, taking comfortable jobs with high pay. After all, there is no better War Symbol than Iron—why not spend a few years getting rich off your *Cor* by intimidating civilian thugs? Only deserters and debtors end up gladiators, slaves once more. Whatever happened to that man, he carries a chip on his shoulder the size of a mountain. He must have been a Praetorian.

Troubled by our interaction, I turn out of the hallway and into the main courtyard. A series of braziers are planted along the second level of wall, burning brightly to hold back the night. These miniature estates provided to the different *domuum* do not have enough *lumos* relics to light the entire exterior, for which I am grateful.

I cast a furtive glance over my shoulder to see if anyone is present, but the space is empty. I force myself to meander casually toward the wall, as if I am merely a maudlin gladiator unnerved by his upcoming matches.

I climb the stairs to the upper walkway of the wall, gazing up at the looming spectacle of Bellona's Arena that blocks some of the night's stars. From Antioch, *Mons* Olympus is further to the east than I am used to, but it still floats above, stark and dead, glowing like a second moon.

As casually as I can, I turn to stand next to one of the burning braziers, trying to mask my movements. Inwardly, my body is raging, my smallest Heart demanding to be fed even though it is full of essence I have not been able to use. My *Cor* burns with the desire to *grow*, and to do that, it must eat. But first, I must empty it.

Slowly, shifting my body to block the view of anyone who happens to enter the courtyard, I lift my right hand and slip it into the flame, giving me a physical link to the element. Heat lashes at me, but my connection to Unrelenting Fire meets it like a delighted host.

I push some of my essence into the fire, cursing as it flares as if I fed it a new log. Gritting my teeth, I force the stream that I am pouring out to slow down to a trickle. My brazier burns a little brighter than the rest, but not so much that I think it is suspicious. As my reserves begin to drop a little, I split my attention, cultivating fresh Fire essence to refill what I am using. A thrill runs through me as I succeed in moving it in two directions at once. I've never been able to manage that before with my new Symbol.

Like the snow in *Domus* Pelias's training hall, it is not the exact form of essence I need. This fire is new and burns from wooden logs. It is not a never-ending fire to the gods. It is only regular Fire, and it must be changed to meet my needs. I clench it with my will, condensing it as if it were a lump of coal, trying to turn it into a diamond. I feel my Copper veins struggle under the pressure of converting the essence, and a wild smile crosses my face. After more than a week of being kept from making any progress, even this little strain feels like a gift from the dead gods.

"It is an ominous sight, isn't it?" a deep voice asks from the night. Startled, I leap back from the brazier, dropping my hand to my hip as I turn to face my master, Senator Varus himself. He stands on the far side of the fire, watching me with his penetrating eyes.

"*Dominus*, I beg your pardon, I did not see you—" I stammer, cursing my inattentiveness. I had been so focused on my cultivation, I hadn't noticed the Golden *electus* sneak up on me.

"*Pax*," he commands gently, an ancient greeting. It means "peace," but I feel none of it. "I did not mean to startle you, Castor. I was just coming to stare at my old foe and found you doing the same." His gaze drifts toward the arena's dark outline.

"Old foe, *Dominus*?" I am surprised by his words.

"Oh yes." He chuckles warmly, amused by my confusion. "You did not know that I also once fought in an arena?" I am stunned by this, unable to imagine him as a common fighter. He laughs again, enjoying my surprise.

"You were a gladiator?"

"No." He shakes his head, his amused expression fading. "I never competed for the Bloody Laurel. The games are not just for entertainment—they are a weapon, a means of control. The Empress and her consuls use them to gather the people in one place, then remind everyone of their power."

"I don't understand."

"I was the third son of my father," he says softly, as if looking back through time. "I was not supposed to be the heir of my family, nor was I sent to the legions to earn glory for my House. Instead, I was merely an extra, kept around in case I was needed." Standing near to the fire and not drawing from it is driving me insane. Its siren call pulls at me like a lover, begging me to come closer. But I dare not risk it in his presence.

"But then I was needed." His tone grows darker. "The son of another family made advances on my sister, and when she refused him, he took what he wanted instead. So, I did what my older brother could not and challenged him *viritim*—man-to-man. Then I cut him into little pieces in front of his family." Slowly, I turn to regard the older man in a new light. Varus destroyed several of the Shadowbound in the garden, but this is a different side of him.

"Who was it, *Dominus*?"

"His name was Gallenicus Valerus."

I know that name all too well.

Brennus Valerus tried to murder me and instead killed my friend Macer in Agogia before being elevated to *Fidelis* in my place. Abruptly, I realize that Varus is not looking at Bellona's Arena, but at the estate just down the street that holds their gladiators.

"I see you've heard of them."

"Yes, *Dominus*."

The senator is silent for a long time, glowering into the darkness. A grim presence radiates off him like a dark flame. During the fight, he tore one of the *sicarii* to shreds, but I did not see how.

"What followed was a short but brutal feud between our families." Varus's mouth tightens, but his voice does not waver. His gray eyes remain fixed on the distant Valerus estate, firm in their hate.

"When enough blood had been spilled, the Empress herself stepped in. She ordered that I stand trial in the red sands of the Mars's Arena for my crime of killing her nephew. There in the eyes of all, Gallenicus's siblings and cousins were allowed to challenge me to single combat. They were meant to wear me down like hunting dogs until I was dead, ending the feud and my life." A hint of dry amusement enters his voice as he continues. "I am still here, so obviously, they failed."

"Forgive me, *Dominus*, but what is your Symbol? I caught only a glimpse of it in the dark." I remember seeing a great disruption as the Shadowbound tried to kill him, and I want to know what that power is.

Varus is silent, and for a moment, I fear I have overstepped. But then he snorts, amused by my daring. "The Enduring Boulder."

A Rock Symbol. No wonder he was able to track the Shadowbound's movements despite their dark shroud. He knew them by their footsteps upon the stone. I shake my head in stunned admiration, trying to picture the palatine cutting his way through the Valerus family one-by-one. It is not hard to do.

"When Diana's attempt with the sword failed, that was when the knifework began." He does not need to tell me what that means; I have seen it firsthand. "My brothers did not survive the next year. My mother jumped from a tower in Forum six months after their deaths. All our enemies were emboldened to act, knowing Diana would turn a blind eye to their treachery. My wife—" His voice cuts off, but there is no doubt that he hides another tragedy in the silence.

"Why are you telling me this, *Dominus*?" I ask after it has been quiet for a long time. Varus does not answer right away; instead, he just stares into the darkness at the enemies that surround him like wolves. He seems less a senator and more a Tribune.

"Perhaps it is because I can." He laughs in derision. "You are oathbound to carry my secrets. There are few that a senator can speak plainly to."

I am quiet at that. Varus is different now. When he first bought me from Dorian's pit, he treated me with the same wariness that a man has for a *tigris*, but now, he speaks to me like I am a trusted confidant.

Yes, I am bound to keep his secrets, but he does not strike me as a man who needs to be heard. No, this is not for his own sake that he tells me this story. This is because I have spilled blood in his name, and that is how his trust is measured.

"Forgive me, but I do not believe that is why." The words pop out of my mouth before I can stop them.

"Then maybe it is because you do not yet understand what is at stake here. What the other *domuum* around us will do to finish us."

"You're saying they will cheat?" The question sounds foolish to my own ears. Of course they will. If they cheat in Agogia, they will do the same here.

Varus's disgusted grunt tells me he thinks the same.

"Are you telling the rest of the gladiators this?"

He hesitates.

"Then why me?"

"The Silver Circuit is the least popular of all the gladiator games. Do you know why?" I shake my head at him from across the fire. "Because it is like watching a gangly, unruly lion hunt a foal. Coppers are amusing in their own way. They're so confident, but they are only at the beginning of their paths. They smash into each other like brave little children. Silvers have begun to see the truth, and it has slowed them down. They are not decisive, they struggle to use their *Cor* Hearts now that it can reach beyond them."

I think of the other gladiators I have dueled. Many of them are guilty of that hesitation. I assumed it was because they were not yet killers, but maybe there is more to it.

"You do not." The senator's eyes bore into me with a calm focus. I remember him telling me that I was the first gladiator he ever bought that he thought might be able to kill him one day. "You use your ice like you were born to it, like it is just another muscle in your body."

I am silent, unsure how to answer a question that he has not asked. Both of my Symbols, Iron and Ancient Frost, feel like they are a part of me. But it is strange to think that this is different than it is for other *electi*. I cannot imagine them any other way.

"Do you have any family?" The senator's voice is probing, but there is no malice in it. Instead, it seems like there is a hint of… understanding? I match his stare evenly, trying to decide how much I dare to lie.

"I see," he says before I can speak, understanding the answer in my silence. "You and I are not so different. We may be bound to different Symbols and grew up in different homes, but we burn with the same cold."

I cock my head to the side in surprise, considering his words. There has always been an understanding between us. Perhaps now I finally know why.

"I hate this place," he tells me, turning to stare back up at the shadow of the Bellona Arena above us. "It is a servant to a sickness, a rot that eats us from the inside. But *Domus* Pelias is currently the worst-ranked gladiator *ludus* in the Empire." The senator's voice is grim as he tells me what I have already surmised. "If we do not improve our rankings before the end of the Circuit, I will lose my license to own one. Doing so will have… repercussions."

"Then why come here? Why participate? Is your yearly quota of *Corda* truly so important?" I cannot understand why he might need more. As far as I know, Alessandra is his only child, and she is already a Silver like me. What other use can there be for them that is so vital?

"Bah, that is a distraction." Varus waves his hand dismissively into the night.

"Then what is at stake?"

"My seat in the Senate. My *Domus*. My child's life. My own."

"You have to have a gladiator house to be in the Senate?" I am baffled by his response. That cannot be possible. There are far more senators than there are *ludi* in the Empire.

"My surname is Pelias," he reminds me stiffly. "I am the leader of one of the great *Domuum*, a descendant of the Iron Lords. My ancestor slew Neptune in his watery home. Already my enemies whisper to the people that my House is fading. My siblings are dead. I am the last." He is silent for a moment, a man in mourning of a legacy lost.

"I have only one daughter. The tree withers, they say. Look at how Varus leads his great line into ruin. It will be an easy thing for them to convince the mob to replace me with someone *stronger*. The Iron Empire loves it when their tyrants are strong." A note of bitterness creeps into his voice.

"How many of the other descendants of Iron Lords have gladiator licenses?" I ask, my suspicion growing.

"All save Delilah, whose family never had one."

"What happens if you lose your Senate seat?"

He gives me a wry look. "Then what little protections I have will be stripped away, and my enemies"—he nods his head toward the waiting arena to make it clear who exactly he means—"will be free to strike at me and mine directly."

I shudder at the thought of the Shadowbound assassins being considered a sign of restraint in the battle between palatines. I also note that I fall under the category of "his." If he loses his seat and the wolves come into the paddock, they will gladly feast on me as well as him.

"And what of the Censors' threat of *Judicium*?" My heart hammers in my chest as I ask my question in a whisper. Antioch is not Forum or Anteforum, yet I am certain it is full of ears that listen.

"It is a goad, a prod." Varus shrugs dismissively, as if the specter of the Empress's judgment is the least of his concern. "They use it to make me nervous, like hunters beating the bushes to make the birds fly up. The danger is elsewhere."

Over Varus's shoulder, I spy a figure emerging from the shadows of the fourth hallway. I keep my face blank as Anas slinks into the pool of light nearby, just far enough to make sure that I have seen him. I give my head a tiny shake, dismissing him. Frustration bleeds through the edges of my concentration. This conversation has come at a poor time. I intended to ask Anas to steal enough torches for me to really be able to cultivate, but I dare not risk letting Varus see the two of us together again.

"So now you know why you must win."

I nod, surprised by how unaffected I am by this. I figured there was more to the game Varus was playing, but it changes nothing for me. I have always needed to win. Now I understand why he needs me to.

The silence stretches between us. I no longer look at Bellona's Arena or the other dormitories surrounding us that hold our competitors. Instead, I stare at *Luna*. The moon's waning crescent hangs above the city like a scythe, a foretelling of the days to come. I feel a kinship to its cold light, and I let myself drift in its embrace. Ancient Frost and Iron seem to relax with me, enjoying this harsh, white specter. Only Unrelenting Fire rages in its cage in my body. It much prefers the warmth of *Sol*.

When the moment has passed, I am only mildly surprised to realize that Varus has vanished, gone as quietly as he arrived. I chuckle as I realize he had no need to stare at his enemies like some brooding adolescent. He only came up here to pass his warning to me.

I stay by the fire for hours, quietly soaking up as much of its essence as I can, straining my Copper veins, forcing them to grow. I cannot shake the feeling that I am being observed, but I cannot see them with my eyes or feel them with Iron and Ancient Frost. Let them watch, I decide after a while. I cannot afford to lose.

CHAPTER 23

The gladiator games begin with a parade.

I can hear them cheering already, the patricians and plebeians that throng the streets outside our quarters, waiting to catch a glimpse of the fighters who will bleed and die for their entertainment. A twisting contempt begins to grow in me like a dark vine as I listen to their delighted screams. Gladiators are not people to them. We are convicts, deserters, and slaves. Once, I might have thought the same thing. But now, I know far too well how blind justice can be to the truth.

"Golds, Silvers, Coppers, Irons, Blanks," Contessa shouts, organizing us as she moves along the courtyard, gesturing for us to fall in line. We are dressed in our *Domus* Pelias leathers, stamped with the symbol of the broken trident. At the *lanista*'s direction, we form three columns of two, nestling ourselves behind the Golden gladiators. Absently, I rub my forearm, resisting the urge to pick at the fresh coat of paint that covers my Copper veins, hiding my secret. It seems like such a flimsy shield to protect my life.

Malus Mors, the big dark-skinned gladiator who was also purchased from Dorian's pit, turns from the rear of the *aureate* column to give me a broad smile. "So, you made it to your first games?" he booms.

"I made it to my first games," I echo, trying to force my face to match his warmth. Inside, I am only cold. Even Unrelenting Fire seems muted, as if that Symbol understands the import of what is to come. The tall man does not have a hint of nervousness about him as he casts his glance over the rest of our column.

"Maybe you will have a name soon too." I remember that the big man already being called "*Malus Mors*" had been a selling point of Dorian's when he showed him to Varus all those months ago.

"What does that mean?" I ask, looking up at him. "How did you earn your name?"

The Strength *electus* looks at me for a moment, then snorts in amusement as he looks away. "It means I killed a man in the Games."

I shudder at the thought of what would have earned him the name "Bad Death" in that context. Then I remember his inhuman strength and decide I would rather not know.

"Stay together and follow the person in front of you!" Contessa roars like a centurion as the double gates of our courtyard begin to swing open. Varus stands at the head of our column, gray eyes watching us with intensity. He sees me looking at him and inclines his head slightly, reminding me of his warnings.

As if I could forget.

I must win.

The Ironbound guards of *Domus* Pelias march alongside us, a single man on either side of each tier. They carry banners bearing the broken trident. I eye them suspiciously, wondering where they have all come from. Varus originally only brought a few of the former soldiers, but their numbers seem to have swelled since the attack at the garden.

With a start, I recognize a blond man who is only a few years older than me. The last time I saw him, he wore the white of the Spartan Guard. It seems that Delilah's personal contingent has folded in with Varus's. I eye the senator as she comes to stand next to Varus, wrapping her arm through his like a lady on her way to the ball. Perhaps that is unsurprising.

We snake our way out of the dormitory and into the cobbled street that runs toward the arena. Other gladiator *domuum* march in front of us, and we join in their wake to form a long, winding parade of warriors. I spy the pile of golden coins that is the Crassus emblem, and the *pegasus* of the Cornelii family, in the distance.

A chill runs through me as I step into the Bellona Arena's long shadow. This does not feel real. It is as if I am about to set foot into another world, another place. Our gods may be dead, but they do not need to be alive to still rule over us.

The end of the street is closed off by a series of long metal barricades. Plebeians cram against the railing, waving to get the attention of the more popular fighters as we pass by. Some have their faces painted in the colors of their favorite *domus*. Vendors move among the crowd hawking their wares.

A pressure builds on the back of my neck, and I glance over my shoulder to see another column exiting their own quarters. My eyes settle on the gray *krakenus* that follows in our wake, and Unrelenting

Fire finally makes its presence known as an old rage rekindles in my chest. It is no accident that the Valerus family follows in our shadow, I am certain. These palatine are nothing if not petty.

I catch Anas's eye at the front of the *Ferrum* gladiators behind the Coppers. I cock my head in the direction of the banners of Brennus's family, and he follows my gaze to take them in. His gaze is hard when he turns back to me. He remembers Macer well.

Varus, to his credit, does not look to the left or right. He continues forward, with Delilah on his arm and Alessandra at his side, remarking on something to the pair of them as we sweep past the assembled throngs and into the arena itself.

The *ludi* enter through a large archway that leads to a tunnel with no other exits. A bright light shines at the far end, and our parade advances steadily. Our footsteps echo off the curved stone ceiling, drowning us in the noise of marching.

But as I draw nearer to the far end of the tunnel, a new sound drowns it out. It rolls in a steady, crushing onslaught, building in power as we get closer. I have just enough time to realize that it is the sound of the crowd before we burst out of the tunnel and into the ring itself.

"**Presenting the *Ludus Domus* Pelias from Anteforum**!" a magnified voice booms, echoing off the stones around us.

Unlike the dream version of Mars's Arena that Contessa trained me in, Bellona's sand is a pure white. *Sol*'s fiery fury shines off it brilliantly, making me squint under the sudden light as we emerge. A deafening wall of sound hammers us as we emerge. I almost stagger under the weight of it.

Thirty thousand citizens of the Iron Empire scream at the sight of us. The *domuum* ahead of us lead us in a slow circle of the entire ring. Even though the pressure of the crowd is different in the real world from the *somnatorium*, it feels familiar. But it is also much more potent than the pretend version. The people are real; their eyes have weight. They chant the names of their favorite gladiators like prayers. It is overwhelming—almost drowning. I imagine being thrown into the waves of the sea that lies just beyond Antioch's walls would feel much the same.

"*Domus* Pelias is currently the lowest-ranked *ludus* in the Empire," the voice continues commentating as we circle, although no longer as loudly. "It has entered with a record-setting *six* new gladiators for this event, including two named *aurum electi*: *Malus Mors* and *Fantasia*. No other *domus* has changed their composition this much in the middle of a Circuit in the last hundred years. The fees alone must be staggering! Senator Varus is really counting on his new conscripts to tip the scales." I resist the urge to roll my eyes, but only barely.

"**Presenting *Ludus Domus* Valerus from Forum!**" the voice booms once more at its increased volume. The cheers of the crowd explode, far louder than they did for us, I note.

"The current Circuit leader, *Domus* Valerus, looks to set a new record in the Games with their fifth consecutive victory spearheaded by the terrifying *aurum* gladiator *Fracti Regis*—the Broken King. Another win will further solidify Senator Xania as the greatest *ludus* owner in the history of the Empire…" The crowd cheers again, overshadowing whatever else the announcer had to say about how great *Domus* Valerus is. I am grateful to be spared.

"Smile," Illy mutters through gritted teeth as we march along the edge of the ring against the edge of the ten-foot-high wall that separates us from the crowd. People crowd at the lip of the ledge, screaming down at us, begging for attention.

"What?" I ask, startled away from my inspection of the people.

"Smile and wave," he emphasizes, raising his own hand to lead by example. "You're new; you have to start getting some fans early." He winks at a group of young women who all shriek in delight. I'm too stunned to do anything other than follow his instructions.

Hesitantly, I lift my right hand and plaster a false smile on my lips. The crowd around us erupts as I make eye contact with a few people. A small boy points excitedly at me while shouting at his father. I am horrified that he is here. My mother would have never let me come to this place.

"They don't even know who I am," I protest through the corner of my mouth to Illy.

"It doesn't matter." He laughs, adding it to his charm. "You're a *gladiator*." His words are mocking but contain a nugget of truth. They have been told to revel in this, so it does not matter who they celebrate as long as they pick someone.

Despite my disdain, I feel myself getting sucked into the excitement. Their exuberance begins to echo in me, warming me like a little hint of fire. There is a sea of people here. Briannus's boasts of the money he makes for the Empire off the Games suddenly don't seem so grandiose.

That warmth dims as I pass under a lone Censor standing on the edge of the wall, glaring down at us with hard eyes. There is a bubble of empty space around him; even the patricians do not dare to get too close to the White Hand of the Empress.

It is not Atticus or anyone I recognize. He is young, only a few years older than me, and his crossed arms are marked by Copper veins. Despite that, he wears the *tellus lorica* and carries a matching sword. I lock my smile in place and keep moving as his watery blue eyes pass over me. I scan the rest of the ring, noticing a dozen other Censors standing at the edge, watching us with hard faces. Their message is clear—everything in this place happens under her eyes.

"Will she be here?" I ask, struck by the sudden thought.

"Who?"

"The Empress?"

"Here?" Illy's laugh is almost scornful. "This is a place of blood and death. Not for one such as her." I say nothing, for what is there to say? In the Iron Empire, our gods are dead. She is the closest thing to holy that we have.

We grind to a halt as all sixteen of the *ludi* in attendance fill the ring from one end to the other. The crowd falls quiet, vibrating with hushed excitement, waiting for the show to begin. A horn sounds into the silence, long and low. The hairs on the back of my neck stand on end as I recognize it as some variation of the legion muster call, but lower and more resonant. A dozen more trumpets begin to blare, their notes echoing off the arena in measured succession.

The sand shakes as a hole opens in the center and a platform rises from the ground. Five figures stand on it, all of them priests, dressed in the ceremonial torn robes of acolytes to dead gods. Four of them hold goats, which wriggle in their grasp. The fifth steps forward, holding a black object before his face, some sort of relic.

"In the days before we became Iron, Bellona was the Goddess of War and Rage. She delighted in the art of combat and the spilling of blood. It was she, along with her husband Mars, who taught us the secret of forging our legions," the priest's voice booms. He is not shouting, but it seems to emanate from a thousand tongues that surround us.

"The *Ferrum* Domini, the Iron Lords, slew the gods and freed us from their oppression. But some of their influence, their guidance, lives on. This is a holy place, for it is the last place that their touch can be felt." I shuffle uncomfortably, drawing an annoyed look from Illy.

"Our ancestors were taught that the Games were called *munera*, which means gifts. These games were our gifts of blood and violence to the gods. The gods are dead; even we priests know that. But this is still a gift, great citizens of the Empire! A gift from the Empress to you! A gift of fire and blood!"

As he shouts, the other four acolytes draw their knives and slit the throats of their goats before dropping the squirming beasts. The animals flee from their captors with their final heartbeats, leaving bright red trails on the pristine sand as they run. The crowd thunders to life, roaring in murderous joy as the sacrifice is completed. One by one, the goats crumple and lie still. I am silent, unnerved for the first time by what I have seen.

As the people shout their approval, the parade begins to move once more. We complete our circuit of the ring, then exit through a pair of giant doors that are wide open. Our path descends down a ramp to the underbelly of the arena, where other *domuum* begin to splinter off as they head to their assigned areas.

In some ways, the facility underneath the arena is more impressive than the towering structure above. Dense tunnels run the length of the grounds, full of machines and industry. Men and women wearing the pale green livery of the arena race in every direction, transporting goods and preparing for the first fight. The Blanks will begin immediately, as an appetizer for the true violence that is to come.

Domus Pelias is assigned a place in the back corner of the complex. Our column pauses, waiting to be let into our sector, but the gate is locked. I am not surprised to discover *Domus* Valerus has somehow been assigned the one across the hall. Here in the far recesses of the arena, there are few eyes to see what happens. Their gladiators point and laugh at us as they pass us, confident in their superiority.

"Ah, Senator Varus," a woman calls, stepping over to accost our line. I see the resemblance to Brennus immediately. Tall and blonde, she reeks of power and privilege, even without the Golden veins that run down her arms. This can only be his mother. Crow's feet gather in the corners of her eyes, and a hint of gray plays at her temples, but she is strong and vibrant, still in her prime. She reminds me of a serpent, the way her tight smile spreads across her face.

"Senator Xania," he replies coolly, stepping away from Delilah and his daughter to meet her in the wide hallway. His face could be made of stone for all the expression it holds. Tension vibrates off them like a pair of cellos. Their hatred shines brightly behind the masks that they wear, peeking out of their eyes like a dark light.

"I'm surprised you agreed to being stabled this far in the rear. Surely the highest-ranked *domus* should be awarded the prime position?" Varus smiles thinly as if commiserating with her. They both know she bribed someone to be able to taunt us. She probably paid for our gate to be locked when we arrived just so she could have this moment.

"Oh, I don't know." The blonde viper smiles. "I like the view from here just fine."

"We'll see," Varus replies calmly, refusing to rise to her bait.

"Six new gladiators? What a bold choice," she continues, game to needle him further. I feel like I am trapped in an alleyway with her son once more. Xania's gray eyes track toward me, noting my *rasa* veins at a glance.

"Is this one of your new crop? I hope you got a discount for his *impurities*." I match her gaze coolly, pulling on Ancient Frost and Iron to balance out the angry response that boils in my gut, egged on by Unrelenting Fire. I feel like a man holding three dogs on a leash, each pulling him in a different direction.

"I got a deal," Varus agrees in the same cool tone. It might have been my imagination, but the corner of his mouth looks like it twitches, barely holding back a smile.

"Mother, let's go up," a man interrupts, his tone sharp with frustration. "It's disgusting down here. Whichever one of those idiot *compositores* put us back with the riff-raff should be whipped—" For once, all my Symbols agree on a course of action, driven into a cold fury by the familiar voice.

It takes every fiber of my self-control not to throw myself at Brennus as he appears to stand next to his mother. Macer's killer is no longer a recruit; he wears the full purple regalia of the Praetorians, complete with gold decurion chevrons on his shoulder. The iron *inhibitus* still glints around his neck, but his exposed arms are wrapped with thick Silver veins. He has become a *Fidelis*.

My hands ball into a fist. We were not allowed to carry weapons during the parade, but thanks to Aquilo, as long as I have Ancient Frost essence, I am always armed. I lean forward, about to take a step, and summon the *Glacialis Falx*, when a hand grabs my right forearm, stopping me in place.

Surprised, I turn my head to see Alessandra at my side, her blue eyes staring into mine. Imperceptibly, she shakes her head, warning me to keep my rage in check. Clarity surges through me like a lightning bolt, reminding me where I am. I force myself to blink several times as I release my Symbols. The fury dims as they retreat. After a moment, I nod at her, letting her know I am back in control. The young woman does not remove her hand from my arm. Its warmth spreads across my skin.

"You remember my second son, don't you, Varus?" Xania asks arrogantly. "He has just been selected as one of the new *Fidelia* for the Praetorians. I convinced Tyrus to give him leave so he can celebrate his new position and witness these *historic* games."

"What an honor it must be to have earned such faith from the legions," Varus replies dryly. Xania's eye twitches ever so slightly at my master's sarcasm. Brennus glances in my direction, and I feel Alessandra's grip on my wrist tighten, but she need not have worried. He only notices my *rasa* veins with a snort before he moves on. His gaze never even flicks up to my face. The Praetorian is not the type of palatine to ever look a slave in the eye.

"Spare me your commentary," Brennus sneers, turning back to Varus. "It's all hot wind coming from a walking corpse anyway." The room goes silent at his threat. Xania's face pales slightly as if she sees a danger that her idiot son cannot.

"I'm not sure I take your meaning," Varus says in a low, slow tone. Something *dark* flickers behind his expression, which makes the matriarch of *Domus* Valerus reach for her son's arm in warning. I wonder if that look was the last thing many of her family members saw.

But the young Praetorian feels invincible, and he steps out of range of his mother's reach, getting closer to the senator. I know the cold thoughts that circle in the back of his mind like hungry wolves. They are the same ones that lurk in mine. He is a *Fidelis*, the most powerful War Symbol in the Empire. What does he have to fear from an old politician?

"It's Legion slang, Varus, dear," Xania says sharply, cutting off her son as he opens his mouth to double down on his threat. I feel a smirk run across my face as I see the fear that lurks behind her eyes. She may have Varus on his back foot, but she still knows what he is capable of.

"Ah yes, I think I remember hearing your brother say something similar." Varus's smile is cold and cruel. He does not look away from Brennus's face as he reminds the boy who killed his uncle. "He was a *Fidelis* too, as I recall, wasn't he, Xania? He must have picked it up there." My eyebrows shoot up to the top of my forehead in shock. Varus dueled a Silver Ironbound and won? My respect for my master goes up by a wide margin.

It is Brennus's turn for his face to go pale. Cruel delight surges in me, relishing in the fear on his face. It is far too little punishment to pay for what he's done, but it is like another stroke of the lash that Gaius whipped him with.

Brennus has forgotten who he's facing. He must have heard the stories when he was a boy, but now he wears the armor of a legionnaire, and Varus has been quiet for a long time. It would be different if he had been the one in the ring, the *Fidelis* tells himself. The taste of violence is thick on the air, metallic like blood. Abruptly, both the Valerus *electi* seem to realize that all their gladiators have passed into their quarters, but all of our *ludus* is standing behind Varus, still waiting to be let into ours.

The tension in the hallway spikes to a heavy crescendo. I can feel my heartbeat pounding in my ears as I lean forward, pulling against Alessandra's grip. The moment Brennus lunges at Varus, she will have to let me go. My oath will compel me to act, and I will do so with absolute delight.

"A thousand apologies for the delay, Senator!" A short man in the green livery of the arena barrels down the hall between the two staring palatines. A giant keyring jingles in his fist as he races toward us. "I told the porters to unlock all the quarters this morning, but they must have missed one. Portunus's Bleached Bones! It's a good thing they can carry heavy things because they can't be trusted with much else." He sticks the key into the gate and unlocks it with a *click*.

"There you are, right as rain!" He steps back from the entrance with a bright smile, gesturing for Varus to enter. The grizzled senator glances at the short man with amusement for a moment before inclining his head to the man with the keys.

"Thank you," he says.

"Enjoy the Games!" the servant replies enthusiastically, unaware of the thick tension in the air between the two *domuum* that stand in the hall.

"Oh," Varus replies, his gaze tracking back to Xania and her son with a knowing glint. "I think I shall."

CHAPTER 24

At first glance, the gladiator quarters seem surprisingly small compared to how many of us are competing. An armory holds our weapons, sharp and polished. A tiny sand square allows fighters to limber up before a match, and there are enough benches for a half-dozen to sit if they are willing to get close. I cannot imagine any senator spending time in this dark, musty place.

"All the way through," Contessa barks from the gate as I enter. Alessandra no longer holds my arm but walks a few steps ahead of me. The *lanista*'s gaze travels from the Pelias heir to me with a thoughtful expression on her face that I do not like.

"Pilus and Tryndus, stay here. Everyone else, on the lift," she orders, gesturing for me to head to the back of the room. I follow the line of gladiators, surprised to discover an elevator waiting for us, made of stone and inlaid with gold. It holds more than a score of us with ease.

I laugh as we begin to ascend. It almost feels like flying. I have never ridden on such a thing before. A few of the gladiators laugh too, although whether it is at the novelty of the experience or at me, I cannot tell.

"You think that's something? Just wait until we get to the boxes," Illy whispers to me as the elevator hums, pulling us along smoothly, powered by unseen relics.

"The what?"

"Just wait and see." The shorter man grins up at me, a hint of delight on his face. "This is one of the only good surprises gladiators can have. Enjoy the moment." After a dozen heartbeats, we slow to a stop, and the doors open, allowing us to file out into true luxury.

We're in a structure that hangs at the top of the Bellona Arena. It is a massive, terraced space that could serve as a ballroom in a palatine's estate. The entire front wall is covered in smooth, flawless glass that looks down into the open ring below.

Tiered seats are arrayed with thick purple cushions for at least fifty people to watch the Games from the comfort of this private viewing space. A feast is laid out on the upper level, and as we enter, servants flow in, carrying flagons of wine and platters of fresh food. The senators make their way to the front seat, where more palatines wait, greeting Varus and Delilah with wide smiles. The rest of the gladiators spread out, uncomfortable to be in such a place.

"Whoa," I whisper in awe at the opulence.

"There are perks to being owned by a senator." Illy grins at me as he heads toward the table. I follow but am distracted by the sight of a large board that hangs on the far wall. A long bar sweeps across it from side to side, holding a flat *graphis* relic up against it as it moves. Names and numbers fill in as I watch in awed silence.

ORDO LUDI, it reads in big letters across the top. This is the current score of all the gladiator *domuum* that are competing in the Circuit. In the first line is the name of the current season leader: *LUDUS VALERUS: LII*—fifty-two. The next closest competitor is the Grus family, who only has forty-three points. No wonder the announcer was singing Xania's praises during the parade—no one is even close to keeping up with them.

There are well over a score of names on the list, more than have come to Antioch to compete. The names of the missing *ludi* are marked with an asterisk, denoting that they will not receive any points for this event.

At the bottom, even beneath the ones that are not here, I find the entry for *LUDUS PELIAS: XII*. A wolfish smile crosses my face at the omen. It feels right that they are at twelve points when their gladiator from the Twelfth Legion joins them. Unconsciously, my right hand raises to rub at the brand on my chest.

Despite my appreciation of the number, it is an abysmal score. The next lowest *domus*, the Belascus family, has twenty-one, leaving us quite the gap to gain, even though they are not in attendance.

I frown as I study the board. Contessa has not bothered to teach about *how* the Games are played. She cares only that I learn how to kill. I suppose that makes sense. I do not need to understand the strategy that she and Varus employ. I just need to win the battles that they choose for me. But it would be wise to learn what I can.

I catch Illy's eye as he steps away from the feast, holding a plate loaded high with fruit and meat. He sighs but comes to me when I jerk my head at the board. His expression sours as he reads the scores for himself.

"It's not a pretty sight," he muses, popping a brilliant red grape into his mouth and crushing it noisily. "What about it?"

"How does it work?"

He stares at me blankly, pausing mid-chew to answer. "The *graphis* relic is made from graphite, which is commonly used in writing materials. This one is linked to the master one so that it copies whatever the *compositores* scribe with theirs—"

"Not that," I interrupt, rolling my eyes at the smaller man. "How do we get points?"

"What do you mean 'how do we get points?'" He mimes my voice in a high pitch. "You don't know how a gladiator game is scored?"

Mutely, I shake my head.

"Mars's Ashes, you are the worst gladiator in the history of the Empire," he grumbles, dropping his grapes back onto his plate. "Fortunately for me and this lovely plate of food, Reese is obsessed with this stuff."

"She is?" I glance at the girl with the horse-mane hair skeptically. She holds a flagon of watered-down wine in her two hands as she stares out at the empty fields contemplatively.

"Watch this," the duelist confides to me before turning toward her. "Hey, Reese, Castor doesn't know how to be a gladiator."

"What?" She turns to look at us, as do half of the other fighters spread across the room. I flush, turning to shoot a glare at my only friend.

"He just asked me how the points work."

"Oooh!" The tall Lightbound *electus* surges to her feet with a bright smile, practically jogging across the giant room toward us. The rest of the room chuckles at my expense, which only sours my mood further. Alessandra gives me a skeptical look from her father's side at the front of the gallery.

"Thanks for that," I mutter.

"Gotta make you seem human somehow." He shrugs, picking up another grape without a care in the world. Reese slides to a stop in front of us, eyes sparkling with excitement.

"Do you really not know how the scoring system works?" she asks, sounding afraid that this was a practical joke at her expense. Someone laughs again.

"I really don't," I manage through clenched teeth.

"Okay, wow, there's a lot to cover." She places her flagon down on a side table so her hands can be free to gesture. "There are only two things that matter in scoring. The tier of the *electi* in the fight and if there are survivors."

I frown, surprised by how simple that sounds. "I'm not following."

"Okay, Copper matches are worth one *marca*. They're just there to keep people interested between the big matches. The same with Iron, because they're basically the same thing." She counts on her fingers as she explains. "Silvers are worth two. Gold fights are three each. Only Silvers and Golds can compete in tournaments that have some other bonuses if you win."

"And the Blanks?" I ask, surprised to hear them left out.

"No points—think of them like an appetizer. They're just there for the story. Who will earn themselves a *Cor* and a chance to become a *real* gladiator?" She waves her hand dismissively. "It's all theater to get the people excited. Every *ludus* is required to field a team of Blanks, but they don't really care about them until they become Coppers." I thought about the group of laughing fighters back in the mess hall of the Pelias estate with a bitter understanding. Poor little sheep are here to be sacrificed.

"What was that bit about survivors?"

"You get two more *marcae* if you kill your opponent." Her eyes lose a little of their glow.

"Wow." I turn back to the board, trying to move on from these grim thoughts. "So, we've won fewer fights than I thought this Circuit."

"Two Copper, one Iron, two Silver, and two Golds," she recites without hesitation. "No eliminations." I decide to ignore the fact that Leon is the only Silver to have won a bout for our *ludus*.

"Right, well, I guess it's time we do something about that," I mutter. "Do the winners of the tournament get more?" A heavy weight has settled over my neck like a yoke. But despite our poor placement, it does not seem hopeless. Varus did not say we need to win, only he must not lose his license.

"Five for winning the Copper one, ten for Iron and Silver, fifteen for Gold." I nod, beginning to see the lay of the landscape.

"We only need nine points to catch up to *Ludus* Belascus," I point out, gesturing at the second-to-last team. "That should be easy to do since they are not here, right?"

"Sure, beating a regional team is *very* impressive," Leon scoffs from where he lurks off to the side.

"Second-to-last place is not last place," I reply flatly, giving the blond boy a cool glance. "That seems like progress to me."

"Generally speaking, the *ludi* that cannot afford to attend all of the Games are viewed more as… entertainment than real competitors," Reese explains, sounding a little embarrassed on behalf of our *domus*. "For one of the great houses to be below them in score is… unusual."

"Of course it is." I sigh, counting the eight asterisks-dotted teams that have more points than us, feeling the weight pulling down on me grow with every name. The next-lowest-scoring *ludus* in attendance belongs to *Domus Crassus*, who has *only* twenty-nine points, but is likely to earn at least a few over the course of the week. We have our work cut out for us.

"Citizens of the Iron Empire, Consul Briannus Nordus is pleased to present, on behalf of the Empress Diana Agrippa, the 312th year of the Games," a voice booms into our box, pouring out of some hidden relic.

"It's starting!" Reese scampers back to her seat, leaving her flagon on the table, forgotten in her excitement.

"Well, might as well see what we're getting into," Illy suggests, nodding his head in the direction the tall woman just fled.

"You just want to sit down so you can eat uninterrupted."

"Is that a crime? I might die in the next day or two, you know. There's no shame in wanting to get in one last good meal." As a former soldier, I had to agree that he had a point.

Illy and I join the rest of the Silvers on the far-right side of the room, nestled away from the rest of the gladiators. Even Leon sticks with us, his normally haughty exterior muted somehow. I'm under no illusions that we have all suddenly become a pack. But the sight of so many other enemies around us has changed all our perspectives.

"The *Spectaculum* is starting," one of the Coppers calls to his comrades, gesturing at the window panes. The rest of the *cuprum* gladiators rush to peer down at the arena. My gut twists in horror as I realize that if I had not been found worthy to be a gladiator, I could have very well ended up among their number. The Spectacles have none of the veneer of nobility that the gladiatorial side of the Games claims to maintain. It is merely carnage—savage entertainment for savage people.

A score of men and women, ranging from Blanks to Golds, are escorted into the ring at the far Shield Gate by a group of legionnaires. At the same time, the Sword Door begins to swing open, revealing the horror that they are about to face.

"Dead gods, look at the size of that thing," one of the Blanks shouts as the *mythus* emerges from the darkness. It began its life as an *ursus*—a bear. But whatever the *Cor* it came into contact with warped it into is something far more terrifying.

It rears on its hind legs like a man as it comes into the light, towering fifteen feet tall over the heads of the poor people who have been sent to face it. Golden metal veins shine brightly among its fur, some of them thicker than my wrist. A white collar that reminds me of an *inhibitus* is fastened around its neck. It lets out a bellow and drops onto all fours, sending a shockwave of dust rippling out from the force of its impact. I am startled to learn that the hidden *sonus* relics relay the sound of their blades crossing as if we watched from only a dozen feet away. It is jarring to hear the noise of combat echoing around our feast.

A horn sounds from the *compositores*, and the crowd erupts in a bloody fervor as some of the victims of the spectacle begin to race forward, swords at the ready. At once, the bear lunges forward, moving at the speed of a Golden *electus*. Its massive paw swats at a Blank, sending him flying in a broken tangle of limbs.

"Surely they can't be expected to kill that *thing*," Illy says, his voice full of the horror I feel.

"They only need to get past it and escape," Reese corrects him mildly, her eyes fixed on the carnage unfolding below. "Although anyone who manages to slay it will be very rich."

One of the Silvers gets behind the bear and decides that it is his destiny to become wealthy. He leaps in the air, dueling blade extended toward the Golden bear's spine. Gasps spread throughout the box as everyone holds their breath, waiting to see if he will succeed.

The *ursus* turns to face the man at the last moment, maw open as it lets out a colossal *roar*. Whatever Symbol the bear possesses is somehow tied to its cry. The *sonus* relics that power the arena cut out instead of carrying its power, but even at our tremendous distance, I can still feel it resonating in my chest.

The poor *argentum* who is caught in its blast evaporates, shaken to shreds by the force of the sound alone. Blood and ichor rain down on the sand, the only remains of the shredded human. A stunned silence descends on the box and the crowd below.

"Was that…" Illy's voice trails off before he says what we are all thinking. In order to have a physical power like that, the *ursus*'s Symbol must be tied to sound, which is not impossible, but it is closely regulated.

"Clearly, it is allowed," I reply dryly after a moment. "The Censors would never allow a *mythus* to break their rules." No one replies to my bait, and I am happy to let it fade. The Golden bear continues its rampage until the rest of the men and women subjected to the *Spectaculum* are dead. Not even the *aurum electi* can match its ferocity and power. None escape. The conversation slowly returns as the *ursus* is led out of the arena by its handlers, leaving the sands bloody and torn in its wake.

"The first match will be between Frontus Loticus of *Ludus* Valerus and Pilus Vestor of *Ludus* Pelias in the Blank Circuit!" the announcer thunders into his relic. A loose cheer spreads its way across the room as we realize it is one of ours, as if the carnage that we just witnessed will be banished by the violence to come.

"People won't start to get really excited until the Coppers, but it's the Golds that everyone really wants to see fight," Reese leans over Illy to tell me as the first match starts. It seems she has decided to become my tutor. Or maybe she's just excited to have someone who will listen. Either way, I am eager to soak up her knowledge.

"Varus told me something similar," I say without thinking. Far below us, the two *Cor*-less men circle each other warily, carrying swords and round shields. Their movements seem slow and languid compared to the high-powered speed that I am used to from *electi*.

"Varus, like *Dominus* Pelias, Varus?" Illy interjects around a mouthful of food. "You spoke to the senator? When?"

"Briefly," I lie, cursing myself for my carelessness. "When he bought me, he was unsure if I was *worthy* of being a gladiator." I narrow my eyes at the shorter boy. "I'm sure you recall that conversation." All five of the other Silvers had been in the Gauntlet against me.

The duelist shifts his leg uncomfortably, probably in memory of the slice I had given him across his hamstring.

"Stick it to him, Pilus!" one of the other gladiators roars as the fight below takes a turn. I glance down at the sand below. New lines of red have joined the dried ones left by the sacrificial goats. The Valerus Blank is bleeding from a slash on his leg as he retreats from our teammate.

One of the Golden gladiators reaches up and touches the glass wall in front of him, sliding his hand up on it. My jaw drops open as the view through it warps and grows larger as if the section in front of him is like a giant spyglass that he has brought into focus.

Pilus presses his advantage. His strokes are fluid and flashy. It's clear that he was trained to fight in a place like this. He would have been of no use in the shieldwall. His opponent retreats under the relentless attack, limping on his cut leg.

"This is over," Leon scoffs, rising to his feet to make his way back to the table loaded with food. Obellius follows like a silent, rocky shadow. My stomach rumbles, but I cannot bear to look away and not witness the first gladiator fight in the Games.

"I'm not so sure…" Reese replies to their backs, but they ignore her. I give her a sharp look that Illy catches over his plate. His eyes narrow as he looks at the fight with more interest. I am impressed—she has noticed the same thing that I see.

Frontus is injured, but he is pretending to be more impaired than he is. I would never have been able to tell at this distance without the wonder of the glass relics, but from our angle, it is obvious. His "wounded" left foot plants too firmly in the sand with each step instead of dragging. He is not retreating, but coiling like a serpent, biding his time before he strikes.

"Damn," Illy says after a moment of study, right before the trap is sprung.

Pilus raises his sword for a ponderous, heavy blow, trying to break through the Valerus fighter's shield. His attack leaves him exposed, which would not matter if his opponent was truly lame. Frontus explodes forward in a sudden burst of movement, dropping his shield and stabbing with his weapon. The tip of his dueling blade slices across Pilus's neck, sending blood spraying. Slowly, the Blank from *Ludus* Pelias falls to his knees, adding to the red on the white sand.

Our box is silent as we watch him die.

"It is nothing," *Malus* booms after a long moment. "That's what they're there for, eh? More blood for the ghosts of the gods!" Several other fighters cheer, raising their drinks in honor of… something. I'm not sure if they know what, or if they're carried away by the heady promise of blood and glory.

My gaze is drawn to Varus, who sits in silence in the front row of the viewing box. His face is hard, carved in granite. From my angle, I can see through his pane of the viewing relic, zoomed in on the body of the boy who has died for him. As the rest of the room resumes its conversation, only he is silent.

CHAPTER 25

More Blanks enter and die. The crowd grows dissatisfied with the violence of normal men.

"*Ferra*! *Ferra*! *Ferra*!" they chant. The plebeians in the bad seats dance as they cheer. Bored men throw empty mugs at other sections. Women throw their clothes. It is hedonistic and wild. I am not sure if this is the Arena of Bellona or of Bacchus. I feel my lip curl in disgust at the sight of their bloodlust.

In the Pelias box, it is the same, although most are too polite to admit why they are bored. The gladiators mill around in groups, talking or eating. In one corner of the room, *Malus Mors* sleeps, his feet propped up in a second chair like a footstool while he leans against the wall. Even the other Golds move past his nest with care, unwilling to disturb the named killer.

Alessandra and Delilah converse in low tones, completely turned away from the sands that have become redder as more men have died. Only Varus still watches with the same intensity, like an eagle at its roost watching the forest below.

Finally, when enough Blanks have bled, it is time for the *ferra* to take a turn. Anas and I exchange a look as he is ushered into the lift with the rest of his group. I give him a slight nod that he copies. Our loyalty is passed between us like a whisper. I know the old officer beside him catches it, but I ignore his stare. If this is truly the last time I may see my Ironbound brother, I will leave nothing unsaid.

"Citizens! The specter of the Bellona has been sated; blood has been spilled on her holy sand. To honor this, Empress Diana Agrippa is pleased to give you a glimpse of the power of the Iron Legions!"

The Iron Circuit is run differently than the others. Instead of individuals fighting duels, a full complement of six gladiators is fielded against another team in a weak mimicry of a shieldwall.

Iron is not a particularly expressive Symbol at the Copper level. Two legionnaires fighting would not look much different than two Blanks. Until they Ascend to Silver, most of the power of Iron is hidden from the naked eye. It can tear shields and break swords, but if another legionnaire uses his own Symbol to prevent that… there isn't much to witness besides two men hitting at each other with *gladii*.

By fielding an entire squad, the *ferra* gladiators will demonstrate a little more of the military might of the Empire to the average citizen. The people in the crowd will be entertained but also reminded to be afraid. My eyes travel to the palatines gathered at the front row of our seats. How many foreign dignitaries sit in boxes like this to witness exactly that power?

Ludus Pelias's first Iron match is against the Grus. My stomach clenches at the sight of the two shieldwalls as they face each other on the red-streaked sand. The gladiators wear the uniforms of their *domus*, but they have been deliberately styled to be reminiscent of the legionnaire's tunic.

As I look at them, I am suddenly back in the line. My skin puckers with the harsh cold of the North. I feel the thrumming of the shieldwall, held together by a hundred soldier's will. My breath comes in ragged gasps. I see the ghost of a dozen faces I left behind to die. I cannot bear to witness my last living brother risking his life while I do nothing. For all my power, I am helpless, and it tears at me.

I cannot watch.

I leap to my feet in an explosive burst, striding toward the buffet table like a man fleeing a fire. Behind me the gladiators hoop and holler as the lines smash into each other. None of the people in this room have ever been in the legions. They do not know what they are watching.

Woodenly, I pick up a plate as I begin making my way around the table, loading up on fruits and meats. I am not hungry—I cannot swallow a single bite—but I am desperate for anything that can distract me from the pressure to *look*. The crash of shields echoes through the relics, and I flinch.

"You should try the white cheese," a soft voice suggests as a delicate hand passes in front of my vision to point. I twitch in surprise, looking up into Alessandra's eyes. They are blue and gentle like the sky on a summer day. The heir of the house stands next to me, almost close enough that I can feel her warmth. Her expression is one of compassion mixed with warning. My eyes flick over her shoulder to the group of palatines that sit around her father and Delilah like a flock of carrion.

She nods, confirming that I have understood her message. I may not yet be in the ring, but this is not a safe place.

Clang. The shieldwalls slam into each other once more. I do not flinch, but something must show behind my eyes, for she reaches out and clasps my wrist in a comforting gesture. Only for a moment, far too brief a moment—then it is over, and she moves down the table, making sure to take some of the white cheese.

I hover around the table like a coward until the match is over, pretending to study the different foods like they are the most interesting thing in the world. The announcer gives a running commentary of the match, which only makes things worse, fueling the horrors of my imagination.

"One of *Domus* Pelias's gladiators is down; his shield is completely ruined!"

"It's going to take a talented *medico* to fix a stomach wound like that. Hopefully, Senator Pelias didn't spend all his fortune on his new fighters!"

But at last, he says something I want to hear.

"He's down! The last Grus fighter is down! It's a victory for the Pelias *ferra*, and unless I miss my guess, they will be seeing more than a few bonus *marcae* for their eliminations! We'll have to wait for the official tally—" Our box erupts in a roar of excited cheering that I shamelessly join in, leaving my plate of uneaten food on a side table as I race to the viewport, desperately looking to see if my friend survived.

I peer down the seating into one of the front panes that is zoomed in on the combatants, leaning to the left and the right to sweep the field. A bearded figure wearing the uniform of a Pelias gladiator lies on the ground, still. For a moment, my heart stops, until I note the figure who comes to kneel over him, checking for signs of life.

It is Anas.

He lives.

"Pelias *Victor*!" I shout with the rest of the room, throwing my head back to roar my relief. I turn to watch as the *ORDO LUDI* relic whirs to life, updating the scores as the judges confirm the eliminations and final points for the match.

LUDUS DOMUS PELIAS: XVI

Sixteen! The Irons have earned us four points. We're still in last place, but the gap between us and the next house has closed. We still have a long way to go, but a win this early on is a good omen.

The palatine hangers-on congratulate Varus, who is smiling for the first time since we entered this place. It seems like a weight has lifted off his shoulders, as if he is just now beginning to hope. My stomach rumbles, and I turn to look for where I left my plate. It feels appropriate to celebrate a victory with a little bit of that white cheese. My smile dies as Contessa appears in front of me, blocking my path to the food with a solemn expression.

"Castor, Illy, into the lift." Behind her, I can just make out the new chant of the crowd.

"*Argenti*! *Argenti*! *Argenti*!" It is time for the Silvers.

Illy's expression is sour and concerned as he joins me at my side. We were not supposed to fight today. There are only three of us in the lift. Pliny tries to ride down with us, but the *lanista* will not allow it.

"This is my time, Magister," she says softly. There is no cruelty to her tone, just the focus of a hunter who has a mission. The squat man accepts her judgment without complaint. They are like *Sol* and *Luna*, the two phases of *Ludus* Pelias. He understands that he must set while we go about our bloody business.

"*Be careful*," he hisses, grabbing my arm as I pass him to exit. I can only nod and promise him that I will. We both know that it is probably a lie. We ride back down into the depths in silence.

"The *compositores* have decided to add a few show matches to today's docket. They want the people to see something closer to real sport before the day is over," Contessa tells us when the lift's doors open to our small quarters under the arena. The walls are filled with weapons and armor. The space seems claustrophobic now, closing in on me on all sides like an ambush.

"So, we're being punished for our victory?" I give the bald woman a wry smile. She frowns, no hint of levity in her now.

"No, you're being trusted with a responsibility."

I square my shoulders at the implied rebuke and nod, trying to copy her tone. Beside me, Illy groans as he realizes that us winning the tournament back in Anteforum has put us in this position.

"I shouldn't have had that second plate," he mutters under his breath.

"This is a special opportunity," Contessa continues, ignoring his complaints. "Individual combat does not begin for Silvers until tomorrow. Today's match gives you a chance to earn extra points. Do not waste it."

I nod in understanding. A tournament has a set number of fights that take place based on how many competitors there were. By adding an extra battle, they have created a way for us to close the gap. If we win.

"Do we know our opponents?" I ask, moving to inspect the armory wall. I would kill to wear a *lorica* once more, but that is the province of the *ferra* gladiators. I worry it would invite too much suspicion for me to choose to wear something so heavy.

"The only perk of being at the bottom of the ladder is the lack of surprises." This time, Contessa gives me a smile, but it is twisted and sickly. "The *compositores* have matched us against *Domus* Valerus—"

"I'm starting to sense a theme," I grumble, but she does not deign to acknowledge my comment. "They have entered a single gladiator to face you."

"A single Silver?" Illy splutters in rage. "Are you serious?"

"I'm missing something," I say, looking between my irate friend and our serious *lanista*.

"They made a deal. If they win with only one, their points are doubled," Contessa explains calmly. Her eyes flash, the first sign of emotion she has shown. There is disrespect in the Valerus's choice, and it is targeted straight at her—and at me.

"They chose me because I'm an *immundus*, didn't they?"

"They argued that it would add to the spectacle."

"That will be their mistake," I promise her.

"Who is it?"

"A named fighter called *Impostor*."

"Mars's Rotting Beard, it's *Impostor*?" Illy demands in horror. "Of course it's bloody him. Who else would they send to murder us? He's going to cut us to little pieces."

"You know him?" I ask.

"He's only one of the most famous Silver gladiators on the circuit," Illy snaps, pulling his long, thin blade from the wall.

"What's his Symbol?"

"It's some sort of Earth one," Contessa says, keeping her cool despite Illy's ranting. "They call it *Locus*—Place, but that's not a real Symbol. It lets him transport himself from one place to another in the blink of an eye." My face goes pale as I try to imagine a way to fight an enemy who can appear behind me at will.

"Well, I see why he doesn't think he needs help," I manage after a moment of thought. I turn to eye the legionnaire armor once more. "Is there a rule that says I can't wear one of those?" I ask, gesturing at them.

"No, they're just heavy and not strong enough to stop a hit from someone with Silver strength unless you have an Iron Symbol to reinforce them," Contessa says, looking at me with a surprised expression.

"But if he can appear behind me at will, I'd rather have it than just leather," I point out. The *lanista* cocks her head, considering my words for a moment. There is some merit to what I am saying. If it gives me the chance to survive even a glancing blow, it is worth exploring.

"Try it on," she instructs, gesturing at the row of *loricae*. "See how your movement feels."

I need no further urging and race to the armor and reach for it with shaking hands. Slowly, I lift it over my head like a tunic, running my arm through the shoulder straps, letting its familiar weight settle on me.

I am home.

I smother a delighted laugh as the familiar awareness of iron sweeps through me. My *Cor* rejoices to have such a robust supply of essence attached to me. My body knows when a fight is coming. Even if my reserves are full now, we will have a need for more soon. I have to stop myself from mentally adjusting how it fits me while they watch. I am not Ironbound; just a sheep trying to fit in a wolf's clothing.

"It feels good. Help me with the straps." I gesture at Illy. There are physical ones to pull for someone who can't just adjust the shape of it at will. My partner fumbles at them, but it gives me the cover to manipulate them with my Symbol, tightening them until the *lorica* fits like a second skin. Behind us, the lift arrives once more, and its doors open to reveal Varus.

In his hands, he carries a pair of *gladii* nestled in white leather sheaths. A thrill runs through me at the sight of the beautiful weapons.

Illy has no use for them; they're far thicker than his thin blade, which leaves only one other gladiator about to step into the ring.

Me.

"*Dominus*," Contessa greets him, bowing her head. Today is a day for formality. It adds to the weight of tension that hovers above us like Dead Pluto's long shadow.

"*Lanista*," he replies, equally as stiff. "Are my warriors ready?"

"Almost. Castor is only missing his weapons." Her tone is thick with anticipation, and all our gazes are drawn to the swords he carries.

"Then I have come at the right time," he says softly, turning from her to face me. Despite my misgivings, my stomach lurches as I understand those are truly for me. His gray eyes bore into mine. It is the first time we have truly spoken since the night by the fire.

My understanding of Domus Pelias's master is deeper than before. I see the coldness that fills him—one that echoes my own. He is right. We are not so different; we are both tempered by the bones of *Terra*—rock and iron are cousins in that regard. Something in me shifts—an understanding, a respect. He is not Gaius, yet he reminds me of the noble tribune who did what was demanded of him. I seek only to do the same.

"When we first met, I asked you to prove that you were worthy to be a gladiator of my house," the senator says, raising one of the sheathed blades to inspect it. "You have not yet bled in the ring for me, but you have bled for something far more important." Illy shoots me a confused glance from behind Varus, but I ignore him. The gladiators who were in the servants' quarters have no idea about the death that visited Delilah's garden a few weeks ago.

"I promised you a boon," he reminds me. Despite the severity of the moment, I have to stop myself from laughing at the stunned expression on my friend's face. "My daughter has admonished me that a promise is not enough."

This time, I don't look at Illy.

"She bade me to equip you with something worthy of your service. To that end, I had Contessa commission these from the greatest ironsmith in the Empire using the gift you were given by Senator Delilah. He charged us a fortune for the urgency." Varus smiles faintly. My eyes nearly pop out of my head as I realize he speaks of the Frost

Iron. I have not seen it since giving it to Pliny. That magister is too sneaky and clever for his own good.

Twisting his grip on the sheaths, he extends the pair of blades toward me, hilt first. "Take this, Gladiator, and carry with you my fury."

My heart hammers in my chest as I reach out to wrap my hands around the *gladii*. My *animus* can sense them; they burn like stars to *both* of my Silver Symbols. The white birch wood of the pommel reflects brightly against the blue stone set in each of their hilts. My hands shake as they settle on the grips that feel like they were made for me. When I hold them, it feels like I have regrown my hands after losing them.

I am whole.

I am complete.

"Draw your swords," the senator commands, watching me with gray eyes. I need no further encouragement. The *gladii* ring like bells as they slide from their sheaths, revealing their secrets.

"Dead gods," Illy breathes in wonder as he sees what I have already felt. The swords have been made in the style of the Iron Legions' *gladius*. The round crossguard is small, designed to fit between the gaps of shields in the wall. The blade is thick and straight, designed to punch through anything in its way.

But that is where the similarity to the uniform weapon of the legions fades. Instead of being the dull gray of iron, my weapons are dark blue. In the center, just above their hilts, both blades are etched with the crown of the Symbol of Ancient Frost. Tentatively, I reach out with my *animus* and try to pull essence from them.

My jaw drops as Iron and Ancient Frost essence pour into me from the two swords as easily as breathing. This is what Julia made for Frigidus, the gift he never received because he spurned her love. Frost Iron is more incredible than I could ever have imagined.

A low laugh begins to echo from my throat as I look up from the blades to the senator. This is a princely gift. More powerful than anyone in this room even knows. With these in my hands, I can keep my two Silver *Corda* full of essence for far longer than I could before. Varus has turned Delilah's mysterious gift into a tool that I can use to carve through my enemies.

"The senator and I thought this would be a suitable use for her family's heritage. And, to my surprise, the *compositores* have approved it for use in the Games," Varus tells me as I inspect my new weapons. "The Censors were horrified to learn that an artifact of the Iron Lords was being used in such a manner, but the consul insisted that it feeds into the legend. But now, no matter where you are, you will carry a bit of Winter with you."

"But Pliny said—" I begin, remembering the magister had forbidden me from using this miraculous element while my Hearts were out of balance.

"Today is a day for risks, Castor," Varus tells me, giving me a soft shrug of his shoulders. "When the Games are done, I suspect that he will insist that you put them away for a time." I nod, willing to accept any terms to get to hold these weapons.

"Alessandra requested that you name them," he suggests softly.

"I can think of no name that would do them justice," I admit after a moment of thought.

"She suggested you might call them *Vindicta*. That *Revenge* is a suitable companion for Winter."

"Then so shall they be." I snort at a host of meanings that no one else in the room would ever know. Finally, I manage to tear my eyes away from the blades and look up at the senator. "You honor me, *Dominus*."

"My daughter honors you. I equip you to fulfill my will." His implication is clear. I have proven myself as someone worth investing in. These swords are not just for me. Every other gladiator or *ludus* master who sees them will know the expectations that rest upon me.

"I understand, *Dominus*."

Varus's lips twitch in the ghost of a humorless smile. He hates this place, I think, but just like any soldier, he cannot always choose his battlefield.

"Good. Then go and teach my enemies fear."

CHAPTER 26

"Whoever's bastard you are, they must be important." Illy's voice echoes off the walls of the dark room we wait in. The roars of the crowd are muted here; they crash against us like a distant storm.

"It's really not what you think." I chuckle, remembering how he thought the same thing Gaius once did.

"I don't need to tell you how much those blades cost."

"They are priceless." I smile despite myself as I glance over at him in the shadows. Harsh light streams through the gaps of the wooden gate ahead of us as we wait to be announced.

"It's just that if we're going to stop holding things back like the *lanista* told us, maybe it would be better if we told each other the truth about—"

"Illy." I sigh in frustration, interrupting his babbling. "Breathe. You're going to need the air soon." The duelist falls silent, but I can feel him vibrating with nervousness. All my fear has fled in the wake of a clarity that can only come on the battlefield.

"Sorry. This is my first Silver fight." I turn my head to study him in surprise.

"Mine too." I toss him what I hope is a reassuring smile, but his shoulders slump more in what seems like defeat. I feel the shade of Durus hovering over my shoulder, watching to see if I learned the lesson he tried to teach me. I'm not Illy's officer, but still, I feel a sense of duty to watch over him. "You're serious? I thought you were a veteran this whole time."

Illy doesn't smile, only shakes his head, making his short dark hair dance through one of the stray beams of light. His eyes are unfocused and wide. I've seen the same expression on men in the shieldwall.

"I fought three bouts as a Copper, then Ascended during my third fight. Contessa put me on the sidelines to get used to my new tier before deciding to bring me to Antioch."

"You Ascended during a fight?" I try to sound as impressed as possible. "What are the rules for that?"

"Once a fight has started, it's started."

"You won, I assume?"

"Only *marca* I ever earned. But that was last Circuit." I understand where his insecurity is coming from. He's never fought a Silver who was actually trying to kill him before. Despite his competence, it feels new and overwhelming. He has all the pieces but needs someone to show him the bigger picture.

"How long were you a gladiator before you first fought in the ring?"

He shrugs, uninterested in the question. "Maybe a month or two."

"How long has it been since you Ascended?"

"Half a year at least."

"So you have almost triple the training against Silvers that you did against Coppers?" I ask. Illy stiffens, lifting his head to look me in my eyes for the first time. I struggle to keep the laugh out of my voice at the blank expression on his face. "Sounds to me like you're more prepared than you've ever been."

The shorter duelist falls quiet, but the silence is now introspective instead of despairing. Free of distractions for a moment, I turn my attention to my own problems. Iron and Ancient Frost curl within me like two snakes, fully sated. But Unrelenting Fire hisses and complains, throwing a tantrum like a toddler angry that its older siblings are given more. My body struggles against the waves of nausea that its temper sends rolling through me. I bury myself deeper in my cold Symbols, using them to numb me to my physical weakness.

I have been here before. I will be here again. My hands tighten around the hilts of my swords, relishing in their firm strength. The cold, hard hunger that follows in the shadow of my Symbols thrums with eagerness.

"He will try to separate us," I tell Illy as the shouts of the crowd reach a crescendo. It sounds like the fight before us is coming to its bloody end. "Stay with me, watch my back, and I will watch yours."

"Sure." The short man laughs in disbelief. "You're good, Castor, but how can you fight someone you can't catch?"

"We'll see," I promise him. I glance down at the nervous gladiator. I can't help but feel like Durus would have one more piece of encouragement before the battle. A smile spreads across my face as I find the words that feel the most like that solid officer.

"No holding back." I hold out my fist for him to rap his knuckles against. He eyes it curiously, as if unsure what I want. It must be a Legion thing. I raise my other hand and tap them together in demonstration. A bright smile dances across his face as he understands.

"No holding back," he confirms, bumping his fist against mine.

"Citizens, rejoice!" the announcer commands again, his booming voice piped into even our waiting area. "This has been a blessedly bloody first day of the Games, but Consul Briannus is not satisfied. On behalf of Empress Diana, he is thrilled to present you with a show match of Silvers as a taste of the art to come!" The people's roar thunders so strongly, the very walls of the arena seem to shake.

"From the Sword Door, welcome the only named Silver gladiator currently in the Circuit, I give you *Impostor* of *Ludus* Valerus." The screams continue as the crowd's favorite emerges. I cannot see it, but I can picture our opponent grandstanding all the same.

"From the Shield Door, come his worthy opponents. Witness Gladiator Illyrius, and Gladiator Castor in his Games debut for *Ludus* Pelias!" The massive gates before us swing open, bathing us in light and sound as the unmuted force of the crowd's excitement pours on us like a flood. It has been a long day. *Sol* has already begun its descent into the horizon, hovering just over the edge of the arena, casting a long shadow. Together we stride out into the ring, where I finally feel the crowd's weight for the first time.

In the parade, there were hundreds of us distracting the onlookers as we circled before them. Now we are only three. In the dream world that Contessa trained me in, the eyes were never this heavy. I feel their gazes pulling me apart, studying me like butchers studying fresh meat.

But despite their noise and their judgment, I have eyes only for one person.

Our opponent stands across the ring, halfway to the middle from the open gates that he entered from. As a named gladiator, he seems entirely unremarkable. He wears a familiar-looking set of fighting leathers, stamped with the eight-armed *krakenus* of his *domus*.

Like me, he wears a pair of swords at his waist, but they are shortswords, not full-blown *gladii*. His black hair is cropped close. He is average in height and build. Only the Silver veins glinting under *Sol*'s bright light marks him as anything special. But I of all people know that looks can be deceiving.

Impostor smirks as he watches us approach. I watch as his gaze makes the tired journey down my arms, tracing the white *rasa* veins of my unused Hearts. Seeing my deformity only makes his predatory smile grow wider. His eyes are flat and cold, the only part of him that hints at the killer that lurks beneath his skin.

In one fluid motion, he draws his shortswords and vanishes in the blink of an eye.

"Fortuna's Bones!" Illy curses as the crowd thunders in delight. We spin to find our rival standing behind us back by the door we entered, blades held high. Even I have to admit it's an impressive trick. Curious at what secrets he carries on him, I reach out with my Iron *animus*, letting the awareness of the area around us fill me. I'm surprised at how many shards of weapons and armor are buried in the sand. I can sense the nails that hold the structure below us up. But more than any of those things, I feel his secret.

Impostor flickers out of view again, and we turn back to the center, where he appears in the space of two heartbeats, smirking at us with extreme confidence. The crowd roars in approval at the sight of a Silver with so much power.

I struggle to hide my laughter, which only irritates Illy.

"We are so dead," my partner mutters, stepping forward to answer the challenge. He draws his short, slender blade and thrusts the tip in the air before moving it in a blinding series of strikes that are almost too fast for my eye to follow. With my Iron senses, I can feel the edge of his blade become so thin that the air itself does not restrict it, allowing it to move faster. I did not know he could do that. Contessa was right—he was holding back.

With a flourish, the duelist sheathes his blade, and the crowd cheers, although not as much as they did for *Impostor*'s demonstration. Lots of gladiators can wield a sword beautifully, but Teleportation is a truly unique ability.

"Aren't you going to do anything?" he calls after me as I start walking toward the center once more. "Showmanship is part of the gig, Castor!" I pause, tilting my head to study the sea of humanity that watches me, leaning forward to see what my trick is.

Teach my enemies fear. Varus's command echoes in my mind, and I start to raise my right hand so that everyone can see when I summon the *Glacialis Falx*. But something stops me, a whisper on the wind. It is not the prickling sensation that I feel when the gods watch me or a command from the oath Varus holds over me. It is merely a simple realization.

This is not how Gaius would do it.

I remember the shock on the faces of the Normans when our tribune cut down their king. The horror that the traitorous Imperials felt when Knut let himself be baited into the duel. That is the fear that I wish to teach those who watch me now. Nothing I could do would be as flashy as *Impostor*'s entrance.

So let them wonder.

Let them see.

I make eye contact with the gladiator waiting for us in the center and slowly turn my head so I can spit on the white sand. Without waiting for my companion, I resume my brisk walk toward the middle. I am eager to begin.

"Dead gods," Illy moans, but I can barely hear him over the thundering of the crowd. My arrogance is like a flame; it catches light and burns as it sweeps through the arena. Some will hate me for it. How dare an *immundus* not show respect to a *named gladiator*? Others will be thrilled at the personal rivalry that now exists between us. But all of them are only here for blood. As long as one of us bleeds, all will be forgiven.

"He's going to kill us," Illy complains as he trots to catch up with my longer stride.

"I think he was already planning on that."

"Okay, well, *now* he really wants to."

"Good."

"Do you actually have a plan? Or is your favorite pastime trying to see how quickly you can make every dangerous person you meet hate you?"

"You don't hate me," I point out.

"Well, no." He's caught so off guard by the implied compliment that he draws up short. "Stop distracting me! If you get me killed by an insane Silver, I'll haunt you in Hades forever."

"Lucky for you, I do have a plan. Here's what I need you to do…"

I finish my whispered instructions before we arrive in the center of the ring, just out of reach of *Impostor*, who glares at me, rankled by my disrespect. I give him a cold smile, full of Ancient Frost. He doesn't twitch, but something in his eyes tells me he does not like what he sees in me.

"Citizens of the Empire!" the announcer booms. As we have been instructed, we turn to face the Prime Box, where Consul Briannus and the other magistrates sit. A dozen toga-wearing men and women look down at us with mild curiosity.

I spy the consul in the center—he alone is beaming. He makes eye contact with me and winks before holding up two fingers in a *V* for Victory sign. I take his meaning and return his greeting with a cold nod.

"Before the tournament begins, we are pleased to present you with this special opportunity to witness the greatest of the Silvers! This evening, witness the power of *Impostorrrrrr*!" The named fighter raises his sword once more as the crowd thunders their approval. I stretch out my *animus*, studying our battlefield.

"This match is a special *marca*-earning fight. If *Impostor* is able to defeat both of the Silvers from *Ludus* Pelias, *Ludus* Valerus will receive double points, adding six to their impressive lead." The crowd "oooohs" in appreciation.

"But first, he must get through the blades of Illyrius and Castor, who seek to arrest the decline of their failing *Domus*!" More cheers. I arch an eyebrow at the consul, who shrugs unabashedly. He said the Games were all about theater. It seems he was not lying. Very well, I have an act to show him.

"Gladiators, are you ready to spill blood in Bellona's name?" the announcer thunders. The Arena falls silent, an unnatural hush descending as thirty thousand souls hold their breath at once. We turn away from the palatines to face off once more. The world has gone cold; I am deep in the current of my Silver Symbols, trusting their guidance.

Impostor lazily raises his sword in agreement. With a glance at me, Illy does the same. I raise my right fist, not bothering to draw either of my *gladii* yet. My companion lets out a frustrated sigh before settling into a fighter's crouch.

Teach my enemies fear.

"Gladiators. Fight!"

Illy charges forward, leaning low, his sword trailing behind him as he races toward *Impostor*. The Valerus Silver does exactly what we expect him to and vanishes in a flicker. My companion slides to a halt as the enemy gladiator disappears. Just like we planned, he immediately begins to backtrack toward me, his eyes scanning all around him in case he is the target. But he will not be.

I do not move.

All I have to do is wait.

My Iron Symbol flares in warning, and I cannot kill the smug smile on my face as I twist, taking a step backward just in time to catch a flicker of movement as *Impostor* appears behind me, shortsword aimed for a killing stab into my spine. His attack slides past me, cutting nothing but air. At the same time, I drive forward with my left forearm, putting all my power into my blow as I bury it into his stomach.

"*Ooof*," he gasps, folding around my wrist. I grab the exposed scruff of his neck and pull him forward, tripping him as I throw him to the sand. The named gladiator lands hard, but he is a Silver—it will take more than that to put him down. He uses the momentum of my throw to continue into a roll to his feet, shooting me a murderous glare before he flickers away, vanishing to safety.

The crowd's roar of approval is so loud, I can feel it shaking the ground beneath my feet.

Illy shoots me a wide-eyed look as he returns to my side, still watching our front like we planned. *Impostor* blinks into being off to our right, sprinting toward us with his blades low.

"He's here!" Illy shouts in warning, moving to meet the attack. The two men exchange a flurry of strikes before the Valerus gladiator leaps backward and vanishes. I turn to my left as he appears a pace away from me, eyes burning with hatred.

I sidestep, forcing him into an awkward turn as his momentum betrays him. Clucking my tongue, I shake my head in disappointment as he staggers. Percy would have beaten me if he ever caught me with such lazy footwork. *Impostor* has grown far too comfortable using the power of his *Cor* to fight his battles for him.

Before he can recover, I am on him, driving forward with my right fist. I punch him in the nose as hard as I can, causing him to stagger. The crowd's roar thunders to new heights as *Impostor*'s head snaps back. I don't give him a moment to gather his wits; instead, I step inside his guard, hammering his face again and again.

New blood splatters on the sand as my fist breaks his nose. My bones are hard as the Iron that fills me. Panic flares in the Valerus gladiator's eyes, and he twists, turning his back to me to run, flickering away. I let him go, directing my scornful gaze at the space of empty air.

Impostor appears in front of us once more, striking at Illy this time. I throw back my head and laugh as loud and as hard as I can at the sight of our enemy. I wonder if those palatines in their boxes can hear me, or if they are only sent the sound of iron striking iron.

"What in the name of the dead gods is wrong with you?" Illy demands as *Impostor* flickers away again. My companion is bleeding from a cut on his wrist but is otherwise unhurt. I wonder how much essence he has left. "Will you *please* draw your sword? I want to live!"

"Soon," I promise him, chuckling as our opponent reappears a dozen paces away, his bloody face twisted as he pants to catch his breath. The crowd is going wild; I can barely hear my own thoughts above their delight.

"…a true spectacle!" the announcer crows into the brief break in the action.

"What are you waiting for?" Illy complains from my side.

"For you to notice, really." I laugh. I have decided that disdain is scarier than being emotionless. Let our enemies see that their greatest fighter is amusing to me. Let that knowledge rest in their mind. Originally, I was planning on besting him without drawing my new blades, but I think when used at the right moment, they will only add to the drama.

"Notice what?" Illy is exasperated by my antics. "I thought we weren't holding back."

"That was when we were impressed." I chuckle. "But he can't take either of us in a straight fight. He's reliant on a trick, and it is no longer working."

"Just remember—if I die—"

"*You will not die*," I hiss, anger from Unrelenting Fire bleeding into my tone. Why will he not trust me? This dancing fool could not kill any of the Silver gladiators of *Ludus* Pelias in a straight fight.

As if goaded by the expressions on our faces, *Impostor* grits his bloody teeth and blinks out of existence, activating his ability once more. As one, Illy and I turn back-to-back to scan the arena. The Valerus gladiator appears nearby, lunging toward Illy once more.

"Left!" I shout, bumping my friend to the side as a shortsword cleaves through where he was just standing. *Impostor* shoots me a frustrated glare. Illy's blade flashes as he catches the next strike. His sword is sharp; it peels a curl of iron from the Valerus weapon. They exchange a dozen quick blows as I circle behind them, closing in on *Impostor* with my empty hands.

The named gladiator glances over his shoulder, tracking my movement, and then jumps back, flickering away before I can close the jaws of my trap. He reappears at a distance, pacing around us, studying us with a frustrated expression.

"Hey," Illy says, studying the Valerus fighter a score of paces away. "When did his face get all bloody?"

"Good enough for me." I chuckle, taking a few steps away from my companion.

"No seriously, I didn't hit him in the face just now. How is it bleeding?"

"I did it a while ago."

"But when he was—ooh." Illy is so stunned, he lowers the point of his sword and turns to stare at me. "You bastard, when did you figure it out?"

"Lucky guess." I shrug as I glare at the bloody mess of *Impostor*'s face. "Now we win." I stride away from Illy, staring intently at the Valerus fighter as I close the distance between us. The crowd's noise fades to a hush as if they, too, can sense that the end is near.

Slowly, I drop my right hand to the hilt of my *gladius*, and I draw it methodically, letting its sound echo through the ring.

I let the blade rotate in my grip as I twirl it once before extending my left hand to point at *Impostor* in a clear challenge. *No more games*, it says. *Let us fight, just you and me*. This is the most dangerous part of the plan. It requires that I leave Illy exposed, which is why I spent so much time disrespecting *Impostor*. I want him solely focused on me in this moment.

The bloody-faced gladiator tilts his head to the left and right, cracking his neck. His eyes burn with hate. With a snarl, he launches himself forward, charging at me. I laugh in delight, breaking into a trot to meet him.

The crowd's bloodlust is loud enough to wake the dead gods, driving us together.

Despite my challenge, I know that there is no honor in the ring. Already I am planning for what will happen, letting my *animus* guide me as I move. He'll wait until we are only a few paces apart, then he will use his Symbol to attack me from behind.

But unfortunately for him, he has no secrets from me.

Just before we get in range, I slide to a stop, throwing off the timing of our meeting. I see his eyes widen as I leap backward, landing on a single knee as I swing my sword behind me in a vicious arc without looking. A jolt runs through my blade and into my hand as my *gladius* meets resistance, then cuts through it, backed by my will.

Impostor screams in horror as his invisible twin brother flickers into view. The second gladiator drops to his knees behind me, blood spraying from his ruined throat.

The crowd's reaction is so deafening, it is painful.

But this is my moment, and I make sure to make the most of it, rising to my full height. I flick my sword to the side, painting the white sand with more red spots, anointing Bellona's temple with my offering.

Impostor is a lie. It was always there in the name, I suppose. *Impostores* would be more accurate, for there was not one of them, but *two*. Identical twins who were both bound to some sort of Light Symbol. They took turns appearing and disappearing, making it seem as though they teleported, when in reality, they never moved.

I felt it the moment we entered the arena. My Iron Symbol sensed the second set of weapons circling around behind us. Then when they switched which of them was visible, I could tell the original stayed right where he was.

Thanks to my practice against Reese, it was easy for me to guess the game they were playing. The hard part was making it look like I figured it out without access to the Iron Symbol. That was why I broke the nose of the one that was still alive, to make him obviously different from his twin.

Hopefully, that will satisfy the *compositores,* Censors, and anyone else watching.

With an enraged scream, the living twin with the bloody face charges me, but I knock his first strike wide. He is slow, and his form is poor. Even before Contessa got her hands on me, it would have been easy for me to cut him into little pieces.

I glance at Illy, who is staring at me like I'm a stranger. I toss him a smile as I block another one of *Impostor*'s wild blows. This time, I twist my longer weapon, locking our blades in place and driving mine forward to slice his wrist. My opponent drops his left weapon with a cry of pain, and I disengage, nodding in his direction as I look at my friend.

"What do you say?" I ask him calmly over the roar of the crowd. "Want a name?" Illy's eyes go wide as he realizes what I am offering him. He takes a step forward, then hesitates, shaking his head and sheathing his blade.

"Not like this," he says almost too softly for me to hear. "I'll earn it on my own."

I nod in understanding, offering him a salute with my *gladius*. I wouldn't want it this way either. But I am bound to an oath, and I must obey.

Teach my enemies fear.

It takes three strokes. I block his high attack, not bothering to draw my second weapon. I counter with a low stab that he dodges before I lock our blades together once more and rip his other shortsword out of his hand. The anger in *Impostor*'s eyes fades, replaced by fear. He uses his last trick, going invisible, but we both know that he is still there.

He no longer carries any iron, but I am too close for him to escape. I watch the sand shift as he tries to run before lunging forward, cleaving into his leg. My cold blade bites greedily into the soft flesh. Blood spurts from thin air before he flickers back into visibility, prone on the ground.

"Pelias Victor!" the announcer roars, his own voice tinted with shock. I'm surprised that the match ends so quickly. I meant to claim another point from Valerus, but it has been taken from me. The crowd is on its feet, screaming in approval. As I expected, they are delighted by the blood I spilled for them.

"Name him!" some begin to shout.

"Name him!" more of them take up the cry.

"Name him!" They chant in unison, over and over, a sea of demanding children, expecting to be entertained. My gaze sweeps up to the Prime Box, where the consul waits. Briannus's eyes glitter as he reclines in the main chair.

"Name him!" The chant builds in volume. Briannus's smile grows to match. He may not be an *electus*, but he is attuned to this crowd like they are his Symbol. At last, he rises to his feet, holding out his hands to either side, gesturing for silence.

Impossibly, thirty thousand people see him and fall silent in waves, their excitement like a pile of banked coals, waiting for the slightest bit of tinder to burst back into flames. The consul beams down at me, showing his delight openly. I know he is already scheming how to use me further.

"My friends!" his voice booms, amplified by the same relic that amplifies the announcer. "Did I not promise you a blessing?" The crowd roars their approval.

"It is traditional for a gladiator to be named after the manner of their first kill in the Games. We all know of storied fighters like *Ignis* or *Umbra*. But my friends, I fear that young Castor here has only shown us a hint of his gifts today!" Another wave of excited cheering sweeps through the audience. What secrets do I hide, they wonder.

Many.

"Perhaps we should call him *Rasa Occisor*, the Blank Killer—that would be a fitting name for such a unique warrior." The crowd's response is more muted, as if many of them had not noticed that I was an *immundus*. A tight smile tugs at the corner of my lips as I feel thousands reassess me once again.

"But that is not worthy. No, friends, I have a whisper of what is to come from this young gladiator. As Consul of the Iron Empire and *imperator* of the Games, I have a true name for you, young Castor." His gaze turns from sweeping the audience to settle on me like a boulder.

"My people, I give you *Frigus Ventus*—the Cold Wind."

CHAPTER 27

Illy is silent as we ride the lift back up from the Pelias armory. I am grateful he does not want to talk because I am caught in a maelstrom of my own emotions.

Frigus Ventus. That is my name now. It will follow me for the rest of my life. The Cold Wind. A chill that has nothing to do with my Symbols runs down my spine as I remember Aquilo once called me the same thing. Who am I that the ghosts of gods torment me so? All because of one foolish oath made in the innocence of youth.

For the first time in many months, I think of Valentina. What have the Censors done to her in their tower? Does she live freely, or have they imprisoned her for what she knows? Despite how our friendship ended, I am sad at the thought of her languishing in the dark.

I shove the thoughts of my childhood aside. Now is not the time to be distracted by the past. If I am not careful in the next few moments, my future will be cut short. There will be questions, I am certain. They will want to know how I did what I did. I must lie well enough to convince them that I am a genius—not an abomination.

The relics that power the elevator cease their gentle hum as we reach the top. My heart is in my throat, and I swallow in fear as I wait for the doors to open. I do not know if my master will be pleased with my performance, with my new name. All that matters is that my secrets stay buried.

"They're here!" someone shouts, and wild cheering breaks out throughout the box.

Contessa waits at the door with a tight expression that tugs at the scars on her face. The bald *lanista* glares at me for a moment before giving us a sharp nod of approval as she steps aside. I make it three paces before we're swarmed by the other gladiators. The Silvers are at the front of the pack, faces flush with their excitement. Even Leon is smiling, our rivalry briefly forgotten.

"Was it because of me?" Reese squeaks, giving me a sharp hug. "Is that how you knew?"

"You saved our lives," I tell her with a broad smile. It's not even a lie. While my Iron Symbol is the real reason I survived, my experience with her made it easy to understand the fiction that *Impostor* was using as a shield.

"You were brilliant too," the woman gushes to Illy, turning away from me to address my companion. "Your sword is so fast. Why do you never do that in training?"

"A lesson I have learned," the shorter duelist says wryly. "From now on, I will."

"Good," Fannia says from where she hovers by the taller woman's hip. "You are more interesting when you're dangerous."

Illy blinks at her sultry tone. She's a strange one, that girl with knives.

"Well done," Leon says when it is his turn. He's stiff but looks me in the eye. I return the favor and give him a nod that communicates some respect. Some of the tension drains out of his shoulders at my acceptance.

"Move!" a heavy voice commands, and the gladiators around me scatter like roaches. *Malus Mors* strides to the front, looking down at me with his dark arms crossed—face serious. I stare up at him, unsure what his reaction will be. A tall, thin woman follows in his wake, bearing the same Golden veins in her arms. This must be *Fantasia*, the other named gladiator that Varus has brought.

After a tense moment, he breaks into a wide smile, white teeth flashing against his dark skin. "Now we are brothers," he declares, wrapping me in a tight hug. "Welcome, Named One."

"Thank you," I manage to choke out, squished against the inhumanly strong man. Even without actively using his Symbol, I can feel the power that runs through his limbs. What a terror he must be in the ring. The woman says nothing, but her fierce eyes study me, dissecting me to see if I am worthy.

A presence cuts through the group, pushing even *Malus* to the side. It is not a physical one, but it is heavier than anything else in the room. The gladiators part for Varus himself, who stands at the far end of the room, studying me with intense scrutiny.

"*Dominus*." I bow my head slightly in respect as the room falls silent. Illy hovers at my side like a nervous shadow. He was in the ring with me, but everyone knows that I am the one under scrutiny. Varus holds my stare for a moment, eyes dark and judging. Then he smiles and points at the wall.

I turn in time to see the *graphis* relic activates to update the *ORDO LUDI*. It moves to the bottom to our line, where *DOMUS PELIAS* currently has sixteen points. It passes over the number once, clearing it before inscribing a new score.

DOMUS PELIAS: XX

Twenty! Inwardly, I frown, regretting not cutting down the second member of *Impostor* before the match was called. With another point, we would be at twenty-one, tied with *Domus* Belascus, the absent regional house.

"A good start," Varus says, raising his flagon in salute. "Pelias *Victor!*"

"Pelias *Victor*!" the gladiators around me echo, lifting their own drinks. Illy and I bear their praise with small smiles, equally uncomfortable with the attention that is on us. Dead Fortuna smiles on us, for after the toast, the guests in the room break back into milling herds. For a moment, I dare to think that is the end of the scrutiny, but I should have known better.

"You two, come." Contessa jerks her head, leading us toward the front of the box. Illy shoots me another nervous glance before following the *lanista*. I am not surprised when she takes us to where Varus waits, standing in front of the glass, looking down on the arena. The other palatines congregate further away, giving us some privacy.

"What in Dead Mars's name was that stunt?" Contessa hisses, turning on me. Now that the eyes of the rest of the room are no longer on us, she is free to berate me. "The *dominus* spent a lot of *denarii* to buy you those swords, boy. The least you could do was use them." I decide not to point out that I technically did draw one, just at the very end.

"How did you know?" Varus's question is softer but much more dangerous. It is the thrust I have been expecting. My shield is ready; I can only hope it is strong enough to deflect his attention.

"It was Castor—sorry, *Frigus Ventus*," Illy says, unwilling to squirm under the senator's intense scrutiny any more than he has to.

"Castor," I say firmly, giving him a dark look before turning back to our master. "It was a guess."

"You didn't draw your sword on a *guess*?" Contessa sputters. She is furious with me for not doing what she trained me to do. I have made her look like a poor teacher. But I do not think she needs to worry. Varus is not angry with her. He wants to know *why*.

"I didn't believe it." I shrug as if it were a simple thing. "A Silver who has an ability, and it is one that lets him teleport? That seemed beyond improbable."

"You are a Silver with an ability," Varus points out, his voice cool and unrelenting.

"Yes, but mine is still bound by the rules of my tier," I reply. I expected his line of reasoning and am prepared for it. "I can only manifest Ice on something I can touch. I cannot affect anything at range. That is the arena of Golds." The senator nods after a moment—he understands my point.

"Reese is also Lightbound," I remind him. "I train against her frequently. It's become instinct when someone vanishes to watch the sand, to track their footsteps. When *Impostor* showed off his ability before the beginning of the match, I watched where he had been. The sand shifted even though he was not there. It made me suspicious."

"Suspicious? You were suspicious?" Contessa is only getting angrier at my explanation. I took too many risks on too small a chance. I do my best to ignore her rage for the moment. She is not the one I have to convince.

"What is more likely?" I ask. "Someone develops an ability that defies all knowledge of *electi*, or their *domus* uses a clever trick to create a terrifying gladiator for their *ludus*?" Both of the Golds' gazes track down to my white *rasa* veins, and I feel my cheeks grow hot as I blush.

"*Impostor*," Varus murmurs. "It was in the name."

"The Valerus would have to be very careful who they used them against," Contessa muses, thinking through the logistics. "An Earth *electus* would be able to sense the two of them immediately. So would any other Lightbound."

"Or make sure that they killed whoever they faced," I point out grimly.

"We will be complaining to the consul," Varus promises. "*Ludus* Valerus has been cheating by using two fighters in single combat. Now that they've been exposed, they must be stripped of the points from those matches." A note of warm hope glimmers in his eyes for a moment, and I resist the urge to smile. I had not considered the repercussions that this would have for the current Circuit leader.

"But why didn't you draw your sword?" Contessa demands, no longer willing to be ignored. "You can be as clever as you like. Well done. We're all so impressed. But clever boys with swords sticking out of their stomachs are still just as dead."

"I wanted to prove that there were two of them," I explain after a moment. "I was worried that if I just cut one's arm, the other would slice their own to mimic the wound, so I had to do something that was not easy for him to recreate."

The two Gold *electi* are silent for a moment, processing my explanation.

"Besides," I say into the silence, "I thought you told me to make them afraid." Contessa's sigh is long and loud as she turns away, defeated for now. There will be repercussions to this, I am certain. But they will be on the training floor, where she can take her anger out on me with a practice blade.

"Well done," Varus says at last, apparently satisfied by my explanation. "You have succeeded in your first task, but that was only the beginning. Tomorrow, the true tournament begins."

"I will be ready," I promise.

"*Valete*," he commands, dismissing us.

"I am *never* fighting with you again," Illy whispers as we walk away from the palatine section of the box toward the rest of the gladiators.

"What's the matter?" I ask, giving him a jaunty smile. "Don't you like winning?" For once, my heart is unburdened. I won my fight and answered my master's questions. This was an unparalleled victory. I am not used to those. A strange euphoria bubbles in my chest, making my feet feel lighter than usual.

"You're impossible." The duelist sighs, turning to eye the feast once more. "But thanks for watching my back out there."

"Anytime." I extend my fist toward him. He looks at it for a moment before his annoyance evaporates a little, and he bumps his knuckles against mine with a small laugh. He steps toward the banquet, and I turn away, a hint of a smile on my lips.

It dies as I stare into the cold blue gaze of Alessandra. The heir of *Domus* Pelias was waiting behind me, her face locked into an expressionless mask that she must have inherited from her father. All the joy that boils in me evaporates under the pressure of her look.

"*Domina*," I say respectfully, giving her a slight bow like I did to Varus.

"*Frigus Ventus*," she says coldly. Her eyes bore into mine, searching for something. I cannot guess what it might be. She is the only person other than Anas who knows my secret. There is no mystery here about how I defeated *Impostor*.

"I understand that I have you to thank for my legendary gift. I do not think even Pelias ever bore a weapon so mighty."

"You do. I expect you to put it to better use." There is no give in her—whatever frigid anger fills her is harder than anything Ancient Frost could ever produce. All the danger that I just thought I escaped now hangs over my head like a dome.

"Forgive me, *Domina*," I say softly, not daring to lose even an inch of formality, "but I do not know what I have done to anger you so. Do you not rejoice to see your father's enemies laid low?"

"It is not that you won. It is the cruelty you showed. The joy you showed in taking another's life. Those swords were meant for a protector, not a monster."

I pause for a moment, considering the truth in her words. I enjoyed cutting *Impostor* down.

I told myself that it was only the demands of the Games, but now, in the quiet of the box, I begin to wonder if that is just a lie that makes me feel better. I was *angry*. It did feel good. That had never happened before. Usually when I fight, I lose myself to the icy logic of Iron and Ancient Frost, which muted any other emotion. But I didn't need much essence to beat the twins. I hadn't even touched my Ancient Frost reserves, which left me far more open to the whispers from Unrelenting Fire.

My face goes pale as I recognize the anger my new Symbol is feeding within me. The danger of my first two Symbols is losing myself to the cold, but now I must also worry about being consumed by rage. Alessandra's expression shifts, and I realize I have been silent for too long.

"It is true, *Domina*," I admit. "Some of it was theater—I was playing to the crowd—but I will not lie to you and say that I was not angry or that I did not enjoy it. *Impostor* was cheating. How many warriors have those twins murdered with their deception? How many points has *Ludus* Valerus gained from their lies? I did delight in making them pay for their deeds." Her blue eyes grow harder with every word as I do not back down from her accusation.

"But more than that, *Domina*, is one simple thing."

"And what is that?" There is a danger in her voice, lurking just under the water like a *crocodilus* waiting for an unsuspecting gazelle to drink from its oasis. Up until now, she has not exposed my secret to protect her family, because she trusts me. But if I am destined to become a monster, then perhaps she should warn the Censors before it is too late.

I step closer so that I can whisper directly in her ear. These words are for her alone. "Your father bade me to make his enemies know *fear*. I am oathbound to obey him. What choice do I have but to be an instrument of terror in the bloody sands?"

Alessandra does not respond as I pull away. Her expression has changed, grown darker and more troubled. I am not sure who she is angry with, me or her father. I give her a small smile as I follow Illy to the banquet table. Winning has given me quite the appetite.

CHAPTER 28

There are only a few more matches after ours.

One more than the rest makes me sick to my stomach. The crowd lets out a long *boo* of displeasure at the sight of the Norman Copper *electus* from our *Ludus*. My heart skips a beat as the barbarian strides into the ring, wearing the same broken trident that I wear on my chest. The anger that simmers just below my surface threatens to boil over as I stare at him.

His arms glint with metallic *Cor* veins. I know that he could not have been with Knut's army, butchering my brothers. But he looks like them, and I find that hard to separate. The blond warrior ignores the crowd's jeers, stepping into the ring carrying a pair of hand axes like his kinsmen favor.

"Who is that?" I ask Reese, trusting her to know everything that goes on inside of *Domus* Pelias.

"His name is Brogi," she tells me excitedly, not noting the shadow of anger that hovers in my expression. "He's Norman but somehow found a *Cor* Heart in the wild! He was caught and sold by the Censors."

My mouth twitches in an almost sympathetic frown despite myself. That tale sounds far too familiar for my comfort.

"What's his—" Down below, the heads of Brogi's weapons burst into flame, which quiets the people watching. My stomach drops at the sight. I know what he is without finishing my question.

Firebound.

"*Ignis*!" Reese replies happily, clapping her hands in delight.

My mouth is sour with fear. Another danger. If his Symbol shares congruency with Unrelenting Fire, I will have to be even more careful to hide it from his eyes. At least he is only Copper. He has no *animus* to extend and feel my secret in action.

Begrudgingly, I am forced to admit that the Norman is well trained. He carves through a Copper fighter from *Ludus* Delos with ease. Brogi's opponent is some sort of Water Symbol, but he cannot seem to conjure enough liquid to keep the flames at bay. He drops in surrender after a dozen strokes, before the barbarian can burn him to a crisp. Another *marca* for *Domus* Pelias.

"Wow, once he Ascends, he might be able to give you a run for your money," Reese says, poking me in the side good-naturedly. The mood in the box is rising as our *ludus* begins to collect more points.

I grunt, crossing my arms. But my gaze is on the blond Firebound as he is escorted out of the ring. I wish his opponent had lasted longer. I would have liked to have seen what he can *really* do.

The final match has a pair of Golden gladiators from *Ludi* Apicius and Grus square off in the ring. I watch spellbound with the rest of the Silvers at the display of violence before us. I understand now what Varus meant when he told me that the top-tier fights are the ones that people truly care about.

They move at a speed I cannot match, relentless as they tear through the sand. Their fight makes our battle with *Impostor* look like children playing with sticks. The arena shakes with the excitement of the crowd. We can even feel their tremors in our feet, high up in the palatine box.

The Grus woman has some sort of plant-based Symbol. Instead of a sword, she wields two whips made of thick vines that curl and snap with her will as they reach for her opponent. I cock my head as I spot the telltale streaks of Copper *Cor* running through them. Has she somehow turned a plant into a *mythus*? My father taught me that they were living things, but I have never heard of such a thing.

The Apicius gladiator is bound to Lightning, calling pillars of white fire down out of an empty sky that thunder so loudly, they rattle the windows.

The two flow around the ring, dodging one another's attacks while striking out. The sand is torn up, mixing the red blood-stained grains in with the ones that are still pure white. Even the other palatines around Varus are silent, watching the battle with a quiet intensity as fighters on their tier go at it.

A thrill of excitement runs through me and my *Corda*. I have come far, but I have so far to still go. These Gold *electi* are dangerous, but what will I be like when I am able to use Iron to its fullest potential?

Like most violence, it ends abruptly. The lightning man closes inside the range of the Grus woman's vinewhips, lunging forward with his *gladius* that crackles with harnessed electricity.

Against someone with a normal, leather whip, that would be an excellent move. But he has misunderstood the nature of her weapons. She jerks her hands backward, and her whips retract, racing toward her like a pair of striking snakes.

One wraps around his right ankle, yanking his feet out from under him. The other coils around his neck. Blood begins to leak out of his leg and neck as sharp thorns emerge from the vine, cutting like knives. I turn away, suddenly feeling sick to my stomach at the sight.

My father kept razorvines in one of his *conservatoriums*, one that my sister and I were not allowed to go into without him. They were a dangerous, meat-eating plant. If a small animal—or child—got caught in its tangles, it would constrict, filling them with toxins from its sharp thorns before feasting on their flesh.

Once, I asked him why he would keep such a dangerous thing in his home. He laughed and pointed out that we had cats that gladly feasted on mice and dogs that would be delighted to bring down a doe. Razorvines protected the plants that grew under their shadow from animals that would eat them, giving them a safe place to flourish.

"Everything has a place, Castor," he told me with a small twinkle in his eyes. "Some predators prey on the weak; some protect it. Nature needs balance. Razorvines are just another beautiful way that life survives."

Seeing it used now as a weapon reinforces to me how twisted these games are. Even the plants are used to kill for entertainment here. I miss my father. He would hate this place. He would hate what I have become. I have done everything he told me not to. I have gone down the path he warned me about.

My hands are shaking.

I look down, stunned by my own body's betrayal. The fear, the shock, the shame, all become overwhelming as the cold logic of Ancient Frost and Iron abandon me. The pain of losing my family drives them away like a scourge.

I fold my hands together and press them to my chest, forcing myself to breathe deeply. I cannot break. Not now. But all I can think about is the expression that would be on my parents' face if they were here to see my fight with *Impostor*. Would they still love me as a son? Or would they only see the monster I am becoming?

"Castor!" I turn away from the wall to look over my shoulder. Illy and the other Silvers are heading toward the lift at the back of the box. "We're going back." The first day of the Games is done, and much of the room has already emptied.

"Go ahead." I wave, trying to force a mild grin onto my face. Something in the way that Illy's own smile dims tells me that I am failing. "I'll be right behind you." My partner hesitates for a moment before deciding not to press the issue.

"See you there," he says before walking away.

I turn back to the wall, where I pretend to study some sculpture of Marcus Iberius, an imperator long gone. I stare at it, but my eyes do not see his cold features etched in marble. Instead, they wade through a path of pain and misery.

"Eyes forward, Legionnaire," a harsh voice grunts at me, snapping me out of my spiral. I glance at my side to see Anas hesitating as he walks by. The former soldier eyes me with the concern of a man watching his neighbor in the shieldwall stumble. His presence reminds me of a different family that is counting on me to walk the path that I am on. My brothers cry out for vengeance, and only we are left to give them peace.

"Eyes forward, *Dominus*," I reply, giving him a tight smile. I straighten my back and force myself to turn away from the statue. I don't feel better, but I am no longer fragile. "Well done today."

"Eh," he grunts noncommittally. "Laertes knows his business, and those Grus Ironbound were lazy fools. Durus would have had an aneurysm if he saw them march." We both smile fondly at the thought of the older centurion screaming at us in drills.

"You heading back to the quarters?" I ask, gesturing toward the lift.

"Yes."

"Let's walk together," I suggest, remembering that I still need the former *captivus*'s help and this would give me the perfect excuse to be seen talking to him. The two of us head to the elevator, moving at a leisurely, unbothered pace. The lift arrives, and together we step in, ready to make our escape.

"A moment," a harsh voice demands as a burly man bulls in to join us on the platform. My heart sinks as three more *ferra* gladiators enter the lift, eyeing me with an equal sense of distrust.

"You almost left without us," the grizzled officer, who must be Laertes, says to Anas, his eyes full of distrust. "Don't do that again."

"Aye, *Dominus*," my friend growls after a moment. I feel my eyebrows arch in surprise without my permission. Anas has never been particularly fond of authority figures. Even Gaius took a long time to earn his respect.

"There a problem, *Argentus*?" Laertes growls, using that familiar uncanny ability of having eyes in the back of his head to turn his glare on me. If I did not know better, I would say all officers are secretly some sort of Silver *electi* attuned to the Symbol of Disrespect.

"I just was under the impression that you *ferra* weren't active duty any longer," I reply after a long moment. I can feel the other two legionnaires' glares resting on me as they hover behind their leader's shoulders.

"Legion is for life, boy. A citizen like you wouldn't understand." My mouth twitches at the insult, but I catch myself before it is too late. "You've never seen a shieldwall carve its way through the enemies of the Empire. These games are nothing but playacting, opium for the masses."

"I watched the *ferra* matches," I lie. Anas winces behind me as the expression on all their faces darkens.

"A travesty." He turns away and spits on the stone floor as the lift arrives at the ground floor. "Ironbound killing other Ironbound is an affront to the gods—even if they are dead."

"I had no idea," I say as blandly as possible, letting my gaze grow dismissive as I scan over the three men who stare at me. "Is that why you all act like you're Mars's gift to the world?"

"We are War's children, boy," Laertes grumbles dangerously. There's a hint of anger in those old, gray eyes. He already doesn't like me on principle, but I am in danger of disrespecting him, which he will not forgive.

"I thought every Ironbound sent to the Games was a deserter or a criminal?"

"And that's why we want nothing to do with you." Laertes turns away from me to lead his men off the lift, back straight as iron, feet moving in perfect time.

"Laertes," I call, stopping him in his tracks. He doesn't turn, but he hesitates, a man hovering on the brink of violence waiting to hear my question. "What legion were you in?"

"What difference does that make?" His question is full of venom.

"I hate Praetorians."

To my surprise, all three of the career soldiers laugh, a hint of tension escaping out of them.

"That's the first wise thing I've heard you say," he says after he finishes chuckling. He glances over his shoulder to give me a measured glance before turning away once more. "I was in the Second." Anas follows in his wake, shooting me an apologetic look.

The basement of the arena has a series of tunnels that connect directly to the quarters of the individual *ludi* so that gladiators and palatines can pass between them directly without being accosted by the excited mob above. The parade today was for their benefit but will not be repeated.

I follow in the footsteps of the four *ferra* gladiators as we wind our way through the complex. I'm frustrated by how difficult Laertes is making it for me to communicate with Anas. My stomach roils as my mismatched *Corda* pull at me. Unrelenting Fire boils like indigestion, threatening to tear me apart as it protests the presence of its older cousins around it.

Using my *animus*, I focus inward, studying the three different Hearts inside of me. They burn against my senses like miniature *Sols*, floating in a sea of white, blank light that must be the *rasa Cor* to which my body has not yet acclimated. Part of me hopes that it never does. I cannot imagine what the strain of having another Symbol would be like on my mind.

I'm so distracted that I barely notice the purple-clad figure who appears down the hallway from us until he is shouting at Laertes and the rest of the *ferra* gladiators ahead of me.

"Out of the way, dogs!" a familiar voice sneers. My eyes snap up to lock onto the face of Brennus Valerus as he storms toward us. "Make way for your betters." Macer's murderer wears his Praetorian tunic, worked with a golden threaded *VI* that marks him as a member of the Sixth Cohort. A single *gladius* hangs from his belt.

Laertes and the rest of the former legionnaires do not even twitch, continuing to take up the same amount of space as they march forward.

For a moment, I consider slowing down to let this drama play out before I am close enough to be caught in it. There is danger for me here.

If Brennus recognizes me, it will be the undoing of me and my master. But my feet continue forward without consulting me. Unrelenting Fire surges in my chest burning brightly in recognition of the object of our hate.

"I said move!" His voice goes up an octave as outrage robs him of his dignity. One of the men who flanks Laertes deliberately bumps the Praetorian with his shoulder as they pass, knocking him to the side.

"Slave!" Brennus screams, drawing his sword in one fluid motion. It sings as it comes free, the only weapon allowed in these tunnels. A vision of Macer plays in my mind, of the skinny legionnaire diving between the Valerus and his blade. I was powerless to stop him from murdering my friend then, but I am not so weak now.

I lunge forward, extending my right hand as I call upon the *Glacialis Falx*. My reserves of Ancient Frost are brimming to the top, untouched from my fight in the ring. The icy *gladius* springs from my palm, its straight blade extending to block the furious Praetorian's swing. Brennus turns to look at me in shock. His Symbol did not warn him of my approach because I carry no Iron.

"You dare raise a blade against me?" he hisses in cold fury, the other legionnaires all but forgotten. "You will pay for that, slave. I am no mere Ironbound." He twists proudly so I can see the Silver veins in his arms. "I am a *Fidelis*, and I will show you how the Iron Lords killed the gods."

I laugh in his face, amused beyond measure.

Brennus dashes forward, bringing his sword up and around as he slashes at me. As a *Fidelis* in all but name, I sense the movement of his sword clearly in the murky hall. My icy blade crosses with his, and I grunt in surprise at the strength of his Iron Symbol.

The hardness of the attuned material has a multiplicative effect on the will of the *electus* behind it. Iron is much stronger than Ice, even ice made from Ancient Frost, which means that even if our wills and reserves are equal, he can exert more force than I can.

I have never crossed swords against a Silver Ironbound with my *Glacialis Falx* before, and the pressure is overwhelming. He cannot reach into my blade with his will and break it, but he can reinforce his, commanding it to cut through something it should not be able to. It takes all my concentration to keep my sword from shattering under his opening attack. Despite how much I hate him and the First Legion, his swordmasters have drilled him well in their craft. He continues his assault, blade flickering like a true duelist instead of the blocky form of a man trained only to stand in a shieldwall.

Cut. Slice. Carve. His will screams to his sword as it tries to ravage my weapon. I grit my teeth as every blow sends vibrations that run all the way down my arm. Essence pours out of me. I cannot withstand his aggression for more than a few more moments. Not without using Iron myself, which would expose my secret here and now.

Instead, I rely on the fact that I am an *uninhibited* Silver and push my *animus* to its limits, avoiding his sword instead of blocking it. I fade away from his attacks, sending mine at angles that force him to give ground to avoid being cut. His frustration grows as he is backed up against the wall. I can feel his composure crumbling. His movements become sloppy as he forgets his form. He will break soon.

Now!

He lunges for a strike. I twist aside with perfect Ironbound timing, stepping in to hold the tip of my *gladius* up against his neck. Brennus freezes as he feels the ice on the edge of his skin.

"You wouldn't dare," he threatens. But his voice trembles as if he suspects that I am a similar kind of man to him. That I might dare. We stand there, locked in place, like statues in the dark as my hand begins to shake. Macer's shade hovers behind me, looking over my shoulder from wherever he waits, unable to find rest.

One thrust is all it would take to avenge him.

My breath comes in ragged gasps. A thousand needles prick on my skin as competing oaths pull at me, reminding me of my duty. The gods watch. As I stare at the Praetorian, his face changes, and he becomes Atticus. The tip of my blade moves forward, pressing in on his skin but not quite breaking the surface. This is madness. Now is not the time for my vengeance.

But I want it.

"Come on, boy." Laertes grunts, stepping between Brennus and me, looking me in the eye with a somber expression. "This cur is not worth dying over." I look at the old officer for a long moment before nodding and letting the point of my sword drop from Brennus's neck.

The purple-clad idiot relaxes, something of his old scorn growing on his face.

"Fool," he hisses. "You'll all be whipped for this."

"No, we won't," I call over my shoulder, walking with the other *ferra* gladiators. "You'd have to tell them why you want us beaten." The former soldiers with me all laugh as we leave the Valerus boy alone in the dark.

As we round the corner, I trigger some of my last Ancient Frost, shattering the *Glacialis Falx* in my hands and letting its tiny pieces fall to the ground. They will melt before anyone notices them.

Ahead of me, Laertes stops to turn and face me, a conflicted expression on his face. The two other legionnaires and Anas huddle behind him, waiting. My friend shoots me a concerned look, which is my only warning before the old officer grabs the edge of my collar and pulls down, exposing the *XII* brand on my chest that marks me as a member of the Twelfth.

"I knew it," he growls.

CHAPTER 29

Dead Mars damn Laertes and his eyes that see too well!

"Knew what?" I spit back in his face, knocking my tunic free of his grip. My right hand curls to hold the hilt of another *Glacialis Falx*. I do not know if I even have enough essence left to summon it, but I must try to keep my secret safe.

"I knew I smelled the legions on you," he growls, looking me up and down once more. His eyes flicker from my collar-less neck to the *rasa* veins on my arms in rapid succession. The lie I told Varus and the other palatines will not work here. Laertes has passed through the forges of Agogia. He knows that no soldier is branded until they emerge from their prisons, ironmade.

"Once," I admit, cocking my head to the side, willing to let this play out a little further. None of them are armed, but they're tough men. I will have to be quick with my icy blade to keep them from pinning me down. Anas stands behind his comrades, his expression strained. He alone knows how deep the water they are treading in is.

"There is no 'once.'" Laertes snorts in derision. "You bear the brand, boy. You're Legion 'til the day you die. The real question is what happened to your Iron?"

"You saw." I jerk my head back in the direction that we left Brennus. "It changed."

"The gods are dead, not me. Save your lies for priests and prayers." His eyes narrow as he takes a menacing step toward me, followed by his two companions. "I watched you fight that Lightbound. I know what a *Fidelis* can do." Something dark flickers across his face. "Too well, I know."

Something on my face must go cold because Anas interjects before I can trigger my ability and cut the old officer down. "Laertes served with Gaius," he barks, shoving between the other two men to close with us.

"You two knew Gaius?" Laertes asks, turning from my friend to look at me with a surprised expression.

"We knew him," I confirm, slowly letting my hand relax as I begin to understand. Laertes told me he was in the Second Legion, the same one our tribune once served in. I search my memory for the banner that hung on his wall, remembering the golden *X* in the bottom right corner.

"You were in the Tenth Cohort of the Second?"

"How did two Twelvies know—" he begins before his own eyes go wide as he puts the pieces together. "Eighth Cohort?" I glance at Anas, who gives me a shrug. It is too late for half-truths now. I look back at Laertes and nod. For the first time, the grizzled veteran seems completely caught off guard.

He is silent for a moment, head bowed as he thinks.

"We were—"

"Silence!" he hisses, looking up in genuine alarm. That familiar serpent of dread that slumbers in the pit of my stomach awakens at the expression on his face, beginning to slither through my guts with its frigid scales. "Not here."

Without another word, he turns away, leading us through the tunnels at a more pressing march. The other two legionnaires follow without complaint. It seems they understand the flavor of the senior gladiator's fear.

Anas and I exchange a glance, and together we follow in their wake. My right hand twitches, feeling empty without the hilt of my *Glacialis Falx*. With every step, my concern grows. This dark hallway is my last chance to kill them. After we emerge from the darkness, my life will be in their hands, as theirs are in mine now.

Do it, my Symbols seem to whisper to me, Ice and Fire united in a common cause. Both logic and fear agree that this is too dangerous. Convinced by my demons, I step forward, reaching for Ancient Frost once more. Anas grabs my left arm with his hand, pulling me back with a firm grip. I twist to glare at him, but he shakes his head, holding up a single finger before adding a second and third.

Wait.

For a moment, we stare at each other as my Symbols demand that I act, but my own instincts are quiet now, muted by the trust forged in deep snow and dark forests. My attunements are to the primal forces of the world, but they pale in might to the strength of the bond between men who have bled and killed for each other.

Reluctantly, I nod, accepting his instruction. Together we follow the rest of the *ferra* gladiators out of the darkness into the light of the *Domus* Pelias quarters. Even though we are coming out of the ground, I can't help but worry that I will be returned to it soon.

Laertes does not stop once we are free from the depths of the arena. Night has fully fallen, but the torches blaze brightly, bathing us in light. Instead, he continues his brisk pace through the courtyard and into the fourth hallway reserved for the Ironbound gladiators. I hesitate at the mouth of the new tunnel, and Laertes pauses, turning to look at me with knowing eyes.

"Come on, boy," he grunts gently. "We have much to discuss that is only for those who have been through the forges." It is not his words that convince me, but his tone. Since the moment he first laid eyes on me, the veteran has always watched me like I'm an outsider. He still looks at me with suspicion, but now it is the glare of an officer who does not know what to make of his legionnaires' actions. I have seen that look in Durus's eyes a thousand times. Now, I belong.

My heart pounds in my chest as we head to the room at the back, as far as we can get from prying eyes. Laertes murmurs something into one of his companion's ears, and the former soldier nods at once, pausing to open the door. The four of us squeeze into the small room before he closes the door behind us, standing watch to prevent anyone from barging in on our meeting.

The moment we are alone, Laertes paces to the far end of the room and whirls, staring at Anas and me with a manic, scrutinizing stare. Out of habit, my spine stiffens as his gaze sweeps over me. He snorts slightly in response.

"You served under Gaius?" he repeats as if he still cannot believe what he heard. My gaze tracks to the second man still in the room, and he waves a hand dismissively. "Lexicus was also in the Second. I trust him."

"We did," I admit, glancing at Anas. "We were trainees together in the Eighth Cohort while he was Tribune."

"How did you avoid getting sent North to die with him?" A tinge of bitterness fills his voice that brings my head up sharply. "Yes, boy, I know. We all do."

"We *didn't*," Anas answers for me.

"You went North?" Incredulity colors his voice. "Then how in Dead Mars's name are you alive and breathing right now?" I give my friend one last glance, and he shrugs. With a sigh, I let my shoulders slump and tell him the story.

Most of the story.

I share how Brodigan gave Gaius a way out. All we had to do was retreat after finding the horde, and the imperator would absorb us into the Sixth. When he heard Anas and I were sent to scout, he interrupts in surprise. "Why'd he send you instead of his *Fidelia*?"

"Other than his brother, Percy, we were the closest thing he had. I was among several trainees selected to train to be a *Fidelis* but was denied by the *Argentum Consilio*." Laertes's face falls in horror at the news. It seems that he had not heard everything.

"Tyrus sent both Marius brothers to die?" he thunders so loudly that I worry the entire *domus* might hear him. "Is he trying to start a war? I always knew he was a pig, but now I see that he is a fool too."

I tell them of the chase, but I imply that we escaped. I do not speak of our time among the Normans, of the *necromanta*, or of what we found in the ice cave beneath the mountain. Those secrets are ones that I dare not offer, not even to someone who shares my admiration for Gaius Marius. When I get to the story of our cohort facing against the might of the Norman host, Laertes's expression becomes grimly amused.

"Let me guess," the former officer interrupts before I can go any further. "He walked out in front of an entire barbarian horde and cut their king into little pieces?"

Lexicus chuckles too, clearly unsurprised.

"His name was Knut, and he was a *berserkir*. Gaius destroyed him." I hesitate once more, deciding what is safe to share with my iron kin. The next part of the story is almost as dangerous as the secret of the not-dead-gods. I take a deep breath and decide to roll the dice. Our Tribune deserves to have his story told. "This High King had Imperial advisors, who warned him about dueling against the tribune. Gaius recognized one of them."

The room is silent as the two soldiers process that. I expected them to be more surprised. It seems they have already learned the truth that I am still learning. This is where the rust of the Iron Empire leads.

"How did you escape?" Laertes asks at last.

I tell him of the pass. Of a fierce winter storm that came out of nowhere. Of an avalanche that swept me away from the rest of my company where I was found by slavers who sold me into the gladiator Circuits.

"That's when this changed," I lie, gesturing at mismatched veins. "My iron went cold when I was buried in the snow. I do not understand it, but it saved my life." The veteran grunts, apparently willing to accept that explanation for now. When I am done, I glance at Anas, who tells his own portion of the tale.

"Gaius lives?" Laertes demands, taking a step toward us in shock.

"He was alive at the end of the battle," Anas growls. "Who knows what the traitors who took him have done with him since." A heavy stillness settles on the room as we all try not to think of the horrors that are likely being visited on a good man.

"You served with him?" I prompt at last.

"Aye," Laertes growls. "Lexicus, Thartus, and I were in the Second under him when he was made the youngest tribune in Legion history."

"You were at Arausio," I whisper. The battle that changed Gaius's life.

"We were," Laertes grunts in surprise. "You know the story?"

"He told me, once. On the way to the North." Anas looks at me in confusion, and so I tell him a quick version. "In the battle, he sent his cohort to reinforce one of the Twelfth's that was getting torn to shreds. He saved them, and maybe the battle, but a lot of palatine sons died for a lot of undesirables." The former *captivus*'s eyes glimmer with understanding.

"You got the right of it. They could only punish Gaius so much, seeing who his parents are. So he was sent packing to the Twelfth and took out the rest of their rage on his officers."

"You were the Prime Spear of the Cohort."

"Is it that obvious?"

"A little." I laugh. He and Durus must have been hewn from the same stone at birth. It makes me miss the man more than ever before. The former officer's rage begins to take shape in my mind as I follow the threads of his story.

Gaius was protected—at least somewhat. But the men who followed his orders, who weren't of the same social strata? They were the targets. Laertes and his men had likely been court-martialed as soon as the tribune was sent to the Twelfth, then sold to die in shame in the Games.

"So we've had a taste of the same knives," I say after reflecting on their story.

"Aye, you might say that," Laertes agrees with an amused snort. "Don't worry, boy, we'll keep your secrets. There's no love lost here for the palatines and their games."

"Or the Censors, I hope."

"Couldn't stand the White Hand before they made us slaves." All four of us laugh, united by a common hatred. A weight slides off my shoulders as I feel less alone. Illy and some of the other Silvers have been kind, but they are not Legion. Here, I am finally among my peers. I must lie to them too, but it feels like I am close to home.

"Would you know their faces?" The Prime Spear's question catches me off guard.

"Whose face?"

"The Imperials who served this Norman High King."

"No, they wore coverings." I hesitate, and he leans forward, ready to hear. "But there was a woman. Her name was Tullia. She was the one that Gaius recognized even with her disguise. I would know her voice. I could never forget it."

"You're sure?"

I nod firmly.

"Tullia," he muses, rubbing his chin in thought. But if he recognizes her name, he does not share it with me.

"We should disperse," he says at last. "There are fewer eyes in these walls than the arena's, but even here they watch closely." He turns to me and gives me a lopsided grin—the first smile I have ever seen on his face. It changes his features from cruel to merely firm, like a stern father watching over his sons.

"You're one of us now, ironbrother. Sleep easy. We'll be watching your back."

CHAPTER 30

WAKE UP!

I jolt upright in my bed. The mattress in my room is hard enough that I am able to sleep on it instead of on the floor.

I freeze in the darkness, ears straining to listen for an intruder over the pounding of my heart. But there is only silence. Seizing my Symbols, I sweep my *animus* forward, hunting for any sign of iron or ice, but there is none. According to my senses, I am alone.

But I know that I am not.

I *feel* her presence, like an oily smear across my mind.

Nemesis, the dead Goddess of Revenge, waits for me. I have sworn an oath to her, but it is incomplete, not yet set like a broken bone. It needs me to do as she has commanded, and the longer I delay, the more likely it is to get infected.

She waits for me in her temple.

I may not be fully bound to her yet, but I am under no illusions about what will happen if I spurn her. I have her attention—the promise has been made; the rest of these steps are but a formality, a test to prove my faithfulness. I have no choice but to obey.

Something tugs at my chest, like a hook around my breastbone, pulling me in the direction I am supposed to go. It is gentle but insistent. It warns me that the next hint will not be as kind.

Damn the dead gods and their games!

I throw off my sheets with a snarl, reaching for my fighting leathers before hesitating. As a gladiator, I am not permitted outside of the compound without escort. Wearing the broken trident of *Domus* Pelias will only draw attention.

Instead, I don a black linen shirt with my leather trousers, hoping that I will look like a palatine out for a late-night dalliance. Mentally, I check my reserves, pleased that I had been allowed to top them up from the *ludus*'s traveling *loci* before I retired for the evening. I am not allowed to carry weapons outside of the grounds of the arena, but if I need one, I have enough essence to use the *Glacialis Falx* with ease.

Tentatively, I slip out of my room, moving the door slowly to keep it from creaking on its rusty hinges. My heart pounds in my throat as I slide out of the hallway, trying to look casual while also staying hidden. There are no rules against me being outside of my dormitory, even in the depths of night. But I have no desire for my excursion to be remembered by anyone watching.

There are no guards in sight, and I move across the courtyard quickly, staying far away from puddles of light pouring off the watchfires that burn in braziers. A low layer of clouds must have come in from the ocean after the sun fell. I can see neither *Luna* nor *Mons* Olympus above, and I find some comfort in the fact that they are hidden.

If the gods cannot see me, then maybe I am free from all eyes.

I hunker in the darkness beneath the stairs that lead up to the top of the wall, letting their shadows shroud me as I wait to see if anyone has noticed my arrival. But there is no one. I am the only soul that appears to be awake at this hour.

Again, I cast out with my *animus* searching for a hint of iron or ice, but the only metal I can sense is in the braziers holding the fires off the ground. Wherever Varus's Ironbound are keeping watch from, they are not here.

Feeling emboldened by their absence, I sweep out of the shadows and trot up the stairs, taking them two at a time at an eager pace. It feels like there is a window of peace that will soon close. Perhaps it is the changing of the guard.

I force myself to move confidently as I reach the walkway along the top of the wall. I cast one last furtive glance over my shoulder, but the courtyard is still empty. The time to act is now.

I vault over the lip of the stone fortification so I can slide across it. My heart leaps in my chest as I slip over the edge. For a moment, I'm in freefall, then my trailing hand grabs the stone crenellation, and I jerk to a halt, dangling two stories above the ground. The Silver *Corda* running through my body has reinforced my body, but being stronger does not simply banish the innate, primal fear that I carry.

No normal man could fall from this height and not break their bones. Every instinct in my mind screams at me not to let go, to claw desperately to the side of the wall and cry out for help. But I do not listen to my fear. It belongs to an older version of me. The Castor who has no Cor Heart, who works in a bakery.

Frigus Ventus lets go.

I land at the base of the wall in a crouch, my *argentum* body easily absorbing my momentum as I pause in the shadows, waiting to see if anyone noticed my brazen escape. But there are no cries of alarm, no movement on the street outside our *ludus*'s compound, only the heavy silence of a cloudy night.

My tension eases once I leave the district surrounding the Bellona Arena. Now there is nothing to mark me as an escaped gladiator, and it should be a simple matter for me to blend in among the other residents of the city.

I make my way down mostly empty streets, walking past taverns that are full of drunks still celebrating the violence of the Games from the day. "Here's to the bloody sands!" they roar as they clink their flagons together.

"The *krakenus* of Valerus will crush you all!" one man shouts in support of his favorite team.

"*Ludus* Apicius will see about that!" another contests, drawing groans from others around him. More plebians shout the names of the *domuum* they support, but I do not hear Pelias among them. Varus was right; the mood of the people turns against him.

I slink deeper into Antioch, trying to retrace the path that the carriages traced when we passed the ruins of Nemesis's temple. I have never been alone in a city like this; I am overwhelmed by the number of streets. It feels like I am in Daedalus's maze—I dread the coming of the minotaur.

Occasionally, I feel the eyes of pickpockets and thugs who watch me from the shadows, looking to see if I am easy pickings. Whatever they see in me, whether it is the *Cor* veins in my arms or the way I carry myself, they decide it is not worth it. There will be better targets on these dark streets later in the night.

This is hopeless, despair whispers to me when I am fully lost. I have only been this way once, during the day. On foot at night, it might as well be another world. How ironic that my defeat is not from an enemy or monster. I am defeated by a poor sense of direction.

I do not even really know the way back to the arena, although that will be easier to find. The massive structure hulks on the edge of the city behind me. A blind man could see it. But the ruins of a dead god's temple are much more hidden.

I am just about to give up and return to the *ludus*'s quarters with my tail between my legs when the prickling sensation on the back of my neck returns. *She is here*. Somehow, I know that Nemesis moves with me.

Above me in the night sky, *Mons* Olympus suddenly blooms into view as the cloud cover that hid it dissipates. The floating mountain shines brightly in the otherwise empty sky, ahead and to my right. A chill runs down my spine as I stare at it, glowing like a beacon. Night itself twists to show me the way.

I am still full of despair as I adjust my course to use the dead home of the gods as a North Star. Seeing the daughter of *Nox* wielding her mother's power to guide me does not make me feel like I am on the right path. The world is not supposed to work this way.

Our ancestors changed everything. They killed the gods to save us from this. In exchange, we gave up our power. The Iron Empire exists to prevent men from becoming gods. The Censors and the *inhibiti* are all safeguards against this world coming back.

Yet here it was. It appears to have never left. The promises of safety from the gods were not kept. But the restrictions and control still exist. I raise my left hand to rub the front of my neck where my own collar used to sit.

Abruptly, Nemesis's temple rears out of the dark in the distance.

I make my way through empty streets. There are no revelers or pickpockets about as I draw close to where she resides. A stillness descends upon Antioch. Every stone home has its doors and windows closed. No lights shine from within. It is as if the people who live here have battened down the hatches, preparing for a storm—a cold wind—to sweep through. Alone, I walk down the middle of the street, confident that we will not be disturbed until our business is complete.

The ruins of the dead god's home take up an entire city block. Its spire has fallen into ruin, pieces of it litter the courtyard before it. Holes have been smashed into its walls, left open like gaping wounds. Her giant, headless statue still keeps watch over the empty street. No lights shine within its crumbling interior. Only a piece of the everflame burns in the brazier at the entrance, one small sign of respect for the vanquished. I eye the darkness with distaste, trying to decide if I am willing to enter that murk unable to see.

This is a test. I have faced so many over the last year that they have become obvious to me. One more being who wishes to know the strength of my mettle. A small smile tugs at the corner of my mouth as I stare at the basin. It is a fraction of the size of the one that I fell into in Delilah's garden, but its Unrelenting Fire is welcome all the same.

Wordlessly, I stick my left hand into the brazier, reaching for my newest Symbol to protect me from the everflame's hunger. The inferno leaps to devour my hand, and I welcome it, gently curbing its bite with a small flick of my will. Instead of my flesh, I feed it essence, keeping it bright and strong. Fire surrounds my fist like a dense swarm of fireflies as I step into the temple. I've become my own torch.

I hold my burning arm high as I enter the darkness, letting it banish the shadows. But something resists my light. It's as if the night that clings to the ruins of Nemesis's temple is alive and angry. I feel it pushing back against me, powered by a will that dwarfs my own.

The nails in the soles of my boots echo on broken stones as I walk through what once was a courtyard for worshippers seeking something from the Goddess of Vengeance. It still serves this same purpose—I am just the only one here.

The darkness grows thicker ahead of me, layering on top of itself in the open doorway to Nemesis's inner sanctuary the same way I condense New Snow into Ancient Frost. I draw short of that murk, holding my burning hand high, feeding Unrelenting Fire into the flame I carry, trying to push it back. But no matter how bright I shine, the darkness does not retreat. This is the domain of one of the daughters of Night, and my light is not welcome here.

I stand just outside of its shadowy embrace for a moment, staring into it as it does the same to me.

Come, it seems to whisper, even as it exudes a challenge that would drive away anyone wise enough to listen. This is not a safe darkness. To enter it is to take my life into my own hands—to walk where monsters tread.

I should leave. Every instinct inside my body shudders in fear at the thought of continuing further into the ruin. I have no desire to face *another* dead god. But the *votum* in my pocket will not let me flee. The blood of my father sings out from the cobblestones it stained when Atticus cut him down. The shades of my fallen brothers watch me from the afterlife, lost and unable to go to rest.

Vengeance has been promised—but first she must be awakened.

I take a deep breath like a man standing at the edge of a cliff. I hold it for a moment, reveling in the silence. Then I release it, and the stream of essence that feeds the everflame curling around my fist. It goes out in an instant, and I am plunged into darkness.

The resistance to my passing vanishes with the light. Somehow, I am able to see, even though it remains shrouded in night. My heart hammers in my chest as I step over the threshold and into the sanctum of the goddess.

The interior is even more ruined than the outside would suggest. A half-dozen stone pews lay scattered and shattered across the floor. But there is a path through the middle of them toward the dais that towers in the back.

A low rectangular altar runs the length of it, sitting under a second broken marble statue of Nemesis herself. The goddess is depicted standing watch over the room, arms extended. In her left hand, she carries a set of scales; in her right coils a long whip. A pair of feathered wings sprouting from her back once stretched the width of the room; now the right one is broken at the joint. The shattered remnants of it lie at Nemesis's feet.

The pull that has guided me thus far tugs at me again, demanding that I approach. The sanctum is quiet and empty, as if it too holds its breath waiting to be released. I feel thrice a fool as I obey the command of the dead goddess. My *animus* sweeps the room as I approach the altar, but I sense nothing. According to my Symbols, I am the only one here.

But I am not alone.

My footsteps falter as I ascend the first step toward the altar. The skin on my forearms prickles with gooseflesh as I feel a familiar pressure exert itself through the room. It wakes like a slumbering lion, shifting in its cage, eager to be free.

It reminds me of standing before the frozen grave of Aquilo in the depths of his icy home. I am not bound to the same Symbol as Nemesis; I do not feel her interference like I did his. But there is a heaviness that is unforgettable.

Did the Iron Lords kill any of the gods?

The silence grows, filling the room like it is being poured in from another place. I am not in the white void where I have faced other of the pantheon before. I am wholly grounded here. The Goddess of Vengeance does not demand that I come to her; instead, she meets me where I am.

I am not sure how to take that.

At last, I cannot stand the tension. "Why have you called me?" I ask the darkness, feeling like a fool. Thousands have stood in this room since the fall of the gods and spoken to Nemesis. If she did not answer them, why would she answer me?

My arrogance grows with my *Corda*. I expect too much.

"To see if you are worthy." Her words slither like the dry scales of a serpent, and a shiver runs down my spine at the sound. It is the parched throat of a skeleton that has not spoken in a hundred years. But now it stirs.

"Worthy of what?" I prompt when she does not speak again.

"Of waking me from the dark." The bloody stone in my pocket begins to burn. I let out a bark of surprise, reaching to dig it out before my trousers light on fire. Its heat is so strong that even my connection to Unrelenting Fire is not enough to mitigate all its wrath.

"But it is already made," I protest, feeling a little stunned by her words. "My brothers and I—"

"I have been considering your pledge," the dark whisper cuts me off smoothly. "I am a prisoner, not a slave. I do not have to obey your call just because you bring me a bloody rock."

I frown as I consider her words. Aquilo did not accept my *votum* until I bled before him. We never made an oath stone. He got what he needed from that encounter. But when Valentina, Marcus, and I swore our first to the gods before the *Sententia*, it was still there when we dug it up to add Felix to our number.

I knew then that if I returned to place where we buried it, that I would not be able to find that bloody stone anymore. Something had come to collect it to seal our oath. I still held the *votum* that my Segestan brothers and I made in the weapon's shed of Agogia, which meant that our oath was in limbo with Nemesis.

My mouth twists in distaste as I lose yet another connection to the boys who had sworn to help me avenge the wrong done to my family and theirs. For months, I have carried the torch of that vow, keeping their flame alive. But now I learn that it was only a fancy—empty words spoken to the wind.

So be it. My disappointment settles into a layer of bitter resolve. They may only have been words. But it was an oath to *me*. I am no god, but I will not let my brothers lie in the dark without vengeance. Without Thanatos or Pluto to guide them, my mother and father may never find each other in the afterlife. My sister wanders alone in the darkness that waits on the other side of the veil. Vengeance is the last thing I can give to them, and I need no goddess to see it done.

I will make my own.

With a flick of my wrist, I toss the *votum* at my feet. It *clicks* as it bounces off the flagstone floor. I turn on my heel, preparing to leave this dead god where she lies. But I am stopped by a dry, cold chuckle that echoes around the dark temple.

"Delicious." Nemesis's pleasure is apparent.

"What is?" I ask, not turning back toward her altar. I do not even know if she is here or how she watches me, but I am in no mood to be polite, not even to a god.

"You burn with the same thing that burns within me, *abominatio*," she tells me. Her voice grows warmer. It seems more human the more she uses it. "For we are both *unrelenting*." I hesitate before turning back to face her.

"What do you want from me?" I repeat, trying to calm down my racing heart.

"What do I want?" Nemesis asks, laughing in disbelief. "I wish to remain asleep, spared from my misery. I wish to be free of the burden of being a shepherd. But none of this has ever been about what I want." I tilt my head in surprise at the goddess's petulant tone. It seems so very… normal of her.

"My onus requires that I act, and so I shall." Her voice grows stronger. "The compact has been broken. The time of peace is coming to an end. The hour of the reckoning is at hand." Goosebumps burst out of every inch of my flesh at her words.

"I accept your *votum, abominatio.* You shall be my cold, right hand as we set the world to rights. Together we shall tear down that which is broken and corrupt and rebuild it in our just image." My eyes narrow at her fervor. I am no builder. I do not seek to right the wrongs of the Iron Empire—just avenge them.

But it is too late now, and if Nemesis's help will stain my blade with Atticus's blood, who am I to say no?

"What must I do?"

"*Release me from this prison.*" Her voice burns with urgency. "It is time that I walk again."

The pressure in the dark room pushes at my back, guiding me. Instinctively, I know what she means. My foot brushes the top of the stairs as I begin to ascend to her, where her altar lurks. I do not kick the bloody rock that I dropped. It is gone, taken by the goddess who slumbers here in the ruins.

My hands find a large chunk of stone in the dark. I pick it up, wielding it like a hammer. The altar stands before me at the base of her statue's feet. I cannot see it in the total darkness, but still, I know it is there, thanks to the divine guidance that Nemesis grants me.

My heart beats so fast that I fear it might burst. I am a traitor to my Empire and people; an *infidelis*—unfaithful. But there is a difference between the crimes I have committed and the one I consider now. This is not just a betrayal, but a blasphemy.

The gods are dead.

Yet I am about to set one free. Unrelenting Fire curls eagerly in my chest, excited by my panic. It delights in the taste of vengeance that it can feel in the air. It wants only to consume, and this is the most direct path toward its goal.

My hand shakes as I raise the rock clutched in my fist. There was already no going back, but after this, there will be no peace. Even if I die, this cannot be undone. There are no Iron Lords left to stand against her. I am about to set a *lupus* free and must pray that it does not choose to eat me.

But Unrelenting Fire would set the whole world ablaze to get its hands on Atticus and Brennus. So I light the match and strike, smashing the goddess's statue with all my Silver strength. Pieces of the marble figure explode under the force of my blow. I raise my left hand to shield my face as I continue to hammer away, turning the ancient relief into dust.

Deep in her stony chest, I find it. A black lump of metal is nestled where her heart should be. My fingers run over the smooth relic, trying to discern what it does. Whatever Symbol the *electus* who carried it was attuned to is a mystery to me. But it has been forged by the Heartsmiths to serve, and with a flick of my will, it thrums to life.

The ground beneath my feet rumbles as the stone flows like liquid, pulling aside to reveal a stairway hidden behind the goddess's statue. I still cannot see, but Nemesis shows me the way.

A long passageway waits for me like an open throat ready to swallow me whole. Steeling myself with my Iron Symbol, I make my way down it, empty hands itching to hold a sword. There is a malevolence to this place that threatens to unnerve me.

"Warning, intruder detected," a flat voice announces in a strange accent as I descend below the temple. It is empty of emotion, and its strange tones send a thrill down my spine.

"Containment breach detected, guardians deployed," the voice warns. "Activating defensive measures." I slide to a halt, casting my *animus* around for any sign of danger. My stomach drops as something flickers at the edge of my domain—a burst of iron moving toward me.

With a thought, I trigger the *Glacialis Falx*, summoning an icy blade in my right hand. My Ancient Frost reserve strains as it manifests the ice, but I do not consume all my supply. As my assailant comes into range, my jaw drops as I realize it is not a guard carrying iron, but a thing made entirely of it.

It moves like a man, with two arms and two legs, but instead of flesh, there is only metal. In its hands, it carries a pair of naked blades. Fear trickles down my spine as I sense two more following behind it. The trio race toward me, like released hunting dogs.

They do not slow down or speak as they come in range. The first metal man simply raises its sword and attacks. My *Cor* warns of the strike even in the dark. Relying on my training, I step forward to get inside its guard, letting my icy blade meet its blow head-on.

Shatter, my will whispers to the sword, powered by the Iron Symbol.

But its weapon does not break. It rebuffs my command easily. My heart skips a beat as my will bounces off an impenetrable wall of authority, much like the *custos* relic that Percy trained us against in Agogia.

No, it seems to say. They are Ironbound! Naked fear blooms inside of me, overwhelming even the cold logic of my Symbols. I have no way of knowing what sort of relics power these infernal automatons. What if they are Silver like me? I am relieved that I choose to use a weapon made of Ancient Frost instead of my own iron. Even though it is a weaker material, it is the only thing that keeps them from being able to work against me.

I disengage my *gladius* from its blade, dropping under its other strike and stepping closer to the trio of guardians. Gritting my teeth, I shove my left hand forward, triggering the *Falx* for a second time, nearly emptying my Ancient Frost reserves. It is worth the risk of running out of essence to be able to fight these enemies with an advantage.

Using my momentum, I stab my left-hand blade forward at the first automaton's abdomen, an old legion favorite. My weapon's icy tip scratches along its metal, unable to push through its defensive power.

I stagger past it, cursing as I become pinned between a triangle of enemies. *Come on, Castor, think!* I curse myself as we exchange a flurry of blows in the dark. Their weapons burn brightly against my mind as my Symbol paints their trajectories cleanly.

Whatever these guardians are powered by, they are a far more advanced creation than the *custos* relic that I trained against in Agogia. But as my blades shudder from the power of their blows, I wonder if they share a similar weakness.

When I tested to become a *Fidelis,* I beat their game by stealing essence from the automaton, relying on the lack of instruction that the Heartsmiths gave it when they forged it. These guardians are more complex, but are they prepared to defend against an Ironbound *electus*?

I duck under the guardian to my left's overhead swing, twisting to slam my frozen *gladius* into the right side of its ribs. As before, my weapon bounces off its armor harmlessly, unable to penetrate its rigid defenses. But this time, I do not try to break in; instead, I *take.*

Come to me, I command, ripping at its essence stores with my *Cor*, relying on the touch between us to serve as a conductor. These guardians were designed to tear through warriors intruding on this crypt, but they were not prepared for someone like me. Its iron essence pours into me in a torrent, and I let out a laugh of victory as the automaton collapses, its armor rattling as it bounces against the stone floor.

Thank you, Percy, I think with a twinge of sadness for the fallen centurion. His teachings continue to save me, even after he is gone. It is only a matter of a few more exchanges before the other two guardians tumble to the floor next to the first. They twitch in irritation, lacking the power to chase me. I do not know the intricacies of how relics are powered, but even if they can self-cultivate, it will be some time before they are back on their feet.

I do not release my grip on my icy *gladii* as I step over the twitching guardians. My reserves are too diminished to summon another pair, and I am using them desperately to try to reclaim some of my missing essence.

I cast around for the source of the voice that spoke, but there is no sign of any living being other than me. Slowly, I make my way down the long hallway, to the doorway that waits. As I draw near, I can just make out words carved by hand into the stone above it.

Hic sunt Fidelia.

Here are the Faithful.

Dread builds between my shoulders as I walk beneath that inscription to descend into what must be the crypt of Nemesis. For hundreds of years, the goddess has slept here, a dozen feet from where the curious have come to inspect the ruins of her temple.

My skin tingles as I step inside the large room, and suddenly, my *animus* senses Iron everywhere. It's as if something was shielding this area from my view, but now that I have gained access, its secrets are laid bare.

A dozen *lumos* relics burst into action, bathing the crypt in light. I raise my left hand to shield my eyes as my pupils adjust to the sudden absence of the dark. When I can see comfortably, I lower it to take in Nemesis's resting place.

The goddess lies in a large iron coffin that takes up most of the room. It is covered in strange markings that I do not understand, but from its sheer size alone, I know that it is what I am searching for. I hesitate for another moment, but it is too late to go back now. With a grunt, I slide its cover off, letting it fall to the floor with a faint ringing *thud*.

I pay it no mind. All my attention is fixated on the goddess who waits within. Like all her kin I have encountered, she is emaciated. Much of her flesh is missing or rotten. Bones stick out of all her limbs, and the bottom half of her jaw is laid bare. Her eyes are covered by a black blindfold that looks like the moths have been at it.

Despite her inhuman size, she does not seem like a god. She seems dead.

Then her head begins to tilt, and the corpse turns to look at me with an expectant stare. My heart skips a beat as I stare at the god, proof of the lie of the Iron Empire. Aquilo was like a ghost. I never saw his physical body move.

But Nemesis *lives*.

"Release me," she hisses, drawing my attention to the chains that bind her. Much of the iron that my Symbol sensed when I entered this strange room curls around her like a serpent. A thick chain of metal is wrapped around each of her limbs, then anchored into the walls of her coffin.

I have seen other gods similarly restrained but never to this degree. Aquilo and Mercury only wore a single ball around their ankles. I stand above this bound, undead god, unsure what to do. Being here is an act of apostasy, of heresy. Our gods are dead! And yet, here she is, and here I am.

Her touch brushes against my mind, eager and insistent. I stagger to the side as a thousand images flash through my mind, memories that are seared into me like the *XII* brand on my chest. In my mind, I watch Atticus butcher my father. My family's estate burns. Marcus dies.

All these pieces of the Castor mosaic cry out and are unanswered. Justice—vengeance—whatever name it wears, has not been delivered. I am owed it and this undead thing before me promises me a path to it. A *votum* is a pact between us, and she is eager to do her part.

My hesitation vanishes, burned up by the fire she stokes. I accept. I need. Together we will right the wrongs.

"Why are you bound more than the others?" I ask, probing her restraints with my senses. To my surprise, they reject my scrutiny, pushing back with a latent sense of will, as if there is something inside of them that holds them together.

"Because I refused their plan," Nemesis's rotting throat groans. "Your ancestors buried me deeper than the rest of them." My eyes flick up to her blindfold, so distracted by her story that I forget to be repulsed.

"What plan?"

She only laughs, a horrifying sound now that it comes from her throat and not her power. "Release me, and I will show you the truth of this rusting world, young *abominatio*. There is much that we must cleanse together."

Once more, I do not hesitate, for it is too late. Nemesis is uncovered. She will be free, whether it is by my hand or not. I cannot put her back in her box. I reach into her coffin and grab the thick iron chain that holds her left leg. To my surprise, the metal is frigid. A dark, cold power pours out of it like a living thing, trying to attack me. I *tsk* in irritation, seizing Ancient Frost and using it to grapple with the strange will.

My mouth drops open as I realize that my cold power is the same as the one that repels me now. Whoever sealed Nemesis in here bound these chains with the same Elder Symbol that I carry. My eyes pop open, and I stare at Nemesis's corpse for another moment. There is a question that I need answered before I continue. "Was it Frigidus or Aquilo who bound you with these?" I demand.

The Goddess of Vengeance's voice crackles as she mocks me. "Both, *abominatio*. It was both."

I begin to understand.

The goddess is still laughing when I break the fourth chain. It is a simple matter for someone who is bound to both of the Symbols that were used to restrain her. It's as if I were forged for this very task. I use my will to reach into the metal and push out the relics that someone—a god or one of the Iron Lords—placed inside of them. Once they are extricated, the iron shatters with a thought.

Nemesis wastes no time. One moment, she is lying in her coffin; the next, she stands before me, looming over me by more than a foot. Fear assails me, but it finds no purchase on my heart. The cold logic of Iron and Ice keeps them at bay.

"Tell me why are you bound? Why the Iron Lords failed! Tell me what you are!" My voice rises in anger as I stare at the freed, rotten goddess. This is yet another betrayal—another stain of rust on the life I live.

The goddess's ruined mouth stretches as she smiles in amusement. "Make me, *Ovicula*."

"You promised."

"And I will deliver. When you are ready." Her voice is thick with promise.

I am silent, holding my hands loosely at my sides, icy blades held low but ready. I am not Frigidus—I do not know if I can defeat her—but she is not what she once was either. Her centuries of imprisonment have eaten away at her. I have made a mistake. She is not an ally, but a wild animal.

Nemesis does not attack. Instead, she laughs. "I accept you as my supplicant now, *abominatio*. Together we shall right this world. Justice requires vengeance. The scales are out of balance, and blood is required." I swallow, excited and terrified. I have broken something foundational. The fire is started.

"What must I do?"

"What any good follower must do." She sounds like she is in pain. "I require essence. Feed me with your vengeance and make me whole." I shudder, but my oath is accepted. I am bound to her, and she to me.

"Are you going to give me your Symbol?" The question comes out of my mouth before I can stop it. Every god who has crossed my path has foisted another burden onto me. I can only assume that she means to do the same. I am terrified what the strain of another Copper *Cor* might do to my mind. She tilts her cadaverous head to study me before chuckling once more.

"No, I will not curse you with this yet." She laughs.

Despite her words, part of me is disappointed. I thought that binding myself to a living god would bring me power, but she denies me. Nemesis must see this on my face, despite her blindfold, for she cocks her rotting skull to study me.

"Do you know what Justice is?" she asks. I shake my head, unsure how to answer. "Justice is a terrible thing, young *abominatio*. I would not wish it on you for the world. It is in every sharp blade. It is a part of every cold piece of ice. Every death belongs to me before it does to Pluto or his ilk."

I swallow, terrified beyond words.

"Do you know who my mother is?"

"Nox," I whisper.

"It is no mistake that I, the Goddess of Justice and Vengeance, sprang from Night's loins, *abominatio*." Her blindfolded gaze consumes me, devouring me from the inside. "Justice can only be achieved once the whole world is blind."

What have I done?

She smiles, enjoying the fear on my face. "Rest well, my supplicant. Together we will do dark, dark things in the name of Justice. I will see you soon." Then, with a flicker of the world, she is gone, and I am alone in the ruined temple of a living god.

CHAPTER 31

I pass a long night alone in my room. No one accosted me upon my return to the Pelias *dormitorium*, and I was able to slip back into my quarters without anyone being the wiser. I have no need of nightmares; my own mind is full of horrors. The shakes that I felt after my fight in the arena return as I relive freeing Nemesis from her prison. It seemed so simple, so right in the moment, but now that the moment has passed, I am only cold.

The world has changed, and I am the only one who knows. The gods walk among us once more. Not just their shades. I am full of a thousand emotions that range from guilt to belligerent anger. Am I a traitor who has set free one of our oppressors? Or is it Atticus who carries the blame for forcing me down this path?

The Goddess of Justice and Vengeance is right—this world and Empire is sick. I have witnessed the symptoms of this firsthand. The rust is everywhere for those with eyes to see. I only doubt that the cure will be better than the disease.

Unrelenting Fire scours at me, complaining at the stress my Silver body puts upon it, even though it is full of essence. I managed to lurk next to one of the braziers in the courtyard long enough to cultivate a full refresh of its reserves, pushing the veins as much as I dared.

My time is running out. It feels like I am trapped in the bottom of an hourglass, watching the last bits of sand pour from the ceiling to bury me. Already too many know what I am: Anas, Alessandra, and Laertes and the other *ferra* gladiators. The Ironbound seemed to accept that I am somehow no longer Ironbound, but they will be watching. The façade will not last forever.

Each of them is something of an ally, although I am worried that I have alienated Alessandra by my performance in the ring. One day, someone who is not my friend *will* discover my secret, and then I will be hunted.

But more than these horrible things that will come to pass in the future, the specter that hangs over me like Thanatos's ghost is the knowledge that tomorrow I will fight in the ring again. Tomorrow, the Silver tournament begins, and I will have to carve my way through more of Varus's enemies to try to save *Domus* Pelias and all our lives.

Echoes of the cheers of the crowd ring in my ears like crashing waves until, at last, they drown out all my other thoughts. Sleep eventually finds me, and I descend into the dark, restless and afraid.

"You did good yesterday, but don't let that draw you into a false sense of confidence," Contessa lectures me the next morning as the lift descends from the Pelias box to the arena's underbelly.

"Yes, *Domina*," I reply by rote, my mind distracted by the sound of the crowd roaring their approval at the fight that rages between a Copper from *Domus* Crassus and *Domus* Grus. Their matches have almost concluded as the appetizer for today and the Silver tournament is set to begin. I do not think that it is chance that I have been chosen for the first match.

Reese was thrilled to explain the match system to me this morning as we trooped through the tunnels. The whole thing is very melodramatic and reeks of Briannus's touch. Apparently, every season, there is a new story that is the setting that we are all participating in. This year, it is some parody or echo of the *Ferrum Domini*—gladiators competing to challenge the gods.

Each house has entered six gladiators that will battle their way to the top. The fights are arranged in groups with one member of each house in each cluster. When a gladiator is the last remaining member of his group, he "ascends" to *Mons* Olympus. *Ludi* get a *marca* for each gladiator from their roster who ascends. Then each of those who make it to the mountain of the gods will fight in a final bracket until only one *ludus* remains in control of the home of the gods. Then they are awarded another set of *marcae* for each gladiator who has not been eliminated.

It seems like a trite thing to die for compared to holding back a Norman horde, but what choice do I have?

"Don't be coy," she snaps, some of her frustration bleeding through as she glares at me. "I fear I have inflated your confidence too much. You're good, but you're no Flamma. You're certainly no Crixus, for that matter." I shrug, unbothered by her comparisons. I have never seen these famous gladiators fight. To me, they pale in the comparison to Gaius Marius.

"Yes, *Domina*," I repeat in exactly the same tone. I twitch in surprise as her fist slams into the stone wall of the lift next to my head, snapping my eyes up to meet her furious gaze.

"I said. Do. Not. Be. Coy," she growls, giving me another glare before storming out into the armory ahead of me. I swallow, unnerved by her Golden speed and power. She's not angry with me, just nervous about the fight to come. In some ways, she is like a mother to us. A horrible, violent mother, but one nonetheless.

"Sorry," I murmur after I follow her out of the elevator. "I am taking this seriously." The bald woman eyes me for a moment before nodding, accepting my apology and promise at the same time.

"Briannus bragged to us that the Games at Antioch would be something new," she reminds me. "We have no idea what the *compositores* have planned for your match. You will need to be ready for anything."

I twist my neck from side to side, stretching it as I listen. She's told me this before, but I think it makes both of us feel better for her to go over it again.

"You're facing a first-time fighter from *Ludus* Grus named Bruttia. Her Symbol is entered as being in the *Domus Planta*, but our spies say she's actually some sort of Poison attribute." I frown, confused yet again by the intricacies of the Games.

"I thought it was unusual for someone to start mid-season."

"Not when she's replacing someone who died."

"Ah."

"We haven't done much training against Plant Symbols. My advice is don't let her cut you, and don't play with your food. You saw the Gold *electus* with the razorvines?"

"I did."

"Trust me, you don't want to let her touch you with anything green. If it gets under your skin, there may be no saving you even if you win the fight."

"I understand." I nod grimly. "I'll keep out of her reach." I reach for my Frost Iron blades, where they hang in their white leather sheaths from the wall. My hands shake in excitement as they touch them, eager to be united with their strength.

"Should I wear the armor again?" I ask, eyeing the *lorica* I wore against *Impostor*. "I have a reputation to uphold."

"You made it work," she says after a moment of thought. "It's unusual in the non-*ferra* leagues, but you already have shown a flair for the dramatic. I worry it might slow you down if the fight goes too long."

"If it lets me take a few hits without her drawing blood, I'm all for it."

"You're strong, and your swordwork is better than most. If you're going to wear the *lorica*, get in close and cut her down. Fast."

"I will. I promise." But even as I do, I feel the oath that binds me constricting around me like my skin is suddenly too tight for my bones.

Teach my enemies fear.

This time, I stand alone behind the Sword Door. Light from the open arena pours in through the cracks, along with the roars of the crowd as the match before me comes to a bloody end. The people grow silent as they wait for the next fight to begin. I can feel their hunger even in the shadows. It is infectious, and my Symbols echo it, eager to be unleashed.

At last, after what feels like an eon, the announcer's voice booms throughout Bellona's Arena. "Citizens! We turn now to the first match of the Prime Bracket of the Silver Circuit, where mighty warriors fight for the right to ascend to *Mons* Olympus and challenge the gods. Rejoice! The Empress and her Consul are pleased to give you, debuting in his first tournament match, the only named Silver gladiator in the competition, *Frigus Ventus*—the Cold Wind of *Ludus* Pelias!"

The giant doors swing open as the crowd thunders its excitement. Men and women are on their feet, screaming for my attention. Look at how they love me, and they have not yet seen what I can do.

I jog forward, eyes locked across the arena where my opponent will soon emerge from the Shield Door. After I cross a quarter of the field, the announcer returns to introduce her.

"And his opponent, also appearing in her first tournament match, representing *Ludus* Grus, Bruttia!" A tall, short-haired woman emerges from the opposite gate, running forward fearlessly. Like most gladiators, she's dressed in fighting leathers instead of iron. However, dozens of different colored flowers cling to her torso, bursting into bloom as she steps out. She carries a long dueling blade in her right and a round shield wrapped around her left.

I'm relieved to see that her sword is made from iron instead of plants, but as I eye the flowers that cover her like battle medals, I realize how little I know of what other *electi* can do. The Iron Legions did not prepare me for the depth of creativity that a fighter can bring to the field.

"Gladiators," a strange new voice booms, rich and deep like a loving patriarch welcoming his guests into his home. "I am pleased that you have chosen to show yourself worthy of entering my house. But I would not be Mars if I did not make you show that you were *worthy*." His laughter is loud and bold. More of Briannus's theatrics, I realize after a moment of pure terror. This is not the true voice of the dead god speaking once more, merely an actor playing a part.

"There are many challenges waiting for those who seek to ascend to my side. But before you can see them, you must pass my first test. Welcome to my Garden of Blades!" The crowd begins to cheer, but their excitement is mild, as if they too are confused about what they are witnessing. But those unenthusiastic screams shift to a shocked roar as the world around us changes.

Trees burst from the ground, growing until they tower over me. Thick hedges emerge after them, rising out of the sand in droves. Last comes grass, growing in thick patches. A half dozen stone fountains full of flowing water erupt around the arena before they are hidden behind the wall of bushes taller than me. I lose sight of my opponent as we are sealed into this green maze.

A rocky pathway rises out of the ground at my feet, pointing me further into the center of the ring. I shiver in awe at the display of power. I do not know how this was done. No relic I have ever heard of can manifest physical trees out of thin air like this. Even my ability with the *Glacialis Falx* pales in comparison. Briannus was not lying when he told Varus that the rest of the season was going to be something never seen before.

Cautiously, I sweep my *animus* forward, trying to gain understanding of the changed arena. I stop short as I sense a dense cluster of iron off to my right, deeper in the maze. It feels like a series of small blades held close together. There are far too many for Bruttia to be carrying on her person, which means that this, too, has been conjured by whatever devilry the *compositores* have created. A trap of some sort, for an unsuspecting gladiator.

It also means that this is not a dream.

Part of me had been wondering if this was a facsimile created by a *somnus* relic, like the one Contessa used to train me, but the things conjured in that room did not really exist. I could not sense my opponent's weapons because they were not real enough.

I can feel the iron in these blades just fine.

"Gladiators, welcome to Mars's Garden of Blades!" the announcer bellows, back at his post. "Only one of you may advance closer on your quest to ascend to *Mons* Olympus. There are two ways to progress closer to the gods. Escape the garden or defeat your opponent. But if you are wise and truly worthy, you may do both for a special reward." It is a testament to how strong the amplification relic he is using is that I can hear him above the crowd.

As he calls for silence, I wonder if they understand the level of power that has been displayed here. Many patricians and most plebeians likely do not. It is hard to understand the limitations of being an *electi* without being one yourself. But the palatines, most of whom bear *Cor* Hearts and watch, will know. The legionnaires are not the only show of strength at these games.

A hush descends upon the arena. A songbird trills somewhere in the garden, breaking the silence. I embrace Ancient Frost and Iron, letting their sturdy calm sweep over and fill me, thrusting me into the depths of their logical embrace. In a heartbeat, I am the cold killer who tore *Impostor* apart—I am the Cold Wind they name me.

"Gladiators," the announcer roars at last. "Fight!"

I waste no time, sprinting forward, casting my *animus* around me, searching for Bruttia. The *compositores* have deliberately separated us from one another, and while I must play their game, I am not required to follow all their rules.

I draw my Iron Frost weapons as I head toward the center of the garden. A hedge wall has grown between me and the middle, but I hack at it with my blades, using my will to keep my edges sharp as I cut at the plants.

Three quick slashes are enough to create a hole big enough for me to dive through. Instead of taking the path to my left or right, I cross it, approaching the next row of hedges. I am not here to prove I can survive their tests, but to beat one other gladiator. The sooner I do that, the sooner I can get out of this nightmare.

I pass through the second hedge, only to be met by another. Snarling in rage, I cut through it, casting my *animus* around hunting for Bruttia, but wherever the Grus gladiator is, she is out of my range.

But not everything is.

I hesitate for a moment as I look through the hole I cut in the hedge, unsure about what is waiting for me. For the first time, I'm not presented with a narrow path, but peering into an open glade. Thirty thousand pairs of eyes watch me as I prepare to dive through. I wonder if their vantage point shows them the danger I am about to face. I cannot see it, but my Iron Symbol is screaming in warning. Whatever is waiting for me carries a great deal of metal.

The problem is that I, *Frigus Ventus*, the Cold Wind, shouldn't know there is a trap waiting. It is made of Iron, not Ancient Frost. Which means that in order for me to keep my secret, I am going to have to do something very stupid. With a sigh, I vault forward, diving through the hole I cut in the hedge, willing my *lorica* to be lighter as I roll to my feet.

I expected to find a tripwire attached to a series of spears or large arrows. Instead, I am presented with a horticultural horror. A massive tree stands in the center of the glade. Its boughs are almost empty, and what few leaves cling to its branches are thin and yellow, as if it is on death's door. A series of thick, black vines wrap around it like the arms of a *krakenus* around the mast of a ship, choking it from its roots to the top of its trunk.

I have just enough time to take in the sight of the corrupted plant before I am attacked by a dozen of its limbs, each tipped with a gleaming iron head. Its appendages flail at me, moving with enough force to gut me through my *lorica*.

I twist to the side, letting the leading vine stab past me. My training takes over, and I cut downward with my left blade, slicing through the appendage, separating the iron head from the rest of the plant.

It falls to the grass with a heavy *thunk*, but there are still eleven more trying to destroy me. Sparks fly as I deflect the second spearhead. I want nothing more than to shatter it with my will, but I dare not make my power so obvious.

I stumble as the third bounces off my chest, but I reinforce my *lorica*, preventing the razor-sharp tip from skewering me. A fourth hammers me as I try to regain my footing, but my will holds my armor together.

"I am *never* coming in here without you," I promise my *lorica*.

I block another of the vine *krakenus*'s attacks in a spray of sparks before managing to cut off a second iron head from one of the tendrils. I grit my teeth in frustration as I leap to the side to avoid being stabbed by a third. There are too many! Even with my Iron Senses, I do not have enough hands to keep up with the pace that the monstrosity sets.

I'm wasting time.

I don't need to kill this thing, only to survive its ambush. Its only purpose is to burn my essence and energy. The *compositores* don't want me to die this early—that's bad entertainment. But if it manages to wound me or wear me down, that only adds to the drama. The announcer said that there was some sort of way to escape, which means that I cannot afford to get trapped here while Bruttia explores.

I cut off a third spearhead, sending it flying. Another shoots straight at my head, and I dive, rolling under the angle of its attack before bursting to my feet and sprinting through the glade where the *krakenus* lurks.

I leap to the side as a long vine tries to sever my spine. It moves with such force that it stabs deep into the ground and becomes stuck, despite the plant's attempt to pull it back. Taking advantage of the opening, I lower my head and sprint a dozen paces until I am out of its range and arrive at the maze wall on the other side of the clearing. The *krakenus*'s vines snap the air in irritation, but it is anchored to its tree and cannot give chase.

I pause for a moment, panting from the exertion, staring back at the monstrosity. From this angle, I can see the main entrance to this glade, which would have brought me right into the trap's jaws. The crowd's roar is distant and muted, as if they have put us in containment like the one they use in the *ludus* training fields. I wonder what is in here that they need to protect everyone else from.

No doubt I will find out soon enough.

Turning my back on the monstrosity that the *compositores* have made, I cut my way back into the maze, hunting for a gladiator that I have to kill.

CHAPTER 32

I jog down one of the maze paths, following the stone pathway. After chopping through a dozen walls, I am no closer to finding my quarry, so I change my approach and follow the guide the *compositores* made for me. I feel like an idiot, a lamb choosing to go to slaughter. They have already shown me that they cannot be trusted. If I had followed the path they started me on, I would have been delivered right into the *krakenus*'s reach.

But not all the mazeways are paved. So reluctantly, I follow this one, hoping it will lead me to something useful. A horn sounds in the garden, and I turn my head in its direction, but I can see nothing over the hedges.

They have not ended the match, which means Bruttia has neither escaped nor died. I will deal with whatever fresh horror the horn is announcing in its own time. Right now, I need to catch up. I push myself to a sprint, racing down the path. Once again, the *lorica* wrapped around me has proven its worth. I have almost completely refilled my Iron reserves thanks to it. Unrelenting Fire twinges in complaint at being neglected, but I ignore the nausea that it brings. Now is not the time for weakness.

My path leads me to another opening, but unlike the last one, the trap that waits for me here is not immediately apparent. Cautiously, I enter a square garden decorated with beautiful flowers. In the center, a fountain bubbles, adding an air of tranquility to the scene. On top of its basin stands the stone statue of a hoplite warrior, an infantry unit that predates the modern Iron Legions. He stands at attention with a large shield and spear. I cast my *animus* about, looking for another vine *krakenus*, but there is no iron or ice present.

In front of the water-filled basin is a small pedestal with a bronze inscription too small for me to read from this distance. Tentatively, I make my way forward into the open, watching the trees for any suspicious movement.

Feeling a little reassured that danger is not imminent, I walk up to the placard and bend down to read the writing. *Only warriors who are worthy may journey further*. That isn't particularly helpful. I shoot a glare up in the direction of where I think the Prime Box is just so Briannus will know I am not impressed by his clues.

Still scowling, I stand up just in time to see the stone figure standing guard over the fountain come to life. A horrible grinding sound emerges as it turns to face me, lowering its shield and raising its spear in my direction. They have made their own *furia*, some sort of stone golem that is set to attack anyone who approaches the fountain.

"You have got to be kidding me," I groan. A rumbling sound behind me pulls my attention. A series of stone bars rise from the ground, closing off the entrance. I might still be able to cut through the hedge walls, but the *compositores'* intent is clear. I am locked in here until I defeat the challenge.

The *furia* does not speak but leaps forward, landing heavily on the grassy ground. Its spear flickers forward at my head, and only my Silver speed saves me from having my skull shattered.

I curse the name of Dead Mars. He had nothing to do with this farce of a game, but it feels good to blame him anyway. The stone hoplite shuffles forward, holding its large shield up to cover itself from eyes to ankles.

I am at a severe disadvantage when it comes to range. I need to get close enough to hammer him with my swords, but first I will have to get past its spear. With a sigh, I move forward as it pulls back its weapon, trying to get close before it can react. I cut to the side, hoping to get around his shield, but it turns with uncanny precision, keeping me at bay.

I knock his thrust to the side with my left blade, stepping into range to hammer my right down on his shield. I reinforce my weapon to protect it, but it makes no difference. My weapon bounces off the shield without even making a crack. I can feel its will resisting me. It feels like a language I do not speak, but its intent is more than clear. It will not let me cut.

I gasp in surprise as it flips its spear around, bringing the butt up in a blindingly quick attack that almost shatters my chin. I retreat a few steps, trying to figure out how I am supposed to defeat this thing. None of my Symbols are particularly effective against stone. Which means the only solution before me is brute force.

I pull on my Iron essence, letting it flow into my muscles and bones, reinforcing the increased hardiness of my body from my Silver *Cor*. Thanks to my *lorica*, it is the easiest of my reserves to refill on the run. With a roar, I throw myself forward, trying to hammer my way through the shield.

My swords ring in distress as they bounce off the stolid stone. The vibrations make my palms go numb. But no matter how much essence I channel into my body, no matter how firm I make my weapons, my strength is not enough to even crack the hoplite's stone.

My world narrows as I strain my veins, demanding their all. In a fit of panic, I throw my left blade down, stabbing it point first into the grass so I can wrap my free hand around the haft of the *furia*'s spear to try to wrest it from its grasp. But I might as well be trying to uproot an ancient tree.

Panting, I continue to press my aggression. The hoplite's spear flicks toward my head once more. I twist to let it pass, stepping in to batter its shield. I draw deeply on my reserve, but even my supply of Iron is running low.

Something within me bubbles, flaring in rebellion. Unrelenting Fire rages, protesting the strain that my Silver body puts on it. As if it senses the weakness of Iron, it strikes, trying to take over. My *Corda* pulse in agony. My Symbols slip out of my grasp like the palm of my mind has been greased.

The strength flows out of my body, and exhaustion hammers me harder than any *furia* ever could. My legs give out from under me, and I collapse on the ground, curling into a ball as waves of nausea sweep over me.

I watch in horror as the hoplite plods toward me. It has enough power to crush my skull like a watermelon underneath one of its stone feet. I have to *move*. It will be on me in just a couple of paces. Desperately, I reach for my Symbols, but there is something between us. The paths to my attunements are jumbled and twisted like the maze of Bellona's Arena.

Obey me! I thunder in my own mind.

With a *snap*, my *Corda* pop back in place like scolded children leaping into their beds. Iron and Ancient Frost pour into me, banishing my exhaustion. I roll to the side just in time to avoid the hoplite's heavy stomp that smashes down where my head was.

I leap to my feet, dancing back a few paces to create space between me and the *furia*. Pliny was right—Unrelenting Fire being *cuprum* is a weakness. I cannot push myself beyond my limits while my *Cor* Hearts are out of balance. I shake my head, grateful to have found the line without dying.

But collapsing did have one benefit. While I was on the ground, staring at the *furia*'s feet, I was reminded of where it came from. I am not completely without options after all.

The *furia* lunges forward again, quick as a scorpion's tail. I flinch away from his attack, forcing myself to give ground, leading my opponent in a circle around the glade. Step by step we travel. We pass by where I stabbed my *gladius* into the ground, and I grab it, relishing in having both of my weapons back in my hands.

The stone *furia* seems to be even simpler than its icy cousin. It follows me in dogged, single-minded pursuit. The Norman shamans use ice from Aquilo's grave to craft theirs. I certainly hope that Terra's or Vulcan's were not disturbed in the making of this thing.

I cut through the middle of the grass, leading the *furia* close to the fountain. As I pass it, I turn and hammer the stone edge of the basin with both of my *gladii*, reinforcing them with the Iron Symbol to keep them from being damaged.

To my surprise, the stone is soft—as if it were prepared for exactly this thing. The pond shatters, and water pours out, flooding the garden. I stand in the deluge, waiting until it is splashing up over my boots. When there is enough to work with, I call upon Ancient Frost and send out my chilling will, freezing the liquid around the hoplite's ankles into ice in a flash.

The *furia* jerks to a halt as the water around its ankles turns solid, rooting it to the ground. It seems confused. Whatever instructions the Heartsmiths imprinted in its stone brain when they made it do not cover this development.

I pause for a moment, pulling some Ancient Frost from my *gladii* to refill my reserves. I dare not risk over-exerting myself and wasting this opportunity. A *crack* pulls me out of my cultivation, and I eye the hoplite with irritation. Some of the ice around its left ankle has begun to give. Growling under my breath, I step forward, extending my left-hand blade to touch the edge of its ice prison directly so I can reinforce the bindings with my will.

The fountain still bubbles behind us, flooding the garden more with every moment. Careful to keep out of range of its spear, I sheathe my left blade before thrusting my empty hand in the water and splashing it toward the *furia*. When it is thoroughly soaked, I reach through the congruency of the water that connects us to freeze it solid like a shell. Laughing, I continue to scoop, adding layer after layer over the hoplite and freezing it until he is covered from head to toe, unable to move even an inch.

Warily, I ease back into its range, watching the tip of its spear, which wiggles but does not move. The *furia* is trapped and helpless. I place my left hand on the frozen cocoon, closing my eyes as I pull my cold out of some of the ice, letting it thaw into water and soak into the pores of the stone.

After a few moments, I clench my fist and send the cold pouring back in, causing those imperfections to expand as Winter's knives dig deeper into the rock. The rock begins to groan under the pressure that grows deep inside it.

Satisfied with the tendrils that have burrowed into the *furia*, I take a step back, giving my *gladius* a flashy twirl. I glance up at the muted crowd that watches above. Many of them are leaning forward, waiting to see what I will do.

Frigus Ventus has never used his Symbol publicly before. Few have probably ever seen the power of Winter this far south. I doubt it ever snows here, this close to the ocean. I smile at them, hoping that Varus and the rest of the palatines have their glass relics magnifying me.

Summoning my Symbols, I hammer my sword into the *furia*'s chest, willing the frost to detonate, tearing the hoplite apart from the inside out. Shards of ice and rock fly everywhere, and I raise my left hand to shield my eyes.

When I lower it, the top half of the *furia* is gone, broken into a thousand pieces. Sticking out of its hips is a large golden key with a black stone set in the handle. I cock my head to study it for a moment. At last, I begin to understand what I must do to escape this place.

Smiling grimly, I reach out to grab it and stick it in my belt. Behind me, the stone gate rumbles open, and I am free to roam the maze once more.

CHAPTER 33

The haunting horn sounds again in the distance. I suspect that it is some new danger, dreamed up by the *compositores* to amaze the crowd. I break into a jog, following a stone path that was not there before.

It seems that by defeating the hoplite, I have unlocked some sort of guidance to my next task. I race along, deciding to trust that the designers of this maze will be guiding me toward something interesting. It may not be for my benefit, but it is better than wasting time lost among the maze.

Judging by *Sol* above, I am heading toward the east corner of the ring. Abruptly, the row of hedges stops, and I emerge into another clearing. A giant stone door is set in the wall of the arena, sealed with three locks.

The first is made of a black metal that my Iron Symbol cannot sense, like the key that was inside the hoplite's chest. The second is made of ruby, and the third is the green of an emerald. I nod my head, understanding what they are showing me.

If I wish to escape, I will need to find two more keys.

I turn and follow the stone pathway as it continues back into another row of hedges. For a moment, my mind flashes back to the maze in the *Sententia*. It feels like I am still a boy, unable to escape the same games. This arena is more dangerous than the one I competed in to try to earn my *Cor* Heart, but despite the drama, it is much the same.

The flagstones lead me back toward the center, and I lean into my speed, hoping to gain time on Bruttia. I do not know if she encountered any traps before she found her first *furia*, but the time I spent fighting the vine *krakenus* may lead to my defeat.

I'm so focused on finding the next challenge that I almost don't notice the danger until it's too late. My *gladii* and *lorica* are worth their weight, giving me easy access to Iron to refill the reserves that I almost completely decimated trying to break through the stone hoplite's shield.

While I am cultivating, the range of my *animus* shrinks, limited by my divided focus. I only sense the iron lurking in the bushes right as I step into striking range. The hedges to my right *ripple*, pulling back like water to allow Bruttia to leap through them unhindered.

The flowers along her armor flicker, changing back to their bright colors, banishing the camouflage that hid her from my eyesight. She lunges toward me, shield extended to knock me backward as she readies her blade to stab. It had not occurred to me until this moment how much more suited to this arena she is than me.

If I were not what I am, her surprise attack would have killed me. It still nearly does. I drop to my knees, letting my shin guards absorb most of the painful landing as I slide under her attack.

Calling on my Silver speed, I leap back to my feet to face the Grus gladiator. My left hand pulls my second *gladius* from its sheath as I lunge forward, matching her aggression with my own. I batter her shield with my right blade, relying on brute force to keep Bruttia on her back foot.

The round buckler is made of oak reinforced with an iron band around the center. It is a simple matter for me to carve through the ring, but the wood stymies me, resisting my sword's edge with a hint of a foreign willpower. It is not overwhelming, but enough to keep my own Symbol from shearing through her shield. I wrench my blade free of the wood before she can twist her shield and rip my weapon out of my grasp.

Bruttia is a tall woman, her hair cut Legion-short. She eyes me with distrust, apparently as confused as I am. For a moment, we are still, until everything clicks for us at once.

Oak is a congruency of her plant Symbol! I realize. That was her will rebuffing my attempt to sunder her shield. Her eyes go wide as they track from my *gladius* to me. I didn't think that she would be able to interact with her shield like that, so I used Iron brazenly. I might as well have shouted my secret to her with my attack.

Which means that I have to kill her.

She must see some of my dark intent in my eyes, because she withdraws a step as I lunge forward, hammering at her with both swords. Panic flares in her eyes as pieces of wood begin to fly off her shield from the power of my assault. I can feel her resistance fading. It cannot be a strong congruency for her, just enough to get an edge over most, but the essence conversion is costing her, even if we are standing in the middle of a garden.

Her shield shatters, and I stalk forward, eager to end this. I am not excited to add another soul to my balance, but to protect this secret, I would do far worse. She parries my first strike wide, twisting into it with her hips, thrusting her upper body toward me. I almost shake my head to see such poor form. The *lanista* of *Domus* Grus must not be cut from the same cloth as Contessa—

The blossoms that cling to the surface of her armor turn bright yellow as they cough forth a cloud of pollen the same toxic color. I try to stop, but it is too late. I sweep through the storm holding my breath, but not before it gets into my mouth, nose, and eyes.

The poison burns as it digs into me. My Symbols panic as they sense a foreign presence sweeping into me, but they are torn out of my grasp. I stumble to my knees as the strength flows out of me. Weakly, I lift my head, staring at Bruttia with horrified eyes.

The gladiator cocks her head, studying me like I am a dangerous animal, before reaching out with her empty left palm and placing it on my forehead. I try to swing at her with my *gladius*, but she disarms me easily. My sword drops onto the stone pathway beneath our feet.

Bruttia smiles a cruel smile, throwing her head back as she pours her will into me, exacerbating the poison that runs through my veins. I can feel its fire spreading. Like lightning striking a dry forest, it takes only a moment for it to go from a spark to an inferno. Lifting her hand, she bends down further to pluck the black key from my belt. I groan, spotting a red one dangling from hers.

"Die in pain, *immundus*," she whispers as she pulls back from me.

I try to mumble a threat, but the only thing that comes out of my mouth is a low groan. She snorts in derision.

"I think I'll keep these," Bruttia remarks, picking up my swords from the ground to admire them. "A memento from the match that gave me my name." I can only watch in dim horror as she turns her back on me and breaks into a brisk jog, content to leave me to suffer alone in front of the thirty thousand souls that watch from the stands.

I can't breathe.

A burning sickness fills me, seeping into my bones. I am lying on the ground. When did I collapse? I remember being on my knees, but nothing after. The coolness of the stone is a relief against my cheek. My eyes are blurry; the world is a smear of green and gray.

I can't breathe.

The pain burns inside me, devouring my will. With what little thought I possess, I reach for my Ancient Frost and Iron Symbols, but they are distant—on the other side of the heat that consumes me. My cold attunements are chased away by the fire of this infection, barring me from them. The end will come soon, I know. I will see what waits for me on the shores of the River Styx.

I cannot tell if the gods watch me. The poison is so overwhelming that I do not feel my skin tingle with their attention. Perhaps they know that I am meant to die, and they have no time to waste on my story any longer. If any of the others live, they will have to fulfill Nemesis's *votum* without me. I let out one last, shaky breath as the darkness comes.

I hope my mother and father are waiting there.

I hope they will recognize me.

With that last bit of acceptance, I stop struggling, letting go of the last of my resistance, clearing the way for the poison to sweep through my body and finish me off.

But instead, a different kind of flame fills the void. The Symbol of Unrelenting Fire leaps free, essence pouring out of its *Cor* like a flood. A second warmth fills me, spreading through my limbs with delightful relief.

It is not the heat of an inferno, but the comfort of hot cider on a winter's night. My breath comes back to me as the pain within me flees, driven out by the purifying fire that chases it through my body. Slowly, I manage to push myself up off the ground, hacking up dark-colored phlegm as the poison is purged from me.

The wall of fiery pain that separates me from Ancient Frost and Iron fades and burns out as Unrelenting Fire casts out the weaker flame. Gasping for breath, I sit on my knees and stare at the world around me with wonder.

I am alive.

My missing strength flows back into my limbs as my Silver Symbols succor me. I channel their essences through my veins, soothing my seared insides with their cooler touch. After a few long, painful moments, I finally feel human. My eyes snap open, and I rise to my feet.

Unpoisoned.

Unbroken.

Unbeaten.

The crowd outside the arena is roaring their approval so loudly, it threatens to overwhelm the invisible barrier between us. I do not look up at my audience as I begin to walk. My eyes are glued to the stone pathway that rearranges itself before me, guiding my steps.

In truth, I do not need the *compositores*' direction. I know where I need to be. There are only two ways to win this match: killing your opponent or escaping. The announcer hinted that doing both would earn the gladiator a bonus, which is why Bruttia didn't finish me off immediately. She needed time to complete the last challenge.

It also meant that I knew where she was going to end up—I've been there once before. I try not to let my fear show as I race toward the gate with the locks. If I am too late, it will not matter that I survived her poison. Her knowledge will kill me as easily as her plants could have.

I emerge from the hedge maze and let out a long sigh of relief at the sight of the three locks that are still sealed tight. I scan the area with my *animus*, looking for any hidden traps or the hidden gladiator, but I sense nothing.

All I can do is wait for my quarry to come to me. I can feel the eyes that watch me, hungrily waiting for the rematch. Boldly, I stride to stand before the gate, waiting out in the open for Bruttia's return.

She will not die to the third challenge, I am sure. Briannus and his *compositores* want to play out this drama all the way to the end. This is what the people pay to see.

Glancing up, I see a part of the crowd on the far side of the ring cheering in reaction to something I cannot see. The *Grus* gladiator must be close to completing the third challenge. I feel the corner of my lip quirk up as I imagine the expression on Contessa's face right now as I wait for Bruttia without a weapon.

I will teach her fear.

The dim roar of the audience punches through the barrier, telling me that the time will be soon. I roll my shoulders and, on a whim, tap into Unrelenting Fire. Ancient Frost squirms in my grasp, as if suddenly uncomfortable. A sharp pain stings in the front of my head, causing me to squint and stagger back a step.

I release the Winter Symbol, separating it from its opposite element. Immediately, my head clears, and I frown, beginning to understand just how difficult it will be for me to manage these two opposite Symbols inside of me. Iron, on the other hand, seems less irritated by the heat's presence. It comes to my call, but reluctantly, as if distrustful of the fire that burns inside of me.

Pushing that thought aside, I sweep Unrelenting Fire's *animus* through my body once more, searching for any remnants of poison that still lurk within. I find a dark spot in one of my legs that I burn away and another in one of my teeth, but nothing else remains of the toxin that she dosed me with.

Shaking my head in wonder, I release Unrelenting Fire, welcoming back Ancient Frost. I roll my shoulders and set myself, ready to face my enemy once more. The crowd above is still, watching intently. I take that to mean that she is drawing close. I sweep out with my Silver *animus*, pushing it beyond my comfortable range. Ancient Frost and Iron spark at the same time as they sense my stolen swords heading toward me.

It is only a moment before she bursts into the garden, moving quickly. All three precious keys dangle from her belt, and she holds my blades in her hands. The brilliant smile dies on her face as she sees me waiting between her and the gate. Stunned, she slows to a stop a dozen paces away from me.

"How?" My smile widens, growing large for the crowd that watches us.

"I am *Frigus Ventus*," I say as condescendingly as possible.

In the distance, the haunting horn sounds once more.

"I—" she begins but cannot seem to finish her thought. After a moment of silence, she shakes her head to clear it, brandishing my cold blades in warning as she begins to march toward me.

"You should have let the poison finish you, *Frigus Ventus*." Her tone makes a mockery of my name. After all, only one of us is armed. Why should she fear me? "It would have been quick. Now all the other deaths left to you are far worse."

She breaks into a jog, eating up the distance between us in seconds. Her right hand swings in a heavy slash, aiming to cut me in half. I smile brightly, raising my empty left for her to see as I call upon the *Glacialis Falx*, and a *gladius* made of ice grows out of my palm before her very eyes.

I catch her blow easily, twisting and knocking it aside with a contemptuous flick. It would be a simple matter for me to destroy her sword thanks to its communion with both Iron and Ancient Frost, but they are mine. I want them back.

Her eyes are wide with fear as she stares at the icy blade that I have manifested. I do not need to look at the crowd to know that they are beside themselves in delight. I can feel their ecstasy shaking the ground of the arena. I will give them something they will never forget. They will tell stories about this for the rest of their lives.

I incline my head at Bruttia, inviting her to attack once more. She hesitates but decides it is her only choice, following up her attack with the sword in her left hand. I repeat the process, summoning a second *Glacialis Falx* to block her attack.

For a moment, we stand frozen as if we are the ice instead of my blades. The tips of our swords touch like lovers holding hands at the beginning of a dance. Then she remembers my will eating into her oaken shield, and she snatches them free, breaking our connection.

I only shake my head slightly, following after her like a predator. She falls back before my advance in terror. There is no fight left in her now. Bruttia is a trickster, an assassin. She cannot stand against me in the open, and we both know it. The same way we both know that she has to die to keep my secret.

"Please," she whispers, but I only shake my head, following her doggedly. I feel no pity for her after her threats and her poisons. I know that if our roles were reversed, she would never spare me.

Ice rings against iron as I press the attack, forcing her to parry my aggressive blows. She falls back, leading me around in a circle in the garden clearing. I am not an idiot; I can feel her trying to maneuver me so she can make a break for the door. I can only smile in amusement at the thought of her somehow being able to turn three locks before I kill her.

The horn sounds again, closer this time. Its notes are low and haunting, reverberating in my chest with an almost primal power. It's a warning, a promise that if we do not make things interesting, the designers of this garden horror have their own ways to up the ante.

Taking their threat to heart, I leap forward, increasing my attacks to catch her before she can flee. Bruttia blocks, eyes roving with fear as she continues to try to figure out how to escape me. But this is the end of the road—there is nowhere to go.

At last, she seems to realize that I will not let her past me to the gate. Desperate for a chance to save herself, she turns and races back toward the hedge maze in the rest of the ring. Cursing Flora, the dead God of Flowers, I chase after Bruttia, trying to catch her before she can disappear into her element.

But I am not the only one frustrated by her lack of courage.

As she reaches the entrance, that horrible horn sounds once more. It is no longer a distant warning, but clear and present. Whatever danger the *compositores* have planned is here. Bruttia looks over her shoulder at me, eyes full of panic. She does not know that she is already dead.

Dark forms leap from the entrance, low and lean. The poisoner goes down with a scream as the first *lupus* slams into her, knocking her legs out from under her. Three more are on her in a flash, jaws ripping. Silver veins run through their fur, marking them as *mythi*. Of all the animals to be given the strength of a *Cor*, I think these must be the most terrifying. Bruttia screams as they tear her to shreds. It is so sudden and brutal that I freeze, rooted in place by the horrible sight.

A fifth wolf pads into the clearing, ignoring the woman that his pack ravages. A head taller than the rest, he watches me, his yellow eyes glowing. He cocks his head at me, staring with far too much intelligence. A chill runs down my spine as I remember the last time I stared into the eyes of one of these creatures. It was in a dream a lifetime ago.

Heat flares in the purple scar that runs around my wrist from the bite that he gave me during the *Sententia*. This is not the same wolf; that one was not real, despite the mark he left around my wrist. But as we stare at each other, I am haunted by the sense of intelligence behind its eyes.

Slowly, the massive *mythus* begins to walk toward me. His head is low, but his teeth are not bared. He does not cower, merely investigates an oddity. It seems to me that he knows me too. I dare not move as he stops just short of me, slowly extending his snout to sniff at my right wrist, where I still carry his kin's bite marks in my flesh. Apparently satisfied, he withdraws, glancing over his shoulder at his pack.

Bruttia is no longer screaming, a mercy for her and me. The other four wolves worry at her corpse, ignoring me. Abruptly, the leader drops to his haunches, opening his toothed mouth wide in a bored yawn.

As one, the rest of his pack obeys, dropping into rigid copies of their leader. Five *mythi* wolves stare at me intently, waiting for something. If they wanted to, they could tear me to shreds as easily as they did Bruttia. They carry no iron or ice to give me an advantage. I cannot hear the crowd. I cannot hear anything above the blood rushing through my ears.

They say that when he lived, Mars kept a pack of *lupi* like faithful hounds. It seems that the *compositores* have decided to restore this tradition. But no matter what their plans are, I can feel the hand of those dead gods resting heavily on the scale. This moment has been planned. It is not for me, but an agent of something bigger than this place and the thirty thousand people in it.

I did not kill Bruttia myself, which will be reflected in the *marcae* earned for *Domus* Pelias after the match. In order to maximize my score, I must complete the keys and escape. The wolves watch me with infinite patience, waiting to see what I will do.

Not breaking eye contact with the leader, I take a tentative step toward Bruttia's body. None of them even twitch, sitting still as stone. Inch by inch, I make my way to the ruined corpse of the Grus gladiator. Even in the depths of Ancient Frost, I feel my insides roil at the sight of what they have done to her. She should have let me kill her; I would have given her a much cleaner death.

The three keys are still tied to her belt. Reluctantly, I look away from the alpha to rip them free, cutting the thong that holds them with one of my frozen blades. Tucking them in my belt, I check once more to see if any of the wolves have moved. They watch me like immobile sentinels, waiting.

Trusting the peace that they offer, I drop my icy sword from my left hand, scooping my Frost Iron *gladius* up from the ground. Casting around, I sigh when I see the second one rests at the feet of the leader. Has it always been there? I am not sure.

Still holding the beast's gaze, I approach him slowly, trying to show this king of predators the respect he deserves. He watches me in silence, yellow eyes unblinking as I draw near. Slowly, I kneel, placing my other frozen blade on the ground to free my hand.

A low growl of warning emerges from the *lupus* as my hand hovers inches from the hilt that sits by his front paws. I freeze, terror running through my veins. But the beast does not move, only communicates his warning.

Steeling myself, I place my hand on the *gladius* and lift it from the ground, rising to my feet in one fluid motion to create some space between me and the wolf. The leader does not growl again. Instead, he looks over his shoulder, back into the arena as if disappointed in me.

I don't know what to make of *that*.

Not turning away from the pack, I take a step backward, beginning to edge toward the door. The leader's head whips around, and one of his ears cocks as if he's surprised by what he hears. My heart races in my chest as I force myself to take another.

As one, the wolves leap to their feet, staring at me with the concentration of hungry predators who have seen a hare. Every instinct in my body screams that I should run, but I am frozen in place, afraid to shatter the stillness. I have become Bruttia, completely cowed by a more dangerous foe. I count my breaths, promising myself I will take another step after I reach five.

Five comes and goes, and I do not move. Neither do the wolves. At last, after fifteen, I can stand it no longer. I swallow my fear and take another step. The leader twitches forward and his pack copies his movements flawlessly.

Growls sound in their throats, a rumbling chorus more dangerous even than a distant avalanche. Even Iron and Ancient Frost cannot keep the fear at bay.

I cannot stay here.

If I stay, I will die. I must escape.

I take another step, even though it feels like I am condemning myself to death by doing so. Once more the wolves pace forward, and their growls grow louder as they express their displeasure. Instinctively, I tighten my grips on the hilts of my blades, drawing comfort from their sturdiness.

I try to hold the gaze of the alpha, but he will not meet my eyes. In fact, none of them are looking at me. The hairs on the back of my neck begin to stand up on end when I realize that all their gazes are fixed on something *behind* me.

Slowly, I look away from the pack to look over my shoulder. There is nothing there, only a door with three locks waiting for me to unlock it. What was it the announcer said? *Whoever does both will receive a special prize.*

I turn my back on the wolves, no longer afraid of them. Now I stare at the exit with a new sense of apprehension. For a moment, I debate simply giving up. I have won; they must let me advance. But the oath that binds my flesh to *Domus* Pelias constricts threateningly. If there are more points to be earned, Varus would want me to take it.

There is a scuffling on the grass behind me, and I whirl, terrified that the wolves are finally attacking. But I am just in time to see the tail of the last one as they vanish back into the hedge maze. It seems the *mythi* want no part of what is to come.

I reach out with my *animus*, reaching through the gate and into what waits beyond. I can feel the mechanisms that move the doors, but beyond is *blank*—not empty. It is a spot of darkness against my senses.

I can only chuckle in dry amusement as I walk back to the gate. This is a terrible decision, and yet I must make it. I reach down and pull out the black key, sliding it into its lock and twisting it. The *click* echoes throughout the entire arena, magnified like the announcer's voice. Next, I insert the ruby key, repeating the process.

Every instinct in my body wants to stop. To turn tail and run away like the wolves that are much wiser than me. But my oath holds me fast, keeping me on the path that has been laid before me. With shaking hands, I put the emerald key in its lock.

Its *click* is deafening like Dead Jupiter's thunder. The last bolt retracts, and I take two steps back as a series of *pops* resound. Slowly, the gates begin to swing open, but whatever waits beyond is shrouded in shadow, just like it is against my Symbols' senses.

I settle myself into a fighting stance, holding my blades forward, ready for anything.

Well, almost anything.

A massive figure, head and shoulders taller than me, emerges from the darkness. In his right hand, he carries a massive maul so heavy I could barely wield it. He is covered head-to-toe in golden armor streaked with black lines that flows as if made of liquid while still hugging him like a second skin. I know without looking that his helm is molded into the snarling visage of a wolf.

It is him.

The one who gave me all these Hearts.

The Golden Wolf.

Far above Bellona's Arena, *Mons* Olympus hovers in the sky, dead and dark.

Watching.

CHAPTER 34

A force I cannot see slams into me. It knocks my probing *animus* back with the ease of the wind carrying a dandelion seed. I am knocked back a dozen paces with casual power.

"Gah," I moan as my back slams against the hard stones. The fear is so overwhelming that I do not feel any pain. I scramble to my feet to face this thing while my mind races. How can it be here?

Terror radiates from him in an aura, like heat from a fire. My hands shake even as I reset my grip on my blades. His power is even stronger than I remember in my nightmares. Now I have a *Cor* to tell me how truly outclassed I am.

Over his shoulder, as the gates finish opening, enough light seeps into the room beyond to highlight the carnage that bathes it. The walls are red, painted with blood. Bodies lie everywhere, torn to more shreds than even poor Bruttia.

No. I realize, looking at the horrific scene before me, this is not a machination of Briannus and the Games. This is something far worse.

"**ATTEND TO ME, MORTALS**," he commands, throwing his arms wide as he looks up at the crowd. My ears pop as the barrier that has contained the arena shatters at a hint of pressure from his will. Screams of terror crash down on me as the people react to his power.

"**YOU HAVE GATHERED HERE TO WORSHIP WAR. WHAT A BLESSING FOR YOU THAT WAR HAS CHOSEN TO ATTEND HIS OWN CELEBRATION**." The blood drains out of my face as I stare at the *abominatio*. Surely, he does not mean that he is Mars in the flesh…

"**I AM PRAECO, HIS HERALD, AND I COME TO YOU IN THE NAME OF ONE WHO HAS LONG SLUMBERED. WAR WAKES! HE IS PLEASED THAT HIS CHILDREN STILL REMEMBER HIM AND BLEED HIS NAME.**" The figure is silent for a moment as he sweeps his menacing gaze around the entire arena, as if measuring each and every individual with only a look.

"**BUT SOME OF YOU HAVE FORGOTTEN YOUR OATHS. A GREAT CRIME HAS BEEN COMMITTED. A FAITH HAS BEEN BROKEN!**" A bolt of fear spikes through me at the thing's words. Can it be?

"**WHERE IS SHE?**" Praeco thunders. "**WHERE IS THE ONE WHO WAS BOUND BUT HAS BEEN FREED? YOU HAVE BETRAYED THE OATHS OF YOUR FOREFATHERS. DELIVER HER TO ME, AND I SHALL SPARE YOU FROM MARS'S JUDGMENT.**"

Nemesis told me that she had been imprisoned by both god and man. Somehow the thing claiming to be a Herald of Mars knows that she is free.

"**WILL NONE OF YOU SPEAK AND TAKE RESPONSIBILITY FOR YOUR BETRAYAL?**" His voice echoes off the walls of the arena, but he is only met by a silence. He waits for a count of ten, then nods once, his liquid gold helm moving sharply.

"SO BE IT. IF YOU WILL NOT CONFESS AND DELIVER THE PARIAH TO ME, THEN MY MASTER HAS SENT ME TO ENACT A SACRIFICE." His voice grows sultry as if he has professed his desire to a loved one. "**FORTUNATELY, I AM ALSO A PRIEST TO COLLECT THE BLOOD HE REQUIRES.**" The wolf head turns down from the crowd to stare at me with a burning intensity. I am driven to my knees by the sheer force of his attention.

"**Have no fear, Ironbound**," the *abominatio* says more quietly, now just to me. The power of his voice rattles my bones inside of my flesh. "**He has not forgotten you**."

Something *thuds* into the ground next to me, followed by a dozen more impacts as warriors land in the ring around this monster. The pressure on me abates as Praeco turns to regard this new threat with mild surprise, and I leap to my feet to discover that I am surrounded by Censors.

Despite my hatred of them, I am relieved at their intervention. Who better to stand against a monster like this than the executors of the Empress's will? Perhaps an entire Iron Legion, but even they might pale before the power of thirteen Censors in their unbreakable armor.

The white-clad warriors spread out like *lupii* themselves, circling the gold-armored giant. Their *tellus* dueling blades glint in the bright sun, sharper than a thought. I am surprised to see old Tartus and Falia among their ranks. I twist, scanning their faces, looking for the one I hate most. Even now I would strike him down if I got the chance. But there is no sign of haughty Atticus's sharp features among the rest. The Censors ignore me, sprinting past me as they hunt their prey.

"**WHAT IS THIS?**" Praeco booms in outrage as he spies the White Hand of the Empress. "**WHAT BLASPHEMY HAVE YOU CHILDREN WROUGHT WHILE YOUR MASTERS WERE AWAY? WHERE HAVE YOU LEARNED TO MAKE THINGS OF NOTHING?**"

"You are an *abominatio* and a false prophet," the lead Censor says, a Golden *electus* who looks to be in her early forties. The bulk of the other Censors align center around her, making her the point of their spear. "In the name of Empress Diana Agrippa, I place you under arrest."

"**Diana Agrippa**." He repeats her name to himself as if remembering something before hefting his mighty maul casually, as if it weighs no more than a thought. "**I am a herald of reckoning, little one. You cannot stand before me; you are an ignorant child. Are you so eager to die? Have you truly forgotten your gods**?"

"You are nothing more than a pretender to a power long dead," she replies boldly, taking a menacing step forward. "We will bury your bones with the rest of the gods."

The wolf head helm tilts to the side, as if surprised for the first time. I cannot see the eyes of the massive man who wears the armor, but I feel his gaze as he sweeps it over us, studying us, looking for something. Whatever it is, he seems to find it, snorting once more before stepping forward to face the Censor.

"**It seems that *much* has been forgotten**," he tells us confidently. "**I shall demonstrate my authority on your corpses**." The Gold Censor needs no more encouragement. She blurs forward, moving at an insane speed that my eyes cannot even track. She carries no Iron or Ice, so there is nothing for my Symbols to sense.

In a blink, she is on top of him, her *tellus* blade flashing. The liquid armor that encases Praeco parts easily under her weapon's sharp edge like water against a knife. But it flows back the moment the sword passes through, refilling the damage in a heartbeat.

The creature looks down at her in wry amusement, the black lines that run through his armor pulsing as he weathers her blows without flinching. After a dozen strikes, the Censor pulls back, staring at him in slack-jawed surprise.

"**I warned you**," he chides reproachfully.

Then he moves.

One moment, he is still, then he is in the center of the Censors, holding the woman by her head, casually palming her skull with his massive hand. I saw nothing, but I am certain he did not actually travel. He is what *Impostor* pretended to be.

"**LET THIS BE A REMINDER TO YOU ALL**," he thunders to the entire arena once more. "**AFTER I HAVE KILLED THESE APOSTATES, YOU WILL DELIVER TO ME THE ONE YOU SHELTER.**" Then his hand contracts, and the woman's head explodes. I turn away, unable to stomach the sight. Above us, the crowd is out of control. At first, they thought this was merely part of the theater, but now they see the danger that has come. I watch as a stampede forms as the people race to flee from the horror that has appeared.

To their credit, the rest of the Censors do not hesitate to surge into action. Most of them are Gold *electi*, and all of them carry the most dangerous weapons that have been forged in the Iron Empire. But Praeco wades among them like a farmer harvesting wheat.

His massive maul swings and connects with a figure in *tellus* armor. The Censor is sent flying, slamming into the arena's walls. I stare in horror at the red stain he leaves behind as he slides to the ground. His white armor is intact, but that is the only thing that is not shattered by the force that hit him.

Praeco dances, never ceasing his momentum. I have never fought with a weapon like his, but it is clear that he is not only inhumanly strong, but a master of it. He twirls, bringing the weapon down in an overhead smash on top of another Censor, shattering him like a piece of pottery.

A brave young woman leaps up behind the monstrosity, swinging her blade in a horizontal arc, trying to slice Praeco's head from his shoulders in one fell blow. The golden armor swirls, disturbed by the weapon's passage, and a few droplets fly from it like a spray of blood. I watch as they fall to the ground. The grass around those golden globs bursts into fire. But despite her attack, the *abominatio*'s skull remains connected to his neck.

The Herald's left elbow snaps backward, catching the woman in her stomach as she slams into his back, unable to arrest her momentum. With a violent wrench, he knocks her to the ground, spinning to bring his giant boot down on her in a terrifying stomp. Bones *crunch*, and the woman lets out a scream of anguish as he vents his rage on her. Not satisfied with one such blow, he raises his foot again before deliberately bringing it down on her head, crushing it easily.

There are only seven Censors left, and Praeco is not even wounded. I glance over my shoulder, eyeing the exit that the wolf *mythi* fled through. I would be wise to follow their lead.

Better late than never.

My feet are full of lead, unable to lift from the ground to flee. That prickling sensation that comes when my *votum* demands I take a specific path flares like a thousand fishhooks, burning from my scalp to my toes. I twitch as they tug me in the direction of the mad Herald.

My mind flashes back to the training armory that I stood in with ten other boys from Segesta under *Luna*'s full light. *The Golden Wolf.* I named him as I cut my own hand to bleed upon the rock. I never believed that I would see him again, yet I swore to my brothers and to Nemesis that I would kill him.

But my oath to Varus *would prefer that I flee*, I point out to whatever cosmic arbiter weighs the promises that I am bound to. *This is an unnecessary risk. Getting myself killed now will only contribute to the fall of* Domus Pelias.

My skin tightens as the binding that sits in my bones from Varus's relic ignites, agreeing with me. For a moment, the two oaths war, trapping me in place. They speak no words, but it feels as if two elemental forces hammer at each other with their wills. I grit my teeth as the pain overloads Ancient Frost and Iron's ability to numb it.

Eventually—and perhaps unsurprisingly—the god wins. The binding in my bones fades, leaving only the tug that demands that I turn and face this thing that is beyond me.

I obey Nemesis's wishes and turn back to face Praeco as he finishes smashing another Golden Censor. What hope do I have to stand against him? I am slower and weaker than almost everyone else on the battlefield. My *animus* cannot sense the armor that he wears.

I do not remember drawing my *gladii,* but they are in my hands. The Iron Frost in the blades blazes with cold, and I drink deeply, refilling both my reserves. There is a strange quivering from my *Cor* that contains my Winter Symbol. It seems to hum, as if exposed to something it has not felt in ages. Unrelenting Fire is strangely silent, perhaps sated by being used in my last fight.

"*Abominatio*!" I step past a panting Lania, who is staring at the crushed corpses of her comrades with wide eyes. I spot a blood splatter that might have been Tartus and almost feel bad for him. The Herald turns from the Censors he is idly pulling apart to stare at me with his wolf mask.

"I owe you," I bark, spitting on the ground to show my disgust. My mouth is dry, but I manage to scrounge up a little moisture to mock this thing. "You killed my family."

"**Are you sure about that**?" he asks, taking a step toward me. His heavy aura hammers at me once more, trying to make me kneel, but this time, I am prepared and resist his authority. If I was not in the firm embrace of Ancient Frost, I am certain my knees would have buckled in fear.

"**A little boy makes an oath with the gods and complains when they keep their end of the bargain**?" His voice is mocking. "**It was you who killed them. You invited the wild creatures into your home. What use is it to be angry at them for not being tame**?" I flinch at his words, burned by the shame that I have thought a thousand times before.

It was our actions that brought them to meddle. I knew when Valentina proposed the oath that it was foolish, but I was too smitten to deny her. Our teachers told us the gods were dead, but my mother always said that wasn't enough. If only I had listened.

"This boy has grown up," I tell him, forcing myself to take a step forward, brushing against his aura like a bull against a fence. "And he has made a new *votum*."

There is a moment of stunned silence before the Herald throws back his head and laughs, an eerie sound that bleeds into a howl the longer it goes. When he is done, he lowers his gaze and stares at me as if he can see the oath written on my flesh.

There is a flicker of movement over his shoulder, and I lift my eyes to see a figure appear in the darkness of the slaughterhouse. Nemesis stands behind him. She is still emaciated and rotten, but more whole than she was before. Her blindfolded gaze bores into me, and I gasp as I feel her *animus* brush over me, injecting me with a trickle of her knowledge.

"**So it was you who freed the mad one**." Praeco shakes his head slowly as if disappointed. He does not seem to realize that his target lurks behind him. "**You have not learned your lesson**." That is the only warning he gives me before he lunges forward, not using his full speed, but still faster than anything I can ever match.

Fortunately, my hands are guided by a god who has been dreaming of this day for centuries.

Praeco darts toward me, but my left hand is already stabbing forward as I set my feet on the ground like a spearman ready to catch a wild boar. I channel as much Iron and Ancient Frost essence into my blade as I can, reinforcing it as I command it to *cut*. The *abominatio* slams into me with enough force to drive me back a dozen steps. My boots tear up the grass in deep furrows as we slide.

My sword is buried in the massive man's stomach when we come to a halt. This close, I still cannot sense him with my *animus*. It is as if he is made of the void. There is only a *null* where I search. The gold liquid of his armor boils around my blade, trying to refill the hole that I have made, but every time it sweeps in, it recoils as if terrified at what it finds waiting for it.

Nemesis's *animus* guides me, like a pair of hands placed over my own. My instincts already know the path. I do not need to be able to sense him with my *Corda* to strike at him. I use my will to shove Ancient Frost essence down the length of my blade, using my ability to create ice *inside* of the Herald. My Heart's resistance to manifesting ice as anything other than the *Glacialis Falx* is absent, cowed by the presence of the god who walks in my shadow.

My Symbol—an Elder Symbol of the god Aquilo—surges into him with immediate effect. The liquid armor around my blade stops, frozen solid. I welcome the cold of my Symbol, letting it consume me like Iron did on a training field, what feels like a lifetime ago. Castor is gone, there is no fear, no anger, only the ice remains.

"**How**…" Praeco asks in shock, tilting his head to look down at the length of my sword stuck in him. "**How did you claim an Elder Symbol**?" He seems frozen, too stunned to react. I ignore him, stabbing forward with my right *gladius*, adding it as a second conduit as I focus all my will on pumping Ancient Frost essence into him. More of his armor turns rigid, locking him in place.

Something is wrong with his insides. I can kind of sense him now, defined by my ice, as it spreads. Winter creeps across his bones like an inevitable ruin, painting them to my senses. I feel his spine wrapped in my will. I count his ribs with ease.

But there is nothing else. My ice encounters no warmth, squeezes between no organs. My eyes widen as I realize that is because there are none to be found. Underneath his strange armor, he is made only of bones. Nemesis's *animus* burns with pride, like a cruel mother.

My gaze falls on one of the black streaks that run along his leg and up to his chest. I have seen markings like them before in the flesh of the woman Vixa. Praeco has no flesh, so the corrupted *necromanta* veins run through his living armor instead—made of *Cor*, not Iron.

"I know what you are," I whisper. "Now you will die."

"**Again**?" His laughter is mocking despite his inability to move. "**You may be the *Frigus Ventus*, but you're not as cold as the grave. You cannot send me there**."

"Let's find out," I retort, reaching out with my will to grasp the ice that I have wrapped around his bones. I cannot sense anything other than my ice; it feels like it is coiled around nothing, but it is good enough for what I plan to do.

"What do the dead need with spines?" There is a *crack,* and the Herald lets out a gurgle as I snap the base of his back with Ancient Frost. His legs give out, and I step back, unable to support the giant as the *abominatio* drops to his knees.

His head is level with mine now. I stare into those glowing wolf eyes as I slowly, painstakingly pull my right *gladius* out of where his guts should be and let the point dangle to the floor. I am not afraid of what I am about to do, even though it seems like madness. I am in the depths of Winter.

"**You think you have won**." His voice is weaker now, fading.

"Not yet. I will not win until the rest of them join you."

"**Join me**?"

"In the grave."

"**You will wait a long time, mortal, until that dream comes true**."

"We'll see. In the meantime, I have a message for your master, from the god I worship."

"**And what is your message**?" Despite his weakness, he manages to chuckle, amused by my temerity.

"She will see him blind." With one vicious stroke, I cut his head from his shoulders. The Frost Iron peels the liquid back and Ancient Frost freezes it like a cold, cauterizing fire as my blade passes through.

The wolf's head drops to the ground, and his body follows. I pull my second *gladius* free and step back, evaluating my handiwork. As I watch, the armor begins to dissolve at my feet. No longer frozen by my Symbol, the molten liquid runs off his fallen form like water. To my surprise, the garden drinks it up greedily. In a matter of heartbeats, there is none of it left.

Soon only a set of blackened and burned bones remains. But as I crouch to study them, they crumble into dust and are swept away by the wind.

CHAPTER 35

Censors tackle me before another moment passes. I'm brought down by the combined weight of three of them. My swords are wrenched out of my grasp as others stomp on my wrists. I struggle as they pile on top of me, struck by how light their *tellus* armor is compared to mine.

"Stay down, Gladiator!" one of them screams in my ear as I curse them, trying to fight them off.

"Stay down or I will gut you!" A heavy boot bounces off my *lorica* as one of them tries to kick me in the ribs. A wave of noise begins to rise as we struggle on the ground. At first, it seems like thousands of voices crying out in fear, but one by one, the Censors holding me grow still as they realize what the crowd is chanting.

"*Frigus Ventus*!"

"*Frigus Ventus*!"

"*Frigus Ventus*!"

They are chanting my name.

"Fools! Get off him," a female voice shouts, joining the fray from the far side. The three bodies holding me down scatter in obedience to the woman who berates them. I pick myself up slowly, collecting my fallen blades as I rise. The White Hand might speak with the voice of the Empress, but the voice of the people is deafening in this place.

I turn to stare at the five surviving Censors, my weapons loose in my grip. To my surprise, the *electi* withdraw a step from whatever they see in my glare. Only Lania remains near, staring at me with dead eyes.

They want to take me. I see it in their eyes, in the hunch of their shoulders. But they dare not. Not here. Not now. I should not taunt the White Hand, but in the depths of Iron and Ice, I cannot help myself. I know that today I have won. An arrogant smile grows across my lips as the thousands that remain in the stands chant in unison.

"*Frigus Ventus*!"

Still staring at the Censors, I lift my right *gladius* into the air, acknowledging the crowd. They roar in delight, an overwhelming sound that would rival Jupiter's mightiest thunder.

"Go," the lead Censor says, her face empty of emotion. There is a promise there, lurking beneath the tough exterior. I only smile wider and bow to the living members of the White Hand, sweeping my blades to the side in dramatic fashion.

The crowd cheers louder. Around us, the arena begins to rumble as the garden dismantles itself. I stare in shock as the green hedges turn pale and fade before collapsing into white dust. Even the grass beneath our feet crumbles to reveal the sand below.

Turning my back on the Censors, I begin to make my way back across the ring to the Sword Door.

"Citizens of the Empire," the announcer begins timidly as if surprised to be alive. "Consul Briannus is pleased to celebrate the victory of the Empress's Censors against a traitorous fiend who came here to kill innocent civilians!"

The crowd shouts, but threaded among the cries are the loud *boos* of men and women objecting to my exclusion.

I keep my back straight as I walk, aware of the eyes that rest on me.

Now that I have surfaced from the depths of Iron and Ancient Frost, I have time to appreciate the danger I am in. I have slain the Herald of Mars. Thirteen Censors could not wound him, but I struck him down with two blows. It was one thing to be a rare and powerful Silver *electus*. But now I have gone and made myself something else.

My eyes travel down to the pair of swords I carry in my hand. *Revenge, indeed.* I snort, disgusted by the strings that pull me in every direction. The Sword Door swings open as I approach, creaking ominously as its maw welcomes me eagerly.

I know that I may never emerge from its depths, no matter what the crowd wishes, so I take one more moment for myself. I plaster a broad smile on my face as I turn to acknowledge the crowd again. I raise my *gladii* into the air in one last salute as they scream my name.

Then I step into the dark. The gates close shut behind me, and I am alone.

To my surprise, no one waits for me. The workers must have fled when Praeco tore through the far gate. How many died down here when he arrived?

Grateful not to discover another set of Censors lurking on the other side of the door, I make my way toward the *Domus* Pelias quarters. I keep my blades drawn in defiance of the rules. Who will chide me today of all days?

The compound beneath the arena echoes with an empty silence. My boots click on the stone as I enter our armory. It is empty. Contessa does not wait for me. Where is she? Even if the house had fled before Praeco, the *lanista* would be the first one back in the building to find me.

I eye the empty lift, wondering how much time the Herald had to roam through the compound before he waited at the gates. Did he stalk through the palatine boxes too? Attuned to the danger around me, I elect to keep my *gladii* with me as I step into the elevator. But as the doors close and the relics begin to pull me to the top of the arena, I sheath my blades to not seem too rebellious.

The doors open to silence.

Food is scattered across the floor as if thrown by the occupants of the box as they fled. Wind whips through the room, stronger than I would have expected even at this height. My eyes stray to the window, which is now just hollow panes empty of glass—not even a single shard remains.

Despite the destruction, the room is not empty. My heart skips a beat in relief at the sight of Varus sitting in the front row, right where I left him. Slowly, his head turns, and he glances at me, his steel gray eyes measuring me shrewdly. After a moment, he nods his head to the seat next to him before looking back out at the unruly crowd below.

My feet feel heavy as I walk through the rows of seats to reach the one next to him. My father was a gentle man in every aspect, but as a boy, I dreaded nothing more than being sent to his study after I had been disobedient.

For some reason, that same fear fills me now as I pad toward the senator. I sit in silence next to him, spine stiff like a soldier at attention, as if keeping perfectly still and straight will somehow appease my master. My eyes track the chaos below as I try to imagine what Varus sees in it. Varus is a perceptive man; I know that whatever current he traces is deeper than the ones that swirl on the surface.

A Censor wades through the crowd, screaming instructions that the masses ignore as they stream toward exits, eager to depart. Legionnaires wearing the blue tunics of one of the Sea Legions scramble around, trying to restore order to the mob.

"*Frigus Ventus*!" a group of plebeians chant as they race over seats, trampling through a cluster of patricians like a stampeding herd of cattle. The silence between us stretches like a hangman preparing his noose. I am not afraid, but that is only because I am too tired to be anything other than resolute.

"Well, they certainly are afraid of you now," Varus remarks dryly.

"Is that not what you commanded me to do, *Dominus*?"

The senator considers my question for a moment before chuckling softly. "I did tell you to teach my enemies fear, didn't I?" He sighs, finally leaning back in his chair to look at me.

My heart skips a beat as his gaze settles on me once more. There is no rage in his gray eyes, only a calm certainty that I find even more terrifying. He looks like a man who has accepted a hard truth and is freer for it.

"I suppose that's what I get for not specifying *which* enemies."

"*Dominus*, I do not—"

"Do *not* tell me that you *do not understand*," Varus hisses, a hint of anger showing in his expression for the first time. I flinch in surprise, caught off guard by his sudden outburst. "I have tolerated your mysteries thus far, Castor, because they have been beneficial to me and my *domus*. But do not think for a moment that means I am blind. You and I both know what it is like to see more than you say. I am not asking for all your secrets, but at least do me the courtesy of meeting me without guile." He says nothing of our conversation by the fire a few nights ago, but he does not need to. It is fresh in both our minds.

I am silent for a long moment as I consider his words.

His request reminds me of another conversation with a man I respect. I pause, caught off guard by that idle thought. Do I respect Varus? He is a palatine, a senator, a man who owns slaves that he sends to die.

And yet, as I have sat with him and gazed into the den of lions that he moves among, I have only seen him behave with honor when his peers have very little. He treats his slaves like humans rather than beasts. He fights to give his gladiators the best chance to survive. If the Iron Empire is a river, then he rides the same rapids as the rest of us, doing his best to stay off as many rocks as he can.

Yes, I realize after a moment of thought, I do respect him.

"You meant the other gladiator *domuum*, not the Censors," I reply at last.

"I care nothing for the Honos-damned Censors," he spits with surprising vehemence. "They are pigeons, fluttering in the wind, carrying messages to the real danger."

"The Empress." Saying her name out loud feels foolish, yet he has demanded that I no longer hold back. He eyes me sourly but does not correct me.

"You and I are two men lost in the dark sea, clinging to the same piece of driftwood to float. Together we may survive and make it to land. But only if we trust each other."

"I understand," I reply softly. His thoughts echo my own. When I decided to fight for him in the arena, I was man adrift, without a chance to earn his freedom. But he has given me an opportunity to earn my freedom. But if his *domus* falls, so will I.

"They will be here soon," he murmurs, cocking his head as if listening to something only he can hear.

"Who?"

"Everyone."

As if summoned by his words, the lift doors open into our windy box and a dozen people pour out, speaking loudly among themselves. Xania Valerus and a few other members of the great families emerge, following the consul, his brows constricted as he shouts at the palatines in his wake. I spy a pair of Censors in their number, and my hand trails down to the hilt of one of my *gladii*, ready for violence. Varus watches my moment out of the corner of his eye but does not react, trusting me to wait until it is time for iron.

"Enough," Briannus barks, rounding on his entourage. He is the only person in the room without a *Cor* Heart, but the force of his will is enough to silence them all in an instant. His power is not over an element, but Empire. Slowly, he turns to face us, face tired and wan. The massacre in the arena has shaken him to the core.

"What in the name of all of the *dead* gods was that?" he asks, looking first at Varus and then at me.

"Consul, the Censors demand to take this gladiator into custody for his actions," one of the Censors barks, inserting himself between the palatines. He's a young man, only a few years older than me. His Gold veins shine brightly against the white of his *tellus* armor.

"And which action would that be, Brody?" Briannus's voice drips with more poison than Bruttia's flowers as he turns on the Censor. "Saving the rest of your brethren from a warrior that was tearing them to shreds?"

"He is only an *argentum*, *Dominus*. It should not be possible for him to succeed where his betters failed. It can only be the result of some trickery or *abominatio* about him." My heart skips a beat as the consul studies me for a moment, frowning.

"To say nothing of how he overcame the *inferna venenum*," a woman volunteers, stepping forward to stand next to the Censor. She wears a brown toga and a pair of round spectacles that give her a soft appearance that is belied by the hardness of her blue eyes.

"*Inferna venenum*, you say?" the Censor asks, looking at me with sharper concern.

"Yes, we approved its use in the match by the Grus gladiator due to his Winter Symbol."

I resist the urge to flinch as I remember the heat of the poison that swept through my body after Bruttia's flowers filled me with their toxin, making it impossible for me to use my Symbol.

"Forgive me, *compositor*," Varus's voice cuts in harshly, rising for the first time to stare up at the group of palatines who stand at the top of the terraced sitting. "Are you admitting that you allowed another *domus* to utilize a custom poison in an *argentum* match?" His posture is relaxed, non-threatening, and yet there is an aura of violence that exudes from him. The woman in the brown toga blinks once, owlishly, as if surprised to be the focus of the senator's rage.

"Well, you see…" she stammers, looking at the consul for help, but Briannus just sighs, holding up a hand for her to be silent.

"Varus, if I swear to you that there will be a *full* audit of the *compositores*'s rulings for this entire Circuit, will that suffice for you to allow this more urgent matter to proceed unhindered?" My master's eyebrow twitches in surprise, which for him is practically a gasp of shock.

It is obvious that things have been manipulated against him from the beginning. If a proper review was conducted and the scoring adjusted, it could have a significant effect on *Domus* Pelias's ranking.

It might even be enough to help them avoid losing their license. He hesitates for a moment, perhaps remembering his driftwood parable.

However, he cannot reasonably pass up such a gift, and everyone in this room knows it too. To refuse it would only create more suspicion. Alessandra's warning that my discovery would lead to the ruin of her *domus* echoes in my ears. Together, he and I must walk a fine line.

"Very well, *Dominus*," he says at last, crossing his arms to indicate his displeasure.

"Thank you, Senator," Briannus replies genially, as if relieved. One-by-one, the heads of the Golden palatines of the room turn back to me, and I rise to stand before their judgment. As I do, I surreptitiously eye the distance to the top of the stands through the broken window of the box.

Could I survive the fall? The drop looks to be well over thirty paces, a distance that gives me pause. Perhaps if I used Iron to reinforce my bones to keep them from shattering? I think there is a chance, but I am not eager to find out. I resolve to keep it only as a last resort.

No matter how many Symbols I have, I know I am not ready to battle two Gold Censors carrying *tellus* blades. Not yet. Even if the fall was twice as high, I would be better off throwing myself over the edge than facing them.

"Perhaps there is a simple explanation for all of these things," Briannus suggests, looking from the eager Censor to me. "Why not ask him?"

"Forgive me, Consul, but we are given complete authority to—"

"Spare me your lecture, boy," the tall consul snaps, turning his dark-eyed gaze on him with a fury. "You may be the Empress's White Hand, but I am her right one. You would do well to remember that no matter what color veins run through your body." The Censor stiffens, inclining his head slightly.

"I beg your pardon, Consul."

"You'll have to forgive young Brody, *Dominus*," a voice comes from the back. The second Censor, a dark-skinned woman, slides through the pack of palatines, eyeing her compatriot with a sad shake of her head. She's older than him, graying at the temples. Despite her age, she is full of the vitality of an *electus*. Golden veins run down her arms, proudly displayed.

"He's only recently been elevated, and it takes the youth a little while to get that pride out of their system." Brody bows again, taking an ashamed step backward to make space for his elder.

"I do remember being young, Claudia," Briannus remarks dryly, a hint of his good humor showing once more. "Do you have any objections to proceeding with our questions?"

"None at all, *Dominus*." She gestures toward me in a sweeping motion, inviting the consul to proceed. A chill runs down my spine as her gaze settles on me. I have seen the cool, calm evaluation that lurks in her gaze before, but only in the most dangerous sort of people.

Her compatriot might be young and brash, but she is not. Claudia exudes the patience of a predator, content to lie in wait as its unsuspecting prey swings closer to its hiding spot.

"Forgive me, *domi*," I interject, tired of being inspected without a chance to defend myself. "I am unfamiliar with this *inferna venenum*." I purposely trip over the ancient words as if my education is worse than it is. "But if I understand the implications of the conversation, it seems as though it is a poison designed to specifically counteract Winter Symbols?"

"Poisoning an *electus* is difficult, even at the *argentum* stage," Claudia offers, her eyes never wavering from mine. "The natural healing and fortitude from our *Corda* make us more resistant to many common toxins."

I nod as if that solves a mystery for me. It does, but I must choose my words carefully. The full truth will see me dead, but a portion of it could save my life.

"That explains the sensation," I murmur, rubbing at my chin as if thinking through a puzzle.

"What sensation?" Briannus demands, eyeing the Censor with some irritation. While she has not defied him, there is an air of disrespect about her behavior that is too subtle for him to complain about. She ignores him, eyes focused fully on me.

"It was as if the poison created a barrier of fire in my mind and body, trying to cut me off from my Symbol," I answer truthfully. I glance up at Claudia, trying to seem truly interested. "I assume that by making my body as inhospitable to Winter as possible, it makes it harder for me to use essence and makes me more susceptible to its poison?"

"That is the basic theory behind it, yes," she admits with an impressed nod.

"So an *electus* with a Fire Symbol would be more susceptible to a poison that lowers the body's temperature?"

"As fascinating as this theoretical discussion is," Briannus interrupts, holding up a hand to cut me off. His goatee twitches as his mouth curls in annoyance. "The question, young Castor, is how did you manage to counter a toxin that was chosen specifically for its effectiveness against someone with a Symbol like yours?"

"Well," I say slowly as if trying to piece together my memories of the fight. "It was very hot. It felt like my insides were burning, and I could feel it attacking my connection to my Symbol."

"And?"

"It wasn't hot enough." I shrug, as if confused how else to explain it.

Claudia's eyes narrow, but she says nothing.

"Not hot enough?" Xania scoffs, leaning forward to look at me closely. "Boy, that poison will kill any Ice *electus* with half the dose I saw you take. You expect to tell the Censors that you are some exception to the rule?" I glare at Brennus's mother as she tries to bury me. Did her son tell her that I embarrassed him in the depths of this place, or does she just hate Varus that much? Claudia must see something spark in my eyes. She leans forward to study me, and mentally, I curse myself for losing control of my anger.

"Senator Valerus, please," Briannus rumbles, not as harsh as he was with Brody. "You are here to *listen*."

"I understand the question, Consul," I interject before the woman can continue her campaign against me. "I suspect that there is a simple explanation for all of this confusion." It is amusing to me that I killed the Herald of a god in front of them, but they ask me about poisons.

"And what is that?" Claudia's voice is soft, dangerous. My skin prickles with goosebumps as I feel the faint caress of something—her *animus* perhaps. This Censor is dangerous.

"My *Cor* is not bound to *a* Winter Symbol, but to *the* Winter Symbol. Ice and Frost and these other attunements that fall victim to *inferna venenum* are but pale shadows of mine. It was the Censors themselves, if you recall, *Dominus*, who discovered that I am bound to an Elder Symbol. I am far colder than anything you have ever encountered."

"An Elder Symbol?" Xania's face is a picture of shock as she turns to Briannus. "You knew?"

"I did." The consul nods. "I was there when they tested him in Anteforum."

"Very well." Claudia shrugs, unbothered by my explanation. "A simple answer to a simple question. But now, we must ask a more difficult one."

"Claudia, if you please." Briannus cuts her off smoothly, arching an imperious eyebrow at the dark-skinned Censor.

"Of course, *Dominus*." The woman inclines her head gracefully, gesturing for the consul to take the reins of the conversation. If she is irritated by his insistence, it does not show on her face in the slightest.

"How did you kill that thing—what did he say his name was?"

"Praeco, *Dominus*," the brown-robed *compositor* offers from his elbow.

"Yes, *Praeco*. How did you strike it down when even our Censors with their blades could not?"

I adopt what I hope is a confused expression. "Forgive me, Consul, but I suspect the answer is the same."

"Why would Ancient Frost be more effective against that *abominatio* than *tellus*?" Despite his question, there is a gleam in Briannus's eyes that tells me he is enjoying rubbing the Censors' failure in their faces. I find myself fervently wishing that he wasn't using me as the fulcrum with which to do it.

"I can only guess, *Dominus*."

"By all means, that is what we are here for."

"He claimed to be a Herald of…"

"The gods are *dead*," Claudia barks, interrupting me before I can speak the name. "You would do well to remember that, *gladiator*."

"Forgive me, *Domina*," I force myself to incline my head in her direction, leaning on Ancient Frost's cool calm to keep my expression neutral. "I merely wondered if my being attuned to an Elder Symbol gave me some sort of power over whatever he was."

"Why?" For the first time, concern grows on her features.

I know the true answer. That there was nothing underneath Praeco's flowing armor for the *tellus* blades to cut. He was nothing more than empty, rotten bones. I could kill him because Aquilo, the God of

Winter, is also attuned to Ancient Frost, and having some authority of a god gives me congruency to the power that fueled him.

But again, I shrug, trying to make sure they think that I am far outside of my depth. "I can only guess, *Domina*. All I know is that when he impaled himself on my blade, I was able to manifest ice inside his armor, which is what allowed me to kill him."

"But how did you cut him when even *tellus* could not?" Claudia presses, her eyes narrowed. "What strange blades you wield, Gladiator." I hesitate, afraid to answer about the nature of the weapons I carry. How do I explain that they are a relic of those who struck down the gods in the first place?

"Is that not why iron was forbidden? Is that not how our ancestors carved out our freedom? He carries the weapons of our ancestors, and they did their duty." Pliny's voice echoes from the back of the room. I have to fight to keep the corner of my mouth from turning up in a victorious smile.

The room is as silent as a grave.

"Where were you trained, boy?" Claudia asks, something sinister entering her voice. I hesitate, suddenly afraid to give this Censor more information about me. The last thing that I wish is for her to look into my past.

"The South, near Segesta," Varus answers for me. He wants them to move on; he doesn't know the secrets that I keep. Claudia stares at me, eyes unblinking as she studies my face. I do my best to ignore her without being disrespectful. She is like a bloodhound worrying around a scent. She has not found her prey yet, but I dread to think what will happen if she does.

"I am satisfied," Briannus says after a moment, nodding once and beginning to turn. The Censor twitches, surprised by his reaction.

"Consul, surely you jest," she suggests.

The second-most powerful person in the Iron Empire turns and looks at Claudia with a slow, unblinking gaze. Tension grows between the two of them like an approaching thunderstorm. I am impressed yet again by how formidable such a man is even without being an *electus*.

"What would you have me do, Censor?" he asks quietly.

"Submit him to us for questioning." Cold hands run up and down my spine as I imagine what being questioned like such a woman is like.

My right hand drops toward the hilt of my *gladius*, moving of its own accord.

"On what grounds?"

"He is an anomaly." She says it like a prefect might say "murderer."

"*Frigus Ventus*!" A few voices choose that moment to chant my name once more. The consul glances out the broken window in amusement before turning his attention back on the woman.

"He is a hero. Who knows how many lives he has saved by his actions today? He succeeded, I remind you, where the Censors failed. He likely saved hundreds of lives. Including my own. What message would that send to the people if they never saw their savior again?" My hand tightens into a fist at his subtle confirmation of my fears. I do not fully know why the consul is protecting me from the Censors. I suspect that he will try to use me in his own way soon enough.

"I do not need to remind you that *Domus* Pelias is under the shadow of *Judicium*, Consul. There will be a discussion about this, by those who sit higher than I," she warns.

"Let them discuss." Briannus smiles warmly. "They do not sit higher than me. Today, we survive."

"Consul, what of the Games?" Xania finds her voice as the rest of them begin to move to the door.

"Oh, they must be cancelled out of respect for the fallen," he replies with a sigh. "The finals in Forum will just have to be even more grandiose to make up for its loss."

When we are finally dismissed, Varus and I descend in the lift alone together. Our shared silence is thick with unspoken thoughts. I can scarcely believe that I have been allowed to escape the Censor's grasp once more. Being caught in the fulcrum of powerful movements is neither pleasant nor comfortable. I am crushed and pardoned by the same hands.

The master of *Domus* Pelias leads me through the darkened hallway, not quite storming, but moving with a power and authority that rolls from him like a storm. The subterranean network of Bellona's Arena is empty, abandoned after the carnage that tore through it. There is a haunted quality to its emptiness—it reminds me of a crypt.

"You begin to see now," he says softly as we are alone.

"You knew about Praeco, *Dominus*?" I ask in surprise.

"That is something else, I fear. I speak of the poison."

I blink as I think back to our conversation in the dark. He warned me that the Empress and *Domus* Valerus would move against him. It seems so small compared to the Herald that slaughtered its way through the arena.

"I begin to understand," I agree, because he is my master, and he is not wrong. Whatever the golden giant was does not mean that he was wrong. Our enemies will not stop hunting us.

To my surprise, the senator pauses, turning to look at me with his heavy gaze. I resist the urge to swallow in fear as I feel the weight of his full attention, alone, in the dark. It is easy to believe that he once carved his way through a generation of the Valerus family.

"I ask much of you," he says softly. His voice is surprisingly… gentle. "I know that. Just as I know you are not *free* to decide to obey."

I say nothing, because there is nothing to say.

"But what choice am I given?" He sighs, and for just a heartbeat, his shoulders droop, compressing under the weight of a heavy, heavy load. It is the first time I have ever seen him look so human. Even by the fire, he seemed more like a statue than a man. The interview with the consul and the Censor must have unnerved him more than I suspected.

"I do not know, *Dominus*," I admit, unsure what is expected of me. I am but a gladiator—a slave—what do I know of his palatine world and the intricacies of the Senate? His enemy is the Empress *herself*. Mine is but a single Censor.

"This Empire is sick, Castor," he says at last, looking away from me to stare into the darkness of the tunnel ahead. "It is rotting and rusting, and no one seems to want to clean it." I swallow a sudden nervous lump that grows in my throat. I know that all too well.

The silence deepens in the bowels of Bellona's Arena.

"And you wish to, *Dominus*?" I ask tentatively, afraid of the answer. He snorts softly but does not answer.

"You did well," he says, ignoring my question. "I am grateful for your loyalty. You have served me in ways the oath cannot compel you. I have seen your faithfulness and will not forget it." I meet his gaze, no longer intimidated by the aura of power that radiates from him, and nod slowly.

His gratitude is sincere. It is not flowery or given in front of others as a performance. It is solid and true, much like the man who offers it. My respect for him grows, and I fall into step behind my master as we continue through the dark tunnels.

He was right—we are not so different.

Varus draws up short as we emerge around the corner into a burst of activity. Acolytes in gray robes scurry around, stacking bodies. The stench hits me a moment later, full of the iron of blood and the smell of offal. I stand behind him, staring in horror at the carnage that Praeco wreaked before he emerged to confront me in the ring. The remains are smashed and torn as if they were crushed by a giant.

Acolytes kneel over individual bodies, cutting at them. My stomach twists as I realize they are harvesting the relics from the fallen *electi*. Even after a tragedy, the Iron Empire will not wait to be paid its due. Not even an ounce of the *Corda* will be wasted—more precious than the lives that carried them.

In the center of it all, a man wearing the torn black robes of a priest directs it all, watching with sharp eyes. His dark hair and sharp nose remind me of a raven, cruel and hungry. The priest turns in our direction as we enter, and his eyes narrow as he recognizes Varus and me behind him.

With an imperious gesture, he extends his right hand and snaps his fingers at a pair of lesser priests, two women dressed in the same black. At once, they approach us, blocking our view of the harvest with their bodies.

"Senator, I am afraid this area is off-limits," the first says in a sharp tone.

"What is happening here that is so secret?" Varus demands, clearly tired of being cut short.

"This creature claimed to come from the gods. We are the ones best equipped to dispel his lies. The Empress herself has given *imperium* to Pontifex Tenebrus," she replies, face full of arrogance. My gaze shifts to the man standing in the center of the ring. A Pontifex! I've never seen one of the heads of the priesthood before. I always assumed they would be old and wise, but he is maybe a decade older than me.

"And your Pontifex forbids me entrance?" Varus's voice is soft and dangerous. He's been pushed too far today, the Stone Symbol that is in his bones has no more retreat left in it.

"Only those sworn to the priesthood are permitted, Senator."

Varus opens his mouth to protest further, but I cut him off. "I think there was another way around behind us, *Dominus*." My master turns in surprise at my interruption. It is not proper for a slave to speak over his master, even a named gladiator like me. His gray eyes narrow—he suspects that I am up to something.

I seek only to protect him. Because he did not see what I did when the first black-robed priest gestured for his underlings to get rid of us. Nestled in the shadows of his clothing were the same dark veins that ran through Vixa. The priest is a *necromanta*.

Nemesis was right.

The Iron Empire is rusting.

Rust everywhere, as far as the eye can see.

PART III

THE FOUNDRY

CHAPTER 36

We do not tarry long in Antioch after the Games are cancelled. Varus loads *Domus* Pelias into our coaches, and the airhorses pull us across the countryside without stopping. The mood in the Silver carriage is strained and silent. The other gladiators watch me out of the corner of their eyes like I am a wild beast. My Copper veins are still covered with Pliny's Silvery paint, hiding the true depths of my differences from them. Even Illyrius is reluctant to talk to me. I find myself wishing that I was in the Iron carriage, among people I understand.

Delilah returns with us. I find that interesting, since she was not present when I was confronted by the Censors and consul. I take her accompaniment as a sign that Varus and his compatriots are bracing for a confrontation. Whatever games the senators are playing against the Empress, they feel more comfortable being together than alone.

Or maybe Anas was right about the nature of their relationship.

As we board the carts, Delilah slips over to me, smiling faintly as she reaches out to clasp my right wrist with her left. "Well done," she murmurs low enough for only me to hear. "I knew I gave Julia's gift to the right person."

I sit in silence, overwhelmed by what I have survived in Antioch. I know now that the gods are not as dead as they should be. That might seem obvious. They have been walking with me since the beginning. But their death has been the foundational understanding of my life—the bedrock that my world is built on. It takes the river of truth time to carve through a valley.

The Iron Lords failed. They did not kill the gods, only buried them. Now, four centuries later, they are returning. Nemesis has been freed by my own hand. Mars sent his Herald to find her. Praeco was once dead but somehow gained a second life. There can be no doubt that they are among us. *Deos excitare*—the gods wake.

Despite this, that is only one portion of the burden that I carry. I have been threatened by the Censors and evaluated by a consul, but not even the returning gods terrify me as much as the sight of the black veins I saw underneath Bellona's Arena.

There is a *necromanta* among the priests.

It makes a certain sort of cold sense. The work of both *necromantae* and priests is concerned with dead things. When we faced Vixa in the cold wastes of the North, I thought of her as a creature of legend, unique and terrifying. But to find another of her order in the open, serving the Empress—as Pontifex no less? I am not sure what to believe. Surely she does not know. Surely no one does. Can it be possible that only I have eyes to notice the darkness that coils around his arms?

I wish that were true, but after what I have seen—after what I know—I doubt it.

But what can I do? I am a Silver slave, no matter what my Symbols are. Who will listen to me when I accuse this Tenebrus, a member of the priesthood, of being a monster that most do not believe in? What business is it of mine what the servants of the Empress do? I have no power—no voice—just a healthy distrust for those who deal with dead things.

Despite my growing fear, I am eager to return to the training facility in Anteforum. It has been impossible for me to find more than a few stolen moments to cultivate any flame essence to feed Unrelenting Fire. No matter what danger finds me in the days to come, I will need to be whole to face them. My reserves are full, but that is not enough to progress through the stages of Copper.

To make matters worse, Ancient Frost has pulled ahead of even Iron and entered the peak stage of *argentum*. My *animus* can sense ice at further distances than it can sword or armor. It is the only one of my Symbols that I can openly practice with, giving it an advantage that I can do nothing to stop. It feels like I am holding three candles, each with a smaller wick, and am trying to burn them down at the same time. And if I fail, if my Winter Symbol tries to Ascend while my newest Heart is still Copper, it could fracture my *Corda* irreparably.

It would be one thing if I only had two Hearts that are at different stages bound to the same Symbol. But I am torn between three that each have their own. I fear that if I were to become both Gold and Copper at the same time, it would fracture my mind.

That is why I am not surprised when Pliny is waiting for me after we arrive in the Pelias compound. As I emerge from the Silver carriage, the short magister stands at the foot of the stairs, a tight, worried smile on his face.

"It is time to get serious," he tells me, turning on his foot without waiting to see if I will follow.

"Were we not before?" I ask skeptically, breaking into a slight jog to catch up to his side. "I think I've been pretty serious this whole time."

"Circumstances have conspired to prevent us from bringing your *Corda* into alignment a priority. Now we have time before the Games in Forum to see to your malady properly." Pliny leads me through the main door of the estate, which makes me stumble in surprise.

I have never been inside the master's house before. It is not what I expected. Varus is a stoic man. I would have thought that his house would have reflected the minimal aspect of his nature. But instead, it is warm and bright. Paintings of foreign landscapes hang from the walls. A fountain bubbles warmly in the atrium, full of bright fish. The magister shoots an irritated glance over his shoulder at my delay, causing me to scurry once more to catch up to him.

"Sorry, I just thought this would look—"

"You expected it to be like the inside of a general's field command tent?"

"Well…yes."

"If it were up to him, it likely would be," Pliny accedes softly, lowering his voice. "But this is how his wife preferred it." I open my mouth to ask the question that has been in the back of my mind for weeks, sensing an opportunity.

"Would you be willing to wear an *inhibitus*?" Pliny's request is mild, casual even. It takes all my self-control to not twitch violently at the thought of being contained by one of those collars again. I am already bound by too many oaths. I will not be a prisoner again.

"No," I manage through gritted teeth.

"I thought not," he admits, unbothered by my terse response.

"Then why ask?"

"It would make things simpler," he explains, leading me through a different entryway into the same library we have seen before. I pause for a moment to stare up at the mural of the Iron Lord Pelias, who looks down on us.

When he and his companions were walking the path before them, did he ever doubt? What kind of man does it take to ascend to a height that his entire race has never achieved before? I search the strokes of his eyes for advice, but I see nothing, only the grim face of a man who refused to kneel. Unlike him, I know all about kneeling.

Pliny opens the passage to his office, and we go down the long tunnel together. I'm struck by how relaxed I feel now compared to the first time that the magister brought me into his lair. I have grown in power and confidence. He collapses into a chair behind his desk and motions for me to sit across from him.

"Starting now, you are forbidden—*forbidden*—from using any of your *argentum Cor*," he says after we sit down. "You are racing toward the peak of your tier, and we cannot risk you tumbling over the precipice until the time is right."

"Contessa is not going to like that."

"The *lanista* would also not like to see our most promising gladiator hobbled by an avoidable mistake. *Dominus* Varus has given me *imperium* over your training until your *Corda* are in harmony. The three of us are in total agreement on this."

I swallow tersely before nodding at the man.

"You are going to sit in that Winter *locus* and cultivate Ancient Frost until your new *Cor* Ascends. Every minute that you are not in the ring or asleep, you are to be in there. Do you understand me?"

"Yes, Magister." I bow my head.

"Now, we need to discern how close you are to the peak of Silver." His brow furrows as he thinks. "It can be difficult to quantify because many elements manifest differently. Elder Symbols are rare enough that little is known about their evolutionary patterns..." His voice trails off, and his gaze snaps toward me.

"You killed the *thing* in the arena with your ability." It is not a question. "You manifested something other than the *gladius* with your *Glacialis Falx*."

"Yes." I nod. "But I don't know if I could do it again. There is still a… resistance to it. I think the circumstances had something to do with it."

"Good," he murmurs more to himself than me. "Mastery of your ability would be a clear sign that you were teetering on the edge of Ascension. Stop using it for now. There will be time to solidify your control of it later. It is imperative that you do not break through that barrier too soon."

"Yes, *Dominus*." The honorific slips out of my mouth without thinking. His eyes narrow, but he doesn't object. My obedience is more important.

"In the meantime, while we are not pushing you toward Gold, there are things we can do to better prepare your body for the Ascension. You are a gifted *electi*, but there is still time to improve your foundation before you build on it." I cock my head in surprise. I have never heard of such a thing.

"Different attunements vary in their essence efficiency." He pulls open a drawer and begins rifling through the ocean of papers and random objects that are gathered there. "Winter Symbols are not a particularly greedy source, although thanks to your ability to manifest Ancient Frost, you have higher demands than most."

He pulls out a pair of bracelets and places them on the surface of his desk between us. They are made of the drab, dull gray metal that most relics turn after their *electus* is dead. Curious, I reach out to lightly touch one with my pointer finger.

I shudder as soon as my skin brushes against the metal. A heavy sensation falls across me, like the pressure of being buried alive. Everything is muted and overwhelming. I can breathe, but it feels a thousand times more difficult than it did before. With a gasp, I jerk my hand back, shooting Pliny a betrayed look.

"What is that?"

"It's called a *pondus*."

"A weight?"

"More accurately, 'a burden,' but yes. It is designed to make the act of cultivation more difficult, to force your *Cor* to become even more efficient at extracting essence from its surroundings." I eye the bracelets distrustfully, imagining how overwhelming it must feel to actually wear them around my wrists.

"Let me guess, you want me to start using them?"

"You excel at pulling in essence. I believe this is due to the extra *Corda* that you were injected with. My hope is that by using this, it will deepen your reserves as well as prepare the other *rasa* inside of you so that we can bind the rest of your unused Hearts."

"You think this will happen again?" I stare at the white lines in my right arm with a sick feeling.

"It seems likely." Pliny shrugs a little as if not bothered. "We don't know how much *Corda* you ingested during your accident."

"I think there were supposed to be… five Hearts," I offer hesitantly. I feel a sudden burst of shame, as if admitting how many I took makes the truth worse.

"Bah, that is a meaningless number," the magister says, waving his hand dismissively. "Until they are fused with a host *electus*, *Corda* are very fluid and unstable. Unless they were specifically inserted into you one by one, there's no way to know how many might have merged or separated into distinct entities. Even I cannot see that with my Symbol. Your *rasa* is a tangled mess."

My eyes widen as I realize what he is saying. "You mean I might have more than five *Cor* Hearts?" I ask softly.

"Or less." He shrugs again. "You are a rather unprecedented case, Castor. I can only guess at what will happen. But I worry if we push you to Gold too soon and then you unlock another set of veins that start at Copper…" He trails off, letting the implication hang between us.

I swallow, trying to keep my fear off my face. My *Corda* already betrayed me in the arena, almost getting me killed against the spearvines. I cannot imagine what the force would feel like if I were already Gold when I bound Unrelenting Fire.

"If I use this, it will help me prepare the blank Hearts faster, so I can bring them all to Copper and then Silver before I Ascend?"

"That would be ideal." Pliny steeples his fingers before his face as he watches my expression. "I do not know what would happen if you have to try to balance a being a Copper and Gold of Ancient Frost at the same time. Copper is a stream, Silver is a river, but Gold is an ocean. I fear you would drown."

I nod along with his plan, trying not to let the panic eat at me. If only he knew how much worse it was.

For a handful of heartbeats, I debate telling him. I can trust him, I think. He's so fascinated by what I am, I think he would only become even more obsessed if he knew the truth. But this is not some trite secret. *Domuum* have been put to the *gladius* for less. Then the moment passes, and he looks away, gesturing for me to take the bracelets.

"What about my Frost Iron blades?"

"Absolutely not." Pliny's head snaps up, and he fixes me with a sharp stare. "You are *under no circumstances* to use them until I give you permission. Do you understand?" His gaze is so piercing that, for a moment, I think he is my *lanista* instead of a magister.

"Yes, *Dominus*," I manage, choking on my surprise. "But why?"

He sighs in vexation, leaning back in his chair to stare at the ceiling before turning his gaze down on me with a sharp frown etched on his face. "Did your teachers in *collegium* like you?"

"*Dominus*?"

"Your magisters, when you were growing up. Were you one of their favorites?"

"No."

"I thought not." He crosses his arms and studies me again, as if deciding whether he can trust me. It takes effort for me to suppress a snort at the irony. Lies within lies, we spin around each other in wheels. Will we make it to our destination, or crash and shatter into a thousand pieces?

At last, he decides. It is going to be trust. "What do you notice when you draw essence from them?"

I frown, trying to dissect what I should and should not know. "I am not fully sure what to make of it," I admit cautiously. "It is unlike anything else I've ever encountered."

Pliny nods as if unsurprised. "That's because you haven't." He sighs, as if regretting going down this path.

I am still, waiting for him to continue. This is not the first time that Pliny has hinted at the secrets of the Iron Lords. If I am going to survive, I will need all the knowledge that he has and more.

"The *Ferrum Domini* were incredibly powerful *electi*. You know this—they teach it to us all. But they were far more powerful than your teachers told you."

"Why?"

"Because the Iron Lords decided it would be better if not all of their citizens could wield the power to challenge gods."

I nod slowly. This feels like a familiar story. It is the same reason that the legionnaires wear an *inhibitus*. Mankind cannot be trusted on a large scale. I shudder to think of someone like Brennus with access to the same kind of power as the Iron Lords.

"Much of what they discovered has been destroyed or hidden, but we still know some things. Julia in particular was renowned for her ability—*Creatio*."

"Creation?"

"Just so. It is hinted at in a dozen ancient texts that I have read that she had the ability to manifest new elements. It was she who first made *tellus* for her Censors."

My jaw drops as I stare at the magister as I finally understand just how rare Frost Iron is. I assumed that it was some sort of relic, a trick. That somehow, Julia had mashed two known things together, not that she had created something that did not exist.

"New elements? How is that possible?"

He shrugs, as if not particularly concerned about this world-altering fact that he has shared with me. "I have only theories, and they would take more time than you have to understand. But I believe that the gift that Senator Delilah gave you is proof of her ancestor's capability. A new element that she created for Frigidus centuries ago."

I can only stare at Pliny for several moments, speechless at the implications. The priests say that the gods created all things at the beginning of time and that ever since then the world has been fixed, completed. There are no new elements, only ones we have not discovered yet. For someone to be able to create one on their own would give them a power that rivals Gaia or Chaos, the long-lost Titans.

"We don't truly know what it is, even if it is congruent to your Symbol. Do you understand why I don't want you pulling essence from a synthetic source while your *Cor* Hearts are in such disarray?"

"I do."

"Take those." He gestures his head at the *pondus* once more. "Fix your *Corda*, and you can begin to unravel the mysteries of Julia Census." Reluctantly, I pick up the bracelets, shivering as they drape their suppression over me. It feels like the world goes gray when I touch them, but I will do anything to continue my journey. Hurriedly, I shove the pair into my pocket, breaking their contact with my skin.

I scan the room as I rise, struck by one last thought, a clue from my friend Illy. "You wouldn't happen to have any books on the nature of Winter and Ice, would you?"

CHAPTER 37

Pliny sends me to cultivate until I collapse from exhaustion, although I am relieved that he does not plan on coming with me to see what I do. I can feel the weight of the *pondus* in my pocket as I walk, and I dread spending time in its grasp.

I make my way to the training hall, pausing only briefly to stop by the dormitories to leave a message for Anas. Many of the gladiators who just returned from Antioch are in different *loci* refreshing themselves after the trip. I keep my head down, trying to avoid attention, as I walk quickly across the sand, heading for the Winter room.

Despite my caution, I can feel the heavy gazes of my peers as I pass them. I sense it even from some of the ones who were not there, who have only heard the rumor of what I have done. I am a named gladiator now; this is only the beginning. I do my best to ignore them.

The door to the miniature blizzard hisses open, letting out a blast of frigid air that I welcome. I crouch on my knees in the deep snowbank, searching it with my *animus* to get a sense of its maturity. It has decades to go before it becomes Ancient Frost, but every day that goes by makes it easier for me to convert the essence than it was when Pliny first activated the relic of this room.

Steeling myself, I reach into my pocket, forcing myself to grab the two bracelets of the *pondus*. Its heavy presence envelops me, holding me down. I shudder even though I am not cold and slip them onto my wrists one by one.

I can still feel my Symbols, but they are muted, distant. It is as if I am reaching for them through a heavy layer of oil. My grip is slippery. I must be methodical with every application of my will, or they will slide right out of my grasp.

I let out a long sigh, forcing my mind to clear of the mysteries that Pliny gave me. They are for another day. My road is long, and I have only begun to walk it. If I am going to make it to the end, I must first fix myself.

Tentatively, I reach out with my *animus*, sending it from my wrists, *through* the bracelets. My will slams against the *pondus* before getting stalled like a herd of cattle coming to a narrow gate. Only a fraction of my spirit can slip out into the world beyond. It is tedious, but at last I am able to connect to the snow and the Winter essence that waits for me to collect it.

Slowly, I pull it into me. Instead of the flood I am used to, it is a trickle. My veins do not burn, but inside my chest, I feel the center of my *Cor* begin to grow tense as it is forced to exert more pressure to drink from the thin supply. It is miserable, but it pushes me in a way I have never felt before.

Sweat rolls down my spine, freezing before it makes it off my body. My breath comes in ragged gasps, but I do not stop. I welcome the pain, thrilled by the sensation of being pushed. My reserve shakes like a weak muscle being strained for the first time.

When I can bear it no more, I release my *animus*, sagging as I struggle to catch my breath. I am cold for the first time that I can remember. I run a hand along the back of my neck, wincing as I peel a thin icicle from my flesh.

As I recover, I probe myself, seeking to understand what I have just done to myself. I cannot see them with my eyes, but my mind knows that there are three *Corda* reserves that burn with essence inside of me. One is small and red; it burns with the heat of Unrelenting Fire. Next to it is a much larger, dark gray Heart, hard and strong. The last is a deep blue, radiating cold like a storm.

Slowly, I compare my two Silver *Corda*, trying to see if there is a difference between them. In the past, they have been largely identical, except for the essence they are bound to.

But now as I study them closely, I notice a darker line that runs around the outer edge of my Winter reserve like a ring of a tree. Curious, I try to inspect it more closely with my *animus*, probing at its exterior with my mind. The essence there seems denser and colder.

Or maybe I am imagining things, looking for success because I need it to be true.

Confused, I open my eyes and stare at the *pondus* wrapped around my wrists. Could it be allowing me to layer more essence inside of my *Cor*? There was only one way to find out. Squaring my shoulders once more, I stretch my *animus* through the relic and into the snow, resuming my cultivation.

Hours later, I am certain that the outer ring of my Ancient Frost *Cor* has grown larger than it was before.

Probably.

My knees ache from supporting me in the snow for so long, but I dare not move. The training hall has emptied out, but I do not trust it. I must be patient. The back of my neck still prickles as if I am being watched. Perhaps it is only Pliny keeping tabs on me.

If it makes my existing Ancient Frost *Cor* stronger, I am grateful for the time spent suffering in this frozen *locus*, but otherwise, this exercise is purely a performance. I must show them that I am an obedient patient, doing as I am told and taking this danger to my progression seriously.

But they do not know what is truly wrong with me, so they cannot fix me. Only I can. Six doors down from me in the training hall is the solution to my problems. For now, I bide my time until it is safe to use.

Midnight, true *nox*, finally arrives, and it is time for me to start my plan. At last, I allow myself to rise from the snow. There is a tenderness inside my chest, as if I have overworked a muscle that is not used to labor. I find some comfort in the feeling, as if my day has not been wasted by meaningless routine.

I twist, stretching my back as I exit from the *locus*. Cautiously, I reach out with my *animus*, sweeping for signs of any hidden watchers, but I find none. Which means either I am alone, or those keeping tabs on me are wise enough to not carry Iron or Ice.

I stand in the dark for a long moment, straining my ears to listen. I hear nothing except for my own deep breaths and the echoing silence of an empty building. At last, I allow myself to relax, confident that I am truly alone.

As if to spite me, the far doors of the training facility creak softly as they open, and a figure lets itself into the room, barely framed against the darkness outside. I resist the urge to hide; I have every right to be here. To scamper into the shadows would only make me appear guilty. Besides, I am almost certain that the interloper is my guest.

"Castor?" a hoarse voice calls as the figure approaches.

"Thank you for coming," I reply with a smile, turning to stride toward Anas. We meet in the darkness and clasp hands, an irony that our old selves would find unbelievable.

"What do you need?" We may be forgebrothers, but that has not made him any more predisposed to small talk. I hesitate for a moment, surprised by my own reticence. It feels pathetic to worry about revealing my new Symbol to him after he already knows the truth. What is one more damning layer upon the pile of secrets he already keeps? He senses my nervousness and cocks his head curiously in the dark, studying me closely.

"I need you to stand watch," I say at last. "There is something I must do, but…I cannot be seen doing it."

"What is it?"

I glance down the line of *loci* to where the red glow of the fire room waits. "When we fought the Shadowbound in the garden, one of them threw me into the brazier of everflame."

"Vulcan's bones! How were you not burnt to a crisp?" Anas starts forward, trying to get a better look at me as if he has not seen me a dozen times since then. I step into one of the pools of light so he can see my expression and give him a pointed stare, afraid to even say it out loud.

"It happened again?" His voice is horrified.

"It happened again," I confirm. I reach over to my left wrist and pick at the paint that disguises my Copper veins. When I have uncovered enough, I hold out my arm so he can see for himself.

"Dead gods preserve us." I chuckle at that, and after a moment, so does he. He was there in Aquilo's halls with me.

"I need to go into the fire *locus*," I tell him, gesturing down the line. "If I do not cultivate essence for this *Cor,* it will eventually kill me or break all my Hearts. I need you to make sure that no one sees me in there. Otherwise, they will be asking questions I cannot answer."

"How long do you need?" Anas's tone is suspicious, like a legionnaire being asked to cover a shift of the night watch. He suspects a trick.

"As long as I can get," I tell him truthfully. "I need to Ascend." His eyes grow wide at that. He is still a Copper, still bound by the *inhibitus*. To hear me speaking so casually of progressing to Silver must seem like arrogance.

"What do you want me to do if someone does come?"

"Distract them and drop your knife." I gesture to where it rides on his belt. "I will sense it and get out."

He blinks in surprise. It's hard to understand the other ways you can use your Symbol until you Ascend. It's like imagining a new color.

"I will do this," he agrees after a moment of thought. "For the Twelfth."

"For the Twelfth," I agree solemnly, clapping him on the shoulder. What a thing to bind us together. The last legion is a place for the dregs of society to die, not for friends to be made.

Anas slides closer to one of the massive support pillars, letting its shadows conceal him as he settles in with a soldier's grace to keep watch. With one last glance over my shoulder to make sure the coast is clear, I stride toward the fire *locus* whose light dances through the glass. The room is a flat space with a metal grid for a floor. *Ignis* relics send tongues of flame shooting up from the bottom in random bursts.

It looks like a glimpse into the depths of Hades itself.

At the door, I hesitate, watching the dancing flames lick at the sky like hungry tongues. Before Unrelenting Fire bound itself to one of my *Cor*, the fire in that brazier burned me with its rage. I remember the heat, the indescribable pain.

I am one with the flame now, but still, as I stand on the precipice, I feel fear. What sane man does not fear fire? Our mothers teach us to stay away from it before we can walk, holding our hands to the hearth to give us a taste of its harsh lick. As I stare into the inferno that waits for me beyond the door, I know I am ignoring all the advice she ever gave me. I am playing with fire and becoming an *electus*.

Angry with myself, I square my shoulders, forcing these invading thoughts to the back of my mind where they belong. Her wisdom is long behind me; I have taken too many different forks on the path since then. There is no way to go but forward, into the fire.

Besides, if Brogi, that Copper Norman *electus*, can handle the heat, what do I have to fear?

I raise my hand to touch the control relic for the door, and it sweeps it open, releasing a blast of heat out of its mouth as if it were a *hydrus* breathing flame. Ancient Frost flees, retreating from the inhospitable conditions like it did when I was poisoned with the *inferna venenum*, but Unrelenting Fire leaps into my grasp without hesitation.

Slowly, I take a step into the *locus,* willing the fire not to devour me. I wince as my foot lands on the iron, half expecting to smell the burning scent of leather as my sandal goes up in flame. A tremendous warmth sweeps across me, but it parts around me, obeying my commands. At the same time, my awareness expands to cover the room, filling it in like part of my body.

I crack open my eyes that I don't remember closing and stare at my foot to make sure that it is safe. But that is silly, I realize. There is nothing about this that is *safe*. That is not what being an *electus* is about.

Living safely will not help me Ascend to Gold.

Living safely will not help me kill Atticus.

Gritting my teeth, I step fully into the kiln, letting the glass door slam shut behind me. Fire swirls around me but does not consume me. It welcomes me as kin—as part of its collective. The tension in my shoulders fades as I accept its hospitality. Taking a deep breath, I reach out with my Copper *Cor,* pulling in as much essence as I can. My Heart leaps in delight as my veins protest, stretching as I work them.

But despite being in the inferno, I am not able to find exactly what I need. Just like in the Winter *locus,* I must condense the essence, layering it upon itself to match the specific quality of my Symbol. It is not a problem of age, like with Ancient Frost. Instead, it feels like a level of determination. Most flames can be kept. It will burn in a hearth or a firepit. But Unrelenting Fire is more determined, hungrier. It demands to be freed, and the pet fire in this room does not quite have the same timbre. I wonder where in *Domus Ignis* my new Symbol resides.

Despite that similarity, I am struck by how different its presence is from Winter's, which seems obvious in retrospect. Iron and Ancient Frost both share traces of cold logic. Unrelenting Fire, however, is a raging river of strength and warmth. Unlike my colder attunements, which numb my pains, this attacks them, burning them out of my muscles. When I first lost myself to Iron, it consumed me and buried me in a place where I felt nothing. No morality or kindness, just the icy determination of an executioner.

But there is a different danger here, I realize as I begin to relax in the embrace of Unrelenting Fire. Its hunger never stops. I feel its desire to spread, to consume. It exists like a feral, starving wolf constantly on the hunt for the next thing that will feed it in its quest. It will only be satisfied when the entire world is fire—when all that remains is ash, it can finally rest. I swallow as a cold touch of fear runs down my spine. Just because the fire does not burn me does not mean that it is my friend.

I am disappointed as I pull in as much essence as I can handle in the heart of the inferno. Part of me was hoping that I would Ascend immediately after coming into this *locus*. I triggered my *inhibitus* the first time they put me in the iron room below Agogia. But Ancient Frost took much longer, even when I was in the depths of the North. In fact, I didn't make significant progress until I went down into Aquilo's cave. Perhaps it was because Iron has less specificity. Any supply of essence can give me exactly what I need.

But my other Symbols require a more particular strain. If I really want to advance quickly, I will need to find a source of fire that matches what I need. If I am going to reach new heights, I'm going to have to earn it.

Turning away from my disappointment, I slide my focus to my Copper *Cor*, studying it more closely. What else can Unrelenting Fire do? I know that I can use it to affect my eyes and body, but that feels like something a child could come up with. Safe under Anas's watch, it isn't just a good time to cultivate, but also to experiment.

Closing my eyes, I reach out with my *animus*, sending it through the flames that I touch, just like extending my awareness through a shieldwall when I was in the legions. Slowly, I reach out with my right hand, palm open wide. With a thought, I command the fire to gather before me in a ball. I cannot manifest fire like I can ice, but it is far easier to manipulate than Iron. Unlike either of my other Symbols, Unrelenting Fire is not a solid—it is *vis*—energy, and it offers me almost no resistance as I shape it with my will.

I contract it with my mind, collapsing it onto itself to become denser. The light grows so bright that I can see it through my eyelids, white hot. I feel the heat, but it passes over me gently.

When I cannot contain it any longer, I release the ball of flame, throwing it forward with my will. I open my eyes, squinting against the harsh brightness, as the attack slams into the far wall, bursting as it encounters the stone. The flames envelop the whole far side of the *locus* before fading, no longer powered by my will. The white wall, which had remained pristine despite the fire that burns day in and day out here, is charred and black.

Whoops. I stare at the burnt stone, stunned at the hunger of Unrelenting Fire. Perhaps I should not be. It is in the name, after all. I walk forward, reaching out with a finger to touch the wall, relieved to find that it does not crumble at my touch. That would be a difficult thing to explain.

What power.

I can only imagine what I will be able to do once it Ascends to Silver and beyond. But first, I must complete the Copper portion of the path. I step back into the center, pulling more fire essence into me to refill the portion of my reserve that I emptied. My *Cor* burns as I push it to grow.

Abruptly, I realize that I have been so focused on Unrelenting Fire that I have forgotten to keep my other senses extended to watch for Anas's signal. Feeling ashamed, I reach for Iron. It is more distant, as if scorched by the heat around us, but comes to my call. I sweep my *animus* out of the room and over to where my friend keeps watch. As my senses become aware of his knife, I stiffen in fear.

The weapon is not on his belt. It is too close to the ground for that. It can only be sticking out of the sand, warning me of danger.

CHAPTER 38

For a moment, I freeze in panic, despite standing in the middle of an inferno. Is it Brogi, coming to top off his reserves in the dead of night? My signal was too clever for its own good. I know there is trouble, but I do not know what I should do to avoid it. Have I been discovered? Should I leave now or remain hidden here until the danger has passed?

Breaking free of my paralysis, I slide to the side of the room, willing the fire around me to billow up, making it harder for anyone outside to see me where I cower. Slowly I inch along the wall, making my way to the glass door, hand hovering over the relic that controls the doors.

The bright light of the blaze I stand in makes it hard for my eyes to see out into the darkness. I cannot make out Anas or anyone else for that matter. My senses probe at his knife, but it has not moved. Damn me for being so careless! If I am discovered, it will only be my own fault.

For a few long moments, I watch but can make out no movement. At last, I can bear to wait no longer. Heart hammering in my chest, I press the panel, causing the glass doors to slide open. Moving quickly but confidently, I stride out into the training hall, stepping into the shadows.

My pulse thunders in my ears, drowning out all other sound. I hover by a pillar, scanning the darkness. There is no sign of another soul.

But Anas's knife is still in the sand.

A solution comes to me at once. Unrelenting Fire leaps to my command as I redirect its essence within me and up to my eyes like I did in the garden. The agony boils inside me again, but I call upon a reluctant Iron to dull the pain and keep it manageable.

At once, my vision shifts, no longer relying on light and shadows but instead using heat. If anyone is here, the darkness will not hide them from me. I turn my back to the fire *locus* behind me that now burns like *Sol* itself. A pair of figures immediately reveal themselves to me, two pillars down.

I recognize burly Anas's outline at once. He appears in various shades of red and orange where heat coalesces in his body. The former soldier is pressed up against the wall, held in place by a second figure who holds something cold to his neck that shows to my vision only in the negative.

Frowning, I sweep my *animus* over them again, feeling for a sense of Iron, but again, I find none. Which can mean only one thing. Anas's assailant bears a *tellus* blade.

There is a Censor here.

Terror claws at me, exacerbated by my Fire Symbol's volatility, but I force myself to breathe. Fear gives my will extreme strength, and I grab Ancient Frost despite its protests while still holding Unrelenting Fire. The Winter Symbol's cold logic sweeps through me, helping to balance my emotions. My heart still races, but I ignore it. Ancient Frost does not take my fear away, merely numbs it, allowing me to think without being overwhelmed.

I move away from my pillar, keeping to the darkness as I begin to circle them. They are frozen in place, as if the Censor is waiting for something. Perhaps they didn't see me exit the fire *locus* and are still waiting for me to emerge.

Regardless, they have given me the opportunity to act, and I am only too happy to take it. My hands feel empty without the comforting weight of my Frost Iron blades in them. Fortunately, thanks to a mad, dead god, I am not without options.

The two of them shift, as if the Censor is trying to get a better angle to watch the exit. I swing further to the right, keeping the pillar between us as I close in on their position. My only hope is to strike fast and free Anas. Together, the two of us will stand a better chance, even if we face a Golden *electus*.

I make my way through the sand, moving my feet deliberately to keep them silent as Percy taught me what feels like a lifetime ago. Standing out in the open with only a pillar blocking their line of sight is agonizing.

If they shift again, I will be discovered in a moment, and the one advantage I have will be ruined. But the younger Marius brother's training is etched in my bones, and I heed his wisdom, not letting panic rush my hunt. For a moment, I am no longer a gladiator, no longer *Frigus Ventus*, but Castor, decurion of the Iron Legions.

Slowly, I round the corner pillar behind my quarry. Reluctantly, I release Unrelenting Fire, returning my vision back to normal. In the dim light, I am close enough to see Anas pinned with his back against the wall. He looks over his assailant's shoulder, tracking my movement. The woman does not notice as she peers around the corner, watching the fire *locus* intently.

As I suspected, she presses a gleaming white *tellus* knife against his throat. His right hand is down at his side, and he opens it to reveal a flat palm, fingers together.

Stop. Warning.

I freeze, giving myself more time to study the situation, looking for the trap that my comrade warns me of. The woman who has him pinned is slight, shorter than both of us with wavy dark hair that blends into the shadows around us.

Fortuna's Ashes! I curse to myself as I realize who it is.

"*Domina*, you can release my friend," I say to Alessandra. She leaps in surprise, turning to stare at me with wide eyes. The dagger does not move from Anas's throat. "I swear to you that he will not harm you."

"He was spying on you. He knows your secret," she replies coolly, already back in control after being startled by me. "We cannot let him live." I blink, surprised by the ice that lies within her.

"No, he was *supposed* to be keeping watch over me." I let a little frustration color my voice. If Durus saw one of his sentries pinned to the wall by a palatine magister-in-training, Anas's back might never heal from the lashes.

"Your lack of judgment does not change the necessity of silencing him."

"*Domina*, pull down the right side of the neck of his tunic," I say, a small smile twisting my face. "You will find something familiar, I think." She follows my instructions and hisses in surprise when she discovers the *XII* that marks him as a member of my Legion.

"The Marius brothers will haunt my family wherever we go," she says with a sigh. But after a moment of reflection, she steps back from Anas, lowering her knife down to her side. "You will keep the secrets you hold, or you will suffer."

"You don't need to threaten me, *Domina*," Anas replies easily, leaning against the wall as if he wanted to be there all along. "My loyalty is bound in blood. Nothing you can say will be stronger than that."

"Dead gods preserve us from the legions and their zealotry," Alessandra murmurs before turning to look back at me with a piercing stare. I return it frankly, understanding that the danger has passed. At last, she twitches, having come to some sort of decision.

"The legionnaire can go. You will stay. It is time we had a discussion."

Anas looks over her shoulder at me for confirmation, and I shrug. I do not think she wants to kill me, but even if she does, what can I do? She holds my life in her hands. My burly friend bends down to pick up his knife before offering us both a mocking salute.

"Good luck," he says.

I'm not entirely sure which one of us he is talking to.

"I told you to be careful," Alessandra snarls as soon as we are alone. She takes a step toward me threateningly, *tellus* knife still gripped firmly in her hand.

"I am trying to," I insist, raising my hands and taking a step backward at her advance. "That's what the guard was for."

"Telling another person your secret is not what I had in mind!"

"He knew before you," I protest. "He was there in the North." Something in my voice cracks through her cold veneer, and she twitches in surprise at her raised knife.

"What did happen?" Her voice is soft. "Plautia has been beside herself since they were sent away…" Percy and Gaius's mother personally blocked my ascent to *Fidelis*. There had been no love lost between her and her sons, but even she is human enough to mourn them.

"We were betrayed and sent to die," I growl, feeling the familiar rage flush through me. This secret is one I have no problem sharing with the world. I should probably be screaming it from the rooftops, so that the cowards that dare turn on the Emp—

A horrible thought occurs to me.

"It wasn't your family, was it?" My voice is hushed even in this empty room; I do not dare to voice my accusations loudly. I want to believe in Varus, but there is a Norman *electus* among his *Domus*, and I have paid too steep of a price to trust any senator blindly.

"What wasn't my family?" Alessandra seems to bristle at the implied accusation.

"Does your father have something to do with the Imperials working with the Normans to invade the Empire?" I cannot keep some of the heat out of my voice as emotion overtakes me. I take a step toward her, despite the *tellus* knife between us. Alessandra's eyes flare, and she recoils in surprise.

"Why would you think that my father—" She pauses as she comes to the same conclusion that I did. "The Shadowbound."

"Why is the Empress trying to kill your family?" My heart races as I feel like a fool for not seeing the threads that connect before me now. Corrupt senators leverage their wealth and power to fund an invading horde to break the Empire so they can remake it in a new image. It seems so obvious that I feel like a fool for taking this long to consider it.

"Castor!" Alessandra's voice is sharp as she pulls me from my rabid plotting. "I swear to you, on the bones of whatever dead god that you wish, that my father had nothing to do with this." She shakes her head softly, a small smile tugging at the corner of her mouth.

"Perhaps you have not noticed, but my father is not a subtle man."

I tilt my head in acknowledgment of her point.

"*Domus* Marius has been a friend of our house for centuries. Even with its current... issues, we have maintained a close relationship with both halves. I know I do not need to remind you who my mentor was when we first met."

She's right—the memory of the whipping that I suffered at her command still stings.

"If Gaius and Percy were betrayed and sent to their deaths, it was not something that was conspired here."

I blow out a long breath, nodding as I consider her words. She is correct once again—it does seem out of character for Varus. Also, if he had killed the Marius brothers, why are his *ferra* gladiators full of men who served under him?

"This is a distraction." Alessandra shakes her head, long black tresses flailing behind her like shadows. "You are being reckless and will get us all killed."

"Then *help me*," I snarl in frustration. "I have been given an impossible task. Pliny watches me like a hawk, convinced that I am just not cultivating Ancient Frost well enough to Ascend my Copper *Cor*."

"Is that not…" Surprise flickers across her face, and I resist the urge to sigh at my own foolishness.

"Alessandra." There feels like no need for formality here in the dark as we conspire together. "You just saw me in the *ignis locus*."

"It could have been for resistance training. Especially after your experience with the *inferna venenum*."

"Then why did you threaten Anas with a knife?" I shout at her in disbelief, but at the same time, I wonder about the effectiveness of such a training method. Ancient Frost faded as soon as I walked into the *ignis locus*. Could I use those harsh conditions like that to strengthen my ability to summon my Symbol like another version of the *pondus*? I will have to try.

"Because he was spying on you and is Ironbound! Just the fact that he noticed you was enough for me to consider killing him." Her voice is tinged with frustration at my stupidity.

"I was in the *ignis locus* because I bound a new Symbol in the garden and I'm trying to figure out how to use it before it kills me!"

Alessandra's blue eyes go wide with disbelief. "But Pliny said the Copper veins were just more of your *Corda* becoming Ancient Frost. That the *rasa* inside of you was slowly being subsumed by your existing Heart and would eventually allow you to be able to become a more powerful *electus* for your—"

"Alessandra, you know that before I found my way to Winter, I was Ironbound." I cut off her panicked babbling. "I do not know how Pliny was fooled, but he is *wrong*. I do not have a second Ancient Frost *Cor*. I have a new one, and I cannot cultivate it safely without people asking questions."

"What Symbol did you attune?" she asks softly, looking up at me through the dim light. I hesitate. I do not know why I bother now. I have already told her too much. Alessandra is right, I am not good at secrecy. It is a miracle from Dead Fortuna herself that I have made it this far.

"Unrelenting Fire."

Her eyes go wide, and she covers her mouth with her hand. "Are you certain?"

"Yes." I snort derisively. "You remember the binding ceremony, I'm sure. Did you get your Symbol's name wrong?"

"No." She shakes her head, lowering her hand. "No, of course not, I just did not expect—although I suppose it is unsurprising in some ways. It definitely is keeping with a theme."

"What are you talking about?"

"Do you know what Unrelenting Fire is?"

And then I understand why she is so surprised. The expression on her face is the same look the Censors had when their relic told them that I was bound to Ancient Frost. I close my eyes, letting the dark shelter me in the calm. "It's an Elder Symbol, isn't it?"

"You knew?"

"Not until now." I sigh, cursing the gods for punishing me for the oaths of my youth under my breath.

"It is also one of the Symbols forbidden by the gods."

I had forgotten that part. She takes my silence as encouragement and recites a rhyme I have not heard since I was a boy, and my father told me stories of heroes now long dead.

"Iron, cold and hard.

Music, sung by a bard.

Last, unrelenting fire.

These will summon Jupiter's ire."

According to the priests, when Prometheus stole the knowledge of *Cor* from the gods, they planned on destroying us all. Instead, in their mercy, Jupiter and the rest of the pantheon decreed that we could use this gift, except for three attunements. That was why I was able to cut Praeco when the Censors could not.

When the *Ferrum Domini* rebelled and Ascended to the peak of Iron, they killed the gods. What more could someone do if they were bound to two of the forbidden Symbols? The prickling sensation on my skin grows as I feel the presence of something *watching* me. I assumed that this new Symbol was still a repercussion for the *votum* I made with Valentina, Marcus, and Felix. Some symptom of whatever the Wolf did to me when he filled me with these blank Hearts.

But now, as I ponder the possibilities that lie before me, I wonder if it is not from a more vengeful source. Visions of the woman wearing the blindfold that followed me through the winter storm flash in my mind, reminding me of the new dead god that I serve.

Nemesis.

Was it her hand that guided me to the basin of fire? What game does she play? I have sworn to her to kill those responsible for the death of my family and the other families in Segesta. Why do I need forbidden fire to do it?

"I'll help you," Alessandra offers abruptly, killing the silence that stretches between us.

"Why?"

"You saved my life. It's only fair that I return the favor."

"And if you keep me from getting caught it keeps the Censors from coming down on you and your family."

"A double blessing." She smiles tightly. "What can I do?"

"Well," I say, glancing around the room at the *loci* that surround us, "if I'm going to Ascend, I'm going to need better fire."

CHAPTER 39

Just because she isn't allowed to push my *Cor* in training doesn't mean Contessa has any intention of taking it easy on me. The next morning the entire complement of Silver gladiators marshals in the training hall under the severe gaze of the *lanista*. I am sweating, put to work as if I had not just survived a set of the Games. All of us have heavy weights strapped to our shoulders on a yoke as we run in circles, carrying more than any non-*electus* could.

"Pick up the pace!" Contessa barks from across the hall. "The games in Forum are in six months, and I swear by the dead gods you will be reborn by then!"

"I was under the impression that process took at least *nine*," Illy grumbles under his breath to me as we move at a brisk trot, shoulders hunched under our burdens. In the center of the room, several Gold gladiators train. *Malus Mors* holds off two other fighters at once, swinging a giant sword I could barely lift even with both hands. Beyond him, *Fantasia* blurs as she passes through solid objects as if they were air. She is like a ghost—a deadly wraith.

"Perhaps the *lanista* wishes us to remember that the impossible is expected of us," I grunt back, feeling sick to my stomach. My mismatched *Corda* twist in complaint, racking my body with pain as I draw from their strength. This challenge is difficult for all of us, but in my condition, it is almost unbearable. What will everyone think of *Frigus Ventus* if he passes out in the middle of a simple physical exercise?

"I'm sure you'll find a way to pull it off," the shorter gladiator retorts. "All part of your budding myth. He can see invisible men, carry more weight than a dozen soldiers, and be reborn in the blink of an eye." Despite the friendly banter of his words, I feel a trickle of sweat run down my back that has nothing to do with the exercise that we are performing.

Illy was the only other person in the ring with me when we fought *Impostor*, the false teleportation gladiator. He has the most reason to doubt exactly how I knew the trick that they were playing. Too many questions about that could get me killed.

"Oh come on," I reply, trying to sound embarrassed. "You and I both know that I just got lucky. Thank the dead gods for putting Reese in our *ludus*. Without her, we'd both be rotting in some unmarked grave while the Heartsmiths cleaned our blood from our relics."

"I'm not sure I've ever seen you get *lucky*," Illy replies, shooting me a wry glance. "I have seen you persevere, but I see no sign of Rotten Fortuna bestowing any latent blessing upon you."

"That's not true," I protest, trying to joke my way out of this conversation. "All of us are blessed to eat at the mess hall here."

"The food is good," he allows, turning to look ahead. The two of us have passed most of the other Silvers; Contessa's lesson about not holding back has been well-learned. Only Obellius is still ahead of us. The massive Rock *electus* powers forward with a load double my own. He's not the sharpest *gladius* in the armory, but there is no denying his strength.

"But you and I both ended up here," Illy continues, turning to fix me with a penetrating stare. "I'm not sure I would call that any sort of fortune." I am silent for a moment, torn between taking an out to distract from this dangerous conversation and… something else.

An instinct left over from another life.

Are you watching, Durus? Looking to see if the lessons you tried to teach me stuck? I remember following in his shadow at Fort Frigidus, visiting the men, learning how to reinforce them with a joke or a casual word. The Iron Legions are only as strong as the men who held it together, and the wise centurion worked hard to strengthen their courage as well as their arms.

Ludus Pelias is not a legion, but we *are* at war. The stakes demand that we win the Games or watch our *domus* fall. If Varus is killed, I have noiallusions about what will happen to us. Those lucky enough to survive will be sold to other houses that will use us with less kindness.

But for me, *Frigus Ventus*, the only named Silver gladiator in the circuit? I had no doubt that I'd find my way into a Valerus dungeon, where Brennus and his terrifying mother could exact their revenge.

My chance at freedom would die with Varus and his house, and then I would die. Nemesis may be free and roaming the world, but I did not think she would protect me. The stories about the gods do not make them sound like guardians, only harsh taskmasters.

If I am going to be free of this place, there is only one way. I must win, and my comrades must win. We must tear through the Forum games like *Fidelia* among normal men. But the rest of the draft doesn't trust me. None of them other than Illy even particularly like me. What could I possibly do to alter that course?

Besides taking a risk and following the example of a better man than me, of course.

"You're right," I admit with a slight chuckle. "Fortuna's ghost does not live in Mar's house."

Illy grunts in acknowledgment but doesn't press. It feels like he is standing across the dueling ring from me, sword held in a low guard, waiting to see what I will do.

"How did you end up here?" I ask the question gently, tossing him an apologetic glance to let him know that he doesn't have to answer. I'm hoping that we have become good enough friends that he will take it as an olive branch rather than an interrogation.

Illy is silent for so long that I fear I have killed the conversation between us. Part of me is relieved, glad to be free of the duelist's verbal probing at a dangerous topic. But I can't help but feel like I have failed, that I have let down Durus's memory.

"My family was patrician," he says abruptly, not turning to look in my direction as we plod through another lap around the training hall. "Wealthy—even for our class. We had a minor estate on the edge of Anteforum, a relic from a bygone era where my great-grandsire was a man of tremendous means. My siblings and I attended a preparatory *academiae* with palatine children to give us an edge in the *collegium* and our *sententiae*." I blink in surprise. I've never even *heard* of an academy for younger students to attend.

"I never really moved in the mixed social circles, between palatine and patrician. But my younger sister was the light of them. Even as a girl, it was obvious that she would grow up to be beautiful beyond measure. The young men of the Great *Domuum* circled around her like sharks." His lips quirk into a frown, flickering like lightning before it vanishes. I keep silent, afraid to break the tenuous surface tension of his story.

"She grew up. Liberties were taken. I took some of my own." His teeth flash in a smile this time, as if he enjoys the memory. It stretches his face into something sharp and narrow, like a vulture's. It's the first time I've ever seen the shorter man look cruel.

"Unfortunately, it was the wrong son of the wrong *domus*," he continues, not looking at me, lost in the memories behind his own eyes. "They dragged me before the magistrates and bankrupted my family."

"Surely you were not convicted as a murderer for that?" I protest, daring to interrupt at last. "For defending your sister?"

"Ah, but it was my word against his family's, and gold gives the most convincing of testimony. What judges couldn't be bought were intimidated. I never stood a chance. Didn't even make it to my *Sententia*. My family was forced to sell our estate and all their belongings. When that wasn't enough to repay the debt, they sold me to the Games." He shrugs, as if he does not blame them for that.

"*Dominus* Varus himself bought me from a stock of Blanks, and I won my *Cor* in the Games."

"Does he know about this?" I ask, eyeing him curiously. Illy's past has a familiar echo to what the senator told me about his own.

"He must." Illy shrugs, a motion that must be difficult under the yoke of all the extra weight. "It is in my writ that consigned me to the Games. Why?"

I hesitate for a moment, unsure if it is my tale to tell. But I think Illy should hear it, and it's not like it is a *secret*. After all, its final scene played out in front of thousands of witnesses. What's one more who knows the tale?

"He told me a similar story once," I allow after a moment. "About his own time in the arena, after his own sister suffered in the same way." Illy's head snaps up, and he stares at me with wide eyes, just as surprised as I was.

"He told you this?"

I nod.

"In a personal conversation that you had, just the two of you?"

My mouth opens to protest, but no words come out. It seems that I have only managed to make myself more suspicious rather than reassure my friend.

"Your turn," he presses, not letting the silence between us build. "I told you my secrets. It's time you trusted me with yours."

"Pick up the pace!" Contessa shouts from the far side of the room, where she glowers at all of us with her arms crossed. I bite back a curse as I turn back to face forward. I have done this to myself. Damn Durus and his teachings. They have only brought me closer to ruin. And yet, part of me yearns to tell the truth. Those who know are not my friends—they are the pieces of driftwood that I have found as I am lost at sea.

But Felix and Marcus are gone, and there are none left for me to share the burden of myself with. To Anas, I am an ironbrother. To Alessandra, I am *Frigus Ventus*, the salvation of her *domus*. Both of them *need* me to be something. They do not care about Castor, the mortal whose flesh holds the *Cor* Hearts that lets me be the thing that I am becoming. I'm not sure that's true about Illy.

"I, too, was patrician," I begin, still not entirely sure if this story will end with the truth or a fiction. My heart seems to see a path, and I can do nothing but follow it.

"My family ran into some trouble with the Censors."

Illy hisses in hatred, making me glance at him in surprise. It seems I am not the only one who bears a grudge for the White Hand and its fingers.

"Like you, there was no justice to be found, and when the dust settled, my mother and father were dead, and I had been conscripted into the Iron Legions. Sent to Agogia to die."

Illy is so surprised that he stumbles, drawing to a halt for a second before he scrambles to catch back up to me. "Mars's Rotting Beard," he breathes softly. My pulse quickens, terrified that I have told him too much already.

"When I received my *Cor*, it went wrong," I continue, feeding him the same half-truth that Varus and Pliny accepted when they first evaluated me. "Thanks to my ice, I ended up here instead of the front line of the Twelfth Legion."

"You were supposed to be Ironbound?" he breathes in wonder. My heart skips a beat at the note of inspiration in his voice. I have become like Icarus and flown too close to the sun.

"But instead, I became an *immundus*." I gesture at my white *rasa* veins with a tilt of my head, trying to remind him that I am deformed.

"A thief of one of the Iron Legion's *Cor* Hearts and in debt to the Empress for what I have taken."

Illy is silent for a few moments as he processes my tale. I can feel the sharp edges of his mind turning as he dissects my story. Despite my concern over his scrutiny, I feel a little lighter than before, even carrying Contessa's heavy burdens.

We do not speak for the rest of the exercise. The *lanista* increases our pace until even *electi* are breathing in ragged gasps. My muscles burn like the veins of my *Corda* when I push them too far. Contessa has found a way to train me without breaking her word to Pliny.

As I sweat and suffer, I think about what Illy told me. His story is familiar; it could be a mirror of my own. The senator seems to collect people like him. How many more of the gladiators in this *ludus* have similar experiences being caught in the rusty machinery of the Iron Empire?

I am sure that is deliberate.

Anyone with eyes can see that there is no love lost between *Domus* Pelias and *Domus* Agrippa. A thread of doubt squirms in my chest, pulling uncomfortably on my patriotic heart. I feel lost. This is not the world I set out to explore. I want no part of this struggle. I am not like those Imperials who hid among Knut in the snow. I do not want to tear down the Empire itself. My revenge is a personal thing.

All my life, I have lived in the Iron Empire, and it has been…good to me. People have enough to eat. The roads are safe to travel. Even in the larger cities, most seem to have plenty. This country reeks of riches and opportunity. I have seen the rust firsthand, but I do not know Diana Agrippa. I have never seen her. I do not know if she is the root or even if she is evil. I hate Atticus and General Tyrus and the small, petty people who abuse their power.

But Varus seems to be heading for deeper waters that I have no desire to swim in. *I need to earn my freedom soon.* A consistent thought slowly emerges from the tangled chaos of my emotions. Not only is it too dangerous for me to be here, under the scrutiny of so many learned *electi* who will eventually ascertain the truth of what I am, but I have no desire to be dragged into some sort of coup against the Empress.

Frustrated, I study my Unrelenting Fire *Cor* with my mind, probing at it like a sore in my mouth with my tongue. It seems no different than when I first attuned to the Symbol in Senator Delilah's garden. While my veins have grown stronger, there is no sign that it is almost ready to Ascend. It is like an anchor tied to my ankle, and the water around me is rising. If I do not get out, I will surely drown.

When Contessa has run us ragged, she releases us from training, eyeing us all like she is disappointed that we did not march a hundred miles inside the training hall. I give her a tired smile, but she doesn't return it. Stress pulls her face taut as she glowers down at me with her arms crossed.

"Forum is less than six months away, Castor," she reminds me, as if I had somehow already forgotten.

"Yes, *Lanista*," is all I say as I reply meekly, ducking my head in a subservient manner.

"Straight into the *locus*," she reminds me. "Pliny won't be happy to see you dawdling." I feel my smile die a little as I realize there will be no break for me. The *pondus*, a weight of a different kind, sits in my pocket waiting to torture my *Cor* the same way Contessa just tortured my body.

"At once, *Domina*," I promise, dropping the last of my weights at her feet before turning toward the Winter essence source. I feel her eyes on the back of my neck watching me as I cross the training hall.

Illy is waiting for me there, his expression guarded. I feel a knot of tension spread throughout my chest as I approach him. I was too honest. I gave him the puzzle pieces, and he put them together.

"Castor," he says softly as I draw close. His voice is pitched low enough that no one else can hear. His brown eyes hold mine fearlessly, like a hunter who knows that he has his prey dead to rights. My right hand curls into a loose grip, preparing to summon the *Glacialis Falx*.

If I am fast enough, I can cut him down before he tells Contessa. I'll be a murderer, but that will just get me sent back to the Games anyway. The truth will see me hung in front of the Empress's Palace.

"I am sorry that you lost your family," he says slowly, not meeting my eyes. "But I wanted to say—"

"Illy, it's not what—" I interject, desperate to convince him, to save his life.

"I know how hard it is to be honest," he continues, looking up at me for the first time. A proud fire burns in the back of his eyes, a boy who is not ashamed of showing his hurt.

The tension in my shoulders fades as I realize that I am wrong. He doesn't know.

"I'm sorry I didn't trust you. Thank you for trusting me. You've saved my life and shown me your pain. You and I are true friends now. No matter what happens, I'll watch your back and one day, I'll help you get revenge for your family."

"I feel the same way," I reply through a mouth full of ash. This is what I wanted, yet I feel guilty. I have not shared my secrets with the shorter duelist. I fed him enough to feel like we were the same, and now he is mine. He is friends with a mask, not the man beneath.

Durus, are you watching?

"What are you going to do?" Illy asks, his eyes boring into mine.

"It's easy," I reply with a wide grin, clapping him on the shoulder. "First, we're going to win."

CHAPTER 40

Slowly, I fall into a routine. By day, I am an obedient patient, cultivating with the *pondus* in the Winter *locus* for all to see. Pliny checks on my progress frequently, growing visibly more concerned with each visit. He is unsatisfied with the progress of my Copper Heart. I am too, although, unlike him, I at least understand the nature of the bottleneck that dampens my progress.

There are some benefits to the work. The darker, colder line on the edge of my Ancient Frost *Cor* is growing. The relic is making me stronger.

After the first day, I take to wearing a *lorica* in the cold. I do not want my Iron Heart falling behind my Winter one. Secretly, I alternate which Symbol I cultivate through the *pondus*. It is the first thing the magister questions me about when he comes to visit me.

"Why are you wearing that?" He eyes the armor distrustfully. "I didn't tell you to do that."

"The iron gets cold," I say, as if that explains everything. "Helps pull the Winter closer to me." Pliny grunts but does not comment further. I feel my skin tingle as his *animus* sweeps over me, checking on my progress.

"Still nothing?"

"I feel some strain, but I have not reached the peak."

"I worry that because your body has already gone through this process, it has built up a resistance."

"Does that mean my *Cuprum Cor* will never advance?" He shakes his head.

"I suspect that it means the threshold for Ascending will increase with each chunk of your *rasa* that finally acclimates." He hesitates for a moment. "If I could, I would forbid you from progressing to Gold until every single bit of your *Corda* has reached Silver. But the world schemes against us."

"What will happen if I gain another Copper *Cor* once I am Gold?"

He shrugs helplessly, but the expression on his face is unpleasant. "I fear we will find out."

By night I creep into the Fire *locus*, using its weaker flames to feed my Copper Heart. Already my veins do not struggle wrestling with the fire. It is too artificial, too relenting, to be what I need to advance. Even using the *pondus* does not make it worthy.

For the first time, I truly appreciate how difficult it can be for different Symbols to advance from Copper to Silver. A rare attunement might struggle to find the right quantity and quality of its element to cultivate the essence it needs. Iron is simple and abundant in the Empire. Ancient Frost and Unrelenting Fire far less so.

Anas watches over me, armed with two knives now. We never speak of it, but I know he is embarrassed about being caught off guard by Alessandra. I am careful to keep my Iron senses trained on him while in the fire *locus*, but no one disturbs our work.

Still, it is painstakingly slow. I begin to despair that I will ever Advance. No matter how many hours I spend in the inferno, there is almost no growth. My *Corda* are too efficient, and the source material too weak.

Contessa is not content to let my other skills atrophy while I try to find balance within myself. Every day, she invents a new training regimen that pushes my physical capabilities beyond their limits, while not using any of my abilities as an *electus*. I thought that Agogia forged me into a perfect soldier, but after two weeks, I can see my muscles beginning to build sharper edges along my body.

I'm in the Winter *locus*, performing my mind-numbing cultivation, when she finds me. "You're taking a break," the *lanista* barks.

"But Pliny said—" I begin to protest.

"*Dominus*'s orders."

There is nothing left to say. With a grunt, I leverage myself off my knees and rise out of the snow. Even though I complained, I am thrilled at the interruption. There is only so long that I can sit here cultivating before I begin to feel like I will go mad. The thick blue line in my Ancient Frost *Cor* grows at a glacial pace, and I worry that I am accomplishing nothing.

The dark-skinned *lanista* leads me out of the training room and deeper into the estate than I have ever been before. We cross through the hallway that leads to Pliny's library, and out the other side. I open my mouth to ask Contessa where she is taking me, but a glance at her face tells me it will only be wasted breath. She is not nearly as loquacious as her magister counterpart.

Behind the Pelias mansion is a garden. It reminds me of Delilah's, where I bound the Unrelenting Fire. I look but do not see any sign of a brazier holding a piece of the everflame. A pity. I grow desperate enough that I might have been willing to throw myself into it to see if that unquenchable fire was strong enough to push my Copper Heart over the edge.

Contessa leads me through the garden to a smaller building that I have never seen before. It is hidden behind a row of hedges, secluded from the rest of the estate. It feels like a home from another world. The building is shorter than the Imperial standard and made of wood instead of marble. A thick thatch roof angles into sharp triangles.

"Listen," she says, breaking her silence for the first time. "When we are inside, keep your mouth shut. If you must speak, be respectful. You have a bad habit of talking to your betters like they are your equals. That will not work in this place. Do I make myself clear?" I open my mouth to protest but realize that it would only prove her point.

"Yes, *Domina*."

She snorts, skeptical.

The whole structure is elevated off the ground by several steps, and as we approach, a portion of the wall reveals itself as a door when someone slides it open. It seems to be made of some sort of light material—barely thicker than the paper on Pliny's books.

Despite not being familiar with the architecture of the residence, I recognize its occupant easily enough. The strange woman who was in the room across from me in Delilah's servant quarters stands in the doorway. She is older than me, but only by a few years. Her hair is darker than midnight, and her eyes match. She wears a shiny tunic with matching trousers made of some silver material that is much finer than the leathers I wear. She glares at me openly, unafraid and unimpressed by *Frigus Ventus*.

I know precious little about the places outside of the Iron Empire's borders. What land does she come from, and how did she end up here? I have never seen anyone like her and find myself fascinated. She looks nothing like the Normans, the pale, blond barbarians in the North. Her skin is darker than mine, although not nearly as dark as Contessa's.

"What?" the woman asks flatly, gaze landing heavily on Contessa.

"I have brought your grandfather another *discipuli*," the *lanista* replies, surprisingly unbothered by the lack of respect in the woman's tone.

"Him?" Scorn ripples across her face as she studies me. I feel her eyes track along my white *rasa* veins and the mismatched Copper and Silver ones. I look like a mess compared to the elite *electi* of the Empire. She has no Heart of her own but seems to understand the implications of my deformity well enough.

"*Dominus* Pelias insists."

"We shall see what *Sensei* says," the woman says dismissively, unimpressed. She steps back from the doorway and turns to head deeper into the home. We follow, but Contessa stops me with a stiff arm as we cross the threshold.

"Uh-uh," she says scoldingly. "Boots off."

"What?" I ask, certain I did not hear her correctly.

"Boots. Off." As if to reinforce her point, the bald woman bends down and unlaces one of hers. "It is a matter of respect."

Feeling more than a little silly, I follow suit with the *lanista*, removing my shoes and placing them next to hers by the door. In my socks, I follow Contessa as she leads me through the house. The same thin, paper-like walls fill the interior, making hallways that feel almost claustrophobic compared to the vaulted marble ceilings of the palatines. Even my own quarters in the gladiator dormitory have more space than this.

The woman does not look back as she leads us through their home and out into an exterior garden that is in a courtyard in the center of the square building, surrounded on all sides by the rest of the home. A deep pond is nestled in a copse of trees I have never seen before. Large, bright fish swim among the lilies, and the pleasant sound of a waterfall undercuts the sound of metal striking metal. A wooden square covers the ground by the water, and my jaw drops as I watch the fighters dance on it.

The older man that I have seen before stands in the center of the ring. He wears a matching black tunic and trousers made of the same shiny material. He is older even than Pelias. His hair, which is pulled back into a bun, is mostly white. But his spine is straight, and he moves with powerful precision. The strangest thing about him is the blindfold that covers his eyes, but he moves like he can see.

Three Gold *electi* circle him like predators, moving at incredible speeds. Each of them carries a dueling blade, and they work together to bring the old man down. He stands in the middle of their pack, holding a sword unlike any I have ever seen before.

It is long and slightly curved, with an edge only on one side. It is almost a cousin to the swords that his opponents use, but far thinner. As I watch, the woman behind him stomps her foot, trying to distract him while a dark-skinned man on the right rushes in from the side.

The old man's curved blade whistles as it cuts the air itself, moving with perfect precision to catch his attacker's strike. They exchange three lightning-fast attacks before the blindfolded man twirls, disengaging with perfect timing to intercept the third *aurum* attacker.

The old man locks his blade with the Gold gladiator, sliding down the length of it to close with his opponent. Then, with a twist, he disengages, his foot lashing out to catch his opponent in the chest, sending him flying. The *electus* ends up outside of the wooden square, and his shoulders slump when he realizes he has been eliminated.

The first man has recovered enough to attack again, but his sword only meets the wind. The old man twists around his blade, jamming his elbow into the Golden gladiator's neck hard enough to leave him reeling. The *aurum* man chokes as he stumbles backward, the tip of his sword dropping.

The blindfolded man's blade flickers to hover an inch away from his chest before it drops, signaling that the second fighter has fallen. The disappointed fighter joins the other *electus* outside of the box, rubbing at his neck with a grimace.

The woman takes advantage of her partner's sacrifice, lunging at the man's exposed back, but he merely flicks his blade to catch hers, turning to face her with a speed I can barely comprehend. He presses the woman with perfect technique, blade flashing. She catches his first two strokes thanks to her own Golden speed, but the third one reveals a power that I have only seen once before.

The blindfolded man's strike comes in diagonally, angled to open her from shoulder to hip. Her own sword flickers to meet his attack, but it does not matter. His strange blade flows like liquid, and I cannot help but gasp in horror as it passes *through* her own weapon the same way that the Censor's blades passed through Praeco's armor in Antioch. She staggers in surprise before the two of them freeze as the sharp edge of his curved blade hovers a hairsbreadth from her neck.

I am stunned. I have seen masters of the sword at their work. I watched Gaius Marius, a *Fidelis*, duel the *berserkir* High King Knut. I do not think either of them could hold off three Golden *electi* as easily as breathing… while blindfolded.

After a moment, the man draws his blade back in a fluid motion, and the defeated gladiator performs a strange bow, bending at the waist and clasping her hands in front of her.

"*Arigatō gozaimasu, Sensei,*" she says. My eyebrows rise in surprise. I do not recognize the tongue she speaks—it is not the ancient language of our ancestors. Frustration boils in me once more at my ignorance. May Dead Minerva damn Vellum and his magisters who taught us so little.

None of the blindfolded man's flesh is exposed to reveal if he is an *electus*, but instinct tells me that he is not. Perhaps he is inked with *berserkir* tattoos under his clothes like the Normans, but I doubt that too. My eyes are drawn to the razor-sharp edge of his strange sword that can flow like liquid. Tentatively, I reach out with my *animus*, extending my senses toward the weapon.

As I suspected, I feel nothing, or almost nothing. There is a hint of iron nestled in the metal, nails in the hilt, and the strange round crossguard. But the blade itself is distant to me, like a light at the end of a far tunnel. It is not made of Iron, but something else, only barely congruent to my Symbol. My eyes narrow as I study the dark metal until I realize why it looks so familiar. It is the same shade that dead Hearts take when their host die. It's the color of relics. A shiver of fear runs down my spine at the blasphemy. Wherever this man is from, they have their own way to use *Cor* just like the Normans. What would the gods think if they still lived? Prometheus stole the knowledge of our art from the very halls of *Mons* Olympus. What does it mean that other people have found their own way to this power? But then, not all of the gods *are* truly dead. Who knows what other mischief the rotting creatures have gotten up to since the days of the Iron Lords.

The blindfolded man responds sharply, speaking in his native language at a rate my untrained ear cannot begin to parse. He points with his sword at the man whom he kicked out of the square.

"Pyrus, *Sensei* says that your weakness is in your footing. You are like a tree with no roots, and any enemy that seeks to dig you up will find treasure easily." The woman who could be his granddaughter translates, her tone imperious and cold. The man continues his lecture. "You will do ten thousand stance changes in the Way of the Tree before you return here." To my surprise, the Golden gladiator merely bows, repeating the same obeisance that the warrior before him gave. He shows no sign of anger at the criticism, only acceptance. He strides from the courtyard without hesitation, his face set in concentration.

The sword moves to the second man, who took an elbow to the neck. The blindfolded man does not turn to look in his direction, but the point of his blade hovers with unerring accuracy. Perhaps that strange weapon gives him an *animus* of his own.

"Zapatar, *Sensei* says that you rely on a shield too much and are useless without one. He wonders if you would rather be a turtle than a swordsman? His pond has space for a new one if you are looking for a home." My eyebrows shoot up at the condescension that runs through her translation.

But the dark-skinned gladiator also shows no sign of indignation. He repeats the same formal bow, holding it while he stares at the ground. "Please tell *Sensei* that I only wish to be a swordsman, not a turtle."

The woman translates his words back to the old man, who cocks his head as if doubtful. He purses his lips, the first expression I have seen on his face, before he nods, issuing a short burst of commands.

"You will perform twenty thousand strikes in the Way of the Wind before you return here."

"Yes, *Sensei*," the relieved-looking gladiator barks, finally coming up from his bow. He too leaves without hesitation; his expression is relieved as he passes by Contessa and me. Part of me rankles at the sight of my fellow Imperials bowing to this man. We are citizens of the Iron Empire. I bow only to the Empress.

Only the woman remains, still standing in the center of the ring where she was defeated. The blindfolded man lowers his sword, studying her intently. The gladiator remains perfectly still like a well-trained dog waiting for its master to release her.

At last, he seems to come to a decision and speaks in sharp tones.

"Katarina, *Sensei* says that you are wise, letting the foolish warriors rush ahead as bait. But your hesitancy only allows you to die last. In a truly honorable duel, there will be no one to hide behind. You are to win twenty matches against other *gaijin* before you return to this place."

"Yes, *Sensei*," Katarina says quickly, bowing once more. "I hear and will obey." She, too, rushes past us without pausing. I eye Contessa, who watches the entire exchange with a hint of amusement. What does she think of all this? She is responsible for the training of all the gladiators in this *ludus*, but this man berates her charges like a tyrant.

The man strides to the far side of the square, picking up a black wooden sheath from a weapon rack and sliding his blade home. He speaks again to the younger woman as he sticks the encased weapon through his belt.

"*Sensei* wishes to know why you are here."

"Please tell him that I have brought him another student."

The woman chuckles, as if Contessa has said something funny. She communicates this to the man, who turns to study me. I can feel his gaze, even though his eyes are buried beneath the blindfold. He says a single syllable which needs no translation, but she does anyway.

"No."

Pride flares in my chest, and Unrelenting Fire feeds on it greedily, burning with indignation. How dare he deny me? Does he know who I am? What I will become? I force myself to take a deep breath and push the eager Fire Symbol away, concerned at how quickly it leapt to my defense.

It does not matter. I am Ironbound. What can some swordsmaster who is not an *electus* hope to teach *me*? I am not like these Golds who flail blindly with their weapons. I see with true eyes.

"The *dominus* requests this favor of his oldest and greatest friend," Contessa replies, sounding not at all surprised by his reaction. But I sure am. The master of House Pelias is a patient and kind man, but senators rarely *ask*—they *imperate*. I study this strange man again, trying to imagine his story. He seems almost from another world; I cannot imagine how he became Varus's closest friend.

The swordsmaster paces toward me now, giving me a closer inspection. My skin puckers as something probes at it. It feels like an *animus*, but it is different too—colder and more alien.

"*Sensei* only accepts those who have Ascended to Gold." His granddaughter does not translate but speaks for herself.

"We wish to make an exception."

"He already has three students. Which would you have him cut to make room for this one?"

"Pyrus," the *lanista* says without hesitation. I can't help but feel a tiny spark of guilt at taking his place, even if he was the first one to be defeated by the swordsmaster.

The old man's hand caresses the hilt of his sword as he studies me, and I am more convinced that I am right. His weapon is his Heart, but he does not carry it in his body. He stops several paces away from me and asks her a question.

"What is wrong with him?" the granddaughter asks.

Another spike of anger runs through me, and I force Unrelenting Fire to stay back, contained in the back of my mind. Despite my irritation, I remember Contessa's instructions to remain silent.

"Nothing."

"*Sensei* says he is twisted, warped." Her eyes track down my mismatched arm veins once more. "He may be blind, but he still sees more than most."

"He is unusual." Contessa says that almost judgmentally. The simmering anger in me threatens to boil as I am needled from all sides. "But he is bound to a powerful Symbol and is in need of instruction."

The translator's face sours at the mention of my *Cor*. "*Sensei* cares not for your inhuman experiments, *gaijin*," she scolds. "That has no bearing on the worthiness of a student."

"Does he care for House Pelias?" Contessa counters, a note of irritation finally entering her voice. There are few in the Empire who would dare speak to a Gold *electus* like her with such disrespect. Fewer still among the people who live in this estate.

The translator hesitates, caught in a trap.

"Because our *dominus* is besieged by enemies and seeks to defend himself from those who would destroy him. Is that not a cause to which his dearest friend belongs?"

The woman scowls but says something in the foreign language to the old man. He responds at once, his voice sharp. The woman flinches, but I cannot tell if it is because he is angry with her or his message is harsh.

"Very well. He will be tested."

"Tested?" Contessa snaps, finally at the end of her own patience. "He is to be trained."

"A blacksmith cannot turn every piece of iron into a sword no matter how much he desires," the translator counters, raising her chin to stare at us. Her dark gaze flickers to me, and I feel her disdain like a physical thing. "*Sensei* will see what can be made of him."

I step into the box eagerly, my pride still burning like a banked flame underneath my skin. This blind old man makes a mistake in underestimating me. I am only too happy to get an opportunity to show him how wrong he was.

But to my surprise, he turns his back on me and walks off the training square, stopping to stand next to the younger woman who translates for him. She stiffens in surprise, before bowing slightly.

"I am confused," I say, breaking my silence at last. I tell myself that I am being polite enough to be obeying the *lanista*'s commands. "Are we to fight outside of the field?"

"No, fool," the dark-haired woman snaps, striding away from her master to the weapon rack where another sword sits. "You have not earned the right to learn from him. I will measure you."

"You can't be serious," I protest, turning to look at Contessa, whose face is impassive. "*Lanista*, she has no *Cor*. What kind of test can this possibly be? Is there a child you would like me to duel after this?"

"As you say," the translator says, lifting her sword. "Then it should be an easy challenge for you to accomplish." With one hand, she pulls her blade free from its case, twirling it with a confident flourish that tells me she is no stranger to holding it.

The blade is similar to the blind master's, although slightly smaller and thinner. It was clearly made for her, a concept I find fascinating. The Iron Empire's *gladius* is made to the same specifications every time. Our uniformity is our power. What would a sword made specifically for me look like?

She holds her weapon in a low guard as she stalks onto the wooden training arena. Now that I am looking for it, it is apparent that her every moment is molded by her training. Her footsteps are smooth and fluid, low to the ground and deliberate. She moves like a dancer that needs no music.

There is a power radiating from her that was not present until she drew her weapon, and despite my confidence, I find it intimidating. Her elder shows no sign of being an *electus* or *berserkir*, yet he easily defeated three Golds. If she has access to the same power, I may be in trouble. Part of me regrets my earlier outburst, but it is too late to go back and undo it.

She pauses a dozen feet away from me, settling into a loose stance, blade still held low. Her dark gaze descends and moves to the pair of *gladii* that ride at my hips with an obvious question. *Can you use those*? Part of me cannot wait to answer her.

"I'm sorry," I say, trying to start fresh. "I do not think I got your name."

"This sword is called a *katana*, *gaijin*," she says, raising it so I can inspect it between us. "I will introduce you to it first."

"What is the test?" I ask, no longer bothering to be polite. My right hand falls to the hilt of my sword, and I draw it slowly. I will only use one; it only seems fair. The old man replies in his language, and a smirk grows on the girl's expression as she watches me. It is not a pleasant thing. I imagine Thanatos might have had one that looked very similar, while he still lived.

"Strike me if you can," she says and launches herself at me, blade rising.

She is faster than she should be. Only my Silver speed allows me to catch her sudden movement. My eyes widen under the shock of her attack. *Something* tears at my blade, trying to devour it. It is not like the will of an *electus*—it feels like some monster from the depths, ravenous and full of teeth. I gasp, burning essence as I reinforce my *gladius*.

Her smile widens, laughing at me. She disengages her *katana* from my *gladius,* and we exchange a flurry of blows. Her sword flickers like lightning, catching the sun as it darts at me relentlessly. Her blade is longer than mine, giving her more reach. Worse still, no matter how hard I pull on the Iron Symbol, I cannot use it to track her weapon reliably. The congruency is too faint. Its warning comes quieter than it should, as if it is traveling a long distance.

I fall back several paces under her onslaught, mind scrambling as I try to figure out how to counter her. Whatever blasphemous art was used to make her *katana* gives her blessings that seem comparable to mine.

I should have used my second sword.

Every time our blades touch, I am hammered by the *katana*'s hunger. It does not steal my Symbol like the power of the *berserkirs*, but it is relentless. It does not seek to destroy my weapon, but me. I feel it tearing at my mind like a wild animal. I'm forced to burn essence at an incredible rate to defend myself from its claws.

Gritting my teeth, I lean forward, forcing my body to take her strong blows head-on. Her form is perfect. She flows like a river, pounding me from every side then dancing away, uncontainable. My pride has vanished, drowned like a flame. Instead, a new hunger burns in the same place.

I too wish to dance like this.

After a few dozen strikes, her cadence begins to slow, and it is my turn to smile. Her strength is impressive, but whatever power the *katana* grants her, it is not a part of her the same way that my *Corda* are. I take control of the tempo, finally able to dish out my own attacks.

She falls back two paces as I hunch my shoulders and stalk forward like a beast. She is faster and more skilled than I am. I am not a true duelist yet, despite my time under Contessa's tutelage. I was taught to fight like a legionnaire, grinding my opponents into the ground with sheer brute force. I weigh at least fifty pounds more than the smaller woman; I might as well put it to good use.

Our swords ring against each other as we push ourselves to our limits. She is entirely on the defensive as I rain blows on her as fast as I can. There is no artistry to me, just pure force. She is a dancer being pummeled by a brute. I move at a reckless pace, trying to push her past her limits.

Clang!

I spot the opening before it arrives, and I struggle to kill the smile that threatens to bloom on my face. I knock her *katana* to the right with as much force as I can, stepping inside her guard and raising my *gladius* for an overhead blow that could split her from breastbone to belly button if I wanted it to.

Desperately, she tries to bring her sword diagonally to block the blow, but the angle is too tight—I will knock the weapon out of her grasp on the way down. I see this knowledge in her eyes in the moment before our swords meet, and now, I do allow myself a small smile.

It dies just like I would have if she wanted to kill me.

A terrifying chill like a bucket of cold water runs through me as her sword *ripples*. The Iron Symbol wriggles like a living thing in my grasp as if it shudders at the touch of her strange power. I can only stare in horror as my *gladius* passes through her *katana* without slowing.

The lithe woman sidesteps my clumsy overhanded blow easily, moving closer to me so the edge of her blade runs parallel across my shoulders, an inch away from my neck. We both freeze, and I feel my cheeks burn with shame as she mocks me. She is not out of breath—she was toying with me. In my focus, I forgot that I saw her master use the same trick. This whole fight was a trap, and I fell into it.

Satisfied with her gloating, she turns to look at the blindfolded man who has somehow watched our fight. His hand still rides on the hilt of his own *katana* stuffed through his sash.

"*Īe*," he says in a tone that needs no translation. I have failed. My eyes close in shame, and I can feel Contessa burning with irritation behind me. I hesitate, torn between making a desperate plea and preserving my pride. I am not used to rejection. Since the *Sententia*, I have excelled at every challenge I have faced. Even when I was sent to the Twelfth, I was *Primus*.

I watched this man defeat three *aurum electi* at once, using only a single sword. My Iron Symbol makes me powerful. It gives me a natural, unfair edge over any opponent who carries a normal sword. But I have sworn to Nemesis herself that I will kill Atticus, who carries a *tellus* blade. I will be as blind against him as Brennus was against my *Glacialis Falx*. Even if he is half the swordsman that this old man is, he will cut me to ribbons.

"Please, *Sensei*." My mouth stumbles over the unfamiliar word, but I do my best to copy the bow that I saw the other Golds use before they were dismissed. "I wish to learn."

He asks his translator a question, and she replies, perhaps telling him what I said. I do not look up, keeping my eyes focused on the ground a short distance in front of his feet. My pride growls in irritation. Even Varus, who owns me, does not demand that I bow! But my need for vengeance weighs me down, forcing me to bend.

You are the Iron Legions of the Empire… Durus's voice chants in my memory. I shake my head slightly, feeling my long hair dance as I do. I was once, but not anymore. Now I must bend, or I will break. I feel the gaze of every person in the room on me, judging me. At last, the man speaks, and my heart skips a beat as I wait for it to be translated.

"You are reckless and angry, like a fire," my opponent translates on behalf of the master. "You cannot be taught because you are not contained." I open my mouth to protest—I am *very* contained. However, she continues on, not giving me a chance to speak.

"Before you can learn the sword, you must first learn to be. Go and watch until you are ready."

"When will that be?" I ask, my confusion bleeding into my tone as I rise from my bow, daring to look at the blindfolded man once more.

"He says you will know."

"I don't even know what he wants me to do."

"Then you are not ready."

Contessa snorts behind me, sharing my frustration.

"The *dominus*—" I begin, like a child appealing to his father.

"Does not own us."

My mouth snaps shut as my protest dies. "Very well," I say, out of ideas, devastated by losing this opportunity that I did not know existed until now. "I will do as he asks."

"Absolutely preposterous," Contessa is snarling to herself as we lace our boots on outside of their home. My feet are relieved to no longer be naked. Fighting without shoes felt *wrong*. "Living on the *dominus*'s land, cared for in every way. Ungrateful cur."

I say nothing, weighed down by the shame of my failure.

"I will speak to Varus," she tells me, seething with irritation.

"You said that the old man and the senator are friends?"

She nods, rising to her feet. "After his time in the arena, Varus went East across the great sea. He came back with Hiro, and they have been inseparable since. Something about killing a *dragon*, whatever that is." I have to trot to keep up with her long-legged pace as she heads back toward the main estate.

"And the girl?"

"His granddaughter. She was just a babe when they arrived."

"I don't think he's going to change his mind."

"I know." She sighs, pausing, shoulders slumping. "But you need to get better."

"Can't you teach me?"

"What do you think I have been doing, *Frigus Ventus*?" she growls, turning to glare at me with the sun reflecting off her bald head.

"Sorry, I just mean—"

"I can teach you to fight, but I cannot teach you *that*. Most cannot even learn it. Those three Golds have been studying under him for almost a year, and you saw how that is going."

"So, what do I do?"

"You heard the *sensei*." Her tone makes the foreign word mocking. "Go learn how to be."

CHAPTER 41

Hiro's challenge reeks of philosophy, so I go to see Pliny. The diminutive magister lurks in his lair beneath the library, and I take a moment before descending into his den to stare up at the mural of Pelias, the founder of this *domus*.

What would the Iron Lords do if they were here? Did they know that some of the gods would stir in their graves? Did they know that they didn't kill them all? They must not have, for it was their decision to hobble mankind after them. They created the *inhibitus* and forbade any Ironbound from Ascending beyond Copper. Why do that if they thought there would be more gods to kill?

I feel an odd kinship with Pelias. I am not the first *electi* bound to the Iron Symbol to become Silver since their decree, but I am the first to not wear the collar. If I Ascend to Gold, I will be the first to follow in their footsteps since the Empire was founded. The Iron Lords saved us from bondage.

What will I do?

Uncomfortable with my own musings, I tear my eyes from Pelias's palatine face and make my way down the short tunnel to Pliny's office. The skin on the back of my neck prickles as I depart, as if the painted eyes on the ceiling watch me leave.

"Did you Ascend?" Pliny greets me enthusiastically, slumping in his chair when I shake my head ruefully.

"Not yet. I'm here because I need your help with something else."

"You should not be getting distracted from your path." His eyebrows form into a narrow V as he scowls. "Is Contessa interfering with your *Corda* training?"

"Yes, but at Varus's command. She took me to meet Hiro."

"Ah." A look of understanding passes across his owlish face. "Let me guess, he refused to train you?"

"How did you know?"

"Because he refuses to train *everyone*."

"He had three Gold *electi* that he was knocking around who would say otherwise."

"Sorry, I should have said he *refuses to train everyone the first time.*"

"They're from the East, right? Across the ocean?"

"Far across the seas is a great island called *Nihon.*" He nods. "Few from the Iron Empire have ever set foot on its shores. Those who have are almost exclusively in the legions." That sounds about right. For good or for ill, the legions are the leading arm of the Empire.

"At my *Sententia*, the Empress said that the enemies in the East were stirring…" I let my question trail off, unsure how to form it. As a boy, the rest of the world was presented to me as nameless, faceless terrors that wanted to crush us. Only the nearby Normans were ever discussed at any length.

"Tensions have escalated…" Pliny admits slowly, his eyes watching me. There is something that he is deciding if he should tell me or not. But having seen Hiro's weapon, I have an inkling of what that might be.

"Does it have to do with *Cor*?" My question catches him off guard.

"Why do you ask that?"

"His sword—that *katana*. It's made from *Cor*, isn't it? The same way that the Normans use it in their ink to parody the gods' power?"

"I had no idea you were such a believer." The magister's lips quirk up slightly in a small smile.

I twitch in surprise. Am I? I would not have said that I was—my mother was far more devout than I. She is the reason that an everflame burned in the brazier by my grandfather's mausoleum. But I have spoken with Aquilo, slain the Herald of Mars, and freed Nemesis from her grave. How could I not be? Hard to be an atheist when you've carried the power of a god in your hands.

"You're right; they use it too," Pliny continues when I do not rise to his bait. "*Terra* is much larger than the bounds of the Iron Empire. Much of our power comes from the Hearts that fall within our borders. But not all of it falls here. There is an entire division of Censors and Legionnaires that are tasked with hunting it wherever it lands." My mouth gapes open at the thought of places far away being plundered by the White Hand and Iron Legions to bring *Cor* back to the Empress.

"I can see how that might cause some tensions," I admit dryly. Inwardly, my mind reels at how small my world is compared to the one that I live in.

"That is only the beginning," Pliny says with a laugh. "If I had been in charge of your education…" His voice trails off, and he sighs with sadness, looking at me like I am lost. Maybe I am. I thought I knew where I was going, but the more I walk down the path, the more I feel like I do not know where I am.

"What would you have taught me?" I ask, my pulse racing in excitement. This feels like treason—flirting with dangerous knowledge. It is not my first time, but I have never been guided in that direction before.

"I would have taught you to question." Pliny frowns, looking away from me. "There is much we do not know and do not discuss."

"About *Cor*?"

"About *everything*." The magister's eyes snap to me, and I lean back, startled by the fire that burns in them. I have often thought of Pliny as different from Contessa and Varus. That where they are fierce, he is mild and patient. But now I see that his fire is just a different one.

"I told you that the Iron Lords kept secrets from us." He eyes me shrewdly, waiting for me to object.

I do not.

"Our recorded history is less than half a millennium old," he says when the silence has grown dangerous. "A hundred years of bondage and four centuries of the Iron Empire."

"I do not understand," I admit softly, ashamed by my failure. I see in his expression that this haunts him, yet it is all I know. The world as it has been given to me. These facts are foundational to how I understand the world. Water is wet.

"Did you see the great spires of Forum?"

I nod.

"The great towers are older than that, built of materials we do not know. In far corners of the world, men find ruins of great cities that are nothing but dust. There are boneyards full of skeletons that no one knows. We have found the names of heroes long forgotten carved into the walls of these desolate places like prayers. There is much that we do not know. Nor do we know *why* we do not."

A chill runs down my spine at his words. He speaks of a world so vast that I feel small. Meeting Hiro and his granddaughter has thrust my ignorance in my face—Pliny magnifies it until it towers over me, a giant I could never best.

After a moment, the fire in his eyes fades, and he lets out a sigh of disappointment. "Forgive me, Castor," he says softly. "I am but an old man, plagued by ghosts."

I swallow a lump in my throat before nodding. I understand that feeling all too well.

"You said you were given a task?" he asks, plastering a smile on his face that seems earnest and pleasant. No trace of his wild questions lurks in his expression, but I feel their shadow still.

"Hiro said that I need to 'learn how to be.' I have no idea what that means." To my surprise, the magister laughs, leaning back in his chair with an amused smile. "What's so funny about that?"

"He's been reading my scrolls again."

"He can read Imperial?" I remember his blindfold. "He can see?"

"No, he makes his granddaughter read them out loud and translate them for him." Despite her haughty attitude, I feel a pang of sympathy for the dark-haired girl. It cannot be easy being in a foreign land, trapped between two worlds. Being forced to translate stuffy magister philosophical texts sounds like a nightmare.

"Okay, so how do I *be*?" I am relieved that Pliny seems to know what that means. Because the only thing that I feel is *lost*, and I think that means that I am failing even before I begin.

"Castor, when was the last time you did anything for yourself?" Pliny leans back in his chair, suddenly studying me with narrowed eyes.

"I cultivated this morning—"

He interrupts me with a disgusted wave of his hand. "No, not like that." He sighs disappointedly.

I am silent because I do not know how to answer his question.

"I am annoyed," he admits.

"Why?"

"Because Hiro has seen what I did not."

"That I am not *being*?"

"That you are pushing yourself so hard that you do not have the time to learn what you are."

"I am *Frigus Ventus*—"

His laugh is sharp and condescending. It slices through my sentence easier than one of my Iron-reinforced swords cuts through leather.

"No, you're not," he says sadly, leaning forward on his desk to study me. "Cold Wind is one of the masks that you wear. But it is not all that you are. It cannot be, for it is a shallow thing. It only kills. It does not love. It does not create. It does not rest. You cannot hope to reach the heights you are aiming for if you don't know who you are."

"No offense, Magister," I say slowly, fully meaning to offend, "but that sounds insane. I am a weapon. I am here to win the Games and save this *domus*. The matches at Forum are in six months, and I am still *broken*."

"Castor, do you know how a sword is made?"

"Of course," I retort hotly. My education may be lacking, but even I am more than familiar with the forging process. I survived Agogia. "They heat iron until it is pliable and then beat it until it is in the shape they want it to be."

"Do you know what happens to a sword that is beaten too much or isn't allowed to cool properly?" His tone is mild, but his eyes are sharp and pleased. I do not know what he plans, so I am silent, refusing to fall into his trap. "It turns brittle and breaks."

The silence that hangs between us is fragile too.

The two of us stare at each other for a long moment as Unrelenting Fire feasts on my irritation and lets it grow. I am so tired of being told what to do, how to feel. I am an *abominatio*—one of a kind in the entirety of the Iron Empire. There is no one who knows what I am going through, the burdens that I bear.

I have bled for these people. Killed for these people. I have done everything they have asked, but I am not *whole*. The white *rasa* veins on my arms bother me. The Copper ones make me angry. They are signs of my failure and theirs. I stand under *the votum* of the Goddess of Revenge. She leans on me like a gristmill, grinding me between heavy stones. Too many of my brothers have died already. I may be the last who carries this burden. I have no time—no patience to cool off. I have people to kill. What do I care if I am brittle? I can shatter after Atticus and Brutus are dead.

And Brennus. Can't forget Brennus.

"Yes," he muses, as if he can see the indignant fires that rage behind my eyes. "You do need to learn how to be." It takes all my self-control and a little help from the numbness of Ancient Frost to keep me from cursing the old man in his own office.

"Do you have any suggestions?" I manage through gritted teeth.

"Go and explore Anteforum," he commands me after a moment of thought. "I will tell Contessa to let you wander as much as you want. Go and cool off—live a little—before we put you back in the forge."

I can do nothing but obey.

I fume in the crowded city on a bright, warm day.

Anteforum surrounds the capital like a collar, spreading as far as the eye can see. I know that now, because I am at the top of the temple to Dead Jupiter, standing on the viewing platform of the ruined building, marveling at the white marble that stretches from horizon to horizon.

The temple is a performative place. The gods may be real. They may or may not be dead. But they are not here. The priests who tend to it wear black togas that are torn to signify their mourning. I eye them distrustfully, looking for a hint of corrupted veins running through their arms, but I see no sign of a *necromanta* lurking among their number. If there are more like Tenebrus, the Pontifex, they are not here.

The building itself has been allowed to fall into ruins, to remind us that its occupant is dead. But if you look closely, you can see the plaster they use to reinforce the edges of the holes in the walls so they do not grow larger. The broken pillars were made that way. The ruin is artistic rather than true. It strikes me as odd that we still worship gods that we killed. Not just because they are dead, but because we killed them.

I will not worship Atticus when he lies in the dirt. I will dance on his grave.

There are no revelations waiting for me in Jupiter's empty home, so I wander the streets until I find a market. My escort, a pair of Varus's Ironbound guards, follow me at a respectful distance. I am trusted to explore, but I cannot go alone. After all, according to the rolls of the Census, I am a criminal.

I wander my way through the crowded stalls, marveling at how different-yet-similar it feels to the market of Segesta, only an order of magnitude larger. There are more people buying and selling here than live in my entire town.

Yet, the cadence is the same. People crowd around merchants who sell fresh food, inspecting their wares with keen eyes. I ignore them; I have no need for it. The *Domus* Pelias mess hall feeds me better than I deserve.

Instead, I sift through the people, wondering what it must be like to grow up in this stone jungle. I see almost no *electi* wandering around. People look at me strangely when they notice my *Cor* veins as well as the guards that follow me. I look like some palatine lord coming to slum with the patricians and plebeians, although anyone with eyes to see would notice that my face does not have the angular edges of higher breeding.

I see more strains of people than I have ever seen before, which whispers to me a truth I have already begun to accept—that Segesta was a place removed from the rest of the world. I feel something inside me crumble, like one of the pillars in Jupiter's temple giving way. *Terra* is different than I know—it is bigger, and I am very small.

Perhaps that is what it means to *be*.

I sweep through the market with my *animus*, curious as to what it will tell me. Iron whispers the knowledge of a thousand things from pots and pans to buttons. A non-descript man wanders past me, carrying four knives. I give him a frank look, and he turns away, looking for an easier mark.

Ancient Frost finds little that it is congruent with, although there is a patch of ice that some butcher three rows over uses to keep his meats cool before he sells them. I sense a passive sort of will reinforcing it, some sort of simple relic aiding him.

Unrelenting Fire is stuck to me, and although it is not alive, it almost feels petulant, like a child not being allowed to go and play with its older siblings. I shove my Copper *Cor*'s Symbol to the back of my mind by embracing my Winter one, trying to ignore its distraction.

"*Dominus*, here!" a man's voice shouts at me. I turn in surprise. No one has called me *Dominus* in almost a year. But as I look, it ignites a firestorm in the merchants around me.

"*Dominus*, I have the softest carpets in all of the Iron Empire!" a woman calls, seeing that I am approachable. "Imported from the wilds beyond reach. You will not believe how plush they are."

"*Dominus*, my leather is the finest in the city!"

"*Dominus*, taste my carrots! Are they not sweet enough to be a dessert?"

The aisle descends into pandemonium, and I lead my guards out, ducking as if they are pelting me with stones and not words. I have fought in the sands of Bellona's Arena, under the eyes of thirty thousand souls, but I find this attention overwhelming.

"Well, that was bracing," I comment dryly to Atrius, the closer of the two guards. The Ironbound is in his late thirties, and I like him even if he was in the Third Legion during his service.

"Try not to make eye contact," he offers, a fairly amused look lurking beneath the professionally blank expression on his face.

"I'll do my best," I promise, turning down another row. Despite my irritation with the vague assignment before me, I am enjoying being back in the mix of society. I have been removed from the normal day-to-day life of a citizen of the Empire since they dragged me to Agogia. There is something cathartic about moving around a crowd of people under the light of *Sol*. It is far different than wandering through the icy waste of the North. I feel like I am part of a body again, after being lost.

"Fresh flour, *Dominus*!" a woman's voice calls as I walk past her stall. "I sell only the finest grains in the Empire!" I pause mid-step, surprised by her words. Something inside me shakes as I turn to face her. A dark-skinned woman, she smiles at me warmly when she sees that she has my attention. She gestures at a row of baskets before her, piled high with various finely ground flours.

"Barley. Rye. Millet. Wheat." My head tilts as I study her wares. I feel like I am outside of my own body, looking, seeing a life that I never got to live. Somewhere far away in a different time and a different place, two boys talked about opening a bakery. A journey of a thousand steps and a lot of blood stands between me and that dream now. But it reminds me of a tall, annoying plebeian who was a better friend than I deserved.

"Where is your wheat from?" I ask, struggling to not let my voice crack with sadness.

"Segesta, *Dominus*, they grow the best in the Empire."

I nod in acceptance of that fact, even though it means I will end up paying more for it. "Give me ten pounds," I say, fishing a *denarius* from my pocket and extending it toward her.

Pliny gave me an allowance to learn how to *be*. I think he expected me to use it on wilder delights, but this is what I want. This is what I need. I feel a faint sense of amusement leaking from my guards, but I ignore them.

My hands shake as I accept the sack of flour from the vendor and cradle it to my chest like a child. I breathe deeply. It smells nothing like bread—yet. But it smells a little like home. I shed some of the pain I carry around me like a snake losing its skin, closing my eyes for a moment in the crowded market to enjoy it. When they open, I turn to my minders with an embarrassed grin.

"I'm ready to go back."

My first stop back at the estate are the kitchens.

"You want to what?" The matron of the Pelias mess hall asks for the third time, still in disbelief. She is a short, squat woman named Palina, who looks like she could stand in a shieldwall without hesitation. I like her. I wish that Unus was still alive so that I could introduce them. Somehow, I know that the one-eyed zealot would love her.

Still holding my bag of flour, I invade the kitchen, a space I have never bothered to explore. It stretches the length of the mess hall. Massive ovens burn, pouring their sweltering heat out into the room. If my Unrelenting Fire *Cor* was Silver, I'm sure I would feel a sea of *ignis* relics set in them. A dozen cooks rush around, preparing for tonight's meal.

"I'd like to bake some bread," I repeat, a broad smile on my face. It is a strange feeling. It twists and stretches my face in a way that it has not done in a long time. It feels nice to wear it when I am not about to kill someone.

Is this learning to be? I think with amused irritation at the two old men who have sent me to toil at what feels like a task with no end. *Am I existing enough yet*?

"We have bread out there." Palina gestures over my shoulder with a long ladle that she wields like it is a *gladius*. She seems to think that I have a problem with her cooking. Nothing could be further from the truth. I have no desire to be this woman's enemy. She might be my favorite person in the whole compound.

"I know." I chuckle softly, trying to defuse the situation. "I *love* your bread. It's not about that. I just want to… make something."

Her brows furrow as she stares up at me in confusion. "Why?"

"I… don't know," I admit after a long moment. "I'm looking for something."

"The bread is out there—"

"I'm not looking for bread."

"You need to make bread to find something that isn't bread?" She stares at me like I am an idiot.

"That is exactly it," I admit with a chagrined smile. I feel mad. Like the whole world has gone insane and they have taken me with them. But I am holding a bag of wheat from Segesta, and I am going to bake bread in memory of my friend.

"The *lanista* insists that I be allowed," I tell her when she still doesn't look convinced. "Just put me somewhere out of the way, and I promise you won't even know I'm here."

Palina begrudgingly gives me a small space right next to the sweltering ovens. It is the hottest part of the kitchen. I have no doubt that is on purpose, but I cannot fault her for it. If I were the chef in charge of feeding this compound, I'd be annoyed at some gladiator coming in trying to bake his own bread too. Fortunately, the Symbol of Unrelenting Fire welcomes the heat, and I do not even notice it after a dozen heartbeats.

I drop my bag of flour onto a table that runs through the middle of the room, grabbing a clay bowl so I can mix my ingredients together. A smile grows on my face as I clap my hands together. I am excited to start. There is, however, just one problem.

I don't know how to make bread.

I mean, I know how to make bread. You mix the flour, water, and yeast together and let it rise. I'm pretty sure you're supposed to add salt too. But how much of each do I use? And where was I going to find some yeast? With a sigh, I look back at the distant form of Palina, marshalling her troops. She is going to hate me.

After much finagling, I convince her to loan me one of her assistants, a young, pimple-faced girl named Callia. At first, my new teacher is too shy to speak to me, but as I begin to do more things wrong, she becomes more irritated.

"No!" she shrieks, shoving me aside with her small, wiry frame. "You have to mix it more before you add more flour; otherwise, you won't know how dry it is!" she demonstrates, sticking her hand into the bulging white mass and twisting it efficiently in her grip. An image of my tall, lanky friend bent over the bowl flickers in my head and makes me smile.

"Of course." I nod along with her instruction. After a moment, she reluctantly lets me take back over, and I twist the dough easily, marveling at its strange feel between my fingers. Felix promised to hire me at his bakery, but I have never actually *baked* before. It is a strange process. Who first came up with the idea of grinding up a plant, then wetting its powder, and putting the paste in fire? A madman, surely.

"That's enough!" Callia shrieks, frustrated once more.

"Okay," I respond quickly, pulling my hands free, showing her that I am listening and will not mix it any further. "Now what?"

"Now you let it rise."

"How long does that take?"

"Until it's big enough."

"Naturally." I nod as if that answer was at all useful. "Then what?"

"Then you bake it."

"For how long?"

"Until it's done."

"You have been a big help," I say with a smile. It's even true. How little about life I truly know.

"Fortuna's Luck with that. *Domina* said I'm to get back to work when it starts rising," the girl says, slipping away without a backward glance. In the distance, Palina glares at us, her hands on her hips. I smile and wave, embarrassed at the disruption my baking experiment has caused.

Left to my own devices, I sit next to my bowl of dough, waiting for nature to run its course. Out of curiosity for a life that never happened, I probe at it with all three of my Symbols, even lightly brushing my fingers along it so that Unrelenting Fire can get a taste.

None of them sense anything of interest. The dough is neither hot nor cold. Ancient Frost could turn the water in its mixture to ice, but it is so thoroughly a part of the *dough* now that the congruency would be quite uncomfortable. Felix had hoped to bind a Wheat Symbol after the *Sententia*. I wonder what that could tell him about the round lump that sits in front of me, *growing*.

It is an agonizing process to wait. Most bakers set it aside for a few hours to let it do its work in peace. A watched pot never boils, and a watched dough never rises. But this is my first attempt, and it feels almost like a healing ritual. To abandon it would be like falling asleep on watch. Some cook might find it and bake it for me or throw it away. I am a mother hen, determined to sit with my large egg until it is ready.

For the first time in quite a while, I am alone with my thoughts. They are more peaceful than I expected. When I was in Dorian's prison, I was alone in a rocky cell, but my thoughts tormented me. They were only of the dead and dying, of failure and blood.

The Pelias kitchen is also made of stone, but it is bright and warm, and the sound of cooks going about their work chases away the maudlin thoughts. I do not think of Atticus and Brennus, or of Ascending.

I think of days spent chasing Agre, our faithful stonehound, through my father's fields. I think of Gnaeus, the old servant who raised me like a grandfather, smuggling me sweets before dinner. For once, Unrelenting Fire is calm, not raging with the anger of loss, but instead, it relaxes in the warmth of pleasant memories. My eyes shine with unspent tears, but I am not sad. Nor am I furious that these moments are gone—I am simply glad to have had them.

"*Dominus*? You can put that into the oven." Callia's voice breaks through my daydreams with hesitation. I start, turning to stare at the girl in surprise.

"What?"

"Your dough—it is risen." I lift the cloth that I placed over the bowl and inspect my round lump suspiciously. Sure enough, it has more than doubled in size. It still looks nothing like bread, but that's what this next part is supposed to be for.

I carve out a small lump of dough and place it on an iron tray that Callia provides me. I roll it a few times in my hand, trying to make it perfect. Eventually, I give up, forced to settle with *good enough*. Carrying my precious cargo, I make my way over to one of the ovens, bending over to slide it in on the grating that sits inside.

Pleased with myself, I lean back, watching my little egg with intense focus. Yet again I wish that I had Ascended with Unrelenting Fire. As a Silver, I would be able to sense and guide the flames that bake it, ensuring that they were even.

Unfortunately, the only way for me to do that now would be to stick my hand into the oven, and I suspect that would only serve to make the cooks even more nervous. No, as much as I want to use my will to meddle with the baking process, I am better off letting this first one run its course.

Although, I muse, eyeing the size of the massive oven before me. *I wonder if I could climb in there and cultivate a better source of Fire essence.* I shake my head, trying to dislodge that stray thought. This is not the time for my dogged obsessions. I am here to bake bread.

My loaf is in the oven for what feels like forever. It is like I am a child on *Adventus* morning again. But at last, the loaf looks done to my eyes. It is gold and crispy on the outside. My mouth waters in anticipation, and I can wait no longer.

I pull the loaf out with my bare hands, trusting the cooks to assume that my Silver body protects me from the heat. I plan on using Ancient Frost to cool it to human-appropriate temperatures. But after a moment of thought, I pause before switching to Unrelenting Fire and using it to draw the heat out. It is easier to use a Symbol that is more congruent to lead the warmth than to drown it with its opposite.

Interesting.

For a moment, my peaceful moment is almost ruined by my mind's desire to experiment with what I have just learned. *Later,* I promise the beast that lurks in the back of my mind, greedy for any knowledge it might be able to use. *Bread first.*

I grab a serrated knife from a block of wood without looking, guided by my Iron senses. Tenderly, I carve into the bread, marveling at how the crust flakes under the pressure. My smile fades slightly as I carve through the meat of the loaf. The bread seems too moist.

Maybe that is only because it is fresh. I cut a few more slices, feeling a hint of chagrin growing as I study them. Something is definitely wrong. I hesitate before picking up one of them, allowing the delightful sense of heat to run along my fingers. I am glad that Callia is back at work—I would hate to have her witness this.

Across the way, Hiro's granddaughter enters the room, dressed in another set of shiny black and silver clothing. Palina intercepts her, carrying a tray of food for the girl. I ignore them, turning my attention back to what I have made.

Closing my eyes, my mind flashes with a vision of a world that will never be. I stand behind the counter of a bakery owned by Felix, proudly presenting the fruit of our joint labor. Valentina is there to buy it, just like she promised in the depths of the arena. Marcus stands with her, dressed in the purple of a Praetorian. It is the dream of a child, but it is a good dream, and I let myself enjoy it for a moment before pulling myself free.

Opening my mouth, I take a bite. It's chewy and a little wet. The salt tastes like it is not distributed evenly. One moment, I get a burst of it, then it is gone, like it never existed. But it is edible—it is bread, technically.

I'm going to have to get better at this. I can almost hear Felix's laughter at my attempt.

I open my eyes and twitch in surprise to find Hiro's granddaughter standing before me, a strange expression on her face. In her left hand, she carries the tray with two large bowls that are full of steaming hot broth. In her right, she holds a slice of my undercooked loaf.

"Bread?" she asks, eyeing my creation with a skeptical air.

"Bread." Despite my failure, I feel a hint of a smile growing on my face. Slowly, she takes a bite, face unreadable as she chews. When she swallows, she gives me a pitying glance.

"It is not very good."

"I'll get better." I laugh. "It's what I do."

CHAPTER 42

My world is consumed by dough. Barred from pursuing most of my normal activities, I throw myself into the science of baking with a relish. Contessa only allows me to perform a light workout every morning to maintain my fighting trim. Pliny, likewise, watches me to ensure I only cultivate enough essence to refill my Ancient Frost *Cor* before banishing me from the *loci* for the day.

Rather than rage against the bars that prevent me from my path to Ascension, I spend my time scouring the markets around Anteforum, looking for new wheat to try. I learn to bake dark rye, to nurture the strange living mess that becomes sourdough. I experiment with grains that have gone through different levels of grinding, resulting in finer or coarser flour.

I do not gain a new attunement to the Symbol of Bread, but I do begin to develop an affinity for the work that is all me. The cooks no longer grumble about my presence, accepting me as a part of their landscape.

With each day, I feel a little closer to my missing friend. A little bit of the guilt I carry for losing him in the snow of the North melts from my shoulders. There is no Thanatos to bring his soul to Hades, no everflame burning at his grave to guide him home. But maybe my newfound appreciation for bread will be enough of a beacon.

Despite the centering I find in this exercise, I know that it will not last forever. My path is not one of peace and tranquility. I may be allowed to visit them from time to time, but I can never stay there. I bring destruction and ruin in my wake. I am in the gaze of the Goddess of Vengeance, and even in death, she follows behind me with whips, driving me forward.

My two Ironbound shadows follow me through the market as I head toward my favorite vendor, Vanta, the woman who first sold me Segestan wheat. I smile at the men and women who call at me as I pass, hawking their wares.

They are used to my presence and know that I will sometimes purchase things that few of my status are interested in. How often does an *electus* come to their market and buy *flour*? They must think I am mad, but my *denarii* are real, so they are happy to indulge me.

In my head, I mull over an idea for a new dough recipe, mixing two different types of flour to achieve something new. I am not quite sure what exactly, but my instincts tell me it will have a different texture, and I am curious to try it.

To my surprise, Vanta is nowhere to be seen. Her stall lies empty, closed for business despite it being early in the day. Peering inside the little shack, I can see several baskets of flour waiting to be shown to buyers. I cannot imagine why she would not be here when the crowds are the thickest.

The danger comes so quickly that I do not notice its approach. I am here as a baker and not constantly sweeping for enemies with my *animus* as I move. Even if I was, I'm not sure I would have been fast enough to save the guards from the sudden burst of violence that erupts in the middle of the market.

A woman wrapped in a heavy cloak and carrying a child passes behind Atrius. As she does, she twists sharply, pulling a shortsword from the bundle of swaddling cloth at her chest and driving it into the back of the Ironbound's neck with uncanny precision.

"'Ware!" I bark to Shotus, the second man, falling back on my legion training in a heartbeat. My *animus* explodes out around me as I embrace my Silver Symbols, focusing on Iron as I sweep for more attackers. My stomach drops as I feel five weapons in the crowd around us, all concealed under disguises like the first *sicarus* wore.

Shotus draws his blade and moves forward to challenge the woman who murdered his partner. She wisely retreats, having no interest in letting the Ironbound touch her sword. I carry no swords with me, but thanks to Aquilo, I am never without teeth.

My hands snap to the side, each curled in preparation to hold the hilts of a *Glacialis Falx*. Ancient Frost essence flows through me as I use my ability to manifest essence into physical form. The power courses through my *Cor* veins and *slams* against a hard, unyielding wall at the surface of my palms, stopping it in its tracks. Something blocks my Winter Symbol with incredible force. I can still feel it simmering coldly within me, but I cannot extend it beyond myself.

I freeze in stupefied terror as my blades refuse to form. I do not know what to do. I am outnumbered and unarmed, far from the safety of *Domus* Pelias's estate. My Iron Symbol warns me as someone rushes me from behind, armed with a similar blade. I hear his feet crunch on the stones. He moves with purpose—to kill me.

I twist without looking, dropping my right hand on his wrist. My fingers dig into his flesh as I twist, snapping the weapon out of his grip. It clatters to the cobblestone at our feet, out of both of our reaches.

I stagger in pain as he drives his left fist into my kidneys from behind in a cruel punch. I let go of his wrist, deliberately stomping backward with my boots to tread on his sandaled feet. He lets out a scream of pain, and I feel something *crunch* under my heel. I turn to my left, driving my fist into his ribs with all the power my *Cor*-infused body can muster. I use Iron to reinforce my finger bones, keeping them from shattering under the force. It still stings when my hand bounces off his bones, but the anger burning in me eats the hurt gladly.

The *sicarus* staggers back, reeling from the force of my strike. Under his sleeve, I catch the telltale glint of Silver veins running through his dusky skin. Whoever he is, he is an *electus* of the same caliber as me. Well, almost the same caliber.

There are no *argentum* like me.

I take advantage of his momentary reset to press myself forward, staying inside his guard. My fists flash as I pummel his body, unleashing the full extent of my strength. There are more rushing to his aid. I cannot afford to take my time finishing this would-be assassin off.

My anger burns like a living inferno, and to my surprise, the Symbol of Unrelenting Fire leaps into my empty mind easily, like a child eager to take its turn. It is not bound like Ancient Frost, only limited by its tier. I cannot use it against anything I cannot reach.

My assailant is well-trained. He weathers my storm of blows, finding the space in my tempo to try to break free and take control of our dance. His hand catches my left wrist, squeezing it with the same Silver strength that I use against him.

Instinct takes over, and I slap him in the face, closing my fingers down to hold on to his head so he cannot break contact. As we touch, I release Unrelenting Fire like a rabid hound, and it hunts. I cannot manifest fire the same way that I can ice. Conjuring a physical element out of thin air is a rare and special ability. However, flame is not truly a solid. I cannot use it to make a sword and stab someone. It exists only as *vis*—energy—and essence has plenty of *vis.* Heat erupts from my hand, powered by my reserves, driven by my will.

I cannot tell what type of Symbol this *electus* is bound to, but I am certain it is not in the *ignis domus.* I can feel his will faintly scrabbling against mine as I shove the fire into him, but his lack of congruency renders him impotent. He lets go of my wrist, clawing at my hand wrapped around his face. But it is already too late.

The assassin's scream is truly horrible. Steam erupts from his mouth as an unstoppable, unquenchable fire devours him from the inside out. The fight around us grinds to a halt as he collapses to his knees, already dead. His eyes are gone, consumed by the fire that rages within him. I turn my back on him to face the other *sicarii,* grateful that I don't have to keep looking at the horror I have created.

Ancient Frost's calming effect is reduced while Unrelenting Fire is my foremost Symbol. Its heat makes me less congruent to my own Symbol. Instead, I rely on Iron, which is not as cold, but it is hard.

The woman who killed Atrius lies next to him, dispatched by Shotus. The lone legionnaire is surrounded by three more killers, but he has been holding them at bay with his *scutum*, doing the Iron Legions proud. All four of them are frozen now, staring at me in horror. The assassins are wrapped in loose clothing, their faces obscured by hoods and veils. Any innocent bystanders have all fled, wisely wanting no part of a contest between *electi*.

A couple of puzzle pieces click together at the same moment. This is a trap meant to kill me specifically, and if I was only bound to Ancient Frost, I would already be dead. Whatever relic or power that is making it possible for them to block me from using my Symbol is absolute in its power. It reminds me of Aquilo's will crushing me in the white abyss where his throne sits.

I stare at the three attackers, bending down to pick up the dead assassin's fallen shortsword without looking. I roll my neck to release some of the tension in it as I straighten up, no longer thinking about bread.

"Now, then," I say into the suddenly quiet market. "I think you three are looking for me?"

None of them respond, but one of them turns toward me, leaving the other two to keep Shotus contained. My smile grows as I step to meet him, swinging my stolen blade a few times to get a feel for its balance. I would do anything for a *gladius*, but it is Iron, and that will suffice.

"Just one?" I laugh condescendingly at the wrapped attacker. "Brave of you." The attacker does not respond, but a tremor of worry runs down my spine as he tosses his sword to the side, like a worthless trinket. I cannot see the *Cor* veins under his clothes, but he moves with a confidence and power that tells me he has Ascended at least once.

A leather pouch hangs from his belt that his left hand moves to adjust, almost a habitual motion. My eyes narrow in suspicion. I'm guessing that holds the relic that blocks me from using Ancient Frost.

"So that's how you're doing it," I say conversationally, taunting him. He shrugs slightly, unperturbed. He thinks I am already dead. But his charred compatriot behind me should be a warning that I still have some teeth. Tired of waiting, I step forward, giving my sword a little twirl as I try to close with the big man.

I stop cold as he draws a long, white dagger from behind his back, holding it easily in a reverse grip. *Tellus*. My heart skips a beat as I stare at the Symbolless ceramic, finally understanding what is at play. I have seen this *krakenus*-branded knife twice before.

Once when it was used to threaten me and my friends in Agogia and again when it was used to kill Macer. It belongs to Brennus Valerus, nephew of the Empress.

I am discovered. My old rival has come to finish me off. But then again, only my access to Ancient Frost has been restricted. If Brennus truly knew who I was, they would have tried to seal me away from Iron too.

I am the rising star of *Domus* Pelias, a chance for the family to escape the trap that has been built for them. I killed one of *Domus* Valerus's favorite gladiators. I embarrassed Brennus in the basement of the arena. Any of those moments make me a prime target for assassination. Especially pricking that idiot's pride. *Stupid*, I curse myself, *for coming to buy wheat without your sword.*

I was a fool for letting myself be distracted by *bread*. It did not fix my life or undo the *votum* that I labor under, but for a little while, I finally felt light again.

But now Brennus and his killers seek to take this peace from me. A grim chuckle escapes from my lips as I eye the *tellus* blade warily. I find it amusing that I have managed to make Brennus hate me enough to try to kill me as *two different people.*

The assassin hesitates no longer, leaping forward, slashing at me with his weapon that is blank to my senses. I still have my eyes, but I feel blind as I catch his weapon with my shortsword, reinforcing the iron as the *tellus* tries to carve it like butter. The ceramic is impossibly strong and sharp. No wonder the Censors guard it so jealously.

A strange numbing sensation flows down my arm, like I have touched some sort of endless void. I try to shove my *animus* through my blade into his, but there is nothing there. All elements share at least the congruency of existing, but his knife is foreign even to that.

My one advantage is that my weapon is longer than his, which means I can keep him at a distance. I know little about knife fighting. From what I have seen, it is more like a fistfight with sharp edges than it is like a proper duel. I have no interest in being educated by this assassin, who clearly knows his business.

We exchange another series of blows at lightning speed. He is at least a Silver *electus*. It takes all my focus to keep up with him. I do not have the time to even consider a counterattack. My Iron Symbol pulses in bruised pain from the numb pressure of the foreign ceramic. If not for the teachings of Durus, of Gaius, and Contessa, I would die in our opening exchange.

Instead, I only bleed. The assassin feints right before dropping his knife underneath my sword and stepping forward to cut at me as he flies past. I understand his move a couple steps too late, but early enough to keep him from burying the *tellus* blade up to its hilt in my chest.

Instead, it scores a long line of fire across my ribs. Even Ancient Frost's chill cannot keep me from screaming in pain as my blood splatters on the stones. I turn, placing my left hand on the wound to check how bad it is, as I continue to drive at him with the sword in my right. He dances out of my range, clearly not willing to let me get my hands on him after what I did to his charred compatriot.

I snarl in rage. I am outclassed by this warrior in every way. He is stronger and faster, even if he does not seem to be actively using his Symbol against me. But more than that—he is better than I am.

My attunements give me incredible power, but without them, I am revealed as a pretender. In the North, I could feel the footsteps of my enemies on the ice, betraying their intentions as they shifted the weight on the balls of their feet. Against anyone carrying an iron blade, it is child's play for me to follow their movements, to read their plans in the angles of their weapon.

But these advantages are crutches. Without them, I am lame, unable to keep up with a real fighter. Contessa is right that I need to become more than this. How am I ever going to kill Atticus if I can't fight on my own?

Heavy certainty begins to build in my chest as I stare at my opponent. I am going to die here. Shotus still battles the other two behind me, but they keep him contained—unable to come to my aid. At the end every man must stand alone. I do so now.

The *sicarus* circles me, confident now that I am bleeding. My demise is a certainty that we both understand—the inevitable end of this encounter. All that is left is to finish the rest of the dance before the song is done. I square my shoulders, thinking of the brave men I have watched go to their end. Marcus showed no fear when he stood against Astrid. I will follow his example, one last time.

"Well?" I ask, extending my blade toward my enemy, meeting his dark-eyed gaze with a ghost of a smile. "I believe it is your move." He shrugs, willing to accept the invitation. There is no fear in him. He closes the distance between us in two long strides, *tellus* knife moving to knock my shortsword to the side.

I steal his move from earlier, dropping the point of my weapon so that his weapon passes over it. I have just enough time to see his eyes widen in surprise before I explode forward, trying to drive my sword into his guts. He leans into his superior speed—he *must* be at the peak of Silver—twisting away from my attack.

I realize my error as he moves closer, getting inside my guard, fists flashing as he drives a powerful punch into the wound on my ribs. I choke down a scream, barely managing to block a stab from his knife that would have opened another hole in my chest.

We exchange a series of frantic blows. It is more like a back-alley brawl than a true fight. Another line of fire sears across my arm as I earn another cut. I lose the tempo of the exchange, falling behind. It is all I can do to survive. Soon, I will not be able to do that.

In a lucky twist of the fight, I manage to grab his wrist with my left hand and unleash Unrelenting Fire. The ravenous essence pours out of me, eager to devour more flesh. But instead of burning into the man like it did with his ally, I let out a gasp as my *animus* slams into a stone wall of will. Whatever his Symbol is, its congruency is more than enough for his Silver *Cor* to rebuff my Copper one. Desperate to escape, I drive my knee into his groin. He staggers back a couple of steps, and I retreat, panting and bleeding from several wounds.

My eyes flicker from his bloody *tellus* knife to the bag that hangs from his belt as an idea begins to form. It is not a good one. In fact, it might be the worst I have ever had. Which, given that I have made three different *vota* with dead gods, is saying something.

There is only one way that I can defeat this assassin. Ancient Frost's *animus* rages impotently at the barriers that lock it within me. I hammer at it with my will, but no cracks appear. The wall is just as unyielding as it has been.

My Iron is useless. Unrelenting Fire is outclassed, unable to find any purchase through his mental armor. As long as the relic that he carries is active, I am denied the Winter Symbol's aid.

Here we go, I complain to myself as I realize that I have already committed to the plan that I do not think will work. I lunge toward the *sicarus*, not willing to wait until I bleed more of my strength out on the stones at our feet.

He meets me easily, blocking my strike with his knife, forcing it high, and stepping back into dangerous range. I welcome him, throwing a punch at his kidney with my left fist while I try to pull my sword back into the fight.

It is a mistake that leaves my chest open for a quick attack. Ready to finish me off, he takes the opening, ducking and bending his wrist inward as he lunges forward with his knife still held in a reverse grip.

Just like I hoped.

I sidestep, rising up on my tiptoes so that the *tellus* blade bites into my upper right chest, far away from my flesh-and-blood heart. I scream as white-hot fire burns through me. Iron numbs the pain as much as it can, keeping me from fainting from the pain.

The assassin's eyes widen as he tries to pull his blade from me, but I lunge toward him, keeping it buried in me. He staggers backward, trying to create enough space to free his weapon. I slam him into the side of a vendor's stall.

My left hand shoots out, reaching for the pouch that hangs from his belt. His free hand reaches down to protect it, but he is too late, distracted by the knife he cannot get free from my chest. I rip the bag free, leaping back from the man. The *tellus* blade slides out of me and I cry out in agony. Its edge is sharper than anything I have ever felt. It cuts through me like I am paper.

I stagger slightly, lightheaded from the blood I have lost, but not without my prize. The *sicarus* tries to follow me, but I throw my shortsword at him, forcing him to duck. I won't need it anymore. Either this move will result in my salvation, or I will be too weak to fight him any longer.

I thrust my right hand into the pouch and grab the heavy metallic object that rests inside. I rip it free, feeling my desperate smile widen as I spy the dark gray of dead *Cor*. Set on the surface in golden lines is the outline of a jagged crown, the sign of Ancient Frost. It is the same design that appeared on the Censor's relic when they tested my Symbol after Varus bought me.

We told her. I remember Xania's reaction to hearing that I bore an Elder Symbol. *We told her exactly what she needed to block*. Suddenly, I am no longer sure if Brennus did this on his own.

The sound of feet scuffling on the cobblestones pulls me from my study of the relic. With a wrench, I pry the golden outline from the surface. It pops out easily, designed to be replaceable. With a disgusted toss, I throw the pieces to the ground, smiling as the weight of the relic's nullification lifts from me.

Ancient Frost leaps eagerly to my call. It has been with me this whole fight, but I have not touched its essence reserves. They are teeming to the brim, ready to obey my commands. I stagger slightly, as my weakened body struggles to hold me upright. I do not have much time left. Shotus still fights with the other two *sicarii* a dozen paces away. Even if I kill this one, it may not be enough for us to survive. A certain kind of clarity descends upon me as I come close to death.

But the grave is cold and familiar.

It is not truly a Winter Symbol, but it is congruent. I feel its icy fingers reaching for me, and I see the path. It is easy for me to seize all the essence within my *Cor*, every single ounce of it, and wrap it up in my will. If being close to fire makes it harder for me to use Ancient Frost, then dying makes it easier. I am united with Ancient Frost in a way that I have only ever been once before. I *understand* what the

Glacialis Falx can truly do. The Frozen Sword is poorly named, for that is the least of its creations.

I now see why the dead God of Winter named me Cold Wind before the consul did.

I trigger my ability, manifesting my frozen essence into ice. The frozen *gladius* grows out of my hand in an instant. It appears in the space between heartbeats. That familiar wall of resistance forms in my mind, restricting what I can manifest, limiting the *Glacialis Falx* to what Aquilo bestowed upon me.

I am so cold.

The power coursing through me cannot be contained by something so frail. I feel it bulge and crack under the force of my power and will. It resists my command, but I cannot be denied. My sword swells as it absorbs the torrent of essence pouring out of my *Cor*. Then it shatters like crystal, exploding into a thousand pieces that shoot out before me like shrapnel.

Freed of its restricting vessel, Ancient Frost sweeps out of me, flowing across the ground. I expect it to form a thin layer of ice, but I underestimate what my Heart is truly capable of. Winter spreads like wildfire across the market. It covers the ground and sweeps up the sides of vendor stalls. The temperature plummets as if the market were transported into the depths of the North. Nothing within fifty paces escapes my cold touch.

All four of the other fighters freeze, stunned by my power. I laugh in delight, despite the monumental cost of essence. I can feel the footsteps of the other combatants breaking through its crust. It is like I am back in the North with my brothers, hunting Normans.

I think my veins are burning with the effort of using all my Ancient Frost essence at once, but I can't feel them very well. My world is numb; the edges of my vision begin to go black. Only the knowledge granted by my Symbol does not fade. It burns brightly in my mind like *Sol* on a cloudless day.

I am not done. I have enough essence left for one more move. My open hand curls into a fist, and I think of Vixa and her stolen Earth Symbol. Nine spears burst from the ground like rapidly growing stalagmites, growing in the blink of an eye. Three of them stab through each of the *sicarii*, impaling them where they stand.

All of them die instantly, unable to fall to the ground, propped up by my spikes. Shotus lowers his shield and stares at me with wide eyes, panting with exertion. Silence descends on the market, like the deep woods of the North buried in winter. My smile is vicious and cruel. Inside of my body, the last of my Ancient Frost essence is consumed, leaving my reserve barren and empty. I have hit the *crassamentum*—the dregs.

"I'm going to need you to carry me," I tell the Ironbound before the darkness takes me.

CHAPTER 43

I come to on a surgery table. The blessed numbness that held me in its arms is gone, leaving me with only the pain as a companion. I jolt awake, ready to fight.

"*Domina*, please!" a woman's voice cracks against my ears like a whip. "Hold him still!" Strong hands pin me down, and I reach for my Symbols, desperate to get free. Something cold and wet falls out of my right hand as I flail.

"Castor!" Varus's strong voice cuts through my panic like a knife.

I go still, no longer sure where I am. Panting with fear and pain, I take in my surroundings. I am no longer in the sea of vendor stalls of the market, but a white room. Bright light shines out of a series of *lumos* relics, blinding me. Pain sparks from my chest as something pinches at it.

"You're okay, lad," Contessa growls, leaning over me to eclipse the light with her dark, bald head. "You're safe." Tension flows out of me as I realize she is telling the truth. "Now will you stop wriggling so the *medico* can finish stitching up your wounds? Mars's Bleached Bones, I thought I taught you better than this. Look at how they carved you up."

I laugh at the disappointed tone in her voice. Seeing that I am back in control, she releases me, stepping back to reveal a thin woman with Silver veins and white robes, who leans back toward me, holding a needle and thread. My eyes track down to the exposed slash in my chest that is only partially closed.

"If it makes you feel any better, *Domina*, they cheated."

"There's no such thing." She snorts.

I tilt my head in acknowledgment before my gaze naturally tracks away from her to where the master of the house lurks in a corner, watching me with crossed arms. He studies me for a long moment, and for once, I keep my mouth shut, following his lead. Pliny stands with him, expression troubled.

The needle burns as it pulls on my wound. Instinctively, I reach for Ancient Frost to numb the pain but stop when I see how critically low my essence reserves are. A shudder runs through my body as I remember the *crassamentum*—the dregs. I have no desire to experience that again.

That was what the cold, wet thing in my hand was for. A literal lump of ice, likely pulled straight from the Winter *locus* to give my desperate, hungry *Cor* something to cultivate from other than me while I was unconscious. Tentatively, I send my *animus* searching and find it on the floor, leaking precious essence. Eagerly, I start pulling from it, but it only makes me hungrier.

The room is silent and tense as the woman goes about her work. Varus's eyes are dark and brooding. He shifts slightly, and I notice that he is carrying a dark gray lump of metal. The relic that Brennus's assassins brought to nullify my Symbol. I suspect he already knows much of what I am going to tell him from Shotus.

"He'll live, *Dominus*," the woman says when she finishes her stitching work. "I've already willed his wounds to seal, but he'll need another session in a few hours to make sure it holds."

"Thank you, Patricia," Varus murmurs from where he stands. "Will you give us a moment with him, alone?"

"Of course, *Dominus*." She gathers up her supplies and makes her way out of the room at a hurried pace. She wants no part of the conversation that is to come. A wise woman, that *medico*.

"Tell me." The senator is not a man who wastes time.

"*Sicarii*," I growl. "There were five of them. They were waiting for me on my regular route. They knew I would have two Ironbound with me and what I can do."

"Do you know what this is?" he asks, lifting the relic up to show it to me.

I start to raise my right hand to wiggle it in a so-so gesture but stop when the motion tugs at the stitches in my ribs and chest.

"I figured it out," I reply grimly. "I was blocked from using my Symbol externally. It had pieces of gold set into it, making the crest of Ancient Frost. I ripped that out, and I could use my power again."

"It is called an *interdictor*, and it is quite… rare," Pliny volunteers from beside Varus. "It is a far more powerful version of the *inhibitus* that they use on legionnaires. It requires several different Golden relics to make it."

"So only someone with tremendous wealth or access to it would be able to get one?" I laugh. "I think *Domus* Valerus has plenty of both."

"That is a dangerous accusation." Varus's voice grows sharp but unsurprised.

"The leader of the assassins carried a *tellus* blade marked with a *krakenus*. I killed *Impostor* and embarrassed Brennus. Xania was there when the consul told everyone exactly what my Symbol was. How could it be anyone *but* them?"

"You're sure it was the *krakenus* on the blade?" Varus asks, taking a step toward me.

Wordlessly, I gesture at the wound in my chest that has only been stitched closed for a matter of minutes. "I got a good look at it. I'm sure it's around here somewhere."

Varus's gaze follows my hand, and his lips compress into a firm line. Varus looks to Contessa for confirmation. She produces the *tellus* blade from behind her back. He rolls it in his hand, brows furrowing as he studies it. I think he expected it to be a fake, but it is not.

"When did you embarrass Brennus?" Contessa's voice is rich with suspicion. I resist the urge to wince, realizing that was a story that they hadn't known about. Only Laertes and his men had been with me.

"He tried to start something under the arena." I shrug offhandedly. "I made him reconsider." The *lanista*'s eyes narrow, but she says nothing.

"It is sooner than I thought," Varus murmurs at last.

"*Dominus*?" I ask in surprise. "Were we not attacked by assassins on the way to Antioch?"

"Bah, that does not count," Pliny grunts, waving his hand dismissively.

"Why does it not count?"

"The Shadowbound were sent by Diana herself. Besides, it was in the country, away from Forum. There are different expectations outside of the capital." Pliny shrugs as if that explanation is obvious.

I resist the urge to roll my eyes. Only the palatine could have different rules for murder depending on the city.

"We assumed that the plan was to wait until the *ludus* placed last in the Games, and I lost my Senate seat." Varus reminds me of the plot that he shared with me in Antioch. "But it seems that your performance has made them reconsider."

"Or maybe, Brennus is just that brittle," I offer, using a legion insult for the Praetorian. To the Ironbound, there is little worse you can be.

"He was not there when Briannus revealed your specific Symbol," Varus points out, rubbing his chin in thought. "But that does not mean his mother did not tell him."

"When do we strike back?" I ask, trying to sit up in my bed despite the pain. "Next time, I will—"

"Strike back?" Varus's expression is incredulous. "The attempted murder of a vassal of a senator is not tolerated. We do not need to retaliate. I am going to file a complaint."

I am incredulous at his response. It all seems so simple and organized.

"There is more," Pliny insists, glancing at his master before continuing. "Shotus says that you froze the entire section of the market with a single manifestation." The three Gold *electi* look at me with blank faces.

"Is this true?" Varus asks softly.

I swallow, trying to buy time to decide what the safest answer is. It felt so natural in the moment, that close to death. But now that I am warm and awake, I know how preposterous it was. But there were witnesses. I can do nothing but own up to my power.

"Yes," I say after finding no way to lie.

"*Frigus Ventus,* indeed," the senator murmurs.

"How is that even possible for him to manifest that much?" Contessa demands, looking to Pliny for answers.

"It should not be. But it means that he is close to Ascending," the short magister replies with a shrug. "Time slips away from us." It takes all my self-control not to squirm under the scrutiny of all three of their intense gazes.

"I didn't want to die," I mumble lamely.

"I have seen men and women perform feats of strength that defy all logic when faced by the end of their road," the *lanista* says slowly, as if she did not really believe what she was saying. "Surely it is possible for an *electus* to do the same?"

I cannot explain what the gods and their servants have done to me. I cannot make it make sense. I can only survive and use it to get the revenge that I have promised. But one thing is for sure: time is running out. I need to Ascend my Unrelenting Fire *Cor* to Silver before it is too late.

They leave me shortly afterward, with strict instructions not to get out of bed until the *medico* gives me permission. I last about fifteen minutes before I cannot bear it anymore. The small chunk of ice has melted.

My empty *Cor* claws at me, and I am convinced that I will get no rest until it is sated. Groaning in pain, I manage to roll off the side of the infirmary bed and onto my feet. I'm still wearing my blood-stained trousers, but there is no sign of my tunic. They must have cut it off me while I was unconscious.

With a sigh of acceptance, I shuffle out of the door, heading toward the training hall. Just a little essence, I promise myself, and then straight back to bed.

Servants eye me warily as I make my way through the compound. Every step sends fire lancing through the half-dozen cuts that have only just finished being sewn together. Even my Symbols cannot completely numb the pain.

Before I have made it halfway to the *loci*, I start to lose my nerve. *There is still time to turn back*. But then Ancient Frost pangs with a deeper pain, and I grit my teeth. The only path to any bit of peace is forward.

"Castor! What are you doing out of bed?"

I turn slowly to face Alessandra, trying to avoid triggering a new wave of pain cascading down my body. Her eyes go wide in horror as she surveys the stitches that cover the front of my chest.

The heir of *Domus* Pelias is dressed in a set of the house's fighting leathers, complete with the broken trident branded on the front. Her dark hair is pulled back into a horsetail, and she glistens like she has just finished a training session.

"Uh, I need to—"

"Does Patricia know that you are *walking*?" She makes it sound like that is some great crime. *Does Patricia know that you are **murdering**?*

"Yes?" I lie unconvincingly. Her gaze travels down from my face to take in my shirtless chest and fresh wounds. For a moment, it feels like she isn't focused on the wounds, but then her eyes snap back up to me and I wince at the heat in her glare.

"You need to get right back in that infirmary before Patricia or Contessa catches you," she hisses, recovering from her shock. "I'm not sure if I should beat you or help you walk."

"I have the dregs," I explain, making her wince with a new type of sympathy. "Need to get to the Winter *locus* before I go insane. Then I'll lie down, I promise." She hesitates, biting her lips as she studies me.

"Come on," she relents with an irritated sigh. "Lean on me. If you tear your stitches, there will be Hades to pay."

I hesitate, but she insists, coming in under my left arm so that it drapes over her shoulder and wrapping her right around my waist. Her touch sends tingles through me where her fingers move across my bare skin that has nothing to do with my wounds. My pulse quickens, which only makes them throb harder.

"Let's hurry," I grunt. "This is not the most comfortable I have ever been."

"My heart breaks for you," she murmurs with a straight face. I cannot tell if she is serious or not.

If I thought that I was getting strange looks before, wandering the compound shirtless and wounded, now people openly stare at the sight of us walking together. Never when Alessandra is looking, but when her head turns, they watch with wide eyes as the beautiful heir of the house walks me toward the training halls. I am painfully aware of her hand, which grips my hip, running low to avoid a line of stitches.

Hot embarrassment begins to creep up the back of my neck, and I realize with horror that it is spreading across my entire body. By the time we arrive, I am out of breath and blushing. I have become a spectacle in more ways than one, and it is mortifying. *So much for the Cold Wind.*

The scrutiny doubles when we enter the long training hall where the gladiators are. A half-dozen practice fights halt as warriors watch us openly, unafraid to be caught looking. I realize with relief that the silver paint Pliny used to disguise my Copper veins is still in place, or the whole room would know one of my secrets. Fortunately, Contessa is nowhere to be seen. I do not have the strength to argue with her.

Illy stares at me with wide eyes, although from the way his gaze moves between Alessandra and me, I'm not sure if he's worried about my health. The heat inside me grows, and despite being bound to Unrelenting Fire, I cannot get it to go away.

"Are you feverish?" she demands, turning to study me. "If you have an infection, I am dragging you back to the infirmary this very second."

"No," I reassure her, holding up my hand to cut her off. "Just hurt. I promise." I continue as her eyebrows rise skeptically. "Just help me into the Winter *locus*, and I will be fine."

We make our way around the outside of the central sandpit, which adds to the time it takes. I try to ignore the room's silent scrutiny, counting down the paces until I will be able to cultivate again. We pause outside the room, and I step away from her embrace, delighted and saddened to be free.

"Thank you," I say, giving her a smile even as I can't quite meet her eyes. "I promise I'll refill my reserves then go right back to the—"

"Oh no," she interrupts me with a toss of her head. "I'm staying right here until you're done and walking you back myself. That's your punishment for sneaking out of the infirmary." A small smile plays at the corner of her lips. She's enjoying this.

"That's really not necessary," I protest.

"And yet, you cannot refuse my command," she says, knowing all too well how true that is. "So, stop complaining and get to cultivating."

"Yes, *Domina*." I sigh, shuffling toward the sliding glass doors to enter my winter refuge. They open at my approach and send a cold wind blasting out. Alessandra shivers, wrapping her arms around herself.

"I don't know how you bear it," I hear her murmur as the doors slide shut behind me, cutting me off from the rest of the world. Any reply I might have made is lost in the sheer joy of being reunited with Winter.

I inhale, drinking greedily from the essence that pools in this room. My Heart lurches like an empty stomach getting its first mouthful of food. I fall to my knees, momentarily forgetting that I am wounded. Agony lances through me, but my Symbol now has the power to banish most of it, numbing the sharpness with ease.

I am not healed, but my pain is greatly reduced, and for that, I am immensely grateful. I close my eyes and lean my head back, savoring each stream of essence that comes to my back and call. Mentally, my *animus* shows me my *Cor*'s dark blue hue slowly returning as it refills.

I am at peace, whole again.

"Okay, that is enough!" Alessandra calls cheerfully as the doors slide open, knocking me out of my almost trance-like state.

"I'm not—" I turn slowly to stare at her in shock.

"You have enough to work off the dregs, and you're not going to be using it up lying in bed. Which is where you are going."

My mouth opens to protest, but her expression hardens, becoming a harsh shadow of her father's. I don't bother. My words will be like the wind rushing along a mountain for all the chance they have to move her. "Okay," I grunt. "Back to bed."

She marches me to the infirmary in the same embarrassingly intimate fashion. I do not lean on her as heavily as I did before, thanks to the numbing from my restored Winter Symbol. But I do not pull away either.

"Thank you," I say as I crawl back into the bed I escaped from without any sign of Patricia. Alessandra nods, tucking a stray strand of dark hair behind her ear as she does, her expression unreadable.

I want to ask her about a hundred things. If she has found a way to help me Ascend Unrelenting Fire. If she will come visit me again so that I am not alone. If she would like to try my bread.

"I'm glad you did not die," she says at last.

"Me too." I give her a half-smile propped up from pillows. I will never admit it, but now that I am lying down, I can feel exhaustion creeping up on me. My body is sated and ready to begin healing. Alessandra is silent but looks like she is trying to decide what to say.

"Please be careful."

I wince with a new kind of pain. I remember what she told me outside of Delilah's home after the shadow assassins attacked. What my life means to her family's safety.

"I will be," I promise. "I know that your family needs me alive."

There's a tug at the corner of her lip that seems almost dissatisfied, as if that was not what she really meant to say, but the moment has passed.

"I will be quite wroth with you if you die." She smiles gently this time.

"If I do, you can light an everflame to keep my soul here and scold it every night before bed."

"I will," she promises. "I swear it on Pluto's Bones."

"Don't do that!" I snap, twitching in my bed enough to make all my wounds sear with pain. She also flinches in surprise at my outburst. "No gods," I pant when I can speak again. "They're dead. Just you and the flame."

"Just me and the flame," she repeats, clearly confused.

After she is gone, sleep avoids me for some time. It is not because I am in too much pain. There is a light in my mind that won't go out. My hands burn with the warmth of holding her. I have been so cold for so long. Iron and Ancient Frost are not Symbols prone to comfort. Even Unrelenting Fire's heat has a wild, rabid edge to it. But not Alessandra.

Not her.

It is madness, I tell myself over and over. I am a slave to her house, no matter how well I am treated. She is a palatine, the daughter of a senator, a descendant of the Iron Lords themselves. Even if the gods still lived, they could never grant a prayer like this.

I know all of this, and yet the light in my mind keeps shining.

CHAPTER 44

The greatest benefit of being an *electus* is the effect that the *Cor* Heart has on my physical body. Alessandra does not come to visit me before I am allowed to leave the infirmary, but that also takes less than two days.

Patricia removes all the stitches from me, except for the deep cut in my upper right chest, where I trapped the assassin's blade. But even that wound is mostly healed, if a little tender still.

Several of the cuts became infected, turning red and inflamed, but to my delight, I was able to burn the corruption out of my body with Unrelenting Fire the same way that I scoured the poison out of me in Bellona's Arena. I do it at night, before any of the *medici* have a chance to see.

I am not allowed to spar, but that hardly makes a difference. I am still under strict orders to *be*. The task which had become so comfortable now chafes at me worse than the bandages I wear. When I first began baking bread, it changed me. For a moment, I was a different man who went down a different path. Instead of breaking things, I made them.

But that is not who I am. It was a fantasy, a fiction that I embraced. I snort in disgust as I realize that I'm doing it again now. Somehow Hiro and Pliny have pulled me into their philosophic game and, for a moment, it made me forget who I am.

In a way, I am grateful for the wounds that I bear. They do not let me hide any longer. Every movement I make burns with the pain of a warrior. I may be baking bread, but I am not a baker. I carry too many Symbols meant for war to be anything other than that.

You are a soldier of the Iron Legion. You do not bend. You do not break. I smile fondly, remembering Durus even now. His words do not rule me like they once did. Like the bread, they are a part of me, but not the whole. I have become something more.

That's probably what this whole exercise is about.

A tremendous moment of clarity descends upon me, stopping me in my tracks. Of course it is. I have Ascended so quickly that my own understanding of who I am has fallen behind.

When I first gained the Iron Symbol, I was Castor the Boy. Then I became Castor the Legionnaire. After finding Ancient Frost that changed again, turning me into Castor the *Abominatio*. Now I am a gladiator with *three* Symbols. What does that mean?

Am I still the Castor who seeks revenge? Yes, I must be—the prickling weight of the *votum* reminds me. When I made that oath with my brothers from Segesta, I had nothing else. I thought that was all that I was. Now I realize that I am not one singular thing, but a jar that holds many.

I am bound by a multitude of oaths. They pull me in multiple directions, and the weight of these things tears at my own weak foundation. If I do not know who I am, how can I bear up under the strain of the gears that seek to crush me?

Who am I?

I am the son of Evander and Julia.

I am Iron.

I am Ancient Frost.

I am Unrelenting Fire.

I am a baker, a legionnaire, a gladiator, a slave, and a friend.

A vision of Nemesis, the tall woman with blindfolded eyes flickers in my mind. There is another piece to my puzzle. Another thing that must be in the jar to fill me up.

I am Vengeance.

All of these things are pieces of me, not the sum of the whole. I have been trying to be all of them with my whole self. But that is impossible—there is only one of me. I cannot be spread so thin and succeed. Something inside of me *clicks*, like a joint popping back into place.

I have done it. A broad smile flashes across my face as I feel—not whole, but less fragmented than I have since I first became an *electus*. Pride runs through me as I realize I have accomplished Hiro and Pliny's task. I have won their game.

Now I am free.

A baker may not be all of who I am, but there is nothing else I am allowed to do. So, I return to the kitchens, using my left hand to knead the dough to keep from tearing open the hole in my chest. The cooks do not comment on my bandages—that is from a world they want no part of. I respect their distance, leaving my violence at the door.

I have begun to understand who I am, but I have also finally learned how to bake a loaf of bread worth talking about. I eye it with a practiced air as I judge that it needs only a few more minutes in the depths of the oven.

Excitement rises in me like dough. I feel like a journeyman preparing his masterwork to prove his worth. This is my proof, my explanation that I have learned what my teachers want me to see. This will earn me my place among Hiro's apprentices.

Now! I use a long, flat paddle to slide under the bread and pull it out. I lean in close, inspecting the round loaf, looking for any visual imperfections. There are none. It is perfect—perhaps the best I have ever made.

Grinning from ear-to-ear, I wrap the still-warm loaf in cloth to keep it warm and scoop it up. I feel Palina's eyes on me as I trot out of the kitchen. I give her a wave that she does not return. She has still not forgiven me for forcing my way into her domain. She has little to fear; I doubt I will have much time to bake any longer.

I follow the path Contessa showed me to the Nihon house hidden in the back of the garden. When the door comes into view, I square my shoulders and fix a smile on my face. My heart races with excitement. When the *lanista* first brought me to this place, I believed that I was unbeatable. My encounter with the *tellus*-bearing *sicarus* has shown me just how much I have to learn. Properly humbled, I approach the domain of a master, eager to become his greatest student.

The bread is still warm.

The door slides open before I finish crossing the glade. Hiro's granddaughter stands in the entryway once more, watching me approach with a small frown. Today, she is wearing a set of red and black silks, embroidered with creatures I do not recognize. Some *mythi* from her part of the world, perhaps. Her expression fails to give me pause; after seeing her a few more times in the kitchen, I've come to suspect that is just what her face looks like.

"What?" Her voice is brusque, but not cold.

"I've come with a gift for *Sensei*," I say, trying to copy the bow that I saw the other *electi* use the last time I was here. A sardonic part of my brain is amused at how much easier it is for me to bow now. I am grateful that the price of that lesson was only a few scars.

The woman's eyes flicker from my face to my bread without changing her frowning expression. After a moment, she tilts her head to the side, inviting me inside. I do not have to be told to take off my shoes.

There are no other pieces of footwear sitting in the entryway, which relieves me a little. I would hate for poor Pyrus to witness me displacing him in the master's training group. I feel bad, but I have Censors to kill.

Without a word, Hiro's granddaughter turns on her heel and leads me through the empty house, toward the garden in the central courtyard. I follow her, distracted as I study the house, full of things from another world. A three-piece painting made of flat panels of wood hangs from a wall, depicting a trio of armed men riding horses through a forest of thin trees.

Golden statues sit on shelves, depicting heroes or gods that I do not know. It is a marvelous thing to see something so different and yet so familiar. I wonder which human first learned to sculpt and then passed the idea through the world, or if art is so ubiquitous that a thousand different people found it on their own? A small smile crooks the corner of my mouth as we pass the wall. I think that such questions are further signs that I am *being*.

"I still don't know your name." I break the silence, speaking to her back several paces away. Her pace does not falter, but she seems surprised. We walk another dozen steps before she responds.

"I am Rin," she says at last.

"It is nice to meet you, Rin," I reply warmly, feeling like I have made some progress. Another good sign for my future. "I am Castor."

"I know." She is almost as cold as Ancient Frost, but there is no malice to it. It cannot be easy to be here, trapped between two worlds, belonging to neither.

There is no more time for questions before we emerge into the center courtyard of the home. I spot Hiro immediately. He kneels in front of the pond, staring into nothing. His blindfold is still on, and I am struck by the similarity between him and Nemesis, the blind goddess to whom I am bound. What more proof do I need that her specter pushes me toward him?

We approach him silently, and he does not react to our presence. Rin stops several paces behind him, and I copy her, moving to stand by her side. She does not look at me, but a solemn weight settles over the courtyard as I resign myself to waiting.

This must be another test.

Before, I was rash and impetuous. I must show that I have changed and learned patience. I square my shoulders and assume the casual stance of a legionnaire on duty. This is not the first time I have been ordered to wait. Once more Durus's lessons come to my aid. I miss that old man like a second father. I hope his end was quick and painless.

The three of us stand in silence for a long time.

The shadows begin to shift as *Sol* moves above us, beginning his afternoon journey toward his nightly rest, and still Hiro does not move. I can feel my bread growing cold as time passes. Surreptitiously, I tap the Symbol of Unrelenting Fire, bleeding a tiny amount of heat back into the loaf, just to keep it fresh.

I glance at Rin to see if she noticed anything amiss, but her eyes are closed. For the first time, her face looks serene and expressionless. Suddenly, I wonder if I am missing part of what is going on here. I have been patient, but I don't think we are doing the same thing. I am enduring, but she is merely existing. There is a difference that I do not fully understand.

Sol fades behind the horizon, and with it, most of my confidence. But my stubbornness remains, and it has seen me through more dire circumstances than this. If the old swordsmaster thinks that he can wait me out, then he will be sorely disappointed. I may be more than just a man bound by an oath of Vengeance, but that is the most important part of who I am. I will not fail; I will not turn away.

At last, Hiro stirs. He rises gracefully from his kneeling pose, not showing the slightest bit of discomfort after not moving in hours. I stiffen, like a soldier who sees an officer coming down the line. I must have finally passed his test. He twitches in surprise, as if startled to find Rin and me waiting for him.

"I have brought you bread that I baked myself, *Sensei*," I announce, extending it forward and bowing at the hips. It is no longer warm; I gave up on trying to maintain it with Unrelenting Fire. It has been so long that at this point it would only be suspicious. But it is fresh, and I am certain that it is my best work yet.

Rin translates, her voice moving quickly in the foreign tongue. I cannot imagine learning something that sounds so different from my own. Our ancient dialect is a mother to the Imperial one that we speak now. In some ways it is easy, many of the words are the same.

Hiro responds with one short question and then begins to walk away, no longer looking in my direction. My heart crumbles before Rin even translates. Somehow, I have failed again.

"Why would I need bread?" she says for him, but her voice is far gentler than it has ever been before. I cannot look in her direction. The loaf tumbles from my numb fingers, and I leave it in the grass.

CHAPTER 45

I stop baking.

Whatever peace I thought I found is lost to me. I spend my days in a haze, training as much as Patricia the *Medico*, Contessa the *Lanista*, and Pliny the Magister will allow me. I bristle under their scrutiny like a teenager trapped in his father's house, ready to escape.

I sit on the side of the training fields and watch the other Silvers train, jealous beyond words. I have tried *being*, but all it has done is make me confused. I feel like a sword that has been put back in the forge and reheated until all its sharp edges turn round and flat.

I was something, and now I am nothing.

Sleep evades me. I am listless like a *tigris* stuck in a cage. Some nights, I sneak back into the hall to cultivate fire while Anas watches over me, but it feels like an exercise in futility. My veins have long since ceased to burn from the strain of that inferior fire. I am trapped in a rhythm I cannot escape from, unable to progress in any of the directions that I want to go, and instead, I sit here, stuck.

Often, I wander the dark estate at night, alone with my thoughts, wrestling with ghosts that haunt me. If Marcus were here, he'd shove me into a wall and tell me to get over it. Felix would make some scathing comment about my melodrama belonging on an opera stage instead of in a gladiator *ludus*.

But neither of them is here to pull me out of my spiral. I have lost them both to the grinding gears of the Empire, and I am no richer for it. Once I walked this path with nine brothers. Now it is only me. Once I told them that I knew where we were going, but now I am lost.

Beyond the *ludus* section of the estate is another massive pond. When I asked Pliny why there are so many on the grounds, he shrugged and said, "What else do you expect from the descendants of the man that killed Poseidon?" A wrecked ship sticks out of the water, and massive, dark fish move below its surface like hungry shadows.

DO NOT SWIM reads the sign at the edge of the water. This place used to fill me with a sense of discomfort from all the creatures that could eat me. Now, I find that that fear is grounding. I make my way along the stone path to an island that sits in the center. There are no plants here, only the stink of saltwater and waves that are created by some *oceanus* relic, recreating the dead god's domain. What would I find if I were to dive to the bottom of this *aquarium*? Some cave full of loot taken from Poseidon's final lair?

The island is a large, flat rock that sits in the middle of everything. A small trail of steppingstones leads to the part of the sunken ship, and another wraps out to the far side. There is a small pagoda made of stone on the northern corner and a couple of benches worn smooth by the people who have sat in them over the years.

Luna's light pours down on the water, and I watch her reflection dance. *Mons* Olympus does not show in the water's surface, and I find comfort in that. I come here to think about the gods less. There is something transporting about the sound of waves that seeks to take me to some other place. Before I went to Antioch, I had never seen the ocean. Now, I understand a little of its strange allure.

The sound of a footstep scuffing a pebble pulls me out of my study of the dark water. I turn in surprise to find Rin approaching. The dark-haired woman is dressed in silver, which shines under *Luna*'s light. In her hands, she carries two wooden training *katanas*.

She tilts her head, studying me like I am a bug she found under a rock. After a moment of inspection, she tosses one of the swords at my feet. It clatters against the stone.

"Come," she says, turning to walk toward the middle of the platform. My heart races as I scoop up the wooden weapon and follow in her wake. She makes it halfway before turning to face me. I watch as she settles into a low crouch blade held low and extended.

I stare at her blankly for a couple of heartbeats until one of her dark eyebrows arches slightly, the first expression she has made tonight. Understanding floods through me, and I copy her stance, surprised at the burn I feel in my muscles from the unfamiliar pose.

She lowers her blade and circles me, clucking in disappointment. Using the tip of her training *katana*, she pushes my left foot back a half-pace. Next, she raises my wrist and straightens my back. My eyes widen at the exertion it takes to hold such a simple pose. My legs begin to wobble after a few minutes, but Rin says nothing, so I dare not move.

When at last she is satisfied, she nods in approval. I relax, groaning slightly in relief. But my new teacher does not let me rest. She falls into the same crouch and adds movement, falling back a step as she raises her blade to eye level where it would be easy for it to block any incoming stroke.

She looks into my eyes to make sure I am watching and repeats the motion. I say nothing but wince as my already stressed muscles complain. I shudder to think how embarrassing this would be if I were not an *electus*. I am a professional fighter. I train every day, and yet a simple pose felt like it was torture.

I resume the form, unsurprised when she corrects my form with the tip of her wooden sword once again. She moves quickly to settle me into the proper posture before gesturing for me to begin. I pull my left foot back, raising my sword in my best approximation of what I saw her do.

She shakes her head and moves in front of me, repeating the movement. I see no difference between what she does and what I did, but I nod as if I have just gained some tremendous insight. I am terrified that if I am difficult or ungrateful, she will walk away.

I drop back into the crouch, ignoring my thighs' protest. This time, she only corrects my right foot's angle before nodding in satisfaction. I smile, proud of my small progress. I fall back with my left foot, and she lets out an exasperated sigh.

"Your hips," she says, breaking her silence for the first time. She pokes my left one with her training sword. "They go first."

"Like this?" I lean into the step, angling myself slightly so I am no longer presenting my front fully forward. It feels strange to me, but she nods, and I begin to understand. Legionnaires are taught to take up space. Together, we are the bricks of a wall. But walls are meant to take hits.

In the ring, I am not a part of a shieldwall. I am not there to take blows and dish them back. That's a recipe for death when I am facing other *electi*. I need to be a dancer—to present myself as little of a target as possible. That seems obvious now, but it is completely different from how I was trained to fight.

When I finally can do the first step correctly, she teaches me how to advance. From the same pose, she steps forward, angling the point of her *katana* toward an imaginary opponent for a simple thrust. It takes me fewer tries to master this one. I am learning. My mind races, trying to understand how to put these pieces together, to use them against my enemies.

As if I read her mind, she shows me how to step to the side, circling an imaginary opponent, while keeping my profile as narrow as possible. Then she has me put them together. She flows through the different poses like water. I follow her routine, awkwardly at first, but finding it after a few tries. Already the steps begin to feel familiar, like a dance to a tune I have heard before.

Sol's light has not yet cracked the horizon when at last she steps back and lowers her sword. I copy her before bowing toward her on instinct. Not as deeply as I did to *Hiro*, but hopefully enough to show my respect and gratitude.

"Thank you," I say as I come out of it. Rin looks away, embarrassed by my response. For a moment, she looks like a hero from a story, framed against *Luna*'s cold light, her black hair dancing in the light wind.

"Why?" I do not need to explain my question further. This time, she looks back at me, and a slow smile plays at the corner of her mouth. I feel one grow on my own face to match it.

"I like bread."

I return to the kitchen.

Over the next few weeks, a new routine emerges out of my despair. By day, I follow the abbreviated training regimen that Pliny and Contessa allow.

Then I bake a fresh loaf. Palina has given up scowling at me when I steal one of her ovens. I am just a part of her life now. At night, Rin and I share my newest creation on the stone benches by the water while she teaches me *kenjutsu*—the art of the sword.

I have learned over a score of forms, the true version of the movements I used in the training hall when I learned how to better manifest the *Glacialis Falx*. Each variation is a puzzle piece I can fit together to form a never-ending dance. Rin insists I learn their names, but she does take pity on me, making translations for them after I prove hopeless at memorizing her native tongue.

"The Water That Cuts!" she snaps from the side, calling out the next set of moves that I must take. I nod, not taking my eyes off the pretend opponent in front of me, flowing forward diagonally in three sharp steps, each punctuated by a horizontal strike.

"The Song That Leaves!"

I retreat, leaning around invisible blows that follow a pattern. The move is different than The Song That Stays or The Song That Is Not. Each of them is designed to follow a series of exchanges that people naturally fall into.

If I swing my sword from left to right, then there are only so many directions that I can move after that. Each variation of the dance takes that into account and is prepared for them. While I understand the vision, part of me—the proud voice of *Frigus Ventus* that grumbles in the darker corners of my mind—is skeptical about this training method's efficiency.

It's pretty, but a fight is not a dance.

When I was injected with my *Corda* and first bound the Iron Symbol, I remember how different actually using my will was from what the magisters had taught me about being an *electus*. I had a lot of theoretical knowledge that was useless until I got my hands on it myself. I worry that all these forms will only be more of the same. But I am willing to do anything for a chance to kill Atticus and Brennus. If Hiro will not teach me, then I will take what knowledge Rin will give me.

I'd be lying if I said that I didn't enjoy the process, regardless of its potential usefulness. The strange woman has begun to come out of her shell, like a lily blooming in the sunlight. I do not know if she is shy, or if I have just finally earned her respect, but I find myself enjoying my time with her. She is demanding and specific, but not unfair.

It is a challenge to keep up with her in this art that she has been learning since she could walk. I am not the *Primus*. It is exhilarating, pushing me to new heights. We only use wooden swords. Iron can do nothing for me here. But I find a strange sense of joy in that. There is a mystery to sword fighting without using my Symbol that makes it feel more like an art than it ever has.

"Good," Rin announces when I have finished the steps that she calls. I let my sword droop as I pant from the exertion. My muscles have begun to grow used to the demands of *kenjutsu*, but I know it will take months before they are truly conditioned for it.

"Bread," the dark-haired woman commands with a small smile, making her way to the stone bench where my most recent loaf sits, still wrapped in a cloth to keep it fresh and moist. *Luna* hovers above us, her crescent shape shining weakly.

My stomach growls, and I accept the loaf to rip a piece from it after she has taken some. She tears into it, sighing contentedly as she chews. I hide my proud smile behind my own chunk of bread.

"You are wasted as a student of the sword," she says between bites. "You were born to be a baker."

No, that was someone else. I am merely a flame keeping some of his light alive. I smile and nod in thanks, not ready to tell her about Felix.

"How old were you when you came to the Iron Empire?" I ask, changing the subject.

"Less than three. I remember very little."

"Why did you come?"

Rin hesitates, lowering what remains of her snack to look at me with discerning eyes.

"To repay a debt," she says at last, troubled by her words. "When Varus-*san* was younger, he traveled to the islands of *Nihon*, where he met my father. Together they—" Her voice hitches ever so slightly, a rare sign of emotion from the cold woman. "My father was killed, and Varus-*san* avenged him."

"I'm sorry."

A heavy silence builds between us. I feel as if I have trod on sacred, painful ground, a private cemetery where visitors are not welcome. It is a place for quiet pain, not to be shared or shown. I recognize it. I have spent a lot of time there myself.

"My parents were killed too." I offer her a glimpse into my own graveyard. She looks at me with a question in her eyes. I hesitate, unsure how much to share. "I have not avenged them," I say at last, raising the wooden *katana* to inspect it.

Rin does not say anything, but after that night, her training intensifies. I do not know why she first chose to teach me *kenjutsu*, but now that she has seen a glimpse of the pain that I carry, she attacks my ignorance with relentless focus.

We meet for over a month before we begin sparring. As I suspected, all the forms and steps that she taught me do not immediately translate. Rin flows through them like a river, her attacks never ending. I am too slow, thinking about my moves before I make them. She is instinctual, and I am a pretender.

Rin ripples toward me in The Rapids, a series of reckless strikes designed to overcome my tempo. I recognize the first steps of her set and remember that The Stone That Does Not Roll is the preferred counter. I set myself, counting on my larger size to weather her storm.

But I am too slow. A true master of *kenjutsu* would not need to think; he would see and act. By the time I am settled, she is already inside my guard, her practice sword thrumming as it cuts through the air, trying to reach me.

Abruptly, she shifts into The Way of Fire, changing her stance to make it easier for pure aggression. Rin's weapon moves in a series of short thrusts that force me to constantly readjust to prevent myself from getting stabbed. She is too fast, too fluid. Once more, I try to shift to a counter to her, only to fall behind.

"Yeowch!" I complain as her sword strikes my left shoulder with surprising strength. I stagger and fail to recover before the point of her training *katana* buries itself in my stomach, doubling me over. She is an enthusiastic teacher, but not a gentle one. My mismatched *Corda* roil, groaning under the strain I am putting them through, even though I am not using my Symbols. For a moment, I think I am going to be sick.

"You know you don't have to hit me that hard," I wheeze when I manage to stand upright again.

"The harder I hit you, the faster you will learn," Rin replies, helping herself to more bread. It is sourdough tonight. It makes me think of Valentina; it was her favorite. What has become of her, the last living member of my original *votum*? Has she become a Censor, bound to the Empress, or have they cast her aside to some fresh horror?

"But the bruises make it harder for me to keep training," I complain.

"Don't get hit then, *gaijin*." She says the term with more affection than she did when we first met.

"Does your grandfather know that you are teaching me?"

The shadow of a frown flickers over her face like an owl flying in front of *Luna* at night. "No."

"What would he say if he found out?"

"That I am being a fool." Rin picks up the loaf and tears another hunk out of it, done with the conversation. I do not think that she is a fool. I think she is beautiful and strong and wise. As we sit together in the dead of night sharing bread, I wonder if this is what old Hiro meant by *being*.

I realize that I don't care. For the first time in weeks, I do not feel stagnant and trapped. It is the closest thing to being happy that I have been in a long time.

CHAPTER 46

Varus's official complaint about my attempted assassination goes unanswered for weeks, until finally, the Iron Empire responds with a show of domineering force. The wheels of justice do not move quickly, but the machine they carry is powerful.

"Castor, come," Pliny's voice echoes through the kitchens, causing all the cooks to panic at the sight of the senator's right hand striding through their workplace. They have only just gotten used to me, but I am an *argentum*. Seeing the Gold magister here is something else entirely.

"This loaf is almost done," I tell him, holding up a hand to slow him down. "Just a few more minutes."

"Now." There is no gentle smile on Pliny's face, only the stretched look of concern.

"But—"

"Leave it with the cooks!" he snaps with an irritated expression. "That is what they are for."

"Yes, *Dominus*." My voice is cold as I toss my towel on the counter with a hint of anger. I feel betrayed, as if he has threatened me with a dagger. Pliny has never spoken to me like I am a slave before. My eyes find Callia, my question obvious. Pale-faced at the sight of two *electi* arguing with each other, she nods emphatically. Anything to get out of this moment.

I follow the magister out of the eerily silent kitchen. Pliny moves at a hurried pace, leaning on some of his Gold strength. I have longer legs than him, but even so, I have to trot to keep up.

"I sent servants to your quarters to collect your finest tunic," he says without looking at me. "You will have to change out here." He pauses, looking at me with a skeptical eye before shaking his head and resuming his march. "There's no time for a haircut."

"Pliny," I interrupt him, feeling like I am an hour behind in this conversation. His fear is infectious, driving my irritation before it like a shepherd. "Will you slow down and tell me what is going on? You're going to give yourself a fit, man."

"They're coming," he says, giving me a flat stare. "They're coming, and we need to be ready. Varus expects trouble."

"Who?"

"The Praetorians."

A full score of the purple-clad legionnaires of the First Legion march through the open gate of the Pelias estate thirty minutes later. My hand curls into a fist as I stare at their hated colors, remembering all the pain their members have caused me.

A Censor, lithe and pale, leads them, her arms streaked with the golden veins of her *Cor*. As one, the troop of soldiers halts, and she continues on her own up the stairs toward where Varus and the rest of us wait for her arrival.

"Senator," she says, bowing her head slightly in respect. "Your complaint has been heard by the consuls, and they are ready to speak."

"I look forward to their wisdom, Censor," Varus responds tersely. He wears a pristine white *toga* and the golden armband of his office. Alessandra and Pliny stand on either side of him, equally as well-dressed. Senator Delilah is also in her senatorial outfit, a match for Varus. She radiates a nervous tension that I can feel in my bones.

I hover a few paces back, in my nicest set of leathers marked with the broken trident of *Domus* Pelias. Pliny had me change behind the hedges while we waited for the soldiers to arrive.

"We have been sent to escort you to their presence and ensure your safety." She gestures at the twenty legionnaires waiting behind her. "I have been instructed to bring you as well as the gladiator in question." Her gaze travels over his shoulder to me, eyes tracing my white *rasa* veins in a familiar dance. "We are to leave at once."

Varus has a carriage waiting, and we climb into it while the Empress's elite watch us with hard eyes. They have made no threats, and yet they do not need to—it is written in the strength of their arms and the edges of their weapons. We move through Anteforum at the slow pace of marching soldiers, not using the *mythi* airhorses that carried us to Antioch. The five of us—Varus, Delilah, Alessandra, Pliny, and I—sit in the ornate coach facing inwards.

"We must stay together. Do not let them separate any of us," Varus commands, hard eyes watching the legionnaires through the window. A chill settles on me at his words.

"You suspect another assassination attempt?"

"I believe in my enemies' ability to take advantage of an opportunity," he replies with a sardonic smile. "Knowing Briannus, this will be a social affair, where he tries to smooth some ruffled feathers."

"Welcome to true society, Castor," Alessandra says, speaking to me for the first time today. A strange light burns in her eyes as she looks at me. "Good thing you have been learning to dance." My mouth goes dry at the coldness of her voice. I have upset her, although I am not sure why.

"Will there be dancing?" I ask the other two men, as if I suspect she is trying to fool me. That seems less dangerous than sitting in her angry silence.

"Hopefully not," Varus rumbles, leaning back in his seat. "But Briannus does love his spectacle."

It takes more than an hour for us to reach the consul's home. No one interrupts our journey, but then who would dare face down a full score of Ironbound?

Briannus's estate is massive. It dwarfs the Pelias compound in height and width. Instead of being a series of buildings built to support the different industries that operate, it is one massive marble building that stretches the length of the entire street.

"He's never been a subtle man, the consul," Delilah murmurs as we roll in through the open gates.

Thick pillars hold up a pristine white roof. More Praetorians stand watch, a sign of the Empress's favor. Their purple uniforms are a bright contrast against the building. I grit my teeth at the thought of being surrounded by them once more, especially given that Brennus is himself a member of their legion.

"Stay with me," Varus says once more when the carriage comes to a stop. He leads us from the coach to where the Censor waits for us along with a sour-faced man dressed in black.

"*Vale* Senator Pelias, *Vale* Senator Census," the servant says, dipping his head in respect to both of the Gold *electi*. "Consul Briannus welcomes you into his home. I am called Duperus. I will take you into the receiving chamber."

"Lead away," Varus says, adopting the cold stiffness of a senator like it is a *lorica*. Duperus nods, turning and walking toward the great entrance. Our group falls into step behind him, while the Censor trails behind us, like a sheepdog herding its flock.

We ascend a dozen marble stairs to reach the door. A pair of purple guards stand on either side of the wide steps, eyes forward, looking more like statues than men. The two by the door have the Silver veins of the *Fidelis*. My eyes clash against the man on the right as we move past. He watches me with a cool disinterest, unimpressed with what he sees. I resolve to keep my *animus* internalized. I dare not risk one of them sensing that I, too, am bound to Iron.

Duperus leads us down a long hallway. Rich tapestries hang from the walls; a thick red carpet is plush beneath our feet. Hundreds of *lumos* relics cast their light, banishing even the hint of a shadow in these pristine, marble halls.

The sheer opulence is staggering, even after the time I have spent living in Varus's house. The consul wealth exists in another order of magnitude. I feel the hint of a frown settle on my face at the sight of such excess. It feels like too much for any one person, even the second most powerful one in the Empire.

We pause at a pair of doors, made of wood and gold.

"You will be announced," Duperus tells us, folding his hands to wait patiently.

I glance at Alessandra, but she is not looking at me. She hovers at her father's shoulder, face forward. None of my compatriots seem surprised by this development, so I resign myself to waiting. After a few moments, the doors open of their own accord, and a voice rings out in the great hall beyond.

"Senators Pelias and Census." Varus leads our party as we stride out into the crowd of waiting palatines. My guts clench as I spy a crowd of Gold *electi* watching our approach with various levels of interest. This must be an assembly of the various *ludi* owners throughout the Empire. A shudder of fear runs down my spine to be the focus of so much strength. I spy Xania Valerus in the back; her expression sharp with brittle anger.

Hic sunt monstra—here there be monsters.

Briannus, the Consul *Quaestor*, emerges from the sea of toga-wearing elites. The tall man smiles broadly, raising both his arms in greeting. His bare skin is a sharp contrast to most of the room. He is one of the few non-*electi,* and yet despite his lack of *Cor*, he is the most powerful man in the room.

"Delilah, it is a wonder to see you again." He takes the senator's hands in his, greeting her first like an old friend, smiling before he turns. "And you, Varus, thank you for coming."

"Of course, Consul." My master inclines his head in respect despite having no choice. "I am honored that you took the time to listen to my complaint."

"What?" Briannus's mouth curls down in the slightest hint of a frown, framed by his black goatee. "Oh yes-yes," he continues as if my attempted murder was no more than a trifle. "I am confident that we will be able to put this matter to rest, once and for all." Something about his tone makes me think otherwise. The bad blood between *Domuum* Valerus and Pelias cannot be cured with some words over dinner.

"Alessandra, you look more like your mother every time I see you."

Varus stiffens imperceptibly, like a bowstring tightening at the beginning of its draw. But the consul continues his greetings, unbothered by the senator's ire.

"Pliny." He inclines his head in respect for his former teacher. "Your wisdom is always welcome in my home."

"No, it isn't," the old man grumbles, a fond smile breaking across his face. Despite the conflict between these palatines, he still helped raise the consul. "But as long as I am, I will gladly drink your wine."

"And you are welcome to it!" Briannus booms jovially before his dark eyes turn to me, and suddenly, I know how a deer must feel when it has been cornered by a wolf. Beneath that pleasant veneer is the shrewd and cold calculation of a general.

"Young Castor, the hero of the hour!" he booms, catching me off guard. To my utter astonishment, the consul throws his heavy right arm over my shoulders as he maneuvers me out in front of the assembled crowd.

"Here he is, *Frigus Ventus*, the man who killed the *abominatio* in Antioch and saved all our lives! Rejoice, for you are in the presence of a demigod in the making!" The other palatines clap politely, but many of their faces remain coldly neutral.

"That's right, lad, you did your Empire and Empress quite a service."

I try not to wince as he shouts in my ear. He is projecting his voice so that the whole room hears his words clearly even though he speaks to me like we're having a private conversation.

Surely this is not his plan. Does he think his public praise will protect me? These are senators who hold the power of the people in their hands. What will happen to them if they kill me? Nothing worth being afraid of. A fine, perhaps, some petty slap on the wrist. The tall consul releases me and steps forward, still speaking to the assembled worthies.

"Now that we are all here, let us begin this conclave."

"The Consul *Electus* Maximus Marius," the voice booms, announcing a new attendant to the party.

The world moves in slow motion.

Briannus twists, a surprised expression on his face. I turn my own head to the door, too afraid to breathe. Goosebumps explode from me as the unseen eyes that watch me open, focusing on this moment. Surely this cannot be what I hope.

Then I see him, and I know for sure.

The Consul *Electus* is older than Varus. His hair is completely white, but he radiates strength and power. He wears the sapphire ring of his station, but it is not needed, thanks to the Silver *Cor* veins in his arms that sparkle under the light of the *lumos* relics. My eyes flick to the base of his neck, where the dark collar of an *inhibitus* curls around him like a serpent. He, too, was forged in Agogia.

Even if I had not heard his name, I would know him. I see Gaius in the set of his jaw in the calm way that he surveys a room of enemies. I see Percy in his long limbs and sharp movements. I see both of their shadows in the quiet sadness that clings to him.

This then is the patriarch of *Domus* Marius, the father of my tribune and my centurion. His cold gaze flicks over our party, not staying on me for more than a heartbeat. In that moment, I am certain that he saw all that he needed to see.

I yearn to run to him. To tell him that I knew his sons and served under them. That they are the pillars of who I want to be. That I would gladly have died for them if the gods had allowed me to. But I do not dare. Not in this room full of knives. To reveal myself to the consul would only get me killed. My heart breaks, but it does so that it can keep beating.

"Maximus," Briannus booms, striding out to meet his counterpart. "I did not think you would join us today."

"Perhaps that was because I was not invited," the older consul says in a tone that I know well. Briannus only laughs—his joviality is his greatest weapon.

"That was only because I thought it was too soon to drag you into all this petty business. It is good to see you, my friend. Your new title suits you."

Despite his growling, Maximus clasps the other consul's wrist firmly. The two halves of the Empress's hands join together in unity.

"I was just about to inform this conclave about the plans for the Forum Games," Briannus says, gesturing for his counterpart to walk with him. Maximus grunts disinterestedly, as if he already regrets coming here.

Varus leads us along the side of the room to join the milling crowd of palatines. For once, their eyes are no longer on us, pulled in by the specter of the new consul walking before them.

"You, my collective worthies," Briannus says, turning to address the room, "represent all the major *ludi* of the Iron Empire. Now that the Censors and *compositores* have had time to go over the tragic events in Antioch, we have made adjustments for the finale of the circuit in Forum." For some reason, as he speaks, his eyes fall on me.

This is no hearing of justice. This is a trap.

"The Empress is concerned," he says, pacing up and down the line of his audience like a centurion in Agogia. "She thinks that the people might draw the wrong conclusions from the events of Antioch. Whatever that madman was, he claimed to serve the gods, which cannot be, for as we all know, they are dead."

"Then where did he get his power?" a voice challenges from across the room. Briannus merely smiles, unbothered by the interruption. This is a room full of politicians, after all.

"The Censors guard their secrets closely, as you very well know, Senator Grus. I do not know what forbidden relic that man used to make himself so dangerous."

"Was he in league with the rebels? There have been other attacks before Antioch! Thebes and Rhodes. Even far-off Segesta was not spared!" another woman interjects.

My blood runs cold to hear my hometown listed amongst the victims; to see the web of lies grow. Praeco did come there, but there was no seditious army with him. Only Censors and Praetorians with their Iron and *tellus*, willing to spill blood to cover their failures.

"*There are no rebels,*" Briannus thunders, his voice echoing from the marble walls of the room.

A heavy, dangerous silence falls. These are the palatines of the great houses of the Iron Empire. They are not men and women to be cowed. Force is not the kind of threat that they respect. The consul sees this, and sighs softly. "It does not matter. What does is that the Empress wishes to reassure her people that the gods are dead. And not only are they dead, but if they somehow *weren't*, our heroes would easily dispatch them." He glances in my direction again, which only increases my sense of foreboding.

"And how will we show them this obvious truth?" Xania's sarcasm is so sharp, I am surprised that the consul does not begin to bleed onto his toga.

"Through a series of performances, of course." Briannus's smile only grows wider as he takes in the room. "No doubt you all took note of the new capabilities that we displayed in the ring. The ability to manifest unique terrain for each battle allows us to create a truly new experience for the masses."

"How is it done?" another senator calls from the back. Apicius, I think.

"Do I look like a magister?" For the first time, Briannus appears annoyed. "It is a new way of using the relics called *utor*. It consumes the relic to power it, allowing it to do things that even the original *electi* could never do."

There is a stunned silence in the room. Even Xania Valerus looks horrified. Relics are a sacred part of the duty of being an *electus*. When we die, we return them to the Empire in gratitude for the loan and the quality of life that they gave us.

Relics are precious and eternal. The *lumos* ones that light this room might have been here for centuries. To consume them, destroying them forever, is a waste beyond my comprehension. Atticus murdered a score of souls to hide the loss of a handful. The foundation of the Iron Empire is built on the bones of the *electi* who matured the *Cor* into something useful. Every generation adds another layer to the base, making us greater than we were. But now they are grinding them into dust for their own amusement.

I feel a sickening twist at the thought of living in a civilization built on bones. Perhaps every single one in the human race has been, but probably not as literally. We are little more than incubators, carriers to hatch the *Cor* inside of us into something usable.

"It is a heavy cost, I know," Briannus says, measuring the mood of the room correctly. "But the Empress believes that the sacrifice is worth it. We are testing, ever testing, to show the people what a true *electus* can do. What a boon!" I feel no better despite his assurances. All *Corda* might belong to Diana Agrippa, but even so, this feels callous.

"We will resume the story of the gladiator groups ascending to the House of Mars. Since these are the final Games of the season, and more of our *ludi* will be in attendance, we have made an adjustment to the tournament. We have added more groups, and the final surviving members of each of those will compete in a large, multi-person melee. They will only need to defeat the members of the other *domuum* to be victorious and earn the Bloody Laurel." A low murmur runs through the room at that announcement. Traditionally, there is only one champion of the season. One last *Primus* to stand above all. Making it a team finale is a major change.

"However, in keeping with the orders of the Empress, there will be new challenges." Briannus continues when the *ludi* owners have settled. My stomach clenches, fearing the worst.

"Certain gladiators will face a guardian of the house between each phase, themed after this Praeco. This champion must defeat them in a special combat to allow the rest of the contestants to continue ascending."

"To make the people believe it was all a part of the theatrics," a senator calls from the far side of the room. Maximus snorts in disgust, a mirror to his sons.

"Precisely." There is a cruel twist to his lips that I have never seen before. "The events at Antioch were merely us setting the stage for the final event of the circuit. The rumors were a part of the theater." A couple of the senators chuckle dryly, familiar with this strategy.

"Which brings us to young *Frigus Ventus*." He stretches my name, holding it out before the room. More of the other palatines turn to study our group once more. For the first time, I realize that I am the only gladiator in the room. Everyone else is a member or advisor of one of the great families. I am the lone patrician swimming with the sharks.

"In order to sell this vision, our famed gladiator will open the Games in a test of defiance against the dead gods." A chill runs down my spine as I remember that the consul wanted to buy me for this very purpose once. "After being victorious against Praeco, he will be the first into the next floor, defeating its guardian to open the way for our Games to begin. A mighty hero, like the ones of old. Although perhaps after he has a haircut."

It seems that the consul will have me for one of his *Spectaculum* after all.

Varus's jaw is clenched as he stares at Briannus. This reeks of political maneuvering. I have no doubt that the guardian of Mars's House will be something truly terrible. In order to sell their lie, he will at least have to resemble Praeco. A shudder runs through me at the thought of facing something like him again. I killed the Herald, but I do not fully understand how or why. The *tellus* blades of the Censors could not harm him. Only my Iron and Elder Symbol had enough power to bring him down. I have no doubt whatever Briannus and his *compositores* create to face me will be designed to hunt me specifically.

"And if he fails to defeat the guardian?" Xania asks the question that lurks in the shadow of the consul's explanation, her voice sharp. My mouth curls into a sneer.

"Then the rest of the quest will be held in his honor, a mighty warband of the Iron Empire's greatest warriors sent to avenge our fallen hero. The minstrels will have songs composed for either eventuality. I am told it will be quite moving. They're calling it the *Ballad of the North Wind*. Quite an accomplishment for someone who is only *argentum*."

Something inside me cracks. It feels foundational, a part of my understanding of the world. My belief that the Iron Empire exists to guard and protect its people does not shatter, but I can feel it shudder as the weight of what I have seen begins to be too much to bear. Is this the price of the world our ancestors built? Lies and death? How much blood is required to hold this dream together?

"Consul, surely you jest," Varus says, stepping forward, unable to contain himself any longer. "*Frigus Ventus* is my House's strongest contender."

"And we are not deaf to your plight," Briannus replies, smiling easily. "After review, we have decided to impose a penalty against *Domus* Valerus for their little *Impostor* trick." My gaze snaps over to Xania, whose face has gone blank.

"They will lose fifteen *marcae* for their deception. Furthermore, any *domus* that competed against *Impostor* under false circumstances has been awarded an additional ten *marcae* in recompense. That includes *Domuum* Apicius, Grus, and Pelias." My mind flashes back to the scoring from Antioch. *Ten marcae* moves us up past many of the provincial *ludi*, closing the gap with the other great houses before the final games begin. Suddenly, Varus is in far less danger of losing his *ludus* license and his senatorial seat even though the Antioch games were cancelled. Our gladiators will still need to perform well at the Forum Games, but it is not an insurmountable lead.

Which means that someone is now more concerned with trying to kill me than they are Varus himself. But why? There are still so many layers to this new world that I do not know how to see. Is it truly just hate for exposing *Impostor*? Perhaps they see me as a barrier between them and Varus and are willing to wait another year while they remove me from the board.

"And what of my complaint?" Varus presses, his voice growing dangerously irritated. For a moment, I think I can hear the anger of the man who slaughtered his way through the Games as a young man. "Already *Frigus Ventus* has been attacked in the streets of Anteforum. I have the weapon—"

"Ah yes." Briannus cuts him off smoothly as if being reminded of a passing trifle. "The reason for this summit is to explain to *all of you* how important our young friend is for the Empress's plans. Now we all know that there is a long history of extracurricular activities in the Games." The room chuckles again. There is no warmth in their laughter, only death.

"In sympathy for the attempt on your gladiator, we have chosen to award *Domus* Pelias another five *marcae*. Furthermore, I must insist on a *moratorium* on any more attempts… at least until after the Forum Games. Have at him in the ring, but the Empress needs *Frigus Ventus* to play his role."

Varus is silent. I can feel his anger rolling off him, but he can say nothing. He has been trapped firm in a golden cage. Briannus dangles *Domus* Pelias's salvation in front of him, buying his cooperation. Thanks to his changes, we have more than thirty *marcae*! And, *Ludus* Valerus is no longer the leader of the Circuit. With this judgment, the Grus will have surged past them.

My head turns back to the corner where Xania Valerus lurks, glaring at me. I hold the Golden senator's gaze easily, unafraid of her. Hate twists her features, and I wonder if she has ever been embarrassed by a patrician before. She cannot touch me; I am protected by the Empress. An irony, given that Diana Agrippa herself sent assassins to kill Varus on the road but now needs me to live.

The formal meeting concludes, and the palatines boil forward, mixing in conversation. Several storm up to Briannus, protesting the changes. Xania does not move from her corner, which tells me that she knew this was coming. The Valerus are cousins of the Agrippa after all.

I stand forgotten, a slave in a room full of senators. Out of the corner of my eye, I spot a flicker of motion. Maximus walks out of the room, alone and without fanfare. My feet are moving before I even make the decision to follow him. I am no one. I do not belong in this room. I may never get a chance to speak to the Consul *Electus* ever again.

"*Dominus*!" I shout after him as I race down the hallway in his wake. "A moment, please."

"Bother me not, boy," he says, waving a hand without turning. "I cannot save you from these wolves." His voice is tired, heavy with age and weariness. I am so stunned that I stop for a moment, watching as he stalks away with a sense of despair.

But a wild impulse bubbles up in me, and Unrelenting Fire latches onto it, delighted by its audacity. I take a risk, stepping forward to call after one of the most powerful men in the Empire, hoping that he is the one who carved his sons into the men they are.

"I knew your sons!"

The consul freezes. For a moment, he is completely still, facing away from me. I worry that he is going to keep walking, to ignore me and leave. But then he turns, his face a mask of pain and distrust.

"Even you, lad?" he asks softly, like a man who cannot believe the depth of the betrayal that he faces. "They send you, the one condemned to die, to mock me? It is not enough that they took them from me, but now they scourge me with slaves?" A hint of that famous Marius rage boils in his dark eyes.

My heart races as I stare at the consul, knowing exactly what I must do but terrified of what it could mean. I carry a host of secrets that will kill me. I share one now, for if I cannot trust the father of Gaius and Percy, there is no hope for me in this place.

I reach up with my hand and pull the neck of my leathers to the side, revealing the *XII* that is branded on my chest above my heart. "*Redemptio in bello*," I whisper, the words of the Twelfth Legion.

Maximus's eyes go wide with shock; his mouth hangs open as he looks from my mark to my face. A thousand questions burn in his old eyes, but he does not even know where to begin. I glance over my shoulder, but no one has followed. We are alone for at least a few moments more. "*Dominus*, your son survived. Gaius lives!"

To my surprise, his expression falls, welling up with deep misery as I have confirmed his worst nightmare.

"I know, boy," he says softly, his shoulders sagging. "Honos damn me, I know." Then, to my utter astonishment, the Consul *Electus*, the second most powerful man in the Empire, begins to weep before turning away, leaving me alone in the hallway.

CHAPTER 47

The conclave only further cements that I will have to be my own vengeance. The sight of Gaius and Percy's father so bent and broken haunts me. In my head, I had dreamed of a Titan, a looming mountain that cast a long shadow over his sons. But it seems that even he has been worn down by the inexorable wheels of the Iron Empire.

If he cannot stand before it, what chance do I stand?

My late-night training with Rin gains a new edge. I push myself harder than ever before. She does not ask me why, but I know she notices. Most days, I forget to bake a new loaf of bread, but she says nothing, only hits me harder.

By day, I hammer my Silver *Corda* with the *pondus*. Both Iron and Ancient Frost continue to swell, adding a second, denser layer of essence upon themselves, showing me that the work is not wasted despite being monotonous.

There is a tension quivering in them, as if they grow restless at being restrained. The weight helps to contain them, to keep them locked in place. But they want to run like wild horses—to Ascend. Their impatience sends a new series of weakness and pain through my body as I am punished for my perseverance.

But I was forged in the Iron Legions of the Empire. I do not bend. I do not break.

Almost a week after the meeting of the *ludi* owners, an interloper appears. *Luna*'s faint light shines overhead as I make my way across the stone steps to the island in the middle of the manufactured lake. A figure waits for me, shrouded in darkness. Rin is always on time—I rarely am.

"I actually brought a loaf today," I call in greeting. I heft the still-warm sourdough in the cloth that Callia, my first bakery instructor, wrapped it in. The sweet plebeian brought it to me in the mess hall. She said it was an extra one that she needed to get rid of, but it is too warm for that to be true.

It seems that some of the cooks miss my presence in their kitchens; I do too. But that was a thing for Castor, and there is no time for him. There is only *Frigus Ventus*. The Forum Games loom large.

"I've wondered where you sneak off to at night," the shadowy figure says, his voice catching me completely off guard. Slowly, I turn to face the amused form of Illy, who is standing just out of reach.

"What are you doing here?" I ask.

"You think you are so sneaky, tiptoeing out after everyone goes to bed, but you're really not a subtle man," the duelist continues with an arched eyebrow.

"Just out for a late-night stroll with my bread." I hoist the loaf toward him in offering. He smiles warmly but shakes his head.

"I thought we agreed to trust each other, friend." He pushes gently but firmly. His face is blank as he tilts his head toward the edge of the island.

My gaze follows his motion to find Rin lurking by the water, watching us like a skeptical alley cat. She makes friends about as easily. "Oh, uh, it's not what you think," I protest, feeling a burst of heat blossoming on my cheeks. "We're here to—"

"—beat each other with practice swords?" he interrupts smoothly, flicking out his own wooden blade from underneath his cloak. My mouth hangs open as I stare at him in shock. His mocking laughter echoes off the stones like waves.

"How—" I splutter, completely dumbfounded.

"I told you; you are not a particularly subtle man." His expression is still guarded.

I've hurt his feelings, I realize. He meant what he said in the training hall, and now I have left him behind. Foolish. I know better. "Well, you caught me," I admit, raising my hands in defeat. "But, uh, what exactly would you like to do—"

"I'm joining you, of course."

"That is not entirely up to me..." My voice trails off as I glance over his shoulder at where Rin watches. I do not know what she will think of this intrusion. Part of me is afraid that the camaraderie between us will be broken; that she will leave and never come back. Illy's gaze turns back toward my strange teacher, and he bows carefully, the same way that I saw the Gold *electi* show respect to her grandfather.

"If you will give me a chance to prove myself, *Sensei*, I would gladly be your student," he tells her. My irritation grows. Was old Magister Vellum truly such a terrible teacher? Even the patricians in Anteforum knew more about the world than I did!

Rin studies Illy for a long moment, her gaze moving from his strange, thin sword to his stance. My friend does not move; instead, he waits for her to pass her judgment. Slowly, like a curious stray, my teacher approaches, giving him another skeptical once-over before coming to a decision.

"We will see if you can be taught," she says at last. "You cannot be worse than him." Her head tilts in my direction. Illy laughs, some warmth returning to his expression as he rises from his bow smoothly.

"I will endeavor to prove you right, *Sensei*."

At Rin's direction, they step into the center of the stony slab and raise their training blades. Illy's is thin like his *rapier*, made of a willow-like switch that allows it to be as springy as the metal version. Rin wields her curved *katana*, which is longer and heavier than his weapon.

"Begin." Rin wastes no time, launching forward at the smaller man with the smaller weapon. She settles into The Way of Fire, which allows her patterns to be used in their most aggressive style. She hammers at Illy, relying on her physical advantages to batter the smaller man into submission.

But Illy is not surprised by her tactics. He's been using that strange, skinny blade against heavier weapons for his whole life. He never meets her attack directly. Instead, he uses it like a conductor's baton, guiding her attacks around him so that they miss him by a matter of inches.

I can't help but be impressed as I watch the two of them dance around the stone island. If I did not know better, I would assume that their fight is choreographed or that they are both *Silva electi*, bound to the wood of their weapons. I have improved much under Rin's tutelage, but I know that both of them are far better at this than I am. Without my Iron Symbol, I am nothing.

I suspect Rin is impressed by his level of control, because she shifts into The Way of Wind, which is less relentless, allowing her to pace herself. She must be worried about running out of stamina before she cracks through his defenses.

As her barrage of attacks slows, Illy flows into the gap, finally trying to land his own attacks on her in the breaks in the tempo. It is Rin's turn to dance, and she dodges his lightning-fast strikes with ease, while her *katana* cuts through the air as she tries to catch him.

Slowly, Illy begins to wear her down. Rin pays for her early aggression. Now he is the one on the attack, while she is forced only to defend. For a wild moment, I think that he is going to beat Rin. But then he falls for her feint, finally allowing his weapon to get tangled up in hers.

Quick as a viper, Rin surges forward, shoulder-checking the smaller man while wrestling her heavier weapon free. He staggers back a step and freezes as the tip of her wooden *katana* hovers an inch from his throat.

"Mars's Rotting Spear, you're good," he pants.

Rin is silent for a long moment as she studies him. Her sword does not shake despite being fully extended. The two duelists stare into each other's eyes, taking something of each other's measure.

"He can stay," she announces, lowering her sword and turning to look at me.

"That's it?" I splutter, almost insulted. "One duel and he gets to join? You made me wait *months*."

"He's better than you," the girl replies with a shrug, scooping up the still-warm loaf from the bench and ripping off a hunk. "I just like your bread."

And then we are three. Every night after Contessa and Pliny have had their fill of me, Illy and I join Rin on the lake and continue to train. I am by far the worst, but between the two of them, I begin to learn quickly. Illy eventually forgives me, but only after giving me a nasty bruise on my thigh.

It takes almost a week, but I finally manage to beat Illy. At first, it is only once, then twice in a row, until eventually, we are trading victories evenly. I am exhausted as I sink into my bed just before the sun begins to rise. Every muscle in my body, flesh and *Corda* is sore.

But it is all worth it. It is working. I am getting better.

A few nights after I finally best Illy, there are four people waiting for me in the dark instead of two. Fannia and Reese hover in the shorter duelist's shadow, alternating shooting nervous glances at me and Rin like two schoolchildren caught out of their *dormitorium* after the night bell has sounded.

"Uh-oh," is all I say, looking from them to the girl who is our teacher. Rin already surprised me once by allowing Illy to join us. She is not from Agogia, but she is like a soldier in the Iron Legions—I do not think she will bend further.

"We want to train with you," Reese says, raising her chin defiantly, stepping forward to challenge me, as if my opinion is the one that matters. I shake my head sadly. *Frigus Ventus*'s shadow is large, but it is only theater. Rin is the real terror here.

"Now who is bad at keeping secrets?" I ask Illy dryly. My friend just shrugs without any sign of regret. I do not think he feels shame often. He is a strange, deliberate man.

"We have to win, Castor, and you seem to be the only person among us who knows the way," is all he says.

I roll my eyes but don't argue his point. I can't. He's right. Yet I can't help but remember what happened to the last group of people who tried to follow my path. Their deaths are a stain on my soul that I can never scrub clean.

"We have to win," he repeats, taking a step toward me, his face earnest. I know he thinks of the changes to the Forum Games. "All of our futures hinge on it. Not just mine and yours."

"You'll have to convince *Sensei*," I tell Reese, nodding my head toward the foreign woman who stands apart from our little gladiatorial group. The shadows hide her expression from me, but her shoulders are braced, like she is prepared to meet a charge head-on.

She is so otherworldly, born in a place I have barely heard of and never seen. I cannot imagine what her life has been like, and yet I find myself grateful that it has led her here. Everything around me is a roiling sea, its waves crashing down on me and trying to drown me. My *Corda* strangle me, my masters push me to do things that will not help me. I am surrounded by secrets like drawn swords, pricking me if I stray from my perfect course.

But here in the dark, all of those problems fade. I am nothing more than the wooden blade in my hands, the rhythm of *kenjutsu*. There is no Castor whose soul aches with loss or whose body is ravaged by forces unleashed upon him by the gods.

Luna's light comes out from behind a cloud, bathing Rin in her pale light. The girl's dark eyes find mine, and for a moment, we stare at each other, having a conversation without words that I do not understand. Then she shrugs sharply, drawing her wooden *katana* and stepping toward the two women who have come to learn.

"Show me why I should teach you," she says, gesturing for Reese and Fannia to engage her. The gladiators exchange confused glances for a moment before doing as they are told. It is a fast, brutal affair. Rin dispatches them easily, but she seems pleased by something I cannot see.

Now we are five.

Contessa knows that I am up to something. It's obvious in the way she studies me with narrowed eyes. It is hard to hide the fresh bruises that I am earning outside of her training. *Cor* allows me to heal faster than a normal human, but it does not make me invincible.

Quietly, our little cabal of fighters ascends to the top of the Silver gladiators. All of us were already on the roster for Antioch, but if Contessa was considering making any changes, we quash her concerns easily.

None of the others can hold a candle to anyone trained by Rin in the training arena. Obellius and Leon are still dangerous, but we carve through the rest of the alternates like a hot knife through butter. The *lanista* is suspicious, but she cannot argue with the results.

I know that she knows what the forms of *kenjutsu* look like—some of her Gold *electi* are trained by Hiro. She cannot be completely confused about what is happening, but we are getting better, and that is all she wants.

Illy's words haunt me every day as we improve. By the end of a week, the four of us are noticeably more dangerous than we were before. I have learned to fight against different styles and weapons, but there are gaps in my knowledge. None of my sparring partners wield the slightly curved dueling blade favored by many heavy fighters—or the Censors. But Leon does.

When Contessa dismisses us, I watch the air *electus* and Obellius walk away together. A long sigh escapes from my lips as I know what I must do, what Durus would want me to do.

We must win.

I walk away from my friends and angle for the retreating gladiators as they head toward the mess hall. Illy barks a laugh behind me. I think he's surprised I'm willing to swallow my pride. Leon's blue eyes narrow in suspicion or fear at my approach. We have barely spoken since I beat him in the dark.

I regret that now—not that I did it, but it will make it harder for me to earn his trust.

"What do you want?" he demands, drawing up short. Obellius hovers at his right shoulder, glowering at me with his broad face. I raise both of my hands to show them that they are empty. Neither of them relaxes, but they know firsthand what my *Glacialis Falx* can do.

"Have you heard the news about Forum?" I ask.

"What about it?"

"That the final will be a team battle?"

"Who cares?" Leon's expression hinges on boredom.

"We do." I nod my head toward where the other three members of my late-night training cabal are watching our exchange with blank expressions.

"Congratulations." His tones are cold enough that they could channel Ancient Frost essence.

"We've been doing extra training at night, out by the old lake. You two should join us." I extend my right hand in a friendly gesture. "We have to win."

"Maybe you do." Leon snorts derisively, staring at my arm like it is a venomous snake in the grass before him. "I could always go join the Censors, *immundus*."

"True." I shrug, trying not to let my face show the chill I feel at his words. They'd love him over there. Atticus would welcome him with wide arms. They are cut from the same cloth, those two. "Or you could help us win the Games."

"Leave us alone, *Frigus Ventus*." His sneer makes my name a curse. Together, he and Obellius turn their backs on me and march off toward the mess hall. Rage boils in my chest, fed by the untamable *Cor* of Unrelenting Fire. *How dare he spurn my olive branch? I will kill him—*

Ancient Frost's cool logic sweeps over me, helping to bank the anger that burns inside of me. I blink rapidly, trying to adjust to the sudden emotional swing that my mind just survived. Pliny is right—I am in danger of losing myself to these elements.

Slowly, I turn back to my training partners, who watched my exchange with Leon and Obellius. Illy shrugs when he sees my expression. "It was worth a shot," he tells me. I feel like I have been whipped in front of the recruits again.

But I should not have doubted, for the seed was planted. My father, Evander, taught me that plants always win. Their creeping roots and vines can shatter the mightiest boulder. They just need time to grow.

Within a week, all four of us are defeating Leon and Obellius regularly in Contessa's training bouts. The *lanista*'s gaze is heavy on all of us, but she does not say a word. Her silence is echoingly loud. I can feel the rest of the Silvers' eyes on us, wondering what we have done to pull apart from the pack.

The next morning, the *Index Gladiatorum Argenteorum* has been updated. Instead of six names, there are only four: *Frigus Ventus*, Illyrius, Reese, Fannia. Leon's and Obellius's have been removed, and the *Quintus* and *Sextus* spots are blank.

The mood among the rest of the Silver gladiators shifts abruptly, like sharks with blood in the water. There are still two unclaimed slots for the Forum Games. A chance for someone new to earn their freedom.

Contessa ignores the *index*, even as the murmurs grow louder. Her heavy gaze settles on me, and I resist the urge to smile. She may not be an officer, but *lanistae* are far too similar to centurions. Realistically, no one in the rest of the *ludus* has a chance of besting Leon or Obellius before the Forum Games. But somehow, she knows that they have not joined with the rest of us, so she gives them a little nudge to encourage them in the direction.

I take this gesture as a tacit blessing of our extra activities. Contessa must be satisfied that whatever we are doing is not putting my *Corda* at risk or exhausting us too much for her training. All four of us have increased our dueling prowess by a noticeable margin in the last month, and Forum looms large.

We must win.

That night, we are seven.

I give the rest of the Silvers a wide smile when I arrive late at the rocky island. Leon and Obellius stand off to the left of the rest of the group, a strange balance to Rin lurking on the right. I hold up my hands, each full of a fresh loaf, the first two I have baked since the conclave.

"Come." I gesture to them, using my bread like batons. "Let us break bread together and speak of the future."

Illy chuckles, although whether he is amused at my clunky attempt to make some sort of peace between us or just that I am trying to swallow my arrogance, I am not sure.

"Bread?" Leon's voice is skeptical, even as he approaches. His shoulders are tight with tension, and Obellius frowns openly at all of us. Contessa drove them here with a whip—it is up to me to make them actually want to participate.

"Yes." I smile, passing one loaf to Reese before ripping a hunk off the other and offering it to the blond gladiator. "Think of it as a chance for new beginnings." I am speaking to the new pair, but my words are for us all.

"When we first came to this *ludus*, we were competing against each other, rivals as well as members of the same *domus*. But that is not working. Pelias is the lowest of the Great Houses and still in danger of losing its license. Now the consul and his *compositores* have changed the rules, forcing us to work together instead of on our own." I bite into my bread, delighting in its soft warmth. It may be my best work yet.

"So we break bread?" Leon's face is incredulous. Obellius just looks confused. I probably should try speaking a little slower for the big guy.

"First, we break bread and make peace. No more rivalry, no more resentment. A blank slate between you, me, and them. Then we become dangerous."

"But we are only Silvers. Our points are only worth two-thirds of what the *Aurum* Circuit can earn," Leon protests. "It's not truly up to us if *Domus* Pelias wins or loses." I see Illy nod thoughtfully over his shoulder.

"That comes next," I tell them with a wide smile, still chewing my delightful creation. "Have some bread first."

We must win.

CHAPTER 48

One night, more than a month after the consul's announcement, Alessandra finds me.

I am in the training hall, cultivating my Unrelenting Fire, even though the exercise is beyond worthless. But ever since I learned about the challenge I will face during the opening of the Forum Games, I have been clawing at my Copper Symbol, trying to figure out how to make it Ascend.

In my current state, it will be easy for them to create something that will kill me. But I do not intend to die. Not yet. So instead, I rage against the stubborn *Cor* in my chest, trying to force it to obey me. I only have a few months to save myself.

My heart leaps out of my chest as the door to the *locus* opens without warning. I spin, mouth open wide to explain what I am doing in the wrong room, only to relax when I see it is her. Anas did not seem to think it was worth warning me that she was approaching.

A chuckle from my fellow Ironbound tells me he enjoyed my reaction.

"Come," is all she says before turning and walking back into the training hall. She is still stiff with me; I hoped that whatever I have done to upset her would blow over. In her hands, she carries my Frost Iron *gladii*. I need no further encouragement, breaking into a trot to catch up to her fast pace. "You too, Legionnaire." Anas detaches from the darkness and follows us, our own personal shadow. I accept my weapons from her and buckle the belt around my waist as we move.

"Did you find me a better source of Fire?" I half whisper, not daring to hope, as she leads us out into the compound.

"I have done what I can," she murmurs, eyes tracking to the left and right. "It will be up to you to take advantage of it."

I am silent, unsure what to make of that.

We make our way to the main courtyard of the compound, where a carriage awaits, drawn by normal horses, not *mythi*. A nervous coachman stands at the front, wringing his hands at our approach.

"*Domina*, are you sure about this?" he asks even as he opens the door. "My master will have my head if he discovers I took a team out at night, to say nothing of the senator's daughter..."

"Have no fear, Timidus," she says sweetly, giving him a bright smile and placing her hand on his shoulder. He sags in delight at the touch. "Look, I have ample guards with me. One of my father's Ironbound and the deadliest Silver gladiator in the Empire." I wince at the accolade. Her kindness cuts like a blade.

"Aye, *Domina*." Timidus seems to grow taller under her bright smile. Together, the three of us climb into the carriage, and he shuts the door behind us before climbing up to the driver's seat.

"Where are you taking us?" I murmur, peering out of the window with a nervous glance. I am trusted, but somehow, I can't shake the feeling that there would be tremendous repercussions if I were caught sneaking off the compound's premises *with* Alessandra.

It's not all bad; we have a former *captivus* as a chaperone.

"There are not many places in the city where fire is left unchecked," she says mysteriously as we spring into motion. The horses' hooves echo off the cobblestones as we pull into the streets of Anteforum. "Fewer still that are secluded like we need for our purposes."

"But you found one?"

"I did, and through no small expense managed to purchase its exclusive use for the night." She looks at me now, blue eyes serious and heavy. "Make full use of it, Castor. I do not think you will get another chance."

I nod, understanding the risk she takes. I am grateful for it, despite the void that stretches between us. "But what is it?"

Her lips quirk playfully at my question. Now that the adventure has begun, she is thawing, caught up in the same excitement I feel in my own chest. Tonight, dead gods willing, I Ascend.

"Leave a girl a few secrets," she admonishes. "You will see soon enough." Anas chuckles from where he sits in the corner. "Something funny, Legionnaire?"

"It's just nice to see him get a taste of his own medicine for once, *Domina*."

Alessandra laughs as she looks back at me, sharing his amusement. I cross my arms and turn out the window, frustrated but unwilling to get sucked into their game. I know I will lose.

Anteforum does not experience true dark. The streets are dotted with light posts, holding *lumos* relics that shine brightly at night. I do not know if someone must go through and activate each one by hand or if they somehow know when it is time to shine.

Either way, it is a marvel and another staggering display of the Empire's wealth. Not even Antioch had anything like this. We move from the residential sector to a more industrial area. Instead of homes and shops built end-to-end, we pass giant stone warehouses that span entire blocks. Smokestacks rise from taller buildings where things are processed and made.

This is the true heart of the Iron Empire, I realize as my nose is assaulted by the odor of bitter chemicals. Here is the domain of the artisans, the craftsmen, the Heartsmiths who make the things that we rely on.

As we wind deeper through this pinnacle of industry, I make out a giant building, larger and taller than any that surround it. Its smokestacks rise high into the night, belching smoke so black, it can be seen against the dark.

"What is it?" I breathe as we begin to draw close. I am awed by its size. A dozen of the Pelias estate could fit within its borders with room to breathe. The gates to its massive compound lie open, and we enter without being stopped.

I scan its yard, counting the mountains of coal that we shoot past as we move deeper into its territory. Thousands of crates sit sealed, waiting to be opened or shipped out. Massive carts sit on rails where they can be wheeled up to sources of fuel or raw materials.

But as we move, I do not see a soul. I do not think that is normal even at this late hour. The air here thrums with the tension of a place that never sleeps. The stillness that has settled on it now is unnatural.

"It is called the Foundry," Alessandra says as the cart comes to a stop. "Its fire has fueled the conquering of much of the world."

"*Domina*, are you sure we should be here?" Timidus asks again as we emerge.

"We won't be long," she promises, giving him another bright smile. "Just wait here. It's all been arranged." The young man swallows nervously but nods obediently.

"How much did it cost to bribe the foreman into emptying this place?" I breathe as I follow her through a mountain range of coal and raw iron ore. The quantity of it is daunting—there is enough here to outfit the entirety of Agogia's legions several times over. Anas and I exchange a glance; I can tell he is thinking the same thing. Above us, *Mons* Olympus glints brightly, reflecting *Luna*'s soft light. I stare at the home of the dead gods for a long moment, wondering if any of them are watching us right now.

"More money than I have," she says grimly. "My father will ask about it."

"What will you tell him?"

"That I was sad and needed to spend something to be happy."

I blink in surprise. Alessandra does not strike me as the type to be irresponsible. I have only ever seen her move with grace and wisdom. "Will he believe that?"

"No. But he won't ask any more questions."

I grunt in understanding. That sounds more like Varus.

She strides boldly, as only a palatine heir can, toward the doors in front of us. Without hesitating, she pushes them open and leads us into the factory that feeds the Empire's war machine.

The inside is more intricate than I expected. A series of belts run in every direction. The room hums with the power of relics as it carries things from place to place. Cart rails run up to bins that spill onto the conveyors that take raw materials where they need to go. It is powerful and awe-inspiring to see the ingenuity that has been used to create this place.

But all those things pale when compared to what waits in the center.

Five stone smokestacks run up the center of the building, exiting out the roof many stories above. On the ground level, they all connect to a long black rectangle. A round porthole, larger than a man, is sealed at the base of each.

Some sort of tempered glass, likely reinforced by a relic, allows me to see what waits on the other side. A white-hot flame, so bright that it hurts to look at, flails against the glass begging to be released. I am bound to Unrelenting Fire, but even this inferno fills me with fear.

Wide-eyed, I turn to look at Alessandra, who gauges my reaction.

"My father is not particularly devout, so we have no braziers like Aunt Delilah," she tells me with a shrug. "Bribing a temple to use their everflame was even more expensive. I checked."

I choke at the thought of her approaching the priests for this venture. She cocks her head, vaguely amused at my reaction. She has swum in these waters all her life. This is not new for her, only me.

"You want me to go into *that*?" I manage weakly, looking at the roaring flames once more. The more I watch it, the more I feel its presence boring into me, as if it is alive and staring back at me.

"The Foundry's fires have been lit for almost two hundred years," she tells me, taking a step toward the furnace. "My magisters taught me that it is more expensive to let it go out and relight it than it is to maintain it. As far as elder flames go, there are few older in the world."

I swallow nervously, understanding why she has brought me here. As a Copper, I cannot feel its essence. I won't be able to until I touch it. To take advantage of this opportunity, I must step into the inferno. If I am going to Ascend, I must conquer my fear. Instinctively, I call upon the strength of Iron, letting it add its courage to my backbone.

"Okay," I manage after a moment of staring. "I'll do it."

"Are you certain?" To my surprise, it is Anas who speaks up. "If you cannot contain the flames..." His voice trails off.

"Then it will be very hot for a very short amount of time," I tell him grimly. "But there are no other sources of Fire pure enough to feed my *Cor*."

His lips compress into a thin line, but he does not protest further. I understand his hesitation; he has only ever been Ironbound. He does not understand the difference, just as I once did not.

"Well, if you are going to do it, you should do it now," Alessandra says at last. "I'm being charged by the hour."

I snort but nod in understanding. Our time here is limited. I must take advantage of it.

"Will you please hold these?" I ask, unbuckling my belt and handing her the swords that she gave me. I have no desire to bathe them in the same flames that I need to baptize myself in.

Slowly, I head toward the center porthole. Each step feels heavy, as if I am walking uphill. My fear surrounds me like a heavy cloak, trying to drag me down, but I grit my teeth and persist.

"The artisans left the furnace banked, but once you are in, I will activate the relic that restores its airflow to maximum," Alessandra calls.

"I'll do my best," I reply dryly, unable to picture what it will look like when it is burning at full capacity.

Pins and needles explode over my skin as I feel the attention of *someone* watching me. That only reinforces to me that I am on the right path. Slowly, I extend my hand toward the glass, grabbing the handle to pull it open.

The heat is so intense that I can already feel it leaking through the barrier to kiss my skin. I close my eyes and grab hold of Unrelenting Fire with all my concentration, welcoming its warmth. I am the Flame. This is my path.

Opening them, I twist the latch on the handle and pull, unsealing the inferno. The heat that pours out of the porthole is like the center of a volcano. I stagger under its assault. Even my connection to Unrelenting Fire seems to pulse for a second before coming back stronger than ever.

Iron and Ancient Frost flee from my awareness, fading to the background like stars faintly twinkling on an overcast evening. Tonight, I am only the Flame. Slowly, I inch forward, heading deeper into the furnace. So far, I have survived my encounter with this heat, but that is not enough to fuel my transformation. To feed my *Cor*, I must touch the fire.

I can bear the suspense no longer. In a moment, I will either consume or be consumed. With a deep breath, I burst forward, sticking my left foot through the porthole. The ground crunches unevenly under my feet as I put my weight on a mountain of white-hot coal. Awareness floods into me as I come into contact with this ancient fire. This furnace is like a sleeping dragon, coiled on its hoard of coal waiting to be unleashed. As mighty as its fury is now, this is but a trickle compared to what it truly is.

Agony sears through me, but Unrelenting Fire meets it eagerly, drinking up the essence and heat that flows into me. My veins stretch, and I scream from the effort and the pain.

But it is not enough.

Gritting my teeth, I lean forward, forcing myself through the hatch and into the furnace. The inferno sweeps through me. Unrelenting Fire gorges on the old flame, sucking down the essence that radiates from it. It is overwhelming, all-encompassing, unrelenting.

It is exactly what I need.

I stumble unsteadily on the loose mound of coal as I turn to face my companions. A laugh rips out of my throat, but I cannot hear it over the roar of the inferno. I raise my hands in victory, but as I gaze out into the dark building, my expression turns to horror.

Three men move out of the darkness with swords drawn.

Before I can shout a warning, the Foundry groans to life. The glass door slams shut, locking me in. Metal gears grind as something shifts, and for a moment, I feel the wind as a new breeze sweeps into the box, causing my hair to dance. I have just enough time to remember Alessandra's plan to power up the furnace before the coals at my feet burst into flame, fed by the influx of air.

Then the world is nothing but fire, and I am plunged into the heart of the inferno.

CHAPTER 49

There is a point where heat transcends itself and becomes cold. This is true of its opposite as well—Ancient Frost can burn. As I stand in the depths of this volcano, I am frigid. I cannot see my hands or any of my body. There is only a blinding light. It does not matter if my eyes are open or closed—the brightness is the same.

It is difficult for me to form thoughts—I am nothing but fire and anguish. Some distant part of me takes that as a good sign. The power of this inferno I stand in is enough to have turned me to ash instantly. If I am still in pain, that means I still exist enough to suffer. I have not been consumed.

So instead, I consume.

My *Cor* pulls in as much essence as it can handle, straining its veins as it races toward the peak of the Copper tier. At the same time, I extend my hands to either side, spewing flames out of them to make more room in my reserves.

For a moment, I am back in the iron room below Agogia again. I feel the awareness of this ancient forge spread through me as the flames shoot fifty paces into the air. I sense its impotent rage at being trapped in this box for hundreds of years, its endless hunger, its desire to consume the world.

I, too, wish to consume. I think of my enemies who still draw breath, of Brennus, Brutus, Tyrus, and Atticus. I gasp as something within the fire shifts, as if it suddenly recognizes me as one of its own. It no longer buffets me but now envelops me. I do not dream of a world of ash, but perhaps an empire of one.

But that's not quite right, I realize, suddenly pulling myself out of the river of Unrelenting Fire's rage. I do not seek to tear down the Empire. I am merely a man on a journey to avenge some wrongs. I am not a world burner. The cracks in the foundation of my faith in the Empire crumble, but do not break.

The system is not broken, just some of the people. I am not a revolutionary, just a janitor. If I am truly honest with myself, I do not even want to be that. I am just a man who is going to get *even*.

More. The fire seems to whisper to me. The elements do not truly speak, and yet they make their desires clear all the same. I shake my head, trying to contain the hunger that pours into me. I thought that Ancient Frost was devouring, but I see now that it is slow and ponderous. It envisions a creeping death for the world as it coils around us like a serpent. Compared to the fury of the Unrelenting Fire, it is patient.

I hesitate, unwilling to capitulate to its demands. I grew up in the wheat fields of the South. I know too well that an unchecked fire soon burns itself out. I have no desire to be like that, rampaging until I am my own demise. Iron and Ancient Frost call to me distantly, reminding me of their different paths. It is as if a trio of *daemons* perch on my shoulder, whispering to me their own variety of temptations.

I am nearing the peak of Copper. My reserve strains to the maximum capacity that its *Cor* can handle in its current state. Wild delight runs through me, joyful and bright. Soon I will be whole! As I grow better at accommodating the inferno around me, I begin to regain more of myself. I can feel my body, hale and unburnt.

But I have forgotten the danger.

I left Anas and Alessandra alone facing the men who were emerging from the dark. I do not know the interlopers' intent, but their drawn swords speak volumes. Anas is dangerous and Ironbound, but as I have learned, there are ways to deal with that.

I must get out! I scream to the flames. The inferno does not listen to me, but it feeds off my urgency, my rage. The light grows brighter; the heat becomes hotter. Like a dog excited by its master's enthusiasm, it reacts.

I stumble forward, banging my fists against the porthole cover, but it is sealed. I might as well try to break through the walls of Agogia with my bare hands. I am trapped. Mentally, I sweep my senses over myself, studying the burning red reserve that is my Unrelenting Fire Heart. It swirls vibrantly, bulging as if about to burst. Its colors are rich and vibrant like a ripe fruit.

I am so close.

My fist hammers on the glass. I feel something in me break, but I do not stop. I will not relent. In my head, I see Anas broken and bloody. I see Alessandra… I cannot bear to look at what my own traitorous mind shows me.

Something is missing. I cast my mind back to the first time I became Silver. I remember what I had to do to finally break through the barrier that held me. I know what I need to do; I am just scared. What if I cannot control it? What if I let it burn me out before my work is done? But fear is just the chain to the anchor that holds me down. To go up, I must be free.

At last, I let go. I welcome the fury.

I Ascend.

Strength flows through me as my body adapts. I have already been remade physically as an *argentum*, and yet somehow, I am remade again. I am already Silver, and yet now I carry another layer, making me *more*.

My *Cor* expands, growing to almost match the size of my other two. A great pressure lifts from my shoulders as the strain of my mismatched Hearts fades. Despite the danger, I throw back my head and laugh as I feel the balance align in my mind and body for the first time in months.

I am by no means free. I still carry three Symbols that pull at me with their disparate natures. But for now, I am as whole as I can be.

Reveling in my new power, I turn my attention to the sealed portholes that cut me off from my companions. I extend my hands, sweeping my senses through the organism of fire that fills this furnace, seeking an escape.

The tempered glass is thick, designed to withstand the blistering temperatures that the Foundry operates at. But what is its limit, I wonder? Gritting my teeth, I extend my hands, pouring my *animus* into the bed of coal that I stand on. Air swirls around me, feeding the flames. Yet I sense there is more potential here, waiting only to be lit.

I reach low, breathing my will into the dormant coals, commanding them to ignite. A rumble runs through the fuel as it fully joins the inferno. I gather myself, pumping more essence into the rising conflagration like a bellows.

Fire leaps up the smokestacks, far higher than it has ever traveled before. The ancient inferno delights in this, like a *captivus* who is one step closer to escaping their prison. Again, I channel my will into the base, feeding it my need, my desperation, and my rage.

The furnace shakes, rattling under the pressure of holding a monster it was never designed to contain. The *hydra* is awake, and it is ready to be free. Something in me senses that the fire is ready. It has grown into what I need: unstable and unstoppable.

I gather it with my mind, forming it into a ball above my right hand. As I did with its weaker cousin in the training room, I collapse it inward, building it into something more. My newly Ascended Silver veins begin to strain as the attack forms. I have never controlled power like this on my own. When I carried the storm of Aquilo, I was only a messenger—now I am the fulcrum.

When I can contain the maelstrom no longer, I hurl it forward. The furnace shudders like a fortress gate being struck by a battering ram as it slams into the tempered glass. The heat dissipates, and I cast my senses over it, trying to evaluate the damage.

I cannot feel the glass, but I can sense the tiny tongues of flame that escape out of the cracks that have begun to form on its surface. A grim smile spreads across my face. I raise my hand once more, beginning to gather another focused blast.

This place cannot contain us.

Me. This place cannot contain me. I have to shake myself to separate from the awareness that surrounds me. I am Castor, son of Evander and Julia. I am *Frigus Ventus,* the Cold Wind. I am the living hand of Nemesis. I am not the Unrelenting Fire, but its master.

My veins stretch once more as I push myself beyond my limits to condense as much of the inferno into a single point as I can. I think I am screaming, but I cannot hear myself over the roar of the fire. My will slams into the barrier once more. Soot and rubble rain down from the tops of the smokestacks as they shake from the force of my attack.

Fire flows freely through gaps in the porthole cover now. Soon we will be free. One more blow.

Panting with exertion, I raise both hands, using them as a combined focus for this final attack. My Unrelenting Fire *Cor* reserve has grown—already it almost matches my Iron one in size and density. This time, I reach through the entire furnace, pulling in every scrap of flame that I can touch.

I push myself far beyond my limits. My veins burn hotter than the inferno around me as they struggle to keep up with the demands of my will, but I will not be stopped. I cannot breathe. I cannot think. There is no room for me to do anything except hold this single working.

I take it all, every tongue of flame, and focus it into a single ball the size of my head. It burns like a second *Sol* above me. Its strength is tearing me apart, threatening to consume me. Its heat is so strong that my attunement to Unrelenting Fire can no longer completely protect me from its wrath.

Grunting with exertion, I throw the ball of fire at the porthole cover. I feel the impact as the glass shatters and gives way. My flames pour through the opening and into the Foundry itself.

For a moment, I stand on top of the coal, catching my breath as the fire reignites and spreads within the furnace. *Something* awakens, and I feel its *animus* rake across me like the hand of a god. The force of its will almost drives me to my knees. My senses push back, following it to the thing that lives within the fire.

My jaw drops as I realize that a *mythi* lurks within this maelstrom. Unrelenting Fire paints it easily, for it is covered in the same fire I am. At first, I think it is a *Salamandra*, a massive lizard the length of a horse. But as I study it, I realize it is more like a serpent. It lurks deep beneath the coals in a cave that it has made for itself, living among the heat. Thick scales cover its body, from its angular head to its tail. Power that far supersedes my own radiates from it.

The creature reminds me of the giant ice worm that came when I Ascended with Ancient Frost in the depths of the North. Like then, this fantastic creature that is also tied to *Cor* does not attack but studies me. For a moment, I consider digging through the floor to its cave to meet this godling of fire. What secrets could I learn from it?

Concern for my companions hounds me, driving me forward like a teamster with a whip. I have no time for the mysteries buried here. I leap forward, ducking out of the exit, and step out of the inferno into the regular world.

Pandemonium reigns outside my fiery cocoon. A dozen little fires have caught on fuel piles as the escaping pieces of the foundry's fire gorge themselves on fresh tinder. In the center of the room, two men stand around Anas, blades drawn as they try to corner the former legionnaire.

My friend bleeds from a dozen shallow cuts, but his *gladius* is still in hand, and he stands tall. My gaze snaps to the side, where another man has Alessandra cornered on the second floor of the metal catwalk. The Pelias heir has my swords in her hands and a defiant look on her face.

As I emerge, her assailant's head turns, and he stares at me in wild disbelief.

The light from my fires is harsh and bright, but I do not need them. I would know his features in the darkest night; they are seared into my memory. His name is written in my mind in blood.

Brennus Valerus, scion of *Domus* Valerus and Macer's killer, stands before me, sword drawn. He and his men must have been keeping watch over the compound and followed us here. It seems not even the word of the Empress is enough to keep him from trying to salvage his pride.

"You!" he shouts, his voice echoing in the empty Foundry. He does not ask where I came from or how I survived my time inside the furnace. He sees only the target of his anger and moves toward it. When we were in the legions, we competed for the same honor. How small he seems now.

He turns his back on Alessandra and leaps from the second story of the catwalk to land before me. His Silver strength allows his knees to absorb his weight from the fall easily, and he rises to his full height as he stalks toward me. Whatever his mission was here, seeing me has distracted him.

"I owe you a thousand cuts, *Gladiator*." He spits as he twirls his *gladius* through a fancy spin. He does not wear a *lorica*, just a set of fighting leathers that almost match my own. But he has a sword, and I do not.

For now.

"That's funny," I reply, tilting my head to watch the *Fidelis*. "I owe you a few more too, Brennus."

"You will call me *Dominus*!" his voice thunders, loud and petulant.

"You don't recognize me, do you?"

"Did I not say that I owed you a painful death?" He laughs as if I am the idiot in this conversation. Above us, Alessandra makes her way along the catwalk moving toward me. It is an easy thing for me to track her progress with my Silver senses as she carries my swords. Brennus does not react, too distracted by our conversation.

"Oh, we met before Antioch." I smile as his expression clouds with confusion. "You murdered my friend Macer in Agogia. I watched Gaius Marius whip you bloody, and I dream of doing it myself."

The Praetorian's face goes pale at my words. His eyes narrow as he studies my face, then widen as he realizes what my long hair has kept hidden. "But you're… you're dead like the rest of them."

"I guess it didn't take." I shrug. Above me, Alessandra tosses my pair of *gladii* down to me. I catch each one out of the air without looking.

"*Abominatio*," he whispers in horror, finally realizing that he has seen me use two different Symbols. The fear in his eyes is almost delicious. I force myself to ignore its savory taste. I am not here to torment him but to execute judgment.

"Come, *Faithful*." I scourge him with the *Fidelis* title he stole from me. "Let us see how you fare in a fight against one of your own."

CHAPTER 50

Brennus wastes no time. He stalks toward me, and I surge forward to meet him, eating up the distance between us in a handful of heartbeats. He brings his *gladius* overhead in a heavy slash that I counter with my left blade. I feel his will hammer against mine as we try to twist each other's weapons.

Relent, it whispers.

Shatter, I command.

I am a little surprised at the strength of his determination. It is too easy to think of him as a fop, who only gained his *Cor* through the power of his name. But as my intent rebounds off the walls of his mind, I am begrudgingly impressed.

Not enough that I don't try to skewer him with my right-hand blade, but I think a little more of his work ethic than I did before. His own Silver Iron senses warn him of the attack, and he twists away, disengaging neatly from me.

My *animus* can sense his will surging along the edge of his sword, repairing any damage that my own inflicted on it. I tilt my head in surprise, unused to the sensation. I have not faced an *electus* using my own Symbol since I Ascended. How strange to be able to feel his *Cor* at work but be able to do nothing to counter it.

He angles his blade toward me and advances, confident in his superiority. As a palatine, he's been trained in dueling since he was a boy. I am a newcomer to the art, but I have learned quickly. Already I can feel Rin's teachings settling into my steps. I flow easily through the forms I have been taught, no longer hesitating. I will bake Rin a hundred loaves of bread for her lessons.

I fall into The Way of Fire, an aggressive stance that lets me use my swords to their full potential. Brennus disengages smoothly, giving ground. Our swords sing as they slice through the air rarely connecting with each other. It would be foolish for him to give me the chance to lock his single *gladius* up and his senses warn him of my plans as fast as I make them.

My frustration grows as the combat progresses. His *Cor* tells him the same secrets that mine does. Yet as much as I have learned, I am no match for Brennus. His form is better, decisions sharper.

A smile begins to grow on his face as we exchange blows. His fear is eroding, replaced by the palatine arrogance that is bred into his bones. I grit my teeth and dig deeper, calling upon my layers of Silver to add more speed and strength to my blows. But it does not matter how quickly I move; I am not faster than a thought, and his Symbol keeps him even with me.

Then it happens.

At first, I think he made a mistake. I feint a strike with my left hand, forcing him to the right. Instead, I step across, closing with his swordless side, trying to use his own body against him. His empty left hand blurs, and a line of fire traces across me, numbed by my Iron Symbol.

I stagger back, my hand brushing toward my side and coming away wet. I stare numbly at the red that drenches my fist, eyes tracking to Brennus, who leers at me, blue eyes sparkling with malice. In his left hand, he holds a familiar white *tellus* knife in a reverse grip. I have fallen for his trick.

How did he get that back? I wonder distantly as shock begins to settle in.

"Do you see now, *Abominatio*?" he sneers, circling me like a predator watching a wounded deer on its last legs. "You were never going to be enough to beat me."

I bury myself deeper into Iron, letting it numb the pain and clear my mind. Using the Winter essence in my *gladii*, I lean on Ancient Frost, using it to push Unrelenting Fire further away. With a grunt, I stand tall and stare at the man who killed my friend. My rage has abated, sent away with the flame.

The only thing left is the cold desire to kill.

I advance slowly this time, not afraid, but giving my opponent the respect he deserves. In some ways, Brennus is the most dangerous man I have ever faced. Even Praeco was not equipped to truly stand before me. Only this man has access to the same power that makes me truly deadly.

A corner of his smile dips at the expression on my face, as if he recognizes the change that has swept over me. He settles into a fighter's stance, still holding his *tellus* knife in his offhand. I watch it warily as we begin to exchange blows. I cannot sense it with any of my Symbols, so I assume that he will rely on it for a killing blow. The unnaturally sharp and strong weapon eats at my swords, forcing me to spend more essence to keep them strong. Each strike from the ceramic is like touching the void that seeks to devour my weapons and me.

Part of me considers dropping one of my iron *gladii* and summoning the *Glacialis Falx* to challenge him in the same way. When I used my icy blades against him in the tunnel under Antioch, he was caught unawares. But something stops me, an instinct telling me to stay the course.

Perhaps it is simply pride. Killing Macer's murderer with a trick feels dishonorable—craven, even. To properly honor my fallen brother, I should finish Brennus as a member of the legion, not the abomination I have become. This is something I need to do as an Ironbound.

No, a foreign presence whispers to me, Nemesis peering over my shoulder. *There is another way.*

I struggle against the next series of blows as Brennus steps in to gut me. He moves fast, his cuts quick and precise. I have not trained against a man with a sword and knife, and my instincts are off-balance.

But there is something there, in the corner of my mind, that pulls at me. A hint, a feeling. I have been here before. Not like this, but close enough. I already know what to do, I just need to release myself to do it. I have already surrendered to one of my Symbols here. Why not another?

I withdraw a pace from Brennus, turning my attention to my own *gladii* for a moment. I have never really practiced shaping them. In the compound, I am only allowed to be Winterbound, so I have spent my time training with my frozen swords.

But why should Iron ones be any different from Ice?

Something fuses in me as the knowledge my mind has gained from training my Ancient Frost *Cor* is applied to my Iron one. A laugh escapes my throat as I realize that all these Symbols are within me. What I learn with one can be used by another.

Understanding *clicks* inside of me, like a joint that is being reset into its socket. I am right; I am whole. The world seems to grow brighter, as if I am suddenly able to see it in its true color. My *animus* extends, swirling with my Silver Symbols.

Brennus studies my amusement with hooded eyes. I shake my head; he doesn't know what I am about to become. No one has been able to do this for four hundred years. Percy told me that the *inhibitus* around a *Fidelis*'s throat will not let them advance beyond the base level of Silver. I have made quite a bit of progress beyond that. The Praetorian may be better with a blade, but he is not my equal with *Cor*. We may both be Silver, but he is still chained—I am free to become a monster.

I raise my left blade in a mocking salute to Macer's killer, then the fight begins in earnest. I steal steps from the different forms but turn them into something of my own. Here I use three moves from The Fire That Devours, then I shift into The Way of Water and the attack becomes part of The Rapids. I do not know if Rin would be proud or disgusted. Our blades flash as we crash together. My aggression is so raw that it is his turn to fall back, resetting our engagement. He tries to pull out of my range, but I do not let him go.

I slash my right-hand blade forward, sending my *animus* into it, reshaping it with my will as it goes. Ancient Frost and Iron work together, commanding the mysterious element created by an Iron Lord to obey my command.

I am not able to manifest new Iron to add to the mass of my *gladius*. But reluctantly, the Frost Iron twists, obeying my command. The sword stretches, growing thinner as it reaches out like a razorvine, becoming almost liquid as it moves.

Brennus brings up his *tellus* knife to block, but his weapon is too small. My swordwhip reaches over his weapon and cuts across his brow. The palatine recoils as I release my hold on the *gladius,* and it snaps back into the shape it was forged into. The Frost Iron resents being pulled from its purpose and is eager to return to it.

I stagger from the cost of using both essences. I will not be able to do that many more times. Regular ice is much more malleable than Frost Iron, and I have trained my Ancient Frost *Cor* to become much more efficient at this task. If only I had worn my *lorica* tonight!

But then I remember where I am.

I reach out with my *animus*, pulling from the raw iron ore that surrounds us, waiting to be processed. Each piece is not a particularly strong source, but we are dueling in the middle of an ocean of the stuff. I hunch my shoulders as I draw it in, willing my reserves to refill quickly while I pull Winter from my weapons.

It is Brennus's turn to reach with a shaking hand to check his wound. Blood flows down his forehead and over his nose. It will not kill him, but it teaches him to fear. I read it on his face, and my *animus* shows me how deep it runs.

Sharpensharpensharpensharpensharpensharpensharpensharpensharpensharpensharpensharpensharpensharpensharpen, a frantic mind seems to whisper. I can feel as his *gladius*'s edge grows thin and keen, reinforced by his eye. I hear him speaking to his blade even though I am not touching it.

Quick as a thought, I throw myself at him. I strike high with my left, and he blocks it with his *tellus* knife. I wince as its edge drags across my consciousness, but my will remains strong, stopping it from cutting through my sword.

I twist my sword free, feinting another ironwhip attack. He winces in anticipation, making me laugh cruelly. In his fear, he has forgotten to listen to his senses. That was not the moment, not yet. I'm saving my essence for a final burst of power. His hesitation buys me time to get in close.

My sword slices along the edge of his right leg before he manages to get his *gladius* between me and his flesh, forcing me away. I dance back, dodging his furious counterattack with the white knife. It whistles as it cuts the air between us.

Now, my fighter's instinct whispers to me as the space opens between us.

My left sword whips forward, and my will twists the Frost Iron without adding ice this time, thinning and stretching it into a wickedly sharp wire. Brennus is ready for it, slashing with his knife, trying to cut my weapon in half while it is in its weaker state.

I activate Aquilo's gift and channel the *Glacialis Falx* along the blade. A protective coating of ice erupts down the length of the weapon. The *tellus* blade bites deeply into the frost before getting stuck. Brennus's eyes go wide as the frozen swordwhip wraps around his knife. He twists, pulling the tension back toward himself, trying to cut his way free, but he is resisted by my will through two different elements.

Something deep inside of my chest *rumbles*—a surging power. Ancient Frost and Iron pull at me like hounds on the leash, begging to be released. *Not yet!* I command, struggling to hold them in place. I have only just managed to get all three of my *Corda* in harmony; I dare not let two of them Ascend and ruin all of my progress.

Brennus tries to force his weapon through the ice to get at the metal below. Which means he is distracted when I flick my right *gladius* at him, shifting it into a second swordwhip. His senses warn him, and he twists, dropping his *tellus* knife to try to escape. But he is too slow. The razor edge of my new weapon slices through his leather and into his chest with ease. Blood begins to leak through, dark on the leather.

We stare at each other in silence, panting with exertion. If I had not Ascended, I know that my body would have been too weak to do what I have put it through. But I am in balance. I am healed.

Despite my increased strength, I still have limits. I can feel my grip on Iron shaking as I struggle to maintain the whips in their malleable state. If I release them, I do not think I will have enough essence to summon them again. It is easier to hold this working than to create it. Some distant part of my mind panics, worried this state will drive me over the edge of Ascension, but I ignore it, too lost in the cold.

I should only need a few more moments to finish him.

I explode forward, driving him with my ironwhips. He retreats under my assault, using his single *gladius* defensively. But no matter how good his senses are, he cannot keep up with my speed as I flail at him.

I cut him to shreds.

Are you watching, Nemesis?

My weapons slice at his legs, his arms, his face. Red blood stains the ground as he retreats madly. One of his companions tries to ambush me, coming to the aid of his master. I kill him with a flick of the whip; the tip goes right through his eye. Whatever his Symbol is, he is not Ironbound. He drops to the ground with a dull *thump* as we continue our duel as if nothing happened.

My vision flickers as my reserves begin to run dry. I cannot keep up with the essence requirements for this. The raw ore around me feeds me as I guzzle from everything I can, desperate to be able to hold the dregs at bay. Despite my advantage, the Praetorian is still trained and dangerous. He baits me, trying to get close so he can go to work with his blade. I keep him at a distance, content to wear him down.

This is for Macer.

In the distance, I think I hear the low tolling of the bells that accompanies Nemesis, as she answers my question. I feel her presence hovering around me like a cloak, sucking in my revenge like it is a *locus* of essence. Her delight is like a starving woman sitting at a feast. With every slice, I feed her.

"Castor, I need help!" a woman's voice screams, shattering my focus. I glance over my shoulder, shocked at the interruption. In the depths of Iron, I have forgotten my own companions. Alessandra flees from the second swordsman, racing along the upper level of the catwalk. She places her hand on the rail, and the man behind her screams in agony, and the air sizzles as she channels lightning into the metal structure. Then she turns and sprints away while he staggers back to his feet.

There is no sign of Anas.

What am I doing? Disgust roils through me as my emotions begin to process again, no longer held at bay by the cold logic of Iron and Ice. This is not what Macer would want. Vengeance should be about justice, not cruelty. I take this risk for nothing other than my own sick delight. I am both a monster and a fool.

It is time to end this.

I step forward, casting my right whip at him. He blocks it with his sword, and I let my weapon coil around his blade. He looks up at me with wide eyes, then drops his sword, turning to flee. He knows what is coming.

My left ironwhip curls around his ankle, yanking him off his feet before he can escape. He falls flat on his stomach and is slow to rise. My foot is on his back before he is even on his knees. I release the working on my weapons, letting them morph back into their original shapes. My simmering anger is the only reason I do not sag in relief as the strain of using my nearly empty *Cor* fades.

"Please!" the Praetorian sobs under my foot. "Just let me go. I'll go back to duty, and you'll never see me again."

"Why did you come here tonight, Brennus?" My voice is cold and hard.

"I… What?"

"You followed us to the Foundry. Why?"

"We were just going to scare—"

"Don't lie to me!" Unrelenting Fire begins to warm up as my coldness fades, filling me with its rage. "You came here to murder the heir of *Domus* Pelias in revenge for your uncle. Just like you murdered my friend in the desert."

His silence is loud.

"Castor!"

My head twists, and I curse, realizing I have let myself be distracted again. Alessandra is on the fourth story of the far catwalk but is running out of levels. The man still follows her doggedly, his hair sticking in every direction. I am out of time.

"Just let me go, and I—urgh!" His voice gurgles as my blade stabs into the back of his neck, severing his spine. Despite my urgency, I lean down as I pull my blade free, whispering so he can hear with his last moments.

"*Redemptio in bello*." I say the Twelfth's motto. I don't know if I believe those words. I do not feel redeemed—just empty. The world is a little more blind than it was a few moments ago. Nemesis's presence fades, like a reluctant dinner guest finally going home at the end of the night.

I have no more time for Brennus Valerus. I leave him in the dust, just as he once left my friend. The gods are dead. I do not know what waits for him on the other side of the Veil. If the ghost of Pluto waits for him anywhere, I can only hope that he is judged as harshly as he deserves.

I am alive, and there are still things for the living to do.

"Castor!" Alessandra shrieks a third time, summoning me to her aid.

"Coming!" I shout, turning to pound up the nearest stairway two at a time. The catwalk rumbles under my feet as I race across it, searching for the path to the next level. A bridge connects my side to theirs on the third level.

I cannot let anything happen to her! That thought is my own, but it is reinforced by the oath etched in my bones by Varus's relic. My body tingles in anticipation and dread. I do not know what it will do to me if I fail to save her.

No! No! No!

There is another sizzling sound, and the man screams again. I race up another flight, leaping over the guardrail to race toward the bridge that connects our two towers. This high up, the floorboards shake under my weight as I sprint recklessly, trying to catch them before it is too late.

I reach out and grab a pole as I race past, using it to aid my turn without slowing down. I am so close. I leap up the fourth staircase two steps at a time, long legs eating up the distance.

"Alessandra, where are you?" I bark as I burst onto the top level, casting about wildly for them. My *animus* sweeps wildly, searching for the attacker's sword among the sea of iron ore and bars.

There! His sword shines like a beacon to my mind, and I race toward the front, praying to any dead god who might listen that I am not too late. As I run, I check my Iron *Cor*'s essence reserves, hoping to be able to lasso him with my sword before he even gets close to her.

I round the corner and slide to a stop in horror at the scene before me. Alessandra stands at the end of the walkway, pressed up against the railing. Her hands are raised, warning off the man who has her cornered.

He turns at my approach; his face is pale and strained, hair spiked in a thousand directions. Silver veins streak his arms. I've never seen him before, but it is clear he knows who I am.

"Stay back!" he warns, raising his dueling blade threateningly toward Alessandra, who has nowhere left to run. "I'll kill her. I'll gut her like a pig!" He shakes like a leaf. Fear governs him—he is little more than a cornered rat.

"Your master is dead," I tell him coldly. I am Iron again. My eyes flicker from him to the space between us, evaluating the distance. Even if I have enough Ancient Frost and Iron essence for my new trick, he is too far for me to reach with a swordwhip. If I am going to strike him down, I'll need to get closer.

"I killed him," I explain, moving a little closer. He shivers, looking wildly at Alessandra before waving his sword threateningly in her direction. "I killed your other companion too. What was his name?"

"Portus." He seems surprised he answered the question.

"Portus," I repeat, as if committing the name to memory. I won't remember him long. He will be washed under the oceans of blood to come. I take another step. Only a few more, and he will be in range. I keep a cool smile on my face, but inwardly I am coiled tightly, a cobra ready to strike.

"Stay back!" He inches a little closer to Alessandra, who looks at me with wild eyes.

"What is your plan?" I tilt my head at him, studying him like a cat. "You must know if you kill her, I will kill you. Well, actually, I will cripple you. Then I will take you to her father."

He lets out another whimper. "But she'll be dead! Blood for blood!"

"Are you a Valerus, then?" I scoff. "Is your blood worth shedding for this palatine feud? Or are you like me, one of their weapons, kept sharp until it is time to be thrown away?" I take another step, but he doesn't notice. My words haunt him, as they haunt me.

"I am not a tool."

I laugh, throwing my head back to mock him loudly. "Risus's Rotting Eyes, that was a good one. Tell me another joke. We are all tools of the masters we serve."

"I am *not* a tool." He grows angry now, turning to face me directly, Alessandra already forgotten.

"Then prove it," I say, stepping forward once more. My right wrist rotates in a small circle as I nudge the Frost Iron in my blade, testing if I can manipulate the sword into becoming a whip once more. I feel it shift slightly, then reject my will as my reserves falter. I need more time.

"Step aside and live. I have no quarrel with you. Live to die another day."

For a moment, I think my words have done enough. His eyes soften and his shoulders hunch as he considers abandoning whatever task he has been given. He sees, I think, what I have been trying to tell him. That to the family serves, he is a game piece and not a man.

I feel his decision before he even realizes he's made it. His dueling blade stops shaking. In one fluid motion, he spins, blade pulling back for one final stab.

I have little Iron or Ancient Frost left to me. In my panic, I release both of those Symbols, reaching for the one I know the least. Unrelenting Fire leaps to my call, hungry to be used. It feels almost jealous that it has not had its turn yet.

My Frost Iron blade clatters to the ground as I extend my right hand, summoning the flame that burns within me. I pour essence into it, condensing it into something real, before I unleash it at Portus's back. A beam of fire leaps from me. It flares bright against the dark upper reaches of the Foundry's bowels.

The man screams even as he drives the point of his dueling blade through Alessandra's tunic and into her torso. I feel him now, connected as we are by the fire. I invade him with my will, commanding my Symbol to burn him.

Alessandra cries in pain but does not lose her footing, taking advantage of her assailant's fatal mistake. He touched her with metal.

Lightning arcs through the sword that connects them, carving a blinding bar on my vision. My mind flickers back to the training arena, where I have seen Alessandra sit in the middle of a storming *locus*, absorbing lightning without a thought.

Now that energy bends to her will as she sends it pouring into the Valerus assassin. The air stinks of burning meat, and he twitches uncontrollably, his body unable to process the power that surges through him. Together we burn him until he can take no more. He collapses to the ground, his body ruined and smoking. Alessandra fixes me with a grim stare as her own knees buckle from the wound she has suffered.

"It's your turn to help me with walking," she mutters before she collapses.

CHAPTER 51

Terror threatens to consume me as I race to Alessandra's side. I discard Unrelenting Fire to reach for Ancient Frost, hoping its cold logic will ground me. With a shaking hand, I check her for a pulse. It is there, strong and fast, praise Dead Asclepius.

Blood pools around her where the sword still sticks out of her chest. Desperately, I cast about, looking for something I can use as a bandage. The Foundry has nothing to offer me but dirty metal and rocks. Out of ideas, I reach out and touch the hilt of the dueling blade, wincing as I see how deeply the sword has cut inside of her.

I cannot let her keep bleeding, but I also have to move her. The sword needs to come out so that it doesn't cut her further. With a thought, I mold the sword, smoothing out its sharp edges, making it easy to pull free. It slides out easily without catching on her flesh.

Blood wells in the open wound, and I curse, not sure what to do. I debate cutting my own tunic into strips, but that will not provide the pressure I need. There is no way to make a tourniquet around her chest. I must find a way to seal the wound, or she will die before I can get her back to the Pelias estate.

A thought emerges from the back of my consciousness, working its way through the barrier of frost that surrounds my mind. Reluctantly, Ancient Frost parts to let this instinct from my hottest *Cor* through. My eyes flicker to the ruined dueling blade that I hold, following Unrelenting Fire's whispers.

It could work.

I switch Symbols, banishing Winter for the power of Fire. Still holding the iron sword, I narrow my eyes and place my right hand on the flat of the blade. With my will, I pour the burning essence that I carry into the dueling blade. It does not manifest as fire, but slowly, the temperature begins to rise.

After a dozen heartbeats, the edges begin to turn pink. A few more, and a handbreadth of the metal glows. I grit my teeth, pulling in more essence from the distance furnace, refilling my *Cor* as it pours out of me. This isn't congruency. I am not manipulating the iron—merely channeling my heat into it.

Finally, the weapon is a cherry-red. The metal is so soft, it bends in my bare hands. Moving quickly, I peel the torn sides of her tunic away from her wound, exposing the flesh on either side. I let out a long sigh as I slowly lower the red-hot blade toward her chest, preparing to cauterize the wound.

"This is going to hurt," I warn, but she does not react. Then the iron touches her flesh, and the air is full of a sizzling sound as the two halves of her wound melt together. I grit my teeth, trying to gauge how long I should wait as I hold it in place. I have only been taught how to take a life, not save one. Alessandra murmurs in her unconscious state, squirming against the pain.

I count to ten then lift the sword, nervously eying the wound that I have seared whole. Her flesh is red and burnt, but as I gingerly wipe at it, no fresh blood emerges. Relieved, I lean back on my heels, dropping the still-smoking blade to the ground. Hopefully, that will buy me the time to get her to the *medici*.

But there is still more to do.

Cursing under my breath, I rise to my feet and eye the man who stabbed her. I've already forgotten his name. He is dead. His eyes have been burnt out of his face by Alessandra's power, his flesh ruined by mine. I cannot just leave him here. Xania might not know what Brennus and his idiot companions decided to do tonight. Leaving the bodies in their condition will only start a war sooner.

I grunt as I bend over to grab him by his belt. Calling upon my Silver strength, I lift him up and over the railing and let him tumble to the floor below. He lands with a sickening *thump* that makes me not want to look. But I have no time to be gracious with the dead.

Alessandra still has my weapon sheaths. I slide my *gladii* into them, tossing the belt around my waist before scooping her up far more gently than I did her assailant. She is light in my Silver arms. I wince as she groans as if in pain but does not open her eyes.

"Hang on, just a little while," I beg softly.

I move quickly, trying not to jostle her too hard, and we make it to the floor in one piece. Her would-be killer is a mess. I ignore him for a moment, scanning the rest of the scene, desperate to find Anas. He has been silent for too long.

Just when I am beginning to fear the worst, I find him. My Twelfth brother is lying on his back, propped against a rail cart in a pool of his own blood. He lets out a sigh of relief at the sight of me carrying Alessandra.

"There you are, *Dominus*," he murmurs.

"You can always count on a soldier to be lying down on the job while the officers are distracted," I say, trying to force a smile.

"Just a quick rest," he assures me. His voice is weak. I set Alessandra down next to him, just outside of his blood, and step forward to check on my friend.

"Come now, you've had worse," I chide him, noting the dozen cuts that cross his arms and legs. They cut him to ribbons. I suddenly regret killing Brennus's other friend so quickly. Relief flows through me as I catalogue his wounds. He's lost a lot of blood, but I see no sign that his organs have been pierced.

"Maybe once or twice."

"Can you walk?"

"Oh sure." He wiggles slightly, trying to rise but failing. "I'll get right on that."

"Okay, sit tight. I'll be back for you both." I rise, intending to go find Timidus, the coachman, and force him to help me. But then I pause, eyeing the three bodies that lie in the middle of the Foundry, and hesitate. The less he knows, the better.

Alone, I commit a crime against the Empress herself.

All three of the Valerus contingent were *electi*. By rights, their relics are now the property of Diana, minus the tithe that would go to their family for their service. That is the oath that each of us swears, Legion or not, when we are given our *Cor* Hearts.

Instead of harvesting them, I feed their bodies to the furnace. The fire rages through the glass porthole that I broke with my exit. It accepts my offerings greedily, filling the empty factory with the stench of burning meat. I thrust myself deeply into the arms of Ancient Frost to keep from vomiting as I move about my grim task.

Part of me finds a small sense of poetry in the moment. Atticus and the Praetorians fed my mother and sister to the flames. Brennus killed my friend. Why should I not feed some of them to the fire as well? An eye for an eye may leave the whole world blind, but I would rather live in darkness than with the vision that has been thrust upon me. Besides, my goddess already cannot see.

Another part of me whispers quietly that this is another step down a road that I will never return from. My mother would not be proud of this. But she's dead; her voice cannot guide me. Only her memory haunts me, distant and cold.

Brennus is the last one to join his comrades in the inferno. There is no one to pray to, but I say one anyway to Dead Pluto, asking him to tell Macer that he has been avenged. It does not make me feel better.

My grisly task complete, I race back to Alessandra and Anas. Both are unconscious but breathing. I let out a sigh of relief as I plan my next steps. There's no point in bringing poor Timidus in here. He will only see things that can get him killed.

Instead, I walk over to Anas and lift him, using all my Silver strength to throw him over my shoulder like a sack of flour. He is heavy. I stagger under the weight but grit my teeth and manage to find some sort of balance.

Lowering my head, I power my way through the expanse of Foundry and out the door that we entered. *Mons* Olympus floats above me, a silhouette against the full moon. I curse the dead gods as I carry the heavy former *captivus* toward the carriage.

"Timidus!" I bellow as I draw close. "Wake up, you sleeping cur!" I am met with only silence. My left hand strays toward the hilt of its *gladius*.

"Timidus?" I repeat, no longer sure of myself. My *animus* sweeps around us, checking for attackers lurking in the yard. But I find no swords waiting in the dark. All I can sense is the iron in the carriage, the equipment around us, and in the ore waiting to be processed.

Slowly, I make my way to the coach and look inside. It is empty, abandoned. A growl sounds in my throat as I realize how the Valerus might have known where Alessandra was tonight. I wrench the door open and jam Anas into a seat.

"Don't move!" I shout at my unconscious friend, turning to sprint back toward Foundry.

Something skitters under my boot as I run through the factory, causing me to stop. Slowly, I bend down to pick up Brennus's *tellus* knife from the dust. The weapon feels strange in my grip, too smooth and light to be made of iron. The only texture on the hilt is the raised pattern of the eight-armed *krakenus*, the sigil of the Valerus family.

I tuck the ceramic blade into my belt as proof for Varus and race back to Alessandra. The young woman has begun to come to, her Silver body working overtime to heal the damage caused by her wound. She opens her mouth to speak, but I silence her.

"Pardon me, *Domina*," I grunt, crouching to scoop her up in my arms once more. She protests weakly, but I do not listen. "We are in a bit of a hurry." Moving as quickly as I dare, I carry her to the cart, loading her into the seat next to the still-unconscious Anas. Worried, I check his throat for a pulse. It is still there but weaker than before. The cushion underneath him is stained red with his blood.

I slam the door to the carriage shut and leap up to the driver's seat, eyeing it uncertainly. As a boy, I would occasionally be allowed to drive the carts in the fields, so I understand the basics of steering a contraption like this. But a pair of oxen pulling a boy through an open field is a far cry from driving a trained pair of horses in the second largest city of the Empire.

There is no one else to do this. It must be me. I do not know how much longer Anas has. My flames have bought Alessandra a while, but he has too many wounds for cauterization to be practical. The only path to salvation is forward. Leaning forward, I grab the reins in my hands.

"Hyah!" I give the tack a light flip, knocking it against the back of the horses, the way I saw Timidus do when we left. At once, the pair break into a trot, pulling against their harnesses. Tentatively, I experiment in the empty gravel yard, pulling them to the left and right, trying to get a feel for their turning radius.

We complete a tight circle, and reluctantly, I aim them toward the exit, which still sits open, waiting for us. The horses' hooves echo off the cobblestones as we burst into the empty street.

At least it is night, I think wryly, glaring back at *Luna*'s full eye that stares down on me as I guide the team through Anteforum's wide streets. The horses can either sense my urgency or lack of experience, for they lean into their task with glee. More than one person shouts at us in alarm as we race past them.

Another carriage veers in terror as we round a corner at high speed, driving up onto the pedestrian walkway to make way. Their drivers shout in outrage in my wake, but I do not acknowledge them. My oath to Varus tingles in my bones, quivering with the same fear that fills me as I race against the clock, trying to save my passengers.

At last, I spy the familiar wall of the Pelias estate. I am surprised that *Sol* has not begun his ascent above the horizon, but when I check his pale counterpart, I am surprised to learn that it has been less than half an hour. It has felt like an eternity as I made my way through unfamiliar streets, trusting the horses' sense of direction more than my own.

"Open the gate!" I bellow as I approach the entrance to the courtyard. A pair of Ironbound guards eye me from the wall, confusion evident on their faces.

"In the name of Senator Varus Pelias, open the gate, or I will open it for you!" I threaten. Something in my voice must convince them, for the doors begin to swing wide open. The team, which had begun to slow, break into a trot at the sight of home.

Please let me not be too late.

We sweep into the courtyard in a spray of gravel as I pull on the reins, forcing the horses to an abrupt stop. The wood of the carriage groans at the abuse, but I ignore it. I'm already leaping from the driver's seat before we're completely at a halt.

"*Medico*!" I shout as my feet land on the ground. It is like I never left the legions. I am a decurion again, ordering soldiers around. Four guards race up to me, hands on the hilts of their swords as they try to figure out if I am a threat. My finger shoots out, stopping them in their tracks.

"You, fetch me every *medici* that's in the compound right now. Tell them we have two combat victims that need immediate aid." The Ironbound's eyes flare wide, and after a moment of hesitation, he salutes and sprints toward the dormitories.

"You, fetch me *Dominus* Varus *at once*. I do not care if he's in the bath, I do not care who he's in bed with. *Bring him to me*. Do I make myself clear?" This one's face pales, but he too salutes me as if I am his commanding officer.

"Yes, *Dominus*," he shouts before racing toward the main house, arms pumping.

"And you." I wheel on the third guard, who no longer looks caught off guard. He's older than the rest, an experienced veteran. "I want every guard in this estate awake on the walls *now*. Full battle kit."

"On whose authority?" he sneers. "You are not my master. Why should I listen to you?"

I do not have time for this. I whirl on him, snarling as I close the distance in a handful of heartbeats. His hand flashes toward his *gladius*, but he never even manages to pull it free from its sheath. His Copper speed is no match for me. My left hand catches the top of his hilt, holding it in place before he can complete his draw.

My right fist connects with his face, knocking him on his back.

"You!" I snap at the remaining soldier. "Every guard. Full battle kit. *Now*." The fourth man looks at his sprawling friend, then snaps to a salute before racing to obey my commands. I leave the groaning guard in the dust, turning back to the carriage and pulling its door open.

"Everyone still alive in here?" I demand, trying to force some levity into my voice as terror clutches at me. Anas is far too pale. He leans bonelessly against the wall, looking more like a sack of potatoes than a man. I check his pulse—it is faint.

"*MEDICO*!" I bellow again, spinning to find myself staring into the face of one of Pelias doctors, a woman dressed in a white nightgown, rubbing sleep out of her eyes. She flinches at my shout but does not flee.

"More are coming, *Dominus*," the first guard tells me, giving me a sharp salute. "*Medico* Jahns was the closest."

"Well done. Hurry the rest of them up. We don't have time."

"What's the situation?" the *medico* asks, sounding almost bored as she slides past me to investigate the inside of the carriage suspiciously. "Surely we do not need to rouse all of the—dead gods, is that the *heir*?" Her voice changes to a squeak. All of the guards stiffen in shock, their wide eyes tracking from me to the dark interior of the carriage.

"Tell them to run faster!" Jahns snaps, turning to shout at the guard who brought her.

"This guard's wounds are more severe—"

"I will see to him after I check on her," Jahns interrupts me firmly, climbing into the cart. I open my mouth to protest but close it silently. It will do no good. What is the life of a slave compared to that of the heir of a palatine house?

"What happened?" Jahns's voice is clinical and cold as she crouches to examine Alessandra's wound.

"She was stabbed by a dueling blade," I tell her, looking at Anas, trying to see if he is still breathing. His chest moves, and I cling to that motion with desperate hope. There is still time. "She was bleeding heavily and unconscious. I cauterized the wound before bringing her back here."

"You did this?" Her head whips around to glare at me in suspicion. I raise my chin as I hold her gaze.

"I did." Something in my stare unsettles her, and she looks away as more people race up to the carriage. Three more *medici*, in similar states of undress, shove their way in, all trying to get a look at Alessandra.

"This guard also need—" I begin, but an older man with white hair cuts me off, waving dismissively.

"He will be looked at next, boy." My gaze travels down to the dark red stains on the cushion of Anas's seat. Fire and Ice move together for once, united by their rage. A cold anger begins to burn in me.

The sound of my *gladius* pulling free from its sheath rings through the night. The temperature of the air plummets as the Ancient Frost in my blade pulses threateningly. All four of the *medici* freeze, slowly turning to look at me with wide, terrified eyes.

"Forgive me, *Domini*," I sneer, the honorific making it clear what little I think of them. "Is it somehow possible that the four of you are so unlearned that it is necessary for all of you to look over the heir? Surely *one* of your attentions can be spared for the man who bled in her defense?"

There is a moment of long, terrible silence.

"What are you going to do, boy?" the old man asks at last. "Kill us if we do not help your friend?"

"He probably *would* kill one of you to make a point." Varus's voice is sharp and clear as the senator arrives like a winter storm. "But you will obey him, for he speaks with my voice."

"Yes, *Dominus*. Forgive me." The *medico* cows at once, bowing his head and scuttling to Anas's side. I turn to the side to make way for him, sheathing my sword slowly. My eyes find Varus's, and he tilts his head in summons.

Reluctantly, I obey leaving my companions in the *medici*'s care and stepping out into the night. A brass horn begins to sound, blowing six short notes in a variation of the legion muster call. Varus's head rises to look in the direction of his guard barracks before turning back to me, eyes dark.

"Valerus?"

"Valerus," I confirm. I draw the *tellus* knife from my belt and flip it in my hand, offering it to him hilt first. He takes it slowly, looking down at his hands for a long moment.

"I gave this to Briannus as proof." His voice is calm and dangerous. Another enemy added to the list. A chill runs down my spine to see him so cold. "So much for the Empress's *moratorium*."

"It was Brennus."

His head snaps up in surprise, and he gives me another long look. "Does he live?"

He had not expected Xania's son to attack us personally. Part of me thinks that Xania wouldn't have either.

I shake my head. "No survivors."

He cocks his head, studying me more closely. His eyes track to my *gladii*, which hang from my belt. I know what he is thinking. The swords are intact despite battling a *Fidelis*. How did I manage to beat him? I say nothing—to be defensive would only increase the suspicion. After a moment, he nods, accepting my word.

"Where are the bodies? How long until they are discovered?" he asks, his eyes flick to over my shoulders, tracking the *medici* that are working on his daughter. A part of him is with her, only concerned with being a father. But he knows that there is more riding on this.

"I burned them," I admit, confessing my crime. "They will never be found."

A stream of guards begins to thunder into the courtyard behind us, shouting orders as they race toward the walls. We stand tranquil amongst their chaos, like a pair of rocks as the tide goes out.

"Burned them," he repeats softly when there is no one around us. He knows what that means for the relics.

I nod without flinching.

"Your idea?" he asks, nodding at the complement of guards manning the walls.

"What would you do?" I reply, tilting my head toward the carriage behind us. The *medici* have begun to move Alessandra and Anas. I do not speak my question aloud, for fear of inviting Thanatos's shade into this house, but he takes my meaning all the same. The loss of his child would trigger a landslide.

His eyes harden, and he glances at the walls again. "Well done," he says after a pause. He claps me on the shoulder, a gesture that is more symbolic than anything. Every eye in this courtyard is on the pair of us. He tells all of them that I carry his favor.

"*Medico*, will my daughter live?" he calls when his hand drops.

"She is stable, *Dominus*," Jahns answers after a moment. "She will have a horrible scar, but the cauterization likely saved her life."

"And her guard?" Varus looks at me as he asks, showing me a glimpse of who he is. How different he is from the drunks who sat on the *Argentum Consilio*. If only all the senators were cut from the same cloth as him, the world would be a better place.

"Too soon to say, but I've seen Ironbound survive worse, *Dominus*," the male *medico* who works on Anas replies. Relief floods through me, I know some of what Anas has already lived through. This isn't where his story ends.

Over Varus's shoulder, Pliny rushes into the courtyard, emerging from his library like a gopher. His eyes take in everything at a glance, but they settle on me with a weight of certainty that tells me he knows what I have done.

For the first time, I inspect my own arms. The paint that hid my Copper *Cor* is gone, burned away by the heat of the Foundry furnace. White *rasa* veins still show among the network of veins that run through my body, but there are more Silver ones than before, plain for anyone with eyes to see.

CHAPTER 52

Xania Valerus comes with the fury of a god.

It takes only a few hours for the senator to arrive. She comes on the back of a white chariot, resplendent in armor that is white but not made of *tellus*. A red cape hangs from her shoulders, and a score of armed Gold *electi* gather behind her, able to match the pace of her vehicle easily.

"VARUS PELIAS," her voice thunders from every direction, as if part of the air itself. "COME AND FACE ME, COWARD." The Ironbound guards along our wall tense, shields raised. I stand at Varus's left hand on the wall, measuring the deadly force that has come and assaults us.

"I am here, Xania," the master of the house replies calmly. His voice is quiet, but it cuts through the night as sharp as a knife. "Why have you come so armored? Is there a feud between our *domuum*? Did not the Empress herself forbid that until after the Forum Games?" His challenge is obvious, daring her to defy Diana in the streets. He seems pure and fearless—a man with no secrets to hide—despite being under the threat of *Judicium*.

"If there is no feud, why do your soldiers adorn your walls?" Xania throws back at him, voice still shaking with fury. "You cower before me like a turtle from the hawk. Bring out my son, or I shall tear you to ribbons and strew your entrails from here to the Empress's seat."

"I have not seen your son, Xania," Pelias replies in the same cool tone, ignoring her threats like he might a child's. "He has not come here. I swear this upon my Symbol."

"LIAR," her voice booms again, shaking with rage. Her retainers mutter among themselves, an echo of dark whispers. Their hands stray to the hilt of their weapons as they glare up at us. The street around them is empty. It is still the dead of night. But I doubt that any passerby would be foolish enough to stay around this congregation of power.

Several of her *electi* stare at me directly, an overt challenge. I take a page out of Varus's book and paste a mild smile on my face as I meet their gazes. They have heard of me, but I do not know any of them.

"So be it," Xania hisses, stepping off her chariot to storm toward our gate. Her red cape billows behind her. It reminds me of the tribune's cloak that Gaius wore, but hers is too large, too red to ever be anything other than theatrical.

In her hands, she carries a long, sheathed sword. She draws it in one long motion, and a low moan of fear runs through the Ironbound standing on our wall. I stare in fascination and dread, for I have never seen a weapon like it before. Even my fantastic blades pale in comparison to this work.

The blade is longer than a dueling blade. It also eschews the normal curve; instead, it is a perfect straight line from hilt to top. It only breaks from tradition at the tip; instead of a triangle, it ends in a square line.

The edges of the sword burn a dark red, moving slowly from the base to the tip as if molten. The very air around the blade seems to warp as if twisted by the heat it gives off. I recognize the flash of dark metal set in its pommel; it is powered by some relic. Something inside of me leaps in excitement as my new Silver Heart shows me the fiery essence that bleeds from it. Unrelenting Fire sees it as a challenge and welcomes it.

The terrible sword's red glow shines off Xania's armor as she holds it before her threateningly. I have no doubt she could use it to shear through our gates. Tension spikes as the men around me hunch their shoulders, preparing for an onslaught. My hands drop to the pair of *gladii* that hang around my waist. I am back on the front lines in the North once more, but without my *scutum* and *lorica*, I feel naked.

Only Varus does not move. His posture remains the same, his shoulders broad and strong. He does not toy with his sword; instead, he cocks his head slightly, as if waiting for something. After a couple heartbeats, he turns away from Xania to fix on a blank spot of the street with focused intent.

The Valerus senator notices his distraction and follows his gaze. Slowly, one by one, the rest of her entourage follows suit, until almost every soul on that street stares at the same empty space of air.

After a long pause something flickers, and three Censors stand exposed with three almost abashed expressions. One of them must bear a Light Symbol that allowed them to slip in undetected. But the stone they stood on whispered their secrets to Varus Pelias. The leader's lips twist into a frown before it vanishes behind the haughty mask all members of the White Hand wear. He steps forward, sticking his chest forward.

"Stop in the name of the Empress!"

"Why would your son be here?" Varus asks, ignoring the Censors and turning back to Xania with a dangerous glint in his eye. The other senator freezes, eyes flickering from her burning sword to the three *tellus*-clad warriors who watch. She seems hesitant now that they are here. In a flash, I understand the game that is being played. The Censors are the eyes of the Empress. Anything that they witness is as if Diana Agrippa were here in the flesh.

Did Xania know that they were there? The Empress has moved against *Domus* Pelias in the past. Do her Censors skulk around behind their veils in an attempt to give the Valerus the fiction of anonymity? By forcing them to appear in a formal capacity, Varus has played their hand. Xania dares not admit where her son went now.

"I said *enough*!" the Censor shouts, irritated that the senators do not submit now that he is visible.

"What is your *Casus Belli*, Senator Valerus?" Varus presses, still ignoring the trio of *tellus*-armored *electi* to focus on his rival. "You can lodge it here in front of these august witnesses." His smile only grows.

I was once told by my old magister, Vellus, that there is a formal way for one house to declare a feud against another. The great *domuum* clash all the time, but just like assassins in the countryside, there are rules that must be followed. The aggrieved party may argue their *Casus Belli*, their "cause for war," to the Censors for judgment. According to him, the Empress believes "soft lands create soft houses." Which means she doesn't like her palatines feeling *too* comfortable.

Under normal circumstances, I suspect that killing Brennus outside of a duel would be a legitimate *Casus Belli*. But since the Empress has placed a *moratorium* on violence, it would be their House that was in the wrong for breaking Diana's peace.

"My son is missing," Xania answers a beat later, her voice hissing with vehemence. A scowl darkens the lines on her face, making her look almost like she was carved from stone.

"That is worrisome," Varus agrees, his voice practically dripping with concern. "I can only imagine how *I* would feel if my own child was gone." Xania's eyes flash as she acknowledges the barb buried in his words. Her son tried to murder his daughter, after all.

"I cannot help but wonder why you have come *here*, brimming with violence?" He glances imploringly to the Censors, as if he were a simple and wounded man. "What do I and my House have to do with your missing son?"

"Our houses have a long and bloody history, Pelias," she snarls, taking a step forward toward the gate. The blazing sword in her hand still casts its evil red glare on the street around her. The three Censors stiffen; if she attacks now, they will be forced to intervene.

"That has long been completed," Varus replies easily, hooking his thumbs into his belt like a farmer. "Our feud ended more than forty years ago, witnessed and recorded by the Censors." He jerks his head toward the trio that watches from the sidelines. "So it seems odd to me that you would immediately rush here, to my home, when he goes missing."

Xania's silence is deafening. She shakes with rage, gritting her teeth as she glares up at us with eyes full of violence. Her son is dead; she must know that. Anger and grief radiated from her like the heat from her relic-powered blade.

For a moment, I think she is going to charge the door despite the presence of the Empress's White Hand. But at last, her eyes go hard and flat. A shiver runs down my spine as she stares at us with an animal cunning. She can wait. This is not over.

"You're right," she manages through gritted teeth. "I will continue searching for him elsewhere. I'm sorry to have disturbed your peace this evening."

"Think nothing of it, Senator Valerus," Varus replies calmly as if he were an old friend and not the man standing at the head of thirty armed and armored Ironbound. "I do hope you find your son." Xania recoils as if he backhanded her across the face but does not reply.

She slides her unholy sword back into its sheath and leaps back into her chariot. Her retinue of Gold *electi* keep pace with her easily, flowing around her like a pack as they race off into the night. I resist the urge to let out a long sigh of relief at the sight of their backs.

The three Censors watch her leave before turning their cold eyes on Varus. The leader doesn't say anything, but after a moment, they flicker out of sight, shielded once more by the Lightbound in their midst. The threat is plain. We may not see them, but they are watching.

The men on the wall slowly begin to relax as the tension lifts like the morning fog before *Sol*'s burning light. It feels as if a siege has just been lifted. I turn to Varus to find the senator looking at me with thoughtful eyes.

"I think it is time we told one another the truth," he says softly, glancing over his shoulder at the blank spot of the street where the Censors last stood.

CHAPTER 53

Pliny waits for me at the base of the stairs when we descend from the wall. The short magister is practically radiating with excitement as he greets Varus and me. His eyes devour my arms as they trace my fresh Silver veins. I shuffle uncomfortably at the attention.

"*Dominus*, I need to examine Castor immediately," he says, stepping forward to block our progress. "If he has truly accomplished…" His voice trails off as he glances surreptitiously around the courtyard. Varus turns to study me again, his brows furrowing as he realizes that I no longer have a Copper *Cor*.

"Very well." He nods after a moment. "We will speak after the good magister has finished with you."

"Aye, *Dominus*." I bow my head in respect. I am still nervous about what secrets the senator wishes to cover. I am reluctant to be drawn into his world, but part of me knows that it is already far too late.

"Come, come," Pliny demands, turning on his heel and making for the training hall. I follow in his wake, trying to calm my dancing nerves. I have not had a moment of peace since I set foot in Foundry's furnace. It still does not feel real that I have Ascended to Silver for the third time.

As we walk, I close my eyes, letting my *animus* sweep around the courtyard. It takes me several tries to get my disparate attunements to play nicely with one another. I cannot hold all of them equally. Ancient Frost or Unrelenting Fire must take the lead. Iron dances to its own tune, mostly unbothered by their squabbling. Once I manage to hold them all, I am stunned by how much my *animus* can see. Unrelenting Fire whispers to me of the torches and bonfires that burn to keep the night at bay.

Iron shows me the soldiers who stand guard, painting their *lorica*, *scuta*, and *gladii* in my mind. I feel the nails in the carriage that still sits unattended.

Ancient Frost has the least to tell me. There is no winter here. Yet even it manages to whisper faint impressions of the fountain that bubbles by the entrance to the main house. Water is congruent but so different that I can barely feel the shape of it.

I open my eyes, overwhelmed by the depth of awareness that fills me like the knowledge of my own body. It is so much! I am burdened by it. Shaking my head, I withdraw my *animus* to a smaller range around me, trying to limit the extent of knowledge to a manageable amount.

"It's just truly marvelous," Pliny said, rambling on in his excitement, "that you managed to finally Ascend your new *Cor* to Silver. What was the final step that pushed you over the edge? Did it happen while you were out of the compound? Did you find a better source of Ancient Frost?" His questions come at a reckless pace; he leaves no pause for me to answer them.

To my surprise, he does not stop at the main training hall with the *loci* in them. Instead, he continues to a door I have not been through before, gesturing for me to follow him. We make our way down a series of halls until we emerge in a second sandy arena.

It takes up the entire room that is otherwise very spartan. A few banners hang from the walls, flanking a weapon rack full of a variety of swords. It feels like I am intruding in the private study of a master.

Contessa waits for us, giving me a sharp nod of approval as I enter. My Ascension means that she can begin to push me as hard as she desires. I will not be protected from her regimen by Pliny any longer. After tonight, I am eager to get back to work.

"Together we will uncover some secrets of the universe, boy," Pliny says, turning to stare at me as he moves into the ring. "Let us start with the biggest issues. Did your second *Cor* merge with your existing one now that they are the same tier? Or do they still remain distinct and separate?"

"Um," I reply, caught off guard by his question. I am not sure I am prepared enough to lie well through this examination. "They are still distinct."

"A pity," he muses, rubbing at his chin in thought. "Although I suppose there may also be benefits to keeping them separate. Tell me, can you now hold your Symbol twice in your mind?"

"No," I reply eventually. "Although I have not had time to experiment much."

"Naturally." He waves off my uncertainty with a dismissive gesture. "We will explore that further. An easier question is this: can you perform a working with each of them independently? Can both *Corda* use your remarkable ability to manifest?" I feel beads of sweat beginning to grow on the back of my neck as I stall for time to answer his questions.

I am not sufficiently versed in the advanced theory of *Corda* to know what the answer to these questions *should* be. I have more Hearts than he thinks, but I do not have two that are bound to the same Symbol. Should both of them be able to manifest the *Glacialis Falx*? I am not certain, since that boon was given to me directly by a dead god.

"There is only one way to find out." He nudges me pointedly, motioning for me to begin my tests.

"Magister, before we begin, I need to tell you that my… oldest Silver *Cor* tried to Ascend tonight as well. I was barely able to keep it in check." Pliny's eyebrows rise in surprise, and he hesitates, studying me for a long moment before nodding once.

"Well, it's a good thing that your Copper Heart Ascended when it did," he says grimly. "But there's only one way forward—we have to know what you have become."

I nod, trying to hide my nervousness as I close my eyes and hold out my hands to either side. Clearing my mind, I seize Ancient Frost with all my will, seeking refuge in its cold calm.

"First use your original Heart," he instructs. "I want to compare what the process looks like inside your body with fresh eyes." Dead Mercury damn his insatiable curiosity! I do not know how I am going to fool his attunement to *Cor* itself. It is a miracle that I have made it this far without being discovered.

I can do nothing but obey. I rotate my right wrist, calling upon my reserves of Ancient Frost to manifest as the familiar icy *gladius*. The Frost Iron blades at my waist have served as a source of essence for me to refill my reserves over the last few hours. The sword grows out of my palm in a matter of heartbeats, settling into my grip as if it were made for me.

"Excellent," Pliny praises from the sidelines. "Your dedication shines in how far you have come." I tilt my head slightly, accepting the compliment silently. Inwardly my mind races, scheming how to stay one step ahead of the magister on this next test.

"Let us see what your new *Cor* can do," he urges. My thoughts freeze, and I force my body to stay loose and light. I cannot show my fear.

I nod, twisting my left wrist and calling upon the *Glacialis Falx*. At the same time, I reach for Unrelenting Fire, forcing it to obey me despite its hatred of being so close to Ancient Frost. I bleed heat into my skin, hoping that whatever Pliny's senses show him will convince him that I am using a different *Cor* to summon the sword. My two Symbols squirm like wet cats, trying to break free from my grasp, but my will does not waver. I cannot afford to stagger on this tightrope.

A second icy *gladius* forms in my hands, slower than the first.

"Fascinating," Pliny mutters as he studies me. I cannot breathe. My body is wound tight like a coiled spring, waiting to break free. "I could sense your new *Cor* activating, but your first one seemed to do more of the heavy lifting, as if it were the one that was guiding the process. Did it feel that way to you?"

"Yes, Magister," I manage through dry lips, relieved that my ruse worked. "It is as if the original *Cor* knows the path, and the other is still finding its way."

"So there is no sharing of knowledge," he muses as if I have confirmed something. "Do they share *animi*?"

I try to reflect on my experience using all three Symbols together in the courtyard. "They are separate, but I can use them at the same time."

"Do they have the same range?"

"I do not know, Magister."

"Let us test. I have some ice relics with me." Pliny fishes into a pouch at his belt, revealing a handful of small dull pieces of metal. Tentatively, I cast my *animus* over them, but I sense nothing. They are inert, devoid of anything that would register to my Symbols.

Pliny twists one of them, and I hiss in surprise as it burns against my senses, leaking a wintery essence. He looks up to confirm that I can sense it now that it is active. "Give Contessa your blades," he instructs. "We can use them to test your close-range capabilities." I shrug and pass the scarred woman my swords as she steps onto the sand with me.

"Aquilo's Bones! These are cold," the *lanista* complains as she grips them. I laugh but stop when she gives me a dark glare. I hadn't meant to imply that I found her pain funny, just how close her curse was to the truth.

"Shut your eyes," he instructs, striding to the far side of the room. "I will place these at various distances away from you. Tell me how many you can sense with each *animus*. In the meantime, Contessa will strike at you *slowly* to see if your Hearts can alternate what they see."

I obey, accepting a plain iron *gladius* from the *lanista* before bowing my head and extending my spirit out from me. It is a simple matter for my *Cor* to cover almost the entire room, but I don't tell him that. I feel as he activates the rest of his relics one by one, placing each of them further from me.

After a moment of consideration, I decide to tell him that my new Heart can only sense three of them, while my original one can feel four. I do not know why I am lying to him more, but my secrets feel worth their weight in gold, and I am reluctant to spend any more today.

"What do you sense?" Pliny calls at last.

"With which *Cor*, *Dominus*?" I ask.

"Start with your original one. Pull it all the way back until you only feel the first relic. We will expand your radius in steps." I acknowledge him silently, eyes still closed as I draw my awareness inward. Across from me, Contessa steps forward, angling a slow slash that would open me from shoulder to hip. I catch it easily with my iron blade, following the Ancient Frost as it burns against my mind.

"I am at the first relic," I tell him as Contessa steps forward in an exaggeratedly slow dance. I twist to match her, letting her lead the pace. This isn't meant to be a test of my dueling skills, but of my senses. Despite my single Ancient Frost *Cor*, I feel my mind stretch as I track the blades before me and the relics that Pliny moves around the edge of the room. It feels a little like I am going cross-eyed, trying to watch so many different things at the same time.

"How about now?" the magister calls from across the room. There are more relics present now, burning brightly in my mind.

"I can sense three. I can keep goi—*urk*." My voice cuts out as something thrums through the air at my back, and my instincts take over. I spin, raising my right blade to intercept the arrow before it can pierce my flesh. It shatters easily, devoid of any will to protect it.

My eyes snap open to find Varus Pelias standing at the entrance to the private room, just out of the range of my *animus*. In his hands, he carries a bow that he lowers as we make eye contact. A triumphant light burns in his dark gaze, and the snarl of rage on my face dies as I realize what I have done.

The arrow that I deflected was tipped with Iron.

This was a setup.

They know.

Fear burns inside of me, fed by Unrelenting Fire's wild energy. For a wild moment, I consider charging Varus. If I kill them all… perhaps Briannus will offer me—but something in his expression stays my hand. No matter what I am, this is the man who carved his way through an entire palatine family. I am already guilty of underestimating him. I cannot afford to do so again.

"I wondered," he says softly, still not moving from the entrance of the room, "how you managed to kill Brennus. You are a dangerous gladiator, *Frigus Ventus*, but even a poor *Fidelis* should be more than a match for you with a blade." He tosses the bow aside. It clatters on the stone floor, loud and unruly in the silence that hangs over the room.

"Perhaps you used your frozen swords," he suggests, descending the stairs to the sand that waits for him. "He would be unable to sense them, and it would give you a chance. But even with the gifts you have, ice is far too brittle to be able to stand up to the blows from a Silver Ironbound for long." I am silent, watching his approach without moving. In some ways, this feels like the closest I have ever been to death.

"Maybe you got lucky," Varus continues, circling me now. Reluctantly, I shift, tracking his movement. "Brennus was young and foolish. Reckless warriors make mistakes, but this is not the first time you have known what you should not."

"*Dominus*, I—" I begin, but he holds up a hand, cutting my protest off with a single gesture.

"You bear the mark of the Twelfth Legion on your chest. When you first joined my House, you told me that it was a ruse used to hide your failures." He pauses for the first time, staring at me with those intense, knowing eyes. "That was a lie, was it not?" I am frozen under his gaze, rendered motionless by fear. It is too soon! I am not ready.

"Yes," I answer at last. A weight lifts from my shoulders as I confess my secret. No matter what happens, I am free of the heavy chains of lies that have been wrapped around me for more than a year. The *electi* in this room see me. The real me.

"You are not only bound to Ancient Frost, but to a second Symbol, Iron."

"Yes."

Varus is still for a long moment, studying me with his head cocked, like a hawk watching its prey before he stops. My heart does not even seem to beat. My whole body is frozen, waiting for his condemnation. I clasp the *gladius* in my hands tightly. Distantly, the oath that binds me to his house tightens against my skin, warning me that I am in danger of violating its tenets. I prepare myself to suffer the consequences of breaking it—whatever that relic will do to me is still better than being given to the Censors.

"You were right." The senator looks over his shoulder at Pliny, who hovers at the back of the room.

The short magister smiles faintly. I am an idiot—of course he knew. What arrogance for me to think that I could keep him in the dark.

"I merely hoped for the best, *Dominus*," Pliny replies.

Varus turns back to me, weighing me with a measured gaze. "Well done," he says at last. A surprised gasp leaps from my throat as I suddenly remember to breathe. Surely, I have misheard him. But Varus smiles tightly before giving his magister another approving glance.

"I don't understand," I manage at last. "Are you not going to tell the Censors?"

"I'm sure they will figure it out at some point," Varus replies calmly. "But by then, it will be far too late." A new kind of terror blossoms in me. Even he sees me as a weapon.

"Why is the Empress trying to kill you? Why is your House under the threat of *Judicium?*" I ask in a whisper. The three of them watch me for a moment, surprised by my question. Then Varus nods approvingly, stepping out into the sand to meet me. Something inside me is breaking. My hands shake, and I cannot make them stop.

"You will speak of this to no one," he instructs. The oath that binds me to his house burns the command into my bones, making disobedience impossible. Varus watches his orders settle over me for a moment, as if steeling himself.

"Do you know how long Diana Agrippa has been Empress of the Iron Empire?" He begins with a question.

"Since… sometime after the death of the *Ferrum Domini*," I answer at last.

"She has ruled since the gods died," Varus corrects me easily.

"But what about…Perseus? He founded the Empire. He was the first Emperor," I protest. I'm grasping at straws. I should know this. Why don't I know this?

"Name one thing that Perseus did other than 'found the Empire,'" Varus challenges, his tone dripping with sarcasm. He pauses, but there is nothing I can say. My education is no deeper than that. "That's because he only ruled for ten years. *Ten years!* Then Diana killed him and took the Iron Laurel for herself."

I don't know what to say. I've known my whole life that she has ruled for as long as anyone can remember. But I have never *thought* about what that must mean. My gaze flicks to Pliny as I remember him complaining that I had not been taught to ask questions. That must change.

"That can't be true," I protest, mind racing. Powerful e*lecti* can expand their lifespan beyond the normal range—but centuries? That is beyond anything I have ever heard of.

"No one knows." Varus shrugs dismissively. "*Domus* Agrippa has long held back secrets from the rest of us."

"What are you saying? That Diana has made herself immortal?" My mind reels as my understanding of the world shudders once more.

"That is exactly what I am saying." Varus smiles tightly, pleased that I understand. "That is too long for a ruler to live. You have taken your first steps on the path of power. You know that it corrupts. Surely you already feel its whispers pulling on you?"

I can't ignore the feeling of dread that grows in my guts at his words. I have changed. It has not even been two years since I became an *electus*, but already I have become something that my mother would not recognize. I have killed. I will kill again. Yes, I have felt corruption's whispers and listened to them easily.

"The Iron Empire is sick, Castor," Varus says earnestly. His gray eyes dance with a long-hidden fire. "It is like a log that has lain in the dirt for too long, and the rot has gotten into it."

"It is rusting," I whisper softly.

"*Yes*!" It is easy to imagine him on the floor of the Senate, orating before a sea of powerful people. But we are alone, scheming in secret. "For too long, Diana has allowed her greed and corruption to spread throughout the Empire. I seek only to cleanse the rot, scrape off the rust."

"You're talking about rebellion."

"Talking about it?" Varus laughs, scoffing at my gentle phrasing. "I have done much more than talk, lad."

"Did you create Knut?" My hands tighten on the hilts of their swords. My oath to *Domus* Pelias holds me in place, but my hands begin to shake as a rage that cannot be contained builds in me, like a volcano close to eruption. Alessandra promised me her father was not involved, but *I must know*.

"What is a Knut?" Varus's brows scrunch as he glances at Pliny.

"The High King of the Normans was aided by Imperials acting against the interest of the Empire. Were those your people?" My voice is cold, and his eyes narrow at my tone.

"High King of the Normans? The barbarians have no kings." A flash of anger runs through me at the amusement in Varus's eyes. "The Lion in the North plays his own games, but the Empire is in no danger."

"There are traitors," I insist, raising my chin to meet his gaze. "They have worked to forge the different barbarian clans into one mighty horde. I have served in the cold and seen them with my own eyes."

"There isn't a force in the world that could break through Fortress Frigidus and into the Iron Empire," Varus tries to reassure me. I open my mouth to protest, but he pushes forward, running over me. "Regardless of what you have seen, I am not a part of any scheme in the North. I do not seek the fall of the Empire. I do not even wish to dismantle it. This is not a true rebellion; we do not seek to overthrow the Empire. The body is good. It is the head that is rotten and needs to be removed."

"And replaced by whom? You?"

He has the grace to look embarrassed, but not ashamed.

"Yes, I will rule," he replies firmly. "I will be a stern but fair Emperor. I will scrape the rust out of our Empire and right it from the course that it is on. But there is something I will do that is even more important than that, Castor."

"What is that?" I cannot keep the skepticism from my voice, and I lash him with it. He accepts my scorn without remark, expression earnest.

"I will die."

I blink in surprise at his offering.

"I am an *aurum electus*—I will live maybe another seventy years. Long enough to right the course. Then I will die. I will fade back to the dust of my forefathers and pass the reins to another. Mankind was not made to be ruled by immortals. We did not kill our gods only to replace them with immortal men." I am silent for a long time, measuring his words. The Iron Empire is sick, but I am skeptical of any man who sees himself as the cure. How many other senators believe that they, too, would be the solution if they wore the laurel wreath of Emperor?

But, something insidious inside my mind whispers, *you know that Varus is a good man*. I frown, trying to balance my understanding of the man who treats his slaves like people with the man who wants to rule the Empire. Is it possible for a rebel to be good? Can you demand power then use it to right wrongs?

Isn't that what you're doing? that little voice whispers again. I flinch, convinced of my own hypocrisy.

If there is a piece of the Empire that has not changed in centuries while the rot around it grows, then perhaps it is time for it to be replaced. I do not know enough about the world to know if that will fix everything, but I trust that Varus cares enough to try.

I no longer believe that of Diana. Either she does not know what her servants do in her name, and she is incompetent. Or she does and is just another of their kind.

"What do you want with me?" My voice is harsh and defensive. I am only a weapon to him. I agreed to serve *Domus* Pelias for a chance at freedom, not to become a rebel. The world has many problems; I am not its savior. I have smaller wrongs that I must address.

"For now? Nothing," Varus says simply. "The Games in Forum begin in four months. There is still work to be done if we are not going to lose our *ludus* license at the end of the season."

"You still want me to win the Games?"

"Removing me as a senator would be an easy way to undermine my legitimacy to challenge Diana. You will win the circuit and save this House."

"How am I supposed to do that? As a Silver, I cannot earn as many points as the Golds do for their matches." The three of them exchange glances that send a thrill running through me, despite the danger. They need me to advance again.

I need that too.

I carry an oath of vengeance on my shoulders that weighs more than I can bear. I want no part of this rebellion. That is for other men, like Varus, to fix. But then I remember the *necromanta* priest who studied the bodies underneath Bellona's Arena, and I remember how pervasive the rust is. I would gladly kill him and others like him. The ones who dig at things that should be left dead.

Nemesis's attention prickles along my spine as she signals her pleasure with the path her supplicant is walking. She, too, has a list of names to feed from, and it is far longer than mine. Varus's rebellion will no doubt be opposed by the Censors; it may guide me to Atticus. Perhaps there is a place for me in it. Time will tell.

"If I am going to Ascend, there is something you need to know," I tell them. A wicked smile grows on my face as I bend over to pick up pieces of the wooden arrow from the ground. Pliny cocks his head, studying me as I extend the dart toward them.

It is childish of me, given the danger that we are in, to take such delight in the expression of shock that spreads across their faces as the arrow erupts into flame with just a touch of Unrelenting Fire's essence. But I do not begrudge myself this one joy. Too much has been taken from me already.

CHAPTER 54

I do not go to bed when I am finally free of Varus and his plots. I am exhausted, but already I can tell sleep will flee from my embrace. My world is still spinning, and the silence only makes it worse.

My family. My friends. Dead gods and stolen *Corda*. It's all too much. I am full of secrets and rage that twists, fighting for position inside of me. I am truly lost and alone; part of a rebellion that I am not certain that I believe in.

Maybe I don't believe in anything.

My feet take me to the infirmary without any prompting.

Anas lies in a bed at the end of the room. The rest sit empty, their sheets folded with pristine, almost military accuracy. Laertes, the Ironbound from the Second Legion, sits at his side, watching over him. He glances up at me before giving me a tired nod. I drag a chair from the front to sit with them.

Anas seems to sleep peacefully. A dozen red-stained bandages are wrapped around his head, neck, and arms. A relic is strapped to his chest with a pair of leather belts, glowing slightly as it does its work. We sit in silence for several long moments, just watching him breathe. He seems at ease, which lifts one of the many weights from my shoulders. I am not ready to lose another friend, another brother.

It is shocking how close to breaking I feel. Brittle, like poor iron or thin ice. Every soul that I have lost feels like a stone tied to my ankles, trying to pull me into the dark with them. I am still a young man, but already my dead weigh me down.

With Anas unconscious, I find myself studying the older centurion from the Second Legion, sitting beside a man from the Twelfth. I do not know why Laertes is here—he did not serve with Anas, did not know him from any other *legionnaire*, but here he is, keeping watch.

His expression is grim and weathered, like a mountain that has been exposed to the wind for hundreds of years. This is not Laertes's first time sitting at the bedside of a fellow soldier. It has taken its toll on him, but it has not broken him, like it threatens to do to me.

"Does it ever get any easier?" I ask, breaking the silence.

"I have lost many ironbrothers, but I still feel it every time."

"You don't go numb?"

"Some do, using our Symbol like a drink to take away their pain," Laertes acknowledges with a nod. "But that doesn't last; it only delays the hurt. Makes the storm worse when it finally arrives."

"I lost a lot of friends in the legions." I do not know why I tell him this. He has certainly lost as many, if not more. Maybe because he is the only conscious man who knows my story who was a part of that world. Maybe it is because I am broken and cannot hold my secrets any longer.

"In the shieldwall, you feel them die," Laertes says, his voice haunted with his own past. "No other Symbol fights like we do—together, even as Coppers. Every time one of us falls, we feel them *ripped* from the line."

I've never thought about that; I spent little time in the front of an actual battle. But even so, it makes me think of the pack mentality of the Iron Legions in a new light.

"I never mourned them," I admit ashamedly. It is tradition for the survivors to build a shrine to the fallen, like we once did for Macer. How else are their souls supposed to find their way to the other side? All the guides are dead. We must show them the way. I did not dare risk doing so while trying to keep my secret.

"Someone did," Laertes promises, turning to fix me with a stark stare. "The Marius brothers did not die in silence. There were those who watched. I know some of the men in the Sixth and Seventh. I promise you they remembered their duty when the Twelfth did not come back from the snow. That is our way."

His words free me of some of my guilt. Not of surviving, but of surviving in silence.

"How do you bear it, then?" My voice sounds weak and small in the empty room. "How do you keep on when you've lost so much?"

The old centurion is quiet for a long moment, as if debating what secrets he is willing to share. "In the legions, they tell us that we are Iron, and so we must endure. But Iron can break. They only need us to last twenty years, then we're no good to them anymore."

I nod in understanding, a cold reminder of another of the Empire's cruel systems. "They do not teach us how to survive, only how to last long enough."

"Too right."

"But how do you last?"

The older man eyes me, something glimmering beneath his gruff exterior as he looks from me to my friend who sleeps in the bed. "You make their deaths worth something."

He makes it sound so easy. Maybe in the Prime Legions, men join for Empress and Empire. But the men of the Twelfth were there to pay for their sins. They died for nothing, killed by an imperator with a vendetta.

Another piece of rust that needs to be cleaned.

"How?"

Laertes just looks at me, his eyes telling me I already know everything I need to. I have seen that look in my officers' eyes a thousand times.

"You know?" I ask. Even here, in the depths of Varus's power, I dare not whisper the word *rebellion* aloud. I cannot, for my oath to this house binds me like a muzzle on a dog.

"Anyone with eyes knows, boy. It's hardly a secret."

"Why?"

"Why what?"

"Why do you care? Why are you here? What business is it of ours if the palatine devour each other?"

"I served my Empire for seventeen years." He shifts so he can glare right in my eye. A fire burns deep in there, buried in the ashes but not out. "In the Second Legion, the best of them. Those Mars-damned Praetorians strut around like they're the heirs of War, but you've been there, you know the truth. Their ranks are full of palatine sons who play games. Not the Second. That's where the real killers are forged. But when I helped Gaius Marius save those boys from the Twelfth, I was beaten, dishonorably discharged, and sent to die in the Games."

I am silent, surrounded by thoughts that I am not ready for.

"And for what? FOR WHAT?" Laertes's voice rises as his rage builds like an inferno. "For saving my ironbrothers? For protecting men of the Empire? For bleeding with the men who bled with us? That is my crime?"

Anas murmurs in his sleep, stirring but not quite waking. Laertes takes a deep breath and leans back in his chair. The two of us watch him sleep for a moment, lost in our thoughts.

"How could I not be here, lad? They sent me here. They told me this was where I belong—and they were right."

I do not know what to say.

In a moment, I feel selfish—foolish. My life in the Empire was easy until it wasn't. But to claim that my family's estate and expansive fields are the norm is a lie. To pretend that many had not been a part of the machine of the Iron Empire, grinding others into dust, was cowardice.

How many of my brothers in the Twelfth truly deserved to be there? Surely the ten boys from Segesta did not. Why was Petrus taken from us? What crime were Antony or Haxus guilty of? What wrong did red-headed Rufus commit that saw him fed to the grinder?

Why did Marcus have to die?

My hands are shaking again as I stare at Anas's bandaged form. The old centurion notices but doesn't say anything. Good officers can tell when silence is more powerful than shouting. We both know that his words have struck home. Now it is up to me to find out what color I bleed.

"Thank you for sharing your wisdom, *Dominus*," I rush out, standing and giving him a sloppy salute that would have gotten me whipped in the legions. Laertes returns it with a wry smile. He's already fought this duel in his own head.

"Get some rest, Legionnaire," he says warmly. "I'll sit with your brother for some time yet."

I nod in thanks and hurry to go, head bowed under the weight of the thoughts that it carries. My eyes are distant, unfocused as I walk. Only her voice pulls me out of my stupor.

"Castor!"

I freeze, hesitating at the entrance to a private room in the infirmary. It is mostly closed, but as I push on it, it swings open freely, revealing Alessandra lying in its sole bed. She is pale, and a large series of bandages are wrapped around her entire torso in lieu of a shirt. I look away hurriedly, embarrassed that she might think I am staring.

But that is not the only reason I look away. Guilt surges in me at the sight of her so weak. It is my fault. I failed to protect her. I took too long in my duel with Brennus and in doing so almost let his accomplice kill her.

"Come in," she asks, her blue eyes holding mine in their grasp. Obediently, I slink in, sinking into a chair that no doubt held her father not long ago.

"How did you know it was me?" I ask, desperate to break the silence.

"I heard someone shouting and assumed it was your fault," she murmurs, leaning back against her pillows as if the effort of sitting up has worn her out. Her black hair fans out around her like a crown. Despite my burdens, I laugh at her teasing.

"Oh, well, I don't know why you'd assume *that*."

Her eyes go flat as she stares at me like I am an idiot.

"I'm sorry I let you get hurt," I say when I can bear it no longer.

"You *let* me get hurt?" she repeats my apology incredulously. "Did you give Brennus or any of his goons permission to stab me?"

"Well, no but—"

"Did you bribe the foreman of the Foundry directly instead of thinking to have an intermediary to make it anonymous, making it simple for the Valerus to find us?"

"No."

"Did you choose the groom who was on their payroll as our driver?"

"No."

"Then how in all of the dead gods' names could you possibly have *let* me get hurt?" She is still weak from her wound, but her glare is strong.

"I took too long killing Brennus. If I had just finished him off faster…"

"You took too long."

"Yes!"

"You took too long killing a Praetorian *Fidelis*. A Silver Ironbound. You were not fast enough killing one of the most dangerous men in the world." We sit in silence, staring at each other in stubborn frustration. I do not know what to say. How to explain that I had failed.

"Yes."

Alessandra sighs and glares at me, her irritation shining bright despite her injuries. I am no *medico,* but I take it as a good sign that she still has so much of her usual fire. "Castor, am I a daisy, a delicate flower?"

"No."

"Am I some poor plebeian wandering the streets, unaware of the dangers that surround my *domus* and myself?"

I think back to our conversation at Delilah's house, where she warned me that my secrets would get her and her family killed. No, she knew the dangers. "Of course not, but I—"

"You are a very gifted warrior. You may be on a path to become the greatest *electus* to ever live. But that does *not* make you responsible for my actions. I am a palatine woman, heir to the house you are sworn to. I am an *argentum electus.* I am educated and dangerous, and I willingly and knowingly chose to take you to Foundry, despite the fact that my own life could be put at risk."

"You knew Brennus was going to attack?" I ask in disbelief.

"No, I had no idea. But I chose to aid you in breaking one of the core laws of our Empire. Treason seems important enough to be concerned about death, don't you think?"

I am silent for a moment, boxed in by her superior rhetoric, but still feeling guilty.

"I wanted him to suffer," I admit at last. Surprise flickers across her expression, and she sits up, groaning slightly as she does.

"Who, Brennus? For what, daring to attack me? I assure you my family has committed equally egregious crimes over the centuries…"

"He killed a friend of mine, in the legions." I swallow, thinking about wiry Macer and his loyalty that I may have earned but never felt like I deserved. "He killed my friend, and they did nothing because Brennus was a Praetorian and my friend was just some Twelfth riff-raff."

Alessandra's eyes go wide, and a hand comes up to cover her mouth. "Castor… I'm so sorry."

My eyes lose focus, staring at a spot on the wall above her head as I tell her the story. I have never told it before. I am grateful to Laertes for telling me how he carries the weight of his burdens, but he was not exactly my first choice for a listening ear.

But Alessandra? I can tell her about Macer.

I tell her how the officers whipped me instead of Macer the day I became Primus. I tell her about how hard he worked to stand in the lines. How he watched my back when the rest of the cohort hated me.

I tell her how he saved my life in the desert outside Agogia.

When I finish, she is silent for a long time. Her eyes brim with tears, although I do not know who they are for. Macer is long gone; his bones cannot see them. There are no messengers left to carry her sorrow to his soul.

"So you see," I half-whisper, not looking at her, "I could have been faster."

"Oh, Castor," she breathes, and her hand reaches toward me in sympathy, but we are too far apart. It flops to the edge of the bed, a genuine gesture that fades under the pressure in the room. For a moment, I consider rising to my feet and fleeing. I cannot bear to sit here any longer and witness the cost of my vengeance.

"You have saved my life twice already," she says at last, trying to absolve me of my guilt.

"But I did not—"

"You and I are on a path of danger," she says with force, cutting me off. She grunts in pain, sitting up to glare directly into my eyes. "My father will not live forever. One day, his enemies will be my enemies. I will be threatened again, and when you save it a third time, you will do better. By the fourth, you will be an expert. Do not let your failings define you, Castor. Without you, I would be dead. If you wish to apologize to me for your perceived failings, then this is how you will do so."

I blink in surprise at her sudden ferocity. Her eyes tell me that she knows that her father has revealed to me the truth. Her words spark against something that Laertes said, like a hammer striking an anvil as it shapes the iron in between them.

I am not defined by my mistakes. Broken things can be repaired. I am not dead yet. If I am going to carry the weight of all these souls on my shoulders, the least I can do is learn from their ends, make their lives worth something.

I can remember them, but change.

My mother and father might not recognize me, but why should they? When they saw me, I was a boy, and Castor the man has passed through the fires of places they could never dream of. Recognition isn't a sacred virtue, nor is change. It is what I am becoming that matters.

Alessandra sees something change in my face because her imperious frustration fades in a heartbeat and is replaced by a soft smile. I return it weakly, unused to moving my mouth in such a manner anymore.

"Scar or not, you did save my life again," she murmurs, holding my eyes with her own. "Last time, that got you a pair of *gladii* worth more than some estates. What can I do to repay you this time?"

I laugh, eyeing the new Silver veins running down my arms. I have already been given all I need.

But there is *something*, that annoying little voice whispers in the back of my mind. I feel more like myself than I have since I left the North. For too long, I have been in the depths of despair, hiding in the shadows and cowering from my enemies.

But that time is coming to an end.

My lips quirk, attempting to form into a broad smile as I hold in a laugh. I know what I want. What I am ready for. What I need.

"I could use a haircut."

The story will continue in

BLOODY SANDS

IRONBOUND BOOK THREE

REVIEWS

So, here we are again. The Cold Wind has come, and we're off to the Bloody Sands next. As always, your support helps keep the series going! If you enjoyed it, please let people know. Millions of books are published every year. The best way to get traction and discoverability is through reviews that readers leave on the platforms where they buy and discover books.

Word of mouth is powerful, too. Tell your friends about it. The better these books do, the more time I can spend working on them, and the more fish I can buy for my aquarium collection. (We're up to four now. I can stop whenever I want.)

But no matter what, thanks for taking the time to read another one of my books. I hope to find you again at the end of the next one!

— Andrew

PATREON

If you're unfamiliar, Patreon is a place where you can support your favorite authors and get access to books while they are still being worked on. You can get everything from my sincere thanks to a chance to give me feedback on the direction of the story. You can subscribe for a day, a month, or a year. It is not required by any means, but it does help me to continue this adventure!

To read the next book of Ironbound, *BLOODY SANDS,* early, as well as my other writing projects, check out the link to the Patreon below or scan the QR code with your phone.

www.patreon.com/AndrewGivler